MEXICO WEST BOOK

A ROAD AND RECREATION GUIDE TO TODAY'S WEST COAST OF MEXICO

BY TOM MILLER AND CAROL HOFFMAN

Elmar Baxter, Editor

Mike Glover, Cover Design

Tom Waters, Illustrations

THIS IS NOT JUST ANOTHER GUIDE BOOK...

The purpose of the **Mexico West Book** is to help you break the pattern of visiting Mexico by asking a travel agent to book you into one resort or another for a long weekend or a couple of weeks. We also aren't telling you to lug a backpack from a $3.00 hotel next to the bus depot to another $3.00 hotel a half-hour's walk from another bus depot.

Rather, we want to help you drive on an independent itinerary to meet the people and see the country as it really is. We will tell you how to locate reasonably-priced accommodations and meals wherever you go. We also want to introduce you to **Playa Ventura** and the beach beyond **El Pabelón**; to **Braulia** at her roadside restaurant where you can buy only one kind of beer and only by the liter; a comfortable little 300 year-old inn on a side street in a colonial town high in the Sierra Madres. Along the way we'll point out fishing and camping possibillities, deserted beaches and awe-inspiring vistas, craft centers and fiestas, historic cities and burgeoning new resort centers.

We hope to show you that it's OK to go beyond the lobby of the resort hotel, to step out of that tour bus, and never look back.

Baja Trail Publications.
PO Box 6088
Huntington Beach, California 92615
Ph. 714/969-2252

ACKNOWLEDGEMENTS...

The first memories which might have energized our efforts toward this book go back forty years to one of our first border crossings and the warm memories of that time.

The list of those who encouraged and facilitated our efforts is long, and many are recognized in the narratives, but we wish to acknowledge a few particularly significant contributors...

To Alvaro Obregón Lukens and Sérgio Estrella Sau of Hermosillo, Sonora who obtained for us a copy of the finest highway, byway and dirt road map yet produced on Mexico; to Roberto Balderrama of Los Mochis, Sinaloa who opened the magnificent Barranca de Cobre up to us not once, but several times; to Gilberto Limón de La Rocha and Benito Millan Sanchez of Mazatlán whose knowledge of the land around that beautiful city opened many doors; to the encyclopedic Robin Lloyd of Puerto Vallarta; and to Laura Camacho Diaz of Tuxtla Gutierrez whose charm and knowledge makes her the epitome of the ideal tourist relations representative.

The writing, design and production brought more individuals and teams together for the final phase of the book. The cover is the inspiration of Mike Glover, who, after his regular job assembled our first Baja Book in the winter of 1973 in a drafty garage with a leaking roof. Since, Mike has embraced Mexico, its fishing and its people. The drawings come from the hand and heart of Tom Waters. An author in his own right, Tom also visits Mexico often, gathering material for his many fishing stories and artistic endeavors. From Carlsbad, California, he operates a graphic design and advertising agency under his own name.

Early conceptual design and the computerization of the special maps came from Kory Jones who is making a name for himself in the creation of movie sets. Cartography concepts and guidance came from Nick Lasarescu, a Roumanian who is proving that the United States of America is indeed a land of opportunity.

We left the editing and proofing in much the same hands as we did nearly 20 years ago: Elmar Baxter, whose many skills include travel writing and photography; Paul "Panther" Pierce, the poet laureate of Baja and broadcast journalist for nearly a half-century; and Pat Brumm of Santa Barbara, who has had her skilled pencil involved in dozens (maybe hundreds) of books over her years in the field.

When we get to the bottom line, design and production, we have several valuable allies... Sandie and Paul Peffer of Irvine, California who operate under the name of Desk Top Designs. Their sharp minds and nimble fingers provided the final massage of the format and the marrying of the copy, maps and artwork. The printer is nearby KNI Inc. of Anaheim. And the result of their collective efforts is in your hand. We thank you all.

IMPORTANT NOTICE AND DISCLAIMER...

The Mexico West Book is a general road and recreation guide to Mexico's west coast. Although every effort has been expended to make this book as accurate as possible, there may be mistakes among the information contained herein. For legal purposes the maps, scales and headings provided in this guide must be considered approximate.

All drivers, owners and passengers of any vehicle using the Mexico West Book are explicitly forewarned that some hazards and obstructions may not have been shown or described, and anything depicted herein is subject to change due to acts of God, political decisions and/or other circumstances beyond our control. The exact geographical location, name, shape or size of features may also have been altered, inadvertently or otherwise, deleted or exaggerated.

Although every effort has been made to depict locations accurately, no warranty, express or implied, is made as to the ultimate accuracy, timeliness or completeness of the information contained herein.

This guide may be used only with the understanding that the information contained herein is subject to errors and/or omissions and that the publisher and authors cannot and do not, make any warranty, express or implied, as to the ultimate accuracy, safety or completeness of this information, nor shall they have any responsibility or liability for any person or entity in connection with any actual or alleged losses or damages caused by the use of the material in this book.

DEDICATION...

This book is dedicated to Tom Miller, Jr., who patiently guided his dad through the pitfall-laden array of software programs needed to translate a year of field notes and maps from laptop PC to Macintosh desktop publishing and on to this final product. Unless you have struggled with it and made the transition, as we have had to do you may not realize the love and patience he had for us, and the project. *Mil gracias, mi hijo.*

THE VIRGIN OF GUADALUPE...

The history of the Virgin of Guadalupe, her role in the Spanish conquests in the New World and her evolution into Mexico's patron saint is an interesting story. It began in the winter of 1531 when an Indian peasant was gathering wood outside of the fledgling village known today as Mexico City...

...He remembered it as **Tenochtitlan**. That was in the years before the yellow-haired giants with the pale skins came to his land, gave him a new name, Juan Diego, forced him to acknowledge the idol brought from across the sea on the floating towers and generally disrupted his life. "*Cristo*," they called him. In ways Juan Diego could identify with that god, for *Cristo* too had suffered, as he and his people had suffered under the new masters, yet there were doubts. After all, Cristo and his mother, *María*, did not look like one of them, they were light skinned...and that bothered him and many others.

On December 12th Juan Diego was on a hillside outside the town gathering wood for the newcomers. As he climbed the hill a woman stepped out from the rocks in front of him...a dark-skinned woman who closely resembled one of the statues in the temple of the newcomers...the one called *María*.

She greeted him in his own language, saying that she was the mother of **Cristo**! Juan Diego listened to the woman and believed her, reasoning that since the living Virgin was dark skinned, Cristo must have been dark too...like him and his people, thus the new God was a real one.

He was elated with his discovery, but how was he to prove to others that this visit with the mother of *Cristo* was real? He had to find a way to prove his encounter. The Virgin sensed his need and created for him a miracle...an armful of roses. Now, when he returned to his village he would have proof, for how else could he have gotten roses in winter except by way of a miracle.

His "proof" was enough for the church and, ultimately, the people of his village. Thus the Virgin of Guadalupe became a vital part of the conversion process to Catholicism of the Indians throughout New Spain.

TABLE OF CONTENTS

MEXICO WEST

1. Sonora
2. Sinaloa
3. Nayarit
4. Jalisco
5. Colima
6. Michoacan
7. Guerrero
8. Oaxaca
9. Chiapas

MEXICO, A SHORT HISTORY...

The first visitations of *Homo sapiens* into the lands known today as Mexico appear to have come about 10,000 years ago when descendants of the nomads who crossed the Ice Age land-bridge between Asia and North America reached the deserts of Sonora and the game-rich sierras of Chihuahua. This vanguard of what was to come consisted of stone throwing hunters and gatherers who found much to sustain their families in these warmer, less demanding lands. As wave followed wave the migrations extended into South America, providing there too, seed for new and great civilizations.

As some of the groups moved into areas of diverse vegetation and abundant water, they discovered plants which could be reproduced conveniently by simply scattering seeds on the rich soil. And it was about 3000 BC, in this environment in the central plain around Mexico City, that corn, beans and tomatoes were first cultivated. No longer needing to roam for their food, the new farmers built permanent homes, wove baskets and domesticated animals. Social units evolved and became larger as the food supply increased.

History became finite about 1200 BC when peoples we now call **Olmecas** created a culture with a high level of technical and artistic skills, including written communications. Their zenith came about 2500 years ago, and reminders of their skills are abundant today.

Out of the ruins of the Olmec culture came new ones: the **Mayas** settled the Yucatan, Guatemala, Belize, parts of Honduras and El Salvador; the **Teotihuacans** claimed the valleys around Mexico City and Puebla, and in turn were displaced by the **Toltecs**; the **Zapotecs**, and later the **Mixtecs**, came into Oaxaca. Each culture borrowed and built upon the technologies of their predecessors to create greater cities and more complex societies.

The Olmec written language was based on hieroglyphics. They also devised a 365 day calendar, carved huge stone heads weighing many tons, and then created ways to move them without the use of the wheel. The Mayans built magnificent cities and understood the use of zero in calculations. Their calendars and observations allowed them to chart and foresee the movements of the planets. *They even predicted eclipses of the sun and moon!*

At the height of their culture, around 500 AD, the city of Teotihuacan near today's Mexico City, had a population of more than 100,000 and is thought to have been the largest city in the world at that time. Records show that it took 10,000 workers 20 years to build the city's great pyramids of the sun and the moon.

The Zapotecs of Oaxaca also produced a calendar, a dot and dash mathematical system and built impressive cities complete with sewers and cisterns to facilitate their complex social structure.

Over the centuries these esoteric people proved to be no match for the waves of fierce warriors moving in from the north and west to ultimately dominate most of what is now Mexico. The last and most powerful of these tribes was the **Aztec** or **Mexica**. They moved into the central plain at the end of the 12th century and, under a perceived divine mandate in the form of a snake-eating eagle perched on a cactus, settled on two islands in the middle of **Lake Texcoco**, the site of present day Mexico City. So powerful were the warriors and their organizational skills that within a hundred years the Aztecs dominated totally, even drawing tribute from far-away Mezoamerica. The Aztecs were probably near their zenith when the Spaniards arrived.

In 1519 a young soldier, **Hernán Cortéz,** brought his 11 ships, 550 men and 16 horses to landfall near what is now Vera Cruz and from there began a march to the land of the Aztecs. It was an amazing feat, this journey of conquest, for within two years the Spanish crown controlled all of the estimated 18,000,000 inhabitants. Working in Cortez's favor was the dislike for the Aztecs by other Indian cultures, many of whom joined with the Spaniards to get their own revenge. The conquest was also influenced by **Emperor Moctezuma's** belief that Cortéz was the **God Quetzalcoatl** returning to share his throne. After one false start, Cortéz entered the Valley of Mexico with 900 Spanish soldiers and 100,000 natives to

2

defeat the Aztecs once and for all on August 13, 1521.

During the first decades of the colonial period the Indian population suffered enormous losses. It is estimated that 16,000,000 died during two smallpox epidemics alone. Millions more succumbed from other diseases, malnutrition and brutal working conditions. The onslaught continued, and despite a high birth rate, there were less than 1.5 million Indians remaining by the end of the 17th century. Even with the losses the Indians still constituted 75% of the total population of Mexico because the Spanish never immigrated in large numbers. Today, *Mexico's 80-plus million citizens are 60% mestizo (Spanish and Indian blood), 25% Indian (often speaking their own language) and 15% Mexican-born citizens whose roots are in other countries.*

Spanish colonization of central and southern Mexico continued, with the conquerors deeding themselves large tracts of land as they went. They scooped up the rich harvests to ship back to Europe and stripped the richest silver mines the world had ever known. The *conquistadores* also took other precious materials such as gold, opals and pearls, and they exploited the Indians to export large amounts of various agricultural products.

As the mines failed the Spaniards moved north, following rich silver deposits and stories of even greater bounties of gold and jewels. Vast areas extending north to Louisiana and San Francisco were added to the domain. Missionaries followed, establishing churches, convents and schools while spreading smallpox, measles and syphilis along with the word of God.

By the end of the 18th century resentment toward Spanish rule began to surface. Finally in 1810, under the leadership of Father **Miguel Hidalgo** and army captain **Ignacio Allende**, the War of Independence erupted and during an 11-year bloodbath a million people lost their lives. For the next 50 years the country was in a constant state of turmoil from civil wars, rebellions, Indian uprisings, changing constitutions and laws, land disputes and hunger. There was also a war with the United States (1846) in which California, New Mexico, Arizona and Texas were lost. The French, under Emperor Maximilian, ruled the country for 3 years as part of a settlement of a Franco-Spanish war before another uprising drove them out. It was truly a time of chaos.

Following his election as president in 1876, **Porfirio Diaz** began to reconstruct the economy of Mexico. For over 3 decades Diaz, in an autocratic and often-cruel manner, pushed Mexico into the 19th century and a form of economic prosperity by building railroads, hospitals, textile, steel and mining centers. By the time he died, all state capitals had electricity and most had public transportation, potable water and modern sanitation systems. He encouraged the export of raw materials such as coffee, cotton, sugar, tobacco, lumber, gold and silver. Copper and coal were mined and crude oil produced for international markets. But all of this progress and prosperity was not without a price.

Too high a price, many feel, for at the end of the Diaz rule the standard of living of the average peasants and workers was one-fourth of what it had been under the Spanish. More than half the country was owned by foreigners and they controlled more of the economy than the Mexicans. The long-festering wounds came to a head in 1910 when the country was again embroiled in civil war.

Over the next six years the tides of conflict ebbed and flowed. Governments came and went, among them, Emiliano Zapata and Francisco "Pancho" Villa, two peasant leaders who attempted to gain control and institute land reforms. After a convoluted series of assassinations, compromises, coalitions and conventions, the **Constitution of 1917** was ratified and a democratic form of government installed. Though giving the president disproportionate powers, it provided for the expanded rights for workers, the restoration of peasant lands and made primary education mandatory. The first major improvements came in 1920 when a strong leader, **Alvaro Obregón**, became president. He instituted agrarian reform and organized peasants and workers into large associations. In doing so he pacified the country and established better international relations, particularly with the United States.

3

In the 1930s the Revolution appeared to have lost some of its drive...promises had not been kept and many peasants were still barely surviving. It was under these conditions that **Lázaro Cárdenas** took office and formed a national political party (the forerunner of PRI) which enabled the outgoing president to pick his successor. Under his leadership further distribution of lands took place through the creation of the *ejido*, a communal land scheme wherein parcels were assigned to members to use but not own. He also nationalized the oil fields when foreign owners failed to improve conditions for their workers. Cárdenas was supported by the workers, the peasants, the army and the small, but emerging, middle class. Though Cárdenas' moves represented progress, they brought on an acute economic slump followed by inflation, a freeze on investments and a currency devaluation. And many say that the only thing which prevented Mexico's total economic collapse was the start of World War II.

WWII was used to justify the end of land reform programs under the excuse that large land plots were needed to produce more food. The heavy exports to the United States and other nations during this period bolstered Mexico's economy. As a result, domestic manufacturing increased, with many peasants leaving the land to work in the factories while others emigrated north to temporary jobs across the border under the Bracero Agreement of 1942.

Miguel Aleman's presidency in the late 40s saw continued industrial growth as he applied his energies to solidifying earlier gains. Alemán was also the architect of Mexico's touristic development. The country prospered and public works programs proliferated...roads, dams, irrigation, electrification and sanitation projects brought prosperity to many through higher food production, increased tourism, foreign investments, etc., but again, not without a price.

The 50s and 60s saw a return to dealing with the perennial inequities of Mexico's social structure. The presidents of this era tried to better define land distribution schemes; encourage the expansion of social security and public health systems; and to build rural schools in their attempt to defuse a growing unrest. In spite of the effort leftist sentiments continued to grow, as did the demonstrations, strikes and assassinations. The population doubled in two decades and rural living conditions worsened, sending millions to the cities in search of work. Corruption too, increased.

The assumption of the presidency by **Luís Echeverría** in 1970 ushered in another era, one of fiscal chaos. In an economy confounded by corruption of mega-proportions and fueled by the discovery of new major oil fields, the peso suffered its first devaluation in 20 years. The 70s and 80s did little to change the trend and the slide became an avalanche. Currently, in early 1991, 30 pesos are worth about one American penny

Today new political parties are emerging and being heard from at the local and state levels. **Carlos Salinas de Gotari**, holder of a business degree from Harvard, comes to the presidency amid accusations of voting irregularities. Since his election in 1988 President Salinas has been busy restructuring the social and economic frameworks of his country. Though many feel that his efforts will be beneficial in the long run, others disagree. Time will tell.

As a Mexican friend said recently, "It is time that we pull ourselves into the 20th century, before it too goes out of date."

BEFORE THE BORDER...

THE PAPER CHASE

The paper trails of contemporary society follow us everywhere, and crossing the border into Mexico is no different...

Tourist Permits...

Travelers to Mexico will need to obtain a Mexican tourist permit. It is required to go anywhere beyond the so-called **Border Zone**. This means that destinations such as El Golfo de Santa Clara and Puerto Peñasco do not require tourist permits unless the stay is for more than 72 hours.

Mexico issues two types of permits. One is good for single visits of up to 180 days and is validated upon showing proof of citizenship to a *migración* (immigration) official at the point of entry. The other, a multiple-entry permit and also valid for 180 days, is required if traveling on business or when using a Mexican hunting license. It requires the submission of three 2x2 inch passport photos. With this document you must log in and out of the country.

In either case, the forms are free at Mexican consulates. Single-entry permits are also available through airline ticket counters serving Mexico, Mexican auto insurance offices, some travel agencies and the Mexico West Travel Club. **(See More Information?.)**

Examples of proof of citizenship (in order of preference) are; valid passport, birth or baptismal certificate, naturalization papers, armed forces discharge or identification, and voter registration,. You must carry such proof for every family member throughout the trip. (It should be noted that U.S. Immigration officials may also require proof of citizenship before allowing re-entry into the United States, and in that case a voter's registration is not recognized.)

Children under 15 may be included on their parent's permit, but separate documents are advisable in case they should return home with someone else. Minors under 18 traveling alone or with persons other than their parents must not only obtain permits but have in possession, a notarized letter of consent from both parents or guardians. If the minor is with only one parent, a notarized letter of consent from the other parent is also required.

Canadians muist present passports or birth certificates when applying for their tourist cards. Citizens of some countries are required to have a visa issued by a Mexican Consulate. For current regulations check with a consulate office. A list is near the end of the book.

Vehicle Permits...

Other than destinations near the border and the Baja California peninsula, any car, motorhome, trailer, boat or motorcycle...any of our adult toys, must be registered when brought into Mexico. There's no charge, but you must show your U.S. driver's license and proof of ownership on your automobile, motor-home, trailer, boat, etc. If you don't own them, be sure to have a **Notarized Affidavit** from the legal owner(s) (*i.e.* the bank or loan company) showing that you have their permission to bring the rig into Mexico.

Hunting Permits...

The quality of wing shooting for dove, quail, pheasant, duck, geese and brant in Sonora and Sinaloa rates with the best in the world. Unfortunately, as good as the hunting is, the regulations are among the worst.

Due to the near-impossibility of getting a hunting license and gun permit on your own, we recommend the use of professionals who know the ropes. Among them is the venerable **Mexican Hunting Association**, 3302 Josie Ave., Long Beach, CA 90808, Phone (213) 421-1619; **Joan Irvine Travel**, 1600 W. Coast Highway, Newport Beach, CA 92663, Phone (714) 548-8931; and **Mexico Services**, PO Box 66278, Los Angeles, CA 90066,

Phone (213) 398-5797. These companies charge a moderate fee for their services and are happy to answer questions.

As guides are currently required for all hunting activities in Mexico, many hunters arrange in advance through Joan Irvine Travel (above). Other companies, but in Mexico, include; **Muy Grande Outfitters**, Celeste #6, Colonia Real de Los Arcos, Hermosillo, Sonora 83250 and the **Plaza Inn**, Leyva y Cárdenas, Los Mochis, Sinaloa. If and when Mexico's hunting regulations get straightened out, hunts of a lifetime await the nimrod.

Fishing Licenses...

Each person 16 years or older on a private boat in Mexican waters must have a fishing license, whether fishing or not.

Permits to fish from commercial passenger-carrying sportboats in Mexican waters are usually included in the price of the trip. However, if you fish from a private boat, or from the shore, you will need to obtain a standard Mexican fishing license. They are available by mail through the **Mexico West Travel Club**, P.O. Box 1646, Bonita, CA 91908, Ph (619) 585-3033, from a few tackle stores near the border or they may also be purchased at fisheries offices in Mexico. In Mexico the supplies can be spotty so it is better done ahead of time. Prices vary as the peso fluctuates.

Possession of cabrilla, lobster, oysters, pismo clams or shrimp is forbidden by law, though you are usually not bothered if a small amount is retained for immediate personal consumption and you have a fishing license. Possession of a totuava is now permitted under certain circumstances but, because they have been declared an endangered species by the United States, they cannot be imported into the U.S.

According to law anglers may catch a total of 10 fish per day, but no more than five of one species. Tighter restrictions apply on some species, for example...two roosterfish *(pez gallo)* or dolphinfish *(dorado)*, one sailfish, marlin, swordfish or giant sea bass. Releasing of uninjured fish is encouraged.

Getting Insured...

Automobile insurance in Mexico is confusing to many visitors, yet it is of vital importance. Simply stated, Mexican law does not recognize **any** insurance except that written by Mexican insurance companies and their representatives, no matter what your American policy might say.

To be protected in Mexico, you **must** carry Mexican insurance on your car, trailer, boat (if trailered) or any other item you may be hauling. If the car, but not the trailer, is insured and you are in an accident, your car insurance is not valid.

Mexican law is based on the legal system known as the **Napoleonic Code**, wherein one is held to be guilty until proven innocent, while our **English Code** presumes innocence. The Napoleonic Code is not unique to Mexico. It is prevalent through much of Europe and most of Latin America.

Therefore, should you become involved in an accident while in Mexico, you are considered liable under Mexican law as both parties are held equally guilty until the matter is legally resolved. Lacking proper coverage, your vehicle can also be impounded and fines levied. Your Mexican policy guarantees, in Spanish, that you are able to pay damages up to the limit on the policy, should you be found at fault.

In the event of an accident and you have Mexican insurance you may be brought to the police station for a hearing. If no one is injured, you will be allowed to leave, if you can pay for any damages and applicable fines. If you are unable to pay, you will probably remain in custody and your car will be impounded.

If the accident involves injury or death to any party, you may be placed in custody until authorities establish responsibility. Legally you can be held for up to three working days before your case is heard. Bear in mind that an accident of any kind in Mexico is considered a felony, not a misdemeanor.

Mexican insurance rates are based on the value of the vehicle and length of stay. Policies can be obtained from a number of designated offices along the border. Once you've a policy in hand, you need only to avoid accidents, but in the event you do have one:

1) Report any accident to the nearest authorities.

2) Be aware that city police have jurisdiction only in cities, not on highways.

3) Do not panic and do not pay anyone.

4) Show your Mexican insurance policy to competent authorities, but do not surrender it without a receipt. *We've never needed it, but we always carry a Xerox copy of our policy.*

Things take time, but we've found the system to be fair in the long run. The thing that spooks many visitors when confronted with an accident situation is the language problem. Sometimes its best to ask for an interpreter. There is often one available for a fee.

Getting Ready...

Some say that planning a trip is half the fun. Fortunately, that's one of Carol's strong points, while Tom seems to survive nicely without any apparent plan. Though our approaches might be different we both believe in researching a destination. Tom's interests take him to references having to do with the land, the water and the people, while Carol strengths lie in facilities, cities and history. A good combination.

There are other considerations besides deciding when and where you are going. Nobody should travel far from home unless they are able to deal with existing health problems. It particularly doesn't make sense to visit a country ill-equipped to handle sophisticated medical procedures if that is what you are likely to need. We recommend medical and dental checkups shortly before leaving on any extended trip.

You might also want to check with your insurance carrier to see what benefits go with you and how they are to be handled. Incidentally, medical, dental, and optical services, as well as medicines, are less expensive in Mexico.

Before you leave be sure to have a good supply of whatever medications you'll need, copies of prescriptions, extra eyeglasses and other common-sense nostrums packed away in a first aid kit.

IT'S THE CUSTOM...

Going South...

Mexican customs regulations are similar to those in other countries, thus expect to have papers reviewed and your vehicle and luggage inspected. It is also unlawful to bring refrigerators, stoves, air conditioners, etc. which are not part of a motorhome, trailer, etc. Recent changes in the laws do allow you to legally import such appliances at reasonable duties, but these papers must be obtained through import companies located near the border. If you try it without the paperwork, you could lose it all, or be turned around.

Time was when the "mordida", which translates as "death bite" and means a small bribe or tip, could help you get across with contraband items, or purchase assistance with minor problems around the larger towns. The Mexican Government has been cracking down on this tradition in recent years, while at the same time increasing the incomes of officials to compensate. Unfortunately, a runaway economy helps keep the practice alive. If an outstretched palm should appear at times, be prepared to part with a small amount of money to speed you on your way. After all, it is part of the culture in most of the world. And when was the last time you got a good seat at a Las Vegas show without slipping the maitre d' a sawbuck or two.

By law each adult may bring one liter of liquor and a "reasonable" amount of tobacco products into Mexico. As for beer, it usually isn't worth it. Budweiser and Miller's are found in many local markets along with the excellent domestic *cervezas*. Mexico's wines are gaining rapidly in quality, especially the whites out of the valleys of Baja California. Domestic rum, brandy, gin, vodka, and of course, tequila, are inexpensive, while imported Scotch, bourbon and Canadian whiskies can cost an arm and a leg.

Though the regulation is rarely enforced, the law limits each visitor is to one still camera and one video camera, plus 12 rolls of film or tape for each.

Coming North...

When returning to the U.S.A. you may bring back up to one liter of alcoholic beverage per person. An American law, it applies to all persons over 21 crossing the border, whether in a car, bus, plane or walking. Currently, each person may bring $400 worth of goods into the United States duty-free. Special exemptions apply to hand-crafted items and certain art objects.

The Ox Muzzle Affair

In the late 70s we took an extended motorhome trip which allowed us to wander as far south as the Yucatan and Oaxaca. The adventure was a wonderful one and the opportunity to buy handicrafts with a cavernous opportunity to get them home was never better. The potential even exceeded our ability to figure out what we were going to do with it all when we got home.

We began by filling the drawers and closet spaces purposely left empty in anticipation of what we were going to buy, but before we were half-way through the trip, everything was jammed. In fact the planning was so poor that by the time we returned to the American border, we had purchased ourselves out of the bedroom and were eating and sleeping in the tiny dining area.

Before reaching the border we had itemized each and every purchase and its price. The list extended well over three pages of a legal-size tablet. It included clothing and hats from the Yucatan; black clay figurines and pots from Oaxaca; wood carvings and bowls from Michoacan and Guerrero; A set of dishes from Taxco; jackets and glassware from Puebla, etc. etc. The list went on and on.

When the customs officer stepped into the coach he took a look around the unit, his eyes hesitating at what used to be the bedroom.. He was surely used to it, and likely already had in mind how much the duty would be. He squeezed into the narrow bench seat at the table and started down the list.

The first item was a wool poncho from Oaxaca. He didn't even want to see it. The next was a machete. Again no problem. The third item on the list, a pair of ox muzzles. He read it aloud. "Ox muzzles?"

"Yes.

"Why? You got an ox?"

"No, they're for two oxen, you always get two."

"Two what?"

"Ox muzzles."

"Where are they?"

"In the bedroom."

"In the bedroom?" he glanced back toward the door, as if to be sure that he could still get out. By this time Tom had walked to the bedroom, reached behind a large box and pulled out the ox muzzles, which looked like nothing more than a pair of woven holders for hanging pots.

The officer sat there, mentally reviewed the conversation and, while scanning the rest of the three pages of imports, asked, "Got any more items like that?"

"A few, want to see them?"

He shook his head and got up from the table. As he stepped down and waved us on, he said to nobody in particular, "Ox muzzles."

AVOIDING HASSLES...

Several years ago, on a multi-day sportfishing trip out of San Diego, a fisherman named Geoff, came down on Tom about the dangers of traveling in Mexico. Uncharacteristically, Tom held his tongue and listened.

The gist of the complaints were that wherever he went he was hassled. At the drug checks, walking down the street, on a beach (he's a surfer), in a bar. Everyone everywhere had it in for Geoff. Even the Aussies put him on their list. He told of spending a night in jail in Brisbane and being thrown off a bus twice "for no reason". Even on the boat, the majority of the passengers, given the opportunity, would have happily dumped him off on the nearest island.

To understand why Geoff wasn't a favorite anywhere, you only needed to be around him a couple of minutes. He had all of the traits which society in general rejects throughout the world...his long hair and scraggly beard were tangled and dirty, his clothes bloody and covered with fish slime. The crew finally had to tell him to change clothes.

Geoff spoke in a loud voice, treated others as inferiors and when he had a fish on, expected everyone to get out of his way. Back at the docks in San Diego he gathered up his gear and his fish and took off, leaving no tip for a patient, hardworking crew. One wonders how he's lived as long as he has.

Here, in one person, were almost all the characteristics which can get you in trouble in Mexico.

ON THE ROAD

Fuel For Thought...

All gasoline in Mexico is sold through the government's production and marketing monopoly, **Pemex** (*Petroleos Mexicanos*). When planning a trip into Mexico, you should consider the following:

Once out of the border towns, plan to buy your gasoline with pesos, as dollars are not always accepted, and varying exchange rates make for confusion on both sides. Prices are set by the government but vary somewhat with the station's proximity to the border.

For vehicles still using leaded gas, Mexico offers the low-octane **nova** For more modern engines requiring unleaded fuel there is good news, Pemex now provides a higher-octane gas, **magnasin**. Look for them in the blue and green pumps, respectively. As **nova**'s low octane rating can cause pinging in older cars we suggest boosting it by mixing in some **magnasin**. Our 1970 Chevy camper is very happy if we add one part of unleaded for each three parts of Nova.

Diesel fuels the country's trucking industry and is common throughout Mexico. Look for it in the red pumps. It is usually off to the side. Diesel owners should be sure they have double filters on fuel lines to pick up stray particulate matter.

Gasoline is becoming more plentiful along Mexico's main highways, but it's still wise to work off the top of the tank. We pinpoint hundreds of Pemex stations in our roadlogs and those designated as "full service" normally carry the unleaded **magnasin**.

As it is now legal to buy liquified petroleum gas (**LPG**) for use as a motor fuel in Mexico, we have also spotted many of these repositories along the way. There are two price structures, one for filling tanks for cooking and heating, and a higher price (which includes a road tax) when it is used for motor fuel. Generally, supplies are good but again, it is well to work off the top half of the tank.

Mexico's Green Angels...

Motorists in need of a helping hand can avail themselves of a service unique to Mexico, the deployment of specially-equipped green pickups for the express purpose of assisting motorists along the country's national highways. Employed by Mexico's Department of Tourism and known as *Angeles Verdes* (Green Angels), each unit carries a crew of two (usually one speaks English), a limited supply of spare parts, gas, oil and water and offers free assistance to stranded motorists. Minor repairs can often be made right on the spot. Parts, when needed, are available at cost.

Though they cover large areas, the *Angeles Verdes* patrol their territory at least once a day. Fortunately, many of the truck drivers are also generous with their time and talent, and can sometimes beat the Green Angels at their own game.

The state of Sonora has, on its own, created their own version to assist tourists on the state highways. Look for the *Angeles Blancos* in their white Nissan pick-ups.

We must emphasize that these services should not lull the motorist into driving into Mexico with a vehicle in need of repair or service. And if you plan off-road side-trips, double check everything, and carry extra water, food, fuel, tool kit, etc.

All in all, travel by private vehicle in Mexico has never been better.

A PLACE TO EAT...

Where to eat in Mexico...it comes as a trauma to so many visitors, yet for us the answer is simple. Our guidelines are brief and have little to do with whether it has dirt floors or electricity. Here's what we look for when selecting a restaurant...

We want the people clean and the kitchen well organized. If the place smells of rancid grease, skip it. If it's popular with the locals it's an almost-automatic OK. So we don't look too oddball when checking this all out, we usually order a soda or beer, even if we don't eat.

Ninety percent of the restaurants we patronize do not speak English, but it's rarely a problem. Somehow the message always gets across. If there's a written menu, something on it will almost always be familiar, if not, they'll usually mention a dish you'll recognize, or you can ask. We rarely get hurt by risking. (See **Cranking Up the Spanish** in back of book) As we go along we will introduce some of these restaurants and their hospitable operators.

*During the many months we spent researching our **Mexico West Book** we had two bouts with the tourista. One came from a green salad in a 5-star tourist hotel in Jalisco. The other time it was the scallops in a restaurant catering to **norteamericanos**, not locals.*

In Case it Happens...

Moctezuma's Revenge.and *turista*...these are two of many names for Mexico's version of traveler's diarrhea. The principal villain in the scenario is a bacteria, *E. coli*. Symptomatic treatment can be made with a long-time standby, **Pepto-Bismol**. This mild, nonprescription medication works 90% of the time, and has few side effects. Additional remedies include Kaopectate, Lomotil, tincture of paregoric, and antibiotics...none of which we recommend because of possible side effects.

Things contributing to a speedier recovery include rest and increasing the take of liquids. Try to take small amounts of of fluids at frequent intervals or suck on ice cubes. Other helps are soups and high-sugar sodas. Try sipping lightly on a Coca Cola (not diet) for many say that something in the syrup sooths the stomach.

Many Mexicans swear by *té de manzanilla* (camomile tea) as a cure. Items to avoid for a few days include spicy foods, milk, dairy products, orange juice and eggs.

If the condition persists beyond a few days a physician should be consulted.

Something we include on a regular basis in all foreign lands, and which may have something to do with our having few problems, is **acidophilus** *bacteria. Purchased from healthfood stores in capsules, we take them on a daily basis to reinforce the natural flora within our digestive systems. For us, it seems to work.*

Much of one's success in avoiding *turista* might also be attributed to not overdoing in strange surroundings. Work up to heavily-spiced dishes and drink bottled water unless you know the water is potable. Ice cubes are no longer the problem whey were 20 years ago as laws now require that they be made from purified water. Enjoy the fresh seafood of Mexico, but be sure it is fresh and comes from unpolluted waters. And always...if something tastes funny, don't eat it, any more than you would at home.

Remember that nearly all medications have side effects, so don't take anything unless indicated.

Many family doctors freely prescribe antibiotics as a preventative for diarrhea, even suggesting that you begin taking it before leaving home. This is fine, but remember that antibiotics can trigger sun poisoning, a potentially more-severe malady than what is being prevented. Think about it.

Remember too that whenever you go anywhere you are changing your lifestyle and your environment. That in itself can cause problems for some people. Most cases occur during the first few days of a visit; after that your system seems to adapt.

Interestingly, visitors to the U.S. also encounter turista. Wonder what they call it?

Making Friends With El Sol...

Sunburn and dehydration are things to guard against in the sunny climes of Mexico. High temperatures or long exposure to the sun with little fluid intake can bring on serious problems, such as sun stroke and heat prostration. Briefly, symptoms include flushed, clammy skin and a rapid, weak pulse. Nausea, headache, cramps and blurred vision are others.

Have the victim lie down in a cool shaded place with the head slightly lower than the rest of the body. Give small amounts of fluids often. Any tight clothing should be loosened and the body sponged with cool water until the body temperature drops. Get to a doctor as soon as possible.

Biters and Stingers...

Few parts of the world are free of noxious animals or insects, and Mexico shares these bedeviling critters with the rest of North America's environments. The major ones, scorpions and members of the rattlesnake clan, are found to some degree in all parts of the country, but rarely in quantity.

Look for scorpions under rocks, in woodpiles, layers of leaves, etc. Clothing, especially shoes, and boxes can be invaded overnight. Before dressing in the morning, make sure the little critters haven't joined the party. They also like to hang out in the shower.

The nature of a snake is also to stay out of the way but they're usually too big to overnight in your gear. *In the nearly 40 years Tom has been going to Mexico he has seen less than a dozen venomous snakes.*

A venomous snake bite or a much less dangerous scorpion sting should be treated with a snake-bite kit. You may also apply a constricting bandage above the wound on the victim's arm or leg. An ice pack is also of assistance. Have the victim move as little as possible until the swelling has stabilized, keeping the injured area below the level of the heart. And get to a doctor as soon as possible, particularly with a snake bite.

And Other Pests...

Noseeums, also known as *jejenes* or *bobos*, are so small they can go through a window screen. They love to lay their eggs in your epidermis along with a local anesthetic of sorts, which often delays the itching for several hours. To residents of the eastern and southern United States they are no strangers, and the marshy areas in Canada also have cousins of these hungry little guys. Look for the Mexican versions along the coasts and around brackish lagoons.

To a Canadian, a Mexican mosquito is little more than a harmless pest, but to those of us who spend most of our lives in a mosquito-free environment, the *sancudo* can be a pain, particularly at night, when they're buzzing your ear looking for dinner.

The best repellant we've found is **Muskol**, a 100% DEET product, while others swear by **Avon's Skin So Soft**! For temporary after-the-fact relief, Muskol also markets a product called **After-bite**. Lacking this, we've used lime juice, ice and cortisone ointment.

A jellyfish can be a real and painful pest during warm water periods. The tiny syringelike devices on their long tentacles can result in painful welts. If you're hit, rub the area well with beach sand and apply meat tenderizer or vinegar to the area. Lime juice, ammonia, even urine, also help decrease the reaction. Occasionally severe reactions develop and further medication is necessary.

The density of irritating critters varies greatly with the terrain, rainfall and time of year, so don't let the above scare you off.

A Weather Report...

To begin with, we're not going to Mexico to play in the snow, or to ski, so we leave the real winter stuff at home. We're down here to get, or keep, warm and travel accordingly. Below is a generalized review of what you might expect along Mexico's west coast...(We see little need to go into greater detail just to fill a couple of pages.)

Sonora: Summers are hot and humid. Little rain, but expect it in Jul-Sep. Balance of year, warm days, cool nights in dead of winter and some wind Jan-Mar.

Sinaloa: Summers in 90s with high humidity. Rains Jul-Sep. Balance, warm days and a few cold nights. Many consider the foothills perfect for wintering (Alamos).

Nayarít: Summers hot, humid and lots of rain. Balance, temps in 70s, 80s, only a few cool nights and scattered rain storms.

Jalisco: Summers in 90s, humid and many showers, chance of hurricanes. Balance, 80s with little rain and few cool nights. Inland—Many claim Guadalajara as the perfect winter climate. Summers there can be rainy, but rarely hot.

Colima: Same weather as Jalisco.

Michoacan: Hot, humid summers with rain Jul-Oct including hurricanes. Balance, dry and warm with few cool nights.

Guerrero: Summers in 90s with humidity. Heavy rains and possible hurricanes Jul-Oct. Balance, high 80s, low 90s with less humidity. Occasional thunder showers.

Oaxaca: Summers in 90s, high humidity, rain Jun-Sept. Balance, in high 80s with warm nights and little rain. Oaxaca City—rain May-Oct, cool winters, warm, not hot, summers.

Chiapas: Hot all year, humidity Mar-Oct. Rain May-Sept. San Cristobal—rain Mar-Aug with scattered T-storms all year. Warm with cool nights and occasional cold snaps.

What to Wear...

Here in Mexico there is little need for concern over what to wear, other than to stick with clothes appropriate to the season. Cotton and cotton blends are best in hot weather as they breathe; a light sweater or windbreaker is handy for evenings and air conditioned buildings; pack a jacket if the mountains are in your plans; and always, a wide-brimmed hat for the sun.

Keep in mind that Mexico's culture still doesn't include bikini-clads wandering anywhere but on the beach or around the pool, so bring cover-ups. Although pants and shorts on women are becoming more acceptable, loose, wraparound skirts for town visits are strongly advised, particularly in non-resort towns.

Dressing for an evening out is simple, just get comfortable. *Guayabera* shirts for the men and casual dresses for the women are almost always appropriate. If you see a tie, it will likely be on the *maitre d'*.

There are few places in the world where one can purchase finer casual clothing at better prices than here in Mexico. Plan to buy some of your wardrobe as you go. You'll be glad you did.

If You Take a Camera...

Take plenty of film...you'll need it. As hot weather plays havoc with film, it is important to store it in as cool a place as possible. The bright sunlight of Mexico makes it advisable to have a polarizing filter. Be extra aware of the need to protect cameras from the fine dust found almost everywhere off Mexico's main highways. Ditto for salt water.

A Pet Problem...

Bringing a pet into Mexico is, frankly, a pain. Not only will you need to have current veterinarian's certificates of health and rabies shots, but you'll need a special visa form from the Mexican Consulate. Once legal, your pet will likely enjoy life along the beaches or in the campgrounds, but if you're hoteling it, you'll find very few that allow pets,

Tips and Taxes...

It has been more than a decade since Mexico instituted a Value-Added tax (IVA) of 15% on many goods and services. Most of the time it is included in any price quoted such as restaurants, goods and fuel. Though some feel that it is a rip-off, it is just another way of raising money. Unfortunately, some hotels are not including it or a service charge in their pricing, so we suggest that you ask, thus avoiding surprises later.

THE PESO STORY

Since September of 1976 when Mexico's economic policy caught up with her and she was forced to devalue the *peso*, it has been one economic crisis after another. And though things have settled somewhat, nobody wants to predict where it is going.

Suffice it to say that Mexico isn't immune to spiraling peso (and dollar) costs. And it surely catches our hosts more than it does us.

Dollars are accepted, sometimes preferred, in major touristic centers, but the outlying regions usually deal only in pesos. We suggest a visit to one of the major banks every few days to restock the peso supply.

Open weekdays from 9 a.m. to 1 or 1:30, they exchange at the going official rate, while hotels, etc., tend to offer a bit less.

Whither Tom's Wallet...

It was some years ago that I and my wallet parted company during a trip to Acapulco. The event was not a sinister one, it just disappeared, but I had to make $40 worth of pocket pesos last for the two days I had remaining.

I made it back to LAX, through customs, and finally home, after talking the shuttle driver into letting me pay him when I got to the house.

The loss had been reported to the police and within a couple of weeks after replacing

the credit cards, driver's license, etc., the incident was forgotten. Then, about four months later a caller from the Department of Tourism in Mexico City asked me if I had lost a wallet and if so would I provide a description. It was my wallet, but neither of us knew how it got to Mexico City...it just turned up on her desk with a note to investigate. There it was on Sara's desk, complete with ID, credit cards and the 200-plus dollars and pesos!

"That's great," I said, "you can send it to my home," giving her the address.

"I am afraid to do that Señor, I will send it up to Los Angeles by courier. The mails are not too safe, you know. I will have someone call you from the Los Angeles Tourism Office when it arrives." I thanked Sara and mused aloud about such a miracle.

Several months passed and no wallet. I wrote it off again. Then a message on my machine was from the Mexicana Airlines office at Los Angeles International Airport. It said that Marta had my wallet and what should she do with it! I called immediately and talked to Marta who said it showed up on her desk with a note for "Señor Miller."

"I could put it in the mail, but I'd rather not." a pause, then..." maybe I could send it over to our Santa Ana office, and you could pick it up from there..."

Feeling that my wallet had already traveled too far without me, I said I'd be right over.

I met the charming Marta and we had lunch in a restaurant with an ocean view. And I paid it for with the dollars still in my parapatetic wallet.

Easy Money, Mexican Style...

Have you ever stayed in a hotel you didn't particularly like because they accepted credit cards? Or eaten in an overpriced restaurant because they too would take your plastic? You need to no more...thanks to one of Mexico's leading banks, **Bancomer**. Bancomer is part of a worldwide network of banks providing instant cash to holders of Visa cards.

In 1988, when we learned about it we stopped buying, and worrying about, travelers checks. Now, with a convenient, ready cash supply, we can bargain in the central markets, eat at the spots popular with the locals, and take advantage of the bargain prices at hotels and restaurants too small to handle plastic or travelers checks.

To start the process we go to a customer services desk in a **Bancomer** branch and tell them how much we want. They verify our card by computer or telephone, check passports for identification and direct us to a line where we are given pesos at the full exchange rate with no service charge! It's wonderful.

When in Mexico for extended periods, we make prior arrangements with the bank at home for our Visa account to be paid automatically, thus keeping our draw high and eliminating interest charges. It's a marvelous system, and it works.

A note of caution...It is now doubly important...Don't lose your credit card.

As we ready the book for the printer, the Bank of America informs us that their ATM card is good in Mexico at any machine that displays the PLUS SYSTEM logo. We haven't had time to check it personally, but it won't hurt to remember your PIN.

Calling Home..

Once off the well-trodden paths of the travel brochures the ubiquitous telephone is rarely on the night stand next to the bed. Should the need arise to talk to the kids, parents or business partners, it may well have to be done from the hotel lobby or one of the long distance phones scattered around Mexico under the banner of *Larga Distancia.* Initially the process in the little phone offices might appear intimidating, but once you learn the system, it's a snap.

First, don't place an international call with the intent of paying for it there. The many taxes and service charges make it much less expensive to call collect, and many smaller offices cannot place international calls unless they are collect anyway. We simply tell everyone before we leave what to expect and ask them to keep the bills for reimbursement. The format below even eliminates a need to know Spanish. You need only print the following information, in the order shown, on a slip of paper and present it to the operator. As to the service charge, it is in pesos and very reasonable.

1. **Name of city and state being called.**
2. **Telephone number, including area code.**
3. **Your name.**
4. Then print: **Quien Contesta** (whoever answers) or the name of the person you wish to talk to if it is to be person-to-person.
5. And finally: **Por Cobrar** (collect).

We've used the format for years with no problems.

Odds and Ends for Happy Travelling...

We carry what we call a survival kit whenever and wherever we travel by car. We try to keep it simple, tailoring it to what we might expect on a particular trip. It usually starts with a cardboard carton from a local grocery and, in Mexico, usually includes the following:

Flashlight with extra batteries
An aerosol insecticide
Insect repellent. W*e stick to Muskol, though Avon's Skin So Soft mixed 50-50 with water is effective over periods of up to two hours*
Picnic supplies-cutting board, sharp knife, eating utensils, can opener, ice pick, Swiss army knife
A few rags, matches and recloseable plastic bags
Paper towels and toilet paper
Wash cloth and towelettes (in glove box)
Large sturdy plastic glasses, coffee mugs
A small electric coil for heating water
Instant coffee, tea bags, and soup mixes
As we're readers, we include a high intensity lamp or a couple of 100 watt bulbs or both. Many hotels have very low wattage lights.

The last piece of equipment is in many ways the most important...a mid-sized ice chest. In it we keep a plastic container for cheese, salami, etc. Juice, sodas and beer are packed in ice.

Guidelines For Off-the-Main-Road Driving...

1) Read the whole log before taking a side trip.
2) Allow enough time and stay within your and the vehicle's abilities. If in doubt...turn around.
3) Pre-run any dirt road with a small vehicle or motor cycle if you're driving a motor home.
4) Always carry a survival kit...extra gas, water food, etc. The Green Angels are on the main highways only.

When It's Dusty...

An old trick to keep dust out of the car when off the pavement is to close the windows and turn the air conditioning on full blast with the lever set to bring in the OUTSIDE air. The intake vent in most cars is in the front and high enough to be away from the dust. By bringing in outside air you will build up a positive interior pressure, thus keeping the dust from seeping the cracks. We've been doing it for years.

A Final Checklist...

Make sure you have the following along and ready to show when needed.

Proof of citizenship
Tourist card
Mexican insurance
All vehicles registrations and/or proofs
  of ownership, notarized permissions

Notarized permission for children other
  than your own if they are under 18
Written confirmations of any hotel
  reservations
Fishing and hunting licenses

The Logs...

We travel for fun. We also write for fun. Though both of us have had other careers which were financially more predictable and secure, we wouldn't trade places with anyone.

It is also a fact that we don't travel, or write about a destination like most other people in this business. Our energies are directed toward enlightening and enticing the driver to cross the border and experience Mexico in a manner rarely available to the airborne tourist who follows the trail of baits laid by travel agents, hotel chains and tourist departments. We want you to meet the people, hear the sounds and taste the flavors of wherever you might travel. To accomplish this we include many miles of roadlogs (nearly 5000 in this case), hundreds of introductions to people we've met during our travels, and invite you to join us in special restaurants along the way. We also include innumerable bits of trivia that might lend personality to what lies around the next corner.

The concept is one developed in 1973 in order to share Tom's wealth of knowledge about Baja California's beaches, mountains and deserts with others at the time of the completion of the transpeninsular highway. Such has been the success of the format that it has changed little since. We've just kept gathering information and data about the people, the culture, the history, the geography and tried to learn more about the plants and animals of each region.

We acknowledge that it's a lot of work, and that entire winters have gone by without touching a jacket or being far from a fishing rod. Our camper and our pickup both suffer from scratches, driftwood slivers and occasional wheel misalignments. We have sweated while digging out of the sand, held our breath fording unfamiliar streams and sunburnt almost every conceivable body part. We've also hauled around heavy cartons of handicrafts and eaten Mexican food for weeks at a time purely in the spirit of research.

You might wonder why we do it. It's not because of the hackneyed phrase, "Someone's gotta do it.", but because it's a helluva lot of fun, and we enjoy sharing it with anyone willing to take the time to read on...

The Maps...

The major federal highways are outlined on the state maps at the front of each state. Our detail maps are designed up to cover the hubs, or activity centers, of the nine west coast states covered in this book. Though we have maps of all of Mexico's roads in fine detail, space will not allow them all to be used. The ones included serve to expand on the roadlogs while the smaller hand-drawn detail maps cover many of the Pacific beaches.

The first two sets of numbers to the left of each roadlog entry are partial and cumulative mileages. The third column identifies the nearest **Kilometer** post. Thus progress can be noted in miles on the odometer and points of interest identified as to a relative position in kilometer increments. All maps are oriented to be longitudinal with the the page.

We trust that you will find adventures in Mexico leading to many happy memories, and that you'll come back soon.

SONORA

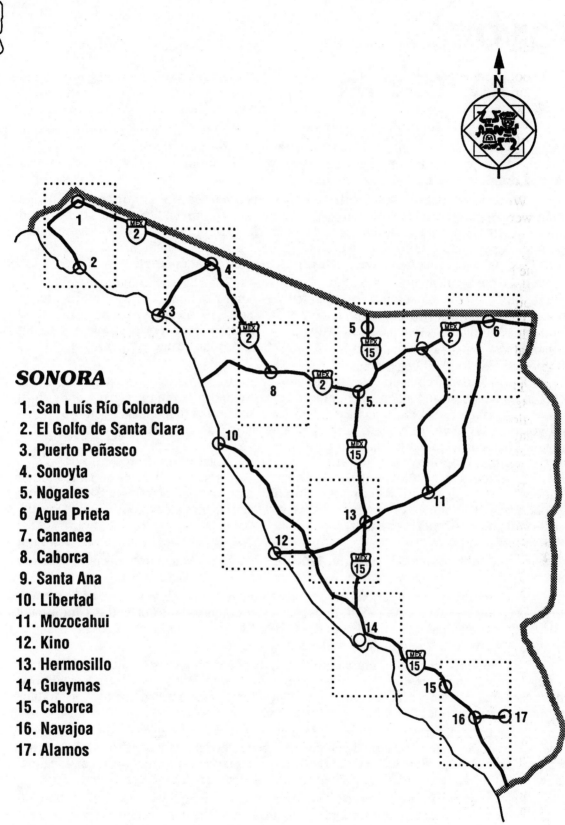

SONORA

1. San Luís Río Colorado
2. El Golfo de Santa Clara
3. Puerto Peñasco
4. Sonoyta
5. Nogales
6. Agua Prieta
7. Cananea
8. Caborca
9. Santa Ana
10. Líbertad
11. Mozocahui
12. Kino
13. Hermosillo
14. Guaymas
15. Caborca
16. Navajoa
17. Alamos

SONORA ...
THE STATE

Sonora, the second-largest state in Mexico, is a desert sandwiched between a living, tranquil sea and scenic, mineral-rich mountains. Until recently it has been largely overlooked...even the traveling Mexican is only now becoming aware of the recreational potential of this magic land across the border from Arizona.

The residents of the past several thousand years...the **Papago, Yaqui, Seri** and **Mayo** Indians...had learned to live in harmony with the harsh environment of Sonora's deserts and near-vertical mountains by adopting a hunting and gathering lifestyle. The closest things they had to permanent residences were the gathering places to which the tribes would migrate annually in order to harvest cactus fruit, acorns, or other edibles.

With the Spanish came agriculture, "civilization," and the requirement that they live permanently around the church. Some adapted well, many did not. The result was pitched battles, starvation and separation of family units. Some of the groups who established mountain strongholds resisted all authority up into modern times. For example, it was not until 1937 that the Yaqui Indians formally ended their resistance and signed a peace treaty with the Mexican government.

The Spanish discovered many things about northwestern Mexico beside the fact that its people were fierce and independent...there was gold and silver in the sierras, and, given water, the productivity of the land was high. They also learned that one had better be a true survivor to make it in the Sonora deserts. Some years it doesn't rain at all and searing temperatures with high winds can decimate a season's crop in hours. The landscape itself is intimidating...volcanic cones, towering, fragmented granitic upliftings, alluvial plains scarred by deluges and endless miles of sand dunes. Rabbits, mice, lizards and a few other creatures have adapted to survival without drinking water, taking their moisture instead from the food they eat. When the desert does receive moisture, it explodes into life, with flowers, insects and small rodents everywhere.

Except in the mountains and at a few select oasis, time moved slowly in Sonora. It was not until Father Eusebio Kino arrived in 1685 that things began to happen. His energy and concern for the Indian brought him a respect most of his contemporaries never had.

The process of "civilization" has not been kind to the original settlers of Sonora. A few Seris live near Bahía Kino and in small beach settlements to the north; the Yaquis have settled around Guaymas and a number of the Mayos live near Navajoa. Even today many of the older Indians refuse to mingle with the Mexicans.

For the *norteamericano* tourist the region has been an almost-exclusive domain of the nearby Arizona resident with a few snowbirds thrown in. But that too is in transition as baby boomers from across the nation begin to look for places to relax, spend their dollars, and maybe retire in a less-demanding atmosphere.

Even today Sonora's coastline is, in the main, remote and little visited. Access is still principally via the water or off-road vehicles. There are dozens of beautiful sandy beaches offering fishing, swimming, windsurfing and other watersports, and another special feature, the luxury and tranquility of an unspoiled beach. At least for a few more years.

Places such as Puerto Peñasco are realizing this and are busy building well-thought-out trailer parks and condominium complexes. The Nuevo Guaymas, or San Carlos, area has proven over the years that investments in Mexico's Sonoran coastline are not only feasible, but desirable. The quality and design of many of the homes in this area is impressive. Bahía Kino too is feeling its oats and will certainly grow over the years.

A good part of Sonora's healthy economy comes from its agricultural development.

SONORA

By harnessing much of the water coming out of the Sierra Madre mountains to the east and applying it to some of the world's richest soils in a fine growing climate, she has created a reputation for quality winter and spring produce. She also grows 38% of the country's grapes and some of the world's finest long-staple cotton.

The introduction, in the '50s, of modern breeding, feeding and processing techniques into Mexico's cattle industry has resulted in a strong market for Sonoran beef, even in the United States and other overseas outlets.

The Sea of Cortéz has also helped Sonora financially and prestigewise. Her Guaymas shrimp set a standard for the industry many years ago and continues to be a valuable export. Other fishery products too have been exploited for years. Unfortunately the extraction of so much sealife has been akin to a rape of the once-rich resources and many scientists are seriously concerned about the future of commercial and sport fishing along the shores of the Cortéz.

SERI INDIAN

We feel that the ingredients are there, and if the positive actions of businessmen and officials at all levels continue an opportunity for unprecedented growth is waiting.

MEXICO 15 — NOGALES — GUAYMAS

NOGALES, ARIZONA, The Town

The southern anchor for **US Interstate 18** and jumping-off point for Mexico, Arizona's **Nogales** is in itself an interesting little city. With a population of about 30,000, it augments rather than duplicates the services available in its cross-border namesake, or *tocayo*. It is Nogales, AZ that offers Mexican automobile insurance. If we had not already made prior arrangements, a dozen offices are ready to serve. Take the #8 exit south off the freeway and drive south through the business district. There are also a number of money exchanges...look for the sign, **Casa de Cambio**.

Nogales, AZ is also the last chance for that symbol of American fast food, the Big Mac. We can also stop at a 7-11 or Circle K, but didn't see a KFC. We fill up on premium unleaded gasoline, for we won't see it again for many thousands of miles. From now on it will be Mexico's new unleaded **magnasin**. A tourist information center located on the right shortly after you enter town gave us all manner of tips on both cities. It was here that we found out about one of Arizona's few wineries, **Arizona Vinyards**.

Owned by Tino and Moira Ocheltree, they probably won't be opening a Sonoma Valley branch for a while yet, but they do have a credible selection. Lois Williams, the lady on duty, not only sampled us liberally but filled us with stories of the region when it was little more than a train stop and perfunctory border crossing. The wines tasted fine, particularly the white burgundy. A rather unique product in today's market, for the Ocheltrees it is a best seller. Most of each vintage is shipped mail order. What may be left over is snapped up within days of its release. Take the **Patagonia** turnoff, only a few yards south of the tourism office and follow it east for 3.6 miles.

NOGALES, SONORA — The City

At 75,000 and growing rapidly, **Nogales** presents the trappings of a border town with a plus...a strong variety of industrial enterprises centered around the burgeoning foreign-owned manufacturing and assembly businesses *(maquiladoras)* and the trucking industry. Nogales was founded in 1880 as a maintenance station and customs office for the railroad. Its name came from the walnut, or *nogal*, tree, of which there were many. During the revolution it was occupied by a variety of armed bands anxious to control the railroad and its access to the United States. Today restaurants, shops, bars and merchandise markets mix with packing sheds, maintenance barns and parts warehouses to make a prosperous, dusty, 4000-foot-high desert city.

Nogales is known for getting very enthusiastic about its **Cinco de Mayo** celebration...somewhat of an oddity in Mexico because most Mexicans look upon the night of the 15th and the 16th of September as their "4th of July." The reason more likely comes down to the economic benefits of promoting the event to their *norteamericano* neighbors. Whatever the reason, many thousands of locals and visitors join together each May 5th and tie on one. ¡**Viva Mexico!**

And Across the Border...

A few meters beyond the border on the right are the **Migración** and **Aduana** offices where they validate our tourist and car permits.

*Bring your positive personal identification in with you, ie: passport (by far the best); birth certificate; notarized affidavit of citizenship, etc. (your driver's license won't work). We also discourage the use of a voter's registration receipt. You must also have the current vehicle registration, and, if you do not have full title, a notarized letter from the legal owner giving permission to bring the vehicle into Mexico. (**See Getting Ready**.)*

We find the officials friendly, though busy. With the car permit, luggage inspected, window sticker in place and validated tourist permits, we're ready for the road. Plan on about an hour for the procedure and double that if it's "getaway time" for a major holiday.

Nogales – Hermosillo Hub Map

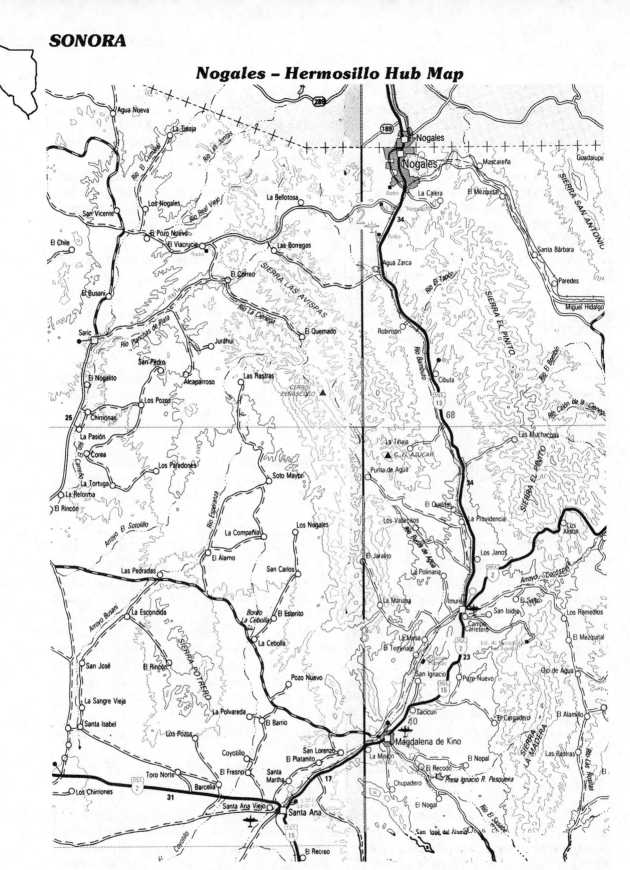

A short reminder on this the first of our hub maps that they are but small portions of the excellent maps we have in our files. By concentrating on the "hub" areas and augmenting them with the highway maps at the beginning of each state and the many individual beach maps, we feel that we are delivering the most possible for the space available. As always, your comments directed to us at Baja Trail Publications will be appreciated.

0.0   0.0   K273   Cross the border, take care of the permits and follow signs south on a one-way street past a full service **Pemex**. A bit farther on the left is a poorly marked supermarket in a large red brick building. It has a fair supply of the basics. *There is a much better selection in Hermosillo*. Several more **Pemex** stations follow, as do some *taquerias*.

1.8   1.8   K270   Just past the statue, the orange building on the left contains the **Las Mesitas** drive-in and a fine plate of tacos made with cabbage instead of lettuce...a sure sign we're in the real Mexico. Continue past several large equipment repair companies and the train station. The area below the station is rapidly filling up with large manufacturing and assembly plants operating under the *Maquiladora* program. There's also a very nice business hotel on the right, the **Marquis de Cima**.

3.4   5.2   K264+   On the right a new, big, top-of-the-line **Holiday Inn**. It is obviously here to serve the businessman working with the nearby *maquiladora*s.

1.6   6.8   K262   Mexico 15 has become a very good four-lane highway between the border and Navajoa...a far cry from what it was even a dozen years ago. We continue south through a broad valley with lots of mesquite and occasional groupings of *matillija* poppies. The train tracks are on the west side, rolling hills backed by the 3600-ft **Sierra El Pinto** peaks are on the east. The Nogales airport is off to the west.

4.4   11.2   K255   One of the drug checkpoints. The northbound lanes are being stopped and inspected for drugs and weapons. Usually a polite question or two suffices, though a full search is possible. These checkpoints do move around...expect them anywhere. Don't be surprised if you are spoken to in perfect English, some of the personnel are (or have been trained by) American DEA agents.

1.5   12.7   K253   We arrive at the ***Migración*** office where the papers we got at the border are inspected. They may also recheck luggage, but when we're lightly loaded they usually wave us through. Continue past a new full service **Pemex** and a mixture of mesquite, small farms and livestock.

7.9   20.6   K240   **Cibuta**, a small town with a school and *Cruz Roja* (Red Cross). Continue south, eventually entering the foothills through a canyon with some running water. Here we can really appreciate the advantages of driving on today's divided Mexico 15.

13.0   33.6   K219   **Estación El Cumeral**, a whistle stop for the train, and one of a number of small towns scattered among the farms and the mesquite. At **La Viguita** we see railroad cars which have been converted into homes for the workers.

8.1   41.7   K206   Intersection with Mexico 2. **Cananea**, **Agua Prieta** and **Douglas, Arizona** are to the east. (**See Sonora Inland.**) A bus depot and a few *taquerias* complete the intersection. There is an impressive monument just after the turn east onto Mexico 2. Continue south over a bridge and into drier land with less mesquite, more ocotillo and other desert plants. At the south end of town there is a stone fountain factory on the left. You can buy 'em right from the *hombre* who makes 'em.

11.4   53.1   K188   Signed paved road (west) to **San Ignacio**, followed closely by a paved road into **Magdalena de Kino**.

A town of 31,000, Magdalena de Kino is one of the mission towns established by Padre Eusebio Kino during the late 1600's. The original site is near the current cathedral of **San Francisco Javier** *in the south end of town. The park fronting the church features a glass-encased crypt containing the bones of* **Padre Kino**. *They lie on the ground, just as they were found about 30 years ago by workers installing a water line. A number of curio shops face the grassy, well-shaded park. Among the offerings are replicas of the poor padre (when he showed less wear) dressed in brown robes and enclosed in glass caskets. The shop owner assures us that they sell very well...in all 5 sizes! Refresco and taco stands are scattered among the gift shops.*

A note on Kino's many mission churches. None of them have survived. Some fell into ruins and disappeared completely while others were replaced by Franciscan churches after the Jesuits were expelled from New Spain in 1767. Return to the highway and continue (left)

past the intersection on a new four-lane bypass.

1.5   54.6   K185   Toll booth. The adjoining parking lot has a touristic display of maps, etc. The road swings east away from Magdalena and into a thick forest of saguaro cactus. This is the first major grouping we've seen.

3.2   57.8   K180   The southern entrance into Magdalena comes in from the right. Continue south on four-lane Mexico 15 through mesquite, saguaro and organ pipe. To the southeast are the **Sierra Cucurpe** mountains.

7.5   65.3   K167+   We have entered the junction town of **Santa Ana**, where Mexico 2 highway comes in from the west. *Beginning in Tijuana, it passes through Tecate, Mexicali, San Luís and Sonoyta before arriving here. The eastern portion to Agua Prieta and beyond begins north of Magdalena de Kino at K206.*

MAGDALENA

In a sense Santa Ana is where it all comes together...Mexico 15. western Mexico's only real north-south highway is crossed by northern Mexico's only east-west highway, Mexico 2. Between the two highways they access all Sonora and Baja California border crossings into western Mexico.

Santa Ana, located on the southeast side of the **Río Magdalena**, had its New Spain beginnings as a rancho in the 1600s. It was visited in 1688 by Padre Kino. Several missions were attempted here but Indian attacks stalled its growth until the end of the 1700s.

*Today's 25,000 residents derive their livelihoods from ranching and farming in nearby arable valleys. Tourism and servicing the many trucks passing through are also major contributors. A full service **Pemex**, a motel or two and a variety of restaurants are along Mexico 15. The biggest fiesta time comes during the celebration of its patron saint, Santa Ana, July 16-26.*

0.8   66.1   K166   An RV park is on the west side of the highway. It has full hookups and looks clean, but not fancy. We leave the outskirts of Santa Ana and head south past a number of irrigated alfalfa fields and a few small fruit orchards.

0.9   67.0   K164+   There is a good-sized rest area with restaurant, police station and overnight parking if necessary.

3.2   70.2   K159+   A new full service **Pemex** is on the west side of Mexico 15. The restrooms are spotless, a welcome relief.

3.3   73.5   K154   Chicken sheds and alfalfa fields are off to the west.

2.4   75.9   K150   We run out of irrigation water about here, thus we are out of the farming area.

2.3   78.2   K146   A full service **Pemex** and a small group of houses.

1.1   79.3   K144   A signed dirt road (east) to **El Peru**. To the west are several mine buildings and tailings on the side of a nearby hill.

2.6   81.9   K140   This portion of the desert is largely made up of mesquite, but as we proceed south it yields to ironwood and *paloverde*.

5.9   87.8   K131+   **Rancho Noria** is signed off to the west on a dirt road. There is a power line extending into the colony several miles away.

3.7   91.5   K126   Road (west) leads into **Benjamin Hill**, a major point on Mexico's railroad system, for the rails from Mexicali and Nogales meet here. There is a full service **Pemex** at the intersection, while a restaurant across the highway sells ice.

1.4   92.9   K123+   A small shrine on the west side of the road.

2.2   95.1   K120   A drug check station for all northbound traffic. A small planting of eucalyptus makes it easy to recognize from a distance.

4.8   99.9   K112   Intersection with Sonora 82 highway to **Querobabi** and a number of ranchos to the east. They are visible out near the center of the valley. The railroad is also down there and we see a train moving north.

6.2   106.1   K102+   A dirt road (east) is signed to **Rancho San Pedro.**

4.5   110.6   K95   There is more ripping up of the desert going on here and it extends well to the south. It is apparently to facilitate the growth of grasses during the rainy season for grazing, but at the cost of a lot of natural vegetation.

3.1   113.7   K90   A sign, *Agua Para Radiador* shows us a tank of water for a thirsty radiator. We don't need it, but it is nice to know that it's available. The clearing process ends for the time being as the road takes a more southerly path.

5.7   119.4   K81   The road makes a slight adjustment (right) and goes straight for a long distance. Just into the run comes **Los Chinos** and a rock chapel with a red roof.

2.8   122.2   K76   A large rest stop is on the right. There are several palm covered *sombras* (shaded areas), parking, a tire repair shop, or *llantera*. Also the restaurant **Guadalajara.** A microwave tower, **Microondas La Colmena** (beehive), is atop a nearby hill, **Cerro La Bandera** (Flag Hill) to the west. The desert off to the east is being cleared. The land is dozed and the trees, cactus, etc., are piled in long windrows for burning.

5.2   127.4   K68   From **El Oasis** a paved road (east) is signed to **Carbo.** There is a small full service **Pemex** on the west side of the road. It is decked out with the new logo and symbol of Mexico's national gasoline industry. The collection of volcanic rock a couple of kilometers off to the right is **Cerro La Cobriza** (Copper Hill).

4.9   132.3   K60   Mesquite and ironwood still predominate with little undergrowth other than grasses and some cholla. Note the at-times heavy infestations of mistletoe on the trees.

3.8   136.1   K54   A graded road (east) is signed to **Rancho Selva.**

5.7   141.8   K45   The desert is gradually working away from the mesquite family and more toward the thick-trunked *copales* and cactus. We also begin dropping slightly toward the 500-foot altitude of the Hermosillo Valley.

4.8   146.6   K37   The highway makes a couple of turns, the first in some time, and continues south with that slight downgrade.

3.1   149.7   K32   A paved road east to **Pesquería.**

7.6   157.3   K20   The mountains in the distance are the **Sierra Madre Occidental.** We are seeing more small varieties of cactus as Mexico 15 continues to descend toward Hermosillo.

6.4   163.7   K9+   The well-signed intersection east on Mexico 21 to **Ures** and the foothills of the Sierra Madre Occidental (**See Sonora Inland.**) and a full service **Pemex.**

1.4   165.1   K7   View of the lake east of **Hermosillo.** The highway continues to drop into the city, finally passing several motels, a cement plant and the **Kino Bay** trailer park on the right.

4.6   169.7   K0   A *glorieta* directs traffic in various patterns to enter or avoid the main section of town which lies straight ahead. Bear left and we go south past a number of businesses and the dam, with a reentry to Mexico 15 after 6 kilometers (3.7 miles). Straight ahead takes us into town along a broad boulevard past hotels, restaurants, supermarkets, **Pemex** stations, etc. The distance through town and out to the *periférico* intersection is also about 6 kilometers.

It is from Hermosillo that many get into the Mexico spirit, for their target will be the **Bahía Kino** *region or* **San Carlos** *and points south. Hermosillo is the last chance for some time to buy a wide variety of grocery products, many with American labels.*

24

SONORA

HERMOSILLO...

The sun shines a lot in **Hermosillo.** Its location in the largest desert in North America would dictate that. Why Hermosillo is here at all is due to the fact that the Jesuits were looking for converts. It has not been a smooth and steady growth since the time when the Jesuit, **Juan Fernandez Cavero** came in 1679. Over the next 60 years **Pitíc** (its Indian name), came and went depending on whether the Spaniards were strong enough to keep the Indians from running away from "civilization" and Christianity. Finally, in 1741, the issue settled itself when there were so few Indians remaining that the new Spanish garrison had nothing left to guard.

In its early days the colony provided much of the foodstuffs needed by the miners in the **Sierra Madre** mountains. Here, where the **Sonora** and **San Miguel** rivers meet, the rich soil and abundant water made the role a natural. It even had its own mint, stamping out gold coins for 30 years. In 1828 Pitíc was renamed Hermosillo and became the capital of the state of Sonora in 1879.

Today more than half a million people take the 110-degree summer temperatures in stride and show themselves to be among Mexico's most energetic citizens. Large amounts of foodstuffs pass through the distribution centers of Hermosillo. Ford Motor Company has an assembly plant from which it ships automobile engines into the United States. The largest cement plant in Mexico is nearby. The hills to the east still contribute large numbers of cattle and many tons of copper and other minerals to the economy. The construction of dams in the foothills and a widespread irrigation infrastructure has added greatly to the productivity of this fertile desert. Grapes, grains and citrus are everywhere.

Old Times in Hermosillo...

How many remember far enough back to when spare tires in Mexico were a rarity? For Tom it went back to the early 60s when he and his group had to stay overnight in Hermosillo while the only retreader in town mixed up a batch of rubber and put a new tread on a trailer tire.

The overnight stay provided them an opportunity for drinks and a huge filet mignon at a tree-shaded downtown outdoor restaurant that had a pet cotamundi tethered near a cement dance floor. The next morning they filled up on chiles rellenos at the Bugambila restaurant, picked up the tire and headed for Bahía Kino and Tiburón Island. The excellence of both the steak and chiles rellenos prompted Tom to stop for a steak and chili rellenos every time he passed through Hermosillo. The tradition continued until the mid 70s.

In 1985 we renewed the stops for the Bugambila chiles rellenos, but could not locate, or remember the name of the tree-shaded steakhouse. It was not until several years later that we asked Matthew, our waiter how long he had worked at the Bugambila. His "Twenty-nine years," answer prompted the question as to whether he remembered the restaurant with the cotamundi. He smiled and said that he did indeed remember the Colores, but that it had closed 15 years ago and the land is now covered by a branch of Bancomer. As to the chiles rellenos...they are still available, but we no longer see Matthew and the quality has dropped dramatically while the price in dollars has more than doubled.

Hermosillo is the home of the **University of Sonora,** and its **Sonora Museum** is highly regarded. An innovative ecological studies center is located just south of town. The **Cathedral** is one of the most beautiful in Mexico and the ornate bandstand in the adjoining plaza is often photographed.

The state's administrative offices are located near the cathedral, lending an impression of organization to the process. Sonora's tourism director is **Alvaro Obregón Luken,** grandson of a hero of the Mexican Revolution and the country's president in the 1920s. Our contacts with him and his staff had much to do with our decision to write this book. Such is the dynamics felt here and elsewhere in Mexico.

Accommodations in Hermosillo are plentiful and wide ranging. They begin at the northeast entrance with two trailer parks, the **Mazocoba** and the **Kino**. Continuing in on Avenida Kino is a **Holiday Inn**, a **Calinda**, several **Valle Grande** hotels and an assortment of independents. A personal favorite from 30 years back is the **El Encanto**. A bit rundown but with thick cool walls, a pool and a comfortable feeling, it is across the street from the **Bugambila**, another old timer. Just past, on the south side of Mexico 15, is **La Siesta**, with its own Sonora beef restaurant.

In Hermosillo restaurants emphasize top quality Sonoran beef and fresh local vegetables. Seafood is also featured, with most of it coming from nearby Kino and Guaymas. We've listed no addresses, only areas, because they're either obvious or the parking is a problem...take a taxi. They know 'em all.

Restaurants we've visited in the highway hotel area include...**Henry's**, fine dining with a good wine list; **Bugambila**, a recent disaster...they must have fired the cooks; **La Siesta**, huge Sonora steaks, but not always "fork tender" and good breakfasts; and **El Potrero**, lots of steaks with a great atmosphere, including **Lencho**, a singing guitarist.

Though recommended, the restaurant overlooking the golf course was a loser...tough steaks and slow service.

In the downtown area we were impressed with the popular **Villa Fiesta** for meats and Mexican dishes; the **El Ranchero** for Argentine-style beef and *cabrito al pastor* (BBQ'd baby goat); a **no-name taquería** (*carne asada, tripa de leche, chilorio de puerco*) under a huge laurel tree at the southwest corner of Rosales and Obregón. It is clean, and cheerful with little tables. If you want seafood, the **Mariscos Los Arcos** has a good selection and high prices.

The main shopping street is Aquiles Serdán. Quality cowboy hats and boots are good buys here.

There are many out-of-the-way places to visit around Hermosillo. We suggest you plan for a few days of touring using the logs in the **Sonora Beaches** and **Sonora Inland** sections. A sunset drive to the top of **Cerro La Capilla** (Chapel Hill) offers some fine views. An ecological center is south of town off Mexico 15. Watch for the sign on the left at K253.

0.0 0.0 K256 Begin at the bridge over the **Río Sonora** near the southern edge of town. Head south past a new-looking, grassy park on the left, a number of services including several beer distributors and a huge new discount store, **Brags**, on the right. The selection here is very wide.

1.9 1.9 K253 Intersection with the Mexico 15 bypass (*periférico*) which skirts the downtown portion of Hermosillo. Continue south onto the divided highway and into open desert. Less than a mile from the intersection is a marked turnoff to the **Sonora Ecological Park**. *We thoroughly enjoyed the well-thought-out displays of native Sonoran plants and animals. Land and aquatic animals are both featured. It is very inexpensive and the self-guided tour takes about an hour and a half.*

3.4 5.3 K247+ A large local **Pemex** for trucks. On the hillside behind the station is a sizable painting of the **Virgin of Guadalupe**. The road has been climbing gently through low hills well covered with ironwood, cactus and a variety of brush and grasses. A few elephant trees (*torotes*) are seen on the hillsides.

8.8 14.1 K233+ **Puente La Poza** (The Pool Bridge), a long bridge across a wash which can easily run full during times of flash floods. This is an indicator of the harshness of the climate. Much of this area is used for grazing cattle during the rainy season. Continue south.

9.3 23.4 K218+ A small rancho with a *capilla* (chapel) bearing the name of **San Francisco**. The many roadside shrines to be seen throughout Mexico are a good indication of the church's influence on the lives of its citizens. Ahead are lots of *chollas*...they come in clusters...sometimes so thick it's impossible to walk through them.

6.6 30.0 K208 The sharp hills of the **Sierra Libre** to the east are full of history for the **Pima** and **Seri** Indians.

Hermosillo Hub Map

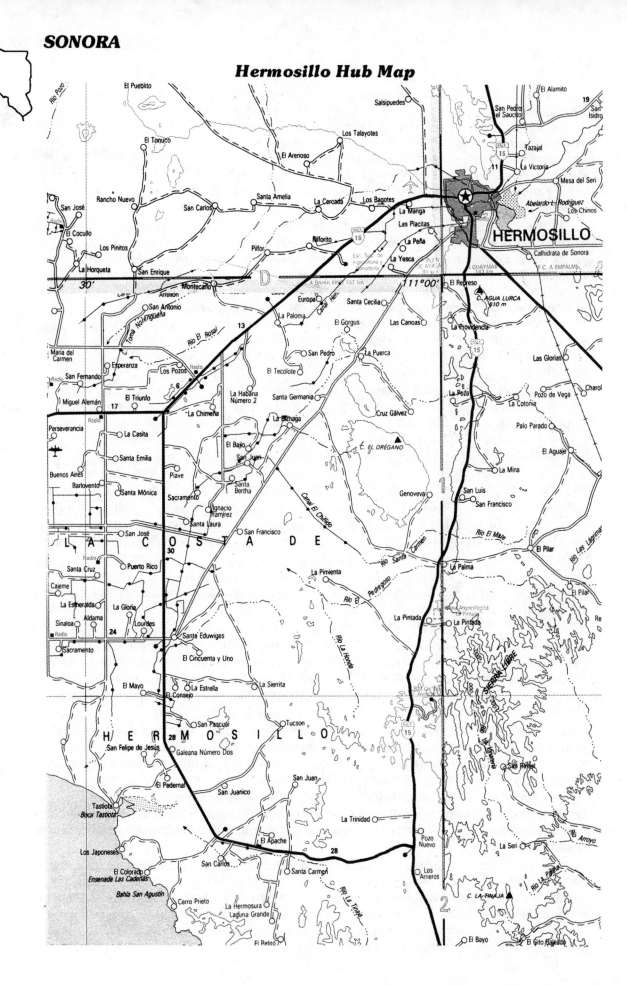

4.1   34.1   K201+ Rest area and **Painted Cave** information center. *To go to the cave cross to the east side of divided highway and drive through the white iron gate. If closed, open and reclose it. At 1.8 miles pass a small, ranch house and bear left. Notice the pinnacled peaks both north and south. Road is a slow one but we see standard cars in the parking area, at 3.7 miles. Don't try it in a motorhome, that would be a loser!*

We take the cement steps toward a small canyon and tiny streambed. At the end of the steps arrows direct us a short distance up the rocks to a viewpoint overlooking a leafy grotto. On the other side is the rock overhang upon which the early people painted their messages. The studies done on the site indicate that they date back to near the birth of Christ. Though not as spectacular as those of Baja's Sierra San Francisco, they do show a number of similarities in design, and are worth the trip. There is no charge, but Alfredo, an energetic and eager young man from the ranch we passed coming in will offer to be your guide. Though he speaks little English, he can take you to the best viewpoints. He works only on donations, so a tip is appropriate. Back to the highway and continue south.

The tree, *Palo San Juan* makes its appearance through here. Short with a heavy trunk, the first branches usually appear at about six-feet. Leaves are elongated, dark green, and rather thick. It is looked upon by many of the rural residents as being of special significance and rarely cut down. Never common, their distinctive color and shape makes them easy to spot.

ALFREDO

7.3   42.3   K190   We are winding gently through low hills. They can be spectacular after the summer rains, their many shadings of green and colorful flowers contrasting against the rock outcroppings. The valley widens as the road continues south.

11.8   54.1   K171   A local **Pemex** (no unleaded). Just beyond, the road from **Kino Bay** comes in from the right. **(See Sonora Inland)** To the south the land is a mixture of desert scenics, tamed and untamed. Cattle graze in the grassy times, rabbits and coyotes, always. We've seen both several times on recent early morning trips.

17.5   71.6   K143   **Puente El Tigre**. The bridge name is indicative of the large numbers of *tigres* (mountain lions) which used to roam this area. The **Sierra Santa Ursula** mountains are to the east.

2.5   74.1   K139   Full service **Pemex** and an intersection with the bypass toll road Mexico 15, to Ciudad Obregón. We continue straight on Mexico 15 for the Guaymas resort areas. **(Bypass log is at end of this log.)**

4.1   78.2   K132+   Turnoff to **San Carlos** on Sonora 17. **(See Sonora Beaches.)**

2.6   80.8   K128+   Road east is to the **airport** and a little-known botanical feature...a desert forest. The name, **Selva Encantada** or Enchanted Forest, overstates the scenic attraction of the place by quite a bit, but it is of interest to plant lovers.

To get there, go past the airport at 0.6mi., and on to the end of the pavement, 2.4 miles. We work our way southeast, following the most used forks into San José de Guaymas, the original site of Guaymas in the 1600's. Once there it is easy to find the brick church which stands on the site of the original (Father Salvaterra, 1701) mission (4.4mi). We then go east from its north side and at about six miles the tall cactus spires are visible ahead. At 7.5 miles we are there.

Here in an area of several acres a hundred or so huge cardón cactus stand almost elbow to elbow with each other and several dozen large senita and organpipe cactus. If you have never been on the road between Baja's Parador Punta Prieta and Bahía de Los Angeles, or around the west entrance into Arroyo de Calamajúe, you might find this of interest. By our observations the claims of some publications that thousands of parrots nest in the cardón forest appear to be outdated...and the lady who directed us here had never heard of them.

SONORA

Back to the highway.

0.9　81.7　K127　Full service **Pemex**. Less than a K beyond is the **Jardines de Xochomilco,** a good *carnes* restaurant with a nice ambiance...but watch for the bugs in the evenings.

0.7　82.4　K126　Turnoff west into **Playa Miramar** hotel and residential area around **Bacochibampo Bay.**

*Let's take a look at the **Hotel Playa de Cortéz,** one of Mexico's oldest resorts that does not lie adjacent to an international border. It all began in 1935 just north of Guaymas at the end of a pair of steel tracks when the **Southern Pacific Railroad** built a deluxe 125-room hotel here on the remote and beautiful* Bahía Bacochibampo.

*You might wonder...why here and why then. Good questions. The here part came because it was near the railroad, at that time owned by Southern Pacific. The why then ties back into the "monkey see, monkey do" syndrome, when rival **Union Pacific** built a resort in Idaho's beautiful **Sun Valley** and brought their guests in by rail.*

*The **Hotel Playa de Cortéz** is an excellent example of the deluxe hotels built during the 20's and 30's. The lobby's vaulted ceilings and the famous wood carvings in the adjoining bar depicting the history of the Guaymas area are part of that era. The Playa's dining room was just that, a dining room. Though formal dress is a long-gone requirement, one can picture the gowns and the formal suits as guests listened to string quartets. Today, dinner music is still a reality, though much more contemporary.*

We get more of that feeling by visiting the suites. Complete with fireplaces and cavernous walk-in wardrobe closets, they are an experience. Advertised rates in 1936 were very high by the standards of the day...$6 to $10 a night American plan! But then, the place was built to have snob appeal, and many were happy to pay. After hard times in the 60s and 70s, the hotel and the grounds are once again well maintained. We and others are finding it fun to return to "yesteryear." Even if only for a few days.

The Playa Miramar area now has a number of deluxe homes sited on the hillsides and along the sandy beach north of the hotel, with more under construction. Another project, a large and modern marina, is well under way and will provide homesites with their own docks. Things are looking up around Playa Miramar. Back to the highway.

Mexico 15 goes to four lanes and curves gently toward the east past the main part of Guaymas. Note the **Zerimar** supermarket. Entrances into the central part of town are marked. They will also take you to the waterfront if you keep heading south.

GUAYMAS

At one time the town of **Guaymas** lived and died with the relative abundance of those lively crustaceans, **shrimp.** For over 50 years the harbor of this busy port was kept busy with the comings and goings of hundreds of the wide-beamed ships with tall booms and decks full of nets known as shrimp boats. It is here in the seas around Guaymas that an especially large and flavorful shrimp lives and reproduces in tremendous quantities. Its qualities were so desirable that the world's most modern processing and freezing plants were imported in order for the world to taste Guaymas Shrimp. To this day the name is a measure of quality in the industry.

No longer does Guaymas have a one-product economy. It is now a shipping port for an increasing number of agricultural products, a shipbuilding center and a magnet for visitors and American retirees alike who find that the good life can be attained here. Satellite developments on sculpted coves, pinnacled hills and sandy beaches have been expanding at a rapid pace, but not so rapid that one cannot still come here and purchase under the the Mexican trust a very adequate home overlooking the **Sea of Cortez** for relatively little money.

Guaymas itself has all of the amenities befitting a modern city of 160,000. Its people are friendly and used to dealing with the American visitor.

The Central city has changed little in the 30 years since our first visit. When visiting the downtown area we park near the harbor and walk the few blocks back to the vicinity of the Central Market. Around here lies some of the finest examples of rural Mexican cuisine to be found anywhere. A few we've tried recently are: **Tacos Cachetón** (someone with very fat cheeks...when you meet the owner, **Aurelio**, you will understand the name) a tiny stand-up eatery across from the Central Market on Avenida Abelardo Rodriguez. Aurelio has never bothered to put up a name, but his window reads, **Tacos #30.** If in doubt, ask anybody.

Off the northwest corner of the *Mercado Central* is a super place for carnitas...**El Flór de Michoacan**. It has sign on the window and is a sit-down. Another, **Lonchería Tony** is near the corner of 20th Street and 15th Avenue *Just north of Banamex, and at the opposite end of the market, it does not open until 6p.m.* They are well known for their *antojitos*, a variety of typical country entrees, including *sopitas, bordos, enchiladas, tamales,* etc. Two of us in mid-1990 had a hard time eating $5 worth of food. All were very good and there are a number of similar-looking little places in the same general area. There are also several fruit and juice stores which offered huge glasses of fresh orange juice.

Continue past power plant and onto the viaduct across an arm of the lagoon.

4.0   86.4   K119+   Paved road south is signed to **Cochorít** and **Playa Empalme**. *At 2.4 miles there is a series of venerable palapa cantinas with lots of cervezas and mariscos, ample parking and a shallow south-facing beach. The area is very flat with only a few dune shapes breaking the near-horizon. A couple of miles to the east we can see several low hills. Empalme beach is probably the coolest place around in the summer. This is no camping beach as such here. Overnight only, with permission.* Back to the highway.

7.8   90.2   K116   Road east and north into Empalme. A railroad and shrimping town of about 70,000, it is lacking in tourist amenities. On the far end of town you see a large collection of "dead" railroad cars from all over North America, even a few switch engines. Continue toward the overpass in the distance.

1.4   91.6   K114   Intersection with Mexico 15D, the bypass toll road we saw above San Carlos.

End of *periférico* bypass log.

Shrimp Trawling...and a Better Way

A common sight along the shores of the Cortéz between September and May are the shrimp trawlers. These 80 to 100-foot boats sporting a handful of long booms to manage the long and heavy nets move laboriously along, dredging the bottom for shrimp. In the process they often bring up large amounts of dead and unsalable sealife such as small halibut, a variety of juvenile corvina and white seabass and other fish plus snails, eels, turtles, sponges, etc., etc. The amount of saleable shrimp taken is sometimes as little as one pound of shrimp for each 100 pounds of sealife which must be thrown away. Truly a waste. We hope that they and other nations which trawl the bottom of the sea for shrimp will soon realize that better shrimp can be raised more efficiently in the controlled environment of fish ponds.

But the unfortunate situation does feed huge numbers of seabirds after the nets are brought to the surface and the shrimp are picked out of the pile. During the moments of separation and dumping of the "trash" fish back over the side a thousand or more seagulls, boobys, man-o-war birds and pelicans may be seen competing for the offal.

Guaymas Periférico Bypass Log...

0.0   0.0   K22   Pass the full service Pemex and go over overpass on to the bypass *periférico* to **Ciudad Obregón** and points south. We can avoid going into Guaymas this way.

3.1   3.1   K17   **Los Faroles** restaurant. *They pour a fine, icy refresco. The place is clean, and the meals look appetizing.* Grapefruit apparently grow well here. Continue through lots a desert with few scars of civilization.

7.8   10.9   K4+   Toll gate. Road narrows to two lanes.

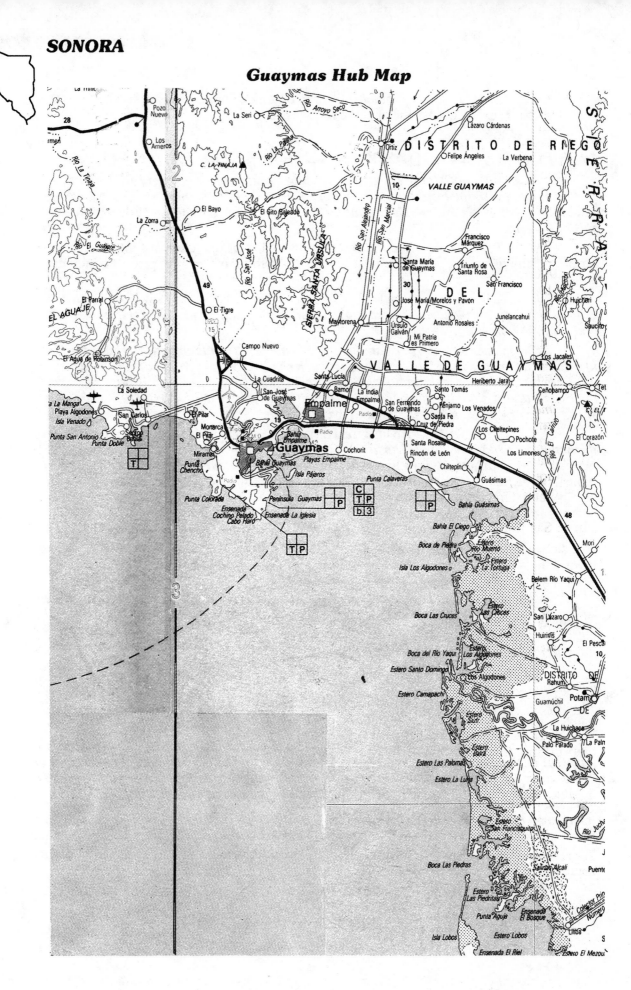

2.2   13.1   K1   Another full service **Pemex** with purified water and ice. We rejoin Mexico 15 just ahead at the overpass at K113.

End of log

MEXICO 15 — GUAYMAS — SINALOA BORDER

This log does not actually begin in Guaymas because of the configuration of the long periférico around the metropolitan portions of the area, including Empalme and its beaches. Instead, we begin at the intersection of the periférico and Mexico 15 about 12 miles southeast of the city center.

0.0   0.0   K108   We are directly under the bridge carrying the southbound portion of the *periférico* and go southeast past a scramble of farming projects, including chickens and hogs.

2.0   2.0   K105   Road (right) goes to **Punta Calaveras**. *We go south on a graded and dusty dirt road. It intersects at 2.5 miles with a well-graded, better-traveled road and we follow it west, then south.*

At 3.8 miles we come to a relatively clean beach. Dirt roads go both directions behind low dunes. There are many opportunities to camp or park. A small fish camp is about a half-mile north, while the road south goes nearly a mile along the beach past numerous opportunities for stopping. The area is quiet, with a tendency to be windy. There are some shells and very little driftwood. Back to the highway.

1.7   3.7   K102   An unsigned dirt road (right) next to a restaurant. *It feeds into the network of roads north of Guasimas. It also deteriorates rapidly.* The hills nearby are of volcanic origin; note the flow lines of the rocks. The area is well populated with the plants typical of the Sonora Desert...cactus, mesquites and a few *copál*. Poultry raising is popular here because chickens like warm weather, don't need much water and a lot of grain is grown nearby, around Ciudad Obregón.

4.4   8.1   K95   A *granja porcina* (hog farm) is next on the left. The steep peaks of the **Sierra El Bacatete** are about a dozen miles to the east. The highway adjusts toward the south, now more closely paralleling the mountains.

0.7   8.8   K94   A dirt road goes southwest toward the Sea of Cortéz.

2.5   11.3   K90   The road (right) across from the cattle-loading pens goes 3km to **Guasimas** while Mexico 15 continues southeast. *The Guasimas road passes through mesquite and cactus accompanied by two lines of power poles over very flat terrain interrupted occasionally by sand dunes.*

It is hard to find the center of Guasimas, but we'll place it in front of the long pier extending out into **Bahía Guasimas**. Most of the people appear to be of Indian extraction, and make their living from the fish, shrimp, crabs, clams and mollusks taken by the many pangas (small boats) pulled up on the beach. There is a pier which goes out about 500 feet. We see a lot of pink murex shells lying about. In fact we end up seeing tens of thousands of them in huge piles along the side roads. These shells sell for a dollar or more in the U.S., while here they can't get rid of them.

A road starts from the pier and follows in a northwest direction for about 0.7 of a mile, then goes around a couple of small hills and back to the water. We can see where others have set up camp and settled in. The area is relatively clean with lots of room...and all of the pink murex shells you might want to carry home. Back to the highway.

9.4   20.7   K75   The hills on the left with the mesa-like formations, form the southern end of the **Sierra El Bacatete**.

7.5   28.2   K68   Paved road (right) toward the **Sea of Cortéz**. We did not check it out.

5.0   33.2   K60   The water from the **Río Yaqui** irrigation system begins to penetrate the desert and we see the results...miles of fields producing two big crops of

wheat a year. Between the harvest and replanting, thousands of cattle feed on the straw and stray wheat.

    1.6   34.8   K57+   The signed road (right) is to **Potam**, from which our map shows roads to **Los Algodones** and **Boca Las Cruces**. (**See Sonora Beaches**.)

    1.5   36.3   K55   The countryside is undergoing a great transformation as the long wet fingers of one of Mexico's most successful irrigation systems reach new tracts of land. Grain is the game here, and it appears to be a winner.

    3.9   40.2   K49   Enter the town of **Vicam**. Thanks to the new four-lane highway project, Vicam now has street lamps and curbs.

    0.6   40.8   K48   A local **Pemex** is on a corner of the paved and signed road (right) to **Casas Blancas** and **Vicam Pueblo**. Beyond are a number of beaches. (**See Sonora Beaches**.) We continue southeast under a pedestrian overpass. Several small hills are off to the right.

    4.0   44.8   K41+   The little clearing signed **Cárdenas** is graced with a couple of stands offering *callos* (scallops), and several more with *cocos helados*.

    1.7   46.5   K38+   Graded road (right) is signed to **Torin**. Continue east with the railroad tracks on the left.

    5.4   51.9   K30   We have dropped toward the river bed and the increased subsurface water is reflected in the larger mesquite trees. We drive past **Jori**, a small intersection with a dirt road.

    2.3   54.2   K26+   More irrigation canals, including one with a small waterfall. We come to a paved intersection (right) into **Bacum**. *Bacum is another one of the Indian villages here in the rich and fertile Yaqui Valley. The valley's network of roads links thousands of fields growing an astounding variety of grains and vegetables.* Continue east through more miles of wheat.

    6.2   60.4   K16+   **Lomas de Guamúchil**, a small group of houses and the **Choffy** restaurant. The sign is visible only to north-bound traffic.

    1.9   62.3   K13+   We turn gradually from east to south and into the flood plain of the **Río Yaqui**. Here huge cottonwoods dominate the scene...some trunks are over six-feet in diameter. Next, the bridge over the riverbed and no water. It's all in the irrigation canals networking throughout the valley.

    3.6   65.9   K7+   We are now in the satellite community of **Esperanza**. To the right a signed, paved road goes to **Cocorít**. Ahead on the left is the Ciudad Obregón golf course. Lined with large trees, it is a bright green despite the heat. Next comes a tank farm.

    2.6   68.5   K3+   On the right are four adjoining open-air restaurants that offer an unbeatable selection of the foods of northwest Mexico. *One features **carnitas**, another, **mariscos** and the third some of the best **carnes asadas** we've ever had, while the fourth has great barbecued chicken. Another excellent restaurant, the **Carnitas Uruapan**, is located about 200 yards beyond. You can also get any of it **para llevar** (to go). The problem is not in stopping, but deciding where to eat.*

    2.2   70.7   K0   The edge of **Ciudad Obregón** is delineated by a full service **Pemex**, a couple of hotels, and a line of traffic signals.

The city of Ciudad Obregón was founded in the 1920s on the site of an old Yaqui village, and is actually located within the Yaqui Indian reservation.

Obregon's explosive growth to more than 400,000 can be traced to the foothills of the Sierra Madre Occidentál and the dams of **Angostura** and **El Novillo**, for it is here the water is stored for the extensive irrigation systems of the Yaqui valley. Even if you had arrived in town without seeing the surrounding countryside, the many storage elevators, grain mills, cotton gins, and associated industries tell the story. Here is some of the richest

33

farmland in North America.

Though we've never stayed in Obregón, inspections and recommendations assure us that the **Valle del Yaqui, Valle Grande Nainari, Costa de Oro**, or the **San Jórge** will prove to be more than adequate. The town has a number of good-looking open restaurants. Our love affair with the restaurants just north of town has limited our in-town eating to only the **Xochimilco**. Located toward the south end of town on the west side of the street, we can stuff ourselves on a mixed grill concoction called a *parilla*, (carne asada, guacamole, green onions in lime water, and salad with vinaigrette dressing) at a reasonable price. The nearby **Mr. Steak** restaurant on the east side of the highway has been recommended. If you're a fried chicken addict, you are rarely more than a few hours from a fix...try **Neil's Fried Chicken** sometime. It is very good, and it's all over Mexico.

The town has few close-in tourist attractions but the surrounding lakes, particularly **Lake Obregón** provides good fishing for bass and catfish. Dove and duck hunting are popular wintertime activities around the canals, marshes and grain fields of the valley and the Yaqui delta. Day visits can also be made to a variety of local beaches. (**See Sonora Beaches.**)

A downtown intersection is signed (west) to **Laguna Narnari**, a popular recreational lake located on the edge of town. On Sundays it is usually jammed with families. *There are several supermarkets and major department stores, so essentials, and many luxuries, are not a problem.*

2.1 72.8 K223 At the south end of the central city area the road makes a jog (left), while a road (south) is signed to **Pueblo Yaqui**. Take the southeast road, it turns south very shortly and goes past another **Pemex** and a whole bank of industrial plants, including flour mills and grain storage sheds. Note the new K markers.

3.0 75.8 K218 A large, new **Modelo** brewery is on the left. A poultry food plant is next, then, in the next few miles, lots of chickens to feed it to.

4.3 80.1 K211 A graded road (left) goes over the railroad tracks and toward *microondas* **La Cabana** relay station on a nearby hill. Just beyond is a small full service **Pemex**, then the entrance to the **Obregón Airport**. The mountains visible off to the east have a number of sharp pinnacles among the many peaks visible...though not unique, they are striking. Continue southeast.

2.4 82.5 K207 A graded road (right) is signed to **Ejido Francisco Villa**. As a symbol of Mexico's internal struggle in the early 20th century for a more representative form of government, there are literally hundreds of cities, towns, villages and ranchos named after this charismatic man. This Villa namesake has several water tanks, unpaved streets and many shade trees. The next group of houses belongs to the community of **El Henequen**.

4.4 86.9 K200 A citrus orchard of sorts with grain fields all around it. The land above the railroad tracks is yet to be cleared, and its scrub, cactus and small mesquite trees are in contrast to that west of the tracks. Ahead comes a new, full service **Pemex** on the right and the little town of **Fundación**.

1.8 88.7 K197 A signed road, Sonora 4, goes right to **Villa Juarez**. Continue southwest past an increasing number of poultry sheds. The scrub and cactus predominate, as no irrigation water has gotten this far.

7.6 96.3 K185 The grain fields are alternately dark plowed earth, growing green, ripening golden and charred black as they go the cycle twice a year.

5.1 101.4 K177 A large poultry operation is on the right. There are at least 20 long sheds in the complex, plus several other outbuildings. The people here have realized the conversion efficiency of chickens in creating meat protein. They far surpass any other popular form of meat-producing animal.

1.9 103.3 K174 A paved road (right) is signed to **Nueva Bacame**.

4.0 107.3 K167+ A paved road goes (right) to **Villa Juarez**. Another road to Juarez also intersects Mexico 15 at K197.

Obregon--Navajoa Hub Map

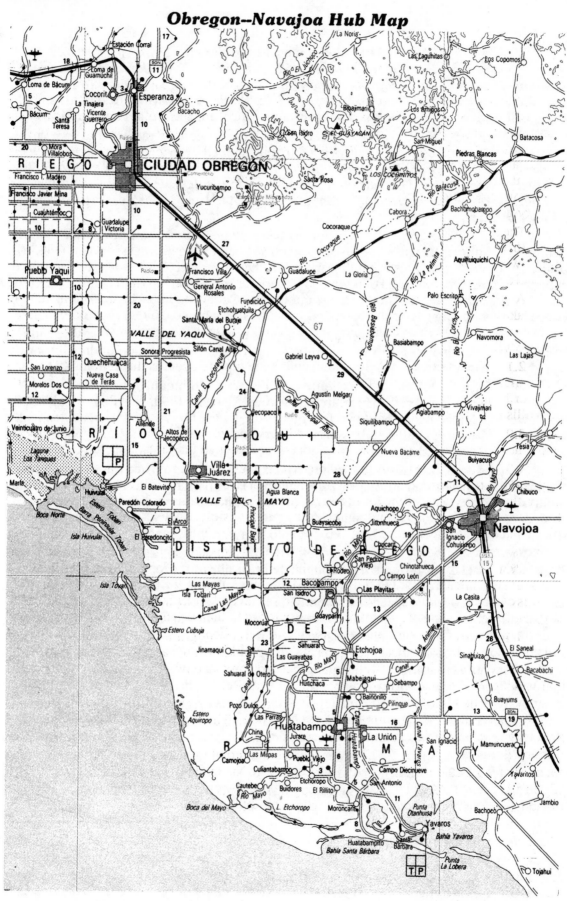

2.8   110.1   K161+   The intersection with the **Navajoa** bypass *periférico. This bit of road is designated as Sonora highway 159 and takes a 13+ kilometer route around Navajoa through fields of safflower, along the riverbottom area of the* **Río Mayo** *and eventually reconnects with Mexico 15 at K153 at the south end of town.* We continue straight past the **El Rancho Motel** (some rooms have kitchenettes) and the bridge over the **Río Mayo**.

1.4   111.5   K158+   The **Motel Del Río** is on the right. A rather large complex of rooms, pool, bar and restaurant, it has a good feeling about it...especially the kitchen. *Where we were able to bring in our own live shrimp to be prepared (Lousiana-style) for only a nominal service charge. (The charge might have been higher had we not shared with the chef and the rest of the kitchen staff.)* Continue south past the **Los Caporales** restaurant and a number of others.

1.6   113.1   K156   Intersection to **Alamos** and **Huatabampito. (See Sonora Inland and Sonora Beaches.)** A supermarket is located on the northeast corner. Continue past a good *pollo asado* restaurant on the right, then a full service **Pemex** and adjoining supermarket. At the south end of town, the **Colonial Motel** is on the right. Mexico 15 turns slightly left and continues almost due south toward Culiacan. This portion of Navajoa is concentrating on large agriculture-related industries, much like Ciudad Obregón.

1.7   114.8   K153   The Navajoa bypass comes in from the right. We continue south on the two-lane Mexico 15 past a full service **Pemex**. This portion of the highway is slated for expansion momentarily, and should be completed before the end of 1991.

1.9   116.7   K150   On the left, a new brewery, **Culiacán Cuauhtémoc**. Poultry sheds continue to proliferate. There are are also more wheat fields, plus some safflower. Safflower is a leafed plant about two feet high with golden brown seed heads when ready to harvest. When it is cut the stubble has a silvery sheen.

5.2   121.9   K142   We are looking at a new development which looks to be in the "that's a good idea" category. It is called **El Trailero** and consists of a number of small family-operated restaurants along the back edge of a large parking area. The place came into being since January of 1990. At this moment the parking lot is hosting several busses and passengers are wandering about, munching on a variety of goodies. There are also several trucks and cars. After Mexico 15's expansion to four lanes this place will surely find more business.

1.3   123.2   K140   69.3 A spot on the west side of the road again might be a sign of things to come...The restaurant, **El Abajeño**, advertises *cabrito* (baby goat) and other favorites and a few trailer spaces for overnighters. It is new, clean and the staff friendly. We wish them well. A short distance past, a dirt road (left) is signed to **Ejido Saniál**. It disappears over the railroad tracks and into the desert. Our map shows the road continuing for many miles back into the arroyos and watersheds of the hills to the east.

2.4   125.6   K136   The small community of **Bacabachi** is on both sides of the highway. The **Sierra Alamos** range is on our left. Behind it lies the fascinating town of Alamos. **(See Sonora Inland.)**

4.5   130.1   K128+   **Huatabampo** is signed to the right on a paved road via Sonora 19 highway. This is another route to get to the beaches near **Huatabampito. (See Sonora Beaches.)**

3.1   133.2   K124   The fishing village of **Yvaritos** is on a signed dirt road (right) which ends up at the lagoon in about 4 miles. The highway approaches the volcanic hills on the left. Note the *microondas* repeater station on top of one of them.

3.7   136.9   K118   The road (left) is signed as going to the microwave tower noted above. The name, **Masaca**.

2.6   139.5   K114   A paved road (right) is signed to **Las Bocas**, a local beach resort and vacation cottage area. **(See Sonora Beaches.)** Continue southeast past more Sonora desert. The railroad tracks are still on our left. *We have been surprised at the rate at which*

the modernizing of Mexico 15 has progressed during the past 18 months on our almost-constant travels though this region. The politicians have promised to have Mexico 15 a four-lane highway from Nogales through the state of Nayarít by 1994.

2.3   141.8   K110   There's a large white **Tecate** beer sign identifying a tiny restaurant. The sign looks bigger than the building.

3.3   145.1   K105   There is considerable roadwork off to the left, shortly to be two more lanes for Mexico 15. *There are five adjoining crosses with new flower wreaths on the west side of the highway. Next to it is a badly mangled car, a gory reminder of the deadly weapons we all drive. Maybe such monuments along American highways would help reduce our nearly 60,000 traffic deaths each year.* Next is the small town of **Rosita**.

Note the numbered markers along the railroad tracks, they denote the distance in kilometers from where the railroad begins in the city of Mexicali, Baja California.

6.8   151.9   K94   **Ejido Tierra y Libertad** (Land and Liberty). It derives some of its activity from being next to the large milling plant just ahead. A cattle feeding and dairy operation is next, then a full service **Pemex**.

2.0   153.9   K90+   **Ejido Juan Escutia** follows closely. *Juan Escutia was one of the teenage military cadets who defended Chapultepec Castle in Mexico City from American soldiers in 1847. Rather than surrender to far superior forces, Escutia wrapped himself in his country's flag and jumped to his death from one of the parapets. Touched by his bravery, the Americans withdrew.*

3.8   157.7   K85   **Ejido Francisco Sarabia** is on the right. It has several water tanks and appears well laid out with lots of open space. There are many shade trees, and the community stretches along Mexico 15 for about a mile. Immediately adjacent is **Ejido 24 de Febrero**, and it extends for some distance before yielding to poultry sheds and desert. Logically, farther from town and downwind, a pig farm. We continue southeast.

6.1   163.8   K75   Here's a rarity for this part of the world...a eucalyptus tree.

3.2   167.0   K70   An agricultural inspection station. No stop necessary for vehicles going south but northbound vehicles will be asked if they are carrying any fruit. There is also a full service **Pemex**.

0.7   167.7   K69   The sign on the right indicates our arrival at the border between **Sonora** and **Sinaloa**. Welcome to Sinaloa.

End of log.

Wash Your Windows Señor?

One of the newer entrepreneurial efforts in Mexico has to do with windshields, or parabrisas. It begins when one or two youngsters begin washing yours without even asking. And it can happen anywhere, a parking lot, traffic signal, Pemex station...even a traffic jam.

Before there is time to react they are at it, whisking away the grime with a big smile. And they don't appear too disappointed if someone refuses to kick in. If our window is clean they sometimes shy away. We found that arm waving and a loud "No!" works about half the time.

Times are tough down here, and it is a fairly harmless way of contributing to the cause. Our usual "donation" is the equivalent of a dime.

MEXICO 2 — SAN LUIS — MEXICO 15 AT SANTA ANA

San Luís Río Colorado, altitude 130 feet, hot, dry and windy. This northwesternmost town in Sonora is rapidly approaching 100,000 population. Its position next to the American border overlooking the **Río Colorado** provides San Luís with its main reasons for existence...a busy commercial life across the border (including maquiladora assembly plants for international corporations) and provisioning the many productive cotton and wheat farms in the river delta. While growing, tourism has yet to become much of a factor in the everyday life of San Luís.

Generally the best place to exchange money around San Luís is at any of the many banks. They are open from 9:30 to between 11:00 and 12:30 (depending on the policy of the moment), Monday through Friday (but watch out for the bank holidays, there are lots of 'em). If they are closed, there are always money exchanges (casa de cambio) on both sides of the border.

We enter Mexico via **San Luís** 25 miles south of **Yuma**, Arizona...**Note:** Tourist and car permits are not required to go to **El Golfo de Santa Clara**.

0.0   0.0   K201   Cross the border and stop at the **Migración** office on the right to get tourist permits validated. Go one block south to the signal and turn east (left). *Do not turn right as that goes to El Golfo de Santa Clara.* **(See Sonora Beaches.)**Continue east on Mexico 2 toward Sonoyta. There are a number of services to the east, including several **Pemex** stations and the **Taquería El Rey**.

2.5   2.5   K197   A full service **Pemex** station followed by the *panteón* (cemetery) and an industrial park. Here a number of foreign, mostly American, companies have built assembly facilities in order to take advantage of Mexico's lower wage scales. The American border is only a hundred yards north of the highway and parallels it for some distance. To the south a small aqueduct brings water into San Luís from the east.

7.5   10   K185   The land is uncommonly flat, maybe a bit like the plains of western Nebraska or California's San Joaquín Valley. Off in the distance ahead are the **Gila** and **Cabeza Prieta** mountains. The vegetation is mainly creosote bush and a few small scrubby plants.

4.7   14.7   K177+   Agricultural inspection station and an occasional checkpoint for drugs and weapons. Ahead is the sideroad to *microondas*, **El Desierto**.

7.5   22.2   K165+   A restaurant popular with passenger busses. The surrounding area has been dubbed "The ejido of the agricultural reform!" They've got a big challenge here.

7.8   30.0   K153   Abandoned buildings of the ill-fated **Ejido Sinaloense**. This is one of several along this stretch of Mexico 2. *One can imagine the heartache the farmers and their families felt as they realized that the dream of their own "little plot of land" was evaporating in the shimmering desert.* Ahead is a paved turnout where you can look at one of the desert's unique plants...the smoketree (*Psorothamnus spinosa*). *Found in low Sonoran desert environments as far north as Palm Springs and south to near Hermosillo, its upright growth, gray-green foliage and springtime burst of tiny purple flowers make a handsome combination.*

9.4   39.4   K138   We pass between the **Tinajas Atlas** mountains on the US side and the **Sierra El Rosario** range to the south. Several species of cactus begin showing, along with increasing numbers of ironwood, paloverde and ocotillo. Note the mistletoe in the ironwood. You will find it also in mesquite and paloverde. A parasite, it may eventually kill its host.

4.7   44.1   K130+   Roadside rest. Marked **Area de Descansar**, they are found sporadically throughout this part of Mexico. They are usually around a shade tree and might encompass cement benches, a table and a place to build a cooking fire. They provide a welcome break. In a short distance there is a little chapel (*capilla*) on a rocky rise, then a small

San Luis Hub Map

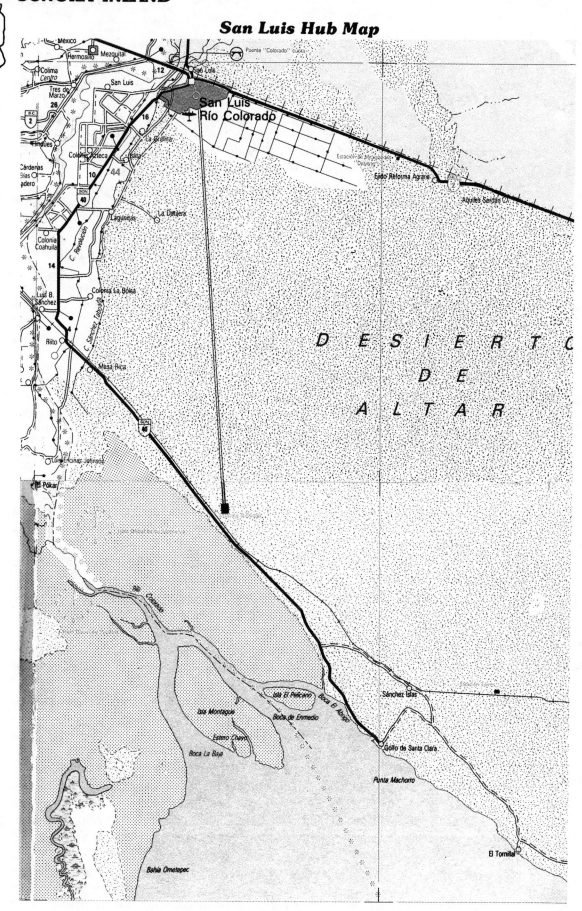

restaurant serving meals and cold "*refrescos.*" Its name...**La Joyita** (Little Jewel).

 2.8 46.9 K126 Road (right) to microondas **Cerro Pinto**. The first saguaro cactus of this log is seen near here. Beyond is **El Saguaro** restaurant. Adjoining is a small, yellow-domed Moorish style chapel. Here we start our climb into the hills.

 5.0 51.9 K118 First of two adjacent rest stops. Note the rough, steep slope of the hills, an indication that they are geologically young, probably less than 250,000 years. As erosion progresses they will become more rounded, thus showing their age. Continue a gentle, winding climb among increasing stands of ironwood and saguaro.

 5.6 57.5 K109 Top of a small pass, altitude 1200 feet. Follow curve to left and begin a descent past increasing stands of saguaros. Road straightens and drops into a valley.

 7.2 64.7 K97+ **La Mina del Desierto.** We were unable to determine exactly what they might have mined, but the ultimate result has been a restaurant. And not a very busy one at that.

 9.4 74.1 K82+ Another small restaurant. The terrain has changed noticeably. More grassy areas, with some trees and cactus. About 3 miles ahead watch to the north for a heavy stand of *chollas*. You wonder...why so many and why there?

 5.2 79.3 K74 Turn southeast past volcanic rocks and the turnoff to microondas **Cerro Lava** through typical desert terrain...*cholla, saguaro, ocotillo.*

 6.4 85.7 K63+ A narrow road south leads toward the **Pinacate** mountains but it goes only a short distance, ending at **Papago Tanks**.

 2.9 88.8 K59 **Los Vidrios** restaurant and a local **Pemex**. To the south is a very poor graded road into the eastern portion of the **Parque Nacionál de Gran Desierto del Pinacate**. We were warned by the *Angeles Verdes*, Green Angels, not to attempt it. They recommended a road 8km to the east.

 4.5 93.3 K51+ A signed road into the **Pinacates**. This is the one recommended by the *Angeles Verdes*. **(See Sonora Inland.)** The road eventually ends up at K59 on the **Puerto Peñasco** road. *We emphasize...**do not** attempt the road alone unless you are **very** knowledgeable in desert travel, as the region offers practically nothing to help anyone survive. You would be completely on your own should you have a breakdown or get lost.*

 4.1 97.2 K45+ A rest area under huge *paloverde* trees here. Road alternates between winding through hills and going straight across small valleys.

 10.6 107.8 K28+ Dirt road south to **Ejido Cerro Colorado**. Some years ago the area was a major source for the red lava rock so popular in landscaping throughout the southwest.

 2.5 110.3 K24+ Enter a valley loaded with mesquite. As it thrives on near-surface water, the valley would be a logical place to dig a well...a wisdom not lost on early settlers throughout the Sonora Desert.

 3.8 114.1 K18+ **El Papilote** (Kite or Windmill) restaurant. It appears to have a good following among truckers.

 8.4 122.5 K5 The town of **Sonoyta** is off to the southeast. The airport is just ahead. Beyond that on the north side of road is a champion junk yard. *Only a few years ago a friend found a Mazda rotary engine here to replace his blown one. It was in perfect condition and showed only 6,000 miles on the odometer. The price...including takeapart, just $150!*

 3.1 125.6 K0 **Sonoyta**. Altitude 1200 feet, population 15,000. Highway north leads to border, 3 km, where tourist permits are validated. Car permits are obtained about 15 miles south of the intersection. Welcome to Sonoyta.

 Many references spell it with an "i" but the residents show a preference for the "y" version. So Sonoyta it is, this elongated border connection for three roads that intersect here...from San Luís Río Colorado via Mexico 2, Puerto Peñasco along Mexico 8, and points

SONORA INLAND

east and south on Mexico 2 and 15.

The town is primarily into trucking and related services. Though tourism is not a big part, there are souvenir shops and restaurants with English menus. For the locals we see at least one *mueblería* (furniture store); a couple of *depositos* (warehouses) for sodas and *cervezas*; several *tiendas* (markets); a *panadería* (bakery) and a tortilla factory. As for the people, they are a cheerful lot, particularly on a holiday...

We are in Sonoyta. It is November 16th, the day children of all ages dress up in costumes representing their national heroes and parade through the streets of Mexico. Our particular parade lasted a good hour. As they trooped and rode by we counted more than 35 Pancho Villas (some too little to walk), two one-armed Alvaro Obregons, several Benito Juarez's and a Carranza or two. One truck even had a diorama of about a dozen of the top heroes all sitting around a table drinking Coca Colas. And there was not a smile on any face...just painted beards and moustaches.

NIÑOS HEROES

Ranchers, bandidos, farm workers and girls in costume are riding on tractors, in the backs of trucks, on the hoods of cars and walking. Even the town taxi brigade is here, loaded with youngsters. Everybody is singing patriotic songs and shouting "Viva Mexico." There are exercise battalions, a bicycle group, several troupes of costumed Indian dancers. We stood with the adults lining the streets cheering everyone who participated. A truly stirring experience.

You might as well get out and watch, because you won't be going anywhere anyway...the cops shut off all of the streets. Enjoy it. We did.

Note: If you plan on crossing the border here, be aware that the US-Mexico border is closed between midnight and 6am. The town of Sonoyta is two miles south of the border.

0.0   125.6   K254   The intersection with Mexico 2. Cross the bridge and look (left) to a tiny white *taquería*...good tacos. A larger *Carne Asada, Aguas Frescas* stand is on the right. We've also had good meals in the **Cafe Excelsior**. Continue past a full-service **Pemex** and up a slight rise.

1.3   126.9   K252   We climb south out of the valley past a lot of *tuna* cactus. The **Sierra Cubabi** rises sharply to the east. Soon the road takes a southeast direction. The rocks are beautiful through here, as are the numerous desert plants.

13.4   140.3   K230+   A small blue *capilla* in a rest area with shaded benches and table.

3.9   144.2   K224   **San Emeterio.** Here is the big immigration check station you **don't** pass unless everything is in proper order. It is here (June 1990) that you obtain your vehicle permit and have your vehicle inspected.

IMPORTANT...We hope that you have read the front part of this book before you left home, for your problems could be big ones if you do not have the proper documentation. It is against Mexican law to have in your possession a car which you cannot prove is yours. You must have a registration which matches up with your identification or, if it is financed, leased or owned by your company, etc., you must have a notarized statement of permission to take it into Mexico in order to proceed farther. You might sneak by here with some sort of story, but if there is a problem later, you may have a terrible time proving that you own the car. These regulations are being more strongly enforced each year, as the car theft problem in the U.S. increases.

The car theft game these days seems to be to steal a car and fence it to someone who runs it past a non-vigilant American customs official and across the border to a ready market for cheap car parts...many of which end up back in the United States.

The Mexican customs system works this way (today at least)...we take our car registration and tourist permit into the second building. The officer confirms that we are the legal, registered owners, and have the proper notarized permission to have the car in Mexico. We next go to the first building, where another officer types out the papers and issues the window sticker. His assistant sticks the permit on the windshield (*parabrisas*) after verifying the **Vehicle Identification Number**, or **VIN**.

The last step is to drive to the third building and park in the shaded inspection area. Shortly someone comes out, inspects the papers, asks a few questions and takes a look around inside. *As we don't have contraband...washing machines, TVs, new computers in boxes, etc., we are told to enjoy our stay in Mexico.*

The whole procedure can take as little as 10 minutes...up to an hour if they are busy. The office is open 24 hours, every day. And if we were to have a pickup full of **contrabando**? That's another story. We might have to pay an import tax based on the value of the merchandise. Or told to go back across the border and return without it.

Continue up the hill toward a new and modern *microondas*, **Cerro de La Silla** (Chair Mountain), another reminder of Mexico's efforts to modernize their country.

0.5   145.2   K223   The altitude at the top of the rise is 1750 feet. The road below is straight for as far as we can see.

5.0   150.2   K215   Cross riverbed. Ahead the dirt road west is signed to **Quitovac**, a Papago Indian village. Ahead, the **Cafe Lucy** is almost hidden by the many trucks parked around it. Note the mistletoe in the trees. The road is still straight.

9.4   159.6   K200   Lots of plants through here...several varieties of ironwood, mesquite and *paloverde*. No turns yet.

11.6 171.2   K181+   The highway makes a slight turn toward the east...very slight. Continue straight on a new course. *As we move from one side of a hill to another, or closer to a watershed, the vegetation can change markedly. Variations in the types of cactus will be noted, ironwood is replaced by mesquite or paloverde. Saguaros come and go, as do ocotillo and agave, etc. You might want to watch for an unusually dark purple-hued nopal cactus. It is found in only a few spots in Mexico and the southern U.S.*

3.7   174.9   K175+   Road makes a slight correction toward the west...then straight again. Just ahead is another microondas, **Cerro Gamo** (Deer Hill), about a half-mile off to the east. There are more specimens of the pencil-type *cholla*.

7.0   181.9   K164   Road makes another slight turn. Altitude now 1100 feet.

11.5 193.4   K145+   Two rest areas, one on each side of a bridge. Ahead is another turn, the fourth in about 50 miles. Mountains off to the left are the **Sierra La Gloria**. The highest peak (toward the south end) is 4300-foot **Cerro El Alamo**.

9.7   203.1   K130   Road begins to wind through the hills. On left is a microondas, **Cerro Basura** (Trash Hill!). Road straightens again after a couple of Ks.

8.3   211.4   K116+   A check point for weapons and drugs for cars going north. As you go by look back and note how well it is marked for approaching vehicles. Nobody should be surprised that one is coming up.

5.9   217.3   K107   We are at the outskirts of **Caborca**. *There are two motels here that we've seen in the downtown area and we chose to stay in the **Posada Caborca**. It was a bad choice. Not only were the rooms dirty but the sheets were threadbare. The other motel, the **Camino Real**, turned out to be much better. If we ever stay in Caborca again, it will be there.*

*Caborca doesn't have much to offer locally but it is a good jumping-off point for the the networks of paved and graded roads south and west leading to all kinds of beaches. (See **Sonora Beaches**.) A quick tour of the downtown will locate a variety of services and the **Padre Kino** church. We cross the railroad tracks, go past the station and the town.* Continue toward Santa Ana. Note the large plantings of grapes and citrus.

7.4   224.7   K95   Road south into **Pitiquitos** at a full service **Pemex**. Continue southeast past another road into town and the railroad crossing. Note the fields of maize or

Kaffir corn. A road leaves the south end of town toward **Puerto Lobos** and other seaside settlements. The amount of agriculture and large numbers of mesquite trees indicate a good supply of subsurface moisture.

13.7 238.4 K73 Enter the town of **Altar**, population, 10,000. Watch out for the *topes*...they are beauties. The paved highway north is Sonora 64, which leads to several new agricultural areas. A bit further into the business section is the *taquería*, **Asadero La Herradura**. Excellent *tacos de carne asada* for very little money. They serve no *cervezas*, only *refrescos*. Back in the car and we're out of town in a moment. Coming up is the microondas, **Cerro Altar**, and back into drier landscapes with lots of *ocotillo*.

14.3 252.7 K50 The road stretches straight to the horizon. No turns, no nothing. More desert cactus and ironwood as we continue southeast. Ahead a graded road is signed southwest 22km to **Las Trincheras**.

5.6 258.3 K41 Another microondas, **Molino de Viento** (Windmill). Road continues straight in a south-southeast direction through rolling hills toward a large broad valley. Altitude about 2200 ft, dropping a bit as we approach **Santa Ana**. Mountains to the north are the **Sierra Potrero**.

19.2 277.5 K10 To the south is a prosperous looking ranch complex. There's lots of mesquite in the bottom of the valley. Ahead is a view of **Santa Ana**. Pass a local **Pemex** for truckers. There is **magnasin** at the **Pemex** stations in town.

6.2 283.7 K0 **Santa Ana** has a reputation for its *taquerias*. We've tried several with good results. There are a couple of hotels here, if you're in a pinch.

Santa Ana, located on the south side of the Magdalena river, had its beginnings in New Spain as a rancho in the 1600s. It was visited in 1688 by Padre Kino. Several missions were attempted here but Indian attacks stalled growth until the end of the 1700s.

Today's 25,000 residents derive their livelihoods from the ranching and farming the nearby arable valleys. Tourism and servicing the many passing trucks are also major contributors. A full service Pemex, a motel or two and a variety of restaurants are along the highway. The biggest fiesta time here comes during the celebration of its patron saint, Santa Ana, July 16-26.

End of log.

LOS PINACATES NATIONAL PARK

*It may sound incongruous to associate a beetle with a national park, but it appears that the Pinacate mountains of northwest Sonora just may have been named after a slow-moving black beetle which stands on its head when threatened, reminding someone alongthe line of the region's many cinder cones. The **Pinacate National Park** represents a particularly unspoiled, yet unique, portion of the **Sonoran Desert**, which in turn is a major part of the **Great Basin Desert of North America**.*

*Encompassing several hundred square miles, the **Parque Nacionál** is centered around **Cerro Pinacate** and the cinder cones and fissures associated with this major area of volcanic activity. Many of the plants here are endemic (found nowhere else) as this is an area much different than that around it...an ecological island, as it were. The western margins of the Pinacates are slowly drowning in oceans of sand blown up from the Sea of Cortéz while to the north, east and south alluvial plains and a few minor ranges of sedimentary origin provide effective barriers to extensive migrations of plant and animal lifeforms.*

There has been little development of the Pinacates, and only two roads penetrate it to any degree. A poor road leaves Mexico 2 highway at K63+ and goes south to **Papago Tanks**, the only reliable water supply in the park. The other leaves Mexico 2 at K59 and K51, the two branches joining some 8 miles inside the park. The area is memorable, and virtually litter-free.

YUCCA

Currently the best northern entrance into the park is at K51. Use of the **Los Vidrios**,

K59, entrance is discouraged by the Green Angels unless driving in pairs and in 4-wheel drives. As this could change, a query would be in order.

   0.0   0.0   The road begins with a topping of volcanic gravel, deteriorating to washboard within a mile or two. *There are no kilometer markers, thus all distances are in miles.* We go south in flat desert terrain with creosote bush, ocotillo and mesquite.

   3.7   3.7   The signed **Peñasco** trail turns off to the west and begins climbing a low hill. The other branch goes to a ranch. On occasions this trail offers alternate routes, but best as we can tell they all come back together. Lava flows are everywhere. Though thousands of years old, they look as if they could have been added to the landscape within the last few months or weeks. Here and there plants are making a small headway in surviving in the black, sharp, intimidating jumbles of rocks. Note the occasional oases of plants and cactus where the blowing sands have collected in pockets in the lava.

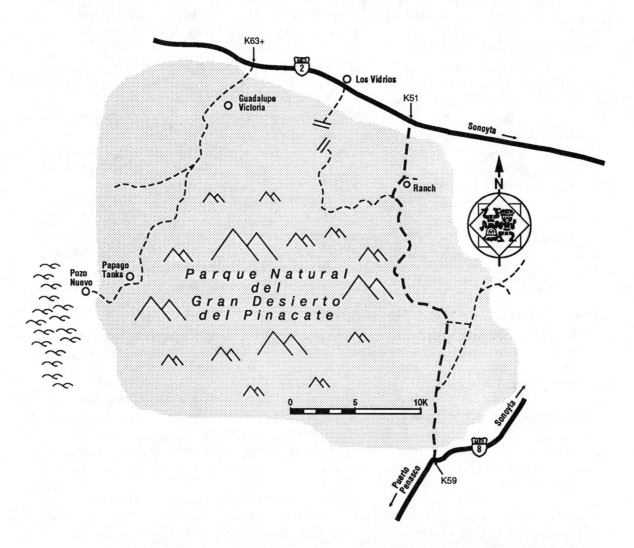

   1.6   5.3   We've gained a bit of altitude and are meandering through increasing patches of vegetation. To the east are black mounds of lava. Large *paloverde* trees are evident. One can look at the black sand and the black rocks and imagine how hot it might get here in the summertime...a good estimate of the air temps would be in excess of 120F. The ground temperatures will undoubtedly exceed that by a wide margin. *Both of our trips into the Pinacates were during "cool" months, November and March, yet we were very aware of the heat.*

2.1   7.4   Note the many fine examples of the "teddy bear" cholla, and the many, many "children" sprouting around them. One wonders how the deserts can resist these prolific plants at all. A good locale for photographs, if you can pick up the silvery-white chollas against the blue sky, black sands and stark, angular hillsides. *The challenge is determining the correct exposure. We double bracket and still haven't figured it out.* Continue winding in a southeast direction.

1.1   8.5   Intersection with roads going west and southeast. We take the west road for **2.5** miles to see what's there...hills and small canyons with little islands of vegetation, plus a couple of pack rat's nests. Backtrack to the intersection.

Here we have two more choices. We decide to follow the most easterly of the options. Ahead are several white cement posts. The terrain varies little, with piles of lava here and there. Most of the trees are *paloverde*, plus ironwood and a few contorted *saguaros*.

On the right at **2.9** miles, a tall sand hill; on the left, an arroyo and a view of the mountains in the distance. The road drifts off even more to the east. We begin to wonder.

At **4.0** miles we come to a fork in the road. The right branch (south) goes upgrade to deadend in a camping area. Return and take the (left) branch east. The farther we go the more it slides toward the north. It gets very dusty and could be a stopper for many vehicles. At **5.7** miles we quit and return to the intersection with the white posts. Total, **10.8** miles.

0.0   8.5   Back at the intersection. A study of the map convinces us that if we had continued the way we were going we would have found ourselves back on the San Luís-Sonoyta highway, assuming that the pickup could make it.

The only road left is the one going south. We take it. The surface is black sand and provides good footing. We begin winding more, but continue south-southeast.

4.7   13.2   An intersection. It comes in from behind on the east side and joins us in our search for the Peñasco highway. The road is now washboardy, and the always-unwelcome challenge of determining what speed is best for the vehicle and passengers.

2.7   15.9   Another road comes in from behind on left. Apparently lost, it too becomes part of our effort to get to Peñasco in time for dinner. Looking at the map, it appears that both roads represent connections with ranches or tiny colonies, maybe **Los Vidrios Viejos, Cerro Colorado #3**, etc. The road broadens as each driver searches out the path with the least washboard. Off to the east on a high hill is a microondas and it's on the map! **Microondas San Pedro** is located 3 km west of the Peñasco highway. Therefore, we know we're on the right track. The prospect of a shrimp dinner is becoming more valid.

1.8   17.7   We've come to the base of a hill. According to our map, there are about five dirt miles remaining. We round a lava bluff and encounter cultivated ground and a small collection of houses.

4.7   22.4   We join the Peñasco highway at K52. It took about two driving hours, and at least three more hours of stopping, looking, photographing and quaffing lots of liquid. With more time, we would like to go farther west on the road at **8.5** and explore the canyons leading to the volcanic cone, **Cerro Pinacate**. But that next time will be in the company of another vehicle. A standard car would likely become a statistic on this adventure. But we see no problems for 4-WDs, pickups, high clearance vans, even VWs if the driver knows what he is doing. And now for that shrimp dinner.

End of log.

AGUA PRIETA — HERMOSILLO VIA THE SIERRA FOOTHILLS

To visit the western slopes of Mexico's Sierra Madre Occidental is to step back in time...to the time when the breadwinner saddled his horse, jammed the day's meal into the saddlebag, picked up his shovel, axe or branding iron, and was on his way before the sun had cleared the horizon. Small ranch houses are seen all along Sonora 12 highway, and this is the scenario many of them reenact every day. It is even more so should we follow one of the switchback trails up a canyon's wall into yet another, and more remote, valley. This is the kind of country we are looking at as we leave Agua Prieta and head south past Fronteras, Nacozari, Cumpas and Moctezuma on the way to Hermosillo.

Agua Prieta looks to be in the middle of nowhere...and it would be were it not for the millions of tons of rich copper and manganese deposits running from **Cananea** to the east and north to Arizona's town of **Douglas**. At 25,000 population and 4,000 feet elevation, the town is big enough to settle the dust, and hot, cold and windy enough to eliminate it as a retirement colony. Originally the site of a **Papago** Indian village, **Father Eusebio Kino** established the **Misión San Miguel de Sonoydag** in 1701.

During the highway logging of the region we stopped off at the modest and clean **La Hacienda** motel. We were directed to a marvelous little restaurant, the **Taquería Cachanillas** (Calle 3, Avenida 5) for dinner. Within easy walking distance, it is clean, busy and friendly and we're the only *norteamericanos* in the place.

0.0   0.0   If you come across the border here, take your paperwork into the *migración* office on the right to get all the permits. Then drive south to the intersection with Mexico 2 and head west. There are several full service **Pemex** stations before reaching the highway.

2.2   2.2   K0   At the junction with Mexico 2 go west (right) toward the intersection with Sonora Highway 12.

1.1   3.3   K2   A junction (left) with **Sonora 12** to **Nacozari** and **Moctezuma**. Expect to see a drug checkpoint here. *Straight ahead (west) would takes us toward Cananea and Mexico 15. (See Sonora Inland.)* We turn south and receive another set of K markers beginning at K194. Go past the LPG station and on into desert scrub...creosote bush, mesquite, ocotillo and yucca. Below on the left are views of the beautiful valley of the **Río Agua Prieta**.

11.6   14.9   K175+   We come to the **Aduana** office. We show our papers, they take a look in the car and we're on our way with a wave and a smile. Cross the railroad tracks (*ferrocarril*) and run parallel to a cottonwood-bordered stream.

While scouting this area before starting the book, an electrical problem lost us several hours. The delay made it too late to travel much farther so we pulled over near a ranch house. As nobody was home we left a note on the door and settled in, finding enough firewood along a nearby streambed for a fire and barbecue. An hour after dark three men came by on their way to the ranch house. We told them about the note and got an OK to stay.

We slept very well, serenaded by a choir of cows with a burro, horse and two dogs alternating as soloists. Orchestral background came from the many frogs down by the stream, plus a few crickets.

18.8   33.7   K145   We are in a beautiful valley with irrigated fields and pastures full of sleek, healthy cattle. Alders and cottonwoods line the margins of the fields. On the other side of the river are tall bluffs. The town of **Fronteras** is just ahead.

There's an interesting collection of old freight cars on abandoned sidings. Some have been converted to housing. Note the many lines represented; several dozen from the United States and at least one from Canada. *We told a railroad buff about the place after our last trip. He wrote down every bit of information and said he was going to Fronteras at the first opportunity.* Continue past **Ejido Ruíz Cortinez**, a small collection of adobes adjoining the railroad tracks. Watch for *topes*. Back to long stretches of highway.

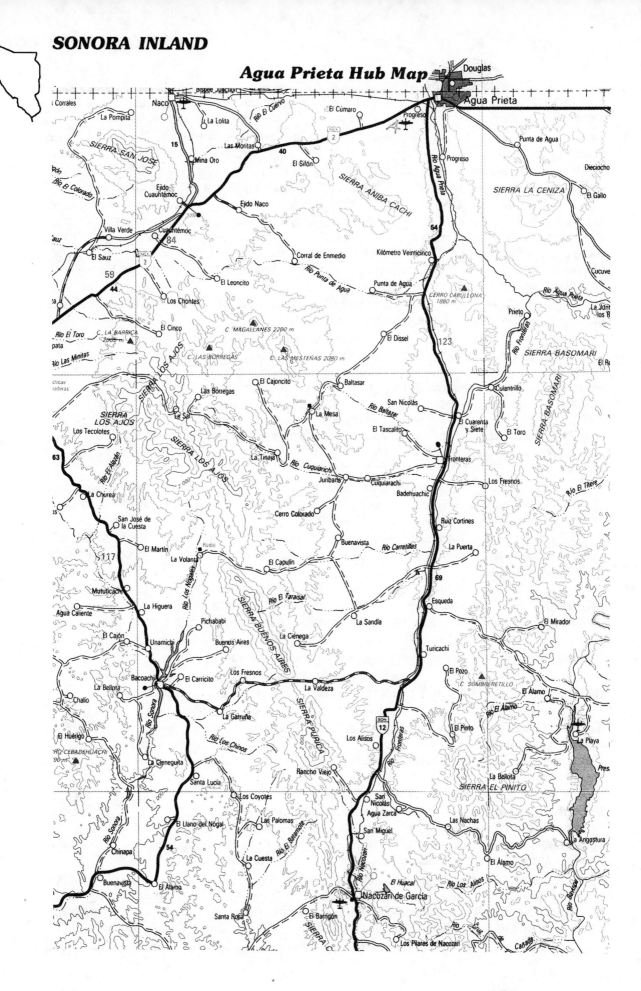

Agua Prieta Hub Map

19.7 53.4 K116+ There is a large *vado* (ford) across a streambed. The banks are lined with cottonwoods while oak and mesquite fill the area above the flood line.

2.6 56.0 K112 We pass the large and prosperous looking **Ranch El Vigía** (The Vigilant), then drive from the river bottom into the hills past lots of oak and mesquite. The area is very beautiful...somewhat mindful of the hills around **San Luís Obispo** in central California. We alternate for some miles between foothills, stream crossings and farmlands.

7.8 63.8 K99 Intersection with the road east to **Lake Angostura**, 45kms. In times past it was considered one of the finest largemouth bass lakes in the world. Though it has slipped a few notches, it still draws a number of the southwest's best bass fishermen. As to current facilities for the angler, we have been unable to determine what they might be, but you will need permits. **(See Before the Border.)** The road ahead becomes more winding as it goes through an *arroyo* toward Nacozari.

9.2 73.0 K84 The remains of an abandoned town, a leftover from earlier mining days. Continue winding through wooded hills.

4.8 77.8 K76+ The turn into **Nacozari de Garcia**, a town which lives and dies on the price of copper and their ability to find and refine it, is not tourist-oriented. *We see several small business hotels, the **Toby** and the **Imperial** are two. The restaurants checked were clean and inexpensive. Many of the homes are of the tract variety, sure sign of a company town. The place is clean and the reddish municipal buildings date back to at least 1913. There is a huge, new smelter nearby which is reputed to belch out thousands of tons of sulfur dioxide. Don't see much reason for returning.* Back to the highway and down a canyon littered with memories of mining operations. Large piles of slag, tailings, etc. are with us for several miles. The road is winding. Watch for traffic.

13.4 91.2 K55 The road leaves the hills and follows a wide, mesquite-filled arroyo. It is places like this that makes one think that there will be mesquite charcoal forever. We return to more pastoral scenes including horses, cattle and grain.

4.6 95.8 K48 Up on the hill is the ranch house, corrals and horses of **La Noria** (The Waterwheel). Ahead is a small town, **Las Hoyas** (The Jewels) with several clean-looking restaurants.

7.5 103.3 K34 To the west is a small abobe town, **Ojo de Agua** (Waterhole). *Incidentally, ojo can mean either a source of water or an eye. In this case, and in most instances where the word ojo is in a place' name, it means a well or spring,*

2.3 105.6 K29 For a town of its size, **Cumpas** must have one of the best-kept ball fields in Mexico. They have a large church, a local **Pemex** and that's about all.

4.3 109.9 K22 Paved road (west) is signed to **Jacori**. The peak to the right is 4500-foot **El Hornito**. Those to the south are the **Sierra La Cienguita**.

13.7 123.6 K0 Enter **Moctezuma**, population 14,500. The small local **Pemex** has a clean little restaurant next door. Their *machaca* is excellent. Another good spot is a small *taquería*, **La Central**, across the street from the bus depot (*parada*) near the plaza and the church.

After intersecting with Sonora 21, we receive a new set of K markers beginning with K164. We head west over a large bridge and begin climbing into the hills. Lots of geological oddities here...rocks and hillsides in a variety of reds, whites, browns and grays. Some have weathered into pinnacles, others have fallen into jumbled piles.

MOCTEZUMA

There is a variety of plants, elephant trees (*torote*), tree *ocotillo*, organ pipe cactus, kapok, pink-flowering *amapola* and palo verde, plus a wide spectrum of brushy scrub. Shortly we have a vista of a deep gorge with panoramic views of small farms, running water and a narrow little dirt road wandering precariously between the cliff and the river.

13.6 137.2 K142+ The **Cafe Lúz**. Out in the middle of nowhere. Here a cheerful

lady with a spotless kitchen opens her gas refrigerator to serve us a couple of icy sodas. Unfortunately, we had eaten a half-hour earlier in Moctezuma. A mile beyond is a band of very pink rocks. Continue winding up and down. Among the stands of cottonwood and alder along the river bottom are several ranches.

14.0 151.2 K120 We reach the bottom of the arroyo and immediately start up the other side.

5.5 156.4 K111 We top out and begin a descent into a broad valley and the western edge of the foothills of the Sierra Madre Occidentál.

8.7 165.1 K97 The outskirts of **Mazocahui** and the intersection with Sonora 118. (To the north is **Arizpe** and **Cananea**.) Continue southwest toward **Ures** (34km) and **Hermosillo** (107 km).

4.7 169.8 K89+ The highway comes out of the canyon of the **Río Sonora** and moves gently into the plains of the western Sonora farmlands. On the south side is a little restaurant which has become popular with the locals, but as yet seems to have no name.

8.9 178.7 K75 Above on the right is a large statue of Christ. It is best seen when driving west out of the *sierras*.

9.2 187.9 K60+ Enter *Ures*, a town with an interesting history. *The spot was picked for a mission in 1644, but it was not until 1665 that the **Misión San Miguel de Ures** was actually dedicated. The town had its innings with Indians both early and relatively late in its history. The most noteworthy occurred in the 1870s when **General George Custer** forced the **Apache** Indian Chief, **Geronimo**, and his warriors out of their stronghold in the Superstition Mountains of Arizona and into Mexico. They eventually holed up in the mountains near here from which they raided the surrounding territory for supplies, etc.*

URES

Ures has twice served briefly as Sonora's capital, in 1838-42 and 1846. A number of the buildings in town, including the church, provide well-preserved examples of 18th century architecture. The church is said to have one of the most complete early records concerning marriages, births, deaths, baptisms, etc. to be found in Mexico, and its archives are well used.

The image that Ures has earned over the years, it's liking for life on the wild side, has remained into the present. Until the fiery **Bacanora** became legal in the late 1970s, much of this distilled product of the maguey cactus was made in the surrounding hills and sold in Ures. *Today the old-time moonshiners of Ures sit around on the benches in the zocalo and tell of their narrow brushes with the "revenooers".*

*The region's big party time is centered around June 24th, **San Juan Bautista**, when horse races and cockfights liven up the inevitable circus, dancing, fireworks, and food stands.* Back to the highway.

3.4 191.3 K55 **Guadalupe**. A good place to find farm-fresh produce. In the fall people come for miles to buy *panocha* (a delicious form of unrefined sugar) and molasses candies from an old sugar factory located nearby.

9.4 200.7 K40 The **Rancho San Judas**. Farms and irrigation are becoming more prevalent. Many small colonies of farm workers are scattered through the region and the smoke from their cooking fires often colors the early morning sky. The farm scene to the west seems endless.

21.2 221.9 K6 The **El Tronconal** village specializes in citrus and grain.

1.9 223.8 K3 The small town of **San Pedro el Sauceo**. Another good place for farm produce.

1.9 225.7 K0 Intersection with **Mexico 15** by the K9 marker. Left into **Hermosillo**.

End of log.

MEXICO 2 — AQUA PRIETA — MEXICO 15 VIA CANANEA

*We begin at the easternmost border crossing that will be covered in this book, from Douglas, Arizona to Agua Prieta, Sonora. The **Migración** and **Aduana** offices are on the right just inside the border. You receive all of your permits, papers and vehicle inspection here..*

0.0   0.0   We cross the border into **Agua Prieta** from **Douglas, Arizona** and go through the paperwork in the offices on the right, then continue straight to the intersection with Mexico 2 past several full service **Pemex** stations. Fill up before getting out on the highway.

2.2   2.2   K0   At the junction go west past the signed **Sonora 12** road south to **Nacozari** and **Moctezuma (See Sonora Inland)** toward **Cananea** and **Mexico 15**. There is usually a drug-check station here. They could be stopping all cars, or waving everyone through. This time we are questioned by an English-speaking officer and a quick wave-on..

9.4   11.6   K15   The area is only lightly touched by mother nature's arsenal of plant forms...short grasses and small bushes seem to be the only things able to withstand the harsh climate of this 4000-foot plateau.

14.3   15.9   K38   Junction with the road north to the rather obscure border crossing at **Naco**. Serving **Bisbee, Arizona,** it is open only during limited hours. We drive southwest toward Cananea. To the north is the 7000-foot **Sierra San José**.

14.1   30.0   K61   An agricultural checkpoint for trucks...we bypass this. We've climbed a bit, but not enough to change things.

12.0   42.0   K80+   Junction with **Sonora 118** south to **Arizpe** and the **Mission Trail** to **Hermosillo. (See Sonora Inland.)** We enter Cananea past several hotels and a shopping center. Note the tall monument. Follow right, then right again around a low hill.

1.5   43.5   K83   A reminder of the tremendous amount of electricity needed to refine copper is behind and up to the right. Note the many distribution towers and transformers. Ahead is a marvelous view of the mountain of copper ore which is the reason for Cananea's existence. It is particularly impressive in the light of the rising sun. Another good view comes just before leaving the valley.

3.2   46.7   K88   A brief view to the rear of the valley leading to Cananea and Agua Prieta. Continue winding through increasingly-wooded hillsides. There are steep grades ahead...check your brakes.

5.1   51.8   K96   After topping out at 5700 feet, we are down to 5200 feet and passing through the tiny village of **Puerto de Cananea**. Note the stands of juniper, cedar and oaks. Continue downward with sometimes-steep descents.

1.9   53.7   K99   View of an observatory high on **Cerro Marquita**, the road to it is just ahead. There are also impressive views of the far peaks and deep valleys of the **Chivato** and **El Pinito** mountain ranges. We continue our westerly descent into rolling hills. Only a few oaks and mesquite remain of the forests above. We go past a tiny village surrounded by oaks and grassy meadows.

5.7   59.4   K108   Note the colors in the rock formations, signs of high levels of mineralization. Continue downward through increasingly fertile valleys.

9.4   68.8   K123   Ahead, a small *capilla* on top of a small rise. Next to it is what seems to be the walls of a much older one...and looks to be under restoration.

4.4   73.2   K130   Continue along the northwest side of this pretty little valley. All the ingredients are here...a running stream with lots of cottonwoods; horses and cattle grazing on lush grasses. On the other side of the valley is the main house and barn of **Rancho El Candelaria**. A final touch...smoke is coming out of the kitchen chimney. Altitude 3100

feet. The nearest neighbor is **El Aribabi** a couple of miles down the road amid a grove of cottonwoods. We've seeing more high desert plants, including agave.

6.2   79.4   K140   Begin a downgrade after a steep climb to 3700 feet. After bottoming out we resume our climb past a rendition of *La Virgin de Guadalupe*. There is also a small *capilla* with the ever-present burning candles. If you find the topography and vistas similar to those in America's western mountains, it is not surprising, for they are part of the same row of ranges...just a bit farther south.

2.9   82.3   K145   We top out on another crest at 4000 feet, then descend out of the oaks into mesquite and cactus along the side of a shallow arroyo.

3.7   86.0   K151   We've a bird's eye view of the valley and the town of **Imuris**. Continue dropping through large groupings of nopal cactus, chollas, ocotillo and yucca toward a small group of brick and block houses.

7.6   93.6   K163   Junction of east-west Mexico 2 with north-south Mexico 15 is at an impressive statue depicting five of the influences on Mexican culture. To the north is **Nogales**, Arizona's main gateway to Mexico. Below is **Santa Ana** and points south.

End of log.

HERMOSILLO — AGUA PRIETA VIA THE MISSION TRAIL

This trip takes us into the foothills of the Sierra Madre Occidental, the Mexico portion of North America's Continental Divide, and up to Agua Prieta, the easternmost of the border crossings which drop naturally into Mexico's western coastal recreation areas. We begin at the Sonora 21 turnoff from Mexico 15, just north of Hermosillo at K 9.

0.0   0.0   K0   We turn east off divided Mexico 15, cross the railroad tracks and proceed through **San Pedro El Sauceo** and its small local **Pemex**. Lots of good produce is grown around here. Watch for it in the roadside stands. We then cross a small bridge.

3.9   3.9   K6   Signed village of **El Tronconal**. Continue through areas of citrus and grain mixed with heavy growths of desert scrub.

11.1   15   K24   There are a few houses around a sign, **San Francisco de Batúc**. Continue northeast. Off to the east is the 1400-meter (4600-foot) **Sierra Mazatan**.

10.1   25.1   K40   **Rancho San Judas** and the **Río Sonora** are off to the right until we reach the bridge, then the river is on the left. *From time to time Sonora 21 will show us some paving irregularities...translation, **potholes**. These roads with little traffic are not high on the government's budget. Not bad, but be aware.*

8.9   34.0   K54+   Into **Guadalupe**, a good truck gardening area. The many roadside stands will offer the best of what is in season. *We have picked up watermelon, garlic, peppers, tomatoes and onions at various times.* A small sugar cane processing plant here. It makes the old fashioned *panocha* (a delicious form of unrefined sugar) and molasses candies each fall.

3.8   37.8 K60+   We come to **Ures**, a fairly large agricultural community. (It is described in the Aqua Prieta to Hermosillo log.)

2.3   40.1   K64   Out the other side of Ures and past the *panteón* (cemetery). We follow the south side of the Río Sonora as it continues flowing toward the **Sea of Cortéz**.

7.0   47.1   K75+   A large statue of Christ on the left side is partially hidden from eastbound drivers. We just happened to look up and back at the right time. Now climb a low pass and enter a higher series of hills. We've got lots of rocks, scrub, cactus and small trees to look at along here.

8.1   55.2   K88+   The road continues to follow the river. On the left (south) is a new little restaurant which has already built a good reputation with the locals but has yet to come up with a name. It is hard to miss as it is the only one for miles.

5.3   60.5   K97   Enter **Mazocahui**. There is a small church on the left. Continue east past the town to the intersection (north) with Sonora 118.

0.9   61.4   K99   We are at the intersection, where we follow the Río Sonora north with a new batch of K markers. On the left are several more entrances into Mazocahui, then past irrigated row-crops and open pastures. Stands of mesquite are down near the river, cactus and scrub on the hills. Pass a small ranch, **El Cahui**. *A first-time visitor to Mexico's hinterland might get the impression that every time a building is built it gets a name and they're about 99.5% correct. just making and installing road signs must keep lots of people in Sonora employed.*

9.5   70.9   K15   **El Milinote** is a signed community off to the west. The sign indicates a small *capilla* (chapel). Walnut (*nogal*) groves share the valley with silage and cow pastures. **Suaqui** is on a bluff overlooking the Sonora river bottom. So does the community of **Las Tortugas**. A look around the pastures along the river shows that the horse is still important here...animals descended from the Spaniards built not for speed or beauty, but utility.

2.9   73.8   K20   We enter **Baviácora**, population 5000, elevation 1600 feet. The church was built in 1639 to bring God to the **Opata** Indians. Baviácora's current populace lives a quiet agricultural existence. It has that "lets slow down and relax" feel. We found a place to stay, **Posada Familiar Baviácora**. It has 6 rooms, one with AC, around a

courtyard of citrus trees. Very clean and very inexpensive.

3.1   76.9   K25   **San José de Baviácora,** a tiny cluster of houses near the river bed of the Río Sonora. Beyond is another little settlement apparently built around a mine. It is probably gold, as the region has been famous for its gold since the 17th century. The trees along the river bank are cottonwoods.

5.5   82.4   K34   **Aconchi.** The church was built in the 18th century and has on its altar a black figure of Christ, the origin of which is unknown. The fiesta time is planned around the 29th of June. *For trivia lovers...the municipality of Aconchi's 358 square miles represents 0.02% of the total area of the Mexican nation! 358 is also the number of square miles in the city of Los Angeles, California.* The town is well known for its *muebles* (furniture). We checked out some utilitarian dining room and bedroom sets at very reasonable prices.

ACONCHI

2.6   85.0   K38   The town of **San Felipe de Jesus,** a small mining and farming center is to the left. Beyond it is one of the most unique spots we've visited in a long time...a hot spring complex. Let us tell you about it...

First, to get there take the road west through town to where it deadends, then left on a graded dirt road. Follow as it gradually turns to the northwest and along a sandy, but negotiable arroyo. The entrance is at 6.9 miles and the office is in the house behind the fence.

*Just beyond the house are a number of camping areas. Most are equipped with cement tables, benches and a barbecue. There are no hookups, but there are toilets and showers. The thermal waters are metered out into a variety of tubs and pools via a series of open channels. The place is spotless. The fees, both daily and overnight are embarrassingly low. It is a weekday, and we have the place to ourselves, until joined by a local family. They help us identify the vegetation and brief us on locating firewood. The thermal baths are operated by a charming German Lady, **Gerlinda Helge,** who came to Mexico in 1976, and couldn't bear to go home. The pool pumps are operated by solar panels, as is her house.*

The place is practically unknown, even to Mexicans. A few Europeans and half a dozen Americans are all of the foreign visitors she gets a year. We truly believe this to be a find. Your comments, please. Back to the highway and continue north.

3.0   88.0   K43   **Huepac,** another beautiful colonial town here in the foothills of Sonora's Sierra Madre mountains. *The small plaza in front of the old **Misión San Lorenzo** is attractively outfitted with white wrought-iron benches under large shade trees. Across the street is a playground with a Cessna and a twin-engine Beech airplane firmly planted so the children can play in and around them. We were told that the planes were caught transporting quantities of marijuana and confiscated on the spot. Our informant said that a number of playgrounds in Sonora have been so outfitted. The American FAA ID numbers are still on the planes.*

HUEPAC

3.6   91.6   K50   The land here is rich and has lots of water, as evidenced by the many cattle grazing in nearly-chest-high grasses. Several nearby ranches have signs touting their bulls for stud services. The popular breeds appear to be sementhal and charolais.

2.8   94.4   K54+   **Banamichi,** with 3000 inhabitants and an altitude of 1800 ft. *A (left) turn takes us to an old mission church in about a mile. Adobe is the most-seen building material and was also used in the church. There is a small posada a block south of the tree-shaded plaza.*

11.0 105.4   K72   We drop to the level of the river and drive past striking red rock formations. Ahead is another of the colonial towns,

BANAMICHI

Sinoquipe. It too has a mission church dating back into the 17th century. We pass the town and climb onto a plateau on the west side of the river. It is dry and barren up here, in sharp contrast to the bright green band down along the river bottom. The colorful hillsides nearby are testimony to the mineral richness of Mexico's sierras. The hills to the east are the **Sierra del Carmen.**

6.9   112.3   K83   More of the red rocks. To the east note the pillar-like formations along the river. The region is known as **Tetoachi.** Ahead some distance is a signed dirt road to **Bamori,** then a bridge with the name *Toro Muerte* (dead bull). The road returns to a gentle climb through the hills.

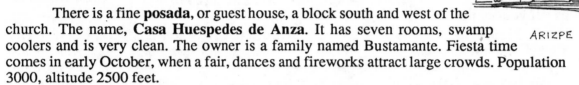

8.4   120.7   K96+   We arrive at **Arizpe.** *It too was founded during the middle 1600s. Its importance in the early days, when it was twice capital of Sonora, came from a rich vein of gold found nearby. When it and a few smaller finds played out, so did the town, until the waters of the Río Sonora were harnessed by upstream dams. The remains of* **Don Juan Bautista de Anza,** *the first Spaniard to land in* **San Francisco, California** *are buried here.*

ARIZPE

There is a fine **posada,** or guest house, a block south and west of the church. The name, **Casa Huespedes de Anza.** It has seven rooms, swamp coolers and is very clean. The owner is a family named Bustamante. Fiesta time comes in early October, when a fair, dances and fireworks attract large crowds. Population 3000, altitude 2500 feet.

3.3   124.0   K102   A stream crossing. *It is here that we meet an elderly gentleman riding a burro. He is of classic design. A face lined with decades of wind, sun and hard work. When he grinned one could imagine hearing a rustling sound, so many are his wrinkles. His name is* **Ramón Ruíz** *and he lives up the river. When asked how far, he gives a "not far" shrug. His burro had no name...apparently it had not occurred to him. It came when he whistled, so no name was necessary.*

We offer Don Ramón an icy Budweiser. He accepts, looks the can over carefully and asks what it is. When informed that it is an American beer (cerveza), he smiles broadly, puts it into his cloth bag, kicks his burro into motion and goes slowly up the Río Sonora.

From the river crossing we climb steadily for 4 miles, top out, then drop toward another valley.

9.5   134.5   K118+   A rather deep *vado* crossing. It could be a problem during a heavy rain. We are in an area of high desert vegetation...juniper, tree yuccas, mesquite, scrub oak, *cholla, nopal,* or paddle cactus. Continue in and out over and past the foothills of the Sierra Madre. The 8000-foot **Sierra Los Ojos** range is to the north.

18.9   153.4   K148   Another of the old towns of the mission trail, **Bacachi.** A *taquería,* **El Retiro,** is off to the right. This mission lacks the character of others we've seen.

Ahead, beyond the stream crossing, is the town of **Unamichi.** To the north the terrain changes. We are now into rolling savannahs, with lots of grass and small mesquite trees.

This hill country of eastern Sonora is famous for its chiles. They are reputed to be even better than New Mexico's chiles. Each fall the farmers make long strings of the bright red peppers and hang them in the sun to dry. Later in the season the lowlanders and city people drive up to buy a string or two. It is akin to visiting an apple-growing region to pick up a box of apples.

We are doing this log in October, a little early, but the long strands are already out drying. At a refresco stop, Tom spies a long line of chile strings hanging behind the store. He offers to buy one, and the lady accepts his pesos. As he takes it from the senora, he notices that it is quite heavy. He puts it down gently on the back seat and we proceed...until...Tom suddenly realizes that in order for those chilies to dry they will have to be hung up, suspended, so that the air and sun can do their job. There is no way you can hang a five-foot, 15-pound string of chiles in a camper, soooo, with tears in his eyes Tom stopped and gave

54

those beautiful chiles to a family along the highway. They really must have wondered who would be so dumb to buy, and then give away, a huge, beautiful string of chiles.

13.7   167.1   K170   We are now traveling north and west in a cattle ranching area. We then drop into an oak-studded canyon and out the other side to more grass and mesquite. The road twists and turns as we drive toward **Cananea**, one of Mexico's major copper mining centers. This part of the road is dull, with little but rolling hills to look at. The 8000+ foot **Cerro Mariquita** is almost straight ahead.

22.2   189.3   K205+   The junction with **Mexico 2**. A mile to the west is **Cananea**. To the east, **Agua Prieta** and the border with **Arizona** at **Douglas**. (See Sonora Inland.) End of log.

SONORA 24 SHORTCUT — KINO — MEXICO 15

When moving south from the Kino region, it is not necessary to go back to Hermosillo. It is much shorter to take Sonora Highway 24 south from Mexico 16 to its intersection with Mexico 15 at K171.

0.0   0.0   K0   Turn south onto Sonora 24 from Mexico 16 (Kino-Hermosillo Highway) at K54. On the right is a ranch with several brick kilns. They were probably used to burn waste and linters from the cotton gins in earlier days.

2.7   2.7   K4   **Rancho El Fundador** on the east side of the road is well centered among large plantings of grapes, citrus and grain. The roads are laid out in a north-south, east-west pattern...much as seen in our Midwest. The desert has almost disappeared in this part of Sonora. Water applied to the desert is producing bounties of grapes, citrus, grains, cotton and other products, at the expense of ocotillo, greasewood, etc. Not a bad tradeoff for *homo sapiens.*

9.8   12.5   K20   Intersection with paved road, **Calle 13**. On the southeast corner is an egg ranch. Beyond is a citrus grove lined with nopal cactus. A fine fence, it also provides some good eating. The young, tender paddles are delicious when blanched, rinsed and then stir-fried with pork and onion slices (Tom's favorite way). The fruit ripens in the fall, yielding an acidic, yet sweet, delicacy. Both are cash crops in the local markets.

6.6   18.8   K30   Intersection with **Calle 12**. On the corner is a small **Pemex**, an even smaller police station, restaurant and **Conasupo**. Largely unseen are the numerous farm workers who live away from the towns on the ranches, and this corner provides them with some amenities. We approach the hills we've been seeing in the distance. Continue south toward Mexico 15 and Guaymas.

6.2   25.0   K40   An egg ranch, **Granja Tastiota**. We've come to the hills and can see the many cactus. Next to the road are fields which are contoured for flooding, such as for rice. Beyond are more grapes, and the first turn in the road since we left the Kino-Hermosillo highway. Lots of water here...the tamarisk have gotten a little out of hand, and are growing alongside the road.

4.4   29.4   K47   Signed graded road west to **Tastiota**, 12 km. (See Sonora Beaches.)

2.5   31.9   K51   An unmarked *vado* (dip). Watch your speed. The sides of the roads are well populated with the mesquite family. Next come a number of poultry sheds.

3.7   35.6   K57   The highway angles more to the east. A graded dirt road goes west to several beaches. (See Sonora Beaches.) We drive past a number of graded entries to large ranches. The growth of the citrus industry in this part of Mexico, and the loss of prime orchards to housing in the USA, makes it likely that some of this fruit will be appearing in our markets in the years to come.

6.3   41.9   K67   We enter a small community with a **Conasupo**, school, etc. A graded road south leads to **Bahia San Agustín**, **Peña Blanca**, **Ensenada Chica** and others. (See Sonora Beaches.) Ahead is another slight turn to the east. Note the sharp pinnacles on the hills to the north. Also check the prominent black lava flows south of the highway. We are passing through a series of dips and changes of terrain as we move toward Mexico 15.

     3.7   45.6   K73   On the north side of the road **Rancho El Chaparral** welcomes us with a brick arch, a corral, a few outbuildings and a pink chapel, or *capilla*. The mountains ahead are the **Sierra Libres**. It is only a short distance north of these hills that we find the painted caves whose artforms somewhat resemble the cave paintings in Baja California Sur.

     8.2   53.8   K86   Arrive at **Mexico 15**. Services include a restaurant and local **Pemex**. We are entering a divided highway, so caution is advised. **Guaymas** is 37 miles to the south, **Hermosillo**, 53 miles north.

     End of log.

NAVAJOA — ALAMOS AND MOCUZORI

     In the did-you-know department...that jumping beans come from only one place in the world...Alamos, Sonora, Mexico. The Mexican jumping bean is a seed pod from a shrub which grows in the nearby foothills. Shortly after the flowering stage a beetle lays an egg in the seed casing. As it grows it eats the seed inside the shell, then settles down to metamorphose inside. All went well in the beetle's scheme of things until someone discovered that people liked to watch the gyrations of the pupae when stimulated by the warmth of a hand. Now hundreds of thousands move across the border to work for the American dollar...without a green card. Come to Alamos, the home of the Mexican jumping bean, and much more.

     0.0   0.0   K0   The log begins in the southern portion of downtown **Navajoa**. A signed intersection, **Alamos, Sonora 10**, directs us east along a semi-divided road across an irrigation canal near the end of town and out into Sonoran Desert scrub.

     4.9   4.9   K8   There are several pig farms nearby...shallow breathing is advised. The air conditioner also helps.

     4.3   9.2   K15   We enter foothills covered with typical small hardwood trees, some cactus and shrubs.

     6.5   15.7   K25+   Still winding and climbing. There is some dry farming of corn. Would imagine it is marginal because we are in a desert environment with often-inconsistent summer rainfall patterns. The road tops out shortly and drops into a valley. Ahead, a hill to the north is being eaten up by a cement manufacturing plant. A large operation, it should be at least a hundred years before they can cart it all away.

     2.6   18.3   K29   A signed road left is to **Lake Mocúzari, 19km.** *Here is one of the better bass fishing destinations in North America. Its age puts it out of the "fantastic" category, but for the average, knowledgeable bass fisherman, there is plenty to toss a spinner at, or drag a plastic worm past. There are no facilities, other than a spot to launch your own boat. Occasionally one can find a boat and guide there, but don't count on it.*

     0.6   18.9   K30+   We come to the rather bizarre collection of doors, windows and protrusions with the building named **Escuela Argentina**.

     4.9   23.8   K38   **El Caracól Trailer Park**. The place is neat and well attended between December and April. There are more trailer parks ahead and in Alamos. Continue winding upward. There are several species of flowering trees here in sierras, and no matter when we visit, something is in bloom. Right now, late November, we're looking at yellow *kapok*, white *osites* and red *poinsettia*. In May there were pink *amapola*, white *plumeria*, the *kapok* and a few others.

     7.4   31.2   K50   Enter **Alamos**, a most interesting town of around 5000. At an altitude of 1500 feet in this latitude, the winter weather fits closely the dreams of many snowbirds from the United States and Canada. Founded early in the 16th century, it is considered to have some of the finest colonial architecture in Mexico.

SONORA INLAND

In 1540, when the Spanish first arrived they came into a land occupied by **Mayo** and **Yaqui** Indians. The first colonial settlers showed up at the end of the 17th century when gold and silver were discovered. The silver veins were particularly rich and the town quickly grew to more than 30,000. The Spanish, and later Mexicans built many beautiful haciendas. It is

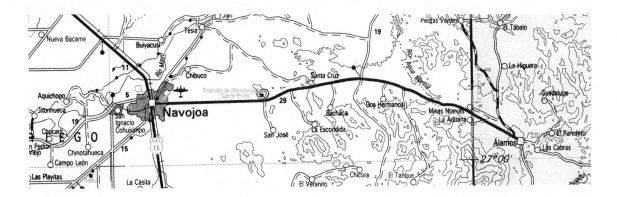

reported that one wealthy patron paved a street with silver bars when his daughter was married. The cathedral was built in 1783 and the china plates imbedded in the tower were donated by the wives of the town.

When the mines were exhausted the town fell on hard times, and by 1920 many of the once magnificent haciendas were in ruins.

Today the town is experiencing its own mini-boom, brought on by a growing cadre of *norteamericanos* who have refurbished a number of the haciendas or built homes nearby. Trailer parks and *posadas* (small hotels) are busy during the winter season, an ideal time to be in Alamos.

One of the people who has made Alamos a part of her life for more than 20 years, is **Veronica Deegan**. She and her husband carefully restored one of the fine haciendas near the cathedral. It gives a marvelous statement of what was here centuries ago, with its high-ceilinged rooms opening onto landscaped courtyards, stone fountains and all. The large rooms of Veronica's home are full of heavy, carved furniture, lending authenticity to the "yesteryear" experience we are having.

Several hotels have taken advantage of the past grandeur of the homes and created intimate posadas. One such is the **Hotel Mansión de la Condesa Magdalena**. Built in 1685, it even has fireplaces in the rooms. Another is the **Casa de los Tesoros**, built in 1700 as a convent. For those interested, tours of the private homes can be arranged. The public library sponsors one for charity on Saturday morning at 10am. For others check with the tourism office in the building to the right of the cathedral for more information.

Veronica, our volunteer guide, says that 300-year old "fixer-upper" homes can still be purchased for as little as 10 to 15,000 dollars. Restored, they range from $85--150,000, and an impressive 3-bedroom, 3-bath home with a high brick fence around 2 acres of fruit trees was built on speculation to sell for $75,000.

She also tells of a silk factory that was operated here by the Japanese between 1911 and 1926. She says that one can see a hint of the orient in the features of some of the locals.

Alamos' main fiesta is centered around December 8th, the Immaculate Conception. Another festive time is a three day Posada before Christmas.

A bus ride back into the sierras to **San Bernardo** is recommended. Visit the mines at **Pueblo Aduana**, take a jeep ride into the Chihuahua wilderness or a boat up the Río Mayo to a hot springs. For before-the-moment information write: Richard Schneider, PO Box 86, Alamos, Sonora, CP 85760, Mexico. We need to come back, and stay awhile.

End of Log.

57

San Luís Río Colorado — El Golfo de Santa Clara...

We begin from **San Luís Río Colorado**, 25 miles south of **Yuma**, Arizona. Note that tourist and car permits are not required to visit **El Golfo de Santa Clara**.

0.0   0.0   K0   Cross the border and go south one long block to the signal, left to the next signal, then right. At this intersection, Mexico 2 continues east toward **Sonoyta**. The Baguette bakery (*panadería*) is on the southeast corner. We continue south on Calle Segundo past a variety of shops, including a number of pharmacies (*farmacias*).

1.3   1.3   K2   Sonora 40 goes southeast past more businesses and eventually into the irrigated countryside.

0.6   1.9   K3   Pass under the large sign indicating El Golfo and Riito straight ahead.

1.4   3.3   K5   A full service **Pemex**, then an LPG station. Propane in Mexico is about half the cost experienced in the USA, and it recently became legal to use in cars and trucks...a great break for propane-powered vehicles. *Note: Not all LPG stations are yet set up to service cars.*

3.1   6.2   K10   Sonora 40 winds back and forth along farm boundaries for several miles. Popular crops include corn, cotton, alfalfa, onions, citrus, sudan grass (a silage for livestock) and grapes. After several miles, the road curves right, crosses a bridge and resumes its southerly direction.

9.8   16.0   K25+   A signed intersection (east) to the pueblo, **Lagunita**.

2.4   18.4   K29+   Local **Pemex** and paved road (right) leading to a small community. *If you are wondering about the small dayglow-green bottles scattered about on fence posts...they are to catch bugs so farmers can better tell what kind of insecticide to use. The practice is common in many parts of the world.*

9.0   27.4   K43   Here is a large outdoor grain storage area next to the railroad tracks and the small community of **Riito**. Watch out for speed bumps, or *topes*. Topes is a good word to learn...it will save a lot of unexpected lumps during your Mexican journey. Continue south, paralleling the tracks.

The farmland has yielded to the scrub and sand of the **Altar Desert**. The feathery-leafed trees seen here and in many other desert environments are the *tamarisk*, or salt cedar. A native of northern Africa, it tolerates high levels of salts.

2.9   30.3   K48+   The small brick and adobe homes of **Mesa Rica** are around us. The landscape remains desert scrub and sand. Shortly Sonora 40 turns straight south through the desert.

13.5   43.8   K70   We can see the trees around the railroad maintenance station of **El Doctor**. They stand out in an otherwise flat landscape. From there the railroad begins its trek across the desert to **Puerto Peñasco**, **Benjamin Hill** and eventually **Mexico City**.

6.2   50.0   K80   The landscape gets flatter and drier and we see areas of small stones. A short hike off the highway yields several pieces of red jasper. To the southwest are the tide-flats where the **Sea of Cortéz** and the **Río Colorado** meet.

3.1   53.1   K85   We top a rise and have our first good view of the Sea of Cortéz, with the peaks of Baja California's **Sierra Juarez** mountains in the distance.

3.2   56.3   K90   The defunct **Samuel Garcia** *ejido*, and just beyond, a dirt trail signed to **Rancho de Tarzan**. *We've lost the logic there somewhere.* Then, another good view of the Cortéz.

6.8   63.1   K101   Enter a long S-curve down to sea level, then follow the shoreline the rest of the way into El Golfo. *The tides are extreme in the north part of the Cortéz...as much as a 28-foot difference between high and low. The result is the exposure of as much as a mile of tide flats twice each day. The locals take advantage of the low tides to gather sacks of excellent clams. It is our view that El Golfo has the best almejas in Mexico.*

SONORA BEACHES

We try never to leave without having a huge plate steamed with garlic, butter, wine and parsley.

    9.4   72.5   K116   The outskirts of **El Golfo de Santa Clara**, population about 1500. On the left is a full service **Pemex**. Just beyond is the beer distributor and across the street, the *supermercado*. You can buy shrimp next door (left) at the home of **Clementina Castro**. Her sons operate a shrimp boat, so they catch 'em and and she sells 'em. A charming family...and friends for 20 years.

    Rudimentary at best, the trailer parks are popular with the ATC and dunebuggy crowds. On busy weekends the action continues most of the night. We prefer turning off on one of several side roads a mile or two north of town. Here we have quiet, few if any, neighbors, lots of beach and great views of the sun setting over Baja's Sierra Juarez. Rooms to rent in Golfo are scarce and marginal. The best we saw were in the El Capitán trailer park...but a noisy choice on busy weekends.

    Boating in the north end of the Cortéz takes special knowledge and skills. The tidal extremes bring strong currents which can propel you along at high speeds. Winds come up with little warning, and then there is the challenge of what to do with your boat when the water's edge is a mile from high tide...particularly if weather threatens. You will also want to be very careful where you park; several misparked vehicles are buried every year by the incoming tides.

    The many miles of uninterrupted beaches backed by high dunes and hundreds of miles of trackless desert make it a playground for those with dunebuggys and ATCs. The beaches still offer a good variety of beautiful clam, murex, auger and cone shells. On occasions a dead whale or porpoise will wash up, providing a feast for the area's coyotes. The high dunes backing the beach some five miles southeast of **Las Cabinas** trailer park are favorites with the sandbuggys. From the top, the world has a different perspective. Behind the dunes are limitless miles of sandy mounds, brushy oases and a treasure of petrified wood and semiprecious stones such as jasper and agate. As always, in a desert environment, take the normal precautions.

    El Golfo has gathered quite a reputation for its fiestas. The celebrations during Easter week and for the **Dia de La Marina** (Navy Day) June 1st, are something to behold. The entire town puts on a food, music and fun-time we will never forget. Dozens of booths pop up, serving every known kind of fiesta food, from watermelon slices to shrimp cocktails. Mariachi bands from Mexicali are here by the dozen, often playing different songs while standing back to back (and never miss a beat). The Tecate brewery brings in an extra truckload to meet the demand. The Mexicali municipal police send down a couple dozen of their finest, to help with parking and to keep order. Not that there was really a problem, but the Mexicali cops figured it was a good way to get in on the party, and get paid for it!

    If you can fit either in your schedule, you won't regret it.

    About twenty Februarys ago we shared a restaurant table with Ken, a scientist from the University of Arizona here in El Golfo to observe the unique daylight spawning behavior of the gulf grunion. A few cervezas later we had an invitation to meet the next noon in front of the beer distributor. After getting well provisioned we drove our buggies east along the beach past all signs of visitors. We then climbed up on a dune, and with the ice chest nearby settled down to wait. Soon several hundred seagulls and pelicans joined us on the nearby dunes. Shortly a few shadowy images appeared in the waves. The birds became restless, but did not fly. "Wait until they make their move," Ken cautioned, "then we can get all the pictures and fish we want."

    After a couple of false starts the birds really got into it when a long silvery wave of grunion rolled up onto the sand.

    It was mayhem with the birds gulping all the six-inch fish they could hold. We got our pictures and a few fish to try. The grunion who dodged the bullet quickly dug holes, laid eggs and deposited sperm, all before the next wave swept them back into the sea.

The runs occur from January through April, three, four and five days after the full and new moons along the Cortéz coast from Bahía de Los Angeles, Baja California around to just north of Guaymas in Sonora. The time of activity is in the afternoon one to two hours after high tide. Check with the locals for more information.

Sonoyta — Puerto Peñasco...

Each year more and more RVers are coming to Puerto Peñasco. Not just for a weekend, but for a season, and the town is doing a fine job of providing facilities for this mobile breed who hail from all over the United States and Canada. Come and see for yourself...

We begin from Sonoyta. It is November 16th, the day the children of Mexico dress up to represent the nation's heroes and parade through town. Our particular parade lasted a good hour and displayed dozens of Pancho Villas and many other of the country's most revered heroes. Bands, bicycles, trucks, tractors and taxis, all stacked with kids singing patriotic songs and shouting "Viva Mexico." A stirring experience. Also, you won't be going anywhere anyway...the police close all the streets.

GOOD FRIENDS

Sonoyta is 3km south of the border at an altitude of 1200 feet. We have our tourist permits validated at the border. A car permit is not necessary if you are only going to **Puerto Peñasco (Rocky Point)**, **Cholla Bay**, etc. but if you are going to follow the coast south and east to the beaches west of Caborca, you will need to have valid car permits. *Note: If you are crossing the border here, be aware that the US-Mexico border is closed between midnight and 6am.*

Cross the border and pick up tourist permits at the **Migración** office on the right. After about a mile, watch to the left for a *panadería* (bakery). The intersection connects the short border road with Mexico 2 Highway. Cross the bridge and immediately to the left is a small *taquería* with excellent *carne asada*. A larger one, and nearly as good, is across from the full service **Pemex,** "Tacos de Carne Asada, Aguas Frescas." The **Puerto Peñasco** road log begins just beyond the bridge where the road curves off to the southwest...

0.0   0.0   K0   Bear right toward Puerto Peñasco past several hotels (no recommendations this close to the border) and gift shops. One shop in particular shows promise...it has a fine assortment of *chimineas* (terra-cotta outdoor fireplaces) outside and good-looking handmade furniture inside. Continue southwest past homes and businesses.

1.3   1.3   K2   Head out of town and into the desert past many mesquite and related trees. The surrounding drainages provide much of the mesquite wood used to make charcoal (*carbon*). The road winds more as it follows various drainages toward the Sea of Cortéz.

7.1   8.4   K13+   Sideroad to *microondas* **Cerro Rojillo** (Pink Hill). Note the sharp granitic peaks off to the east. Large chollas are scattered along the highway. Shortly we come upon the first organ pipe cactus of this log.

4.1   12.5   K20   The highway leaves the hills for awhile and traverses a long alluvial plain.

6.3   18.8   K30   Much of this land is used to graze livestock following the rainy seasons. Keep an eye out for wandering animals, especially when there has been rain.

5.9   24.7   K39+   This area shows volcanic activity, and in its sandy soil, the presence of ancient seas.

6.6   31.3   K50   Just beyond is the first of a series of short bridges. Lava vies with sand for dominance in this area. The plain widens and continues its gradual descent toward the Sea Of Cortéz.

5.6   36.9   K59   A graded road (right) follows the line of power poles off to the

Sonoyta Hub Map

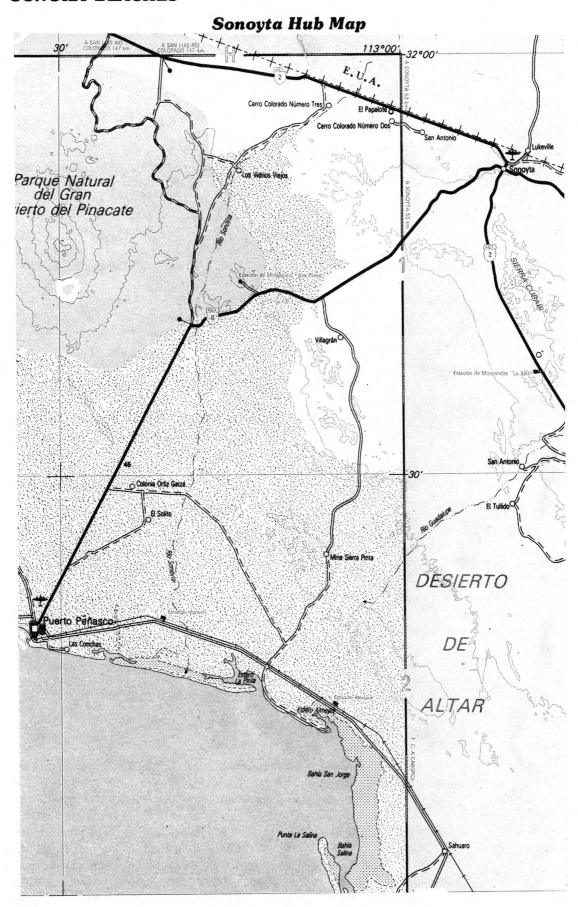

northwest. It is the southern end of the road through the **Los Pinacates National Park. (See Sonora Inland.)** *There are several varieties of paloverde trees; a closer look at them, even from the driver's seat, shows some differences. One has very sharp spines, another has tiny leaves and is willowy in appearance, while the third has many small branches and a relatively normal leaf arrangement.* On the right we come to a large sprinkler system, a new kind of irrigation in this part of Mexico.

9.0　　45.9　　K72　　A road (right) is signed to **Dunas**. It leads 10km northwest toward a horizon full of sand dunes. *The area is an absolute wonderland for duners. It is an easy road to follow, taking care to go around to the right of a ranch. At six-plus miles a broad area is suitable for camping. From here a trail leads up through sand and lava to the dunes beyond. The place was surprisingly clean, considering the use it must receive. Several friends who regularly ride the Glamis and El Golfo dunes would go nuts here.*

7.2　　53.1　　K85　　A couple of well-kept houses (they have the water) and a number of abandoned ones. Soon comes the small paved airstrip serving Puerto Peñasco. Handling even small jets, it gets a good play over holiday weekends.

5.8　　58.9　　K94+　We pass a small motel as we enter **Puerto Peñasco**. In about a half-mile a tall billboard outlines the advantages of turning right and heading for **Cholla Bay**. We take the 5-mile drive over a well-maintained dirt road.

The first portion contains all of the stores the weekend visitor might want to visit...curio shops with T-shirts, shells of all sorts, carved ironwood figures, stacks of mesquite firewood and fireworks. Other nearby gringo services include a *panadería*, several beer distributors and a small *tienda* (grocery store).

At **4.0** miles a road branches south to **Sandy Beach**, an open camping area with few amenities except for the **Reef** bar and grill. Popular with the ATC crowd because they can run their little three-wheelers on the beach, it is a lot of fun if you are one of the crowd. The quieter RV parks are in closer to town.

Continue another mile and we're in **Cholla Bay**, an improbable assortment of about 800 ramshackle weekend getaways, cavernous boat storage garages and stylish, comfortable-looking homes. The ambiance is good, especially if you are from the Phoenix-Tucson corridor. It has grown a lot over the past 20 years and much of it is very good. The people who come here have done a lot for the local community and are publicizing it in a positive manner. In general the visitors and their wide variety of toys (boats, catamarans, windsailers, ATCs, dunebuggys and macho 4X4s) are well behaved and treat the town with respect. San Felipe in Baja California and its visitors could take a few lessons from this group.

The center of the action around Cholla Bay is **J.J.'s Cantina** and the **Cholla Bay Yacht Club** where fishing is spoken in at least two languages. Because of the wide tidal variations, a lot of thought has been put into the launchng and retrieving of fishing boats. The result is a special launching rig where the engine and driver are a good six feet above the ground. Called "giraffes," they go into deep water to handle the boats. The club has three major fishing tournaments, in February, July and October.

Though the fishing quality has suffered mightily over the past two decades, the optimism has changed little. Summer weather still brings sailfish, dorado and occasional yellowfin tuna in limited numbers. Other pelagics, such as sierra mackerel, put in appearances around high spots within boating distance. White seabass and corvina are two other catchables, though their numbers have diminished greatly. Reef dwellers such as cabrilla and grouper still show up, but because of their scarcity even a triggerfish can win a tournament.

Today, little is heard of the totuava, the fish which, in the 50s and 60s, was the springboard for starting the Cholla Bay colony. Nearly fished to extinction by commercial netters, these huge members of the croaker family are making a slow comeback and are listed as an endangered species. It is not legal to transport totuava back to the United States, though an incidental catch is permitted. We'd suggest that if you catch one, throw a BBQ and talk

about the old days.

Several charter operators offer fishing trips...one promotes three boats...the **Nina**, the **Pinta** and the **Santa María**. Ask for **Martín** or **Chino**. The dive shop also advertises sportfishing charters.

Accommodations here are minimal, with the moderate priced **Vista del Mar** providing most of the rooms...four 2BR apartments with kitchen, and 13 rooms on the water. Write them at Cholla Bay, Puerto Peñasco, Sonora, Mexico. Back to the intersection into Puerto Peñisco

Peñasco itself is a fast-growing destination for the proverbial "snowbirds" who are finding the combination of climate, cost and ambiance a great reason to spend a winter in Mexico. The growth of touristic services in the area is little short of astounding. *As first-time totuava fishermen in the 60s we were lucky to find a working light bulb*. Today, it is becoming a magic land.

The major growth has been in the trailer parks along the beach southeast of town. The **Playa de Oro** is the one the rest are trying to emulate. Operated by Americans, the place is spotless and well organized. Restaurants and clubhouses, most with satellite dishes turned toward American sports programming, are popular with both the winter and weekend visitor. Fishing charters are easy to arrange, check with the park management. Want shrimp? Again, ask around. *Mike at the Playa de Oro favors Mario in Stall #6 on the malecón.* Other names of RV parks in the vicinity: **El Mirador, San Rafael, El Senorial** and **Miramar**.

A growing cadre of hotels include water-facing ones such as the **Viña del Mar, Costa Brava, Playa Bonita** and **Granada del Mar**, while the large **Senorial** and smaller **Costa Brava** are cityside. For dining, the easy-to-find **Reef, Posada de Leon, Puesta del Sol** and **Costa Brava** are recommended. So too is the **La Cita Cafe** near the **Pemex**, the **La Curva** and the scenic **La Gaviota** inside the Hotel Vina del Mar. We also like the looks of several of the small stands offering shrimp and octopus cocktails.

Another top-notch park is the **Playa Bonita** west of the harbor. Its 300 spaces are full most of the season (mid-October through Easter) and over major holidays.

All in all Peñasco is coming of age. Back to the highway.

Puerto Peñasco — Desemboque Via the Coast

Over the past 20 years friends have told of driving their dunebuggys from Peñasco south and east along the coast to explore the beaches and lagoons. They talked of the richness of the sealife, windrows of seashells and the thrill of standing on beaches that held no other footprints. The desire to emulate their experiences has been with us since the first report. And when we heard that the coastal trail from Peñasco to the paved Caborca-Desemboque road was being improved (maybe eventually paved), we decided to jump the gun and try to get through.

Well, it worked and it didn't work. The log is as follows...(One last reminder...if you plan to continue south of **Estación Almejas** into **Caborca**, etc., you must have your vehicle and tourist permits validated, meaning that you have to go to the immigration station located at **San Emiterio**, south of **Sonoyta** on Mexico 2 at K244.)

0.0   0.0   We leave **Puerto Peñasco** by driving east from the south end of the plaza on **Avenida Fremont**. We go past the **Cruz Bomberos** fire station and out into the **Desierto Altar**. The paved road roughly parallels the beach and is about a half-mile back. Any of the several dirt roads south will take us to the main trailer park section of Peñasco.

1.2   1.2   Road right is to **La Concha** , a *norteamericano*-oriented development of modern homes. *At 1.5 miles we come to a guard gate and ask to look around. Permission is granted and we drive past about a hundred very nice houses during our three-mile tour*. We continue south and east under, then paralleling, power lines. A hundred yards to the left are the tracks of the **Noroeste Mexico Railroad**. Beginning in Mexicali, it eventually ends up in Mexico City.

1.8   3.0   A dirt road (right) takes off in a perfectly straight line.

1.6   4.6   A well compacted sand road leads south to several commercial oyster operations. *At mile 1.0 it becomes washboardy, then curves left past a marsh. Once to the water the road parallels the shore of a small estero. At 2.1 we come to a small point with room for several shaded tables and a couple of cars.*

Meet **Gerardo Cota**, *a new, young and eager participant in Mexico's entrepreneurial society. We bargained for several dozen of his best oysters and ate them almost as fast as he and his wife could open them. In front of us are the floats upon which the oysters grow. The cost, under two bucks a dozen! And they surpass anything found in a stateside oyster bar.*

The Cotas are not in the restaurant business, so we used our own cups, limes, salsa, crackers and cold beer. What we didn't eat were iced down and eaten the next day...breaded and fried in butter. Excellent.

The long, narrow lagoon hosts a year-around assortment of shore birds, plus many ducks and some geese during the winter. Gerardo says they catch corvina, sierra mackerel and small cabrilla. This might be a fun place to launch a small cartopper or inflatable, but be well aware what the tides will be and plan accordingly. Tide tables for the northern Sea of Cortéz are available from the University of Arizona, Tucson, AZ 85721. At last reading they were $8.50, and well worth it. We heartily recommend a visit to the oyster lagoon. Return to the paved road and continue southeast.

3.3   7.9   A sideroad here goes **4.7** miles south to **Playa Encanto**. Graded and sandy, it intersects with a more-used road from the northwest at **4.0**. It appears to parallel the oyster lagoon and is probably the other end of the road mentioned above. After another **0.7** miles we reach the beach.

Playa Encanto's introduction is less than auspicious...there's a trash dump, a couple of huts and several dead cars closeby. Its only redeeming feature might be that one of the residents has a large pile of beautiful ironwood for sale...for firewood! We turn to the northwest toward a number of impressive homes facing a beautiful, sandy beach. A stop at the beach revealed not shells, but dozens of ATV tracks! It is as if every one for miles around had nothing to do but drive their ATVs. We are impressed with the several homes under construction. We checked several out; large rooms, great views and deluxe fixtures. The road continued even beyond our turnaround point at **7.5** miles. The area is indeed beautiful. Back to the paved road.

We now follow the railroad tracks and power lines east past a railroad work camp, **Estación Irigoyen.** Across the road is a sign directing us to visit **Playa del Sol,** a beach development. *Another sign indicates that it is on ejido land, meaning that renewable 10-year leases would be the best expected on any land purchased (or leased) here.* The road then redirects itself slightly south. The two mountain ranges off to the northeast are the **Sierra La Espuma** and **Sierra La Comancha.**

6.9   14.8   A few houses and people are struggling among very parched plants, even the few cactus look thirsty. Ahead in the distance are reflections from **Bahía San Jorge.**

4.2   18.9   The road leads south toward the shore. *As of December, 1989 the paved road ended here, but grading equipment was working ahead.*

Now...in case they stop construction completely, there are a couple of things you should know. If you are driving a passenger car, turn around. If you have a pickup, van or VW, unless you are an old hand at going through deep, soft sand, turn around. If you have 4-WD, don't worry, just be careful and don't stop in a sandy spot...piles of buried brush mixed in the sand over the next mile testify as to what will happen. Once past that mile, the rest is easy.

4.6   23.5   A dirt road (south) must be the the 10-mile trail leading to the northwest corner of **Bahía San Jorge.** *Unfortunately we were running late, and missed seeing it. A number of stories from the past are of fine corvina, cabrilla, pargo and pompano*

*fishing to be had here, on a flyrod! The late **Bill Valentine** of the **Cholla Bay Sportman's Club** went on several trips to San Jorge exclusively for flyrodders.*

     5.3   28.8   As we approach **Estación Almejas** we can see no sign of life...dead buildings and a number of grey-painted busses hiding a house. We almost went

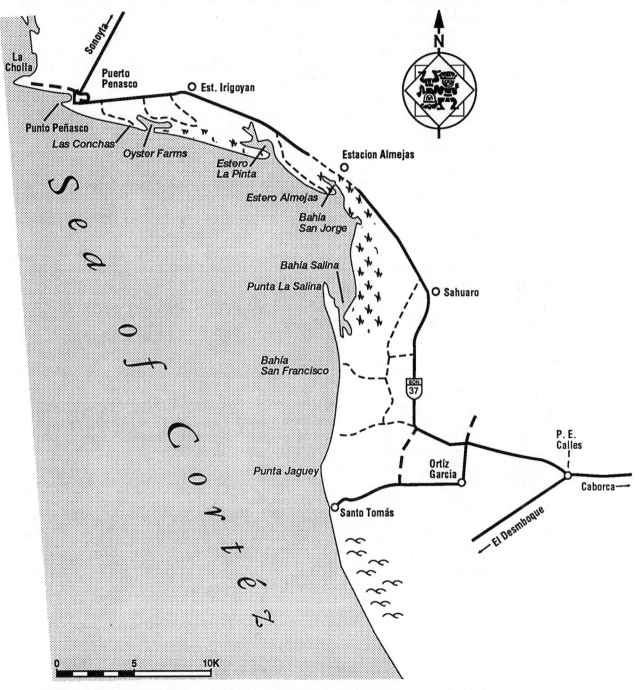

on by, but were flagged down by somebody in uniform. A surprise...the house is not only inhabited, but is a **Mexican Customs Office!** *The oficina de migración is manned by two very jolly gentlemen and they are joined by another equally -jolly fisherman, **Jesus Castro**.*

    It is the job of the officials to check permit papers for the cars and inspect luggage. The work here is not too demanding, only one or two cars a day pass by, and very, very few foreigners. (We are the first **norteamericanos** in two weeks!) The officers, **Jorge** and **Manuel**, are assigned here for 15 days at a time, then rotated to other offices. They might be back once a year.

We find Jesus of particular interest. He claims to be the best fisherman around, though he has no boat. He wades out into the bay at low tide, sets his gill net and returns on the next low tide. Jesus then brings the fish home and cooks them for his guests. You see, Jesus owns the house, and he rents himself and the house out to the government. Both Jorge and Manuel are a bit on the paunchy side, and Jesus happily claims it is due to his culinary skills. When you stop to have your papers inspected, say hello to Jesus. You might even drop off a cold beer or two...it is a thirsty job, taking care of government business. By the way...If your papers aren't in order, you'll be turned back.

1.5   30.3   **Poblado La Zinita** is a small fishing camp near the shores of San Jorge. Just beyond are a series of empty impoundments. They appear to have been built in an attempt to farm shrimp. Continue southeast into increasing amounts of desert vegetation...stands of *senita* cactus and a few *saguaro*. We are now several hundred feet above sea level.

7.7   38.0   A sand road angles south into the desert toward some unseen destination. The senitas here are the largest we've ever seen.

2.8   40.8   The small railroad maintenance station, **El Sahuaro**, stands on the beginning, or end, of the pavement coming from the southeast.

5.1   45.9   **Colonia Coahuilla**, a farming center for a variety of products including, rice and other grains, olives, cotton, and melons. Just ahead a graded road goes off to the west and **El Soccoro**.

2.7   48.6   Here's a road west to **Campo Domico** and **Oriba de Alba**, followed by a road to **Los Hermanos** and **Santa Anita**.

4.0   52.6   The paved road turns east at a small *ejido* colony. From here a dirt road leads west to the sea. *This camp itself is a mess, but the beaches in both directions are beautiful. Here would be a good place from which to begin a dune buggy or ATV odyssey along endless beaches. Free camping is easy here. As always, it is best to try and get acquainted with your nearest Mexican neighbor before settling in. It is only good manners, but it will give each a chance to size up the other.* Return to the paved road and go east from the ejido through vineyards, olive orchards and some citrus. On both sides of the road, but back a distance, are several prosperous farm complexes. Obviously things are working for these people. The bounty of an irrigated desert.

12.1   64.7   A small community, **Las Enchilayas,** and a signed road (south) to **Ortíz Garza**, another farm settlement. Across from the intersection is a small power transformer station. Continue east past a graded road (south) to **Colonia Oeste**, then bear slightly left before swinging south near a grape distillery (left) and under some power lines.

9.9   74.6   The community of **Plutarco Elias Calles** is at Sonora 37's intersection with the **Desemboque** road. Here we find a small local **Pemex** and a few services. Sonora 37 continues east into **Caborca**.

End of log.

BEACH TO OURSELVES

SONORA BEACHES

Caborca — Desemboque...

El Desemboque is one of those destinations which will surely have its day, for the beaches are beautiful, but we don't feel that it is yet ready...you be the judge.

0.0   0.0   K0   Leave the signed intersection in the center of **Caborca** and head west on Sonora 37 past a variety of businesses.

3.4   3.4   K5   Note the large dairy on the north side of Sonora 37. It is unusual to see such a modern milking operation in Mexico. Its presence is an indication of the growing centralization and standardization of such food products. There is an ice plant to the left (south).

1.1   4.5   K7   A **Pedro Domecq** distillery, home of **Presidente** brandy. It is fueled by the more than 35,000 acres of Thompson seedless grapes grown around Caborca. Incidentally, there are no wine grapes grown in this part of Sonora. All of the production is for table consumption, raisins, or conversion into alcohol.

An important intersection occurs at the west corner of the Domecq property...the road south (signed **Primavera**) is to **Puerto Lobos. (See Sonora Beaches.)** Another mile and the Caborca airport appears. We were surprised at the number of private planes hangared here, indicating the overall wealth of the area's citizens. Continue west on a slight downgrade past stands of mesquite, open fields and a grape packing plant.

3.0   7.5.   K12   Enter a pass between two low hills. Note the large painted image of the Virgen of Guadalupe. Judging from the size of the parking lot and the many viewing areas, it is a popular spot. In the hills to the left we can see the cuts and tailings from recent mining activity. Also note the markedly vertical north-south lines of rocks on the right. We pass through the hills and past a target range for the local sportsmen's club. The open ground beyond is typically "peopled" with creosote bush, ocotillo, ironwood, mesquite, paloverde, saguaro and cholla, and out in the middle of it all, a large distillery.

6.3   13.8   K22   Graded gravel road (south) to **Bizani**. It also joins into the Puerto Lobos road.

3.0   16.8   K27   Another road to Bizani, and beyond, another distillery, **Embotelelladora del Desierto**. Sideroads are rampant here, with many merely providing access to the vinyards and orchards. *When the desert does show through, we find sahuaro, senita and cholla, plus the mesquite family and creosote bush.*

7.2   24.0   K38+   Graded road (south) to **Laguna Prieta**, an *ejido* located in the lower slopes of the **Sierra El Alamo**. Just beyond is a roadside community of perhaps 60 houses. The road bends slightly north and heads past several houses, vineyards and another distillery.

6.6   30.6   K50   Sonora 37 swings back west and a bit south past rice fields, olive trees and vineyards at **El Coyote**.

5.0   35.6   K58   Power lines lead into a bank of transformers for further distribution through the area. Adjoining is an ice plant while a small *ejido* struggles for recognition across the highway. We are out of the cactus zone and are now relegated to creosote bush and small leafless scrub when there's uncleared land.

2.5   38.1   K62   Sonora 37 continues north toward **Puerto Peñasco** via **Campanas del Desierto**, etc. **(See Sonora Beaches.)** The road to the **El Desemboque** beaches continues southwest past more grapes and the good-looking ranch, **El Piñito**. We are also seeing several orchards of peaches, plums and citrus. There is still some raw desert, but probably not for long.

5.5   43.6   K71   Paved road (south) to **La Alameda**. Just past that is one of the most modern-looking vineyard operations we've seen. Agriculture is obviously winning the battle of supremacy over the desert here. Even during a trip to El Desemboque in 1982, there were barely signs of *homo sapiens*, much less miles of grains, grapes, etc.

7.0   50.6   K83   Graded road (south) to **El Cerrito**, a small community hidden in a stand of trees.

      1.8   52.4   K86   A large modern home surrounded by several acres of well manicured gardens, sited in the middle of many, many acres of grapes.

      2.4   54.8   K90   A graded road (right) leads to **Playa Los Dorados**. *The road goes northwest through dunes covered with small plants and grasses. Take the signed fork west at **1.0**. Shortly another fork leads us to a ranch house (left) or to the playas. We stop short of the dunes (**6.2 mi**) and climb past several seasonally-occupied shacks. The beach extends for miles. It sports a fair number of shells and some driftwood. Rudimentary trails behind the dunes should lead to other attractive camping spots. While we are having a bolillo (Mexican roll) and queso (cheese) break, large numbers of pelicans are lambasting a huge school of baitfish only about 50 feet offshore. A walk to the water's edge next to the activity didn't even get their attention. Dinner was at hand. Retur*n to the highway and drive southward past several ranches and irrigated lands. A mile before the road ends it turns toward the dunes and the sea.

      6.8   62   K102   **El Desemboque**. On this third visit in 7 years, Desemboque continues to be a disappointment. *It is still one of the dirtiest fish camps we've encountered anywhere. Rotting fish are piled on more decayed carcasses. Trash abounds, and the people don't seem to care. The distant views are marvelous, as are the dunes away from the village. With all of the water available nearby, it seems strange that the residents must still get their water from trucks and store it outside in uncovered barrels. Fifteen years ago the other El Desemboque (El Desemboque del Seri) had similar conditions, but they took an interest and today El Desemboque del Seri is clean by the standards of this trash heap. It would appear that the attraction for visitors from hot, inland Caborca would be great if it were cleaned up. We've seen it happen elsewhere...hopefully here someday.*

      End of log and back to Caborca.

Cabora Hub Map

Moctezuma

Tres de Enero

38

102

Rio Asunción

SON 37

San Isidro

El Tepeyac

El Sahuaro

El Papalote

La Alameda

Adolfo López Mateos

San Juan

Jesús García

Caborca

22

9

Caborca Viejo

El Yaqui

San Martín

La Huerta

SIERRA EL ÁLAMO

El Mexicano

Rio Asunción

Mejoqui

El Delirio

Las Calenturas

Josefa Ortiz

Emiliano Zapata

El Deseo

San José

Constitución

San Juan

Ruiz Cortinés

Santa Rosa

El Molino

Emilio Carranza

Santa Martha

Santa Mónica

Guillermo Prieto

Pozo Prieto

Aquituni

A L T A R - P I T I Q U I T O

La Verruga

Bamuri

SIERRA EL VIEJO

Puerto Lobos

Rio San Lorenzo

El Plomito

Zapori

Rio El Julio

Rio El Carbón

El Carbón

Pozos de Serna

La Primavera

El Americano

El Caracol

La Golondrina

El Dátil

Campo Julio

Rio El Dátil

Santa Rita

El Testerazo

Puerto Libertad

La Tinaja

San Jesús

Punta Tepoca

P

Victoria y Libertad

El Destierro

El Pocito de los Cazadores

San Francisquito

Las Estrellas

Punta Cirio

69

Caborca — Puerto Lobos...

The desert region south and west of the town of Caborca was, and still is seldom touched by all but the most dedicated adventurer. People who really want to go into the thousands of square kilometers of Sonoran desert and experience the beauty which exists in such an environment still have it virtually to themselves. Only along the coastal margins was there much of an opportunity for the early people to survive, much less eke out a living. Today the desert is shrinking and the difference is water. The introduction of electricity has allowed pumps to bring water from deep in the earth to produce a cornucopia of marketable produce. Today the Desierto Altar is accessible through a network of rutted trails, effectively binding the region together. We headquarter in Caborca for this adventure.

(Note... The **El Camino** is the place to stay in Caborca..We tried the **Posada Caborca**...a big mistake.)

0.0   0.0   K0   Leave signed intersection in the center of Caborca and head west on Sonora route 37 past a variety of businesses.

3.4   3.4   K5   Note the large dairy on the north side of Sonora 37. It is unusual to see such a modern milking operation in Mexico. Its presence is an indication of the growing centralization and standardization of such food products. There is an ice plant to the left (south).

1.1   4.5   K7   The **Pedro Domecq** distillery, home of Presidente brandy. It is fueled by the more than 35,000 acres of Thompson seedless grapes grown around Caborca. Incidentally, there are no wine grapes grown in this part of Sonora. The grapes of Sonora are for table consumption, raisins, or conversion into alcohol.

At the end of the property we take the signed road (south) to **Primavera** and on to **Puerto Lobos**. It begins by traversing fields of cotton and grains, including rice, through the valley of the **Rio Asunción**. The shallow ground water encourages large stands of mesquite.

3.1   7.6   Intersection. The paved road (east) leads eventually to the dirt road to **Puerto Libertad** out of **Pitiquito**. This road is signed to **Colonia Emiliano Zapata**, but the Zapata road is not paved and branches off the paved road after a couple of miles. Continue south toward low, rocky hills, and as we get closer we can see tailings from a small mine.

2.6   10.2   Top a little grade and descend into terrain covered with greasewood, and scatterings of a variety of cactus. To the south is the **Sierra El Viejo**. As we come more into the center of the valley the mesquite increases and we lose the greasewood.

3.1   13.3   The graded dirt road (west) is signed to the ranch of **El Deseo** (The Desire). Continue along the valley floor through healthy stands of desert flora. Then come more farms, a large power transformer and the road turns west.

5.6   18.9   Watch for the unpaved vado, or dip. This one seems to take a beating during heavy rains. Chances are that it will be unpaved for some time to come. Beware, and slow down.

1.0   19.9   The pavement ends here with little indication that it will be extended in the next few years. Take the left (south) road to Lobos. Obviously the end of the road does not mean the end of the ranches. Some well-kept ones are just ahead.

1.9   21.9   We rattle across a cattle guard and proceed south into, and out of, the little settlement of **Primavera**. (You won't find that on many maps!) The roadbed is coarse sand with a bit of washboard and an occasional sandy high center. Not much traffic here...we just scattered a covey of quail, and at midday.

3.3   25.1   Another cattle guard and sign prohibiting hunting and the gathering of wood. Shortly we climb a rocky ridge...use caution. Then back to the sand and a sign, **Lobos**, 48km. The road turns a bit to the right. On the left a corral and windmill, and the first elephant trees of the log. Another cattle guard follows. Altitude 1000 feet.

4.1   29.2   A sandy road north is signed to **Santa Rosa**. Southeast of us are the 3000-foot **Sierra El Viejo**. A bit earlier we went by a poor trail which took off in the direction of **Pozo Prieto**.

2.8   32.0   Another road sign. It says we can be in **Puerto Libertad** in 85 kilometers if we take the road to the southeast. It doesn't show on our maps...Look for a very large cardón cactus right at the junction...the first we've seen on this log. *The road from here to Puerto Libertad is covered under another beach log.* **(See Sonora Beaches.)**

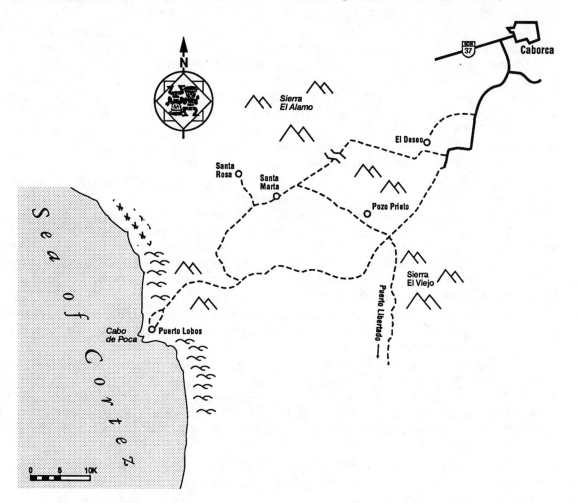

For now, we go straight down a long hill through scenery seemingly out of a botanical garden, so perfectly placed are the rocks and plants. We stop to look at a purple-paddle (*nopal*) cactus sporting spines fully three inches long on a paddle measuring no more than five inches.

5.8   37.8   A cattle guard and another sign about hunting and wood collecting. The road splits briefly...left is sandy, right is dusty...your choice. We are now almost to sea level. Quail everywhere. A narrow road marked with a big tractor tire veers off to the northwest. This a good place to check out the differences between the **sahuaro** and **cardón** cactus. Take a moment and compare the bulkier trunks of the *cardón* and the fewer, narrower and shorter branches of the *saguaro*. Note too the stands of organ pipes cactus.

We have not misspelled saguaro/sahuaro in the paragraph above. The two are perfectly interchangeable, and nobody seems to care which is used.

3.5   41.3   One more cattle guard. Then we follow the one-lane road off to the southwest. We can see the road climb toward a low pass into the coastal plain. More quail and a lonesome windmill. Here in the lowest part of the valley the mesquite grows to huge proportions. Note the size of the trunks of some and speculate how old they might be. Two miles beyond are a number of abandoned buildings.

2.6   43.9   Civilization! The road passes under high tension wires, probably originating from the **Puerto Libertad** power plant.

3.3   47.3   A sign says that **Rancho El Costeño** is off to the northwest. The name indicates it is probably on the coast...we mark it for exploration another time. The next few miles are like a roller coaster as we go in and out of gullies.

4.1   51.3   At last, a view of the **Sea of Cortéz**. The road separates for a left-right choice. We go right. They rejoin and we take the right branch again, bringing us to the dunes north of town. *To the right is a seemingly abandoned camping area. It has about 16 sombras, or thatched palm shades and two central shower/toilet buildings. Free camping here should be easy. The beach sand is very flat and firm with a few shells and a few clams on low tide.* We angle south (left) past what might be a landing strip, and the town dump.

5.6   56.9   The branches reconnect and we proceed into town. A sign, "For Fishing Guides see Rocky in the Stone House where the flags are flying," is on the right as we enter town. A better sign might be, "Bienvenidos a Puerto Lobos."

We've definitely arrived. And so has the Caborca Lions Club. Their official logo and name is on a bus parked under a tree. And it's been there for some time. The school is on our right. A few substantial buildings are scattered around among a number of minimal houses. It is obvious that water is scarce...nothing grows that doesn't take care of itself. We see several signs offering cabins for rent. On the beach are dozens of pangas, back from their morning of tending nets, etc. Off to the side, having gotten their share earlier, a thousand gulls and pelicans are digesting their lunch and waiting for the next dole. The road goes northwest over hard beach sand toward the houses and lighthouse out on the rocky point.

Here on the point we seem to have an American colony, judging from the license plates and the general demeanor. Some nice looking houses and cabins; several appear to be occupied much of the year.

The town sports a number of miniscule *tiendas*, but no restaurants or cold *cervezas*. The bay is well protected and at one time was considered one of the best fishing spots in the Cortéz. Today's catch goes little beyond small sharks, *corvina* and little halibut (*lenguado*). There are several launch ramps. The name, Puerto Lobos, indicates that sea lions (*lobos del mar*) are, or were, found nearby...likely on the rocky west face of the point. There is no gasoline except out of a drum.

How would we rate the road to Lobos? Better than many Baja roads that we drive a standard car on. The sand is not too bad...high centers on occasion, thus clearance is very important. Back to Caborca.

Lobos Road — Puerto Libertad...

To some the thought of immersing oneself in a desert environment is very intimidating. We will never forget the reporter for the New York Times *who came west in early 1974 to do a story on the new Baja Highway. He flew to San Diego, arranged for a car and headed into the new land.*

A couple of weeks later he returned to the United States and filed his story. The essence of his report was summed up in one sentence..."Mexico 1 is a dangerous road through a dull, dry desert with no redeeming features." Even the deserts of western Mexico are not for everyone, and we hope it stays that way. If you like Baja, you'll love it here.

This log begins at the 31 mile mark of the **Caborca/Puerto Lobos** log. **(See Sonora Beaches.)**

0.0   0.0   The sign here says that we can be in **Puerto Libertad** in 85 kilometers if we take the turnoff ahead. The sign is a bit premature...the turnoff is a full hundred meters beyond. *It should provide plenty of notice since there is little need to slow*

down, change lanes or use the turn indicators. Look for a very large cardón cactus right at the junction. Puerto Lobos is straight ahead to the west. We turn south for **Libertad**.

SONORA DESERT

> *The sign indicating an intersection with a road into Puerto Libertad was a pleasant surprise as it was not on any of our maps. We had anticipated having to go east of Caborca to Pitiquito in order to drive to Libertad. This way we are cutting off about 50 miles of dirt driving.*

2.7   2.7   A large, padlocked gate and a railroad-tie fence, then a cattle guard. Someone obviously has plans for this part of Sonora. The surface is coarse granitic sand...almost like crushed gravel. Lots of ironwood, paloverde, ocotillo, saguaros, chollas and a variety of leafy plants. Our direction appears to be southeast.

2.9   5.6   Another gate. Big and white, it is sealed with what has to be the largest Master padlock ever built. On the other side of the gate, a long straight road goes off to the west. We continue southeast.

1.3   6.9   Cross a small, rocky arroyo and a few moments later drop into another one and follow it **0.2** milesbefore climbing back onto the plain.

2.8   9.7   Another cattle guard, then a large, new sign, **El Rancho San Francisco y Corpus Christy** (sic) with a number of livestock brands painted on it. We're impressed. The sign alone is a knockout. It is very easy to follow a trail through here, no choices. The desert could not be more beautiful than what we are seeing right now.

4.3   14.0   A sturdy corral and a house near the road. Above on a bluff, are several more buildings... one of which looks to be large and modern. A signed intersection indicates **El Carbón** and **El Caracól** to the southeast. They are on our map, and on the way, so we follow. We come to low hills, move through them and onto a rolling plain sloping gently east.

6.4   20.4   Another cattle guard. The soil is red and dusty. Altitude, about 1000 feet. Some of the chollas are a good 10 feet high. The sand and rocks change back to granite. The ground here does not support as much plant life so the creosote bush takes over.

3.6   24.0   Another small ranch with one of the nearly-solid wood corrals and a working windmill. Nearby a sign indicates we are over half way...**Puerto Libertad, 40km.** According to our rough mapping, we should be at El Carbón, but there is nobody to ask. Continue south southwest through marvelous stands of ironwood and mesquite. The whole narrow valley is full of it.

5.4   29.4   A house by the road. Up on the hill are a number of garishly-painted cabins or small houses. The yellow-orange and yellow-red combinations, plus the landing strip just past the access road guarantees that this is what is marked on the map as **El Americano!** And that makes El Carbón the ranch 5-miles back. *(Sometimes you have to use deduction.)* What a hideaway. The hills to the left show property(?) lines laid out on a north-south/east-west grid. Continue south.

2.5   31.9   Another ranch, windmill, corral, horses, etc. It is like suburbia after the previous 50 miles. This is **El Caracól**. A left branch east and south wanders off through the desert, undoubtedly with a number of ranches on its itinerary. We follow the most-traveled southwest branch.

5.4   37.3   Some power lines, presumably from the Libertad power plant, but the direction is not correct. We pass under and are shortly presented with a view of the **Sea of Cortéz**. The long piece of land far to the west is Baja's **La Gárdia Angel** island. Directly behind the island is **Bahía de Los Angeles** in Baja California. Continue west by southwest through a gradually-descending alluvial plain toward the sea.

10.8   48.1   We touch pavement for the first time in a long time. To the right (northeast) is the airport, left is the town of **Puerto Libertad**.

A short distance beyond the turnoff into town is the reason for this paved road, the airport, many of the residents and the power plant. An oil-powered thermoelectric, it uses the oil pumped in from the tankers offshore. The heat generated is also used to make fresh water through the flash distillation method.

The paving ends at the plant but a graded dirt extension continues north around a hill, generally following the shore. A short trail branches to the water before the main road continues on north of the rocky bluff.

We arrive at **Campo Julio** (3.4 mi). Open to the north, it has a nice beach and enough room for a dozen or so rigs. There is one trailer here in late November.

Libertad's gasoline is from a drum today, and leaded only, but that will soon change, as a small **Pemex** is under construction...presumably with a pump for unleaded. There are very minimal touristic services...a couple of rooms are for rent near the movie theater, and a **Conasupo** grocery store. For what it is worth, a **Tres Estrellas de Oro** bus leaves the downtown area for Hermosillo each morning at 7:30.

The waterfront shows the degree of effort put in by the fisherman to make a living from the sea. Their open 25-foot pangas, nets, lines and other paraphernalia are scattered everywhere. Some in need of repair, some obviously abandoned. It's a tough life anyway, but when the fish are about gone...it's really tough.

End of Log.

Hermosillo — Bahia Kino...

Note: Mexico highway 15 passes through Hermosillo via three different routes. We begin from the signed intersection of Mexico 16 and Sonora 16 on Calle Rosales in the south part of Hermosillo. Adjacent is a full-service Pemex, and just to the south is a bridge over the Río Sonora.

0.0   0.0   K0   Turn west from **Calle Rosales** at **Bahia Kino** sign and proceed through several miles of businesses.

3.6   3.6   K6   The **Babos Motel** on the right looks interesting...it advertises jacuzzi, satellite TV, phones, etc.

2.6   6.2   K10   The divided highway ends just beyond the entrance into the Hermosillo airport.

1.2   7.4   K12   A **Pedro Domecq** distillery, one of the homes of **Presidente Brandy**. Another is just outside Caborca. Together they take a good amount of the thousands of tons of white seedless grapes grown around here. Also getting their share is the **Viejo Virgel** distillery down the road on the right.

5.0   12.4   K20   The large factory (right) is for the making and storage of chicken feed.

3.5   15.9   K26   We go through a low pass between two hills. Just beyond is the local gun club's skeet and target range. Where farmers have not cleared the land, the desert hosts members of the mesquite and cactus families. Chicken and egg production is big business around here, if the number of long chicken sheds are any indication.

8.9   24.8   K40   The road makes a slight adjustment west. There are large vineyards on the right. Citrus acreage too, is expanding rapidly.

5.1   30.9   K48   We pass a cotton gin on the south side of the highway. Today the seeds, even the linters, go into feed for cattle and chickens instead of the incinerator. Continue between the hills and past a series of abandoned buildings...gas station, several restaurants and a grocery. In the early 1960s this was the end of the road. They died when it was no longer the last outpost.

3.1   34.0   K53+   The paved road south is **Sonora 24**, which provides a handy

Kino - Isla Tiburón Hub Map

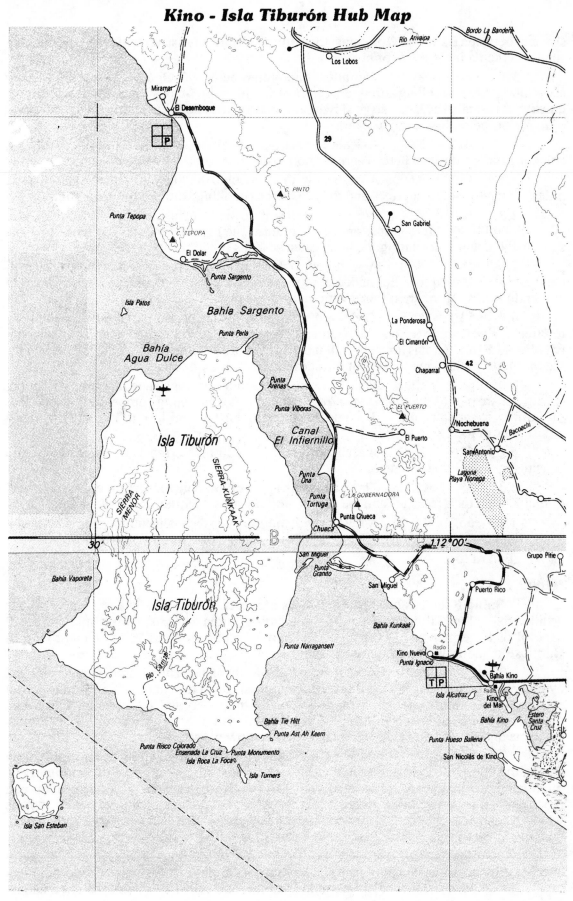

Bordo La Bandera

Río Arivaipa

Los Lobos

Miramar

El Desemboque

P

29

C. PINTO

Punta Tepopa

San Gabriel

C. TEPOPA

El Dolar

Punta Sargento

La Ponderosa

Isla Patos

Bahía Sargento

El Cimarrón

Punta Perla

Chaparral

42

**Bahía
Agua Dulce**

Punta
Arenas

EL PUERTO

Punta Viboras

Isla Tiburón

**Canal
El Infiernillo**

Nochebuena

Bacoachi

El Puerto

SIERRA KUNKAAK

San Antonio

Punta
Ona

Laguna
Playa Nonega

SIERRA
MENOR

Punta
Tortuga

C. LA GOBERNADORA

Punta Chueca

Chueca

B

30'

112°00'

Grupo Pitie

San Miguel

Bahía Vaporeta

Punta
Granito

San Miguel

Puerto Rico

Isla Tiburón

Bahía Kunkaak

Punta Narragansett

Radio

Río Kunkaak

Kino Nuevo

Punta Ignacio

T **P**

Bahía Kino

Isla Alcatraz

Radio
Kino
del Mar

Bahía Tie Hitt

Punta Ast Ah Keem

Bahía Kino

Estero
Santa
Cruz

Punta Risco Colorado

Punta Hueso Ballena

Ensenada La Cruz
Isla Roca La Foca

Punta Monumento

San Nicolás de Kino

Isla Turners

Isla San Esteban

shortcut between **Kino** and **Guaymas. (See Sonora Inland.)** Just beyond is a grape packing shed and then a large grove of nut trees.

    5.1   39.1   K62   The rather shabby community of **Miguel Alemán.** It has many stalls along the road selling almost everything...it's like a 365-day swap meet. People move quickly, especially the kids...so go slowly. Beyond are the adobe, brick and tar paper homes of many of the regions farm workers.

    1.1   40.2   K64   **Avicola Teresa**, one of the many *Huevos de Oro* (Golden Eggs) chicken ranches through here. There is another on the right a mile down the road.

    3.1   43.3   K69   A large, new **Vides** alcohol distillery is on the left amid more miles of grapes, some nut trees and the prosperous-looking **Rancho Santa Isabel.**

    2.8   46.1   K74   We pass a series of power transformers across from a group of ranch buildings. More grapes and some grains. The region also grows a lot of melons, squash and cucumbers during the high-value seasons in the United States.

    2.6   48.7   K78   A well-kept older ranch with worker's homes and a small capilla are all nestled together under large trees. Also on the south side is a peach orchard and grain fields. More grain fields with many large pecan trees in back.

    4.4   53.1   K85   The paved road (north) is the beginning of the new highway to **Puerto Libertad. (See Sonora Beaches.)** The paved road south also leads to a beach, **San Nicolás de Kino,** but it is not paved all the way. We are looking at about the last hurrah for the mesquite in this area as the salt intrudes into the soil. Continue west.

    3.0   56.1   K90   This is the third half-mile-long egg shed in a row, with more ahead. All are part of the *Huevos de Oro* (Golden Eggs) marketing company. We soon lose the farming as the salt build-up becomes apparent. Even the ocotillo, chollas, organ pipe and creosote bush look stressed.

    6.2   62.3   K100   Just ahead (left) is the entrance to the dead/dying **Montecito** beachfront condo development.

    3.3   65.6   K105   The road (south) past **Pulpo Nuevo Restaurant** is to several of Old Kino's local beaches and the busy **Condominios Jacqueline** development.

    1.1   66.7   K107   A **Pemex** with **magnasin** at the main entrance into **Old Kino.** The gringo community of **New Kino** is another couple of miles to the west.

    End of log.

KINO BAY...

    Bahía Kino has been part of Tom's life since 1962 when he and several friends decided to explore **Tiburon Island.** In those days the area was unknown to all but a small handful of fishermen and adventurers. The paving stopped about 50 kilometers west of Hermosillo, along with electricity and other services.

    That September trip was a memorable one thanks to a hurricane which prolonged by several days their stay in Dog Bay on the southeast end of the island. Finally, hungry, wet and tired the five nort*eamericanos mad*e it back to Kino, safety and a celebration of life. And that part of Kino has changed little...the storms still visit, the Tiburon camping spot looks the same and life is still being celebrated. Here is how we see it today...

    The region comes across as a quixotic mixture of modern and primitive, an amalgam of Seri, Mexican and gringo lifestyles scattered along four miles of shoreline. The mixture begins at about K107 on the outskirts of **Old Kino,** a crosshatch of dirt streets and block and tarpaper dwellings. At one time the majority of the inhabitants were Seri Indians who had been displaced from their ancestral home on Isla Tiburon in the early 1960s. Today they might comprise one-fourth of those living here.

    If you have ever looked at the polished ironwood carvings offered for sale in nearly every tourist center in Mexico then you have seen the product for which Kino has been famous since Jose Astorga of El Desemboque made and sold the first ironwood carving in

1961. The craft has become the major industry in this community and Old Kino is a great place to buy some special treasures. Thousands of visitors do so on a regular basis.

The beaches fronting the town are usually not too clean but there are two restaurants near the water...**El Marlín** and **La Palapa del Pescador.** The Marlín quickly became one of our favorites as they serve excellent beefsteaks at reasonable prices along with very fresh fish. We've also had good midday *tacos de carne asada* from one of the carts on the main drag.

The area's accommodations are in the relatively-new development several miles to the west, **Nuevo Kino.** This portion is made up of some hundreds of private homes and scattered condominium complexes, trailer parks, hotels and restaurants. Activities include sunning, swimming, fishing around the offshore reefs and islands, shelling and exploring the vast desert wilderness both to the north and south of the bay. We also recommend a visit to the Seri Indian Museum located in a tiny park near the center of town. The elderly gentleman who watches over it is friendly, cheerful and very proud of the display. Donations are put to good use here. *There are also a number of worthwhile beaches to the south of Kino which we've visited several times in years past but didn't get logged for this book.*

Our stops here have included the **Kino Bay Motel and Trailer Park** (both parts) near the west end and the **El Cactus** trailer park a mile or so above the highway on the dirt road north to El Desemboque. (In 1962 we slept on the sand in front of the **Caverna del Seri.**) The El Cactus has two bungalows to go along with a the trailer spaces and pool. It is a fine environment for relaxing and transcribing our notes. Other accommodations the bungalows at the **Santa Gemma.** On the beach near the center of the settlement, they cater to families and are popular weekends and holiday periods. **Hector**, the manager, also operates a small store and his office has the only *Larga Distancia* telephone in the area.

Other trailer parks in the area are the Caverna del Seri at the far west end of the road. The restaurant there also serves as the region's only night club, providing a Mexican fiesta atmosphere on Wednesdays and country western music on Fridays. (These times may change, so check before putting your cowboy boots on.) There is also a boat ramp. The Bahía del Sol is another RV park, but is several blocks back from the water.

The restaurants we've tried have been friendly, but the quality and service in most were quite variable. We enjoy the breakfasts at **Abraham Valenzuela's** La Hacienda (*Watch for the sign near the Seri Museum directing you a couple of blocks inland.*) and the dinners at **Saro's** and the **Pargo Rojo** (*on the main drag*). Saro's is operated by a couple...he is from Italy, she from the United States. The place is busy and offers a good Italian menu. They also have three rental suites overlooking the Sea of Cortéz. We celebrated a homestyle Thanksgiving at the Pargo Rojo among many new friends...the owners, the workers and the guests. Another gathering spot for the regulars is the clubhouse for the Kino Bay Yacht Club.

The area plays host to a lot of snowbirds from all over North America between November first and the middle of April. Temperatures can get very hot during the summer and it takes a pretty durable *hombre* to stick it out.

Libertad — Kino Via Paved Road...

This road was built to accommodate the construction of the new power generating station in Puerto Libertad. The site was chosen because it is one of the few places in Sonora where the inshore water is deep enough to accommodate tankers. The area also needed an economic boost due to declining catches of fish. The highway opens a number of once nearly impenetrable mini-destinations. We will look at them as we go along.

0.0   0.0   K167   Leave **Puerto Libertad** on the new, paved highway and turn south toward **Bahía Kino** and **Hermosillo**. The paved road to the airport and the trail northeast toward **Lobos** and **Caborca** is next. (**See Sonora Beaches.**) The terrain has only scattered creosote bushes and an occasional cactus, the rest are small annual grasses and plants.

1.9   1.9   K164   On the right is the entrance into an abandoned campground. Well, almost abandoned. There is a herd of goats and four youngsters watching us. As we stop, they wave and, goats and all, come to welcome us. We meet **Isidro, Jesus, Pancho** and **Esteban**. As the sun is about to set, we excuse ourselves to watch it drop into the islands and mountains of the Baja peninsula. Dinner is a slab of halibut brushed with butter and garlic and grilled over mesquite charcoal. Our evening's entertainment is supplied by the youthful quartet, who were fascinated with the sounds of their tape-recorded voices. Two of the kids live in the small house a couple of hundred yards south of the camp. If you stop here they will probably drop by.

The camping area itself has the same appearance as the one at Puerto Lobos and none of the facilities are serviceable here either, but the location is perfect. A long sandy beach with some pebbles and a few shells. It is open to the breezes...a good thing during the warm months.

In the morning we return to the highway and go south past a signed graded road (left) to **Victoria y Libertad**. Continue on up a slight grade past hills on each side of the highway. Those on the right form the northern edge of the 1400-foot **Sierra Cirio**. The range got its name from a small colony of *cirio*, or *boojum*, trees which live nearby. Originally thought to be found only in Baja, they were discovered here some years ago.

8.8   10.7   K150   The hard-to-see road into **El Coloradito** is here. Watch for it 200 yards north of the K150 marker. (It took two passes to find it the first time.)

*We enter a single-lane dirt trail past teddy bear chollas, cardons, and ocotillos, then wind sharply up and down toward a crest somewhere ahead. At **1.7** we see the Sea of Cortéz. A little-used road goes to the left at **3.1**, followed by a much better view of the Cortéz. We pass one of a number of dark purple rock formations. At **4.2** that little-traveled trail is back with us. At **4.6** we are on the beach.*

El Coloradito. A beautiful spot. The beach is divided by a large rock in the center. There is a variety of fish to be caught around the rocks and over several offshore reefs. It is easy to launch a cartopper or inflatable here. The road is a bit iffy for campers in a couple of places (tight turns and a pretty good tilt) but a snap for pick-ups, 4WDs and vans. There is enough room for a dozen or so rigs without getting into each other's hair. The years ahead will see many more coming here. Back to the highway.

3.0   14.4   K144   An unsigned dirt road (right) disappears into the hills and on to **Las Cuevitas**. *Following this winding single-lane trail is like taking a tour through a botanical garden, so well placed are the rocks and plants. Good clearance is a prerequisite for this sidetrip. At **1.5** miles much of it comes together with many large plant specimens highlighting the bright red cliffs with small caves (cuevitas) scattered throughout. A check of a couple of the caves show that the local packrat association is very strong here. One cave is full of sticks and the mesquite pods. Another is occupied by a rat obsessed with saving the little round cholla branches...there must be half a pick-up load in there. At **2.5** miles, hundreds of ocotillos large and small, shrubs with purple flowers, elephant trees (torote) and barrel cactus (biznaga) vie for space among bright red rocks. We continue winding*

*toward a crest at **4.9**, then a twisting drop to the water through ironwood, copál, torote and cholla.*

*The beach is at **7.2**, where a small fish camp is trying to make it on sharks, rays and triggerfish. Most of the fishermen appear to be **Seri** Indians. There seems to be no objection should someone wish to camp here, but we would probably put it in the day visit category. Return to the highway and south to the top of a small grade. The road goes straight for several miles.*

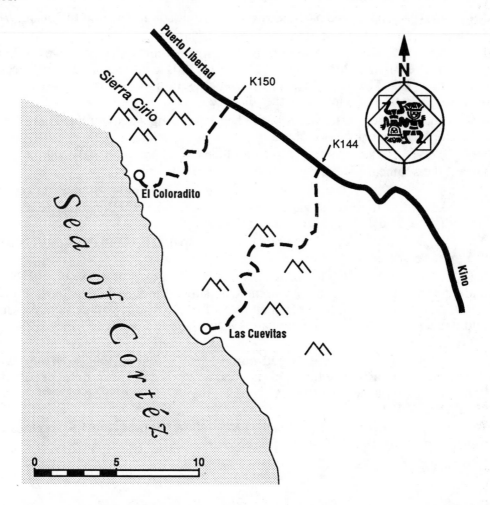

1.3   15.7   K142   Here's another signed road (right) into Las Cuevitas. We'll have to check this one another time, though it does not look well traveled. Ahead a few miles, an unsigned road east appears well used and likely goes to places like **El Desierto, El Pocito de Los Cazadores, Santa Rita** and **La Tinaja**.

7.5   23.2   K130   It is mountain-naming time...those ahead and to the west (right) are the **Sierra Tordilla**, while the ranges some distance to the east and northeast are the **Sierra Batepito** and **Sierra Jojoval** respectively. Nearby, the ocotillo predominate, followed by cholla, a few cardón and saguaro.

1.9   25.1   K127   A ranch to the right has several hundred acres planted in nopal cactus. *They may be intended to act as a host for the **cochineal** bug. The cochineal is a very tiny fellow who lives on the nopal. When processed they yield a natural red dye which is in great demand in several parts of the world. Two less likely possibilities are for the harvest of **nopalitos**, young leaves, or the **tuna** (fruit), both of which are part of the latino cuisine.*

4.3   29.4   K120   A dirt road intersects from the left (rear) and crosses to go southwest toward the hills.

7.7   37.2   K107+   A particularly large *vado* showing recent flooding. Just beyond is a small *refresco* stand. Not a spot we'd pick to start a business, but it's surely within walking distance of the owner. The *cardón* cactus have just about disappeared as we move out of their environment.

6.3   43.5   K97+   The graded road angling right is an entrance onto the dirt road to **Desemboque del Seri, Chueca,** etc. **(See Sonora Beaches.)** For now we continue on the paved highway.

5.9   49.4   K88   We pass a dirt road straight southwest into the bush. Where to? *Quién sabe.*

13.1   62.5   K67   The peaks off to the south are quite tall. One is over 3000 feet, but they seem to have no name. Most unusual. Behind the hills to the west are **Punta Sargento** and the north end of **Isla Tiburón. (See Sonora Beaches.)** As we pass the cleft between the hills we can see the peaks of Tiburón in the distance.

4.4   66.9   K60   The *vados* take a beating during a heavy rain. There are two trucks and a skiploader clearing one as we pass.

5.6   72.5   K51   The highway continues straight, with only minor adjustments, toward the southeast.

6.9   79.4   K40   The highway intersects and we angle to the right on a due south course. According to the highway sign, we are on Sonora 29. We come back into the the land of irrigated fields. On the left is a large vineyard.

3.0   82.4   K35   A chicken ranch, **Santa Rosita,** is off to the west. Then continue through more grapes.

8.1   90.5   K22   It is amazing how much the vegetation can vary, often within a few hundred yards. Right here the plants indicate subsoil moisture, thus part of a flood plain. A short distance back the plants looked like leftovers from a garage sale. Ahead are ranch buildings and a double row of date palms leading toward where a house used to be, then come irrigated fields.

3.4   93.9   K16+   **Topes** (speed bumps) and a school, then a **Pemex** with a surprise, unleaded **magnasin** gasoline. This is good news. We pass a number of paved and graded farm roads over the next 10 miles. Grapes are big. At times one wonders if the world can absorb them all.

10.3 104.2   K0   We have reached Mexico 16 Highway at K85. **Hermosillo** is 53 miles east, **Kino Bay** 13 miles west.

End of log.

Bahía Kino — Desemboque del Seri...

There are two entries onto the road north along the coast to Desemboque del Seri and eventually to the paved highway connecting Kino and Puerto Libertad. The first (we call it the launch-ramp entry) begins at the end of the road through Nuevo Kino at the Caverna del Seri restaurant and trailer park. The second is back in town and, though easier driving, is harder to find. But first, lets do the launch-ramp log.

Launch - Ramp Log...

The first turnoff is at the end of the **Nuevo Kino** road, **5.6** miles west of the **K110** marker. We take the road north across from the entrance into the **Caverna del Seri** trailer park and restaurant. *The restaurant provides the area with essentially its only taste of nightlife and has since the early 60s. There's dancing to a live band several times a week.* Follow the graded dirt road (north) around the rocky promontory and past the launching ramp at **0.5** miles. Continue north to the top of a hill for a fine view of the **Sea of Cortéz** and **Tiburón Island**. Just beyond is a marine research laboratory and shrimp larva propagation facility.

At **1.2** a road (left) goes west to **Windy Point**, a popular camping area. Continue to the top of a short, rough hill (**1.5** miles), then drop back to a small arroyo and a road out to a south-facing camping beach. We bear to the right and north on a terrible trail across an alluvial plain toward the hills. Plants in the area include *lomboy* (a type of *copál*), ironwood, paloverde, greasewood, *torote* and cactus.

The left fork goes toward the beach at **2.2** miles. We take the right fork up the arroyo and around the south end of a small ridge to rejoin the main road to **El Desemboque del Seri** after a very long **3.4** miles. Expect sand, rocks and high centering on this route.

The Downtown Entry...

The sign marking the turnoff to **Punta Chueca** and **Desemboque del Seri** is hard to find because it is partially hidden by a palm tree. Look for it **1.9** miles west of the K110 marker in **Nuevo Kino** on the east side of a small rocky hill. The well-signed **El Cactus Trailer Park** is on the same road.

0.0   0.0   Follow the graded road as it curves right (east) for a short distance. Go under the power lines, past the water pumps and begin bearing north.

0.8   0.8   Continue past the El Cactus.

1.1   1.9   Ahead and to the right is an attempt at a vacation home development, **Sierra Kino**. Continue north past the entrance. The range of hills to the west are known locally as the **Sierra Cuevitas**, due to the many small caves to be seen in the steep slopes. Our road climbs, then descends into another watershed.

3.1   5.0   We are at the intersection with the launch ramp road from Kino (described above). *Another entrance to that road is ahead about a half-mile.* As we work our way in and out of the hills ahead we catch glimpses of the Sea of Cortéz and Tiburón Island. There are numerous trails which branch both up and down the dry streambeds, most of which are made by the *leñeros* (wood gatherers), but few reach to the water.

2.3   7.3   A narrow, rough trail comes in from the east. Continue northward past more views of Tiburón.

2.9   10.2   Road (left) is down toward a beach area. Continue (north) downhill through a stretch of fairly soft, but passable, sand. We are back near the beach after going around a small range of hills.

1.8   12.0   We pass a locked gate and a private property sign out in the middle of nowhere. It even lacks a fence on either side of the gate! Maybe that comes later.

1.1   13.1   Intersection with a dirt road (left) to the coast. *It descends quickly past a small crossroad (0.4 miles) before arriving at the beach and an unoccupied house at 1.5 miles. There are a number of camping spots. The map indicated that we should* *name this spot **Punta San Miguel**. So be it. There are also some tanks and other parapher-nalia indicating attempts to locate and store water. The current through here can be strong and dangerous, as indicated by the name of the channel in front of us, **Canal Infernillo**. (Channel of Hell, or Devil). Though probably not appropriate here, infernillo also means chafing dish.* Back to the main road and continue north.

2.8   15.9   A good view of the north end of Tiburón and a few small houses for the people who monitor the island. Closer, on our side of the channel, is a small cluster of houses, **Punta Chueca**. Just ahead is the road into the town.

0.7   16.6   Road (left) leads past a school and basketball court, **0.6**. *This Seri Indian colony of about 1000 is principally a fishing community, but they are relying more and more on the skills of their people in making ironwood carvings, necklaces and a very unusual kind of **canasta** (basket).*

These thick and heavy baskets are made by the women from fibers derived from the small branches of the copál, a small, common, pithy tree. It is said that when tightly woven they will hold water. When you hear the prices asked for their work, they may appear high (several hundred dollars and more for the larger pieces), but you need only watch them gather, prepare and weave the fibers to realize that it can take months to complete just one basket. Many of the designs are traditional and all colors come from natural dyes. The Seri baskets are in demand from collectors and museums worldwide.

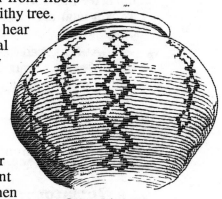

SERI BASKET

The Seris are not much for living inside the block houses the government constructed for them. Most have chosen a cooler alternative, a brush and tarpaper lean-to tacked onto the government housing. The Seris are a dark and handsome people, and the women have a well developed sense of how to sell their handicrafts. This will become evident as soon as you stop.

If we get out of the car, even open a window, we are fair game. In a wink we are backed up against a fence, tree, even the car, by as many as a dozen or more women offering necklaces (**collares**), baskets (**canastas**) and ironwood carvings (**figuras**, or **monos**). Though they rarely bargain on price, they may offer increasingly better-made items at the same price. Take your time and look things over. There are museum-quality treasures here in the hands of the ladies of Chueca. The pushing and shoving is done good naturedly, but until you leave they are likely to continue.

The value of bringing clothing to the Seris for trading has been written about so many times that most Seris are up to their ears in clothes. On today's market don't expect a couple of jackets or dresses to be an "open sesame" to great bargains. The best thing is still cash on the barrelhead. We recommend bringing clothes to Mexico, for it is welcome anywhere, but an offering of new Levis in early 1990 failed to get an exchange even closely resembling their retail value. Save the jeans for the shrimp fishermen.

*The necklaces here are unique to the Seris. Using limpet and other shells, dyed shark vertebrae, fish bones and seeds, they create an attractive variety of **collares**. We have about a dozen styles on display in our home.*

In years past these people and those in El Desemboque and Puerto Libertad were the only ones who carved the animals out of ironwood. To a degree it was an extension of their culture, for they used to make arrowheads and harpoons of this wood. (We have two museum-quality harpoon points for capturing turtles in our collection.) In those days all of the work was done with hand axes, files and a variety of abrasives. Today the large majority of the production comes from Bahía Kino and is done with electric saws, drills, routers and sanders. Only a few of the old maestros remain. When you see some of their work...think seriously about a purchase. They will not be around forever.

SHELL NECKLACES

We return to the intersection and continue north. Good views of **Isla Tiburón** are off to the west. It's a big island...30 miles long by 20 wide. For the next mile or so the road follows close behind the margins of the beach, then turns inland and climbs.

2.4   19.0   We now border some hills and are several hundred feet above the water. The quality of the road has deteriorated to a degree, but should still be passable to experienced drivers of all but large trailers and motorhomes.

0.3   19.3   A road (west) goes about 150 meters to the water. *The beach is beautiful and has several excellent camping spots on a bluff overlooking the water. Swimming should be good, bearing in mind the possible heavy tidal currents. The view is magnificent. Though we didn't stay here, experiences in similar spots would lead us to expect good fishing for corvina and spotted sand bass on the high tides. Give it a go with either silver spoons or small scampis. Failing that, put shrimp pieces on a two-hook dropper rig.*

1.6   20.9   A road (left) goes over a couple of small ridges (**1.2** mi) to a long curving beach protected from the north and open to the south. It is a beautiful location. Return to the highway and on past several small arroyos leading to the water. Several show faint tire tracks, but we tried none of them. This is ideal 4-WD and ATC country.

The green-gray bushes along the road are a variety of daisy. In the spring they are bright with hundreds of yellow flowers.

1.2   22.1   Road (left) down an arroyo to the water past ironwood, cardón, organpipe, paloverde, elephant tree *(torote)*, lomboy, etc. A mile farther north there is another road to the beach. There are several broken bridges and stretches of roadbed. With the new paved road to Puerto Libertad, we doubt that this road will ever be restored. The prominent peak some distance ahead is **Cerro Pinto**. The road continues straight north a mile or so back from the beach.

3.3   25.4   A fence. Civilization cannot be far away. Continue over the deteriorated roadbed and through a number of short detours. We have moved closer to the water and are now bordering a mangrove lagoon. This should be an interesting place to launch an inflatable or cartop boat, but watch the tides.

3.8   29.2   Road (west) to an attractive camping spot (**0.3** mi). *There are several palapas left over from the commercial fishermen. The beach is sandy with a few pebbles and shells.*

There are also a few small arched tent-like affairs made out of ocotillo branches over which one might throw a tarp to create a sleeping area. Built by the Seri fishermen, they are covered with brush to give shade and ventilation. If it gets cold or very windy, they add a tarp. These structures are common in this part of Sonora. Back to the road and continue north.

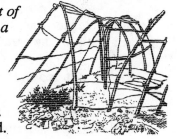

SERI CAMPGROUND

Off in the distance we see the conical peak of **Cerro Tepopa**. Though a part of the mainland, from here it looks like an island. Directly west, and much closer is a sandy point identified on the map as **Punta Arenas.**

3.1   32.3   A road (west) *0.5* miles to the beach and more of the Seri ocotillo tent frames just above the high tide line. *There are several nice camping areas and the road, though sandy, is firm enough for our pickup. A walk along the beach reveals some driftwood and shells. The place has a good feel.* Back to the main road.

3.6   35.9   We are on a straight road going north. Cerro Pinto is now much closer and directly ahead. Turn slightly northwest and another straight beach.

2.1   39.4   Signed road (left) is to **El Sargento** and more beaches. *Drop down off the hill past paloverde, cardón, cholla, ocotillo and lomboy. We drive past one of the small Seri seasonal fishing camps (**0.7** mi). The dirt road continues ahead to **El Dolar** at the foot of **Cerro Tepopa**, then past the sand point of El Sargento and a small offshore rock,* *a distance of several miles.* Back to the main road and north up a hill. From the top of the grade there's a good view of **Punta Sargento**'s mangrove-lined estero.

3.2 42.6 Another road angles back toward Punta Sargento but we continue north on a very straight road which no longer goes near the water. The terrain and plantlife varies little from what we have become used to.

11.6 54.2 A slight turn. After this stretch, even a small change becomes an event. The shore line is coming back toward us.

2.1 56.3 We arrive in **El Desemboque del Seri**.

Meet **Antonio Lopez**. He is a Seri who looks to be in his seventies. His skin is a very dark mahogany. Don Antonio was born on Tiburón Island and lived there until the Mexican government forced him and the rest of the Seris to relocate on the mainland in the 1960s. He is one of the few old-timers who still fashions ironwood into carvings of animals, objects, etc., entirely with hand tools. *While we talk he is using a machete to rough out a replica of a machete. Already easily recognizable, it will be two more days before it will be ready to sell. Its value...about $30. The Machete's lines look good and the gold and coffee hues of the selected ironwood will make it a keepsake.*

When asked what he would like if someone were to visit him, Don Antonio replied that he is in need of metal files and wet-or-dry sandpaper. Sr. Lopez is a quiet man who appears happy in the tiny tarpaper lean-to he and his wife share a few yards from the Sea of Cortéz. When we return we will bring some files (limas or escofinas) and sandpaper.

We met our new friend by chance. As we stepped from the car we were surrounded by the lady vendors and Tom retreated into Don Antonio's yard (with his permission) to take some of the pressure off. The women respected his property and waited for him to step back outside. And when Tom did...the good natured melee began again.

When and if you come this way, put a few files and some sandpaper in the car for Don Antonio Lopez, or someone like him. It's a small price for the opportunity of meeting an interesting person.

0.8 57.1 We are at the north end of the town and, after asking directions to **Puerto Libertad,** are poised to take the sandy road northeast between two hills. The road divides, then comes back together and passes a few minor intersecting trails. Continue on the main trail.

2.5 59.6 The road moves up onto a bluff and winds its way through the hills. We pass many cardón cactus along with the other vegetation typical of the region. We see quail, or their tracks everywhere.

2.3 61.9 A small abandoned house, a palm and a few other bits of civilization remind us of the price of living in these parts.

3.2 65.1 The road separates and we take the right branch. Shortly, they reconnect, just before dropping into a narrow valley with a small ranch, corral and several outbuildings. A number of saddles are straddling the veranda railing. Mesquite trees shade the front yard and a soccer ball lies waiting for someone to kick it. A garden patch indicates some surface water at least part of the year.

1.7 66.8 A fork in the road. We take the one to the right and it goes straight past an abandoned house, cement tank and well with water 75 feet down. *(How do we know? It took 2.5 seconds for a dropped rock to reach the water. That's about 75 feet.)* Off in the distance are several small ranches. We pass a small abandoned brick house.

2.9 69.7 We stop at a ranch with several boats in the yard. There is evidence of trucks coming and going, and we see several large piles of charcoal (*carbón*). *The charcoal is made in huge pits 10 by 40 feet and at least 10 feet deep. One of the pits is cooking, another is in the process of being emptied and two others are empty. A look at the wood scraps lying about shows that they are making charcoal out of ironwood! The same wood which has become so scarce for the carvers around Bahía Kino. According to the map,*

SONORA BEACHES

*the name of this place is **Rancho San Ignacio**.* Continue east toward the highway.

      0.7   70.4   We come onto the **Libertad-Kino** highway at K120+. The road which branched left back at 66.8 appears to connect with this highway about two miles north of our entry point. Libertad is 30 miles north, while the Kino-Hermosillo highway, Mexico 16, is 75 miles to the south.

      End of log.

Kino — San Carlos Beaches...

Peña Blanca, Etc.

*There are many beautiful beaches along Mexico's western shores: there are dozens between **Puerto Vallarta** and **Manzanillo** and many more little bays along **Oaxaca's** coast, for example. And here, between Kino and Guaymas, hidden from all but the few with a boat, sturdy pickup or 4-wheel drive, are dozens of rocky points, protected coves and sandy beaches which easily match those and other already-discovered beauty spots. If there was a ready water supply, many of these places would be overrun with getaway and retirement homes such as are found today around Bahia San Carlos to the south. Perhaps it is only a matter of time until this happens. In the meantime, enjoy.*

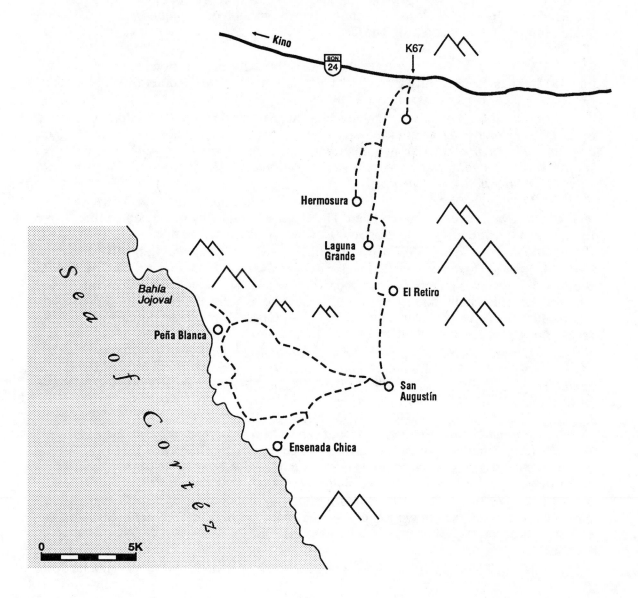

*The journey begins by driving south on Sonora 24 from the **Hermosillo-Kino** (Sonora 16) highway. Proceed along the highway to the graded road (right) at K67+. The trip is not for motorhomes. Sturdy camper and van types only. It is a breeze for a 4-WD as long as the clearance is good.*

0.0   0.0   The road south is signed to **La Hermosura** and **San Agustín**. Graded and dusty, it passes through fields of alfalfa, grapes and other produce. Stay with the road and the most traveled forks.

4.2   4.2   Farm buildings are off to the right. The soil is a rich, dark brown. Most of the product is irrigated wheat. We make a 90-degree turn (east) past eucalyptus trees, then go back south.

2.4   6.6   **Rancho El Augustín,** a fairly large operation with large, clean living quarters. Just downstream from where a pump is spewing large amounts of cool, sweet water, a young girl is washing clothes on the side of the cement ditch. *(This could be one of the water sources mentioned in the introduction.)* The valley begins to narrow as we continue down the watershed. Ahead is a small cluster of seasonally-occupied farm worker shacks. Continue south.

2.2   8.8   A fork in the road. Go across the cattle guard, not around it.

1.0   9.8   Another cattle guard at the other end of the property. Cross it and head west by southwest over a semi-graveled, washboardy, single-lane road. Climb gradually out of the watershed. The desert plants include greasewood, organ pipe and cardón.

1.3   11.1   We take the road (right) at the intersection because it is better traveled and has been recently graded. The left trail may well go to other beaches south of Ensenada Chica. Hopefully, we'll find out later.

0.9   12.0   A sign indicates that **Ensenada Chica** is 3 kilometers ahead on the left. The road is rocky and winds quite a bit, but is passable to most vehicles with good clearance. *The small arroyo is full of life, ironwood, a spidery-looking cholla, copal, torote, several kinds of ocotillo and, nearer the water, some narrow-leafed agaves. There are also signs of rabbit, quail, and rodents.*

At **2.2**, someone has dressed a small saguaro with armlike branches in a hat and shirt and put a Budweiser beer can in its hand. The effort will probably not become famous. We finally top a last little ridge and drop into **Ensenada Chica** at **2.6** miles.

Here we see four or five well-kept little houses along the margin of a perfect little, rock-sided cove. There are actually two small coves, with a common entrance. As it faces southwest, it receives protection from the winter winds. The reefs around **Isla San Pedro Nolasco** are only about 8km to the south. A favorite spot for the boats out of Bahia San Carlos, they are actually closer to here than to San Carlos. There are a number of camping areas, though permission should be obtained.

While feeding this data into the computer, a dozen pelicans are diving on baitfish schools about a hundred yards in front of us; three redbilled oyster crackers are pecking at the barnacles on the rocks; and several curlews are hunting for lunch in the sand. A good place for an inflatable boat, for fishing or to visit other, even more remote, sandy coves. Snorkeling should be superb, and we would expect to catch a variety of rock-dwelling fish almost anywhere. Be sure to bring lots of the small Scampi-type tails for your leadhead jigs. It is a natural for here. What else can we say...the cove is stunning. Return to the junction at **12.0** miles.

0.0   12.0   Here we turn north toward more beaches. It goes uphill to a crest in a half-mile, then down steeply for the first few yards before gradually dropping toward the northwest. When the road forks, take the best-traveled branch, as they do reconnect.

1.6   13.6   Cross a dry stream bed. It is obvious that water is not far down

because the plants in the stream bed are green while the same species only a few yards above are parched. A good view of the Cortéz, the reddish hills and the many caves ahead.

        0.9   14.5   We see a fence...news in this part of the desert. About 200 yards back from the beach a small road goes **0.3** miles south over a ridge into another small beach. *This bay is almost perfect. There are actually two beaches separated by a 30-foot high rock. One is pebbly while the south one is a tiny sandy crescent. The sand beach has several pangas on it and a few small buildings. Access for camping other than tenting is poor. A very beautiful spot.* Back **0.3** to the junction, and continue toward another beach over the sometimes-rough, rocky trail and eventually down a slope toward the sea.

        1.1   15.6   This beach is a good 250 yards long, and most of it campable. A large rock juts out into the water about one-third the way up from the south end. Its sides have been eroded, leaving cave-like overhangs around most of it. A sand bar extends back to the main beach, affording a calm side in almost any weather. *Again, the water is crystal clear and there are abundant lifeforms around the rocks and over the water. We spent several hours exploring the beach and snorkeling around the nearby rocks and spotted several sizeable cabrilla and triggerfish among the many damselfish and wrasses.*

    At the north end of the beach is another, much smaller, cove with several houses, a large palapa, outbuildings, storage tanks and satellite dish.

    From here the road takes off north along the coast just behind the building described above. It goes over a low ridge into **Bahía Jojoval**. The name suggests that jojoba bushes grow near here, and it turns out that there are several nearby jojoba bean enterprises.

    Jojoba beans have been found to provide an oil which replaces whale oil in many applications. Curiously, its chemical composition is almost identical to that created by the sebaceous glands of the sperm whale. It has materially lessened the demand for whale oil, thus helping to reduce the take of these unique animals.

        .5   16.1   A short side road to the beach, **0.3** mile. *One word describes* **Peña Blanca** *very nicely..."wow." Again, the two cove formula with rocks in the middle. There are several spots for camping...a place to remember. These are a bit more open than some of the others, thus more caution in launching boats. We have to come back to this one.* Return to the road and north past Peña Blanca. It goes about 200 yards before pooping out in the rocks. Return to the beach and back past Ensenada Chica and, eventually, the highway. This trip would be ideal for one of the 4-WD minivans.

Bahía San Augustín, Etc.

    The rough dirt road leaving the Kino-Guaymas cut-off at K57 brings us to another cluster of jewels in the chain of beaches bordering Sonora's western extremities. We also learn that it may have been possible to drive from Peña Blanca northward to reach these beaches. (We had given up earlier, feeling we were overmatched.)

    Head west from the K57 turnoff through irrigated fields. It doesn't last too long...a mile after starting we are in the desert. The roadbed is a bit sandy, but it should not bother most vehicles with competent drivers. We find all three of the region's large cactus species here...organ pipe, saguaro and cardón, plus cholla and greasewood. In short, a stereotype Arizona-Sonora desert mix.

    At **4.0** a road branching slightly left is signed to **Bahía San Agustín** and **Cerro Prieto**. We take it. This section is sandy and soft with opportunities to high-center. We reach the top of a small rise and descend into the narrow coastal plain.

    At **2.5** miles we arrive at the beach and follow the road south past many camping areas and eventually a tarpaper shack at **3.1**. The road continues south around a prominent, dark hill, Cerro Prieto (Dark Mountain). Keep following the road past an unsigned chainlink fence and through an open gate. At **3.8** we are on another beach, *La Cocina* (The Kitchen). *This one is also a lovely crescent with several camping areas, beautiful water and lots of possibilities. One difference is that it could be more open to the weather. According to a* *fisherman we met in Cerro Prieto, Cocina offers very good fishing, thus the name.*

The road branches again at **4.3** with the left side going on past the beach, then up and out the southern end of the small depression. The road continues south along the coast past several more coves before connecting with the road north out of Peña Blanca. At **5.2** miles, we turn around and retrace our route.

We go back past the Cocina intersection and on to **Bahía San Augustín**, a two-mile long beach with some rocks here and there. *The sand is gray, rather fine and blows into dunes in places. A road parallels the beach down to the other end, but provides no Augustín access through the soft sand. The best places to camp are to the south.* We headback inland to the intersection noted at mile **4.0**. *We also tried a short road at **4.6** which died after some hundreds of yards. (Caution: It is not easy to turn around out there.)*

0.0   4.0   From this intersection, we now go north on a poorly signed trail toward **El Colorado**. The land is beautiful. The rock formations blend perfectly with the many desert plants, as if to a master plan.

3.2   7.2   At the remains of a cement-block house the road turns decidedly west to another intersection (**0.6**). The north branch is signed to **El Choyudo**, 12km. We continue west toward the water.

2.9   10.1   Another intersection. The branch (right) goes north through the hills. We follow the (left) branch toward a red, rocky hill, which turns out to be on the water. *We are in the fish camp of El Colorado (0.7). It is clean and well organized. The catch is principally trigger fish and small shark. As we look around, our eyes keep coming back to the tall, red rock. It is red, very red, with a bright blue spot about a third of the way up the side. We thought it might be a shrine until we got much closer, when it turned out to be a sombra (sun shade) for a trailer.*

Anchored by the huge red monolith, the beach swings south. A few rocky patches break up the mile-long sandy crescent. According to those we queried, camping here is no problem. El Colorado is definitely on our "return" list. Back to the last intersection and north, then east, through the hills and the beautiful Sonora desert.

1.3   11.4   We have a crossroads. The one coming in from the east appears to be a continuation of the road signed to El Choyudo (see above). We turn west (left), drive up a canyon, then down into a very small cove that contains a defunct fish meal plant, and **Luís Lopez Ruíz** (**1.2** miles)...

We had no sooner stepped out of the pickup when from across the sand came a loud, "Hola". At first we couldn't even place it. Then a very short man came bounding along the rocky path toward us. With a huge smile he reaches to offer his hand in greeting. Luís Lopez Ruíz is at our service. Whatever our wishes we need only ask. During the preamble he bounced around energetically, showing us his boat and his net. Nearby was a small pile of supplies including a dozen large, fresh red chiles arranged over the top of a gasoline drum to dry. Luís has been a fisherman for 42 of his 51 years. Somewhere he has picked up a bit of English, but he does not appear to be able to read. (When we show him our map he recognizes the coastline and speedily names off the landmarks without even taking notice of the written names (He says we are in Ensenada Las Cadenas.) He also drew trails in the sand, trails we did not know exist, but later found them to be highly accurate.

When asked where he lives, he points to the tar paper leanto, and says, "Today I am here. Next month I might be south of Guaymas, or around Mulegé." He smiled broadly and added, "Wherever the fish go I go." It shouldn't take him more than a few minutes to load up and shove off.

When we left he said we would meet again. Carol and I agree...we will meet again. Luís Alvarez Ruíz is truly one of the few remaining vagabundos del mar (vagabonds of the sea), and he couldturn up anywhere in the Sea of Cortéz, at any time. Back to the intersection.

0.0   11.4   On our return we head north toward **El Choyudo**. Shortly the road branches again and we take the left branch (southwest).

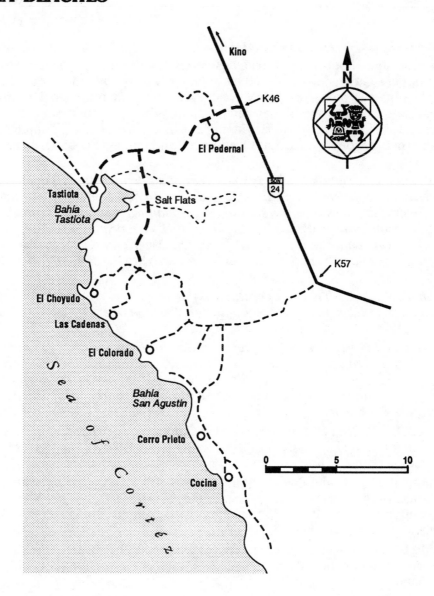

3.4   14.8   We find ourselves in a nothing-appearing town with little or no access to the water, but El Choyudo's importance should increase greatly in the years to come. *Shrimp farming is coming in a big way, as it is in many estuarine environments in western Mexico. We talked to a young engineer who told us that over 500 acres of the estero will be made into ponds to raise premium blue shrimp. Privately financed, it will have its own hatchery where the eggs are fertilized and hatched into larvae. Food will come from the waters introduced from the estero and also from fish meal products. It's an operation we'd like to revisit.* We backtrack a short distance and head north.

3.8   18.6   An unmarked intersection. To the west 2.1 miles is **Tastiota**, a once-busy fishing port, but lack of product has made it rather quiet. Here too, shrimp farming might provide new prosperity. Back to the intersection and east toward the highway.

1.5   20.1   Intersection. **El Pedernal** (The Flint) is on the right and **San Felipe de Jesús** is to the left. Continue East.

1.9   22.0   We are back on the Sonora 24 Highway, but at K46+.

San Carlos and its Beaches...

Take the signed **San Carlos** road west at K132+ north of Guaymas. Prominent on the horizon is **Teta Kawi**, a twin-peaked mountain named for what it resembles...the teats of a goat. The highway proceeds straight west. At K7 note the unfinished high-rise on the beach. It was supposed to be the El Presidente Guaymas but a lack of funds did it in. There's talk of a new effort, maybe *mañana*. Beginning at K9 businesses begin popping up, ending at K12 and the marina. Beyond are roads leading to residential viewpoints, resort hotels and camping beaches.

*The community of San Carlos is somewhat of a phenomenon. In the late 50s it was little more than a few leveled spots along a south-facing beach. Behind was a lovely little mangrove-rimmed lagoon. Here, at a spot where the mangroves (mangles) had been hacked away, we used to launch a small boat into the beautiful bay. A primitive trailer park operated by an American was on a small protected cove. The American seemed to be everywhere: owner, operator, clerk and trouble shooter...his name was **Stu Bryson**...the park, the **Shangri La**.*

By then the Yacht Club was in operation, but there were no houses. It was a full hour's drive northwest in a pickup to reach a beautiful palm canyon where a high-rise hotel is today under construction.

*A few years later we came down with 10 families for Easter Week (Semana Santa). The adventure included crowded camping, very little ice, and shrimp for less than a dollar a pound. The fishing too was excellent. Yellowtail were plentiful over the deep reefs outside the harbor entrance and around **Isla San Pedro Nolasco**. We barbecued, fished, sunned and ate shrimp for a week. A marvelous time.*

Today San Carlos has more than 1000 vacation or retiree homes. This, along with a thousand hotel rooms and an equal number of trailer spaces allows San Carlos to host up to 10,000 visitors at a time.

Among the hotels, the **Posada San Carlos** is still the tops, with the small **Creston** a viable alternative. Another lively, happy spot is the **Fiesta San Carlos**, while the **Solimar**, a condominium/hotel above the golf course has nice grounds, pools and jacuzzis, but the rooms and suites need maintenance.

Add gift shops, laundromat, beauty parlors, bank, hardware store, several small "supermercados" and lots of restaurants and San Carlos has the makings of being a topflight resort destination.

Some thoughts on eating...the restaurant at the **Shangri La** is good. The **San Carlos Grill** (decorated to look like part of the Carlos 'n Charlie's chain, but isn't) has a good a reputation but we never found out how good they really are. The service was so bad that we walked out.

If you have your own kitchen facilities and want do do your own scampi, watch for the shrimp vendor outside the supermarket. An older man, **Alejandro Zavada** has great pride in the quality of his shrimp. They might be a few pesos higher, but we've never had the tiniest problem with his shrimp.

There are now six trailer parks totaling around a thousand spaces. A note on the trailer parks...the largest, Shangri La, has seen better times, but is still a factor for it certainly has the best location. Currently the **Teta Kawi** (near the entrance into town) is at the top of the heap along with the adjoining **Totonaka RV Park**. Another beautiful one, is the **San Carlos Trailer Club**. More of a mobile home development requiring membership, it is located 3km north of the highway. Take the signed, paved road on the east side of the golf course. Facilities include clubhouse, pool and jacuzzi.

Diving around San Carlos is very good. A number of international diving championships have been held here. The area's three dive shops, **Gary's, San Carlos Dive Center** and **Cortez Seasports** all offer equipment rental, air, trips for diving, sightseeing or fishing. Windsailing and ATC exploring are also fastgrowing pursuits among the younger

visitors.

The recent years have greatly extended San Carlos beyond its marina cove and surrounding environs. Residential and marina developments have sprung up at **Algodones**, **Catch 22** and **Palm Canyon** beaches. Beyond those bounds Club Med has appropriated a kilometer-or-so of beach for their purposes. And the end is not in sight...

0.0   0.0   We leave the community proper at the entrance to the **San Carlos Bay Marina**. Bear right around the yacht harbor, across the top of the outer bay and into the residential area. Here magnificent homes look down on crystal waters and dozens of yachts bob at anchor. Above the rooftops a forest of toadstool-like satellite dishes make a statement for contemporary living. Continue up to the top of the short grade and down onto the beach at Algodones.

2.0   2.0   On the left is a close-up view of the **Teta Kawi** peaks. Ahead is the new **Algodones Marina** project. *Once thought to be impractical, it is proving the skeptics wrong. Already a hundred slips have been installed and a dozen homes completed and more under construction.* Follow the paved road (right) past the graveled entry into the marina.

1.2   3.2   We top a small rise to view a wide sweeping beach. On the near end surrounded by that once-remote grove of native palms, a **Howard Johnson** hotel is under construction. Just past the hotel, several trails lead to the beach. Camping is behind the dunes. An advantage in the winter, disadvantage in summer.

1.3   4.5   Entrance to the **Costa del Mar** resort condos on **Catch 22** beach. *The name comes from the fact that the 1960s movie, Catch 22, was shot here. Remains of the sets can still be seen above the beach near the runway.*

From there it is a short drive to the entrance into **Club Med**. *Reportedly gaining in popularity, we were twice refused admission to even inspect the grounds. "Write our New York office for an appointment," they said. They've done well without us so far...they'll likely continue to do so.*

0.6   5.1   This is where the fun begins...the pavement ends at the entrance to Club Med. Drive a hundred or so yards north and follow the shoreline for numerous campsites. This is the end of the road for motorhomes and trailers.

0.5   5.6   A small fish camp. Maneuverable rigs with good clearance and standard cars should be able to continue without problems. Another mile brings us to a seasonal fish camp.

We now have you enmeshed in a web of trails. Pick any well-traveled one. *We spent most of a day exploring, relaxing and walking a dozen beautiful beaches.* To the north along the hills is a well-traveled and graded road which takes us around a large fenced tract. *What lies off that road probably includes the palm canyon, cave and beach we started out to visit 8 hours ago. We'll have the answer in our next Mexico West Book.*

It is an easy, shorter run back to San Carlos on the above-mentioned road than the way we came. We go up to the new road and work our way back through Catch 22 to San Carlos. It's been a good day.

Beaches South of Guaymas...

For over 30 years we've been driving south of Guaymas to a variety of destinations as far away as Puerto Escondido, Oaxaca. And for those three decades we've nearly always done the same thing...tank up and head for Mochis, Mazatlán and points south.

Our work on this book is causing us to look more closely at what lies along the coast between Guaymas and Navajoa. Aside from a tremendous amount of farming and a few trails across the salt flats there is not much that will be put on our "must return" list, but that doesn't mean it will not fire someone else's imagination.

In addition, by checking out the areas and writing about them, maybe we can satisfy someone's curiosity about what lies beyond that next row of dunes. It's not all good, and it's not all bad. Please read on...

A paved road west at K57+ is signed to **Potam**, 10km. We start by paralleling an irrigation canal and gradually swinging south. It is hard to realize just how much agriculture there is in this part of Mexico until you begin traveling the side roads.

At **6.1**, just before entering Potam a paved road goes west to **Algodones**. At **8.1** we arrive in the unsigned little town of **Rahúm** and the paving ends. We follow the main road until it angles north more than it should, then back-track to a ranch house and ask.

The answers saved a lot of time...first, we are on the wrong road. We were headed for **Huirivis**. The **Boca las Cruces** road is a half-mile from the ranch house, but it has been closed for more than two years. They also told us how to find the Algodones road...it leaves from the center of Rahúm and bears left where we had borne right. Then one of them added, that it too had been abandoned for several years and that dune buggies are the only things that could make it through. So much for Algodones and Boca Las Cruces. Back to the highway.

South and West of Obregón

0.0   0.0   We turn off the highway next to the local **Pemex** (K48) on a paved road (south) through the town of **Vicam**.

3.0   3.0   The signed community of **Casas Blancas** follows. Just beyond we cross the riverbed of the **Río Yaqui**. *At one time it carried water year around, but the dams, wells and irrigation canals keep it dry except during times of heavy runoff.* Continue toward the community of **Vicam Pueblo**. This town is one of several communities located within the Yaqui Indian reservation. These tribal centers are governed through a system of elders, councils, etc. Other communities on the reservation include **Potam**, **Yaqui Pueblo**, **Pueblo Nuevo** and **Cocorít**.

1.1   4.1   We are in Vicam Pueblo, standing in front of a semi-abandoned church. *The entry is through the cemetery past a hundred or more graves. Inside there are no pews or candles burning, but the main altar and two smaller side ones are relatively intact. The floor is dirty and we hear rats scrambling around in the false ceiling.*

We walk around in the dim light and inspect the place. There are eight statues of Christ on the three altars, and all of them are clothed in clean, long lacy white dresses! Some have bodices, others are covered only from the waist down. An eerie feeling. Our descriptions of the garb to others later brought forth no explanations.

The town appears to be almost deserted because of the Yaqui's habit of putting distance between themselves and their neighbors. *Tract housing would never go over with these people.* We continue through town and head south and west through delta land jammed tight with mesquite. It is almost as if the road is enclosed between high green walls, so thick is the vegetation.

7.4   11.5   Through the brush we see a bit of farmland off to the right. Several houses and outbuildings are beyond.

92

2.0   13.5   The small town of **El Tapiero** (Adobe Wall Maker) also appears to be a Yaqui settlement with the same open-housing format. There are canals going in all directions, sometimes crossing each other via bridges or tunnels. Continue southwest. By the way...we lost the pavement a mile or more back.

2.8   16.2   The road swings right (west) and is paved again. A mile beyond, a small community (**Pueblo Nuevo**), then what appears to be a secondary-level agricultural school. Soon we are heading south again, still blessed with pavement. The soil of this delta region is incredibly productive...up to four vegetable crops a year. They have the heat, the water, and the markets to make it worthwhile.

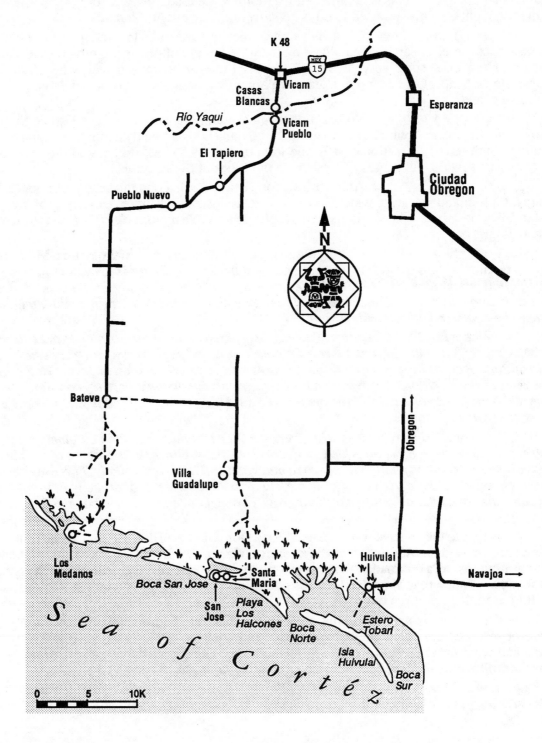

12.6 28.8   The town of **Bateve** is off to our right, and the pavement ends for good this time. Continue south over an increasingly difficult road. Large potholes, sometimes with water in them, begin cropping up as we continue through mesquite scrub and marshy areas. This is definitely not a rainy-season road...this clay makes some of the stickiest mud you can imagine.

4.4 33.2   A fork in the road...we take the graded, better traveled, (right) side.

2.6 35.8   The road turns to the right. A long line of sand dunes are ahead. This is definitely not a motorhome road...but OK for vans and campers...all you need to do is go slow and stay out of the mud.

2.0 37.8   We arrive at the dunes. A road forks left and goes behind the dunes. These piles of sand are stabilized by the wide variety of plants growing on them. As we go south we see some very tall ones. There are little roads running everywhere, and all appear to be heading for the point ahead. We are now among mangroves and driving over solid wet sand.

1.6 39.4   We are at the water, with the main channel of **Estero Santo Domingo** directly in front. The other side of the channel is a long sandy peninsula which goes off in a southeasterly direction. A **0.7**-mile-long branch road goes southeast along the mangroves past several camp sites. We return to the fork out by the dunes.

0.0 37.8   Another little road heads north along the beach for about 200 yards, then inland toward a water tower. The road is sandy at times, especially if we go inland. The best road right now is just at the high tide line. We try to stick to the trails showing the most traffic.

1.6 39.4 63.9   We arrive at the southeast side of the **Estero Melagos**, and "downtown" **Los Medaños**. The entrance into the **Sea of Cortéz** is to the left. *Medaños is a fishing camp obviously in a struggle to survive. A number of houses are abandoned, boats lie about unrepaired, and few people are down by the water, despite it being midday when the boats should be coming in.*

Where Los Medaños fishermen once prospered on the taking of snook and a dozen other kinds of fish, plus large numbers of clams, crabs and scallops, the town's remaining inhabitants process little more than small sharks and 15 to 18-inch-long corvina and, from the piles of shells, colonies of murex snails for the small amount of meat they contain. There are few options remaining for these people. It's sad. It's inevitable. And it's happening all over the world.

There is no denying the attractiveness of the beaches, bays and channels around here. And there are some spots which look especially fishy. Dinner-size catches of members of the bass and corvina families, plus sierra mackerel and halibut are likely. There may even be a few snook (robalo), left over from the old days. With a small boat the way is open to explore the sand islands and fish the mangrove channels. We must come back and explore this area.

Return to the intersection on Estero Santo Domingo, then north to find a road running far enough east to provide access to **Playa Santa María**. We do this by returning to Bateve and turning east on a dirt road. After about 3 miles we are back on pavement. We then zigzag east and south to a road signed to **San José de Bacum** (north). We go south until we reach **Villa Guadalupe** and run out of pavement.

We continue on dirt, working our way south about 15 kilometers, past a variety of enterprises...pig farm, grain fields, melon patch and a fish farm. We finally get into the saline flats and wind through them until reaching the water. Our key to finding Santa María was that we followed the power poles. Without them it would have been a lost cause.

Actually, it still was a lost cause, for Santa María and nearby San José de Bacum are virtual cement junk heaps with about 10 livable houses between them, plus at least 50 with

VICAM

no windows, doors, and in some cases, walls or roofs.

Back we go, past the melon patch, the pig and fish farms, etc. to move about 20km east to pick up Sonora 119 Highway. The road continues south some 15km kilometers, to **Huivulai** and **Estero Tobari**. At the estero there is a causeway jutting out into the water toward a long sandy island. *The causeway was built some years ago as part of an attempt to create a tourist mecca on the island, **Barra Peninsular Tobari**. It never made it. In fact it does not look as though they even finished the causeway.*

We drive out on this manmade finger of rocks to watch the sunset. The calm waters margined by tidal mud harbor many lifeforms. Waterfowl are everywhere. V's of ducks pass overhead, as do staggered lines of cormorants and pelicans. Shorebirds are getting a last crab or marine worm before calling it a day. *We stop and talk to four fishermen who show us their catch...crabs, clams, a few corvina and shrimp. They also had two ducks.*

We exchange pleasantries and as we start to move farther out onto the causeway they give us their shrimp. A gracias is extended, but they will accept no money. We watch a fiery sunset (*puesta del sol*), perhaps in celebration of the warmth we feel at this moment.

With the sky still a mass of glowing embers we drive back past the fishermen cooking the evening meal over a small fire. We stop for a moment, reach into our ice chest and leave a gift of friendship. Here on the lagoon, the fire flickers as our friends eat clams, fish, crab and duck with tortillas, a plate of beans and generous chunks of **Martin's New York extra-aged cheddar cheese**. That is probably a first. We head for a restaurant in **Navajoa**, and hopefully an accommodating chef. Back to the highway.

Navajoa — Huatabampito...

The trip to the beaches west and south of Navajoa begins at the intersection that also leads us to Alamos. This time we go west, then south out of town.

0.0   0.0   We leave Mexico 15 at K156 in downtown Navajoa and head west toward **Huatabampo** on Sonora 149 highway. Note the many beautiful homes as we drive west. At **Avenida Talamánt**, turn south.

2.3   2.3   K3   A full service **Pemex**.

5.2   7.5   K11   On the right is a fairly large college campus...**Colegio del Pacifico.** The land is flat, very rich and well utilized in all manner of agricultural endeavors. We are on a straight southwest course.

2.5   10   K15   The road heading due west here is to **Bacobampo** and more lettuce, tomatoes, corn, etc. etc. Continue southwest. The horizon is broken only by an occasional line of trees.

5.6   15.6   K24   Sonora 149 swings due south. Another kilometer brings us to **Etchajoa.** *We were just stopped by the police for a donation to a benefit circus being held sometime later in the year. We won't be here, but the officer promised to give the tickets we bought to a deserving family. We hope the kids have a good time. (In Huntington Beach, California, we are "encouraged" by our local police and fire departments at least three times a year to purchase tickets we will never use either.)* Continue (south) out of town and back into the farm country...miles of it.

6.2   21.8   K34   A big grain mill and storage area on the left. On the right is a large **Ley** Supermarket. These landmarks are as important as the beer distributors when traveling for extended periods in Mexico.

.5   22.3   K35   A sign declares that we are now entering **Huatabampo**, population 45,000. On the left is a full service **Pemex**, including *hielo* (ice). To get out of town on the Huatabampito road, take the main street east past the **Pemex** several blocks to **Iturbe** street. Then follow the traffic pattern south to **Juarez** (0.7 mi). Continue east **0.5** miles, then take the signed road (south) toward **Huatabampito**. We also lose our K markers.

4.4   26.7   We've entered the pueblo of **Batantahui**. Watch the **topes**...they are dillys. Note the roofs of many of the more primitive houses...they are dirt plastered over crisscrossed layers of bamboo, or *carrizo*. Continue straight.

2.5   29.2   Intersection. Yavaros is off to the east (left). Continue (south) toward Huatabampito. In **Moncorít** we run out of pavement (**1.4** miles).

It's **4.2** miles, and we are near the water. We take a short road over the dunes to the beach (**0.4** mi). This is an estuary, thus no waves, etc. A road goes along the shore to the west and north. Camping is very easy here. If you pick a spot near someone's *casa*, ask permission.

High, unstabilized dunes precede our entry into **Huatabampito** at **9.8** miles. Once past the dunes the town unfolds itself as what it is...a hot weather destination with a good ambiance. There are some permanent homes here, but the majority of the action has to be during the daytime and around the palapa restaurants on the beach. *We had a good talk with Clemente, whose family owns two restaurants. (Both have the same name, El Mirador, and are across from each other.) He showed us a menu and gave us a tour of the kitchen. The food was reasonable, the kitchen clean, and the help amiable. If you want to come to a busy family beach, and none of them gringos, come here on a Sunday.*

There are areas where one can camp...but self-containment is essential. Check with Clemente if you have questions. There are several nice residential homes near the south end of the beach. Clemente had one tip for visitors...Easter Week (*Semana Santa*) is a zoo here. Avoid it if you can. Otherwise things are pretty quiet, especially during the week.

0.0   29.2   Back at the intersection to **Yavaros**. Go east from here. In **2.1** miles the paved road begins a wide, gentle curve toward the south. As we enter the town there

are several fish processing plants to the left...a precursor of things to come. Wait until you enter town...fish factories everywhere. Not only is it a principal processor of fish for reduction into fish meal, but many tons of shrimp are packed and frozen here too. *Frankly our opinion has changed little over the past 9 years...Yavaros still has little to offer the tourist. If we're wrong, we'd like to hear it, and why.*

    End of log.

How to Buy a Shrimp...

A good reason for visiting Mexico's west coast fishing ports between September and May is shrimp. During this time every village that can dock a boat will have shrimp for sale somewhere...

In El Golfo de Santa Clara, Sonora, it is Clementina Castro, whose sons catch the shrimp; in Puerto Peñasco the merchant stalls along the Malecón provide the action; Guaymas has shrimp markets outside the packing plants and at the cooperativa. In Aguiabampo it might be a panga operator just returning from a night of casting a hand net. The opportunities are widespread.

In the larger towns the shrimp vendors are often located in one area, and vie with each other for business. Honed by years in the business, their hawking skills are considerable. A murmured, no gracias will rarely get one off the hook. And don't expect to find jumbo shrimp at super bargain prices...like anywhere in the world, you get what you pay for.

Check the shrimp for freshness by being sure that the meat is firm and does not have a strong, fishy smell. Shrimp from large ocean trawlers are more likely to be bruised and of lower quality than shrimp taken from shallow estuaries. In the deep-water ports check carefully. The vendors will often show several samples, then sell you an already-packaged kilo. Remember, you can always ask to have the bag opened...if they refuse, try elsewhere. Take a good look at where and how they are stored and feel the temperature of the product on display. If they are not icy, forget it. Above all, as with all seafood, be aware of the odor. If you have any misgiving, call it a day.

Lastly, don't try to carry any shellfish far without good refrigeration. They may be perfectly good when purchased, but spoil on the way to the skillet. It is for these reasons that we rarely buy shrimp unless we can cook them almost immediately.

Las Bocas — Agiabampo...

The beaches located below Yavaros are quite similar to those above...many square miles of estuaries and long lonesome beaches, if one can get to them. This series of roads appear to traverse some 12 to 15 miles of beaches. We shall see.

0.0   0.0   We go south off **Mexico 15** at K114 below **Navajoa** toward **Los Bocas**. The road is signed and graded. Agriculture has not gotten here yet. The low sand hills are great for cactus and the like...mesquite, organ pipe, ocotillo and lesser plants. We also see a number of the unusual tree, *palo San Juan*. After a bit we add cholla and lose ocotillo. The road continues almost straight south. It then drops toward the sea through heavy brush and a series of *vados* before coming to the water.

7.4   7.4   Arrive at Las Bocas. The area is a getaway destination for the people of Navajoa. There are several hundred homes through here. The area's exposed position for hurricanes is reflected in the liberal use of natural wood and rocks in construction and in the thickness of the walls, etc. The fact that large, new power lines parallel the coast tells you something...the bigwigs expect this area to grow.

The continuity of the shoreline and the area immediately behind is interrupted by channels of brackish water, or *bocas. The amount of water and degrees of openness to the sea varies, but it is easy to see where the name comes from.* At one point we watch several 8-10 year old boys throw nets in an effort to catch shrimp. And they did.

The beaches stretch for miles and are very beautiful. Camping locales are not obvious, as most of the frontage areas are fenced. We see several likely spots to the north and would expect more to appear as we work our way south. Again, a question directed toward one of the residents should provide some insights. No motorhomes past Las Bocas.

0.0   7.4   Back to the intersection...take the south fork past more homes, plus several under construction. We also see a few small *tiendas* and what looks like weekend restaurants. The road continues south near the beach. We stop and check the beach and several homes under construction. Everyone is friendly.

3.2   10.6   We turn away from the beach and into heavy brush. The road twists and turns avoiding soft spots, or trying to. The going gets sandy.

1.6   12.2   We are now in a beautiful forest of things that grow in this environment: mesquite, saguaro, cholla, etc., plus some large and unique-looking barrel cactus, or *biznaga.* We pass several shore-bound roads, taking one occasionally to find more houses and possible campsites. Cross a sandy arroyo and into a tiny, nameless village, then more roads to the water.

1.7   13.9   This graded stretch ends, so we head back to the sea and homes with hurricane-proof cement roofs. There is no problem stopping here...just ask permission and for their recommendations. We turn inland around a marshy area with a dozen homes visible on the beach side. Here the power lines end. It's time to move on...

2.7   16.6   We have worked our way inland about 2 miles to a fairly-well-traveled road which will take us south toward **Agiabampo**. Shortly we cross a cattle guard.

2.3   18.9   An intersection of two dirt trails. The best traveled is the right. We follow, stopping in the village of **Plutarco Elias Callas** for directions. Here we find that Agiabampo is 20 dirt kilometers ahead. Continue southeast, ignoring for the moment all of the side roads.

3.7   22.6   Here is one we can't ignore. It goes southwest and finally ends up at a shrimp farm on an estuary. *There's no way to the ocean, but the farm is interesting. They anticipate producing 50,000 pounds or more of premium blue and brown shrimp annually from the 100 acres of ponds.* Return to the intersection. Total distance in and out...**7.3** miles.

Several more exploratory side trips got us nothing but *esteros*. A check of the map

shows no more likely beach trails. The road becomes better traveled as we work our way southeast toward farmland. The road finally makes a break toward the south. We see some irrigation canals here and there. Cross a vado and the town of **Agiabampo** is directly ahead.

    3.8   26.4   Enter Agiabampo. This dusty town has several roads leading to frontages on **Estero Bacorehuís**. Small cabins are on some pieces of land, others are only openings in the *mangles* (mangroves). The area is generally dirty, unkept and certainly buggy during much of the year. *The estero has had a good reputation for snook fishing...an*

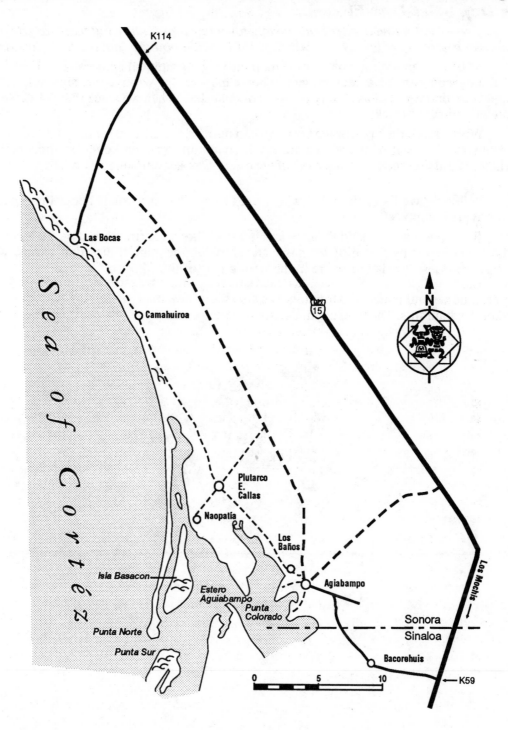

80-pounder was said to have been taken here many years ago...today a 10 pound robalo is considered exceptional. Such is progress.

We begin thinking about heading out to Mexico 15 so we ask a group of men at the plaza. They direct us east about 2 km, then south and east until we reach the highway at about 29 kilometers (18 miles). We do as they say, and wearily drive onto the Mexico 15 roadbed at K59. Total miles, counting side-trips, about 65. The time...nearly 6 hours of driving.

End of log.

The Don't-Get-Lost Elixers...

If you cannot find a particular beach, town or other feature but feel that you are in the neighborhood, here is a system which will find what you are looking for, if it exists...

At times converting a name on a map into a geographical spot you can visit, enjoy and photograph can be a real project. The maps can be wrong, the sign might have disappeared, or the place has simply gone out of business. When we reach that point, we look for a Coke or Pepsi truck.

While doing the logs for the book we had noticed cases of soda bottles stacked along the highways in front of houses where small roads intersect and even in the middle of nowhere. We also discovered that most of the cases were accompanied by pesos to cover the sodas.

Suddenly we had a thought...who would know the back roads better than the soda truck drivers? Nobody!

We immediately tested the idea and it works like a charm. Since, we've located all kinds of places just by repeating the name and showing the map. If they don't know where it is it either doesn't exist, or we're in the wrong part of the Mexico.

RIDE SHARING

SINALOA

1. **Los Mochis**
2. **Culiacán**
3. **Cosalá**
4. **Mazatlán**
5. **Copala**
6. **Guamúchil**
7. **Esquinapa**

SINALOA...
THE STATE

Like its neighbor to the north, Sonora, Mexico's state of **Sinaloa** is a large, fertile piece of land squeezed between the **Sea of Cortéz** and the mountains known as the **Sierra Madre Occidentál**. It too was long-isolated from the rest of Mexico by these natural barriers.

Very few artifacts have been found to show the culture of the pre-hispanic Indians except for a few petroglyphs. In the north the **Mayo** Indians still preserve some of their ancient culture, art and social order. Survivors of a fierce and independent race, many are still ruled by old traditions. They produce excellent handicrafts for their daily use rather than the tourist trade. However, their baskets, woolen blankets, ponchos, pots, weavings, sombreros and wood carvings can sometimes be found in local stores, for example, in **El Fuerte**.

During the colonial times Sinaloa was part of Spain's *Nuevo Galacia*, and included California, Arizona, New Mexico, Texas and Sonora. Mining was the principal industry in the colonial period and El Fuerte, Cosalá and Copala were silver and gold centers. Though Sinaloa became a state in 1824, even today it remains relatively isolated.

Only one narrow road, Mexico 40, connects Sinaloa with its eastern neighbor, the state of **Durango**. A long and twisting railroad track labors from sea level to cross through 8000-foot passes to provide a thin freight connection with **Chihuahua**. Seaward, Mazatlán, Mexico's second-busiest harbor, and Topolobampo provide commercial windows to Baja California and the Pacific Rim. For north and south traffic, only Mexico 15 and a railroad are conduits for Sinaloa's commercial resources.

A widespread series of dams and irrigation projects have given the state's fertile, tropical desert the consistent water supplies it needs to be one of Mexico's most valuable agricultural centers. As we drive down Mexico 15 we see sugar cane, grains, fruits and vegetables throughout the year, for the growing season never ends in Sinaloa. Many of North America's winter vegetables come from the Culiacán valley and the plains of Los Mochis.

A pioneer in the art of catering to the airborne tourist, Mazatlán has an international airport dedicated to receiving the vacationing *norteamericanos* and whisking them off to their hotels. They still do a fine job, and those who appreciate the laid-back style of hospitality unique to Mazatlán return year after year, not only to soak up some rays but to renew their friendships with **Rogelia** the maid, **José** the bartender and **Pancho** the beach vendor.

During the past few years a resource Sinaloa shares with neighboring Chihuahua is being discovered by the gurus of the travel industry, the **Barranca de Cobre**. Visitors from all over North America are coming to see a canyon four times larger than the **Grand Canyon** and populated with 40,000 or more **Tarahumara** Indians whose running ability and stamina are legendary. More often called **Copper Canyon** in the brochures, it may be experienced only by taking what **Reader's Digest** has described as the most spectacular train ride in the world. The scenics, the people, and the uniqueness of the adventure are attracting growing numbers to the Barranca de Cobre. **(See Sinaloa Inland.)**

And Sinaloa is feeling her oats in other ways. New highways are opening fresh travel destinations for both the domestic and international traveler. Her 600-plus kilometers of seashore, old colonial mining centers and world class largemouth bass fishing are all gaining in popularity with the knowledgeable Mexico traveler. And she shares with Sonora the finest whitewing dove hunting in the world.

102

SINALOA

What could be the salvation of recreational and commercial fishing in the Sea of Cortéz may lie in the brackish lagoons of Sinaloa's western shores...the expansion of aquaculture to its true potential. Literally thousands of square miles of untapped estuarian habitat are potential sites for the controlled production of oysters, clams, mussels, food fish and, most important of all...shrimp.

With the potential of annually producing many thousands of tons of valuable crustaceans, these water farms could relieve the terrible pressure placed on the Sea of Cortéz and other intensively trawled regions along Mexico's continental shelf.

The ingredients for growth are here in Sinaloa, Mexico's gateway to the tropics.

There Used to Be a Law...

It was in the mid-fifties that Mazatlán tourist facilities began to expand beyond the confines of the harbor and Olas Altas beach. They had even planted coconut trees along the new road that followed the beach north toward the distant Playa Mazatlán.

1957 was our first family to Mazatlán and we never dreamed that the "skills" learned during Tom's trip to Hawaii in 1947 would ever again find an application, but they did, with almost disastrous results...

On the last day of our memorable first vacation at the Playa Mazatlán, Tom and the kids were looking for something new to do and he had noticed the gardener trimming the hotel's palm trees. "Why not see if I can remember how to make coconut hats," he said.

After a few false starts the system fell into place and soon son Tom and daughter Diana had beautiful palm-frond hats. Within an hour, half the hotel guests were asking where they could buy the hats. The kids were thrilled and wanted to take orders. For a moment it looked as though Dad might be forced into a new profession...until young Tom returned with one of the beach attendants. If I could teach him and his partner how to make the *"sombreros de palmas,"* he promised to handle the problem, and the family would be allowed to return to *Los Estados Unidos.*

The pair proved to be excellent students, and the next morning when we left for the airport they were already filling orders.

In 1958 we didn't go to Mazatlán, but friends told us that the palm hats were everywhere. In '59 we landed expecting to be inundated with hat vendors. We saw none, in fact there weren't even any palm trees on the road in from the airport, or on the hotel grounds. We were later told that there were no palm trees left in Mazatlán. The town had been picked clean by the hat makers and there was a law against making a coco palm hat!

*Today, with an enlightened eye to their survival, the coco palms of Mazatlán flourish, as does the business of making **sombreros de palmas**.*

MEXICO 15 — SONORA BORDER — CULIACAN

*This portion of Mexico 15 takes us through more of Mexico's breadbasket. Because of its tremendous agricultural capabilities and transportation needs, Mexico is busy with the modernization of Mexico 15. By the end of 1992 it is expected that all of the highway within the state will be four or more lanes. Sinaloa also brings us together with descendants of the original settlers, the **Yaqui** and **Mayo** Indians. The feeling you get in some of the towns is similar to visiting the Indian towns of the American Southwest.*

0.0   0.0   K69   The sign on our right indicates we are at the border between **Sonora** and **Sinaloa**.

2.7   2.7   K65+   A mandatory stop for a drugs and weapons check. Everyone here has been courteous and efficient. This is for northbound traffic, but southbound vehicles may also be stopped upon occasion. Do not speed by.

1.6   4.3   K62   **Chavez Talamantes** is a rather strung-out line of houses amid miles of grain fields.

4.0   8.3   K55+   **El Carrizo** is to the left. At the south end a paved road goes (left) to **El Naranjo**. Next comes a marshy area with some standing water and lots of reeds.

3.4   11.7   K50   A farm-worker community, **Poblado Numero 5**. The variety of plantings through here...grains, beans, truck crops, safflower, etc. presents a broad spectrum of greens, particularly in the late fall when a wide variety of crops are under cultivation.

4.4   16.1   K43   The signed town of **Chihuauita** begins here and extends for nearly a mile. We approach a low line of hills and the end of the fertile soils of the extensive floodplains around and below **Navajoa**. The plants in the non-irrigated areas are back to the Sonora scrub, consisting of paloverde, mesquite, cactus, and small hardwoods.

6.0   22.1   K33   We seem to have seen the last of the irrigation system for awhile. The pueblo to the left is signed **Ejido G. Calderón**. The few miles ahead is a bear for slow traffic as stretches invite passing, but not without a high level of risk. Soon the road will be widened and the problem will be solved. In the meantime...*Cuidado!*

7.0   29.1   K22   We come out of the hills into the Los Mochis valley.

3.9   33.0   K16   Turnoff right to Higuera Zaragosa goes along the north side of the **Río Fuerte** and follows a large irrigation canal. *According to one of the farmers we met at the intersection, the names of the four beaches west of here are **La Biznaga**, **La Salida**, **San Juan** and "No Recuerdo (I Don't Remember)."* (See Sinaloa Beaches.) It is also the turnoff to the popular **Río Fuerte Trailer Park**. *On the left about 200 yards off Mexico 15, the park has 60 spaces with full hookups, plus others offering only water and electricity, etc. A pool, clubhouse, barbecues and a jacuzzi round out the facilities.* Continue south across the **Río Fuerte** and a full service **Pemex** (left). On the right a restaurant makes its name that of the product, **Carnitas, Estillo Uruapan**. *Their supply of succulent deep fried pork was diminished by a half-kilo upon our arrival. Very, very good and priced right. A lot of the local farmers gather here to talk over the day.* We continue south past scattered houses and more fields.

2.7   35.7   K11+   A military encampment is on the right, then more farms and many *paloverdes* along the roadside. Continue south some distance toward the city.

7.2   42.9   K0   The turnoff into **Los Mochis,** with a road also going east from here to **El Fuerte. (See Sinaloa Inland.)**

*Los Mochis has none of the prehispanic or colonial aura about it that is so common in most major Mexican cities. It was founded in 1872 by an American, **Albert Kinsey Owens**, who wanted to establish an American colony, raise sugar cane and build a railroad to Chihuahua. The American colony never really got off the ground and the railroad was not completed until ninety years after the fact. (See Copper Canyon Side Trip, Sinaloa Inland.)*

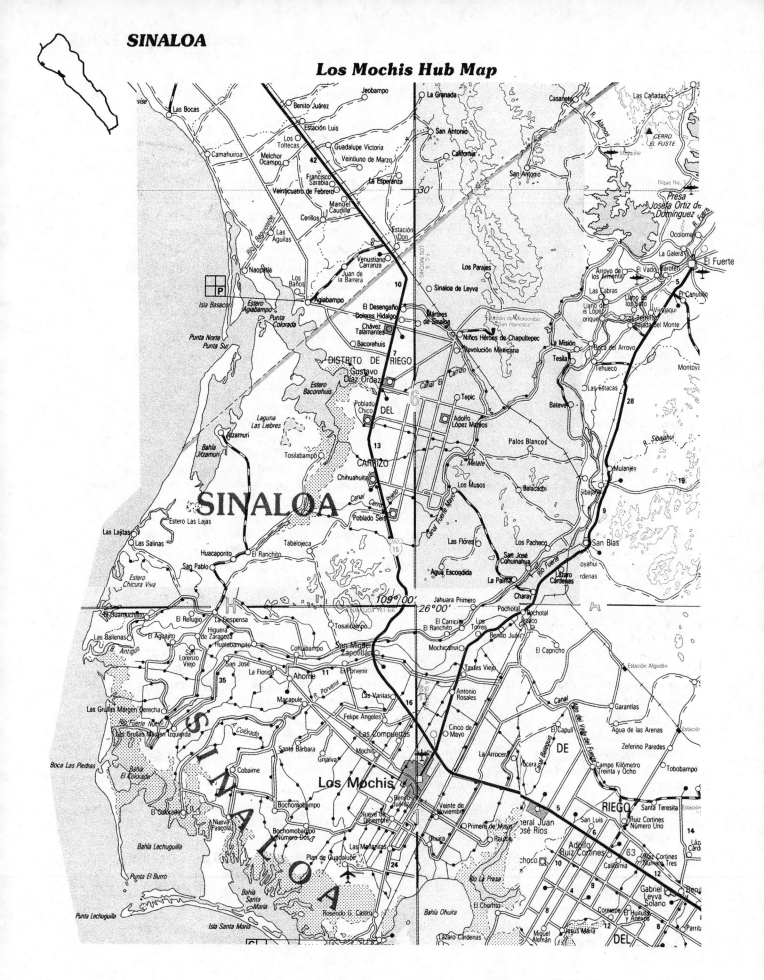

But Owens didn't strike out on all counts. Mochis does have one of the largest sugar refineries in Mexico.

In some ways, thanks to its late start, Mochis today is a well-planned, modern city with wide streets, greenbelts, even a golf course. It is the home of one of the largest palm collections in the world. Only two others compare...one in Florida and another in Brazil.

Mochis is the starting point for the Copper Canyon train trips, leaving at 0600 every morning. Largemouth bass, whitewing dove and ducks attract sportsmen from all over North America and Europe. Two hotels, the 4-star **Santa Anita** and the equally nice **Plaza Inn** have capitalized on this and offer a variety of hunting and fishing packages. For more information write Bob Balderrama, Plaza Inn, Leyva y Cárdenas, Los Mochis, Sinaloa, Mexico.

Mochis hotels, beside the Plaza Inn and Santa Anita, include the less expensive **El Dorado** in the downtown area and the Holiday-Innish, and expensive, **Colinas** out on Highway 15. Cityside trailer accommodations are available at the **Copper Canyon Trailer Park** located on the eastern outskirts of the city.

You won't starve in Los Mochis. One of the best bets is the dining room of the **Santa Anita**...ask for their house-special shrimp. For breakfast we like the **El Taquito** across the street and a block west of the Santa Anita. It is inexpensive and excellent. Try their special *salsa casera* with your entree. Fresh-made and heated on the stove, it is one of the best.

*The **Los Mandilones** across from the Plaza Inn makes a great plate of tacos from grilled beef marinated in their own special sauce. The recently-opened **Mr. Owens Cafe** at the Plaza Inn serves a food-mix similar to its sister-hotel, the Santa Anita. A block south of there is **Los Cazadores**, a steak house with excellent meats. One block to the west is **Pizzeta La Pizza Pizza**. A block behind the El Dorado at Angel Flores and Ramirez is **La Calle**. A young man, **José Ibarra**, with a degree in hotel and food management from the University of Arizona is doing a great job in an attractive outdoor setting. Try his ribs **(huesitos)**, beef brochettes, **alambre** (beef strips) with bell peppers, onions, bacon, and cheese or a specialty, **molcajete**, chicken or beef, onions, cheese and avocados in a spicy broth. The latter comes to the table boiling in an oven-heated stone pot. No wine or beer, but you can bring your own. Two top-notch seafood menus are at the **El Farallón** at Flores and Obregón streets and the **El Bucanero de El Fuerte** at Allende #828 Norte. We give the Bucanero an edge here. **El Platanito**, small, clean and busy, serves **pollo asada** and is located on Indepencia just north of A. Rosales. Here you select your beverage from a long list of **aguas frescas**. Back to the highway.*

0.0   42.9   K204   We're back at the overpass. Note the new K markers as we head south on the four-lane divided highway, passing the hilltop Hotel Colinas on the left. *The Colinas has a rather stark 54-space trailer park at the bottom of the hill off the entrance road to the hotel. Guests at the trailer park can use the facilities of the hotel, but you have to walk some hundreds of yards up a hill to get to them.*

2.6   45.5   K200   Pass a large outdoor grain storage grounds. As with many economies where funds are limited, permanent storage facilities are not always possible. There is some loss, but it cannot be helped. Just beyond is a bridge over an irrigation canal and an access road to fields on the other side of the highway.

4.3   49.8   K193+   A large grain processing plant to the west...**Asgrow**. Over the next few miles we see a number of the small agricultural communities which provide workers for the many square miles of cultivated fields.

4.6   54.4   K186   Intersection with road, (right) into **Juan José Ríos** and a small full service **Pemex**. Most of the fields here are dedicated to the growing of wheat...two crops a year. Each spring and fall they burn the stubble and the process generates a sometimes-heavy pall over the countryside.

4.3   58.7   K179   A paved road goes southwest to **Bachoco**, 8 km. Ahead is **Volkart** cotton gin on the west side of the highway. One of many through here, it processes

106

some of the finest cotton in the world. The local long-staple variety and equally-fine strains grown in Sonora bring premium prices on international markets. Two miles beyond, a graded road goes (right) to the town of **Miguel Alemán**, 12 km. Note also the increasing numbers of fields devoted to vegetables. These fields produce almost exclusively for the off-season markets in the United States and Canada...tomatoes, peppers, squash, green onions, parsley, etc., etc.

For Lettuce Lovers...

If you like the crisp and flavorful lettuces which used to grace our tables only in the early summer, you will appreciate what this portion of Mexico does to keep red leaf, bib, arrow, etc., in the produce sections of North America's supermarkets. From late November through March thousands of acres of the finest farmlands in the Los Mochis-Culiacán corridor are filled with tens of millions of lettuce heads, big and small. Thousands of workers are picking, packing, hauling and replanting all of those delicious little morsels just for us. We thank you.

6.8   65.5   K168   We now see more citrus, bananas and papayas growing in the yards of the towns. Such a typical town is **Gabriel Leyva** on the west side of the highway.

2.6   68.1   K164   Intersection with paved road west to **Huitussi**, 25 km, a fishing village on the shore of a lagoon.

5.1   73.2   K156   Graded road west to **La Entrada**, 4km. A short distance ahead, Sinaloa 24 leads east to **El Naranjo** and into the foothills of the *sierra*. In another two miles we pass the new Corona beer distributor. They are always significant landmarks, even if you don't drink beer. Just beyond is a plain-looking little restaurant with icy *refrescos*.

3.9   77.1   K150   The farming diversifies a bit here, with contoured fields of wheat (and maybe rice) becoming apparent. Cottonwood *(algodón)* is a dominant tree in the area.

2.3   79.4   K146   Ahead is what used to be a toll station for the bridge over the **Río Sinaloa**. There are usually people below relaxing, washing cars, or shoveling sand into pickups. The center of **Guasave**, a city of nearly a hundred thousand, is about 2 kilometers off to the right.

*Guasave was founded in 1595 by the missionary, **Bernardo de Villafane**, who built his first mission among these Indians. The strong Indian heritage is still be seen in the faces of the residents. Good times to visit Guasave are on the first and last Sundays in October when **Yaqui** and **Mayo** Indian dances are featured as part of the **Santo Rosario** fiestas. Two churches from the 18th century are still in use in the Nio and Pueblo Viejo sections of Guasave.*

The area is reported to have a number of petroglyph sites nearby. Inquire locally. The road to **Boca del Río** and **Las Glorias** beaches leaves from Guasave's main east-west street.

We follow south, zigzagging as shown on the Los Mochis Hub map. There are doves everywhere...by the thousands. At the margins of the lagoon are a number of shrimp-raising pens. The beach is at 36.1 miles.

*Las Glorias serves the Guasave area and has a number of private homes in varying stages of disrepair. The **Congrejo Mojo**, a hotel listed in several guidebooks as being of 3-star quality, is a disaster. The restaurant appears to be busy, but the kitchen looks disorganized and smells of rancid grease...sure indicators that we will eat elsewhere. The shoreline is singularly unimpressive with few shells and little driftwood scattered along a gray, hot, sandy shallow beach. We see no reason to return.* Back to Gusave.

If we go the other direction at the same intersection we would be on our way to the colonial town of **Sinaloa de Leyva**. Founded in 1540, it is 44 kilometers to the north. *The unique rectangular base design of the original church is of interest to architecture-buffs.* We continue southeast through town.

2.1   81.5   K142+   Mexico 15 bears to the left, the road straight ahead is to **El**

Burrión.

5.4   86.9   K133+   Toll booth. The charge is minimal.

4.1   91.0   K127   **DeKalb** is another of the American companies with seed growing operations here. Their plant is on the left, while another, **Northrop King,** is just ahead.

4.3   95.3   K120   Intersection with Sinaloa 1D, a beautiful, four-lane toll road. We go straight through the overpass. If we had kept to the right and gone over the overpass we would have stayed on Mexico 15. This route, however, is but two lane and goes through congested **Guamúchíl** before reaching **Culiacán.** But should you decide to take the "scenic" route, the log for the Mexico 15 road follows this one. The route of the toll road generally follows the train tracks toward Culiacán. Our entry onto Sonora 1D gives us a new set of K markers.

0.0   95.3   K0   Beginning of the tollroad. It is a pleasure to drive through attractive farmlands without having to deal with traffic. This *autopista* is typical of what may become standard for many of Mexico's arterial highways. We are told that Mexico 15 and Mexico 200 will be among the first to be revamped. The improvements are expected to attract many new American and Canadian drivers to Mexico.

7.5   112.1   K27   On the left is what at first looks to be a very small town. Look again, it is a *panteón* (cemetery) and those are shrines. Some hills are beginning to show on the south and west horizons. Far to the east are the foothills of the **Sierra Madre Occidentál**.

5.2   117.3   K35   Large plantings of young mangos. In front of us is a sharp-pointed volcanic cinder cone. When the cultivation stops, the land goes back to the usual desert plants...mesquite, cactus and scrub.

7.0   124.3   K46   Another overpass with a couple of tiny roadside restaurants on the east side. Pecan orchards are to the side of the highway. Mexico is a major producer, and consumer, of pecans.

2.8   127.1   K50+   Here we have a little restaurant on the west commited, in writing, to provide "*Pescado Frito*" and "*Gasolina*" from a drum. Hopefully, a winning combination for the owner.

3.4   130.5   K56   On the west side and just beyond the overpass, is a clean little restaurant. There are usually several cars parked there. They also offer *cocos frios*.

3.2   133.7   K61   Turnoff and overpass leading to **La Reforma** (west) and **Tapatío** (east). Then comes a little restaurant with cold sodas and good looking *antojitos* (typical Mexican dishes). We come into more vegetation with tall specimens of *pitahaya* cactus. In the fall the sweet fruit is gathered and eaten fresh, or cooked and preserved in a variety of ways.

11.8 145.5   K79+   We go under a highway overpass and past a road maintenance station, then over a small river. Continue southeast.

8.4   153.9   K93   Sinaloa 259 exit to **La Palma** (west) and **Vitaruto** (east). The land continues to fascinate us with its ability to produce crop after crop...sometimes 4 and 5 per year on certain varieties. Far to the east are the shadowy forms of the Sierra Madre Occidental.

11.3 165.2   K111   Here is the Sinaloa 280 exit to **La Curva** and **San Pedro**. The highway now swings east toward **Culiacán**. Sugar cane is a big crop along here.

7.0   172.2   K122   Toll gate and just beyond, a big full service **Pemex**. New and shiny, it offers ice, restrooms and bottled water. There is a small restaurant adjoining. To best enter Culiacan's central business district, take the **El Dorado** turnoff here and head northeast. The highway itself continues east as a two-lane road until it rejoins Mexico 15.

7.3   179.5   K134   We reach Mexico 15 south of Culiacán at the K209 marker for the Culiacán-Mazatlán leg of our journey.

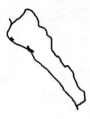

SINALOA

Los Mochis - Culiacan, Staying on Mexico 15...

This log starts at the southern terminus of the Sonora 1D toll road but we continue the cumulative mileage and K markers from the Sonora border.

0.0   95.3   K120   Start this log from the top of the overpass.

4.5   99.8   K113   The fair-sized community of **Benito Juarez**. The houses are brick with cement roofs. Irrigation canals of varying sizes are everywhere...these are the life-giving arteries for the **Río Sonora** delta.

3.9   103.7   K106+   First a Pemex tank farm, then a full service **Pemex**. Next up is the **Motel York** on the left. It looks clean and well organized, with satellite TV. Watch on the right for a complex of six little league baseball diamonds together in a large field. *Next to soccer, baseball is Mexico's premier sport.*

0.9   104.6   K105   Enter **Guamúchíl**, a city of 60,000, and follow the road (south) past many small businesses. If you wish to find something to identify with...there's a **Pollo Loco** about mid-way through town. Guamúchíl stretches itself along the highway for some distance past its official center, the plaza...and the turnoff to **Mocorito**.

*Guamúchíl and neighboring Mocorito are given credit for creating **chilorio**, a dish almost synonymous with Sinaloa. It is a mixture of shredded pork in a spicy chili-based sauce. We buy it canned in the markets to take home. Excellent heated and spread on a warm bolillo or in tacos.*

On the way out of town we pass a Corona beer warehouse and the transformers of a power distribution station. To the south are low hills with abundant cactus and mesquite-type trees in the noncultivated areas.

8.0   112.6   K92   Reach the top of a gentle ascent between two hills and follow a straight, but hilly, stretch southeast past dirt turnoffs to a host of *pueblitos* and *ranchos*.

2.3   114.9   K88   A little restaurant on the top of a rise sells a fine *pollo asado* (barbecued chicken) and cold *refrescos*. The landscape varies much between October (end of the rainy season) and May (the driest month). It can resemble the tropical mountains of the south seas, or a brush-laden tinderbox dreading the thought of a match. This is one of the reasons we choose to travel this part of Mexico during the late fall months.

9.7   124.6   K72   A small community of **Terrero de Los Guerreros** (Land of the Warriors). Rolling hills and cornfields join the natural vegetation in catching our eye for the next few miles.

7.5   132.1   K60   A dirt road (left) goes north toward the foothills of the *sierra* and **El Tancote, Bacamon** and **Aguajito de León**. There are many great views on this sparkling day. Soon we top a small grade for another panoramic view of the mountains to the east. Then comes a bridge over a small seasonal river and the signed, **Rancho Viejo**.

9.1   141.2   K45   A paved road (right) to **Pericos**, a locally important farm center. A few hundred meters beyond a paved road (left) goes north to **Badiraguato** and on to the mountain town of **Santiago de Los Caballeros**, 71km from Mexico 15. Past Los Caballeros, dirt roads of one kind or other extend at least 60km more to *ranchos* and *pueblitos* near the Chihuahua border.

Until the roads were completed a few years ago that region's only contact with the outside world was through a network of dirt landing strips. Most of the fields are still in use, needed because of washouts and landslides on the roads. The economy of this wilderness depends upon cattle, mining and drugs. Law enforcement officials do not recommend "beyond the pavement" travel around here, period!

2.1   143.3   K42   A small banana plantation is on the right. On the left ahead are a number of well-kept houses. Another kilometer brings us to a packing shed. The rolling hills and thick vegetation continues.

    8.5   151.8   K28   **La Campana** (The Bell), a village whose dry-season greenery indicates an abundance of water. A kilometer beyond a signed, paved road (left) goes to **Presa López Mateos**. The lake behind the dam is a big one, and contains large numbers of black bass, mojarr a and catfish.

    5.5   157.3   K19   A graded road (right) to **El Tamarindo**, 15km, and next to it, a prosperous farming operation. Continue southeast through **El Limón**. Notice the bluffs around the mountain tops to the northeast.

    3.4   160.7   K14   Here's a toll gate...and a minimal charge. If you wish to buy oranges or mandarins, the little stands on each side of the booths have good, clean fruit. Another two kilometers and the **Restaurant Valle del Sol** is on the left. It is clean and organized with good *antojitos*, tasty *carne asada* and cold *Pacificos*. A kilometer down the line is a full service Pemex.

    5.0   165.7   K4   We've entered the outskirts of **Culiacán** past new government-built apartments, the regional fairgrounds and a bull ring, Carta Blanca/Tecate brewery and another full service Pemex.

    1.8   167.5   K1   We are on the causeway leading to the bridge over the **Río Culiacán**. Welcome to Culiacán, a **Nahuatl** Indian word meaning, "where the waters meet."

CULIACAN...

Culiacán lies in a fertile valley attended by two rivers, the **Humaya** and **Tamazula** that meet just upstream to form the **Culiacán**. The combination of abundant water and rich, alluvial soil is the alchemy which makes Culiacán, at 500,000 residents, the largest city in Sinaloa and its capital.

Early **Toltecs** migrated to the area about 500 BC, and the Aztecs are believed to have passed through here in the 12th century on their way from **Mexcaltitan, Nayarít** to **Tenochtitlan**, the site of present-day **Mexico City**. It also was one of the first Spanish cities to be established this far north (1531) and quickly became a center for explorations into Sinaloa, Baja and Alta California, etc.

Culiacan's economy is based on a long list of agricultural products and related industries such as food packaging, bottling, cold storage and cattle and poultry-feeding operations. The downtown section sports a fine 18th-century **Cathedral** facing the plaza, or *zocalo*. In the civic center an archaeological museum displays many valuable **Nahua** ceramic pieces.

Also near the plaza are the **San Marcos** and the **Excelsior,** two clean, moderately-priced hotels that suffer from traffic noise. On the hill to the south is the **Capilla de La Guadalupaña**. Adjoining it, and offering a particularly fine nighttime view of the city, is the **San Luís Hotel**. Newly refurbished, it is a favorite. Another popular one, the **Tres Rios**, is located on Mexico 15 near the northwest entrance into town.

Southeast of the plaza area, near the state government buildings is the **Plaza Fiesta**, one of the best shopping centers in northwest Mexico. Nearby is the **Carreta de Los Colín**, a **campestre**-style restaurant serving a host of meats. Their *parilla* for two comes with beef, pork, lamb and chicken on a table-top brazier plus *quesadillas*, fried potatoes, deep-fried pearl onions, tomatoes, cabbage, cucumbers, red onions and stacks of *tortillas*! There was hardly room on the table for the serving plates!

Other good places to eat are the **El Acueducto** for carnes, and next door the Villamar for mariscos (both are on Niños de Los Heroes facing the river); the **Los Arcos** (seafood) on Xicotenacatl; **Mr. Fish** and **El Chaparral** on Avenida Obregón and Ganaderos for steaks on Niños de Los Heroes. **La Esquina** near the Excelsior Hotel is reported to have excellent *cabrito* (baby goat).

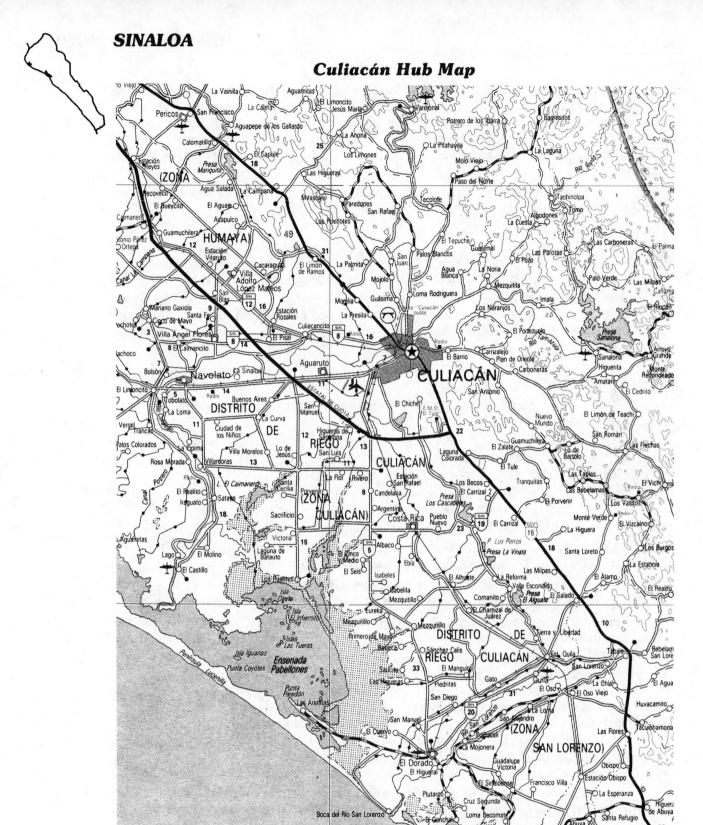

Culiacán is a popular jumping-off place for hunters and fishermen. Dove and duck are thick in the surrounding farmlands and the lakes behind the irrigation dams harbor bass, mojarra and catfish. Near the **Presa Sanalona**, 36 km to the east is the **Imala** resort with therapeutic sulfur springs and picnic areas. Another of the thermal areas is around **Carrizalejo**. There are also a number of beaches and fishing villages nearby. (**See Sinaloa Beaches.**)

*The best fiesta time in Culiacán is centered around the week of **Carnivál** with parades, fireworks, flower-throwing contests and ethnic dances on the last Sunday.*

End of log.

MEXICO 15 — CULIACAN — NAYARIT BORDER

A glance at the map of Sinaloa will show why we are splitting the Mexico 15 log into two pieces for this state just as we did for Sonora...it's a long one.

0.0   0.0   K230   Leave the center of **Culiacán** via signed Mexico 15 and head south through considerable traffic and many businesses. A number of full service **Pemex** stations are along here.

5.1   5.1   K222   Several restaurants and a half-dozen *refaccionarias*, or parts stores, specializing in truck parts.

3.7   8.8   K216   A full service **Pemex** and a sports complex with a variety of fields and buildings.

2.7   11.5   K211+   There's a large produce market on the west side of the highway, then a storage area with wide gates. Next comes the **LPG** gas station and the **Costa del Sol**, a clean-looking businessman's-style motel.

1.6   13.1   K209   Intersection with Sinaloa 1. Proceed south past the clean and inexpensive **Campanas del Rey** motel, then several long chicken sheds. The **El Tule** *microondas* is on the hill to the right.

3.7   16.8   K203   **Los Ponchos** restaurant. Famous for its meats, it is clean, popular and offers *antojitos Mexicanos* in addition to the *carnes*.

3.8   20.6   K197   The **Elefante** restaurant, with a marvelous hand-painted elephant on their sign, sells icy **Coronas** on a breezy, shaded patio.

2.6   23.2   K193   Intersection right with Sinaloa C-19 to the farming village of **Costa Rica**, 17 km. Adjoining is a full service **Pemex**.

2.8   26.0   K188+   Small community of **El Carrizál**. There are several signs along here advertising purebred semental bulls at stud. The semental have proven an efficient and profitable breed of cattle in the hot and moist regions of Mexico because they are resistant to hoof diseases. Heavy stands of brush, cactus and mesquite line the roadbed and covers the hillsides.

9.0   35.0   K174   **El Salado**. A signed and paved road leads west to **El Dorado** (**See Sinaloa Beaches.**) followed by well-attended open-air restaurants offering the usual fare. A kilometer beyond, a full service Pemex.

5.6   40.6   K165   Bridge over the **Río San Lorenzo**. Lots of water in the fall and very little before the summer rains. Just past the bridge is the small town of **Tabala**. On the left are the remains of a picturesque old church and adjoining *panteón* (cemetery). To the east are the prominent outlines of the **Sierra Madre Occidentál**.

6.9   47.5   K154   Small town of **Los Flores**. The inhabitants apparently like fruit...we see banana, mango and papaya trees are in almost every yard. In the fall the roadsides are covered by vines with pink and red flowers resembling those of a miniature bougainvilla. Called *San Miguelito* (Little St. Michael), it is not so obvious in the dry season, but, given water, it can completely cover, even kill, small trees. It is also found in the Los Cabos region of Baja California Sur.

112

6.6   54.1   K143   **Higuera de Abuya** is the site of a mango tree nursery. In the years to come many mangos will come from this area. The road continues southeast through low hills covered with brush and cactus. Much of the flat area is planted to corn.

8.4   62.5   K130   **El Avión** (The Airplane) a small town with the beautiful *sierras* for a backdrop.

5.0   67.5   K122   **Ejido 26 de Enero** is off to the east. Bananas do well around here. Just down the road is **Vida Campesina** (Farmers Life), another community of farm workers.

3.1   70.6   K117   Several hundred nice looking, well-maintained painted brick houses are to the north of the highway. Beyond, on the other side, is a clean little restaurant, **Guille**. The family serves up plates of excellent *machaca* for very few *pesos*. Farther along is **El Grillo** (The Cricket) restaurant. It is larger, and well populated with truckers. Both are neat and clean.

6.9   77.5   K106   Intersection with highway leading east to **Cosalá, El Salto** and **El Comedero** lakes. **(See Sinaloa Inland.)**

0.6   78.1   K105   A small restaurant is at the paved intersection southwest 18km to **La Cruz** and on to the "resort" area at **Playa Cuetla**. We went and wasted our time. *The area is a windblown beach with several dozen houses in various stages of collapse. None appeared habitable. Should you wish to camp here, there should be no problem. The place puts us in mind of a Rod Serling* **Twilight Zone** *story about the death of the world through atomic radiation. It is hard to find even one redeeming feature here. The road is paved most of the way, with dirt for but 5 of the 27 kilometers to the beach.* Back to the highway.

8.8   86.9   K91   Paved Sinaloa D-3 road goes east 1km to **Elota**. If you wish to go beyond Elota, a graded road continues through two small pueblos before coming out on the **Cosalá** highway. A half-mile farther is the bridge over the **Río Elota**.

4.3   91.2   K84   Off to the left, **La Minita**, a small, well-maintained mine.

2.5   93.7   K80   A paved turnoff (right) is to the town of **Piaxtla** followed shortly by the bridge of the same name.

3.8   97.5   K74   **Crucero Piaxtla**. Mexico 15 does a bit of winding and dodging through low brush-covered hills.

1.3   98.8   K72   Paved road west goes off to **Estación Dimás**. Beyond is **Barra de Piaxtla** and some interesting rock carvings. **(See Sinaloa Beaches.)**

3.1   101.9   K67   A signed paved road east goes to **San Ignacio** and a dozen other communities and ranches extending into the western sections of the state of **Durango**. *Again a warning...drug activity is high in the remote portions of the sierras and enforcement personnel warn against travel beyond the paved roads in this area unless you have a good command of Spanish and are "clean."*

4.4   106.3   K60   The highway winds, sometimes sharply, through low, heavily vegetated hills. Morning glory vines are so thick they are smothering other plants. We don't remember seeing them before the past few years. Here may be an example of an introduced plant dominating a native environment in a destructive way. The road continues through miles of sameness.

16.8   123.1   K33   Paved road east to **El Quelite** (The Green Spot) and **El Quemado** (The Dark). A kilometer farther a graded road west leads to the railroad junction of **El Marmól** (The Marble or Onyx) and a fishing village. We didn't make it out there, but friends swear by it for a day's *panga* fishing. Heavy vegetation continues. Cross a bridge over the **Río Quelite**. There are vines everywhere...over trees, cactus, bushes, cornfields. Even telephone poles seem about to succumb to the double attack of morning glory and San Miguelito vines.

7.2   130.3   K21+   The white cement globe on the low rise to the right marks the

Tropic of Cancer. At 23 degrees, 27 minutes north latitude, this is the farthest north the sun reaches at the summer solstice, June 21st or 22nd. From now on we are officially in the tropics. Dry-farmed plots of corn are everywhere, even spreading up onto the low hills.

    3.4   133.7   K16   A large dairy on the left is followed by extensive plantings of mangos.

    3.2   136.9   K11   Here is the paved road right to Mazatlan's beaches. This 11-kilometer road brings us in at the top, or **El Cerritos**, end of the complex of condos, trailer parks and hotels which make up a majority of the city's beachfront destination housing. Continue south on Mexico 15. Just past the intersection on the right is a small *carnitas* stand, **El Habaleño**. It has a good local reputation. The surrounding hills are home for large numbers of the *amapola* tree. When at their peak in December, their hot-pink flowers are a photographer's delight.

    4.5   141.4   K4   **Rancho San Juan**. Another kilometer and we pass through the satellite community of **El Venadillo**.

    1.7   143.1   K1+   An interesting-looking restaurant, **Los Arbolitos**, features *Cabrito a la Maya* (???). No time to check it, but we'd be interested in hearing on this one.

    0.6   143.7   K0   Intersection. Right fork goes into Mazatlán at the southern end of the main hotel zone. The left branch is the *periférico* around the city.

MAZATLAN...

Coming to Mazatlán is like coming home. It is easy and natural to drop by for a day, week or month. Much of the flavor of the city remains as it was a decade or a generation ago. Despite its growth, we trust that this part will never change.

The earliest visitors, the **Nahua** Indians, called it the land of the deer, who became a welcome part of their diet, supplementing the region's abundant fish, crustaceans, seeds and fruits.

In 1531, the Spanish arrived to establish a small colony and port. It later became a provisioning stop for the Manila Galleons, a supply center for the burgeoning gold and silver mines in the nearby Sierra Madre, and, because of the success of those endeavors, a target for pirates. *Stories of buried and sunken treasures still make the rounds in Mazatlán.*

After the mines collapsed and Mexico became independent, the town welcomed a variety of immigrants from Europe and the United States while continuing as a farming and fishing center.

The tropical sun here in Mazatlán is the same today as it was in 1957...but that's about all...

*The hotels **Freeman** and **Decima** were the flagships of the sleepy little fishing town. Top restaurants included the **Shrimp Bucket** and the **Copa de Leche**. The horse drawn "calándrias" (open, fringe-topped surries) were the big item and a trip from the Copa de Leche to the top of Icebox Hill was a highlight of every visit but when we tried to get the driver to take us to the **Playa Mazatlán** hotel, he refused, saying it was too far for the horses.*

*The Hotel Playa Mazatlán of 1957 was located near the end of a dirt road (just before the **Los Cocos** trailer park) and sported 28 rooms and its broad sandy beach was almost empty. Several times our dinner was supplemented with pompano Tom caught off the rocks south of the hotel. The tab for two adults and two children in two rooms, American plan, came to $20 a day!*

*The favorite evening meal for the kids was **hotdogs flambé**...pieces of frankfurters alternated with pineapple chunks on a long skewer and doused with brandy. The staff would turn out the lights in the dining room and carry a yard-high mass of flames across the dining room to our table. (After the first night, son Tom realized that it would make a better show if we sat as far from the kitchen as we could get). They ordered the same thing every night.*

114

SINALOA

Just getting here was an adventure. It began in Mexicali with $62 round trip tickets and half price for the kids on an airline nobody had ever heard of...Aeronaves de Mexico. The flight began early, and we stopped at least twice on the way to the promised land. And each time we stopped everyone got off, went into the "terminal" for maybe an hour while mechanics worked on the plane. Then, following a shouted announcement, the pilot and the crew would troop out to the old DC-3 and stop. There at the bottom of the stairs, each in turn would solemnly genuflect, cross themselves and climb aboard. As the passengers all followed suit we, surely the only protestants aboard, decided it was prudent to do the same. It worked...we arrived without mishap.

Much of Mazatlan's business community is centered around its waterfront. Its shrimp fleet is the largest in Mexico. From here grains and other products from Sinaloa's rich agricultural plains are exported throughout the Pacific Rim. Cruise ships are hosted almost daily along its modern quay and large ferries provide service between the mainland and the Baja peninsula.

Mazatlan's first tourists might have been the American sailors who occupied the town during the Mexican-American war in the 1840s, and the Mazatlán of today still is being invaded by *norteamericanos*. These invasions, though, are much more benign...and 99% have return plane tickets in their pockets.

The city's 21 kilometers of beaches make for many of water-oriented activities, including the perennial "working on a tan." There is good diving and snorkeling around the offshore islands of **Los Venados, Los Pajaros** and **Los Chivos. Aqua Sports** at the **El Cid Hotel** has equipment for rent and can arrange boat trips to the islands. Boats to **Isla de Piedra** (Stone Island) leave from the docks near the intersection of Avenida del Puerto and Calzada Gabriel Leyva. Actually, Isla Piedra is not an island but a peninsula, and can also be reached by car. This area is slated to become another mega-resort, with hotels, condos, etc. **(See Sinaloa Beaches.)** Surfing is good in several locations, including the reef at the south end of the **Olas Altas.**

Deep sea fishing remains a top draw. Tuna and dorado augment year-around billfishing (striped marlin, December-April; sailfish, April-December). Blue and black marlin are uncommon, but the best opportunities occur during the summer. The region's record marlin is a blue weighing 988 pounds. To arrange for fishing, it is best to make an early-afternoon visit to the docks and check out the catch and the boats. Don't hesitate to ask a returning angler how he liked his boat and captain. Make your reservation with the landing, it is sometimes possible to negotiate a better price this way. Recommended landings are Mike Maxemín's **Flota Faro**, Bill Heimpel's **Star Fleet** and **Dorado Sportfishing**. Major billfish tournaments are held each year in June, August and October. *Tom's first billfish were taken here in 1957, a marlin and a sailfish on the same day.*

Turtles Everywhere

In the early 1960's Mike Maxemín and Bill Heimpel operated Mazatlan's Flota Faro and Star fishing fleets, respectively. Great rivals, they kept the quality of the Mazatlán charter fleet among the best in the world. The taking of sailfish and striped marlin were commonplace, even among inexperienced tourists from Hastings, Nebraska and "Noo Yawk City," my partners on an early marlin trip out of Mazatlán.

The trip was a memorable one. As a California boy who had rarely been east of the Colorado River I was fascinated by the "foreign" accents of two of my own countrymen. The early morning water was like glass and the air was clear. The fish were a long way out, so after giving up on following the conversations of the two "foreigners", I started watching for sea turtles.

There were dozens in view at almost all times. The traditional green sea turtles predominated, but the sightings also included some of the huge leatherbacks and several of what the crewman called "concha". (We know it as the hawkbill and its shell was used for combs, belt buckles, and other jewelry items.)

I had counted to just over 300 turtles when the Noo Yawker hooked a sailfish. Within seconds the farmer did likewise. The fish took off in opposite directions. Both reels were emptying fast as the magnificent animals streaked toward freedom. Suddenly the anglers realized their plight and began yelling at **Isidro***, the captain, to move the boat toward their fish. Knowing he was in a no-win situation, Isidro responded by doing nothing. A wise move, for both fished stopped their plunging runs at the same time, leaving less than 5 yards of line on each spool.*

Not realizing their strokes of luck, the anglers continued to yell at the captain and each other. Calmly, Isidro moved the boat slightly to one side or the other, keeping the boat precisely half-way between the fish so that when two yards were gained, each reel wound on a yard. Little by little the fish came closer together. Eventually both were gaffed and everyone shook hands, then we broke out the cervezas.

Today it is rare that even one turtle will be seen during a full day of fishing. Both the beautiful hawkbill and mammoth leatherback are highly endangered, and the green is heading that way.

Fortunately for the turtles, the Mexican government recently banned the taking of turtles or the use of its meat. There should be better days ahead.

Tired of the beach? Rent a bicycle or a horse, play golf or tennis, take a harbor cruise or tour the Pacifico Brewery. Watch a baseball game, a rodeo or a bullfight. Visit a disco or two, or a dozen. When you've finished that list, here are some more...

City tours (arranged or on your own), the **Aquarium**, the **Archaeological Museum** and the old section of town with its **Plaza de la República**, its 19th century **Cathedral, City Hall, Teatro Angela, Capilla de San Jose** (the oldest building in town) and the central market are all viable endeavors.

Vista points include **Cerro de la Nevería** (Ice Box Hill), where the wealthy locals dug tunnels in the 1800s to store ice imported from San Francisco and Alaska. From **Cerro del Vigia** (Watchman's Hill) you can see the sunrise over the distant Sierra Madre mountains, or watch the sun set into the Pacific from **El Creston**, the highest lighthouse in the world at 515 feet above sea level.

At first sight one might think that shopping in Mazatlán is little more than perusing innumerable T-shirt shops. If you don't wish to go anywhere to shop, don't worry, you'll still have a chance to buy. Just go to the beach and try to read. The vendors will give you innumerable opportunities...to buy that is. If you like Mexico's folk art, clothing and jewelry, check out the displays at the **Designer's Bazaar** and the lively **Arts and Crafts Center**.

Where to stay? Every price range is found in Mazatlán. For the every-so-often, self-indulgent stay you can't do better than the large, luxurious **El Cid**, whose amenities include an excellent golf course, huge free-form pools, a number of restaurants and a disco. *We once sat out a hurricane at the El Cid in an oceanfront room. Two days of wild weather were softened with several bottles of wine and a couple of good books. We had a front row seat for Mother Nature at her worst, or most spectacular.* In our opinion, this is one of the best-operated large resort complexes in all of Mexico and provides excellent value at all levels.

Several of the "Do it for Less" travel guides recommend various budget hotels in the old section of the city, but we didn't see one we'd choose to stay in...and we aren't that fussy. There is an almost unbroken line of suitable, inexpensive hotels extending north through the **Golden Zone** and **Playa Gaviota** on up to **Sábalo Beach**. We've used the **Oceano Palace**, the **Tropicana** and the historic **Playa Mazatlán**.

Another way to go, and tops with us, are the suites with kitchens and bedrooms. A good value is the **Linda Mar**. We've used Rocky Mar's units as our work headquarters for this book, and couldn't have had a better environment. Rocky's address is: Linda Mar, RT Loaiza # 226, Mazatlán, Sinaloa, Mexico. Phone 3-55-33.

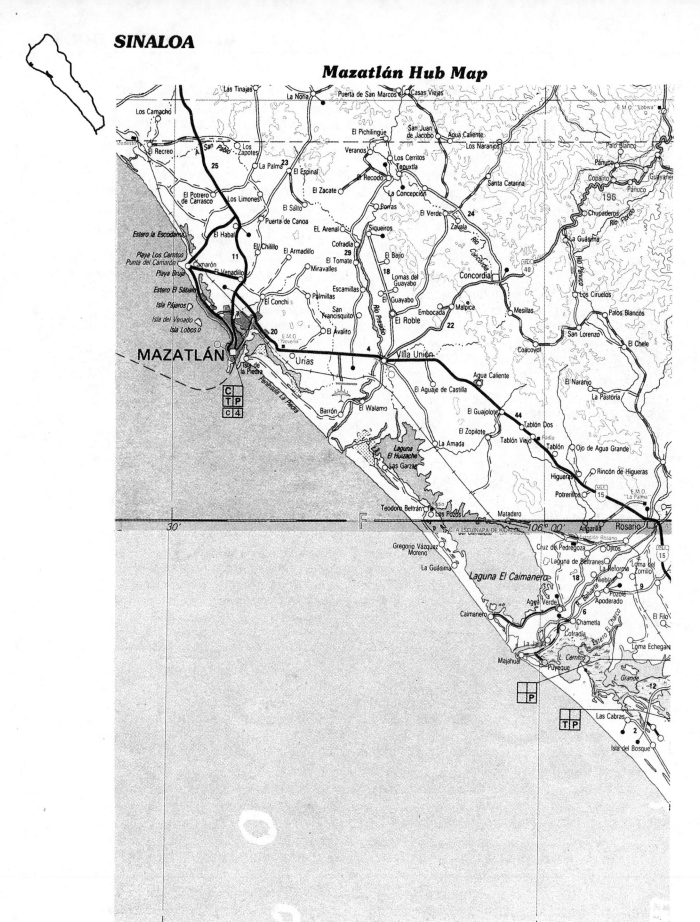

Beachfront trailer parks in Mazatlán are disappearing due to the rapidly escalating value of oceanfront property. Rare is the trailer park operator who can resist the high bucks being offered for his or her under-utilized land. As of mid-1990, here is what is still there. The **Mar Rosa** just north of the Golden Zone, then the **Playa Escondida** and **Mara Villas Trailer Parks**. If you go 0.6 miles north of the Sabalo Beach road back to Mexico 15 on a dirt there is a free-camping area (at least it was in mid-1990).

As with the hotels, food choices are broad. A good value, and very popular, is the **Mexican Fiesta** held at the **Hotel Plaza Mazatlán**. It includes domestic cocktails, Mexican beer, live music, dancing, floor show and Mexican buffet for a flat price. For *antojitos mexicanos*, we enjoy **La Negra** on Gutierrez Najera, four blocks north of the Fishermen's Monument and just past **La Brocheta Loca**.

The grand fiesta of the year for Mazatlán is their famous *Carnival*, or Mardi Gras, celebration. The event dates back to 1898 and is considered one the of the finest in the world after Río de Janiero and New Orleans and both locals and visitors put their all into this pre-lenten extravaganza. Only the most hearty will even consider trying to attend all of the events, which include costume balls, parades, fireworks, mock sea battles and wandering Mariachis playing long into the night. Reservations for this are a must.

Lesser fiesta times include December 8th (The Immaculate Conception), *Dia de Guadalupe* (December 18), fishing and golf tournaments, and an increasingly-popular Los Angeles to Mazatlán yacht race. Mazatlán is truly a busy, lively town and we love it.

FIESTA OF THE VIRGIN

Back on the highway we follow Mexico 15 southeast toward the intersection with the road in from the city's harbor area.

3.4   147.1   K287   Here we inherit a new set of K markers as we make the turn (left) onto a divided four-lane highway and past many businesses and billboards hyping hotels, airlines, suntan lotions, car rental agencies, etc.

5.6   152.7   K278   To the left is a large area surrounded by a tall block wall. Little cupolas resembling guard towers are prominent along its perimeter. At first glance it looks like it could be a prison. Perish the thought, the sign says it is only a **Centro de Rehabilitación Social**! That may be a better name than some of ours. Call them what you will; *carcél, jail, calaboose, klink, pokey, slammer...whatever. In Mexican jails it is not the responsibility of the jailers to provide tasty meals, only the bare essentials (maybe beans and tortillas) but families or friends can bring inmates meals twice a day. (A Domino's Pizza franchise could be a winner here.) They also do not provide TV, but they do allow connubial visits on a space-available basis.*

2.8   155.5   K273+   **Mazatlán International Airport** is on the right. This same road goes to **Isla de la Piedras. (See Sinaloa Beaches.)** Mexico 15 reverts to two-lane just past here but its widening to four should come during 1992 with plans for expansion clear to Puerto Vallarta shortly thereafter. Continue southeast over the year-around **Río Presidio**. Look to the right for an excellent view of the church in **Villa Unión**.

Tonicol is a name seen on a lot of soft drink bottles in and around this area. We've given it a try several times, but the jury is still out. The flavor is somewhere in the cola-rootbeer-Dr. Pepper ballpark. Could it be another Coca Cola?

A side road to **Walamo** and miles of beautiful beaches (plus a turtle hatchery) begins on the right at the white building with green lettering advertising farm supplies. **(See Sinaloa Beaches.)**

4.4   159.9   K266+   Intersection (left) with Mexico 40, the highway to **Concordia, Copala, Pánuco, Villa Blanca** and **Durango. (See Sinaloa Inland.)** There is a full service **Pemex** (right) with stores selling ice and bottled water across the highway. There is also a permanent drug check here. Sometimes they stop all cars, sometimes none.

2.8   162.7   K262   The area is busy with a variety of seasonal truck crops and corn. Farther on the highway winds past a large mango orchard. Watch for oncoming traffic.

5.0   167.7   K250   Enter the small town of **Agua Caliente**. Despite the name we can find no mineral baths, etc.

3.8   171.5   K248   **El Guajolote** (The Turkey), sometimes spelled, *huajolote*. The dirt road here goes west to **El Zopilote** (The Buzzard). Small ranges of hills flank the highway here. Well in the distance is the towering **Sierra Madre Occidentál**.

6.9   178.4   K237   **El Portezuelo** (The Pass). On both sides of the road are examples of what may come to be large scale, diversified orchards. **Conafrut** has planted a variety of citrus, mango, papaya, avocado, etc. over several square miles. Just beyond comes a large egg farm. The land not under cultivation has cactus, mesquite and tropical shrubs.

8.1   186.5   K224   We enter the outskirts of **Rosario**. Just before the Pemex a road left goes inland to **Cacalotan**. **(See Sinaloa Inland.)** Next comes the clean and air conditioned **Motel Yauco**.

A Fling at Mexican Baseball

*During one of our stays at the **Yauco** we met **John Ludy**, a tall, blond American of 25 years. John is a pitcher for the **Rosario Mineros** (Miners) and a good one, good enough to play almost anywhere in the world, except in the big leagues (so far). John is one of three American players on the Rosario team as part of a baseball winter conditioning program.*

Ludy's view of his future in baseball is a healthy one. He knows that short of developing a knuckler that jumps a foot, he won't make it into the majors. But today he is making a good living and seeing a lot of the world in the process. So far he has been to several Caribbean countries, Mexico three times, Japan and a half-dozen spots inside the USA.

LOS MINEROS

There are two other Americans on the Mineros who are younger and here to learn and play every day. All three are staying at the hotel. If you stop by during the winter, check the Yauco out, you might meet a future multimillion dollar superstar.

The town is off to the right with the 19th-century cathedral **Nuestra Senora de Rosario** dominating the visible buildings. Its carved wood altar covered with tens of thousands of sheets of pure gold is reputed to be the most valuable found outside of Guadalajara and Mexico City. The church also has a fine collection of religious icons. Another oddity is the relationship that busy Rosario has with Panuco, a ghost town located in the mountains near Copala. **(See Sinaloa Inland.)**

Founded in 1655 and at one time considered the cultural capital of "La Frontera," Rosario is located on the north bank of the **Río Baluarte**. The town's history connects it to some of the earliest Sea of Cortéz explorations through its position as a supply center for the seaport of **Chametla**. Today it serves as a trading center for the sierra villages and ranches to the north and east, thus its central market is a busy one, and often has some excellent examples of native crafts. *The number one singer of folk ballads in Mexico, **Lola Beltran**, is from Rosario.*

ROSARIO

From Rosario, a road leads west to **Agua Verde** (Green Water) and on to **Agua Dulce** (Sweet Water) along the north side of the Baluarte. **(See Sinaloa Inland.)** Continue south on Mexico 15 past an ice plant and across the long bridge. Next, at **Chilillos**, K221, a graded road inland leads to **Matatan** where they make *machetes* and beautiful and unusual furniture

119

out of palm leaves. **(See Sinaloa Inland.)**

    1.8   188.3   K213   Sonora Y-1 road (west) along the south side of the Baluarte is to **Chametla** One of the first seaports on the west coast of Mexico. **(See Sinaloa Beaches.)** Continue (south) through farmland and past a series of low hills

    6.8   195.1   K202   The **La Palapa** restaurant is on the east side of the road. It has a good menu, and a surprise...a *Larga Distancia*, long distance telephone. And it works.

    0.6   195.7   K201   Entrance to **Esquinapa**. The trail of one-way streets in Esquinapa makes it a challenge to get through without making a wrong turn. We try and follow the sporadic signs. If you want dried shrimp, this is the place to come...everyone has it for sale.

    About a half-mile into town watch for signed road to **Teacapan**, and Sinaloa highway Y-104. **(See Sinaloa Beaches.)** In another mile we pass a bus depot and large local **Pemex** amid a smelly jumble of fruit stands, *taquerias*, etc. No recommendations. Something better is bound to come along. Continue southeast.

    3.8   199.5   K195   **Gas Pacifico**, an **LPG** station. Continue toward the nearby hills and their spectacular cliffs. A beautiful sight during the rainy season, rather bleak during dry times.

    10.6 210.1   K178   Dirt road left is to **La Campana** (The Bell). Nearly all of the houses here have thatched palm roofs. Note the steep pitch of the roof-line. Lots of rocks with brush and grasses trying to establish themselves wherever there is a bit of dirt. Two miles south is a rather unusual rock formation. Make of it what you will. Continue winding through low hills.

    3.8   213.9   K172   The short fan palms have shown up again. They seem to thrive when there is open land. A couple of miles ahead is the town of **Palmillas** and more thatched roofs.

    6.3   220.2   K162   We are at the top of a small rise. To the west is a very large swamp. The water is sweet here but as we move west it blends into the large brackish lagoon surrounding Teacapan. **(See Sinaloa Beaches.)** On the left side of the road are beautiful granite cliffs. Mexico 15 becomes more winding. Watch the oncoming traffic.

    5.6   225.8   K153   The road has returned to low, flat farmland. Mangos, corn and forage crops lead us into **Copales**. To the east are the foothills of the Sierra Madres.

    4.4   230.2   K146   The signed community of **La Concha** and an agricultural check station. Occasionally it also serves as a narcotics and gun inspection station. Just ahead, at the center line of the **Río Las Cañas**, is Sinaloa's border with **Nayarít**.

    End of Log.

MEXICO'S COPPER CANYON

It's four times the size and 280 feet deeper than Arizona's Grand Canyon and accessible only via what a May, 1974 **Reader's Digest** article hailed as "The Most Dramatic Train Ride in the Hemisphere." Those are some pretty strong reasons why the tourists outnumbered the locals in the **Los Mochis** train station waiting to board the **Chihuahua and Pacific** passenger train. We are all headed for Mexico's famous **Barranca de Cobre** (Copper Canyon), the state of **Chihuahua** and one of the most fascinating trips we have ever taken.

BARRANCA DE COBRE

Briefly, we climb from tropical Los Mochis to the Sierra Madre pine forests on a train track which took over 90 years to build and has been recognized as one of North America's finest engineering feats. Along the way are 86 tunnels and 37 bridges. At the **Estación Temoris**, we will see three levels of track, one atop the other, and connected inside the mountain by 360-degree tunnels.

As we proceed into the foothills, the farms, cactus and mesquites gradually yield to oak, pine and manzanita during the 85-mile, 8000-foot ascent from **El Fuerte** to **Divisadero**.

More background...The Barranca de Cobre is actually a number of canyons, products of a long series of cataclysmic shifts in the earth's crust coupled with severe volcanic action. For many millions of years major river systems have worn their way through the mountains. The distance from the canyon rims to its river beds is over 6000 feet in places. Climatic conditions range from native ponderosa forests with heavy snows, to the tropics. At Divisadero we stand among the pines and, with binoculars, are able to identify banana, mango and papaya orchards below.

Here, in an area which is yet to be fully charted, live around 40,000 (nobody really knows) of some of the most durable and resourceful people on earth, the **Tarahumara** Indians.

Only peripherally assimilated into Mexican society, these amazing people live in a culture which has worked for them for centuries, through subsistence farming (corn, beans and squash), foraging, and the hunting of wild animals (from deer to mice). They live easily throughout the area in the many caves or in primitive rock houses built precariously near the edges of mile-high cliffs. There is little doubt that these people enjoy the most spectacular residential views of any society in the world.

The Tarahumara also prefer a solitary existence, rarely going much beyond their extended families. The diet consists almost entirely of corn and beans. They do not catch enough game to add much protein, and squash is used sparingly as flavoring in various soups and gruels.

But there is another ingredient which cannot be overlooked...tesguino. A beer made from corn, herbs and spices, it is part of the family diet. Not high in alcohol, its weakness dictates that they drink large quantities in order to feel intoxicated. And they do...a full 20-liter clay olla (pot) can become history in a few hours. It is from this unique brew, some scientists theorize, that come many of the nutrients needed to thrive in Tarahumaraland. A note...from what we've seen and heard, the hangovers are horrendous...curable, according to one Tarahumara, only by drinking another few liters.

A FEW NOTES...

Were you to make your own tesguino, you could expect to soak, then cook for several hours, as much corn as could be spared. Next, drain and grind the kernels to a mush, reintroducing the liquid and your own special mixture of herbs and spices into a especially-made clay *tesguino* pot. The last step is to fill the pot with water and stick it in the back of the cave.

The first tasting takes place at 24 hours. Most never get beyond that, but connoisseurs are known to hold out for the magic 48-hour mark. You'll have to be the judge. We found a 40-hour vintage to be "interesting," and better than the one-day variety.

Because of the lifestyle the Tarahumara babies are at high risk...infant mortality is close to 50%. But once able to take part in family activities, their health level and longevity picks up dramatically...a phenomenon which is still under investigation by sociologists.

It is a popular notion that the Tarahumaras are the world's greatest marathon runners. It is more likely that they should be recognized as the world's greatest long distance runners, for it has been shown over the years that the Tarahumara barely gets warmed up by the time he completes a marathon (26 miles, 385 yards). His best races in his mountain homeland begin at 50, and often exceed 150 nonstop miles. There is a well-documented instance of a Tarahumara carrying mail from Chihuahua down to Batopilas in the Sierra Madre. He would make the 300-mile round trip in six days, take a day off, then set out again!. And he did it for many years.

The ability of the Tarahumara to adapt to his surroundings has carried over to religion. Since 1607 the canyon residents have heard the recruiting efforts of the missionaries. Little by little they have accepted portions of the dogma, but it has not been a clearcut victory for the church. Most Tarahumaras saw a way to accept the new teachings without offending their own Gods...they just added the new ones to the old and increased the number of celebrations each year. The results are some of the most colorful Christmas and Easter celebrations to be found anywhere. Accommodations throughout the barranca are reserved years in advance for these week-long, nonstop celebrations. Another, December 12th (Virgin of Guadalupe) celebration is also of special interest, and nearly as well attended.

*Handcrafts abound, particularly baskets woven from yucca and coarse grasses found in the nearby hills. Look for them along the way and wherever you stop. Clever versions of violins, leather drums (**tambor**), dolls, terracotta pots or **ollas** and **collares** (necklaces) are among the things for sale. There is little or no bargaining with the quiet and gentle Tarahumaras. They have a price and stick by it.*

The Trip Itself...

By leaving and returning to **Los Mochis** you have the advantage of seeing all of the Barranca de Cobre and the rolling plains of the Chihuahua highlands in the daylight...the canyon going up and the highlands coming back.

We recommend that you take one of the package tours offered for the Copper Canyon, giving yourself time for extra day trips if you find something of special interest. Ask your travel agent at home, or from the *Flamingo Travel Agency* in the **Hotel Santa Anita** when you arrive in Los Mochis. (They speak excellent English.) In this way, at the critical locations of **Cuauhtémoc** and **Chihuahua**, you will be assured of seeing areas of interest which are not often available to the unescorted visitor. For the return trip, you may take the train or fly.

When reserving seats for the train, try to get on the right side on the way to Chihuahua, on the left coming back. You may also stand in the vestibules of the cars and look out the open windows...this is essential for photographers. Look for specifics on what to see and do in the log following.

Tasty meals are available in both directions, and refreshments, including *cerveza*, plentiful. We had excellent service from all of the personnel on the train, and their comments and good nature added to the experience of the trip. The kilometer markers used in the log begin at 268 kilometers northeast of the city of Chihuahua.

SINALOA INLAND

K920   The train is leaving the **Los Mochis** railroad station right on time...6:00 AM. The sun has just risen, throwing a bright light on the receding suburbs. The fields along the tracks are typical of the area...grain, marigolds, vegetables and silage.

K883   At **San Blas** the **Chihuahua and Pacific** tracks intersect with the north-south tracks and shuttles passengers and cargo between Mexicali and Mexico City. The land is still flat and dotted with trees and patches of cactus.

K830   The old town of **El Fuerte** (The Fort). Founded in 1563, it became permanent in 1610 and served as the state capitol in the 1820s. Many fine homes are here. Plan at least a day visit. **(See Sinaloa Inland.)**

K781   The bridge over the **Río Fuerte** is more than 500 feet long. (It seems to sway a bit as we go across.) The countryside is beginning to change. More trees and cactus are evident as we go deeper into the foothills of the **Sierra Madre Occidental**. Soon come veritable jungles of huge trees, vines, tumbling steams and tall cliffs and spires.

K755   The **El Descanso** (Rest or Relief) tunnel is the first one we encounter, and is the longest tunnel (5966 feet) of the 86 in the line. Each tunnel is numbered so we can keep track.

K748   *Tom will never forget the **Chiapas Bridge**. Several years ago he plastered himself on the cow catcher of the engine for the trip across the 335-foot high, 950-foot long bridge with a video camera to get footage for a Los Angeles television show. His heart still pounds when he thinks about it.*

There are several varieties of *agave* plants on the canyon walls along with many, many species of shrubs, annual flowering plants, and small trees. Even the variations of plant forms from one side of a tunnel to the other is fascinating.

K708   It is in **Temoris** that the symbolic moment of completion was celebrated with the driving of a golden spike in 1961. A lovely spot, with a waterfall cascading at the far end of the dead-end canyon. It is here that the train makes three passes along the sides of the canyon walls. At the end of each pass the tracks form a loop inside the mountain as it goes higher! An amazing feat.

K668   **Bahuichivo** is a small logging community and supply center for the mining operations located in the canyons to the south and east. Twelve kilometers from the depot lies the town of **Cerocahui**. A primitive village of nearly 1500, it began as a mission outpost in 1680. A few years later its gold-colored tiled dome and the red rock walls were completed, creating one of the most beautiful churches of the era. Across the street is the **Hotel Misión**, a modern hotel providing a variety of services to visitors. The hotel has a rustic charm which grows on you very quickly. The meals are excellent and the staff cheerful. They are truly privileged to live in such an environment.

Cerocahui is the starting place for a variety of fascinating adventures, highlighted by a 30-mile drive to **Urique** along one of the most difficult roads we have ever seen. From the mile-high hotel we climb to nearly 7000 where we stop at a mir*ador* (viewpoint) overlooking the world! It seems so, anyway.

From our perch we look almost straight down on the village of Urique, 5400 feet below us. Our driver, Luís, assures us that there is indeed a road down through the jumble of shadowy peaks and vertical cliffs. First completed in the early 70s, it took bulldozers and hundreds of workers five years to get there from where we stand.

TARAHUMARA WOMAN

With his foot ready to apply the brake and the transmission in compound low, Luís worries his pickup down through an incredible collage of rocks, cliffs and trees. It was not until the last mile or so that we find a roadbed more than about 10 feet wide. (If you have an acrophobia problem, perhaps you'd better skip it. But if you don't...go for it. The experience will never be forgotten.)

We are finally in Urique. Altitude 1200 feet...a full mile below our high point earlier this morning.

First visited by the Jesuits in the early 1600s, its existence has depended upon the bounty of precious metals found in the area. From panning the Urique river to working stopes perched halfway up a vertical 3000-foot cliff, the region still yields gold and silver. *We were shown some beautiful nuggets taken "only a few feet" from the town's basketball court.* In many ways the adobe town has changed little. There is electricity (4 hours a day), a school, clinic, and a twice-a-week a supply truck that grinds its way up and down the incredible trail. Lacking much traffic, the cobbled streets serve more as gathering places for the town's citizens, their horses, goats, pigs and chickens.

Gold and silver is still a major topic and mantelpieces are dotted with samples. The old ways have not left these people. They still make their own saddles. Their lariats are made from leather strips, while ropes plaited from the tail hairs of horses, burros and cows are seen hanging from every pommel in town. Most of the corn, beans, wheat, fruits and vegetables come from the canyon. Urique's goat cheese has been made and sold for over 200 years. The aura of the town makes its dozen-or-so pickups look out of place.

Our visit is in late October, yet the water of the Río Urique is clear and cold, the air hot in the bottom of this mile-deep canyon. Two hours earlier at the rim of the canyon a sweater had felt good.

OUR AMIGA IN URIQUE.

We are eating in the **Restorante Plaza**. The owner, **Virginia** has lots of smiles and does a fine job on beef stew, Urique style. There are 3 hotels in town offering a total of about 20 rooms. While they do make sure you have plenty of candles, don't expect room service or a private bath.

The adventure also includes a visit to the cave dwelling of a Tarahumara family, a stop at a spring and more vistas than you can imagine. The trip is not always available, but ask for it...if you have have the chance, take it. You will not be sorry.

Actually, a walk around Cerocahui is an adventure in itself. This morning we watch a steer being slaughtered, skinned, cut up and sold in the street in front of the small square. The senior *rastrero* (butcher) makes the first incision and then solemnly oversees the work of his *ayuderos* (helpers), assisting only when it seems necessary. The hide serves as the table for the meat, protecting it from the sandy street. Surely a most of old Bossy will be eaten by tonight, for refrigeration out here is rare.

A step into one of the several *tiendas* revealed the usual galvanized buckets, lengths of rope, candies and foodstuffs. And one other thing...a do-it-yourself shoe kit.

Slabs of tire treads were stacked next to lengths of leather thongs. You could pick your brand, Goodyear, Winston, Michelin, select a pair of thongs, and with the punch laying on the counter, have yourself fixed up in minutes. You did have to provide a knife sharp enough to shape the soles. The cost? Less than $2.00!

K662   **Cuiteco**'s mile-high climate has proven very good for apples and peaches. Both are excellent and are shipped to many Mexican markets. Cuiteco was founded in the 17th century by padres **Juan Salvatierra** (founder of Loreto in the Baja California peninsula) and the prolific **Eusebio Kino**. The **Hotel Cabañas Piñar de Cuiteco** has 20 *casitas* with fireplaces, private baths, a restaurant and museum.

TARAHUMARA LADY

SINALOA INLAND

K624   After a short halt at **San Rafael** to unload supplies and get a new crew, the train pulls into a cantilevered wooden platform built to accommodate the guests of the **Hotel Posada de Barranca**. It would be hard to find a more peaceful location than the Posada...here in the crisp clean air of 7800 feet we are eating crisp sweet apples from the trees in the courtyard...We are relaxed: listening to the train whistles; watching the clouds form and dissipate over the nearby peaks; walking a quarter-mile to the canyon rim to sip *margaritas* while the sun sets over the canyon.

A fifteen minute walk to the north is **Divisadero**, (also a train stop at K622) another beautiful site for views of the Barranca. The **Hotel Cabanas Divisadero Barrancas** sits right on the edge of the canyon. To the east a number of trails lead to the caves and stone houses of the Tarahumaras. Several years ago we rented horses and hauled camera equipment into several of these sites. Using video cameras and a battery-operated color monitor, we showed the families what they looked like. It blew them away.

Across from the hotel is a sizeable field for recreation and ceremonial dances. If you like baskets, you will love Divisadero...it is here that some of the best Indian basketry in Mexico is found, and at reasonable prices.

Tom talks of a very moving experience his first morning at Divisadero. He was watching dawn break over the barranca when the Tarahumaras began calling back and forth across the canyons. Their shouts echoed, sometimes many times as they took turns discussing the day's itinerary. After 10 minutes, everything was settled, and the sun resumed its quiet penetration into the gigantic canyon.

K585   Railroad buffs will like this. Here at **La Lazo** (The Loop) the train makes a complete 360 degree turn in order to gain enough altitude to make it over the crest at **Los Ojitos**. At 8071 feet, it is the highest point on the route. It is not uncommon for passengers to report seeing mountain lion, bighorn sheep and golden eagles in this wilderness area of the Barranca.

TARAHUMARA

K564   To most the appearance of **Creel** comes as a surprise, for here is a town of 16,000 in a desolate setting little different than the precipitous country of the past several hours. Named for an American engineer it was first busy as the Chihuahua-leg of the railroad, and later as a lumber town. Finally, faced with diminishing logs, Creel became the single most important supply center for the Tarahumara. Today, with the completion of a paved highway, it is even enjoying a modest tourist boom. There are a number of hotels, ranging from the three-star **Parador de La Montaña** to a charming Mexican B&B, **Casa de Margarita**.

There is much to do around Creel. Lakes with largemouth bass are within a half-day hike. All day bus or van trips can be arranged into **Batopilas**, another of the very old and remote settlements in the *barranca* of the **Río Urique**. Visit **Cusárare Falls** and stop at the **Misión de Cusárare**. Shop for fine examples of native crafts, maps and historical pamphlets in both English and Spanish.

It is on the last leg of a drive into Batopilas that we watch a group of six young Tarahumaras run up and down long hills while knocking carved wooden balls ahead of them with sticks. They move like the wind, and we are driving like mad over bad roads to get far enough ahead to get pictures. The driver says that they are coming to Batopilas for the day and will be returning home that afternoon...and home is 12 miles away high on the side of the canyon!

K401   The farming community of **Cuauhtemoc** lies just east of the continental divide at 7200 feet. The town of 60,000-plus, it lies in a fertile valley and is well known for a variety of products, including cheddar cheese, beef, wheat, beans and corn. It is the home

125

for some thousands of German Mennonites. Once described as "hard-working, cheese-making, carriage-riding, German-speaking, God-fearing fundamentalists," their lifestyle has changed little since they came here from Canada and Pennsylvania in the early 1920s. Incidentally, the *Mennonitas* produce most of the apples grown in Mexico.

A short distance to the north is Casas Grandes, the single most important archaeological site in Northern Mexico. A visit is a walk through history as you view the remains of amphitheaters, temple mounds, and six-story adobe apartments complete with T-shaped doors and indoor plumbing. We found a local guide through the **Hotel Rancho La Estancia** and have rented him and his car for a day. It is well worth it, especially since we have been joined by a couple from British Columbia.

Another worthwhile trip is said to be to **Basaseachi Falls** and **National Park**. Partially paved, the road takes you to the foot of the third highest free-drop waterfall in the world, 1016 feet. Hunting for duck and geese is a popular program and here, and stories about the excellent nearby trout streams is spreading. We need more time here.

There are several fine hotels in Cuauhtemoc. The **Estancia** boasts a sauna and pool, and we liked the looks of the **Hotel Tarahumara**. The **Rancho Viejo** serves fine steaks and typical Mexican dishes.

K268   The last spot on our tour is **Chihuahua**. A city of more than half a million, Chihuahua is a city with a lot of history behind it. Located on the edge of the hot and dry **Chihuahua Desert** it has large and important agricultural, livestock, mining, industrial and commercial interests. Headquartered here, the Chihuahua and Pacific Railroad serves as the only major freight link between north-central Mexico and the Pacific Coast.

Founded in the early 1700s Chihuahua first became a seat of government in 1824. The cathedral, completed in 1758, is of classic Colonial design. Built in 1751-54 by the Jesuits, a four-mile aqueduct brought water from a dam in the foothills into town. Some of its 80-foot stone arches are still intact.

Chihuahua is a city of murals. Some of the best are in the governor's palace, the **Instituto Cientifico y Literario** and the railroad station. Many places were part of the revolution of 1910. The home of **Pancho Villa** is here, so too is his tomb, which he has never occupied, and isn't likely to. Bullets are still imbedded in the walls of the prison where revolutionaries tried to free some of their leaders. **Father Hidalgo** was executed there in 1811...the cell where he was held may be seen along with memorabilia from the era. Plan to visit the never-occupied mansion built by a mining magnate for a would-be bride who refused to marry him. The furniture is priceless and the story fascinating.

Fiesta time in Chihuahua comes during the latter part of May, centered around the city's Saints Day, Santa Rita. Waterfowl hunting is popular and each winter many American nimrods came for the excellent duck and geese action.

Nearby lives a sizeable Mormon community which was formed early in the century when polygamy was banned in the United States. Their many descendants are influential in Chihuahua's political, social and business circles.

TARAHUMARA GIRL

We've traveled the routes *outlined above, portions of it several times, and have never had enough time. Recently, when asked how much time to allot for a comprehensive trip up the Barranca de Cobre and on into Chihuahua, we replied that two weeks would not be too long.*

End of report

EL FUERTE...

El Fuerte has been around for a long time, having its beginnings during the 16th-century search for gold in the sierras. Today its attraction lies in excellent nearby hunting and fishing. It is also a trading center for Indians living in the canyons to the east.

0.0   0.0   The turnoff from the Mexico 15 highway to the colonial city of **El Fuerte** is at the overpass leading into **Los Mochis**. Marked to **San Blas**, the road goes east on a road signed as Sinaloa 1-24. We pass a number of small *ejido* settlements and lots of sugar cane.

4.9   4.9   Now we're in bean country, with fields in all directions. The soil here is the fine alluvial type, which has made many parts of western Mexico such good farmland. Here, if you wanted a rock you'd have to import it.

0.7   5.6   On the left is the town of Antonio Rosales. Beyond Rosales come a string of little settlements, some with water towers, some with basketball courts.

1.0   6.6   Cross a large irrigation canal.

0.8   7.4   A paved road left, then across another canal. What little ground not under cultivation here is covered with heavy stands of *paloverde or carrizo* (cane). **Mochicauhi,** a good-sized town follows and we skirt its southern edge.

3.0   10.4   Constancia is strung out along the highway on both sides. Beyond, we are escorted by rows of huge cottonwood trees. They are so well aligned they had to have been planted, yet most are at least 8-feet in diameter.

3.513.9   **Camajóa** has two basketball courts within a block of each other. Just beyond in **Charry**, the road forks and we keep to the signed, right branch.

6.0   19.9   A large canal, then into the pueblito of Lázaro Cárdenas. After a railroad crossing there's **Macoyahui**, a scattering of houses and several cattle loading pens next to the tracks.

2.0   21.9   The highway forks.

go left to **San Blas**, right to **El Fuerte**.

1.1   23.0   A paved road right to **Sinaloa de Leyva**, another of the colonial cities which grew up around the mineral riches of this portion of the Sierra Madre Occidental. The church in San Blas is visible off to the left. We then pass the eastern access road into San Blas.

5.0   28.0   Cross the tracks of the Chihuahua y Pacifico railroad. We can see a K marker for the railroad. It reads 630, meaning that it is 630 kilometers from its beginning somewhere beyond Chihuahua City. We now pass a relatively-large brick-making operation. There are 7 or 8 kilns and lots of bricks in various stages of completion.

9.5   37.5   **Santa María** is a good-sized ranch with a number of out-buildings. We then recross the RR tracks. The gravel turnoff on the left is to **Tehueco**. The hillsides are covered with deciduous hardwoods prized as plant stakes, fences, etc. When cut they are called barras.

A new wrinkle for aluminum can collectors...we recently drove past a small ranch with a huge pile of beer cans in the yard — thousands of them. As we watched, a large dual truck begin to roll back and forth over the cans, flattening hundreds with every pass. He was finished in less than five minutes.

9.6   47.1   **Cabanillas** is a small town on the edge of an arroyo, then comes a state prison.

2.3   49.4   **El Fuerte** is on the left. We go under an arch, past a local **Pemex** and into the center of town.

The town of El Fuerte had its beginnings in 1564 when it became a stopping place for

127

the **conquistadores** on their way north to New Mexico from Durango. It also served as an "education center" for the Indians and, as such, it had its shares of Indian problems. Finally, in 1610, fortifications were built and it became known as **El Fuerte** (the fort). After subduing the Mayo Indians, it flourished as a commercial and farming center, then as a major trading post for the gold and silver mines in the nearby sierras. For a brief time in the early 1820s it was the the state capital.

Today El Fuerte benefits from irrigation water from nearby lakes **Dominguez** and **Hidalgo** and crops (principally corn, beans, squash and cotton) have never been better. The lakes also provide good bass fishing and duck hunting, while the surrounding farmlands attract hundreds of thousands of whitewing and morning doves daily during the season.

The town itself is low key, with a number of the old colonial homes still standing. One had been extensively restored by a Los Mochis businessman, **Roberto Balderrama**, and turned into a small hotel, **La Posada de Hidalgo**, with a fine dining room. It is worth a visit even if you do not plan to stay in El Fuerte. Tours can be arranged through the hotel to visit other old homes in the area. Take a walk around the **zocalo** and a look at the colonial-era buildings and church. You will also see a government shop featuring handicrafts from the foothill ranches. The displays of baskets and masks are especially good.

An important date to the locals is June 24th when the Mayo Indians perform their famous deer dance. Other busy fiesta times are Christmas and Easter. Back to the highway

SINALOA INLAND

COSALA...

When we first announced our intentions to do a book on western Mexico a friend in Los Mochis, Roberto Balderrama said, "If you don't include Cosalá you will have missed one of the most beautiful colonial towns in Mexico." A couple of days later we were speeding down the highway with Roberto and his wife Vilma.

0.0   0.0   K0   Turn east on Sinaloa D-1 from Mexico 15 at K106 north of Mazatlán onto a paved, signed road to **Cosalá** and go straight east toward the hills.

1.9   1.9   K3   A cattle ranch, **La Papalota** is on the right. Many of the hills around us are sharply peaked, indicating relatively-recent uplifting and/or volcanic activity. **Nuevo Salto Grande**, a small community off to the right, is next The pavement has many dips and could cause instability in large vehicles.

2.4   4.3   K7   The cluster of buildings to the north is signed **Japuio**. The mountains show many rock bluffs with vertical cliffs extending 100 feet and more. Continue northeast to the top of a small rise and a view of **Laguna Salto**. *Only recently completed, it promises to be another one of the bass-filled lakes of Mexico. Already several outfitters are open on the lake, with peak fishing for big bass expected through the 1990s. This lake, coupled with* **Comedero** *to the north of Cosalá bring bass fishermen in from all over North America.*

1.9   6.2   K10   The road turns left at the "Y." The right branch is closed as it, now ends up in the lake. The newly paved left branch skirts the lake at a distance and we catch occasional glimpses as we move north.

2.6   8.8   K14+   There are some imposing granitic mountains off to the left. Cross a small bridge and continue north.

4.3   13.1   K21   The paved road coming in from the back and right is the old roadbed.

0.7   13.8   K22   **El Sabinál** is a small collection of houses and a one-room school. The road continues to wind and gain a little altitude.

1.9   15.7   K25   Some of the nearby hillsides have been cleared of the small trees and cactus typical of this area and will be planted for the rainy season.

3.2   18.9   K30   Several of the mountains exhibit high, vertical planes of rock framed by heavy stands of brush. We climb a bit then drop into a little valley with a few houses signed as **El Rancho**.

3.4   22.3   K35   **Ipucha** is a small community consisting of a number of houses, a *panteón* (cemetery), a school and no basketball court. A couple of graded roads branch from here into the hills and a series of ranchos.

3.0   25.3   K40   We move past more hills and follow a stream-bed past large *higueras.*

3.1   28.4   K45   The cut on the right seems to be dropping a lot of rocks...watch for slides.

0.6   29.0   K46   There is a sharp turn (right) with a flight of stairs going about a hundred feet up the steep side of the rocks to a small shrine on the top of the cliff. We top out on our climb and start to wind into the large valley to the north.

1.8   31.8   K49   The valley floor and the few houses at **El Potrero** (The Caretaker). Farther along we see more irrigation and some large mango trees.

1.5   33.3   K51   We pass the local **Pemex** station and an ore processing plant on the left just before entering the outskirts of **Cosalá**. Beyond about a quarter-mile a graded road left bypasses town and joins the graded road coming from Cosalá to go north to **Comedero** lake.

0.9   34.2   K52+   Once across the small streambed we are officially in town.

Cosalá. One can go up and down the streets of this little town of perhaps 10,000 and by selecting various houses create a diorama of the history of colonial Mexico. Stone lintels, fountains and even benches appear in and around quiet courtyards with great, old trees providing shade. White walls 2 and 3 feet thick are topped by handmade *tejas* (roof tiles).

When and how did she start? How about in 1550 with the impressive name of The **Royal and Ancient Site of the Immaculate Conception of the Eleven Thousand Virgins of Cosalá!** Even in those days the name must have drawn attention. (*And how could the travel industry have missed that one?*)

As for the **R.A.S.I.C.E.T.V. of Cosalá**, it did become one of the most important mining centers in northwest Mexico, even serving briefly as the state capital shortly after Mexico became an independent nation.

The two 16th-century churches were joined two hundred years later by the **Santa Ursula**, which is sited on the tree-shaded plaza. The bells from Santa Ursula sound out the hours in loud, clear tones. The interior is embellished with silver donated by miners of the era. A History and Mineralogy Museum is housed in an old colonial mansion facing the plaza. There are numerous photographs, mining tools, documents and weapons depicting the early history.

Just out of town past the airport runway there is a small sugar mill. It operates as one would have a hundred or more years ago. The cane is delivered from the fields by burros so loaded that all we can see are legs and an occasional nose. The juice from the crushing goes into the troughs cut in the cement and stone floor, ending up in huge copper kettles to be heated by burning the *bagase* or dried stalks. As it boils the evaporative process is hastened by men lifting large, sieved ladles of the hot liquid into the air. As it thickens it is moved from one kettle to another by means of other, portable, troughs. At a critical stage of completion the material is ladled into large wooden pitchers from which the maestro fills square-cut pockets in long wooden molds. The visuals, the smells and the beauty of the completed product, piloncillo, creates a marvelous chemistry. A never-to-be-forgotten sight. It is in operation from November through March.

COCA-COLA TRUCK —
SIERRA STYLE

On the road out to the sugar factory we pass a lumber mill which processes the wood from the nearby mountains. If you like the exotic woods of Mexico, here is one place to stop and look around. We have seen wood here which will make magnificent furniture.

Cosalá is also home base for one of the world's finest saddlemakers. Several years ago when the presidents of Mexico and the United States met, this man was commissioned by the president of Mexico to create the "saddle of saddles." The presentation was made and it now resides in the tack room of ex-president Ronald Reagan's Santa Inéz rancho. If you wish to meet the maestro himself, **Arcadio Garcia's** little shop is on the right as you enter town. He will usually have at least one finished saddle, plus several in process. A charming man who is justly proud of his work.

The town currently has two small hotels, the **Colonial** which replicates closely what one might have had as a hotel room a hundred years ago with only one exception...a light bulb. The facilities are down the hall, including any water. The other is the **Conde**. It is in a more modern building with the rooms facing into a central courtyard, and each room has a fan. Sorry, no swimming pool here either. We hear that another hotel is in the planning stages and will overlook the plaza.

The food situation in Cosalá is somewhat limited, but there is a good cafe, **El Pueblito**. It is owned by **Eduardo Marino**, who is also the cook. He comes with fine credentials, having spent eight years in the Camino Real hotel system. We were impressed with the selection, presentation and quality of the meals.

Less formal meals can be picked up around the plaza. At midday we head for a

130

cheerful lady on the northwest corner. She has 'em standing in line for plates full of small tacos, beans and salsa. At night we've found the young man on the east side to provide great *quesadillas* stuffed full of *carne asada*, chopped *repollo* (cabbage) and sauteed onions and heaps of *rábanos* (radishes).

There is one more restaurant we'd like to tell you about, even though the owner has moved away to be with her family. She is that much of a special person...

*She is **Francés Padilla**, a marvelous lady who operated one of the most unique eateries we've ever run across. Her home was the restaurant and identified only by a very small sign, **Cafetería Francés**. La Señora Padilla served breakfast and midday meals only. Her menu was whatever she happened to have in her kitchen. For very reasonable pesos we received large plates full (with seconds), all of the coffee, sodas, etc. we wanted, and huge helpings of hospitality. Since we met, we seem to have adopted each other. A number of her children live in the United States, and we've had the pleasure of talking to one who lived in Southern California. While in Cosalá her casa became our casa. We wish her health and happiness in her new home.*

The big fiesta day here is **San Juan Bautista** when regional dances, horse races, cockfights and home cooking abound. The date, June 24th, or the nearest weekend.

Only 20kms to the north over a graded dirt road lies **Lake Comedero**, one of the best bass fishing lakes in North America. A new reservoir, it is just coming on stream as a bass lake where not only quality but quantity have anglers coming from all over the United States and Canada. We took a day and caught enough largemouths to fill the back of the Toyota pickup, if we had kept them. A great time in a new-to-us-fishing environment.

One of America's top marketers of quality bass fishing, **Ron Speed**, has established the **Comedero Sportsman's Lodge** on the premises. Offering packages including rooms, meals, boats and guides, he may be contacted at S&W Fishing and Hunting, Inc., PO Box 1013, Malakoff, TX. Phone (214) 489-1656. He also operates a fishing camp on the new **El Salto** lake. El Salto's strength seems to lie in size rather than high numbers as six to ten pounders are already becoming commonplace.

Roberto and Vilma Balderrama are right, Cosalá is a must for any travelguide to Mexico West. Back to Mexico 15.

COPALA AND BEYOND

Here, as in many parts of Mexico, a turn toward the mountains is a turn toward its colonial history.

0.0   0.0   K292   Turn from Mexico 15 just north of Mazatlán at K266+ onto the signed **Durango** highway, Mexico 40. Head east toward the mountains in the distance. Much of the pork consumed in Mazatlán must come from the three or four hog farms along here. Shallow breathing is recommended.

3.1   3.1   K287   Road begins winding up into the hills. This is a particularly good area for the bright pink blossoms of the ama*pola* tree. Blooming around December in this area, it puts on a spectacular show of color. A short grade follows, then drop into a small valley.

3.2   6.3   K282   Cross a small bridge and into **Malpica** (A Bad Trail or Path) where the paved road (north) to **La Embocada** (Narrow Passage) takes off. Continue upward out of small valley and top another rise.

1.8   8.1   K279   Begin descent into another valley through a large grove of mangoes. The ruggedness of the sierra escarpments show well in the views to the east. Ahead is the first of many furniture factories or sales sheds between here and **Concordia**. The styles to be seen are unique to the region and are typified by the name "colonial."

2.5   10.6   K275   The outskirts of Concordia. Cross the streambed and past more factories and shops. Aside from furniture Concordians also make and sell terracotta pottery. The baskets we see are made in the nearby ranchos. The best road into Concordia is just ahead. Take a left past a garish new stone building.

Concordia was originally **Villa de San Sebastián**, the name given the Indian village found here by Francisco de Ibarra in 1563. It was changed in 1828 due to a *concordia*, or agreement...

During the early days of settlement and pacification of the local tribes of New Spain, the Spanish brought in mercenaries from all over over Europe to assist them in the process. In this region the foreign troops were largely French, German and Prussian. A group was stationed in San Sebastián when the Spanish decided they had things under control and ordered the troops out of the country. Many of the soldiers, rather than return to the tumultuous Europe of the era, simply melted into the countryside, worked the land and established businesses. This was fine until Mexico's land reforms of the early 1820s. Claims and counter claims flew until a meeting was arranged in San Sebastián during the year of 1828. A settlement was reached and to commemorate the event, the name was changed to Concordia.

Todays 20,000 people are still in the process of change from a commercial mining and farming center to an economy which includes furniture manufacturing. Always a rather pretty collection of white buildings with red tile roofs, the town has begun repaving (or simply paving) many of her main streets. The beautiful 18th century **Iglesia de San Sebastián** is worth a visit, particularly during the town's major fiesta, a four-day wingding built around its *dia da Santa* and founding anniversary, January 20th. Back to the highway.

A few meters east of the **Pemex** station a paved road signed **El Verde** goes north past the edge of Concordia to several small foothill communities. El Verde is located on the edge of a lake, **Laguna Caimanero**. *The lake's name tells a story of the past. A caimanero is one who catches and kills caimans, a variety of alligator. At one time this part of Mexico was well populated with these toothy fellows. Growing to 12 feet, they were a part of the food supply for the early settlers, and visa versa.*

Another town, **Tepuxtla**, is famous for the *machetes* produced by its *herreros* (blacksmiths). Located north **15.2** miles (24 kilometers), Tepuxtla is a fair-sized collection of houses. Locating the *herreros* is easier than finding them at work. According to **Sr.**

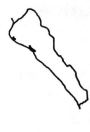

Concepción Portillo, a buyer and seller of machetes, they work early over the forges, then adjourn to other tasks, returning late in the afternoon for another session. The *machetes* of Tepuxtla are built for use...that is obvious from their historic design. The men of this village are reproducing a true piece of yesterday at their forges. The one we bought will be kept and used in our Baja home. Back to the main highway, Mexico 40.

From Mexico 40 we go south at the **Mesillas**-signed junction a few meters west of the **Pemex** station to look for more furniture factories. The road takes us through a portion of Concordia before coming out into farm country. Mesillas (Small Table) is reputed to be good for a variety of handcrafts, including furniture. We find a factory but find nothing we haven't seen in Concordia. One point of int*erest...a first...house walls made from fired bricks, but with adobe mortar. It would appear the idea is proving to be a washout.* Back again to the highway and continue eastward into the hills toward **Copala, Pánuco, Villa Blanca** and **Durango**.

3.1   13.8   K270   Cross a small streambed and up through increasingly-dense stands of small trees, many of which flower profusely at various times of the year. Watch for a sign, **Cerro El Elefante**. On the right, the huge granitic monolith does bear a resemblance to its namesake.

3.7   16.0   K264   Sign, **El Zapotilla**, has been erected in honor of the nearby ranch. A mile ahead we top a ridge and another magnificent view of the *sierra*.

1.3   18.8   K262   A dirt road right 3 kilometers to **La Guasima**. Another mile and **Magistral**'s handful of houses are upon us, then through a streambed.

4.3   23.1   K255   Cross over the **Río Pánuco** and past Chupaderos. It too has a past rich in prospecting for gold, mining claims and the inevitable boom-bust cycles. Today several hundred people live from the cattle and the nearly-vertical cornfields on the hillsides. A fine native sculptor lives here in Chupaderos. You can ask in the village for the "*Artesanía de monos*," or check with **Dan Garrison** at **Daniel's** in Copala. He often has a few in the gift shop.

3.2   26.3   K250   A road right is signed into **Copala**. Arrive at the town's entrance less than a mile later.

Copala contains little more than a thousand people today, yet its history ties together Spanish dons, incredibly rich veins of gold, presidents of Mexico, and the love of the town by a number of well-to-do Mexicans and Americans. And it is this last group who have been instrumental in preserving a number of the historic *haciendas* built during the town's heyday.

Copala was another of the mining sites selected in 1565 by the Spanish engineer, Francisco Ibarra during his whirlwind tours of Mexico's mineral-rich Sierra Madre Occidentál ranges. Its success was sustained over several hundred years and during that time many of Mexico's most influential families were able to trace some of their wealth back the silver mines of Copala. A president of Mexico, José López Portillo president from 1976 to 1982, was born here and spent some of his youth in Copala. A plaque to that effect is on the familial home near the church.

Today the town revolves around the mystique of a tiny colonial mining town changed little over the centuries. Tour busses come so people can inspect the church, see the old jail, look at the fine homes, shop in the little shops and have lunch at **Daniel's Restaurant**.

Daniel's is a story in itself...it began about 20 years ago when oilfield worker **Dan Garrison** and his mother, **Chavala**, journeyed to Copala to visit her birthplace and claim the family estate. The paperwork took some time, and while waiting the pair fell in love with the place. Soon mama began to share her excellent cooking with others, and they had a restaurant. Not much of one, but enough for Dan to begin promoting in Mazatlán, Los Angeles and elsewhere. His pitch included the beauty of the town, its historic sites and his mother's cooking, especially her banana-coconut cream pie! Mama responded by enticing repeat visits just for the food.

Our first time in Daniel's was in 1974 when Chavala was still cooking over charcoal on an outdoor hearth. The lunch we had that rainy afternoon lived up to every bit of the hype, plus the two hosts shared their love for the area and their dreams for its future.

A big break came in 1972 and again in 1980 when National Geographic featured Copala in their fine color essays on western Mexico. The Los Angeles Times travel editor, **Jerry Hulse**, has been here several times and stories of his enchantment with the region have fired the imaginations of many. Today up to seven tour busses a day visit this quiet little time-capsule.

There is even a small hotel in Copala, the **Posada San Jose**. We've stayed there several times. Located on the zocalo facing the church, this 400 year old building boasts 12 sparkling rooms, but keep in mind that the town rolls up the sidewalks very early and one must make arrangements through the **Butter Company Restaurant** before 5 p.m. All rooms are upstairs off a broad well-hammocked veranda.

The whole town is surrounded by bucolic nostalgia...piglets running around like puppies, roosters continually tuning their pipes. Our room this night opens out on a tiny street where a burro is tethered for the night. His lonesome brays are only unnerving the first few times. Back to the highway.

0.0   26.3   K250   Continue winding upward. Over the centuries many miles of tunnels have been dug into the mountainsides throughout the area and some can be seen ahead.

1.2   27.5   K248   Signed road (left) north to **Misión de Guadalupe** and **Pánuco**. **(See Sonora Inland.)** Continue climbing. Note the scatterings of wild poinsettias and small trees bearing white daisy-like flowers...at least in the Nov-Jan period.

3.8   31.3   K242   A restaurant with lots of trucks. It is also the only wide spot for some distance.

1.3   32.6   K240   The road (left) is the entry onto the upper **Pánuco** road. **(See Sinaloa Inland.)** Ahead a signed dirt road (right) leads to **El Coco**, 1km. Continue winding uphill. When catching up with a truck keep a sharp eye on both the road and the driver ahead. He will make every effort to help you get by and his knowledge of the road is invaluable. Their courtesy is consistent with truckers we've seen all over the world.

1.8   34.4   K237   **La Mesa de Carrizál**. A tiny collection of homes, whose residents raise corn on the super-steep mountainsides and maybe a bit of tree cutting. We have now climbed to where small oaks have replaced most of the tropical species. A few more miles and we're in the pine forests of the **Sierra Madre Occidentál**.

2.5   36.9   K233   The left turnoff is into the **Motel Villa Blanca** while Mexico 40 continues toward Durango.

Should you wish to go a few miles farther you'll find the small cliffside village of La Petaca. Its green-painted church can be seen from the highway a couple of miles beyond the Villa Blanca. A bird, the tufted jay, is found in only a few square kilometers nearby. Their rarity attracts birders from all over the world.

The Villa Blanca itself was brought to our attention about three years ago during a dinner discussion of where to find ethnic food in Mexico. The specialties of many cultures are common in centers such as Mexico City, Chihuahua, Monterrey and Guadalajara, but we agreed that aside from Mexican, Italian and Chinese cuisine, Mazatlán was a culinary wasteland. A member of our party jokingly said that what he really wanted was a plate of sauerbraten, red cabbage and potato pancakes...and right now.

No sooner had he finished his lament when a local at the next table offered to direct us to just such a restaurant an hour's drive from where we were sitting! His instructions led us high in the mountains behind Mazatlán and the exact menu requested!

134

SINALOA INLAND

The Motel Villa Blanca was built and operated for some years by **Rolf Richter**, a German national and his Mexican wife. During this time he trained several of the local residents in the intricacies of German cuisine, thus allowing him more and more extended visits to the fatherland. The place has 12 rooms in an alpine atmosphere befitting it's mile-high locale. The setting among the pines is impressive, even without the spectacular view.

The building is located on the edge of a high cliff overlooking the world. From the roof we have an unobstructed view of the Pacific coast and Mazatlán. To watch the sun fall into the ocean from such a perch is worth the trip and the overnight stay. Our goal is to return during a July-August thunderstorm season and watch the fireworks from this vantage point.

End of log.

Pánuco and the Lost Mission of Guadalupe...

We ran across the story about the Misión de Guadalupe during a lunch conversation with Dan Garrison of Copala. His account was so intriguing that we set aside a day, or two if necessary, to follow up on Dan's story. And we're glad we did...

0.0　　0.0　　　　　We turn (left) north onto the signed Pánuco road at K248 on the Durango highway, Mexico 40. The first hundred yards show evidence of a paving effort. We wind sharply uphill on a semi-graded roadbed. The hills are a bright green with many flowering trees, shrubs and annuals in the fall. April-June reveals a landscape of little greenery, a few flowering trees, (*kapok, amapola* and *palo blanco*) and stark, rocky hillsides hidden earlier by vines.

1.1　　1.1　　　　　Top our first rise. Surely only one of many. The roadbed has deteriorated a bit, but still easily passable. The road narrows as we move down along a cliff face. The steepness of the hillsides becomes more apparent when you are clinging to one side and face a similar cliff only a few hundred meters across the abyss with a road scratched onto its side too. Off the cliff, we come to a hairpin turn with several small trees covered with a large flower closely resembling a daisy.

1.0　　2.1　　　　　Signed road (left) leads to that road on the other side of the cliff and to **Mina Los Pajaros**. Continue winding past a small banana orchard behind a wood-railed fence. Soon we cross a streambed. The road is still a good one, though it continues up and down.

1.7　　3.8　　　　　We are at the home (left) of **Don Francisco Quintero** and his family. It has a sign fronting the house which says "*peligro*," a leftover from when the building was used to house dynamite for the local mines. We park here for one of the most interesting walks we've had in some years...a visit to the lost **Misión Guadalupe**.

HOME OF DON FRANCISCO

The mission's history is rather sketchy in that it lay forgotten for perhaps centuries in this remote canyon. Its beginnings came with the gold seekers of the mid-16th century and, by its size and number of outbuildings, must have been intended as a major site.

Our hike begins behind Sr. Quintero's *casa* and proceeds roughly along the path of an ancient stone aqueduct carved into the side of the canyon. At about 500 meters the brush opens to reveal a narrow suspension bridge across the **Río Pánuco**, a harrowing 50 feet of swaying wooden slabs and rusty cables that bring heartbeats to a near-panic pitch. (On the return we wade across the river.)

Now we meet Sr. Quintero, who is waiting for us. It is difficult to guess his age, so full and dark is his hair. His hands are large and muscled for such a slight frame. Sr Quintero is the government-appointed guardian of the **Misión Guadalupe** and he takes his charge very seriously. He owns about five acres adjoining the ruins, upon which there is a tiny house

135

and a wide variety of fruit trees, including coffee.

Our tour included passage through the church, the walls of which remain in surprisingly good shape. The roofs, of course are gone, for they were of wood and tile. There are remnants of several outbuildings...a granary, living quarters and cooking facilities. Behind are extensive gardens with portions of the original irrigation system in place and usable. Don Francisco repeated what is known about the mission and when we leave, he loads us with as many grapefruit as we can carry across the river and back up the canyon. (*They were extremely sweet and flavorful, but with a couple of hundred seeds in each.*)

Senor Quintero does not charge for his services, but will accept a modest **propina**. *In similar situations we have found that a kilo package of* **manteca** *(lard) and something like a few fresh tomatoes and onions are welcome additions. This trip we are leaving the above, plus a large box of holiday cookies for the children.*

Back to the car, we cross a small running stream and begin a steep, winding climb with many sharp turns. Remember it is still one lane, so speed is not a priority. If you begin to falter, keep in mind that a bus comes this way every day.

1.1   4.9   We've probably climbed a thousand feet since the stream crossing. Now in view are pinnacled peaks off to the north. Huge trees are around us and we see springs along the side of the road.

0.3   5.2   Intersection. The road (left) is to **Pánuco**, the (right) branch is back to Mexico 40 (the Durango highway) at K240.

But first to Pánuco...the turn is sharp, and steep. A few hundred yards later we reach a pass into another valley and begin a descent. After the second curve we are treated to a marvelous bird's-eye view of a waterfall, a collection of buildings, a small blue and white church, the cemetery and schoolyard. The voices of the children carry to our cliffside perch. Smoke angles gently upward from several chimneys. And in a little clearing to our right, two burros loaded with firewood are having a loud disagreement. A special insight to centuries past.

The road divides gradually into several alternatives for the final drive into town. Fortunately a youngster directs us straight ahead to a very narrow cobbled street. Four blocks later we are parked at the town square less than a mile from the last intersection.. Several horses are tethered while their owners stand talking. An elderly woman and a dog slowly move out of sight around a white building with bright red doors. The municipal buildings, a couple of homes, two tiny **tiendas** and **Rosy's Restaurant** form the outer quadrangle of the town's center. Usually facing the **zocalo**, the Pánuco church here is on a bluff several hundred yards to the north.

Rosy has no menu, but did rattle off a number of dishes should we be interested. No meal now, but she finds a couple of **refrescos** to fortify us for the hike to the church.

We've never seen or heard of anything like it. We call 'em the Petrified Pigs of Panuco...Maybe a reader has an explaination...

HE'S EARNED A REST

On our walk up the hill to the small church of Pánuco we came around a turn to step into the middle of about a dozen pigs. They were everywhere. Lying down, standing, sitting...and they were all motionless! This gaggle of porkers appear to have been frozen in time. We stood and watched them for a couple of minutes, then walked on up to the church. When we returned they had moved only slightly. Any ideas?

The church appears not to be the original but its interior trappings show considerable age. Over the altar is the famous virgin statue which came to Pánuco by mistake.

The Immovable Virgins

During the colonial days, as the mission stations developed their own commerce and

became villages, it was the practice of the Jesuit missionaries to build bigger and more lavish churches. Altars, vestments and statuary, instead of being fabricated on the spot and blessed by the local padre, were brought in from Mexico City or imported from Spain and consecrated by the highest ranking priest available.

*It was into this atmosphere several hundred years ago that two prosperous mining towns, **Rosario** and **Pánuco**, set out to improve their temples of worship. Both progressed well with their building programs, and both ordered statues of the Blessed Virgin from the cathedral in Mexico City with requests that they be blessed by the bishop.*

In due time the statues arrived and, with great ceremony, were placed upon their pedestals. Over the years the faithful found great solace in placing their problems at the feet of their personal virgin.

As the centuries progressed Rosario grew and prospered while the rich veins of gold and silver petered out around Pánuco, yet the faithful still had communion with their personal virgins, until...someone reviewed the church records and discovered that the virgin built and blessed for Pánuco was in Rosario, and Rosario's was in Pánuco!

As the story goes, the problem was turned over to the respective town elders for a solution. Their decision was to switch the statues. Plans were made and the date set.

On the appointed day a cloudburst forced a cancellation. Later, men came to move one of the virgins off its pedestal, but were unable to budge her. On another occasion she was carried to a waiting truck, but the truck refused to start, despite the efforts of the town's best mechanics. Finally they gave up and put the virgin back in the church. As soon as the did, the truck's mechanical problems disappeared!

Today Pánuco's virgin remains in busy Rosario, while her counterpart is lovingly attended by the few residents of the ghost town of Pánuco.

By the time we return from the church the school is in recess and we have several dozen kids around us, laughing and chatting. Few have heard of California, much less Huntington Beach, but almost all of them know of Dallas and the Cowboys! (Later we discover how they know...on a hanger just inside the door of one of the stores is a Dallas Cowboy football shirt!) One boy offers to take us to the church. As we have already been there, he quickly offers to organize the kids for a photo. After a group shot of about 30 kids, **César Lizarraga**, our 12-year old unofficial Pánuco host leads us to the exit. Less than a mile later, we are back in the real world.

¿UN AMIGO?

After a return to the intersection, take the uphill trail to the east. The road deteriorates markedly in places during its climb back to the highway. The 2-plus miles takes nearly 30 minutes. Several times we decide to forbid any standard car from attempting the journey. Then in the worst part of the trail we meet a large-sized late model Chevrolet crawling and squeaking along, its stereo turned high.

Just before reaching the highway we pass several houses and a number of friendly, shouting kids. Obviously there's not a lot of tourist traffic through here.

    2.1   7.3   Back on Mexico 40 at K240. To the right is **Mazatlán,** left is **Durango**.

    End of log

ROSARIO — CACALOTAN

We have been told that in Cacalotan we might find someone who makes the round wooden chopping blocks we see in the taquerias...

0.0   0.0   Take the paved road east at K224 of Mexico 15 at the north end of the **Pemex** station in **Rosario**. We proceed east along the north side of the **Río Baluarte**.

1.9   1.9   **La Urraca** (The Magpie), a rancho consisting of a couple of houses and a few outbuildings. The road winds through low hills past a few more ranches until it tops out, then drops into a beautiful valley. In the distance are the foothills of the Sierra Madres.

2.9   4.8   Our road turns right toward **Cacalotan** while the straight-ahead dirt road is signed to **Chele**, 20km, and eventually **Concordia**.

0.7   5.5   Cross another bridge over the Baluarte and enter the town. We park by the church and begin asking about the people who make the "*tablas para cortar carnes*." One recommendation led to another and our search turns up a family who live on a side street south and east of the church. It is here that we meet **Enriqueta Arminta de Gonzalez** and she amiably answers our questions.

Yes, her husband does make *tablas para cortar carnes*, but he is not home.

Yes, he makes them from the finest of materials, the trunk of a large amapola tree...preferably one with white flowers.

No, she does not know what they would cost, nor are there any on hand.

Yes, she will accept an order, and deposit, for any number of the *tablas* we wish.

Enriqueta now has some of our pesos, and we have her written receipt and a commitment for several to be ready when we return.

We can't wait. Back to the highway.

*For those who follow up on things like this...we did return and we do have our **tablas**. Two are for friends in the USA and the other two will reside in our Baja home. Also...we have learned to coat the tablas with mineral oil right away, otherwise they tend to crack.*

ROSARIO — MATATAN....

We are looking for some of the artisans who live in the hidden ranchs of the sierra foothills and still make the furniture and implements much as they did centuries before...

The graded dirt road to **Matatan** leaves Mexico 15 below Mazatlán at **Chilillos**, a small town just 100 yards south of the bridge over the **Río Baluarte** at K221. Follow northeast through brushy terrain, gradually gaining altitude. Cultivated plots are here and there, much of it in corn. The Baluarte is off to the left.

At **3.3** miles a dirt road goes (left) straight into the tiny village of **Copales**. In dry periods the locals drive across the riverbed to **Cacolotan** on the north side of the river. We don't recommended it. Just beyond we come into an construction area. Eventually it will be part of a major new irrigation project for the valley and delta area below. The infrastructure follows the river bed to a dam being built some miles above us.

The few houses of **Los Habitantes** is next at **7.0** miles. *Valentín Ayala, one of the residents along this piece of the road to Matatan, is about sixty with strong hands and broad feet. He is thin and looks to be made of wire. Valentín has a watermelon patch off somewhere and each day he brings his sweetest melons in and stacks them under the huanacaxtle tree by the road. We stop and let him pick out a small one for us. He smiles and walks unerringly to one particular melon...as if it had our name on it, picks it up, dusts it of and carries it to our car.*

If you have a few moments he will tell stories about the gold in the hills. He is also prepared to show his collection if there's interest. And it's for sale. And the melon was excellent. The road continues to follow the river.

There is a view of the church tower at **9.2** miles, than we drop into a small arroyo and up into the village of Matatan. Inquiries at the abarrotes (grocery store) for the local maker of machetes (*machetero*) points us to **La Casa Tamarindo** and **Sr. Pilár Martinez Espinosa**. A tall gentleman of about 70, he displays a number of the uncompleted machetes and knives. He is not working this afternoon, but he shows us the hearth with its charcoal, hand-operated leather bellows and anvil. Over his half-century as a blacksmith *(herrero)* Don Pilár has acquired a considerable reputation. His clients extend as far as the sea at Agua Verde and to "ranchos y minas" near the Durango border. We will return soon and place our order. "Give me time," he said, "and I will be happy to make you a fine machete."

We also meet **Ignacio Ibarra Luna** and his sister, **Auralia**. The house number is 43 (on the left as you enter town). They are one of about twenty families in this part of the sierras who make chairs and other furniture out of palm leaves! It was as we were leaving town that a casual glance through an open door revealed one of these incredible objects.

The chair might be best described as a wooden frame whose form is dictated in part by the shape of the branches cut. They then take the leaves of a native fan palm, which come from ranchos farther up in the mountains, soak and twist them into a tight, strong cord. The coils of cording are then woven between and wrapped around the wooden frame. We are especially intrigued by the *vuelos* (rocking chairs) and placed our order for two, one with a high back called a *pavo real*, or peacock, and one with a shorter, wider back called a *guajolote*, or turkey. They will be given an honored spot in our Baja home.

We also remember Sr. Ibarra for his intense interest in gold mining. His lean-to workshop holds a number of hand made tools for the extraction of gold from the sierra. Wooden gold pans, a curious device made from a cow's horn, a pair of rocks ingeniously assembled to finely grind ore, a couple sturdy bags for carrying the ore, and one more item...a baby food jar containing a bit of color. A fascinating day. Back to the highway.

The Beaches of Las Lajitas...

It is sometimes amazing how far people will go to recreate. Here is a stretch for even the most durable adventurer...

The intersection comes at K16 of Mexico 15 north of Los Mochis goes west and is signed **Higuera de Zaragoza**. The **Rio Fuerte Trailer Park** is to the left. The road moves easily west through a number of small communities and miles of farmland.

At **5.3 El Guayabo**, a small community with very large, shady cottonwoods. We continue on past a paved intersection from **Ahome** to the south (**7.2**) and then on to **El Tule** at **12.5** and a mango packing plant. At **14.8** a red sign with a shrimp and the word **Terramar** tells us to go right on a dirt road. We do, and follow it west and north to another intersection at **18.6** miles. We continue straight on the best-traveled road until reaching a three-way split at **21.3**. Stay with the north road paralleling the canal. Once on this there's no problem finding the beaches beginning at **26.8** miles with the private community of **Las Salinas**...and no entry allowed.

We move about a half-mile north to the *playa libre*, **Las Lajitas**. The area is a trash heap with garbage all over the place. Even the beach is a mess, not only from flotsam but because of erosion. The residents of Las Salinas look to be fighting a losing battle to keep their sand. We can see large rock breakwaters and bolsters, some of which have been undercut and are disappearing into the encroaching water. There is a huge pile of old tractor tires and sacks of cement piled up in one place inside the compound.

Such movement of sand islands is not uncommon as the residents of the coastal islands of Florida, Georgia and the Carolinas will attest. And it's happening here, too. A probable cause is the change of the water flow patterns of the Rio Fuerte a few miles to the south. With reduced water flow, less sand comes downstream to be pushed ashore by the prevailing winds and currents.

We saw items of interest on this side trip, but can't recommend the playas. As to the other beach names we had been given...**San Juan** is the name of the general area and nobody at Las Salinas has heard of **Las Biznagas**. As to **No Recuerdo**, we don't remember. Back to the highway.

The Topolobampo Area...

Someday we might have a brighter report on Topolobampo, but for the moment this is how we see it...

The road to **Topolobampo** begins in **Los Mochis** at the signed intersection of G. Leyva and Alvaro Obregón. Turn left and follow it until it dead ends at **0.9**, then turn right (west) toward Topo. **2.1** brings us to the railroad tracks and more farms. At **6.6** make a slight adjustment toward the south past a road (right and **8.9** miles) to the airport. At **12.0** the salt flats are on both sides.

A signed, graded road to the right (**12.4**) heads across the flats to **Baviri**, 11 km. *It goes along the mangrove-lined north side of an arm of the Topolobampo lagoon system. (We can well remember **robalo** (black snook) fishing forays along here in the mid-60s. The action on fish to 3 and 4 pounds was fantastic, even from the bridges.) We cross causeways at 2.0, 2.9 and 3.5 miles respectively. A one-lane wooden bridge at 5.6 brings us into Baviri and the beach variously known as **Animas**, **Medano Blanco** and **Baviri**.*

*The collection of small restaurants is singularly unimpressive, but we've learned that's not a criteria for good food. The largest, cleanest and most organized restaurant is the **Hawaii** and would be our first choice for a meal out here. The beach extends in both directions. It's clean and shallow, making it a great place for families as the kids would need a minimum of supervision. Overnighting out here is not a problem and longer stays could probably be arranged. Return to the Topolobampo highway and west toward the town.*

At **13.5** miles from Mochis a **Pemex** tank farm is on the left and, at the end of the

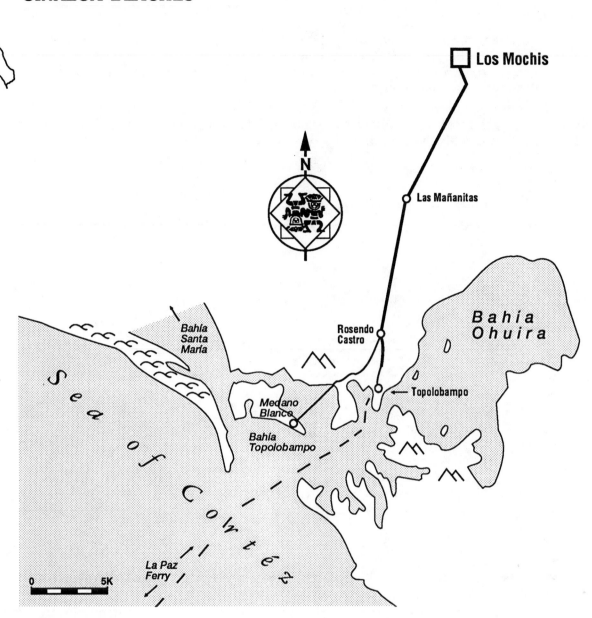

property, a paved road (left) up the hill to the boat-shaped **El Yate Hotel**. An experimental concept of nearly 30 years ago, it will never sink, perched as it is on solid rocks, but it is in danger of crumbling to an ignominious end. Our visit brought in the only set of tire marks to be seen in a parking lot covered with a layer of undisturbed sand.

Back to the main road and an intersection into the central part of town at **15.2**. The ferry terminal to La Paz is on the road to the right. Follow about two miles and you can't miss it.

Topolobampo's claim to fame is her port. It is unique in that here in an area known for its sandy beaches and long shallow undersea structures we find the third deepest natural harbor in the world. This means that any ship in the world can find protection, or cargoes, here in Topolobampo. *The reason for this anomaly lies in the movements along the terrestrial fracture line known as the San Andreas Fault. The result of this bumping and grinding is seen in the the collection of rocky hills, including the offshore **Isla El Farallón**.* Topo is also a terminus for the Baja California ferries.

We find the town dirty and unappealing with as-yet very few redeeming features.

141

Even the waterfront restaurants have piles of trash nearby. There is seasonally-excellent sportfishing out around El Farallón and boats take people to nearby barrier islands and the clear ocean beyond. There are all of these possibilities and more, but we've found no good way to arrange for anything on the spot.

Should you wish to fish or explore the bay and the islands it is best to make arrangements in Mochis...the only place we know is **Flamingo Travel** in the **Santa Anita** hotel. Back to Los Mochis and the highway.

Playa Altata and Beyond...

*It was about 15 years ago that we became aware of **Altata** but it wasn't until 1980 that its natural surroundings and its people became a reality.*

0.0   0.0   We begin in **Culiacán** at the **Cuauhtemoc statue** where the

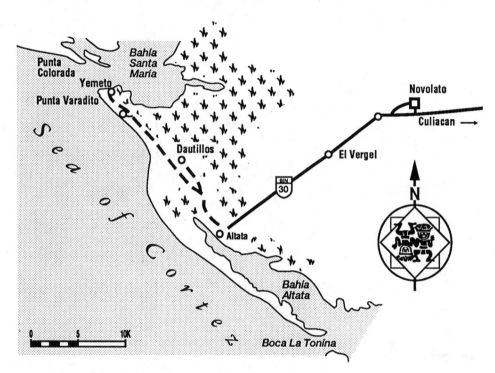

road west is signed to **Navolato** and go past the Sinaloa state government buildings and Culiacan's **Ley** shopping center. This is also the road which leads to the Sinaloa 1 toll road and Los Mochis.

2.5   2.5   We are on Sinaloa Highway 280 and go west past a large ice plant and the airport (right). Continue through the businesses district and several residences. If you like pecans, this is the country. Lots of 'em grown near here, and many vendors to sell 'em.

1.2   3.7   K0   The kilometer markers for the **Altata** highway begin here.

5.6   9.3   K9   A fork in the road. The right branch is signed to Altata. For the next several miles we are looking at many mangos and pastures. The road goes under the bridge carrying Sinaloa 1D toll road but there are no ramps here. The small town of **El Batallón** is next.

6.7   16.0   K20   **Los Mangos Restaurant**. A sizeable family restaurant with a playground for the kids. Note the large mango trees along the right side of the road and the miles of sugar cane. *The state of Sinaloa is the 4th largest producer of sugar in Mexico.*

2.3   18.3   K24   We have a full service **Pemex** at the intersection into **Navolato**.

142

SINALOA BEACHES

We go straight ahead toward the sugar refinery, bearing slightly left around some very large steel tanks. Once around Novolato the road goes southwest over a bridge.

2.9   21.2   K28+   Cross a bridge over a small river. Ahead is a five-point intersection. Take the marked road angling slightly off to the left. Row crops such as tomatoes are a big item here during the winter and the activity supports a large population of *campesinos* (farm workers)...pickers, weeders, sorters and packers.

5.6   26.8   K37   **El Vergel**, a small, well established community of farm workers. Beyond is a similar-looking, unmarked town.

5.0   31.8   K45   We start into the salt flats and marshlands which characterize the *estero* regions of this portion of Sinaloa's coast. Gone are the land farms, and coming up, water farms, or aquaculture. Here in Sinaloa's brackish *esteros* lies a grand opportunity to add to Mexico's foreign exchange credits through the production of shrimp.

Already **granjas de camarones**, *shrimp farms, are popping up here and there along Mexico's west coast. Prime habitat and warm temperatures, along with the addition of proper nutrients, are producing huge blue shrimp weighing an ounce or more in less than 9 months. (A check at our Huntington Beach, California, fish market just before press time had these babies selling for $14.29 a pound!)*

On the surface the system looks simple. Dikes are bulldozed around a portion of marsh-land and pumps installed to provide unpolluted fresh or salt water. Next they add several million larvae and a carefully monitored food supply. Between now and the year 2000 some biologists have estimated that the entire world's demand for premium shrimp could be provided through shrimp farming...thus freeing the world's oceans from the hoards of shrimp trawlers (over a thousand in the Sea of Cortéz alone!) and their incredibly-destructive fishing methods. A nice thought, even if it doesn't all happen.

Trawling is the technique of dragging a large bag-like net along the surface of a shallow, sandy ocean bottom. During the trawl it scoops up all life in front of it, including its target, shrimp. Its destructive nature comes from the fact that it: 1) Indiscriminately dredges up the many benthic (bottom-dwelling) species of worms, snails and crustaceans, 2)Kills immense numbers of small fish for which the shrimp fishermen have no use. A large percentage of these wasted fish are juveniles of varieties which, if left to mature, could provide millions of kilograms of excellent, and valuable, food.

In Tom's visits to these trawlers he has watched as a thousand pounds of fish are destroyed in order to gather as little as 50 pounds of shrimp, then watched them repeat the process. He also tells of small sea turtles brought up dead or dying. The fishing, both commercial and sport, for corvina, totuava and halibut have all but disappeared in large measure because of the desturction of the juvenile forms of these species by the shrimp trawlers. It would appear that farming of shrimp in enclosed areas would give some hope for a dramatic turnaround in the ailing Sea of Cortéz.

4.4   36.2   K52   Graded road (right) is to **El Tambor**. At the intersection, a small **Pemex**, with **magnasin** yet.

2.0   38.2   K55   Entrance to **Altata** and **Bahía de Altata**. To illustrate how close the town is to the water, the main road is on the tide line and a dozen or more restaurants literally move in and out with the tide, dragging their portable counters and supplies of mar*iscos* along as the tide changes. An interesting touch...we need only to bend over to rinse our hands.

We are loading up here at the **Restaurant Loreto** on shrimp, clams and octopus...*camarones, almejas and pulpo*. The owner is a charming lady by the name of **Loreto**. She is also the chief shrimp peeler, chef and telephone operator (the town's telephone is in her kitchen). A charming lady.

*A coincidence of coincidences...***Norman Strung**, *a fellow journalist from* **Montana** *and his wife,* **Syl** *have a winter home here. They aren't expected for another six weeks but*

143

Loreto said she'd deliver a message if we wrote it out. Great idea...an excuse for another shrimp cocktail.

Tom was but a minute into the letter when the waitress asked him follow her to the kitchen. Loreto handed him the phone, and on the other end, Syl Strung! She was calling from snowbound **Bozeman** for no reason other than a touch of Altata homesickness. Long distance telepathy.

There are lots of pangas, the shoreline is covered with them. Seasonally they trawl for shrimp, trap *jaiba*, (blue crabs) and fish for sharks, bonito, pargo, corvina, etc. They also gather oysters, scallops and clams. Several *panga* operators will take you fishing, for a ride around the bay or across to the sand bar and the open ocean, *olas altas* (Meaning "high waves," it is their name for the beach on the distant sand bar facing the Pacific Ocean.). Altata is the principal beach destination for the people in the Culiacán region and is a busy place on Sundays and holidays, especially *Semana Santa* (Easter Week) and *Návidad* (Christmas Week). Informal camping is allowed where you can obtain permission, especially along the beach to the north. There are no hotels. Return to the El Tambor turnoff.

0.0   36.2   K52   Back to the turnoff and we go north along the power lines over graded, washboardy gravel.

3.4   39.6   Signed intersection (left) is to **El Tambor**. As we go farther into the salt flats the travel options broaden. Trails appear along the billiard table-smooth flats, pleasant alternatives to the wet-weather trails through brush and sand. Take whichever path seems to be the most traveled.

2.4   42.0   We come to a fence, then a cattle guard where the road divides. The (left) option leads to a small ranch and windmill. A run to the south on that road brought us no closer to the ocean so we doubled back to the cattle guard, this time following the power lines while zipping along over the salt flats.

3.9   45.9   A road (left) over the dunes is sandy...we get almost to the top, then walk over to a beautiful beach and a nearly-completed building complex. *Its purpose remained a mystery until the manager of an El Tambor restaurant told us it will be used to raise larvae for the shrimp farms planned for the region.*

0.8   46.7   Take the fork (left) into **Playas El Tambor**. A sandy beach open to the *olas altas* (high waves) with a few coco palms, a couple of restaurants and an appealing, laid-back ambiance. The *cervezas* were cold and the fried *lenguado* (halibut), excellent. There are no facilities for campers but there's no problem, according to one of the locals. One thing for sure...the place abounds with good seafood, fine beaches and a friendly atmosphere.

After returning to the fork we are headed farther north along the beach to **Punta Baradito** and the community of **Yemeto**.

4.2   50.9   Arrive in Yemeto, with its fleet of open *pangas* rigged to take shrimp from the shallows of the large **Bahía de Santa María**. We buy beautiful big blue and brown shrimp from one of the fisherman in front of the small processing sheds. They are still alive...until **Jesus Ochoa**, the fisherman, pulls the heads off before weighing. They come in with their catch each afternoon somewhere between 2 and 5 o'clock, September to May, weather and tide permitting. We now return past Tambor, Altata and Novolato to Culiacán and the kitchen in the Hotel San Luís where the chef, **Don Magdaleno** has promised to cook them for us.

Beyond El Dorado...

One thing the dedicated beachcomber has to learn is to expect the unexpected. And then there's the unexpectedly unexpected, as our trip to Boca del Río San Lorenzo demonstrates...

While preparing for our big swing through the beaches of western Mexico, Tom mentioned that we were going out to view one of the finest pieces of wildlife habitat anywhere in North America...the marshes in and around the mouth of Sinaloa's Rio San Lorenzo. He had been there in the early 80s and was blown away by the tens of thousands of ducks and other waterbirds living it up in the marshy habitat. He also talked of the mangrove channels, the rambling dunes of the sand bar and buying shrimp from a lad with a throw net. He made it sound pretty good...

  0.0 0.0 K0 We turn off Mexico 15 at K174 north of Culiacán in **El Salado**, a small, bustling farm town and head southwest. The farms here are busy with grain and cattle.

  6.4 6.4 K10 Entrance into town of **Estación Quila**. Its beginnings were with the railroad as a maintenance facility. Today farming is the big thing. Warning...there

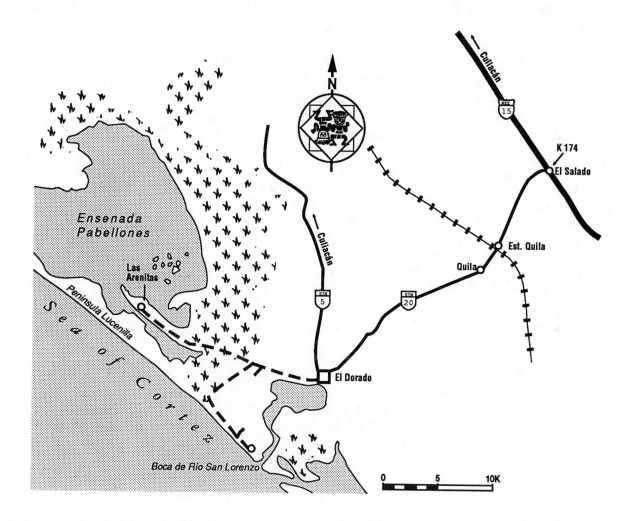

are large, show-stopping *topes* here (speed bumps). About four sets of 'em. Stay on the one paved road through town. The gazebo in the plaza center is impressive, as is the church.

  1.2 7.6 K12 Out of town and southwest past pastures of fine-looking cattle.

  1.7 9.3 K15 The region is checkered with small collections of houses with names such as **La Compurta, Huanacaxtle, El Camalote, Santa Cruz** and **Navito**. All share an interest in the many row crops and abundant sugar cane in the area.

    8.8   18.1   K29   Entering **El Dorado**, a town of more than 30,000 which will need to get its act together before a stranger can find his way through. The town is putting in sewers, water pipes and paving all at one time. But even such a mess has its good side, for in the middle of it all we meet **Jesus Torres**.

A young man standing under a huge cottonwood is talking to friends when he spots us across the street studying a map. He comes over and offers his help and his name. Hearing the problem, Jesus jumps on his bike and leads us through the maze of streets. We follow for a good 10 minutes, ending up at the right road. He then tells us about the beaches, the shrimp farm and **Las Arenitas***, the fishing village famous for its shrimp. Refusing any pay, or even a soda, Jesus remounts his bike and disappears down a side street. "Gracias a Jesus."*

The street renovations should be completed by early 1991, and this log reflects the changes. Follow the main road into town as far as the huge sugar mill. A paved road (right) north goes through the complex and out the other side.

    6.0   24.1   We bear west on a graded road marked **Las Arenitas**. The first mile or two is pure sugar cane, then yielding to pastures and row crops.

    1.6   25.7   Road left to **Campo El Real**, a chicken ranch. The power lines follow that road, though we didn't. Continue west toward Arenitas.

    0.6   26.3   A signed intersection indicates that Las Arenitas is 12km ahead with **La Boca de San Lorenzo** 13km to the left. A small ranch, **Ponce**, was also signed at 5km. Continue northwest toward Arenitas

    1.7   28.0   Enter onto a viaduct over marshy flats. To the right, a large pond is part of a shrimp farm. Owned by a cooperative, it has full-time guards and maintenance crew. On the other side we climb to the top of a 10-foot hill for a view of mangrove channels and dunes to the southwest. Back down to swamp level.

    5.1   33.1   Entrance into **Las Arenitas**. *Our welcome to town is a fun one...half a dozen teenage girls have roped off the road into town and will kidnap us if we do not come with a donation for the church. A thousand peso coin paid the ransom and we went on our way. Tom was sorry to have been released, the girls were very beautiful.*

Las Arenitas is on a very slight rise above the surrounding waters. Here mangos, bananas, papayas and other tropicals grow in profusion. We continue west until coming to the fishing portion of town. A *cooperativa* packing shed is fronted by at least 50 pangas outfitted with booms for netting shrimp in the estuary. There are fish, *jaiba* (blue crab) and shrimp being weighed in as we arrive. The shrimp are less than $8.00 per kilo for the big ones. Return to the intersection to **La Boca** with tonite's dinner assured.

    0.0   26.3   Turnoff to **La Boca de San Lorenzo.** The road goes southwest across the flats. Shortly it leads onto a viaduct a few feet above the marsh around us. Ducks and shore birds are everywhere; doves are resting on the scattered cactus and scrub; rails, are busy scurrying around on their super-long legs stabbing at creatures unknown. The air is still...mirrorlike reflections of birds, brush and sky surround us. We stop to take a picture. Five seconds out of the car shows the foolishness of that move...mosquitos. We drive on.

    4.3   30.6   The trail turns sharply southeast through low brushy sandhills toward the shoreline and the dunes.

    2.6   33.2   Road (left) is into the swamp and the shrimp farm Jesus was telling us about.

    1.5   34.7   The road ends at the edge of the dunes with a lighthouse in the distance. There is an open mangrove channel on the left. We could keep busy here for days. When we reach the end of the road we're greeted by a strange sight...at least 30 people are jumping up and down slapping at themselves and each other with shirts and towels! A fascinating sight.

With the car stopped we discover why. Mosquitoes in uncountable numbers! By the thousands they land on our windows, nearly blocking the view. It is like an Alfred Hitchcock movie! With the windows tightly shut we watched the embattled would-be picnickers scramble into their truck and go flying down the road, still slapping and swinging.

Later we see them parked in a much drier spot eating salsa and crackers. From the nets in the back of the truck it was obvious they had planned to catch shrimp at the river's mouth and have a feast on the spot. If the normal breezes had been blowing, chances are they would have had hundreds of shrimp to wade through, rather than hundreds of bites to scratch.

We'll try again, on a windier day. Back to the highway.

Estacion Dimas and Beyond....

The side road to the ocean west of Estación Dimás is more than just a trip to several nice beaches...

0.0　　0.0　　K0　　The paved road west from Mexico 15 at K72 north of Mazatlán is signed, **Estación Dimás**, a maintenance station for the railroad. The terrain is rolling hills, many of which are planted in corn each summer. This portion is not irrigated, except by Jupiter Pluvius. Cross a small bridge.

2.4　　2.4　　K4　　Paved road north to **Piaxtla de Abajo**. The asphalt goes as far as the tiny town, then poops out. Likewise with the road back to the highway via **Piaxtla de Arriba**. The only reason for going that way might be to check out some unique poinsettias in Abajo. There are many more red leaves in the "flowers" than we've ever seen on their north-of-the-border cousins, and they're incredibly healthy-looking. Continue southeast through irrigated fields.

2.6　　5.0　　K8　　A papaya orchard, **Rancho La Paloma** is on the right. Ahead we climb out of one valley and go through several small ones with a mixture of irrigation, dry farming and brush.

3.1　　8.1　　K13　　Cross over a small riverbed. Dirt road ahead goes north to a several small farms on the bank of the **Río Piaxtla**. Continue winding gently past a number of low hills. Estación Dimás shows up in the distance.

5.1　　13.2　　K21　　Intersection left with road to beaches. Continue into **Estación Dimás**. Population 4000. We see a twin-spired blue and white church. End of K markers.

2.2　　15.4　　　　Turn onto a signed, graded road to **Las Barras**. It proceeds briefly south past fields of sorghum, then gradually redirects itself southwest through heavy brush containing cactus, agave and guamúchíl trees.

5.2　　20.6　　　　Cross the railroad tracks. Immediately beyond, an ungraded trail branches (left) south along a barbed wire fence. For the moment, continue straight. Road immediately swings north, then west.

1.8　　22.4　　　　Road branches (left) toward ocean. Just beyond we enter the tiny fishing village of **Barra de Piaxtla** at 22.9 miles. *Complete with lighthouse, but no electricity, it is home for about 100 anglers, their esposas (wives) and muchos niños. We spend about an hour checking out the beaches and tidepools. The fishermen and the kids are friendly, and carefully explain how we can get to more beaches to the south. The homes are primitive, and with no power everything must be left open to catch the breeze. The beaches around the town are spectacular with several likely campsites nearby. Now, back to the turnoff located just out of town.*

0.0　　22.4　　　　Turn south on an ungraded trail and follow **0.5** miles to the beach. In front of us is a magnificent sight...rocky headlands on each end of a mile-long crescent of perfect sand. Camping is a possibility right here but don't block the trail over the sand to the beach. On low tide almost any vehicle with decent flotation can go down and stay

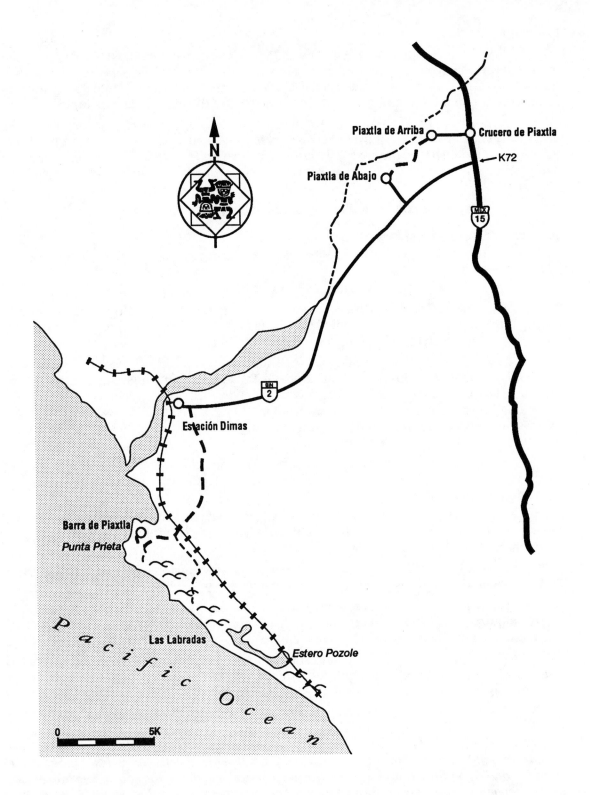

anywhere they want. There is driftwood, and while the sand above the tides is soft, one could unload camping gear and take the vehicle back to solid ground at the end of the beach. Something to think about.

While we are checking things out several divers come out to gather oysters and lobsters. A jolly lot, they have invited us to stick around and join in the harvest. And you know

148

what they say, never reject hospitality in a foreign land. We couldn't wait, but left each of them a cerveza. We salute the ostioneros. Return to the graded road and back towards Dimás.

       0.0   20.6   We are now back to the railroad tracks and the road bearing south along a barbed wire fence. Part of the road maintenance along here appears to include dumping oyster shells in the potholes. It is a mess in wet weather, dusty when dry.

          At **1.6** miles the trail gets more bumpy, then deadends at the ocean. There are several camping spots fronting on the rocks at the north end of this mile-long stretch of sand. We follow the road another 50 yards to a sandy ramp down onto the beach. On low tide it is an easy run to the other end and the carved rocks known as **Las Labradas**.

       The Labradas are little known beyond this part of Sinaloa, yet these large, smooth black rocks are of scientific interest. The surfaces of as many as 75 boulders have been inscribed with a variety of spirals, abstracts and animal forms. The site is believed to have been a meeting place among the early nomadic tribes of the region. It was here that they may have left messages and prayed for hunting success. The markings are located near the mid-high tide line, and are deep enough so that they make excellent photo subjects in the right light. Return to the highway.

Isla De La Piedra...

       The spot known as Isla de La Piedra is an anathema in several ways...

       It is not an island, yet it is. **Isla de La Piedra** is as it is named...an island of rocks in a sea of sand and bordered on one side by an ocean. Were it not for the sand it would be an island, just as its sister rock at the entrance into Mazatlan's harbor, **Isla Venado** is an island.

       Piedra has a reputation for being a place to get away from it all...boats take people across Mazatlán harbor to a landing a half-mile walk away, or you can drive by skirting the large lagoon to the south of the city. There is no electricity and the excellent *huachinango, mojo de ajo* is cooked over wood. However, there's a plan afoot involving Isla de La Piedra and a dozen or more miles of sandy beaches and coco palms to the south...and 800 million dollars. The story is that a consortium of Mexican and American investors is proposing to build eight high rise hotels with 3200 rooms, 1800 villas, two golf courses, a shopping plaza and exposition center plus all of the appropriate infrastructure.!

       We've all heard those dreams before, yet some of the more knowledgeable people around Mazatlán are excited about the possibilities of this one. If it comes about we'd like the coconut hat concession. In the meantime we'll stick to writing.

       The driving entrance is at the airport turnoff from Mexico 15 at K273+ south of Mazatlán. Watch for a paved road branching (right) at about 1 kilometer. Take the north fork and cross the railroad tracks at **1.2** miles. The paved road continues west around the lagoon. At **5.0** miles a graded road (left) is signed to **Barrón**. The road turns northwest and up the coast into many, many coco palms at **6.6**.

       The paving peters out at **8.3**, just past a guarded entrance into a residential development. The area has only a few completed homes behind the tall walls, according to the guard. He knows of no major work going on right now. The rest of the way is a sandy, lumpy ride, ending at **23.4** miles. *Presumably there will not be the problem of sand all of the time, for work was being done on a parallel road which had apparently washed out.*

       The beach here is beautiful. Next to the rocks on the right the water is calm and a number of families are splashing about. The restaurants are deserted, though it is a warm December Sunday. Over an iced *cerveza* the woman whose family owns the restaurant said that fewer and fewer people come to visit her beach. It is a long, hot walk from where the boats now let the people off. *Apparently a closer landing was destroyed by a hurricane several years ago.* The place is pleasant with its warm, calm water, uncluttered beach and its own rocky "island" covered with cactus and small trees. Maybe too quiet for the people who live here. Back to the highway.

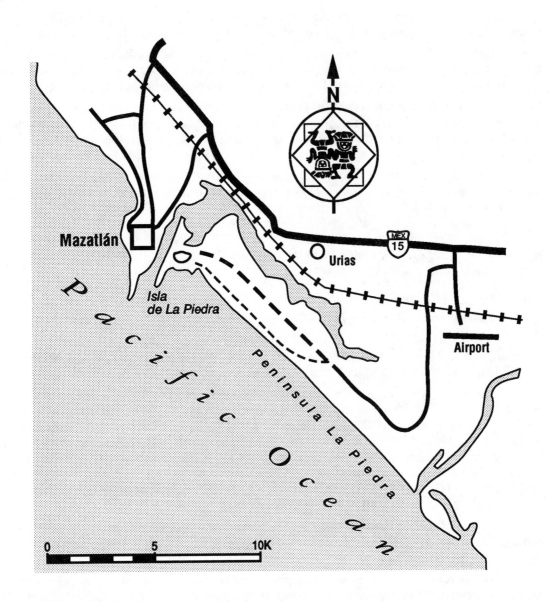

In Search of Turtles...(See Mazatlán Hub Map)

   There are numerous opportunities to reach beaches and/or points of interest in the Mazatlán area. In some instances we end up combining both, such as in this log. The dirt portion of the road can be a bit of a mess after rain, but the locals make it in standard cars. We'd suggest a fairly high clearance on a car and no motorhomes.

   0.0   0.0   Turn southwest off Mexico 15 in **Villa Union** on the dirt street next to the feed and seed store, a white building with green and yellow lettering, past numerous small homes and a first...several fairly large, healthy-looking *hairless* dogs.

   0.4   0.4   An intersect with the paved road heading west toward **Walamo**. The countryside is well-dotted with avocados and coconut palms (under which they've planted beans). Shortly, a railroad crossing and a mango orchard.

   2.6   3.0   Pastures of well-blooded sementhal cattle lead up to **Walamo**, a town of about 8000 We lose the pavement in town, but find it on the other side, a common condition in small towns because the town has to pay for the paving. The name, Walamo, comes from a large tree which once grew in the area. Continue west past mangoes that have

150

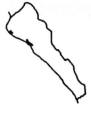

been apparently regrafted with new and more productive varieties. There are also dozens of fields of table vegetables; beans, squash, peppers, tomatoes and eggplant.

5.2   8.2   Cross over a brackish channel. The road is now leading us southeast into the swampy, northern edge of the **Laguna Caimanero**. The region hosts many shore birds, ducks and large numbers of medium-sized flocking black birds. Shortly we swing more inland through similar terrain.

3.3   11.5   Cross a viaduct past **Las Garzas**, a tiny fishing village. The boats here are very small and without motors. They take *jaibas* (blue crabs) in traps from the *laguna* for the Mazatlán market.

0.8   12.3   We work our way inland and onto higher ground. A few homes are off to the northeast. Coco palm plantations and cattle are the money makers here.

3.6   15.9   Pavement ends. Continue through more coco palms and a series of tiny settlements. One of the predominant plants is the *guamuchíl*, a dark green small-leafed plant which can get to tree size. It gave its name to the town of Guamúchíl north of Culiacán. To the best of our knowledge it has no food or medicinal value. We work our way back toward the ocean.

3.2   19.1   Arrive at the beach, a beautiful light gray crescent of sand which stretches from the mouth of the **Río Presidio** 30 miles southeast to the **Boca del Río Baluarte**. The beach is firm and sloping. Surf fishing is reputed to be good for snappers, corvina and an occasional *robalo* (snook). There is driftwood everywhere. Nearly all of the more than ten miles accessible by car could be camped on. Would suggest that you be prepared for bugs if the breeze is from the land, or stops entirely.

*Meet Hector Contreras. Scientist Hector Contreras, one of a handful of dedicated marine biology students from the **University Autonoma of Sinaloa** in Culiacán. At about the midpoint of this long sandy crescent the students have built a rudimentary sea turtle research station using lumber gathered from the beach and sheets of black tar roofing material. Hector and his associates have spent the past year monitoring the sea turtles as they come in to lay their eggs. Daily they run the 30 kilometers of beach between the rivers to locate the clutches of eggs laid the night before. They then dig the eggs up and bring them into a closely-fenced area where they are reburied. 45 to 50 days later the little fellows are clambering out of the sand and milling around, ready for their cycle of life in the sea.*

HECTOR CONTRERAS

After a thorough check by the biologists and a few days to settle down, the fledglings are taken to the ocean and released. On December 9th the records showed they had gathered 11,817 eggs during the '89 season, and by carefully transferring the eggs into places of safety, the hatch rate has risen dramatically, from 50 percent to 80 percent. Hector also gave us some encouraging data on a Oaxaca turtle preservation program,.

The group is entirely self-funded, right down to food, gas, shelter and technical supplies. Though he did not ask for a donation, he accepted whatever pesos could be spared. It could make a difference in the success of the project, at least in what they might eat.

10.4   29.5   The paved road reappears just past several beachfront *balnearios* (palapa-type restaurants) at **Agua Caimanero** who cater to weekend and holiday visitors. Cross a bridge and on the left is a large, diked shrimp farm. This section of the laguna is due to have another 500 acres of its surface cordoned off for more shrimp. One of the workers said their shrimp will be available in quantity through the *cooperativa*'s offices in **Agua Verde** by the end of 1990. Hopefully this, and programs like it, will help retire some of the 800 shrimp trawlers now operating out of Mazatlán. Pray for their success, the sea

151

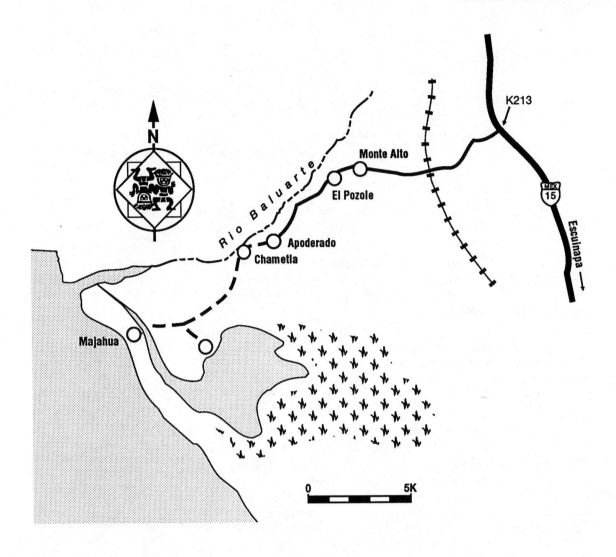

could use a rest. We head inland through marshes and backwaters, then back to farming as we leave the salt flats.

     15.3   44.8   **Los Ojitos,** then the train station on the outskirts of **Rosario.**

     4.0   48.8   We arrive in downtown Rosario... then east through town and back to Mexico 15 at K224.

Chametla and Playa Majahua... (See Mazatlán Hub Map)

At times the trip to and from is more interesting than the intended destination...we put Majahua in that category.

     0.0   0.0   K0   At K213 of Mexico 15 turn right on a paved road signed to **Chametla.** and drive past a small collection of houses and a fruit packing shed. The countryside is a series of hillocks rising out of a variety of farming enterprises.

     3.2   3.2   K5   Cross railroad tracks and a small irrigation canal. Mango trees are everywhere. The trees along the road are a mixture of small tropicals with *guamúchil* and *huanacaxtle* predominating. The hillsides are a mixture of the same varieties, plus amap*ola* trees which turn the hillsides a bright pink each December.

     1.4   4.6   K7   A cement *vado* (dip) across a small arroyo and into a *pueblito* with *topes*, **Monte Alto.** Apparently they're not used to much traffic through here as we see

152

several dogs sleeping in the streets. We weave our way through and continue southwest. This beehive is followed by another sleeper, **El Pozole**, and yet another, **Apoderado**.

Pozole the name given of one of Mexico's many fine stews, or soups. Made with a meat stock, hominy and a variety of vegetables, it is served with shredded pork, chopped cabbage and fresh onion. Muy rico! (Very good!)

5.1   9.7   K15   We enter the town of **Chametla**. The street divides to accommodate a building containing a fruitbar store, **Paletería Graciela**. *Chametla is also considered to be the site of one of the oldest pre-Hispanic settlements in Sinaloa. Recent excavations indicate Indians lived here as early as the first century AD. And it was from Chametla that Hernán Cortéz left on April 15, 1535, to explore the Baja California peninsula.*

Though it still fronts on the riverbed, dams and siltation have removed Chametla from any list of current seaports. Today there is barely enough water to float an innertube, much less Cortéz and his soldiers. (But it is still listed as a seaport in several pieces of Mexican tourist literature and in at least one "current" Mexico travelguide published in the United States.)

The pavement ends as we continue southwest past a *ciruela* (tropical plum) orchard. Those are the scraggly gray-barked, leafless trees on the left. Sometime in late May or June, after the fruit has matured, the trees begin to show leaves in anticipation of impending rains. To the right is the river bed for the **Río Baluarte**.

2.8   12.5   We dodge a little south and follow the power lines, then past more mangos and a fish hatchery with a sign saying that they raise 12,000,000 *tilapia* per year here.

The tilapia is a family of food fish native to Africa and Indonesia. They grow very rapidly to a marketable size. Under favorable conditions a tilapia egg can hatch and grow to a mature fish weighing a pound or more in less than a year. Principally vegetarians, they are relatively inexpensive to raise and are gaining in popularity as a food fish in Mexico and other nations. The hatchlings from here undoubtedly go to other ponds for their final growth.

At the hatchery the dusty road goes toward the west through fields of grain and mangos. We have flushed several coveys of quail, despite it being midday. The typical scrub is yielding to the salt flat biota.

2.4   14.9   Intersection and in a half-mile a dirt road (south) is to Puyeque. We continue west toward the ocean and a single-lane bridge over a canal. Mangroves and salt bushes predominate.

1.5   16.4   We are at the water and Playa Majahua, but not at the ocean. The beach is across a tiny floating footbridge where several somewhat disorganized palapa restaurants face the olas altas. The sand is a reddish gray and trash is everywhere. The place would be worth a return trip, were it not for the paper, bottles, cans, etc., lying about. Back to the highway.

On the way out we pass several fishermen with long stringers of fish apparently taken with the net that one of them is carrying. The fish are black snook, one of the finest eating fish to be found in any ocean. They are also prized as a game fish, with world-record-size fish ranging to 50 pounds and more. There's only one thing wrong with the scene described above...none of the fish are more than 8-inches long! A terrible waste! Protection of some portions of these nursery lagoons is a matter which must be addressed soon, before such fish populations are beyond recovery.

Teacapan...

The southernmost town in Sinaloa is Teacapan, a seedy resort and fishing center. Several attempts to get off dead center have been made, but it has yet to catch on.. One of these days it will, and those in on it will be glad they stuck it out.

153

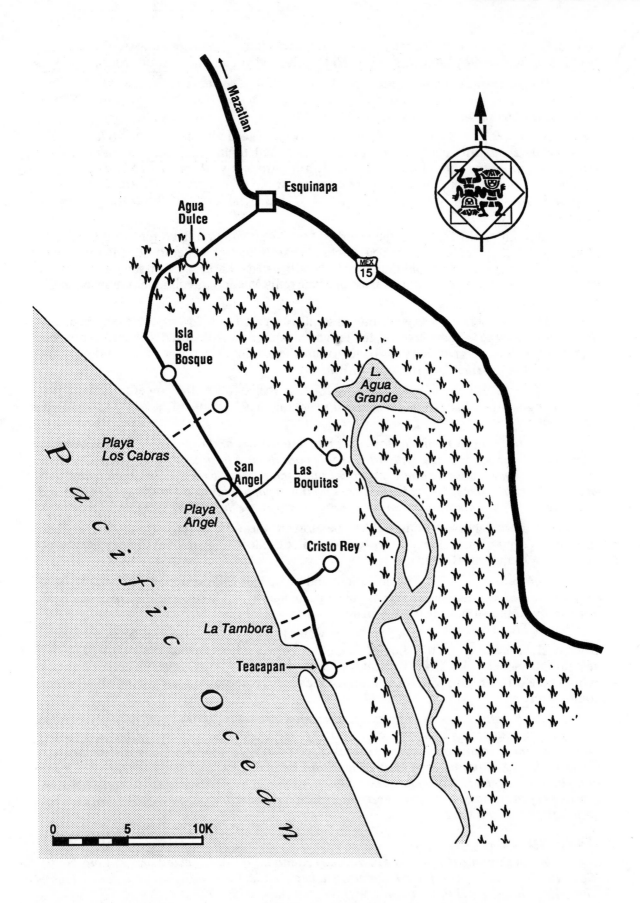

0.0   0.0   The signed turnoff to **Teacapan** is located about 0.4 miles in from the northern entrance into the town of **Esquinapa**. It is a right turn off the one-way route south and east through town.

0.5   0.5   An intersect with the signed highway toward Teacapan . Here, after taking a right, we are going southwest across the railroad tracks and past some scrub and small bits of cultivated land. Mangos seem to predominate.

2.6   3.1   K5   **Agua Dulce** is a signed community of several hundred. The road swings (left) at a small collection of houses and an arm of the lagoon around Teacapan.

3.1   6.2   K10   We curve back to the south and across a bridge. There is a particularly large *tabachín* (flame tree) here at the turn.

1.3   7.5   K12   Drive past a small community with a water tower and a ball field. The stands are well shaded by a huge *huanacaxtle* tree. And so is third base.

1.1   8.6   K14   A large processing plant is on the right, then a paved road going into a coconut plantation. Across from the plant is the prosperous-looking **Rancho El Rodeo**.

1.6   10.2   K16+   Another town is on the left, this with thatched roofs. A quarter-mile farther a paved road (right) goes to **Playas Las Cabras**.at **2.0** miles where there's a busy little *palapa* restaurant and a number of temporary shelters. The place is a winner, except for the trash.

4.3   14.5   K23+   Next to a very large *higuera* with many air roots, a dirt road west is signed to **Playa Angel** and **Rancho San Angel**. Here they are bulldozing shallow excavations much in the style of a shrimp farm, *granja de camarones*. Overnight camping down at the beach is possible.

2.0   16.5   K26+   A housing compound of some sort is followed by another road to the beach. The high water table allows for rapid growth of silage grasses among the miles of palms and many cattle, mostly sementhals, feed in the brisket-high pastures.

6.1   22.6   K36+   A large planting of mangoes. Beyond are more thousands of coco palms. Next comes a paved road (left) to Cristo Rey, a small farming community which also does a bit of fishing in the adjoining mangrove channels. (We are told that panga fishing trips can be arranged at Cristo Rey. We'd appreciate knowing more about this.)

1.0   23.6   K38   **Playa La Tambora** is signed off to the right. The mile-long road to the beach goes past several houses which have been built under the coco palms. Owned by Canadians and Americans, they serve as winter havens for several dozen snowbirds. There is also a house or two under construction. In front of them on a long shallow beach is a p*alapa* restaurant with lots of shade.

0.5   24.1   K39   A small RV park, the **Las Lupitas**, is on the right. It is not close to the beach, making it not all that attractive to many, but it has a following among Oregonians.

0.8   24.9   K40   There is a small **Pemex** at the entrance into **Teacapan**. Officially Teacapan is the southernmost port in the State of Sinaloa and a commercial center for fishing and copra. Unofficially it is trying to flex its muscles as a tourist resort and has had several tiny bursts of success over the past 20 years. The principal attraction here is fishing, which, though better than average, is diminishing. The many miles of mangrove channels provide opportunities for anglers, especially those skilled at casting swimming lures next to the mangrove roots for *robalo prieto* (black snook) and *pargo* (snapper). There are also niches for bird and alligator watchers but you have to make your own deal. A Teacapan jungle trip is still being promoted in Mazatlán but nobody down here seems to know anything about it. The abundant water makes the climate equitable, but humid and buggy.

The town is small and frankly, nondescript. The Oregon Trailer Park closed when

Bob, the owner, died and his widow was not able to keep it open. There are no other tourist facilities other than a few *palapa* restaurants depending on weekend and holiday trade from Esquinapa for survival. There are several new, modern homes near the water.

Not far south of here are a number of large *manmade mounds. As much as 45 feet high, 150 feet wide and 1600 feet long, they are made of millions of oyster shells that date back to the 16th century. Apparently the story that the Spaniards were very fond of oysters has some basis in fact. We also understand that several archaeological sites are located about 7 kilometers south of town. They are accessible only by boat, then a long wet, buggy walk. Back to the highway.*

The House On The Rock...

We step out on the point to look at the beautiful little beach and the rugged cliffs which bracketed it. It is magnificent, and a very special place on Mexico's west coast. Then we look below us and gasp in amazement and envy...someone is building a brick house complete with arched windows and lanai on the cliff face overlooking the tiny beach. What sunsets, what views of the sealife directly below, and how private. This Shangri La has to be one of the most unique we've ever encountered.

This narrative has been located well away from its actual geographic location out of respect for the owner's ingenuity and perception in building here. They have a right to their own world, if only for a few years. (*In the mid-70s we built a home on a remote beach in Baja, and though we wrote of our adventures there many times we never revealed its location other than that it was "south of La Paz."*

It worked, we never lost the privacy we were seeking. Though today it is covered with homes and beachfront lots, without electricity, are selling for a lot of money. We wish the house on the rock equal success.)

NAYARIT

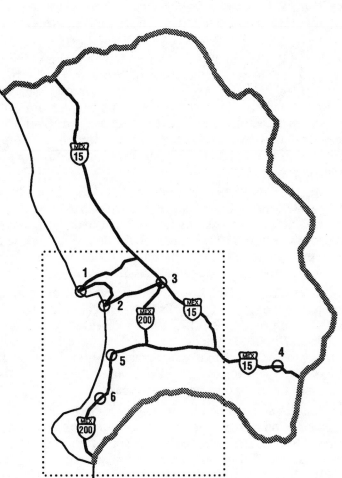

NAYARIT

1. **San Blás**
2. **Santa Cruz**
3. **Tepíc**
4. **Ixtlan**
5. **Las Varas**
6. **Rincón de Guayabitas**

NAYARIT...
THE STATE

Though **Nayarít** is one of Mexico's smallest and least-populated states it is very big on nature. From lofty mountains still harboring puma, deer and raccoon to steaming jungles with jaguar, wild boar, river crocodiles and parrots (including the rare *guacamayo verde*, or green macaw). There are also the coastal marshes with their ample stocks of *caimans* (the Pacific version of an alligator), raccoon-like cotamundis, storks, herons, cranes, ducks and geese. Nature's bounty is everywhere. There are also all manner of unique plant forms, including orchids and bromeliads under solid rainforest canopies.

It was in this environment that some of *mezoamerica's* earliest cultures evolved. Even today significant numbers of the **Huichol** and **Cora** Indians dwell high on the mountain plateaus where the states of **Nayarít**, **Durango**, **Jalisco** and **Zacatecas** meet. There they live in stone or adobe houses in a self-sufficient environment, much as they have for centuries. Many of their customs remain as they were over 450 years ago when the Spaniards marched into their land. Even the Jesuit priests were unable to obtain many converts for the Huichol's complex mythological religion, centered around the psychoactive drug found in *peyote* cactus, was very strong.

Instead, the Indians assimilated the symbols of Christ and the cross into their already-well-defined religion and artforms. An example is the popular God's-eye cross made from colorful yarn asking for God's presence and invoking His protection for their children. The Huichols are a proud group and jealously guard their customs and religious practices, sometimes ignoring Mexican laws in the process.

HUICHOL INDIAN

Many of the Huichols still make annual pilgrimages of up to 500 kilometers to the state of **San Luís Potosí** to gather the peyote buttons for their religious ceremonies. The rites culminate a few days after the December full moon in the town of *San Blas* when they gather for three days and nights of dancing and feasting. On the fourth day the priest, or *maracame*, makes his appearance carrying offerings of beans, fried and roasted maize and peyote for **Papa Naacahue** the tribe's principal god. They then return to their mountain homes for another year.

San Blas became the west coast's first ship-building center when Hernán Cortéz ordered ships built to explore the vast ocean to the west. For a short time, she also shared the lucrative Oriental trade and the harbor was often filled with ships laden with porcelain, silks and spices from China and the Philippines. Later, after the China trade was centered in Acapulco, San Blas became a hideout for English and French pirates preying on the Manila Galleons.

Today fish, shrimp, oysters and produce from the coastal regions provide most of Nayarit's income. Though narrow, thanks to a year-round rainfall pattern these warm and humid plains produce nearly 2 million tons of agricultural products annually, including limes, coconuts, bananas, sugar cane, corn, coffee, chiles, beans, tomatoes and melons. The state also grows 60% of the nation's tobacco and its quality draws buyers even from major American cigarette manufacturers.

Though not a major source of income, there is mining activity near Ixtlan, Santa Maria del Oro and Jala. Around Tepíc and Compostela efforts are afoot to expand on an industrial base currently limited to sugar refineries, cigarette factories and flour mill.

In contrast to the wet, west-facing coastal plains the mountain valleys and plateaus are relatively dry, being deprived of moisture by the high Sierra Madre mountains. Here cattle and goats graze while corn grows on the hillsides during the rainy season. Other crops not needing much water, such as *nopál* and *maguey* are also common.

The coastal regions of Nayarít have much to offer the tourist...and a lot of it the tourism people don't yet appear to realize what to do about it.

The beaches north of Puerto Vallarta are only now being discovered. Drive around and explore the beaches; try a San Blas jungle river cruise. Stay a few nights in Rincón de Guayabitos. Surfers have many choices as do snorkelers and birders. Almost a must is a visit to the island city of Mexcaltitan, the original home of the vaunted Aztec civilization.

The future for greater prosperity would appear to lie in aquaculture in the lagoons to the north of San Blas and in the careful development of touristic facilities along its beautiful, often rugged coast.

BRICK FACTORY

MEXICO 15 — 200 — BORDER TO BORDER

The state of Nayarít is one of Mexico's smallest states, yet it holds a disproportionate amount of the country's finest seashore. Banderas Bay and the Mita Peninsula to the south presents one beauty spot after another to those who will take the time to look. Its rainfall, among the highest in Mexico, is reflected in the jungle-like vegetation in the west-facing valleys and hillsides. The rains also make for high yields from its tobacco and sugar cane fields. We will be going by the cradle of the Aztec civilization, a jungle paradise and a beach with its own bus line. Join us in Nayarít.

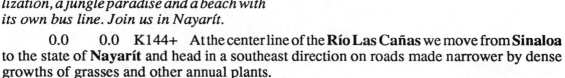

0.0   0.0   K144+   At the center line of the **Río Las Cañas** we move from **Sinaloa** to the state of **Nayarít** and head in a southeast direction on roads made narrower by dense growths of grasses and other annual plants.

1.0   1.0   K143   Signed road north to **Cerro Bola**, 10km. It also goes to **Las Casitas, La Palma, La Hacienda, El Tacote, Salitre** and **San Francisco del Caiman**. Tiny farm communities all.

4.4   5.4   K136   Turn left for **Acaponeta**, a town of about 25,000 that is busy with cattle, tobacco and sugar. Some gold and silver were mined around here many years ago. A big holiday is August 15th, **La Asención de la Virgen**. A few hundred yards ahead is the turn southwest toward **Tecuala** and **Novillero**. **(See Nayarít Beaches.)** Cross a bridge over a large river and past a paved road southwest to a number of farming centers which never make it to the ocean, just to the swamps.

4.3   9.7   K129   Signed graded road north to **San Diego de Alcalá**, 38km. This is the exact name the Franciscan priests gave **San Diego, California** in 1768. It is likely that this is the first San Diego de Alcalá. The main crop around here is tobacco. Sheds and drying racks of various sorts are evident as we pass. Nayarít is the largest tobacco growing state in Mexico.

5.6   15.3   K120   Note the large granitic formations jutting above the dense deciduous vegetation. Several side roads ahead take off to farms, etc. Continue through low rocky hills.

5.8   21.1   K111   A nameless little village. Watch for the to*pes*. Need a coconut? Here's the place to get 'em.

6.3   27.4   K101   Graded road west to **El Pescadero** (The Fisherman)...*we took the bait and ended up in a little valley miles from an ocean or a river. So much for that.* Back to the highway and continue south through low hills. Farther on the small fan palms come back. The leaves are used for roofing, and can be seen not only in the villages, but on the fancy *palapa* restaurants in such places as Mazatlán and Puerto Vallarta. Well-fed cattle are seen grazing through here...most appear to carry the blood of the sementhal line.

5.6   33.0   K92   Paved road left into **Rosamorada**. A high steeple shows over the trees. The town must have been prosperous in times past. Continue through lands under

160

Tepíc - San Blas Hub Map

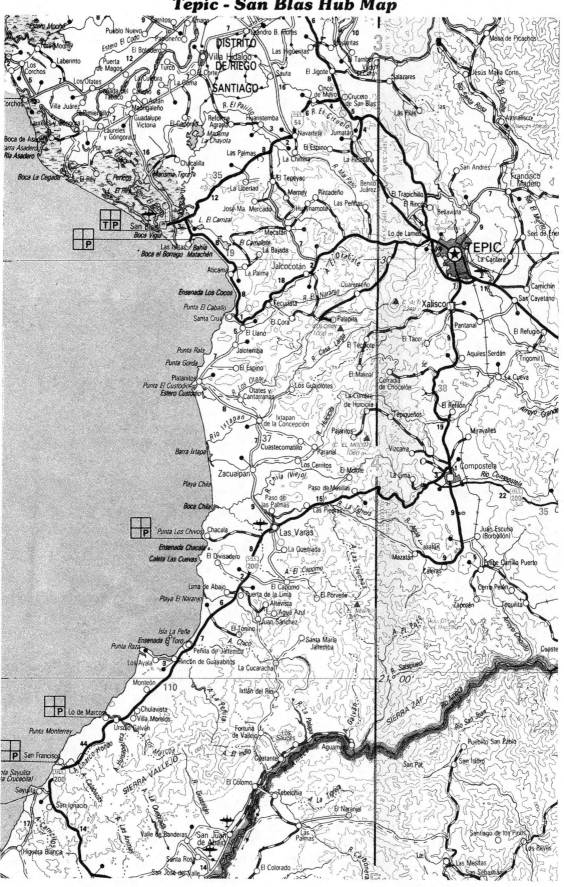

cultivation while other sections are being cleared.

11.6　44.6　K74　A banana plantation on the east side of Mexico 15, followed by large plantings of mangoes and other orchard types.

1.0　45.6　K72　Signed paved road west to **Mexcaltitan**. The area presents a fascinating premise...that the **Aztecs** came from this island community to the high valleys of central Mexico and founded **Tenochtitlan**, the administrative center of the Aztec empire at the time Hernán Cortéz invaded Mexico. **(See Nayarít Beaches.)** Follow Mexico 15 over the long bridge and the **Río San Pedro**.

1.3　46.9　K70　Signed paved road right to **Tuxpan**. This has been an important intersection for at least the past 15 years. Our first recollection was that *cocos helados* were the only things offered and we always stopped. Then came *carnes*, *pollos*, and a variety of other stuff. The corner is now a jumble of vendors, *taquerias*, a messy **Pemex** with **magnasin** and ice, and trucks and cars parked in every available spot. Where we used to stop and relax after filling the tank, we now hurry by and take a break down the road. As for Tuxpan...there's undoubtedly an undeserved prejudice here, but we've never visited the place. To the southeast, several roads branch to small farming communities.

8.9　55.8　K56　Paved road west to **Santiago Ixcuitla**. Beyond are several beaches. **(See Nayarít Beaches.)** Continue southeast past farms and stretches of true jungle-like scenery with huge *huanacaxtle* trees, vines, tall palms and an almost impenetrable layer of small trees and shrubs.

2.5　58.3　K51　Cross the **Río Santiago** on a long bridge. *It is fascinating to watch the activities in the river bottom. Families washing cars, moms doing laundry and washing kids; kids paddling around or chasing a couple of dogs; men standing around a barbecue drinking beer; and two men filling a pickup with sand. All winter this region offers watermelons for sale...and the several we've purchased have been excellent. Coconuts and papayas are also good roadside commodities. We've also taken a liking to the **ciruelas**, a tropical plum. Numerous orchards and roadside stands make it easy to pick up fresh ones all during the season. The sweet/tart taste of the yellow ones has nearly made Tom an addict. Look for them and the nearly leafless trees around the K39 area.*

2.0　60.3　K48　The paved road right is signed to **Guadalupe Victoria**, 27km. From there it is 16 more kilometers into San Blas and we see very few curves. This could be a good back door entry into San Blas, particularly for people driving motorhomes or with trailers.

9.5　69.8　K33　Intersection with paved Mexico 54 to **San Blas**. **(See Nayarít Beaches)** There is also a small local **Pemex**. Continue uphill through more jungle, including several exceptionally large *huanacaxtle* trees. Note the heavy infestation of vines (mostly morning glory) into the trees. There are several signs announcing the new 4-lane toll road coming up.

2.5　72.3　K29　Here the road splits...the old Mexico 15, a 2-lane headache, goes left to Tepíc, the modern and speedy toll road Mexico 15D takes off to the right and down a hill. We take the toll road. No longer will we have to follow long lines of smelly diesel trucks up that narrow, old stretch of highway. Hooray!

10.2　82.5　K13　Top a low rise. Just beyond the road is a small town which appears to have been split in two by this wide piece of asphalt. Continue to ascend via a number of ups and downs toward Tepíc.

5.6　88.1　K4　**Toll gate**. The facility is clean and modern with clean restrooms (May, '90). Continue toward Tepíc through a forest dotted with wild banana plants.

2.4　90.5　K0　End of 15D and intersection with a two-lane *periférico* (bypass) road around the main portion of Tepíc. Follow south toward Puerto Vallarta and toll road to Guadalajara. For Tepíc head east into the central portion of the city.

A busy overgrown-looking city of about 350,000, **Tepíc** is the capital of the state of

NAYARIT

Nayarít. Its location in the cooler highlands with plenty of water made it a target for early Spanish settlement, and in 1542 it became a staging area for explorations throughout the Spanish territories of northwest Mexico and the American west.

Previously it was home base for a **Toltec** settlement beginning sometime between 559 and 619. Today it is one of the centers where **Huichol** and **Cora** Indians from the nearby sierras bring their crafts to sell. It is the remoteness of the Huichol **pueblitos** which has enabled them to preserve much of their heritage and it shows in the designs of the yarn paintings (originally used as offerings in religious rites), wands, or **murvieri,** wound with yarn and dangling feathers and the well-known God's eye, **tsiduri,** to protect the children. Ceremonial masks are also made of yarn or bead work. Embroidery and weaving too are very important and a man may choose a wife based on these skills.

On Avenida Mexico, #19, the **Museo Regional de Nayarít** has a good display of Huichol art and clothing. There are several stores that sell Huichol artwork located near the downtown market and the **zocalo.** One, **Casa Aquiar** is located behind the downtown market at Zaragosa and Puebla Norte.

The **Convento de La Cruz** in Tepíc is the home of the famous **Cruz de Zacate.** Made of straw some hundreds of years ago it is credited with many healings. The soccer stadium has a monument to **Juan Escutia**, the boy hero of the defense of Chapultepec Castle in 1847. *He wrapped himself in a Mexican Flag and threw himself from the top of a parapet rather than surrender to invading American soldiers. Upon realizing the dedication of these children the soldiers stopped their attack.*

Todays Tepíc thrives off sugar, tobacco, textile and cotton products. The region is also strong on cattle, pigs, horses and poultry. During the last 2 weeks of May there is a fair with exhibits and cultural events.

There are a number of scenics in the area...**El Salto** is a beautiful waterfall west of the city; **Atonalisco** is another, 10 km to the north. **Laguna Santa Maria de Oro** is a volcanic crater lake 53 km south-east of Tepíc. **San Blas** is the nearest beach resort. (**See Nayarít Beaches.**)

The top hotel in town is the **La Loma** motel a half-block off Mex. 15 at **Loma Park.** The top restaurant, **Robert's International Restaurant** is just a few doors north of the motel. They do some fine things with **ostiones** (oysters) and robalo (black snook). Their red meats too are excellent. Two other excellent restaurants featuring *carne asada* and *carnitas* are the **Los Bandilleros** and **El Jardín.** These two are also within walking distance...go north to the highway and walk east on the north side of the street. A breakfast stop we enjoyed was the **Altamirano** on Avenida Mexico a couple blocks south of the cathedral. We return to the periférico and go south.

0.5   91.0   K7+   Another road (east) into Tepíc signed **Centro.** To take it, keep to the right and go over the overpass. To continue south go straight ahead through the foothills and past a large rock quarry. The road is 2-lane each way and its path along the foothills provides an overview of the town.

4.6   95.6   K15   For **Puerto Vallarta** we take the signed Mexico 200 turnoff from the 4-lane Mexico 15 *periférico* uphill and south toward Puerto Vallarta. Our new K markers begin with K4 on Mexico 200.

1.7   97.3   K7   Enter **Xalisco.** Watch for *topes.* **Pemex,** no unleaded. Xalisco dates back to the seventh century when the **Toltecs** established an outpost among the **Nayarít** Indians.

The nearby village of San Juan is famous for its caverns. There are seven separate and distinct entrances which were supposed to have been used by one of Mexico's most infamous outlaws, Manuel Lozada. Inside the cave an intricate network of corridors provided almost unlimited avenues of escape. Lozada presumably hid his supplies, horses, wagons, even the treasures he "liberated" from the wealthy, in the miles of tunnels. There is a large cold-water well in the shape of a bathtub which refills itself every time water is removed. But Lozada was not the first to visit the caves...shards of very old ceramic pottery and other artifacts have been recovered.

After a miserable mile of narrow Xalisco streets, Mexico 200 continues past sugar, banana and tobacco fields. The volcano, **Sanganguey** to the east is one of several in the area. At over 7200 feet, it is the tallest of the lot.

4.7 102.0 K14+ Enter the small town of **Aquiles Serdán**, then back to the sugar cane. With its tall green mountains, sugarcane, bananas and pineapple the area is reminiscent of Hawaii.

2.8 104.8 K19 We reach the top of a winding ascent, then back down through banana and corn fields and a few scattered patches of tropical forest.

5.9 110.7 K28+ Pass a small stream bed and begin a steep, hairpin ascent. Watch for very slow trucks...coming and going. Top out after a climb of about 500 feet and continue up an easy grade.

2.2 112.9 K32 Many, many turns as we go through beautiful scenery but the road requires all of our attention. The number of crosses along the road attest to this. When someone puts a toll road through this stretch of country, we'll be the first to take it.

2.2 115.1 K35+ **Restaurant Campestre** on the east side of Mexico 200 at the edge of **Compostela**. A good stop after a hot drive...cold *refrescos* and great *quesadillas*. The road to Vallarta goes (right) just ahead at the sign. Compostela itself is a city of maybe 20,000. It began in early colonial days and the nearby mountains still yield some gold and silver. Agriculture and the manufacture of cigarettes are important parts of the economy. Its big fiestas come on **Corpus Cristi** day, the Thursday before Easter and December 1-10 in honor of **Senor de La Misericordia**. A full service **Pemex** is just ahead on the left, then cross a bridge over the **Río Compostela**.

0.7 115.8 K36+ On the east side of the road a clean little restaurant, **El Duende**, appears to cater to *vaqueros* (cowboys) and their horses. The first time we noticed it several cowboys were sipping sodas and a horse was drinking from a bucket. This time, four horses are talking outside while their riders are talking inside.

1.3 117.1 K39 This intersection east through the valley is for the Mexico 200D toll road. It is the preferred route to Guadalajara from Tepíc or Puerto Vallarta. It connects with Mexico 15 some 50 kilometers southeast of Tepíc and saves a lot of slow, winding and dangerous driving.

Continue toward a large granite monolith not unlike the one in California's Yosemite National Park, but a lot smaller. In the fall and winter wild poinsettias, *(noche buena)* are blooming in little groups over the hillsides. As you may know, they are native to Mexico. In out-of-the-way villages we have seen absolutely brilliant displays.

Along this section of highway are what look like original stands of forest containing numbers of the *palo papelillo* a tall red-barked tree which might be called a *madrone* in California, the large and feathery huanacaxtle, wild palms *(cayaco)*, *higuera* (wild fig), etc. with their compliment of vines, including philodendron, bromeliads and orchids. An hour or so spent a few hundred yards into this magnificent canopy should also reveal dozens of varieties of birds.

11.2 128.3 K57 On the west side of the road is a small restaurant featuring *Pollos Asados al Carbon*. Primitive, clean and a big stack of charcoal...one of these days we'll give it a try.

8.1 136.4 K70 To the right, a small, clean, *mariscos* restaurant, **El Río Viejo**. Offering *ceviche*, oysters, shrimp, etc., it always seems to be busy and it should be worth a stop. Next is the small town of **Las Varas**. To go to the beaches northwest of Varas turn right through the center of town and follow the paved road to **Playa Platanitos** and beyond (to

Santa Cruz and San Blas if you have the nerve). **(See Nayarít Beaches.)** There are several more restaurants and many fruit stands. A good place to stock up on pineapples, papayas and several types of bananas.

    2.6   139.0   K74   A graded gravel road right goes to **Chacala, Chacalilla** and **Punta Los Chivos. (See Nayarít Beaches.)** It is sometimes hard to find the kilometer markers along here due to the rapid growth of the weeds along the road. Visible today, overgrown tomorrow. Tobacco production continues, plus mangoes and bananas.

    4.4   143.4   K81   Road right to **El Divisidero** and **Caleta Las Cuevas**...

We take the dirt road west through pastures and mango orchards, with papayas and bananas showing up at 1.7 miles. The red clay soil makes for dusty driving.

The 50 or so houses of El Divisidero surround us at 3.0 miles. A lady tells us that a beach lies off to the west but that the road is bad and we will never make it. We smile and said we would head that way anyway in the hopes that we could take some pictures. She wishes us well.

The first mile is rough but negotiable. We begin thinking that the lady had underestimated our trusty little pickup. Then the road gets less used...the weeds are growing to two feet on what is supposed to be the road! That should be telling us something.

We are at 4.8 miles and accept the fact that we will not even get back up this steep, twisting, grassy hill unless we turn around. Suddenly, finding a turnaround becomes the priority, and one opens up about 50 yards ahead. But now we can hear the surf, and catch tiny glimpses of the beach. we must go on.

With towels, snorkel gear and ice chest we walk down the now-almost-extinct trail through a primeval jungle of trees, vines, bromeliads, orchids, birds, butterflies and mosquitos. More and more of the beach becomes visible through gaps in the vegetation. Surely Caleta de Cuevas would be the most private beach yet. Only a turn or two and it will be at hand.

Then two things happen...we see a clothesline filled with laundry and the mosquitos decide they are through with the ankle hors d' oeuvres and ready for the main meal. At this moment we wisely choose to keep Caleta de Cuevas for another time and return to El Divisidero where we will tell the lady she was right. Back to the highway.

    1.3   144.7   K83   A couple of Limas here...**Lima de Abaja** to the right and inland to **Puerta de la Lima.** Continue past more tobacco sheds, large plantings of bananas, corn and mangoes. The pesky morning glory vines are everywhere turning some of the smaller trees into shapes resembling topiary. Then comes a small **Pemex.**

    3.4   148.1   K88   A dirt road takes off southwest to the home of **Nicolás,** an older gentleman we picked up at the entrance and will be taking into **Rancho Los Cocos.**

The graded portion dead ends at a paved airstrip. We go right on the sandy trail paralleling the strip. Unfortunately this area is a popular spot for everyone to dump trash and we go through several hundred yards of it. At the end of the strip one trail goes sharply left toward some trees while the other goes north through low grassy dunes.

We continue north to a beautiful, deserted, long sandy beach at 1.6 miles. Nicolás, who is the caretaker of Rancho Los Cocos, says that anyone can camp anywhere, but suggests that you introduce yourselves first. (He would likely accept a small token, and introduce you to his dog.) The beach itself has some driftwood, shells and sand dollars.

This is not a motorhome or trailer road, but most pickups and vans should have little trouble with the sometimes-soft sand. It looks to be windy at times and the drop-off would discourage swimming over most of the range. Nicolás, a 30-year resident, says that fishing is good for pargo and a variety of small croakers and jacks.

Nicolás is a nice old gentleman who has a dog that loves him very much. Back to the highway and continue south past a local **Pemex**. (*A right just past the gas station goes to another beach.*)

    2.2   150.3   K92   **La Peñita Trailer Park** is on the right. Terraced on a bluff overlooking the Pacific, it is only a few yards off the highway. To the north is the long sandy beach which includes Rancho Los Cocos. Next, cross a small bridge into the town of **Peñita de Jaltemba**. Just past the bridge on the west side is a marvelous *pollo asado* restaurant, the **Kariña**. The owner is **María Guadalupe** and the place is named after her daughter. They don't serve *cervezas*, but don't despair...Maria owns the little store next door, and it has a refrigerator full. You will like this jolly lady with a special touch on the marinade for the *pollo asado*. She uses a mild pepper called *achiote*, orange and lime juice, oil, oregano, garlic and a couple of spices we didn't recognize. A road (right) goes to the beach from the center of town.

    The street toward the beach has lots of small stands, several service-type stores and a fair-sized supermarket (about 5 blocks in on the left). The area includes several restaurants including the **Azteca** who claims anything you can think of to eat to be a specialty of the house. Don't know about that one. Or, how about a **Nebraska Ice Cream** parlor!

    The best bet for a hotel in Peñitas is the Siesta. It is located toward the south end of town near the estero. The town looks as though it might have been organized into a tourist destination the same time as neighboring Rincón de Guayabitos and just never really got off the ground. There are some beautiful homes along the beach front, but one block back, shacks and overflowing sewers are evident. There are also homes, nice looking ones which appear to be abandoned...windows broken, no furniture, etc. Is it all a part of the trail of broken dreams which has laid a pall over this portion of Nayarit's coast? Someday it will blossom, it is too beautiful not to...but not yet.

    A last note...with the amount of obvious pollution, swimming at Peñitas would not be our choice, nor would we eat the local oysters. Back to the highway.

    2.0   152.3   K95   Turn (right) into the **Rincón de Guayabitos** resort complex.

RINCON DE GUAYABITOS...

    Rincón de Guayabitos is a well-marked enclave of touristic developments extending both north and south from its entrance at K95 of Mexico 200. To the north are numerous homesites, many with homes on them. Most appear to be owned by *norteamericanos*, as we see license plates from all over the U.S. and Canada. Some are large and well cared for, though quite a few have "for sale" signs on them. (The most common reason for leaving here, and most retirement communities, is failing health on the part of the retirees.)

    We look down the canals built past many of the homes to give the owners a "waterfront" location. Unfortunately, most of the canals are now choked with weeds and trash.

    The southern part of Rincón de Guayabitos is dedicated to businesses...hotels, restaurants, stores, condos, trailer parks, etc. The **Peñamar Hotel** is large and attractive with air conditioning in the better rooms but the tennis courts are dead. Nicer, more expensive with a disco upstairs is the **Fiesta Mar**. Not recommended on Friday or Saturday nights.

    One thing going right now in Guayabitos is the **Club Cocos Hotel**. It is part of the new Club Cocos concept which has proliferated in this portion of Mexico. The concept is to take over management and marketing of hotels which are not doing too well and present them as one-price-for-everything partytime destinations through travel wholesalers in the United States and Canada. Right now the Guayabitos operation is accepting walk-ins on a space-available basis for a very low price. It is located at the south end of the complex.

    As we see it, apartments, suites and bungalows are the way to go here in Guayabitos. The area caters to visitors who stay for extended lengths of time. Except for the holiday times, there is usually a wide choice. All the units we've seen are acceptable to one degree or another. These types of accommodations provide an opportunity to relax in your own space for very little money. If you want to do any cooking you may have to have your own utensils, etc. *(We keep a small box of essentials tucked away in the trunk.)* Some of the names are...**Maria Teresa, Costa Alegre, Gallo Oro, Posada Mexico, Posada Jaltempec, Anai Bungalows.**

Our one eat-out experience was at a fine little restaurant near the south end of the plaza area. The food was great, but the lady told us it was closing in a few days and she didn't know what was going to happen. Things change so quickly in such areas, we'd suggest asking around.

For many *norteamericanos* the trailer parks are the attraction. Located on the beach toward the south end of town, they cater to fishermen by providing launch ramps, fish cleaning tables, etc. The fraternity here is quite strong...some have been coming back to the same park and space for 10 years and more. The trailer parks are: **El Dorado, Fisherman's Paradise, Villa Nueva** and **Tropico Cabaña.** There are also spots for overflow, but with few amenities. The places get full in November and usually remain so through Easter.

Nearby fishing can be excellent, particularly for the "table" species...sierra, dorado, tuna and pargo. Blue and black marlin, sailfish and roosterfish are also taken. Back to the highway.

A large field of vine-festooned boulders of varying shapes and colors are on the left ahead. Another beach access through here is at **Los Ayalas.** *In some ways these beaches are part of the Guayabitos complex, for Playa Los Ayalas is directly south, separated only by a rocky point. It can also be reached from Guayabitos by taking the short dirt road past the Club Cocos hotel to join the main access road.*

*This is more our kind of beach, with its laid-back atmosphere, palapa restaurants among the coco palms with music blaring out of a 50-year old jukebox. The half-mile beach is uncrowded, with clear water and a gentle slope. Several small vacation homes are at the south end at the foot of the tree-laden rocky point. Here just above high tide line, we enter a short, narrow walking trail up and over the point to a beautiful, secluded beach. Variously called **Playita de Beso** (Kiss Beach) and **Caleta de Ayala** (Ayala Cove), it is calm and crystal clear with a gentle slope. Snorkeling along the south wall is good.*

Add a bottle of wine and a couple of burritos to the ambiance of Caleta de Ayala...a perfect combination. A note on the trail...it's about 200 yards long and slippery and steep in places. Back to the highway.

8.0   160.3   K108   Road west to **Lo de Marcos.** *From the corner a cobbled street goes a half-mile to a grassy plaza with a rather unimaginative cement kiosk. Continue straight through town on a cobbled street to the ocean at Playa Latracadero, 1.2 miles. Several trailer parks are off to the right...the homey-looking **Mi Pequeño Paraiso**; the large, clean **Los Corales** with bungalows; the smaller, upscale **Las Brisas Suave** and an unmarked one. The beach is better here at the north end. Surfing looks to be a good bet during the summer season when the storm waves should come in at a good angle.*

*A kilometer to the south is **Playa Las Minitas**. Here a palapa restaurant of the same name serves the usual and keeps its dozen or so tables busy on holidays. The west-facing beach is little more than 50 yards wide, with rocks buttressing each end. The surf here and at Los Venados to the south can be heavy with strong currents so caution is advised. Winter months are likely to provide the best swimming.*

***Playa Los Venados** at 2.1 is another of the small, inlet-type beaches of the region. It has a good-sized parking lot, but no restaurant. There are three fishermen with handlines on the rocks at the north end. A family has a fire going and are getting ready to cook something. The beach is very clean...a sign of respect.* Back to the highway.

6.2   166.5   K118   Paved road (right) is into **San Francisco.**

*When **Luís Escheverría Alvarez** was president, he had a home here and the govern-*

ment poured a lot of money into cobbling the streets, building a school, several large packing sheds and a modern hospital. Little of it seems to have worked, for Escheverría is gone (though his daughter is reported to visit occasionally) and the buildings are in various states of disrepair. The hospital, however, is the best along the coast.

The beach at San Francisco has several good palapa-style restaurants. A couple of small hotels are several blocks back from the water. A family restaurant, the **Chalupa**, has quickly became a favorite. It stands about two blocks back from the beach. To keep it going, Pop and the boys fish while Mom and the daughters fix a wide variety of dishes, including a favorite...very fresh huachinango mojo de ajo.

A road from near the center of town leads a mile north to another attractive beach. Here, about 10 years ago, a man from Guadalajara built **Club Playa de Costa Azul**. Apparently marketing and promotion were not among his strong points, for very little has happened since.

The place has suites and rooms at reasonable rates. Our stays have always been pleasant, but we can see upcoming problems if maintenance is not stepped up. Several beautiful homes are being built now on the slopes overlooking the club and beach. Hopefully signs of better times to come.

We like San Francisco. Back to Mexico 200.

2.4   168.9   K123   A paved road (right) goes to **Sayulita**, an almost-still-sleepy village. A camping area is marked off to the right at **0.8**. Continue to the beach at **1.1** mi.

Several restaurants overlook the beach, with the **El Ranchito** our favorite. The place is run by a jolly lady named **Victoria** who not only puts together a mean breakfast of **huevos rancheros**, but her **huachinango frito mojo de ajo** makes a mockery of the highly-touted dish in Puerto Vallarta's best restaurants. It is family operated and includes one grandma, plus sisters, kids, cousins, etc. It is quite a group. Take the street that goes to about the center of the beach and look to the left.

One morning while having a late breakfast at the El Ranchito, the fishing boats began coming back to the beach and we were able to choose between flopping-fresh fish, crabs and oysters.

The town is changing rapidly. In only two years a number of large homes have been built on the wooded hill overlooking the Pacific at the south end of town, with more under construction. Up at the north end we find a trailer park, (about 30 units) with the **Villas del Palmar**, a bungalow complex, next door. Nearby is another development, **Las Gemelas**. These appear to be private homes set in a common, park-like setting.

On the bluff above the developments are a number of homes which look to be permanent residences. Out of a dozen homes, two had cars with California plates, and two were from Texas. A Canadian pickup rounded out the census of those visible. Hopefully the building will continue in the form of private homes, not as hotels or condos.

Our first time in Sayulita was in 1978. At the time we met an American who had just moved into a house his landlord had built for him for $500. On top of that he was paying $50 a year in rent!. Tried to find the house but couldn't. At the time, he was the only foreigner in town. Back to to the highway and continue southeast to climb inland through a tall, noisy, jungle.

5.7   174.6   K132   **Club Arena Blanca** is ahead to the right on the paved road out to **Punta Mita** and **Cruz de Huanacaxtle**. **(See Nayarít Beaches.)** There is a closed tourism office at the intersection.

5.8   180.4   K140   Road (right) is to all kinds of residential buildings, condos, hotels, hotel-condos, apartments, etc. and extends from here back toward Cruz de Huanacaxtle. The area is about a kilometer long. All front the beach and there are but a few spots for individual access to the water. A couple of the names...**Vista Vallarta, Vista Bahía Suites**

and Trailer Park. The park is small and full (mid-January).

    0.6   181.0   K141   Enter **Bucerias**. *The town is coming into its own in a pleasant way. Foreigners are moving in and buying property but not in such Americanized ghettos as found in PV. The small restaurants and friendly little hotels still flourish and have not yet been preempted by a Holiday Inn. A nice trailer park, the Bucerias, is on the beach at the south end of town. It looks to have about 50 spaces and is nearly full (mid-January). The Bucerias town beach is a nice one with circular palm sombras in front of several beachfront restaurants. Another plus...living costs are less here.*

    The closer we get to PV the more signs there are promoting everything from condos to airlines, discos to shopping centers. They have learned well the American philosophy of saturation advertising.

    1.6   182.6   K143+   Road right leads to a hotel and a road west along the beach. After several beach access spots we are back in the outskirts of Bucerias. On the inland side of the highway we see the **Restaurant Famar**. It is recommended as having the best hamburgers for a hundred miles in any direction. Pretty heady stuff, even though the statement was made by a couple from North Dakota.

    0.6   183.2   K144+   An interesting-looking restaurant on the right, **Las Casuelas**. It is casual and clean with outdoor seating.

    0.3   183.5   K145   The **Flamingo Golf Club** is off to the right, along with signs directing us into the development zone known as **Nuevo Vallarta**. *The zone extends along about 4 miles of sandy beaches, including a marina which has been constructed at about the half-way point of the beach. Jack Tar Village, Marina Fiesta Vallarta, Costa Vallarta II and Villa Varadero are among the most ambitious building programs. All list as attractions, the beach, the marina and golf course.*

    Facing the beaches are a number of posh homes, with more on the way. Streets wind everywhere, but few come to the ocean without something being built around it. There are lots of things for sale here...timeshare, condos, lots, marina slips and homes. We'd suggest that you take time and look at the homes. Some of Mexico's finest architects have outdone themselves. If you are contemplating a contemporary Mexican-style home sometime in the future, there are many ideas to sketch or photograph. Back to the highway.

    4.2   187.7   K152   Paved road south to **El Chino** and **La Jarretadera**. The road quickly turns to cobbles, then dirt. It goes on to a couple of difficult-to-get-at, not-too-clean beaches. *(It is also the back way into the Nuevo Vallarta development, but we recommend the signed entrance back at K145).*

    0.1   187.8   We cross the bridge over the **Río Ameca** and into the state of **Jalisco**. This is a time zone change...it is now one hour later than it was on the other side of the bridge.

    End of log.

Mexico 15 — Mexcaltitan

*Here is an opportunity for deja-vu, if you're an Aztec. This is a tongue-in-cheek introduction to **Mexcaltitan**, an small city located in the middle of one of Mexico's largest system of lagoons. An island measuring only about 50 acres, Mexcaltitan is home for around 4000 people in an atmosphere which, when you hear the story, lends an eerie glow to the entire experience.*

0.0   0.0   K0   We leave Mexico 15 at the K72 marker on a paved and signed road northwest through irrigated farm land. Crops include grain and other seed crops. It also has a number of tobacco fields with their attendant drying sheds.

5.4   5.4   K9   This spot is shared by a box factory, a mango packing shed and a road (left) to **San Vicente**. The road continues in a westerly direction through intensively cultivated fields, many of which are currently in tobacco.

0.8   6.2   K10   The road continues west, dropping gradually toward the lagoons ahead.

5.8   12.0   K19   A paved intersection (left) with a road going southwest. Just beyond, a signed road (right) is to **Pericos**.

2.0   14.0   K22   A cemetery, then the town of **Pimientillo** and its water tower and *topes*. Continue west past several small ponds with water hyacinths and on into scrubby vegetation with only a few cultivated patches. After a mile or so, this changes and we see many fields dedicated to melons, at least during the winter, and a packing shed.

3.1   17.1   K27   A box factory is on the left. We follow the paving to the right at the intersection indicating **Union de Corrientes** as straight ahead.

1.7   18.8   K30   The end of the pavement. (*The K markers give up here.*) It is now graded gravel and we soon have water on both sides of the raised roadbed. Shortly we begin to see mangroves, indicating the presence of salt water. There are a few boats scattered here and there. Water birds are everywhere. Cranes, egrets, stilts, ducks, mudhens, etc.

2.9   21.7   Off to the left the water covers a number of graves. Only the headstones are showing.

0.9   22.6   The dirt road left is signed to **Mexcaltitan**. The sign is mounted on two posts stuck out in the middle of the swamp. We are now going almost due south over a relatively-good ungraded dirt road. Both sides are pure lagoon with lots of *mangles* (mangroves) and water. Every so often we see people wading along with *tirayas* or circular throw nets. They use them to catch shrimp or small mullet *(lisa).*

2.5   25.1   We cross a small bridge and then several "islands" a foot or so above the water.

2.5   27.6   Here is the landing connecting Mexcaltitan with the rest of Mexico. Our guide is be **Cruz Fermín**, a man in his 50s who was born on the island, as was his father, and his father's father, etc., etc. We hop in his pole-propelled boat and head toward a nearly-circular village of about 4000 which seems not to be sited on an island, but more like it is the island.

CRUZ FERMÍN

Mexcaltitlan is located in a huge lagoon complex fed by the **Río San Pedro**. The "island" is so low that its streets are under water during the summer rains. But even that is not the most interesting part of a visit to Mexcaltitlan...

Until recently, anthropologists had not known the origin of the Indians that took over the **Valley of Mexico** in 1325. Calling themselves **Aztecs**, they had come with ready-made technologies and societal systems. Quickly assimilating the locals, they built a city,

170

NAYARIT INLAND

Tenochtitlan, to serve as capital of their soon-to-be extensive empire.

But that mystery is beginning to unravel as more is gleaned from the Aztec's chronicles of their early travels. This, added to a mounting trail of artifacts, makes it reasonably certain that the Aztecs actually left this little island in 1111 AD under their Chief/God, **Huitzilopochtil,** and his priests. Then, over the succeeding 214-years, they (or more properly, their descendants) journeyed through Nayarít, Durango, Jalisco, Michoacan, Guanajuato and Queretaro to their new home in the valley of Mexico.

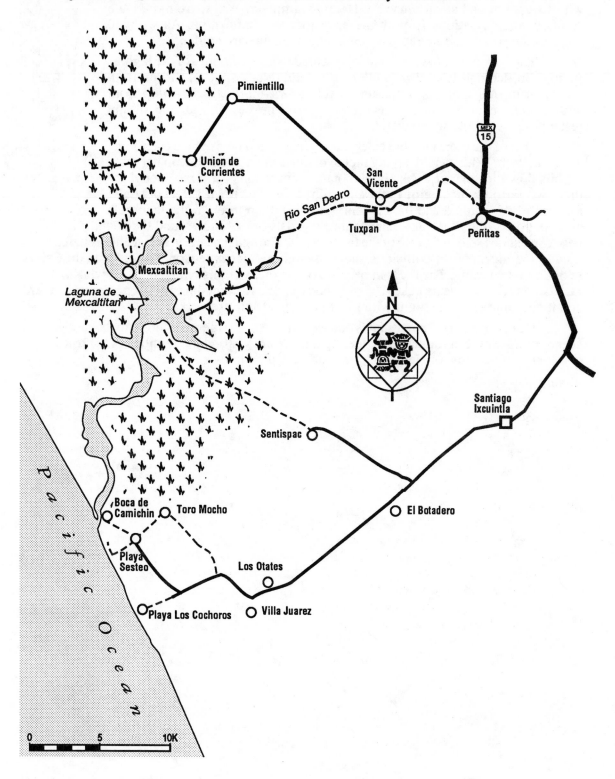

And there are other bits of evidence... Several come from early hand-painted manuscripts wherein the Aztecs set out from an island in canoes. The illustrations show an island with street patterns dividing the village into four sections, almost identical to the way that both Mexcaltitan and Tenochtitlan are laid-out. And an old map drawn by Ortelius in 1579, shows **Atzlan** to be precisely where Mexcaltitan is today. Fascinating!

After circumnavigating the 400 by 500-meter island, Cruz Fermín takes us along the streets that become canals with the summer rains, and on to the *zocalo* with its church and small museum. Here, in simple displays, are more statements of their relationship with the ancestors of Moctezuma. As we walk through the streets the Indian features of the residents are evident.

The island is noted for the meals created from the bounty of the lagoon, such as broiled and fried *lisa* (mullet) or *robalo* (black snook), shrimp turnovers, shrimp meatballs, shrimp pate, as well as *Tlaztihuil*, a thick shrimp broth with chiles and corn meal. We opted for shrimp ceviche at one of the restaurants overlooking the water.

MEXCALTITAN

One of the most unusual celebrations in Mexico takes place each June 28th and 29th. With an underlying theme of ensuring a good shrimp harvest, it boils down to several weeks of elaborate preparations for a race between their two patron saints, **Saint Peter** and **Saint Paul**. The town's fleet of boats are brightly decorated and the citizenry parades them through the lagoon in anticipation of the great race. The contest consists of one lap around the island between canoes selected to carry the two statues. Though the action is fast and frenzied with much shouting and near-collisions, the winner is predetermined, or "fixed," with the Saints taking turns winning. The fix is in because of the many fights which occurred during postrace celebrations in years past. Today nobody seems to care, the excuse for a party is there and it continues into the night with plenty of music and fireworks

Our journey to Mexcaltitan is one we will always remember, not only because of the scenes of the day, but for that eerie feeling that we are visiting the families of the true rulers of Mexico at the time of Hernán Cortéz. Back to the highway.

Mexico 15 — Novillero Beaches...

The terrain through the northwest portion of Nayarít is dominated by the siltation of the many rivers which come from the rainforests to the east. The beaches, therefore are made up of sand bars backed by extensive lagoons. The region is also open to heavy winds, thus discouraging heavy investments in oceanfront developments. The beaches of Novillero are the best the area has to offer.

    0.0   0.0   K0   We head west off Mexico 15 at K136 on a paved road signed to **Tecuala**. The turnoff is a few hundred yards south of the intersection left into the town of **Acaponeta**. We go by several fruit stands and cleared, but not irrigated, farmland. Watch for wandering livestock. The ranchers use the roadway to move cattle from field to field. Continue in a southerly direction.

    5.2   5.2   K8+   On the left is **Rancho Ariviana** with its several large buildings and many acres of mangos. Next comes the small town of **Agua Verde**. It has a small church, a crumbling zocalo and a basketball court.

    2.3   7.5   K12   **Tecuala** has a carnival going on. Apparently the only space big enough for all of the rides spans the highway, so that's where it is. We are directed to detour through a vacant field to get around it. A road, right, is signed to **Novillero** several blocks after entering the cobbled main street. Continue through town in a westerly direction.

    1.2   8.7   K14   We are back to the pavement and passing through fields, some of which are irrigated. Cattle and mangoes appear to be the most popular products with some corn, coco palms and papayas.

    5.6   14.3   K22+   A paved road left is signed to **Quimichis**. Also on the left are a number of small houses with large, equal-sized yards, much in the manner that the *ejidos* divide up their holdings. There is a little town off to the south...**Paso Hondo.**

    3.4   17.7   K28   We are coming into the lagoon environment now with some cattle still around but with salt tolerant plants more apparent. Next come a few mangrove channels and an occasional fisherman's shack or small boat. The quarry here would probably include shrimp and *jaiba*, or blue crab.

    1.7   19.4   K31   A paved road right is to **El Perico**. The mangroves are taking over as the salinity of the water increases. We see a dozen varieties of water birds including

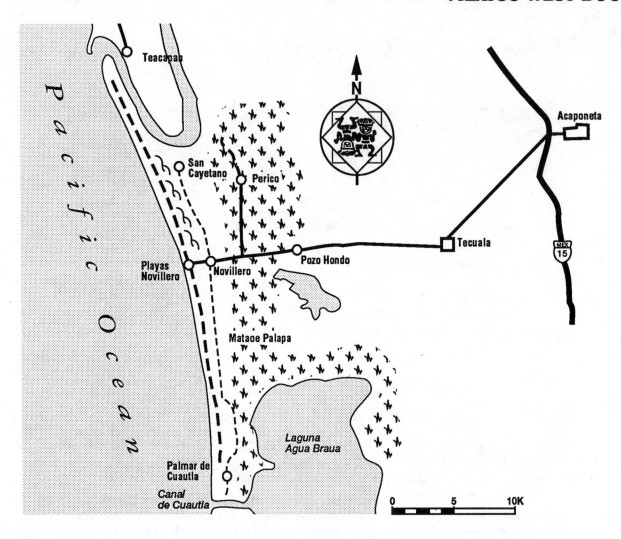

the roseate spoonbill and blue heron. We then go over a broad channel with a few houses and a number of boats lining the shore.

2.9   22.3   K36   We come to **Ejido El Novillero**. Watch for *topes*. At the intersection next to a small **Pemex** the right branch is to **El Cayetano**, the left (south) one goes to **Palmar de Cuatla**. At best, both roads are a mess, yet they are served by busses...read on.

2.0   24.3   K39   We are at **Playa Novillero**. The accommodations are limited, and marginal. But it is worth it to us, for there is a wonderful 45-mile beach offering all kinds of opportunities for new experiences.

At low tide you can drive the whole thing on the moist, hard-packed sand (about 20 miles in each direction). Not only do we do it, but everybody else, including the local busses, does too. They say you can buy a ticket and get off where you wish for a private (almost) picnic and swim. The beach abounds with driftwood (most of it is to the north), clams and a variety of shells. The water is generally of a benign nature, meaning that many families are out on Sundays and holidays. Camping is a breeze...just run along until you find a spot you like and park above the high tide line. Be careful on this because it is sometimes a narrow line between high tide and soft sand. (We also suggest parking on an incline facing the ocean...in case you get stuck, it is easier to get out.)

*Playas de Novillero has several palapa restaurants specializing in fish and shrimp. One, the **Posada del Sol** serves an excellent shrimp dinner and we enjoy talking to Carlos, the owner, and his wife. Carlos' grandfather on his mother's side was an Englishman named Freer who came over to make his fortune around the turn of the century and never went home.*

NAYARIT BEACHES

*We said at the start that the hotels are marginal, and the old **Playa Novillero** fits well into that category. The next morning we were told that the **Casa Blanca** on the south side of town would have been a better choice. (The Playa Novillero now has a new hotel on the beach on the right as you reach the beach on the paved road. As yet there is no sign and it has not been painted, but the rooms have fans, are clean and the plumbing works.) Several miles north of town on a sand/dirt road is a vacation home development, **El Delfín**. It has suites for rent by the day or week. They appear to be well done and crowded on weekends. It can also be reached by driving along the beach should you want to check it out first. The accommodations at El Novillero might be second class, but the beach is a five-star beauty. Back to the highway.*

Playas Cochoros and El Sesteo (See Hub Map)...

0.0   0.0   K0   Turn from Mexico 15 at K56 at the signed intersection to **Mexcaltitan** and **Santiago Ixcuintla.** The land around us is dominated by tall scrub with fan and the majestic *cayaco* palms with a few houses and mangoes scattered about.

1.9   1.9   K3   A power distribution complex is off to the right. The agriculture through here is gaining almost daily as a new network of irrigation canals nears completion. Permanent plantings of fruit trees such as mangos also indicate a regular supply of water.

1.2   3.1   K5   A fruit processing plant is on the right. A mile later we bounce over *topes* and enter the town of **Santiago Ixcuintla** and onto a cobbled surface.

1.8   4.9   K8   At the zocalo, follow the sign, right, to **Los Corchos**. We come off the cobbles in a half-mile and head west on smooth asphalt.

1.5   6.4   K10+   A (turn) left and we regain a general southwest heading past cultivated fields, some with mangoes.

2.0   8.5   K14   The town of **Amapa** is just off to our left. Pass the *topes* and continue southwest past an increasing amount of grain fields.

1.6   10.1   K16+   Road right is signed to **Mexcaltitan**. It goes about 25 kilometers (16 unpaved) to the landing where boats will pick you up for a ride of some miles to the island town. The history is a fascinating one. Access to Mexcaltitan is much better from the north and is recommended. **(See Nayarít Inland.)**

1.2   11.3   K18+   **El Botadero** is signed to the left about one kilometer. Grain fields continue to predominate with scatterings of mangoes and coco palms.

4.2   15.5   K25   A paved road (left) into a grouping of houses and trees. Shortly we come to more speed bumps (*topes*), big ones, and a box factory on the right.

2.8   18.3   K29+   More *topes* and then the town of **Los Otates** with its shady, little *zocalo* and neat, white benches.

1.0   19.3   K31   Intersection with **Villa Juarez** is to the left. We bear (right) toward the ocean on a straight line.

1.9   21.2   K34   A graded road (right) to a ranching area out in the middle of the swamp, **Toro Mocho** (Hornless Bull). At this point we swing back to the southwest. Sweet water is abundant here, as evidenced by the lush vegetation, including thousands of pink *San Miguelito* vines along the roadsides.

1.5   22.7   K36+   We are now into the salt marsh environment, with only a few cultivated areas on the higher spots.

1.0   23.7   K38   A signed intersection, with **Los Corchos** (Fish Floats or Corks) indicated straight ahead. Shortly we cross a bridge over a wide mangrove channel. Below two men in pangas are using handlines to cast chrome lures to the edges of the mangroves in search of a hungry snook or pargo. *If they are willing to spend their time fishing for them in this manner, it must mean that there are quite a few fish around.* Continue on a graded gravel surface.

We arrive at the ocean in 1.3 miles to find a couple of restaurants offering **mariscos**. *The beach extends as far as we can see. It has a fair amount of driftwood and some shells. We see tracks where people have muddled through the dry sand to the moist sand and then taken off to the north. This could be a way to get off by yourself and locate a camping spot. The same option exists to the south, but that is shut off after about a mile by the mouth of the* **Río Santiago**. Return to the intersection at K38.

We then continue north past mango plantings and marginal pasture land to arrive in **Los Corchos** in **2.0** miles. Here, a signed dirt road (left) directs us past a large flame tree, or *tabachín*, and on to **Playa El Sesteo** at **1.3** miles from Corchos. There are several restaurants with lots of shade including spots for cars. There are a few nice houses back a bit from the water, plus several about to collapse. We see lot markers and vestigial roads running past the coco palms. We are looking at another example of an organized real estate **non**-development.

Did we mention the hotel? You won't want to miss this one. *Just before the beach a large, fairly-new sign advertises a pool, discotec, bar, restaurant, mariscos, botanas and in big letters, "oyster soup," at the Hotel El Sesteo. As we inspect the beach area, we wonder where the big hotel is, and why anyone would want to invest so much money way out here.*

The answer came when we found the El Sesteo several hundred yards back from the water. It is virtually abandoned with broken screens nailed over blown-out windows. There was someone there and he waved a greeting. We stopped the car, only to have several dozen mosquitoes land on our windshield within seconds. That took care of that. What is needed now is a great big wind to come along and blow the sign down. Back to Los Corchos.

This time we go north **1.0** miles to a fishing and oyster-farming camp on the edge of the lagoon. A couple of shacks sell oysters to eat or carry away. There are shells everywhere. The name of the spot is **Boca de Camichín**, and it has a basketball court. No real need to return unless we're looking for raw oysters. Back to the Mexico 15 Highway.

Mexico 15 — San Blas...

Were it not for poor timing, it is possible that today San Blas, Nayarít would be a major international destination. The problem came about because the push to put San Blas on the map came about two generations ahead of its time.

0.0   0.0   K0   We make our move toward **San Blas** from the K33 marker north of Tepíc on Mexico 15. The road takes off west and immediately hints what is to come...a winding trail through tropical mountains. The red soil is volcanic in nature. The ridge along which we begin this log offers a fine view of the mountains and valleys ahead. Even in June, just before the rainy season, the mountains are green, In October and November after the rains, they are spectacular.

2.7   2.7   K4+   We pass a small community, **Ejido Cinco de Mayo**. It sports several hundred houses a small zocalo and numbers of colorful flame trees (*tabachín*) and bougainvilla. We cross a small bridge and follow left up the other side.

4.3   7.0   K11   We come into the outskirts of **Navarrete** and several *topes*. Next comes a dirt intersection, right, to **Huaristemba**.

1.8   8.8   K14   **El Palillo**, (The Thin Person), a family resort complex using a pool, streambed bathing, etc. There are some large trees through here, giving some indication what might have been in this part of Mexico many years ago... *Cayaco* palms, a dozen varieties of huge trees, bromeliads, orchids and long vines reaching down a hundred feet and more.

1.6   10.4   K16+   A dirt road (left) goes south to **Colonia Tépeyac**. We continue onward through hills and some banana and mango

176

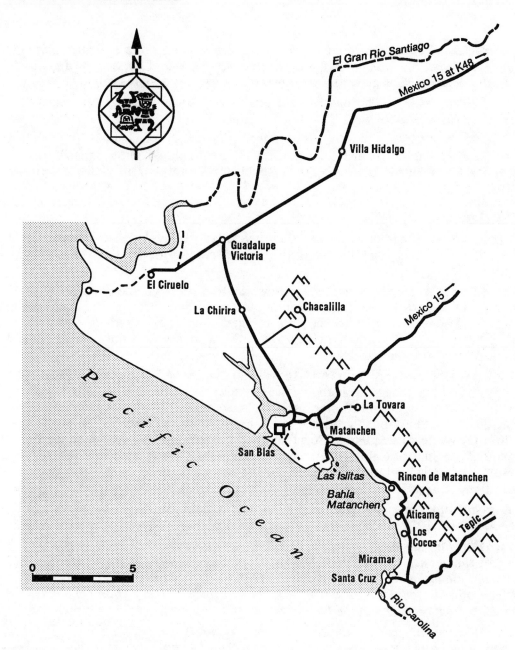

operations. The hillsides across the valleys also show banana plantings. And wherever there's shade you'll usually find coffee trees...some say the best coffee in Mexico is grown here in Nayarít.

    1.0   11.4   K18   **Las Palmas** is off to the left with several *topes* guarding a basketball court. We clear town and wind past large fields of agave, or maguey cactus. A bit out of place we would think but somebody knows something we don't.

    1.8   13.2   K21   Graded dirt road (left) to **La Libertad**. The road drops more sharply and we overlook extensive banana plantings.

    2.5   15.7   K25   Here we have more of the pure jungle terrain. *One hopes that the owners or the government will make more concerted efforts to preserve what little is left in this region. It is so beautiful and unique.* We continue down another canyon.

    We bounce over several *topes* and enter the outskirts of **Singayta**. *The combination of the jungle above and the watery delta areas below has provided Singayta with a singularly*

177

large number of avian species within its boundaries. There are said to be more than 400 varieties of birds either residing here year around or moving in and out according to their own personal timetables. Continue to drop down to sea level and then straight west.

      5.1   20.8   K33   The paved road left is to **Santa Cruz, Los Cocos** and **Matachen. (See Nayarít Beaches.)**

      1.2   22.0   K35   Cross the bridge over a wide mangrove channel. To the left is the main departure point for the boat trip up to **La Tovara**. To the right is a paved road to several beaches, plus **Chacalilla. (See Nayarít Beaches.)** We are now officially in the town of **San Blas**.

SAN BLAS...

      Despite considerable energy expended some years ago to develop **San Blas** as a tourist center, it remains a small fishing village and sleepy beach resort. But San Blas is a town with a busy past.

      According to those who study such things, the first people came about 4000 years ago. Here they made arrowheads, chipped cutting tools and lived off the abundant sealife. Much later the **Toltec** Indians used the area for gathering food for their cities in the neighboring hills. One, **Chacalilla**, may prove to be a major find once an organized archaeological effort is mounted.

      San Blas came into being in the mid-16th century when the Spanish established a fort on the hill behind the entrance to the lagoon. It was a major port, first with the Manila galleon trade, then for sending cargoes into Sonora and the Californias. In 1768 Padre Junipero Serra sailed from San Blas to establish missions to the north. With the founding of his second mission, **San Diego de Acalá**, Father Serra initiated the string of events which led to the development of the State of California. About that same time a detachment of the Spanish Armada was garrisoned here to fight off French and British pirates.

      We mentioned earlier that there had been a push to put San Blas into mainstream Mexico tourism some time ago. Here is the story as related to Tom some years ago by **Maurice Cockshott**...

      *It was the mid-50s and the people of San Blas felt they had everything going their way. The government had encouraged investors by paving her streets and installing water and electrical systems. A new luxury hotel, the **Hermosa**, was to be officially opened by **President Alemán** himself. The world was invited in the form of a large band of journalists and dignitaries from Mexico and the United States.*

      The citizenry, flushed with the success that was surely around the corner painted their homes and got the town ready for the world. The big day came and tables were set out around the pool of the luxurious new Hotel Hermosa for the big event. The schedule called for the dedication ceremony, a tour of the hotel and a wide-open happy hour before a sunset buffet of lobster, shrimp, baked whole snook, clams, oysters and octopus (all of it brought fresh into the docks that day). The weather cooperated and the supply of seafood was enormous. Everybody had a great time until the sun approached the horizon...

MIGUEL ALEMAN

      *It started first in the back rows near the hotel and spread toward the beach. Someone slapped at their arm, then the back of the neck. Next came a scratch, and another, and another. More slaps and more scratches. One said it was mosquitoes, another said they were mangrove **noseeums**, like the ones in Florida.*

      Suddenly, with little fanfare President Alemán made a short speech and left the podium. Several more brief acknowledgements followed and the dinner broke up, everyone fleeing for their rooms. Here, after the hotel had dispatched workers to each with bug sprayers and complimentary bottles of tequila, the guests found some relief.

NAYARIT BEACHES

The next morning, early risers discovered that the noseeums of San Blas were ready for breakfast, and that the dawn patrol is almost as insidious as the evening flight. They also discovered that the president and his entourage had slipped out during the night to a more friendly climate. Needless to say the foreign journalists had little positive to say about San Blas.

The Hermosa hotel is located a mile or so south of town. It is crumbling toward oblivion, but the polished bronze plaque commemorating that evening is still in the entryway.

It is a shame that the repellants available today were not around two generations ago. It might have meant a whole new ballgame for San Blas.

There are two beaches within walking distance of town, **Playas Hermosa** and **El Borrego**, which end at **Estero San Cristobal** to the south-west and **Estero El Pozo** to the east..

There is little argument that the **Las Brisas** hotel is the best in town, and its **El Delfín** restaurant serves creditable meals. The **Posada de Rey** has small clean rooms and the management is friendly. Their roof-top bar is a good spot to watch the *puesta del sol* (sunset). We find good food at **La Isla** (also known as **Tony's**) and **McDonald's** (not the golden arches variety). The **Tornino** looked inviting and clean with good recommendations. All are within 2 blocks of the plaza. Just off the plaza next to the old church, is the central market.

A few meters west of the bridge into town a road goes to the top of the hill and the old Spanish fort variously called **Fuerza San Basilio** (the sign at the bottom of the hill) or **La Contaduría** and its/their nine cannons. There are also remnants of a very old church. Down in the town, we find the walls of the old custom house, built in 1770.

At that same junction with the highway, a sharp left goes to the side of the river. Here a number of *pangas* offer trips up the **Río La Tovara**, a not-to-be-missed journey to where a sparkling freshwater spring flows out of the side of a hill.

As we park, several guides offer to take us up the river, promising a memorable trip. We selected a young man named **Elisario**. Our choice was a good one for he showed a comprehensive knowledge of the many varieties of mangroves and other plants and animals along the 90-minute trip up-river. The amount of wildlife was a surprise, despite the fact that it was promised by the guides. *Caimans* (alligators) lay basking on sand bars, three to four-foot green iguanas lay motionless on sunny branches. We saw several raccoons peering out of the mangrove roots, while turtles gathered in small herds around partially submerged tree trunks. Birds are everywhere, from oyster catchers to herons, humming birds to ospreys. We even heard a few parrots.

The trip ends at a crystal-clear pool fed by a large spring which comes right out of the lava hillside. A restaurant, bathrooms and warm, crystal waters makes this a perfect spot to take a swim or sit in the shade and sip something cool. The guide allows up to an hour layover before heading back.

The town of San Blas, surrounded as it is by such a wide variety of habitats, from jungles to saltwater lagoons, is well known to birders. More than 400 avian species have been identified around here. The San Blas jay, mangrove cuckoo and pygmy owl are but a few found almost nowhere else. A bird-watchers paradise.

There is a lot to see and do in and near San Blas. Come and stay awhile, but be sure to have the bug juice handy.

How to Beat the Bugs, Almost...

What do we use in Mexico to keep the bugs at bay? It is called **Muskol**, and originally came from Canada where it was developed to repel northern critters such as giant mosquitoes, black flies and noseeums. We tried it a dozen years ago on the sand fleas and/ or *jejenes* of Baja's Bahía Concepción and it worked beautifully...even on Tom, who is a moveable feast for all manner of nibbling critters. It really works, and for up to six hours. Most outdoor stores in the United States and Canada carry Muskol, but it's not found in Mexico.

Another material with a strong following is the improbable, **Skin So Soft**, manufactured by the Avon Company. An after-shower skin oil, it is surprisingly effective for as much as two hours. Personal experience has it good for not much over an hour but long enough to get in a sunset without problems. And it is a less-chemical way to avoid the little beggars.

San Blas North, Plus Chacalilla...

*The paved road north to the beaches, etc., begins a few yards west of the bridge into San Blas. It takes us through miles of low, almost-swampy land which is being exploited in a variety of ways. We will also take a sidetrip into a town near an ancient **Toltec** City.*

0.0   0.0   We leave San Blas and go north on a paved road past some apparently-abandoned aquaculture enclosures. There are a number of them and one wonders why, when so much effort is being expended elsewhere in Mexico to build the same thing.

1.4   1.4   More nonfunctional enclosures. The question reoccurs. We pass a few low hummocks which are being farmed. There are also scattered drainage channels to dry up more of the swamp.

2.1   3.5   Pass a large white building and a pump house, then jog west briefly before returning north. Then we see shrimp pens, some in use, others not.

1.2   4.7   A dirt road (right) is signed to **Chacalilla**, 4km. *We have been told about ruins near the town, so we go looking. The semi-graded road is dusty, rocky and rutted. We go past a number of large shrimp ponds under construction.*

At **0.6** there are several large *higueras* with many trunks, or air roots. The climb to the top of the low hill begins at **2.1** via a rough and rocky road. It's not impassable, just slow going. There are more higueras along the climb to the top where we can see banana and papaya fields.

Houses begin appearing around **2.6** and the streets become organized rocks, or cobbles. There is almost no one around, and the zocalo area is deserted. We finally run into **José Navarez**. Actually we run into his mother. She had seen us coming from a distance and waited by the side of the street with a bag of **ciruelas**, a delicious little tropical plum. We accept a small bag as a gift and are introduced to Jose.

*It turns out that Sr. Navarez has been around the site of the nearby (and as far as we know, unnamed) Toltec city all of his life and can point out some of the geographical aspects and several carvings. The ones he showed us from his personal collection were impressive. He can act as a guide should you wish. His English is non existent, but he speaks an easy-to-follow Spanish. When you come through the town ask in the tienda for the location of the house of José Navarez. Incidentally, Jose's neighbor, **Socorro de León** showed us some nice shards of fired clay figures which she had picked up in the nearby corn fields. Return to the paved road and continue north.*

1.7   6.4   **La Chirira** is a wide spot in the road with three *topes* and a number of brick houses. A lot of the land nearby is cultivated, but we'd guess that salt intrusion from the high water table limits what they can grow. About all we can see are salt-tolerant *ciruelas* and coco palms.

3.3   9.7   We enter the town of **Guadalupe Victoria** after passing the *panteón* (cemetery) and a school.

0.6   10.3   At the intersection the road east goes back up to Mexico 15, coming out at K48, about 15 miles below Tuxpan. We turn left and head west toward **El Limón**. The plants along the highway are all green and vigorous while the cultivated fields look to be having problems, probably from salt.

NAYARIT BEACHES

1.9   12.2   K32   Here's a K marker, apparently from a series leading from Mexico 15 into Guadalupe Victoria and points west.

0.7   12.9   K33   A dirt road (right) angling back a bit is signed to **Isla del Conde**. Just beyond is **El Ciruelo** a small town with a cobbled entrance, a water tower and a very bright blue tienda highly visible down one of the side streets. As we leave town the pavement disappears.

3.8   16.7   There are quite a few cattle, but the pastures don't look all that good. Ahead is another small town on our bumpy rock and dirt road. Continue past the basketball court and on to the water.

0.8   17.5   We are looking at a half-dozen restaurants and a bunch of pangas pulled up on the beach. We are at a lagoon, not the ocean and would guess the bugs would be a bear late in the afternoon. We can see no real reason for returning. Back to the highway and San Blas.

San Blas — Tepíc Via Santa Cruz...

0.0   0.0   We leave from the San Blas highway by the K33 marker and head south on a signed road to **Los Cocos**, **Matanchen** and **Santa Cruz** on a raised road bed through a mixture of open water, clogged mangrove thickets and scrub brush.

1.3   1.3   We arrive at Matanchen and note the *pangas* which will also take us through the swamp and upriver to **La Tovara**. **0.2** miles farther west the road swings sharply left while a dirt road goes straight to **Las Islitas**.

If you need a reason to come to San Blas it could be to take the jungle boat ride up to La Tovara, or to spend a day or two sampling the beaches and the moods around Play Las Islitas. *The area is a stunning combination of small beaches ranging from shallow calm to boiling cauldrons and sharp pinnacles. There are a number of restaurants offering all sorts of Mariscos, but with a twist...almost all include banana bread on the bill of fare. One combination surf shop and store announces that it is the home of the original banana bread. The story goes that it was invented here by (or for) surfers on a health-food kick.*

The calmer Islitas beaches face south and southeast while the more active ones look to the southwest and west. Yes, surfing is a big thing here, with long rights showing off the points during certain wave patterns.

We have gone past at least four distinct beaches and there are lousy roads to several, but all we've seen are winners. Don't miss Las Islitas. Back to the highway to continue in a southeasterly direction past an airstrip (the would-be jetport of the 50s.) and a number of roads (right) to the beach. Some are softer than others, but all seem to get their share of attention during family beach time, Sunday afternoons and holidays.

2.7   3.9   We continue along the coast line of beautiful **Bahía Matanchen** as it curves to the south. A mile beyond, we encounter (left) a blue and white-painted fish culture school. The beach on the right is a busy one. The sand is solid here and we see cars parked near the water to give their passengers the maximum cooling from the ocean.

1.5   5.4   **Rincón de Matanchen** is at the corner where the beach and rocky bluff meets. At this point we turn inland for about a mile to emerge on top of the cliff some 500 meters from the *rincón* (corner) but well above it. There are several restaurants on the right, and signs of more to come.

1.8   7.2   **Aticama** is the next signed town along the ocean. The low cliffs provide good views and a bit of extra height to catch the breezes, but not too high for narrow stairs or trails to bring those wishing it, an opportunity to visit the small beaches at the bottom. We stopped at the **Mariscos Los Siete Mares**. They specialize in cocktails made with the warm broth taken from the very light cooking of whatever is going into the large cocktail glasses. The combination of the shrimp, the broth and several freshly chopped

181

vegetables was a knockout. Highly recommended.

1.0   8.2   We pass a couple of smallish adjoining trailer parks, then continue past a number of small places offering rooms, suites, or apartments. There are also a number of vacant lots and we are told that they are still very reasonable in cost should we wish to buy.

1.2   9.4   A small motel, **Casa Mañana** is off to the right. It is less than a year old and looks it. Everything is neat and clean. It is owned by a Mexican woman and her Austrian husband. It has only 7 rooms (2 with kitchens) and even during its first season it was full much of the time. The restaurant here is reputed to be excellent and the husband does much of the cooking. The current guests are very happy with the place.

1.4   10.8   Road (right) to **La Manzanilla**. *We come to the water 0.3 miles later. It is on a cliff overlooking the ocean with a number of spots to stop and look or enjoy the breeze. We found the palapa where the road meets the ocean to be clean, well organized and efficient when we ordered a refresco. It is a family place with areas for the kids to run around and even play in small freshwater pools. To the south along a dirt road a hotel-looking place turns out to be a vacation spot for the employees of the Sabritas snack food company.* Back to the highway.

0.8   11.6   K47   A set of K markers begin here at the intersection. The right branch leads to **Santa Cruz** and **Miramar**. *The Miramar entrance is located only 0.3 miles toward Santa Cruz and is a sharp drop (right) to several friendly little restaurants who serve some of the best mariscos in the area. The ambiance is marvelous, especially if you like Mexican folk songs played at full volume. The fish is fresh...it comes daily from the pangas pulled up on the beach. The road continues southwest another 0.5 miles and the somewhat-of-a-nothing town of Santa Cruz. There is access to the beach by going west along the north side of the zocalo 0.5 to a pebbly beach with a bedraggled palapa restaurant. We follow the sandy road another few hundred yards to a river mouth. We see several families picnicking and swimming in the fresh water. Aside from the little beach with the fresh water and a few very small stores, for us there is little reason to revisit Santa Cruz.* Back to the intersection and east toward Tepíc.

0.4   12.0   K46+   A signed dirt road goes right into the hills beyond to take us to **Jolotemba** and eventually to **Las Varas** and **Puerto Vallarta** via Mexico 200. It is quite a road.

*Once we drop off the pavement it is 12 kilometers before the paving begins again with any assurances that it will continue. The course is as bad a one as we would ever want to attempt without 4-wheel drive **and** someone else along to commiserate with. We went through streams and dust bowls, over boulder piles and hairpin turns, plus near-vertical ascents and descents. Among it all are a number of banana operations and several houses, including Jolotemba (5 houses). Why and how they get back and forth, we don't know.*

*And all of the above came in the first 6 or 7 kilometers...after that it levels out and is merely washboardy, potholed and dusty. It was so miserable we even forgot to record a log. (For the rest of the road see the **Platanitos** log in the **Nayarít Beaches** section.)* Now, on with the highway to Tepíc and a rapid climb into the forest.

1.4   13.4   K43+   We continue in an easterly direction.

1.8   15.2   K40+   Here is a small forest glen on the left with several tiny white orchids growing out of the cut in the hill. Continue upward, topping out for a moment, then back toward a valley.

1.7   16.9   K38   **Tecuitata** is a *pueblito* on a ridge. From here we descend again past a small dilapidated-looking *balneario* (bathing place) with a pool and splashing facilities for kids in a small stream. The road then begins to climb past jungle growth and scattered views of the hills off to the right.

4.5   21.4   K30+   From the crest of another winding grade we see the first straight stretch in 8 miles. It is short-lived. A few hundred meters later we're back to winding, climbing and descending.

0.9   22.3   K29   Another straight section before entering **Jalcocotan**, another banana town with a *zocalo* and fair-sized business district. We continue through the hills. The volcanic origins of the area shows well in the pinnacled hills and the black rock formations along the highway.

3.0   25.3   K24   We find a short stretch of passable road, then a paved road north to **Mercatán**. This road connects with the other San Blas road, Mexico 54, at K16+ and is paved only part of the way. The coffee plantings we've heard about are now obvious...some adjoin the highway under the tall trees.

2.5   27.8   K20   Off to the right is a line of cliffs which should create hundreds of waterfalls during a good rain.

1.5   29.3   K18   The town of **La Yerba**. It is obviously a coffee town...there are even bushes growing in front yards and under a roadside tree. Just past town a road left is to **El Pintadeño**, 16km, and probably coffee all the way. We seem to have come out of the winding phase of the highway for awhile. What a relief.

2.7   32.0   K13+   A cobbled turnoff left is to **Lo de Garcia.** *After wondering during this whole logging episode about why someplace would have the name of Lo leading it off, we finally figured it out. Later we asked someone and they confirmed it...the words* **Lo de** *signify that it is the place of...therefore this is The Place of Garcia.*

1.1   33.1   K12   We have now climbed high enough to have a scattering of pine trees around us.

1.8   34.9   K9   Swing around a curve and toward a small church and community of **Villa Carranza**. Then comes **Platanitos** (Little Bananas). From here we see nothing but mountain peaks.

1.7   36.6   K6   **El Izote**, and a few topes. We drop sharply toward the valley below. **El Ahuacate**, (The Avocado), is next as we continue to drop.

3.4   40.0   K0   The road left goes into downtown Tepíc, the road right is part of the Periférico which takes us on to **Puerto Vallarta**.

End of log.

Las Varas — Playa Platanitos...

0.0   0.0   K0   The road to **Playa Platanitos** begins from K70 of Mexico 200 northwest through the center of **Las Varas**. The road starts out cobbled and divided, but quickly reverts to paved and narrow. The action here is tobacco and bananas. Large drying sheds are everywhere. Nayarít is Mexico's premier tobacco-growing state and its burley is among the best in the world. A portion of the crop is exported to the United States.

3.4   3.4   K5+   The road redirects itself north past more tobacco.

1.8   5.2   K8   Enter the town of **Zacualpan** and a series of *topes*. A new-looking church and a *zocalo* with its beautiful roses are next. At this point we turn southwest from the east side of the zocalo to continue our journey. *We checked with one of the townspeople to ascertain the correct turn for* **El Custodio** *and he walked a full block in the blazing sun just to be sure that we are on the right road. He then stood there for several minutes reviewing the directions again and telling us to be sure and stop at Playa Los Platanitos.*

2.3   7.5   K12   A small settlement of high-peaked thatched houses. This is another one of the many places in Mexico which has extensive plantings of the red-orange flowering tree with a number of names...*tabachín, flamboyant* or *arbol del fuego*. When not in bloom, they can be recognized by their two-foot-long black seed pods.

2.5   10.0   K16   Go past a technical school on the left, then follow a short *periférico* (right) around the small town of **Ixtapan de La Concepción**. Then come more tobacco and pasturelands. Around us are low hills with fair numbers of the tall *cayaco* palms. The road continues to skirt the hills forming the north end of the valley.

6.8   16.8   K25   Mangrove-lined channels of an estuary appear on our left. **0.2** miles beyond, a dirt road goes left and down 200 meters to **Playa Platanitos**. The 250-meter wide beach is south-facing and quite shallow. The water is only chest deep a good 50 yards out, making it popular with families with small children. (We're here on a Sunday and kids are everywhere.) There are five small restaurants to choose from and all feature *Ostiones en su concha*. The place is thoroughly charming and well worth a visit. Overnighting should be OK with permission.

The road continues some hundreds of meters beyond the beach, then turns inland toward Santa Cruz. *See the Santa Cruz portion of the San Blas-Tepíc log for a description of this road*. Back to the highway;

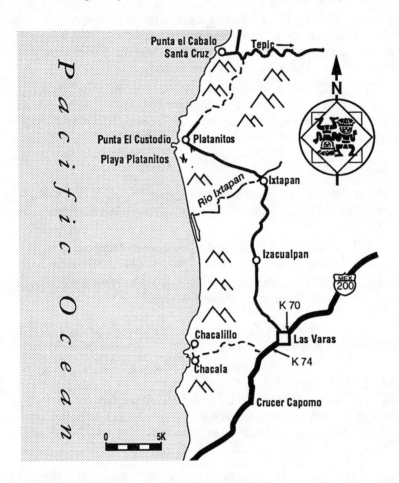

Chacala and Chacalillo...

0.0   0.0   Turn west off Mexico 200 at K74 on the signed semi-graded road to **Chacala**, 9km. It is a typical farm road with pastures on each side, followed by mangos, bananas and pineapple.

2.2   2.2   A small ranch with several outbuildings, then more pineapple. If we were driving a motorhome we would have to be very motivated to come in here. For other classes of vehicles, even passenger cars with good clearance, just take it slow.

3.2   5.4   We are at **Chacala**, a small collection of houses fronting on a beautiful 500-yard sandy crescent with rock promontories on each end. Snorkeling and free diving is particularly good off the south end. The calm water of January is reputed to build to good surfing conditions during the summer. Fishing for dorado, sierra, pargo and roosterfish is good much of the year, with the roosters occasionally patrolling the beach in about 4-feet of water.

A coconut grove provides shady areas for free (or almost free) camping. There are no facilities as such, though several *palapa* restaurants have primitive toilets. At the the south end a small complex of buildings is being used as a language school. Between there and the coconut grove are several cabins which have been rented in times past, but at present look to be permanently occupied. *One inhabitant is a young adventurer from the U.S. who married a local girl and opened an adventure tours company. It has a name, **Nomad Adventure Expeditions**, but he hasn't yet decided on a mailing address! His intent is to take clients kayaking through the coves and tiny beaches of the region. One could imagine that such a group could live almost entirely off the land and the sea, during the adventure.*

Just past the bluff forming the north end of the beach is a tiny rock-enclosed cove which was used for shipping grain more than 200 years ago. At one time wheat was sent from here to Salina Cruz, then across to the Yucatan. The walls of a church and several warehouses are still standing. For more details check with the elderly gentleman who lives in the house across the road. A retired railroad employee in his high eighties, he is dedicating the remainder of his life to preserving the historical integrity of the buildings across from his home.

At the north end of the line of houses, where the road forks, we take the right branch to **Chacalillo**, or little Chacala. It leads up a small hill, then over a miserable, rocky, downhill "slalom" onto one of the most pristine coves we've ever seen. The camping area is **0.5** miles from Chacala. It too is shaded by coco palms. The only residents are a couple from Canada who are touring Mexico in a beat-up passenger car. Their tiny tent looks incongruous among all of the tall coco palms. The cove's 150-foot sand beach is perfectly offset with brushy promontories at each end and enough intertidal rocks to attract an abundance of marine animals.

Camping at Playa Chacala would be heaven for the person looking for isolation. The road in is not good...in fact dicey at times, but almost any skilled driver should be able to take a van or pickup in. It would also appear to be a perfect spot from which to launch a cartop or inflatable, particularly since the magic 100-fathom line is not far away. Back to the highway.

Punta Mita Beaches...

The peninsula of land known as **Punta Mita** and which forms the northern reaches of Vallarta's **Bahía Banderas**, will surely be one of the next to tumble into the category of a major tourist destination. Here are examples of what might be in store for the region.

Though some of the circuit is rough and dusty, an experienced driver with good clearance should be able to take almost any vehicle the entire distance. There's a lot to see and experience on the Mita peninsula...(We start at the south, paved end, and return via Sayulita.)

0.0   0.0   The Mita road begins at K132 of Mexico 200 just north of Puerto Vallarta. Head south and west past a closed tourism office and on toward **Cruz de Huanacaxtle** and **Punta Mita**.

1.2   1.2   The community of **Cruz de Huanacaxtle** is on the left. *We take the road to the small harbor. A rooftop restaurant and bar using a whale in its sign is nearby. Another, **Felipes**, is well recommended. Other restaurants are scattered around town. Another, back from the water but high to catch the breezes, is the **Miramar**. We've seen a few marginal apartments near the east end of the beach.*

A walk around the town and along its beaches makes it pretty obvious that it has some real sewage problems. As the pressure for development increase, so will the incentive to put in modern treatment facilities. Back to the peninsular road.

0.5   1.7   **Piedra Blanca** trailer park is down to the left. *The beach is sandy with rocks scattered around. There are several palapa restaurants.* Back to the highway and up a hill. All along here we can see small dirt roads branching toward the ocean...most of them make it, though several don't. One forced us to back nearly a quarter-mile because of a locked gate. You take your chances on the little ones.

1.4   3.1   A steep, narrow road goes left about 200 yards to the beach. *The layout should make for great camping but the entrance is not suitable for large rigs. The south-facing beach has light surf and offers good beachcombing. Puerto Vallarta's skyline is in the distance. A relaxing spot. Be sure the insect repellant is handy come late afternoon, for the critters are hungry.* Back on the road we come to a little restaurant on another beach. "*Ostiones en Su Concha,*" says the sign. Oysters on the half shell are always hard to turn down. The turnoffs continue, some to the water while others go to view points, or a lot someone hopes to sell.

0.5   3.6   A stone and cement arch marks the entrance into **Playa Destilladeras** and a number of private homes. *There is beach access shortly before reaching the homes.* To continue on the highway, go right and up around the property.

2.0   5.6   A road left leads several hundred yards to a southwest-facing beach. The word is that it is one of the better surfing beaches in the area. The summer hurricane season should bring some great right breaks. The parade of beaches continue. Some can only be hiked, others are 4x4 territory, and all are little-visited.

1.6   7.2   The dirt road (left) is signed, **El Paraiso Escondido** (Hidden Paradise), and goes past underbrush containing numerous agave plants. Obviously shade-loving, they have long, narrow leaves up to 7-feet long with sharp spines along some of the sides. *We stop in a large, clean parking area at **0.3** miles. The beach, **Playa Pantoque** (Bilge Water Beach!), is one of those that you might have trouble deciding whether to tell the world about, or say nothing.*

A large palapa restaurant faces a perfect 300-yard crescent of white sand broken by a jumble of granite boulders and bracketed by large rock formations. The east end has several good tide pools, while the other is more vertical. The normal surf pattern is small here, thanks to reefs just offshore. Snorkeling is good when the water is flat.

The restaurant is clean, efficient and well attended. Offering the usual mariscos, they also serve very cold Corona Extras.

There is one blight on the perfect aura of the moment...courtesy of two American couples...

There are politely-worded, printed signs in English and Spanish asking that no one bring their own food and beverages onto the beach. As we leave, two older couples with midwestern accents walk past us with beach chairs, towels and an ice chest.

They stop at the sign and read it. One of the women pointed to the chest and said, "Oh George, it says we can't bring that onto the beach."

Good old George replies, "To hell with 'em. They're just trying to make us buy food and beer." And with that they walk through the restaurant and onto the beach! We quietly gag and leave.

7.2   Back to the road and past a restaurant (right) with a reputation for serving local foods. If you like armadillo, iguana or snake, you won't want to miss this one. Its name, **Fonda Las Amapas.**

The number of rental Jeeps we see here are indicative of the high interest tourists have for out-of-the-way-spots.

1.7   8.9   Another road (left), this one going to a building site with a marvelous view. Next comes a signed road to **Playa Plumeros** (Beach of the Feathers). *At 0.7, the Restaurant Palmas sits on a south-facing beach with rocks on both ends. More open*

186

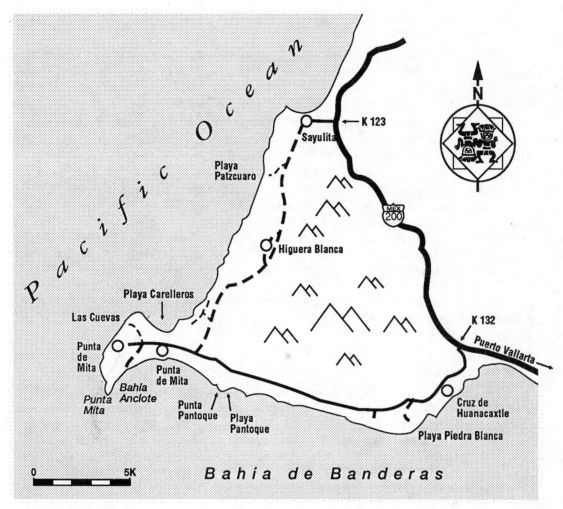

to the breakers than El Paraiso Escondido, it is sporting a number of pelicans working baitfish outside while shorebirds are sharpening their beaks in the sand to the left. It is quiet, and has a good feel. Back to the paved road and on toward Punta Mita through scattered vegetation.

      0.6   9.5   A road (right) goes north toward Sayulita. (This is the direction we will take after visiting Punta Mita, etc.) Just beyond and off to the left is a residential project signed **Punta de Mita**. *There are a number of streets laid out and a plaque commemorating the date the President of Mexico came out to dedicate the area. Some houses are up and occupied, others remain uncompleted and threatening to return to rubble. The cobbled streets are becoming overgrown as a dream fades. The site is beautiful and should be breezy enough to be comfortable much of the year. Maybe it just wasn't its time.* Back to the highway.

     Road (left) at **1.2** miles is to **Playa Anclote**. The clutter of signs at the entrance...**El Anclote, El Dorado, Rosios, El Coral** and **Miguel**, assure a choice of eating places. *About a mile long, and sandy with a few rocks here and there, this beautiful beach is well protected from the northerlies. It is a popular destination for land and sea travelers alike. We can count at least a dozen sailboats at anchor. The wind whips through here much of the time, if the stunted and windblown trees are an indicator.* Back to the road and west to the point.

     At **2.4** miles from the intersection we reach the end of the road at **Punta Mita**. The physical end and the lighthouse are about a mile to the left. *Mariscada* restaurants featuring shrimp overlook the rocky beach. *The intertidal sealife here must be great. We are here on*

187

a low tide and see acres of exposed rocks with several dozen people busy gathering limpets, oysters, clams, octopus, etc.

While the water was flat and the wind light as little as a mile back, here it is blowing hard with whitecaps as far as we can see. One might describe the point as "air conditioned". It is easy to see that when it gets hot and sticky elsewhere, it should be more bearable here at Punta Mita. We head back to the intersection and up the north side.

0.0   9.5   We have returned to the Y, the upper side of which leads to **Sayulita** and back to Mexico 200. It begins paved and holds well for a half-mile before turning into hundred-yard intervals of dirt and crumbling asphalt.

1.2   10.7   A dirt trail goes north (left) toward the ocean. We follow a set of power lines until they turn left, then drive straight out to a graded point overlooking several small sandy beaches. Houses are visible both to the left and right, each one appearing to be on its own point of rocks. The scenery is spectacular. Several locations look as though they should offer excellent winter surfing. It is reminiscent of Hawaii's north-facing beaches. *While we are looking around a van comes out of one of the houses and heads toward the road. It has California plates and two very tan surfer-types inside. Fishing should be good off both the rocks and the beach. As we survey the fishing potential, a school of bait fish surfaces about fifty yards offshore, prompting a passing line of pelicans to peel off for a meal.* The point we are on is fairly level and shows signs of having been a campsite. An excellent spot for a pickup or van.

Back to the road and on to a thick forest of the giant *cayaco* palms. A road leads into the forest on the left. We continue past a few thatched houses.

1.7   12.4   We follow a piece of the paved road briefly, then turn left into **Higuera Blanca** as the bridge ahead is washed out, (and appears to have been for several years). Chances of repair, nil. *Be careful going down into the town. Work your way north and east, following the most traveled path. We get lost twice, but have only to call out the window to whoever we can find, "Sayulita?" The response is a hand pointing the way.* We're back out to the paved road in a half-mile. Continue northeast through an ever-thickening jungle.

1.9   14.3   A small banana plantation and a house.

0.9   15.2   Another detour off the paved road for a short distance, then back and past a couple of houses, a small corn field and a drying area for the oily nuts harvested from the *cayaco* palms. *The kernels are sold in the tiendas in this part of Mexico, and they taste terrible!*. Continue through the jungle.

1.2   16.4   Road left is to **Playa Patzcuaro**. *The trail rambles through the jungle, then down the bed of a running stream past mango orchards. Just before reaching the beach there are several large gates with guard houses, and dogs. The trail drives much longer than the 0.7 miles it turned out to be.*

The reasons for the gates become apparent when we walk out on the beach. On each end of this beautiful little cove are recently-built, palatial mansions. We are told they are owned by people from Mexico City. This could be another sign of what may come about on the Nayarít coast. There is no camping area, but a day trip to swim, check out the driftwood, and relax is a winner. Back to the road and on through more jungle past occasional gardens hacked out of the heavy underbrush. The signs of civilization are around us in the form of trash piles.

2.2   18.6   We enter **Sayulita**, coming to a view of the ocean and views of a number of very nice homes built on the hillsides overlooking the Pacific. Continue on the now-well-paved road east out of town.

1.3   19.9   Back to the Mexico 200 highway at K123+.

End of log.

JALISCO

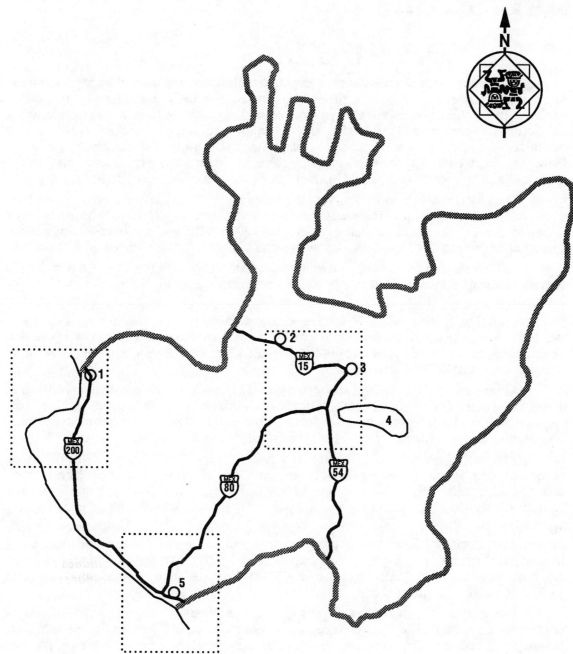

JALISCO

1. Puerto Vallarta
2. Tequila
3. Guadalajara
4. Laguna Chapala
5. Barra de Návidad

JALISCO...

THE STATE

When one looks at the outline of the state of **Jalisco** on a map, it appears to be the ultimate in that peculiar political pastime of drawing boundaries, known as *gerrymandering*. There is no practical geographical rhyme or reason for giving Jalisco the borders that it is saddled with. From rugged mountains to dusty plains and indented shorelines, the state's perimeter is touched by eight other states: Nayarít is to the north; then, in clockwise order, Durango, Zacatecas, Aguascalientes, San Luís Potosí, Guanajuato, Michoacan and Colima, plus the Pacific Ocean! Its capital, Guadalajara, is the second largest city in Mexico.

The oldest indigenous findings are the rock carvings located in different parts of the state...near Puerto Vallarta and Ciudád Guzman. There are tombs similar to those discovered in Ecuador and Columbia at Acatlán de Juarez and El Arenál. These tombs consisted of deep carved chambers reached by staircases where many offerings were buried with the dead.

Jalisco, along with Nayarít, Durango and Zacatecas, was the pre-Spanish home of the **Huichol** Indians and many still live in the mountains to the north.

Other Indian groups shared the area and together left rich cultures excelling in pottery and ceramic figures, particularly in the region around what is now Guadalajara. Elsewhere we find evidence of thriving communities in this temperate climate as early as two thousand years ago, and remains of pyramidal platforms, patios, terraces, plazas, ball fields, and other structures are still being discovered.

At the time of the Spanish conquest, a group known as the Chimalhuacanos lived in the region. Their leader was a woman, Chihualpilli and she initially accepted the Spanish but, upon seeing their harsh treatment of her people, recanted. In the ensuing confrontation they were defeated and suffered greatly under the tyrant, Nuño de Guzman.

The state played a vital role in the expansion of New Spain (Nuevo Galacia) to the north and west. It was not only a corridor for travel but its mining and agriculture centers contributed significantly to the coffers of New Spain. By the 1700's its population was equally divided between descendents of Spaniards, Indians and the Negroes originally brought over as slaves.

The people of Jalisco were deeply involved in the struggles for independence during the early 19th century and several of their citizens were key figures in the Revolution of 1810, when the Spanish were finally overthrown. To this day, the state is a prominent force in Mexico's national political scene.

Contemporary Jalisco has a prosperous and diversified economy, with major contributions coming from agriculture and livestock, tourism, mining, manufacturing, forestry and native crafts. Another important, and unique, industry is the growing of the maguey cactus and its distillation into the national drink, tequila.

A still-expanding beach scene around Puerto Vallarta, plus portions of the state's other 350 kilometers of coastline, offer both high-living destinations and quiet hideaways. These regions will benefit greatly with the expansion of Mexico's highway system.

Guadalajara and environs provides a variety of cultural experiences, with its opera house attracting music and theatrical companies from all over the world. Museums also abound, and the large English-speaking population lends even more to the internationalism felt in this city of 5,000,000. Several satellite communities, among them Laguna Chapala, are popular with *norteamericano* retirees. This region hosts more foreign retirees than any other in Mexico, with the large majority from the U.S. and Canada.

Jalisco, a happy, lively state, is the home of the Mexican Hat Dance, mariachis, charros, rodeos, bullfights...and tequila. Salúd!

MEXICO 200 — BORDER TO BORDER

The state of Jalisco has been a center of Mexico's touristic development for nearly a half-century. Tourism spread from Guadalajara to Jalisco's coastal treasures, beginning with Puerto Vallarta. Today you may venture to Yelapa or Tehualmixtle, Puerto Vallarta or Barra de Navidad. You are in for a treat; there is something here in Jalisco for everyone,

0.0   0.0   K153   We cross the bridge over the **Río Ameca** and into the state of **Jalisco**. And there's a time zone change...move watches and clocks ahead one hour.

2.0   2.0   K156   The paved road inland is to **Ixtapa** and **Las Palmas**. (*By chance we stumbled onto a tiny hotel, the **Alamos**, about a hundred yards in from the highway. It has a pool, the rooms are clean and inexpensive. If all else fails, here might be a stop for the night.*) Ixtapa has some reputation as a center for *barro*, or terra-cotta pottery; however, they keep it well hidden...

*Good friends **Gloria** and **Ken Hansen** are building a house overlooking the beach about a dozen miles north of here at the **Club Playa Costa Azul**, and they had run across some unique terra-cotta light fixtures (ollas para lamparas) made by a man (whose name they didn't know) in the town of Ixtapa. Despite the paucity of information, the beauty of his work is driving us to ferret him out.*

*Ixtapa is a dusty, nondescript town of about 10,000 located just off Mexico 70, the paved road leading northeast into the long and fertile **Valle de Banderas**. At 2.5 miles we followed the signs into Ixtapa, inquiring of a lady in a **farmacía** where we might find the potter for the ollas. She didn't know but suggested it might be out by the cemetery. After a bit of chasing we found the cemetery, and ultimately, the home of the potter. Unfortunately Sr. Sanchez was not home but the many terra-cotta objects around the house...pots, dishes, even planter boxes, confirmed his skills. The wife, **Adela Sanchez**, was charming but could not much help. Everything had to be done through her husband, **Miguel**, and he was at his ranch near K11, off highway Mexico 70 beyond the town.*

Having come this far, we take off on a hunt for Miguel. A bit of wandering finally bring us to his rancho, but he is not there. Two huge dogs are vocal and effective defenders of the considerable numbers of terra-cotta pots, etc. lying about. We will give it another try.

2.0   4.0   K159   To the right is the **Puerto Vallarta International Airport**. Ahead and also on the right is a huge shopping complex under the pelican logo of **Comercio Mexicano**. Typical of a new wave of shopping centers springing up in many areas of Mexico, we've found them to be clean, amply stocked and well organized, with some of the merchandise coming from the USA. Their opening will add measurably to the convenience of shopping in Puerto Vallarta. And if that isn't enough, the Commercio Mexicano people have enticed **7-11**, **Denny's**, **Price Club**, **Woolworth's**, **McDonald's** and **Carlos and Charlies** to open stores and restaurants here.

The nearby **Marina Vallarta** project is shaping up much better than many had anticipated and looks to be a winner. According to several residents, the docks appear well run, with regulations on dumping in the bay, etc., similar to those in American yacht harbors.. Someone has started a private, American-style, elementary and high school here, and it is off to a rousing start, with about half the students coming from well-to-do Mexican families.

Three large luxury hotels totaling about 700 rooms are now on stream in the development, bringing to 8500 the number of rooms available in PV. The **Isla Iguana** program, which appears to be directed toward slightly less affluent visitors, is not quite as elaborate, but should also do well.

1.9   5.9   K162   The cruise line docks are to the right with an attendant jumble of vendors, taxis, etc. Welcome to PV! We follow Mexico 200 south past a variety of hotels, including the **Playa de Oro, Posada Vallarta, Holiday Inn, Fiesta Americana, Los Tules, Plaza Las Glorias, etc.**

1.9   7.8   K165   We turn left at the signed intersection to Barra de Navidad.

This road goes around behind the town and through a cut in the hills, several tunnels and finally spills us back into town on cobbled streets a few blocks before exiting Puerto Vallarta.

Puerto Vallarta...

Perhaps we owe her an apology. Beginning with the first visit 15 years ago Puerto Vallarta showed us her beaches, her hotels and her high-rise condos. We ate fine food at fine restaurants, rubbing elbows with people from all over the United States. We took trips to Yelapa, Mismaloya, did the sunset cruise and parasailed. She had shown us her best, at least in the view of travel agents, tourism officials and ad agencies. But there's one thing Puerto Vallarta had not shown us, until our last trip...her heart.

Why it took so long must lie with our own prejudices against highly-touted tourist destinations. It also has to do with well-meaning agencies and officials who keep visitors insulated from the local people by housing us in remote 200-room chain hotels with their three restaurants and so-so Americanized food, private beaches, and air-conditioned tour busses.

What we really need as travel communicators, and as tourists with an interest in the country we visit, is the time and the opportunity to meet the real people of this, or any, destination. Today we are taking the time to meet them on their terms, in their restaurants, shops and streets. Here is the heart of Puerto Vallarta. And we like it.

The first written record of the region came from a journal written by one of the priests who accompanied Francisco Cortés de San Buenaventura (nephew of Hernán Cortés) in his exploration of the Pacific coast in 1524. During the trip the party looked from a high pass down into a large and beautiful valley. After two days of marching they reached the valley floor only to have their way blocked by an army of some 20,000 Indians. The natives of "**Tintoque**" carried cotton flags, or *banderas*, of assorted colors and sizes tied to their bows. The valley was thus dubbed "**Valle de Las Banderas**" by the Spaniards and so it is known today. Another party visited the area from the sea in 1541, and English pirates are reported to have hidden in the bay between 1557 and 1570.

According to official property records, it was in 1851 that **Guadalupe Sanchez** brought his family here, cleared a plot of land near the **Río Cuale**, built a house and planted the rich soil. They and their children had a good existence. Their produce went to the mines in the *sierras*. Supplies for the mines also came into the bay, and it became a port. But it was not until after World War I that a cartographer gave it an official name...Puerto, because it was a port, and Vallarta, in honor of a former governor of the state of Jalisco.

Puerto Vallarta remained a small agricultural center until after WWII when a few yachtsmen began to stop off in the calm bay. Some returned by private plane to continue their romance with the tiny village. Eventually a few rooms became available. In 1948, the **Rosita** hotel opened its doors in hopes the trickle would grow. In 1954, the first commercial airplane landed on the dirt strip on the south side of the Cuale. The first to "discover" PV were residents of Guadalajara and Mexico City. Things were looking up for the citizens of the small town formed by the extended family of Sr. Sanchez.

Mexicana Airlines had opened the doors, but it was **John Huston** who started the chain of events responsible for publicizing Puerto Vallarta to the world when he selected it as the location for his movie version of Tennessee Williams' play, "**The Night of the Iguana.**" And we also remember that it wasn't the movie which did the trick, but the tricks turned by **Elizabeth Taylor** with the film's star, **Richard Burton**. Nothing has been the same since. Incidentally, Taylor was not in the film; **Ava Gardner** was Burton's co-star. (If you missed it, or want to see it again, there is a screening each night at the La Jolla Mismaloya Spa and Condominiums.)

Probably the best known section of today's Puerto Vallarta is **Gringo Gulch**. Actually a street, Cuauhtemoc, it contains only 10 houses, though now most of the residents on the north side of the Cuale claim that they are part of the famous Gulch. As one owner put it, "Why not, it helps the resale value." (Liz's non-Gringo Gulch house recently sold, but not for the cool million bucks she was asking).

Our introduction to the Gulch came through **Robin Lloyd,** a resident for 16 years. His home has a commanding view of the river, the upper end of Isla Cuale and the Colonia Emiliano Zapata portion of old Puerto Vallarta. Why the Gulch and not the beach? is a question often asked of Lloyd. His answer..."On the beach you have a big blue expanse of water all day and a black hole at night. Up here everything changes minute to minute: a burro crosses the Cuale, protesting all the way; roosters crow; children play along the river while their mothers wash clothes; a father sings to his family. And it goes on all of the time," he mused.

Lloyd and another freeway fugitive, **Tony Stubbs,** are partners in **Vallarta Today,** one of the most informative tourism tabloids we've seen anywhere. They recently bought all manner of new computers, scanners, printers and presses to further improve their product. Look for Vallarta Today when in town. It is far better than the material in the local tourism office.

How big is PV today? Best estimates put it at about 300,000, up from 70,000 a decade ago. Where do they all stay? One need only to drive from Mismaloya on the south to the airport on the north. The shoreline is practically wall-to-wall hotels, condos and restaurants. Many are innovatively designed to compliment the environment, such as the **Ocho Cascadas** condos in **China Cove** and the nearby **Camino Real.**

We see some of the growth as overkill. *An example is the twin-towered eyesore at Mismaloya Beach. Here, rechanneling of the river has virtually destroyed the beach and dislodged the people who for so many years had made it one of the most charming destinations in the Vallarta area. There's a lot of controversy over this one.*

At the other end of the city, last rites have been said over an estuary which used to be the home of *caimans* (alligators), fish and many waterbirds. It is now a bustling marina, condo and shopping complex. Unfortunately, economics and our survival are an unavoidable factors our world's environment...the residents do need to eat and Mexico can use the foreign exchange.

With our finger on the newly-discovered "pulse" of old Vallarta, we go in search of local restaurants, downtown hotels, sights and shopping...and like the results...

This time we headquarter out of the **Encino,** but visit, and find very acceptable, the **Molino de Agua, Rosita, Posad a Río Cuale, Oceano** and **Oro Verde.** Especially appealing was the Encino's open, interior courtyard, but the bar and restaurant service was a loser.

PV's two trailer parks are located between the ferry terminal and the downtown area. **Tacho's Trailer Park** is a short distance off Mexico 200 east of the terminal, while the **Puerto Vallarta Trailer Park** is a dozen or so blocks south and also east of the highway. Both are well organized, well-shaded and well populated with mosquitos. How long they will last, because of escalating property values, is a moot point.

From almost any of the downtown hotels one can walk to the restaurants mentioned below, and many more.

A welcome variation from the ordinary the Oriental specialties of **Archie's Wok and Deli** on Francisco Rodriguez. Archie, a Filipino, was for many years the personal chef of John Huston. And if he is not too busy, can share some fascinating stories and insights into the lives of Huston and his guests.

South of the Cuale on the beach is El Dorado. This place has been here so long that the palapa roof has been repaired many times, a sign of permanence. It offers a good variety of dishes at fair prices.

Just beyond, **El Farolito** offers the usual with a bit of a switch. The owner, **Fernando Cosio** is an artist, and customers can watch him work in the back, and even haggle over one of his paintings. Fair prices, good midday meals.

We found **Quino's** restaurant on Aquiles Serdán (opposite the pedestrian suspension bridge) to be one of the finds of the season. Their specialty are dishes called *"Casuelas,"* various seafoods baked in a selection of excellent sauces. The green chile and the diablo are favorites. Prices, very fair for what you get. The best seating is upstairs overlooking the street.

Go up a block or two past Quinos and angle over to the river. Turn right up the dirt road about 400 yards to where it joins a paved road. On the far side, look for **Los Arbolitos**, a small place with an upstairs dining area overlooking the river and a busy street. Lala Araiza and his family operate in a marvelous atmosphere. Everything is good, but try the filet mignon for a tender and filling steak. Another favorite is the taquitos of barbecued pork. A plate of eight, plus beans and salad, stuffed Tom to the point of bursting for very little. Nice people, good food and inexpensive. Get a balcony seat and watch the world go by. When through, grab a ride on a combi bus and be back at the beach in minutes, for pennies.

Lázaro Cárdenas, #454 is the home (downstairs) of a stationery store and (upstairs) the restaurant **Los Faisanes**. It's international menu has a good reputation among the locals. We ran out of time for a personal visit.

Another one we missed, but Lloyd guarantees the quality and ambiance, is **La Hacienda**. On Aguacate avenue, it is owned by one of Vallarta's oldest families, **Carlos** and **Elena Mungía**. Back in the 50s, an American had built a huge traditional Mexican colonial hacienda. With its walled courtyard and maze of outbuildings, it is a statement on the elegance of Mexico's early days. The Mungia's extensive art collection, plus their own works, are everywhere. Sr. Mungía is also the official historian of Vallarta, and loves to talk about it. The Hacienda is best reached by taxi. And do call for reservations.

A spot out of the area, but still definitely one for the locals is **Caza Mar**. Located across from the **Plaza Las Glorias**, it has excellent prices on large and tender servings of filet mignon. Its broiled fish is also excellent.

We can't put names on the various carts we tried, but one on the corner of Morelos and Serdán is jammed from about 9:30 each evening. The cart is clean and the lady is charming and efficient.

Shopping in Puerto Vallarta has been judged to be second only to the Guadalajara area in the diversity and quality of its shops. The main shopping area, aside from the usual T-shirt and novelty items (they are everywhere) and the hotel gift shops, is located in the downtown area just north of the river. Here are found a good selection of period furniture, hand embroidered native resortwear, crafts from all over Mexico, jewelry, designer dresses and artwork. Other shops are located in **Isla Cuale** and the area south of the river.

There is one source of handcrafted arts that merits individual mention...**Galería Olas Altas**. At Olas Altas 509, it has one of the widest varieties of indigenous folk art we've seen anywhere. Its display of **Huichol** Indian yarn and bead paintings is superb, as are the wood carvings, masks and woven articles. *When we walked out the door with our treasures, we couldn't believe that 90 minutes had gone by.*

The cathedral in Vallarta, **Nuestra Senora de Guadalupe**, is one of the most photographed in Mexico. Its unique crowned steeple was modeled after the crown worn by Mexico's Empress Carlotta before Emperor Maximilian's and her deposition in 1867 at the hands of Benito Juárez. The church was completed in 1951. The downtown also has the old central market, half of which is now souvenir shops. A walk through will show little more than what has already been seen in the streets or on the beaches...and the vendors are just as aggressive. The other half offers vegetables, meats, and the usual "essentials" of housekeeping in Mexico.

An unique area is the island in the center of the **Río Cuale**. Several years ago, the Isla was developed to feature shops, restaurants, a couple of small parks and the *Museo Arquelogico,* a collection of interesting artifacts of the region. It is a popular attraction for local and visitor alike. Downstream entrances are at the traffic bridges, while a pedestrian cable bridge off Aquiles Serdán provides access above.

In some ways, Puerto Vallarta's fishing has been taking a bad rap...there is some good action here, but it is not found as close in as some of the other Mexican angling centers. The contours of the Bahía Banderas puts the magical "100 fathom line" some 30 miles from the harbor. Today, with a greater awareness of the challenge of fishing for the smaller sportfish, i.e., roosterfish, jack cravalle, amberjack, tuna, etc., there is less push to go that 30 or 40 miles each way for a billfish. We have seen a number of fine catches of 25 to 30-pound roosters, nice pargo ranging to 40 pounds and a dozen amberjack over 50 pounds during a four day January visit. Unfortunately nothing is released, thus the quality of this newfound fishing resource will have to be monitored. Our experiences with snorkeling here have been poor, but new areas around the arches and near Yelapa show promise.

Water-oriented activities will surely draw more attention as the marinas come into their own. With hundreds of American and Mexican yachts berthing here, new fishing, and diving spots will be discovered, talked about and become common knowledge.

Cleaning the Cuale

Robin Lloyd, publisher of the **Vallarta Today** *tabloid and resident of the storied Gringo Gulch portion of downtown Puerto Vallarta, tells this tale about how the foreign and local people get along...at least around the Gulch.*

Recently, after mounting a successful campaign to clean up the streets of the Gulch, a number of the residents decided they were tired of looking at the mounting piles of trash in the riverbed, particularly the bleach bottles, and decided to do something about it. A Sunday was selected and abut 30 Mexicans and norteamericanos from the north side of the river showed up. Shortly, a sound truck was heard echoing from the south side of the Cuale, "Look down to the river, the gringos are picking up the trash." it said, "This is embarrassing! Let's go help..."

Within minutes there were several hundred people along the river filling big plastic bags amid shouts, music and singing. Everyone had a great time and there is talk of making it an annual affair.

3.5   11.3   K214   Arrive at the full service **Pemex** just before skirting the southern edge of **Banderas Bay**. Watch carefully, as it has the last **magnasin** for nearly 100 miles. Beyond, the road is steep in places, narrow and always slow. We just take our time and look at the many beautiful houses and vistas along the way.

4.5   15.8   K206+   The impressive **Hotel Garza Blanca** sits on one of the finest hotel sites in the world. Around a few more curves come the series of small islands with arches etched into their sides, appropriately named, *Los Arcos*.

5.3   21.1   K198   **Hotel La Jolla de Mismaloya**, another upscale development which is catching on big. Around the next turn, we overlook **Mismaloya** itself, "*a narrow beach backed by a sharp canyon and stream. A half-dozen seafood palapas serve the locals who come by truck, bus and burro to enjoy the gentle surf and their own particular style of a day in the sun. Don't miss it.*" That is how we described the beach in a magazine article in May of 1982.

Today it would read..."*Misamaloya, a narrow, manicured beach covered with toweled loungers, backed by 300 hotel rooms stacked one upon another in dual eight-story towers. The running stream has been shunted off to the side, destroying part of the beach. A number of nearby deluxe restaurants provide the guests with expensive seafood, steaks and Mexican food.*" And what about our friends with the seafood palapas? They are trying to hang on, but in the end they will be squeezed out. Regretfully, a lot happens in eight years.

The only thing we can say is that hopefully someone has learned something from this destruction of Mismaloya Beach and that it will not be repeated.

1.3   22.4   K196   **Le Clif Restaurant.** In our view one of the most spectacular restaurant settings in the world. The food is good, service friendly and prices in line with the overall picture. It is hard to pass Le Clif without stopping, no matter what time of day...and impossible at *puesta del sol* (sunset).

In a half-mile we come to a little village cramped between high cliffs, **Boca de Tomatlán.** The narrow beach is home port for the panga fishermen who each morning check their nets or handlines for bottom fish. Life is easy here, for the sea and the land provide almost all one needs to live, and with little effort.

It is hoped that Tomatlán will learn from Mismaloya's experience about the impact of the modern world. A few cracks in the facade have already appeared in the form of a large *norteamericano* home perched on the cliff and another under construction.

Just before the bridge, the entrance into Tomatlán is to the right. To the left is a road to some homesites and, 2 kilometers off the highway, another of the unique restaurants around PV, **Chino's Paradise.** Here in a riverside setting the entire family does a fine job of providing excellent meals without using modern conveniences such as electricity. They are open from 11 to 6 daily.

Cross the bridge and begin climbing into the **Sierra Lagunillas** mountains. Orchids and bromeliads are common on the large trees lining the highway. The **Río Tomatlán** comes tumbling out of the hills ahead and presents ideal photo opportunities, but no turnouts.

2.4   24.8   K192   The famous **Chico's Paradise** restaurant is off to the right. Terraced down the face of the arroyo, it overlooks the Río Tomatlán as it cascades over and past huge rounded granite boulders. The food represents the simple fare of the Mexican rancher and is exceptionally well prepared. Parking is very limited, no motorhomes, please.

A note...Chico's has apparently tumbled to the quick buck. Friends who took a bus tour of the region were hit with a lunch bill for about three times what the same production-line enchiladas would have cost in PV's tonier restaurants.

4.4   29.2   K185   Cross a stream and continue upward. We are now in a pine forest. It looks strange to see log cabins, piles of firewood and bananas sharing the same yard, but it happens here at 2000 feet above sea level.

5.6   34.8   K176   We reach the summit at 2400 feet, then descend gradually through the forest. The trees are a long-needled variety which has little or no piney scent, and don't appear to get bigger than about 18 inches in diameter...hardly enough for good lumber, but we cut a few boughs to decorate our Barra condo at Christmas.

3.7   38.5   K170   **El Tuito.** An agricultural town just to the west of the highway. *From it a secondary road proceeds through the sierras to the ocean where it joins a road coming up from the south and proceeds to **Aquiles Serdán.** (See Jalisco Beaches.) Another road used to reach the sea is via **Las Guasimas** and **Chacala** at El Chimo, but it has been closed since 1987. Incidently, the **Río Tuito** passes through here on its way to the ocean at **Yelapa.*** The highway continues to wind in a southerly direction. The hills to the east are the **Sierra El Tuito,** dominated on the south end by 3600-foot **Cerro El Portezuelo.**

6.3   44.8   K160   Cross the **Río Las Juntas** and continue winding. Cosmos grow wild here and after the summer rains the roadsides are loaded with color. *At home we can' hardly get them to bloom.*

3.1   47.9   K155   We are now down to around 500 feet and the forest has been cut down, leaving open, gently rolling hills.

4.4   52.3   K148   A graded road goes east to **El Tigre,** another goes west to **El Piloto.** We continue south.

4.1   56.4   K141+   Graded road east to **San Rafael,** 12km.

2.5   58.9   K137+   **El Tequesquite** and another road to San Rafael. Lots of plantings of grains and other rotated crops through the irrigated flatlands. To the east is the 7000-foot **Sierra Cacoma** range.

3.0   61.9   K132+   A graded road (right) is signed to **Cruz de Loreto**. It is not a good road, a better one is at K124 (**See Jalisco Beaches**).

1.6   63.5   K130   The ranchers here are going in for mangoes in a big way. There are many new plantings, plus a *vivero*, or nursery, containing thousands of small trees. Mixed in are several sections of citrus.

3.1   66.6   K125   **José Pino Suarez** settlement. A half-mile beyond at **K124**, a graded road leads to the ocean through **La Gloria** to many beaches. (**See Jalisco Beaches.**) We've now got a stretch of easy driving, straight through rolling hills.

5.6   72.2   K116   Cross the **Río Tomatlán** on a high bridge at **La Cumbre**. Then pass a signed, paved intersection to **Tomatlán**, 12km, and a local **Pemex**. A dirt road west here goes to an estero, but no beaches.

2.0   74.2   K113   We return to the hills for a moment, then back to flatter terrain, with cactus and mesquite among the many tropicals. Marshy patches are seen here and there. Continue southeast through alternating marshy and arable land.

> *Some of the ponds are covered with a tiny, bright green plant called duck weed. This little fellow hitch hikes on the feet of ducks (hence the name). It is a pest and can materially affect an aquatic ecosystem by shutting off light from the plants and animals below.*

8.0   82.2   K100   A few houses signed **Campo Acosta**.

7.5   89.7   K88   **José María Morelos**. A small settlement from which a graded road leads east toward the hills, and two roads go west toward the Pacific, and different beaches. The first takes off near the northern edge of town at the *refaccionaria* with **Quaker State** painted all over it. The name of the beach is **Playa Chalacatepec**. (**See Jalisco Beaches.**) The second goes south and west from the south end of the zocalo. Its name escapes us, and we have to save it for another time. Ahead we reenter the hills and wind southeast until reaching the bridge over the **Río San Nicolás**.

3.1   92.8   K83   **Quemara**...a road (west) here does not go to the ocean.

1.6   94.4   K80+   We come back to the ocean in a region known as **Chamela**, named for the bay on which it borders.

1.6   96.0   K78   Road west goes beyond a locked gate to a private beach. **Mezcales**.

1.4   97.4   K76   Road southwest to **Playas La Fortuna** and **Perula**. (**See Jalisco Beaches.**)..

2.5   99.9   K72   A large sign indicates that the **Villa Polinesia** motel and trailer park is ahead. The entrance is well marked. (**See Jalisco Beaches.**) In case you miss the brightly painted tiki statues, keep an eye out for the **El Tejaban** restaurant. It offers fine *antojitos* in a clean and friendly atmosphere. Then comes a local **Pemex**. There is also a small, on-the-road trailer park, the **Chamela**.

2.2   102.1   K68+   Ahead, on the hill overlooking **Bahía Chamela**, is a building complex. Obviously not in use, it appears to be in good condition, even to street light standards and paved roads with curbing. When we come closer, the area is well marked with signs announcing that it is federal property, and to stay out.

> *The Chamela behind the chain-link fences goes back to the presidency of Luís Escheverría Alvarez. It was a victim of the peso devaluation. The principal backer of the huge project was one of Mexico's major banks, and when it was nationalized, this area became the property of the government. We hear that several groups have considered taking the project over, but none have...in the meantime, the decay continues.*

1.4   103.6   K66+   Two adjacent roads go west a half-mile to adjoining small apartment-type mini-resorts. *The northernmost, **Centro Vacacional Chamela**, is owned by a teachers society. You are supposed to be a member to stay there, but the manager says that they rent the units out if they are not occupied. The left one is **Club Chamela**, and it does have bungalows for rent. An interesting thing here is that both roads begin at the highway together and both end up at the same piece of beach and separated by less than 50 yards of sand. There must be a story there somewhere. The beach is beautiful, with gentle waves and somewhat protected by a series of small offshore islands.* Back to the highway and past a series of roads leading to small evaporative salt ponds.

0.6   104.2   K65   A dirt road slants (right) to the beach, going past more salt works and a fenced piece of property with a "for sale" sign on it. *It covers several acres and has some bedraggled buildings on it near the beach. If you are in the market for Mexican resort property, the phone number in Guadalajara is 38-52-61.* Back to the highway.

0.4   104.6   K64+   **Mariscos La Viuda** (The Widow), a popular seafood eatery with a *parabolica*, or satellite dish.

0.9   105.5   K63   Another seafood restaurant, the **Mariscos Don Lupe**. No parabolica, and less customers. Better food or better programing, or both??? The road begins winding as it enters the low hills forming most of the region between here and **Melaque**, where Mexico 200 returns to the ocean. No use trying to make time through here...it isn't safe.

6.0   111.5   K53+   Turnoff into the **Playa Careyes** complex. (**See Jalisco Beaches.**) Here **Hotel Plaza Careyes** and **Club Med** share some of the most picturesque beaches and rocks in Mexico. Coves, headlands, islands and more are there to enjoy. A perennial favorite destination for us. *Careyes is a name for the sea turtle, and the nearby beaches used to host thousands of them. Today few remain, but with a new national ban on the capture or sale of all sea turtles, they might eventually make a comeback.* At the bottom of the hill is another part of the Careyes property, a shallow lagoon and a nature preserve of sorts.

THEY ARE NOW PROTECTED

1.2   112.7   K51+   A dirt road (right) goes through a gate signed as Costa Careyes property and onto a beach with a palapa restaurant fronting on a beautiful 300-meter-wide strand. It is here that we once photographed turtles digging nests and laying eggs. This is on private property and no overnighting is allowed, but should you wish to watch the turtles a check with the hotel usually results in an OK.

5.3   118.0   K43   Cross the **Río Cuitzmala** and into the outskirts of **Cutizmala**. A sign warns about *vibradoras*, a speed control device similar to *topes*. The road continues to wind through the low hills, in and out of jungles and across small clearings. *The occasional large black blobs we see in the trees are termite nests. They look somewhat like a large lump of mud...and are basically that. The termites haul the dirt up bit by bit, mix it with a mucous-like secretion and build an entire, self-sufficient colony right in the middle of their food supply, the tree. It is essentially a temperature and humidity-controlled biosphere with somewhere between 25 and 50 thousand inhabitants, including an egg-laying queen who replenishes the supply of workers at the rate of a hundred or more a day.*

4.5   120.5   K36   A signed dirt road goes west to **Arroyo Seco**, 4km. (**See Jalisco Beaches.**)

1.8   124.3   K33   At the little cement lighthouse, a paved road (right) goes into **El Tecuan**, 10km, is one of the most interesting places along any of Mexico's thousands of miles of coastline. (**See Jalisco Beaches.**) Continue east through the hills past **Miguel Hidalgo**; a clean restaurant, **Yoli's**; and the small town of **Agua Caliente**.

2.8   127.1   K28+   Cross the **Río Purificación**, then a signed dirt road south to **Playa Tenacatita**. Aaaahhhh, Tenacatita. Here is one of those places where the beauty of the people and the ocean scenery match up well. **(See Jalisco Beaches.)** We are tempted to keep this place a secret. Continue winding up and down in an easterly direction.

4.7   131.8   K21   Turnoff (right) onto a cobbled road leading to the **Hotel Fiesta Americana** of **Los Angeles Locos de Tenacatita**, a rather large hotel on the so-called "all inclusive" plan. They do not accept walk-in trade, nor will they allow anyone through to the beach. "It is exclusively for our guests." said one of the managers when contacted by phone.

Our understanding of Mexican law is that all beaches are open to all visitors, so the exclusion might be illegal, but the armed guard at the entrance has an effective argument...a big **pistola** and a very firm "NO."

2.6   134.4   K17   Signed, **Boca de Iguanas** road is on the right. *The roadbed is a lumpy gravel washboard which goes past the entrance to the closed **Hotel Bahía Tenacatita**, 0.9, and to the trailer park area at 1.5 miles. There are two trailer parks, the **Tenacatita** on the left with marginal facilities, and the **Boca de Iguanas** at road's end across a small viaduct. The Boca facility is well conceived, the people friendly and the reports of services excellent. There is also a small hotel located just inland from the trailer parks, the **Campamento Palmeras**. The beaches here are south-facing with light swell conditions during the winter months. Though we didn't try it and didn't ask, the area on the far west end of the beach past the trailer parks looks fishy...there should be some action along those rocks.* Back to the highway and continue over several small bridges.

2.2   136.6   K13+   The signed road west takes us to **La Manzanilla**, a small beach town **0.8** miles in from Mexico 200. *Its economy is centered on fishing and the trade its beaches and restaurants bring in. Oysters are featured in many of the dozen or more restaurants, along with huachinango and shrimp. In January the town celebrates its saint's day in a big way with rodeos, dances and lots of good eating.* Back to the highway. Just past the intersection, note the dark reddish-purple rocks in the cuts for the roadbed.

¡OLE!

2.8   139.4   K9   After a series of rolling hills we top the grade and begin a descent into a broad valley past **Aguacatillo**.

5.6   145.0   K0   Intersection with Mexico 80 to/from **Guadalajara** at K257. We go (right) on Mexico 200, which continues south to Guatemala. On the left is a full service **Pemex**. Continue south toward Barra de Navidad.

0.7   145.7   K258   The Mexico 80 highway ends here at the intersection into **Melaque** and **San Patricio** straight ahead. **(See Jalisco Beaches.)** To the right is **Bahía de Cuastecomate**.

*Cuastecomate is one of those unexpected little spots which show up every once in awhile near other, more visible destinations. It is located 1.7 miles behind the short set of hills west of the highway. The narrow beach faces almost due west and is protected by jutting fingers of rock on each end. The waves are generally small and shallow. An afternoon wind-chop makes the water dirty, but we've some reports of fair snorkeling on calm mornings. Eight palapa restaurants attend to the day-visitor's needs and the southern end of the beach is the site for the **Coco Royale Costa Sur** hotel, a "total package, couples only" resort. On weekends, chartered busses from inland cities such as Autlan and La Huerta bring families here for a day at the beach.*

In the town itself a growing number of Americans and Canadians are renting or leasing property and building palm shelters for motorhomes or trailer for their winter stays. Back to the highway.

We turn east and follow Mexico 200 toward Manzanillo. The new series of K markers begins here with K61. Follow east (left) for Manzanillo.

1.4   147.1   K59   Road south (right) is to **Barra de Navidad** (See Jalisco

Beaches), a friendly little village with a great potential as a major resort destination. Continue to head east toward Manzanillo on Mexico 200. A local **Pemex** is at the corner.

    1.8   148.9   K56   We pass mangos, limes, bananas, peppers, coconuts, corn.

    1.3   150.2   K54   **El Aguacate** (The Avocado). There's a fruit stand, but we've never found an *aguacate* for sale here. Watch the *topes*.

    0.9   151.1   K52+   Bridge over a small river bed which drains into the lagoon behind Barra de Navidad. The tall trees bordering the highway are the *primavera*. Their light white is prized for cabinetry and the springtime show of yellow flowers is spectacular.

    1.3   152.4   K50+   The paved, signed road (right) leads to **Ejido La Culebra**. Also on that road are **Isla Navidad**, the rocky point undergoing development, and **San Francisco**, the small community with a number of palapa restaurants serving Barra de Navidad via water taxis. **(See Colima Beaches.)** *The Río Cihuatlan is the border between Colima and Jalisco. It swings north, draining into the lagoon which empties into the ocean between Barra de Navidad and the peninsula of Colamilla.* In front of us is a wide valley fully planted in coconuts. It is quite a sight. Though the product from here might appear to be all coconuts, a variety of other foodstuffs are grown under the tall palms...bananas, limes, chiles, melons, squash, tomatoes, etc.

    2.8   155.2   K46   The signed entrance to **Cihuatlan**, population 25,000. There is a detour (right) around the center of town. To do business in Cihuatlan you must drive to the east end of town and come west on a one-way street. There is a full service **Pemex** just north of the bridge...It is on the right where you turn around to go back into the business section.

    1.3   156.5   K44   Enter the long bridge across the **Río Cihuatlan**, which serves as the border between **Jalisco** and **Colima**. A good sized river during the rainy season, it empties into the ocean about 10 kilometers to the north. The hills behind this area are the **Sierra Pirote**. Pirote is the name given the *huanacaxtle* tree in the southern portion of Mexico. Both names mean a fine, dark wood for cabinetry and one that is highly prized throughout Mexico.

    End of log.

DUGOUT CANOE

MEXICO 15 — TEPIC — GUADALAJARA

The road ahead, from Mexico 200 near **Tepíc** *in Nayarit and southeast to Guadalajara, Jalisco, is probably the slowest remaining section of Mexico's major highway system. The government has assigned a high priority to its improvement and there are signs of activity. But while bureaucrats plan and bulldozers push rocks and dirt around, we are all poking along inhaling the fumes of the trucks and busses as they struggle up and down this antiquated, winding road. Everyone will welcome the change...*

0.0   0.0   K35+   We begin this log at the signed turnoff east through a long valley from the K39 marker on **Mexico 200**. The new road designation is **Mexico 68-D**. Though only two-lane, it travels well with a minimum number of curves. The terrain varies only slightly as we proceed through the valley.

1.5   1.5   K33   An interchange with a road (right) leads to one of the many small towns in the hills. A few yards beyond is a small full service **Pemex**.

0.9   2.4   K31   The toll gate is upon us. Here we find clean restrooms, a small food service area and a little park with playground equipment. Continue northeast.

0.5   2.9   K30+   Cross a bridge over the railroad tracks. The jungle we have become used to during the past couple of hours has yielded to a more open savannah dotted with members of the mesquite family and a small, reddish-barked tree which looks like a member of the *papelerilla* family. As we gain altitude a few oaks appear on the hillsides.

3.7   6.6   K25   The road to **Milpias** branches off to the south. Continue east and north to begin the climb out of the valley.

4.9   11.5   K17   The turnoff north is to **San Pedro Lagunillas**. There are sizeable lakes near its northern and southern portions. The northern one is visible from the highway after about a mile. *The lakes drain into a tributary of the **Río Ameca**, which eventually forms the boundary between Nayarít and Jalisco before emptying into the Pacific.* Begin a gradual descent into a broad valley heavily planted in sugar cane. Ahead on the right is a tall mountain, the 7500-foot **Volcán Ceboruco**. The name reveals its volcanic origin, and its system of vents has spewed lava over much of the region in recent centuries.

4.4   15.9   K10   We break out of the valley in a spectacular way...go around a corner and onto a bluff overlooking a huge, deep canyon. Below are patches of sugar cane and other crops. Beyond are rows of hazy mountains. Begin a gradual descent.

1.6   17.5   K7+   The *mirador* on the right provides a panoramic view of this part of the world. *The spot carries memories...some years ago we stopped here during a hellacious lightning storm. While we ate lunch in our motorhome, Mother Nature treated us to a spectacular lightning display across the valley.* Ahead is a turnoff (right) to **Guasimas**. Continue east to Mexico 15.

3.4   20.9   K2   Ahead (right) are the spires of an old church. It looks to have been built in the 1700s. The town's name, **Chapalilla**.

1.3   22.2   K0   Intersection with Mexico 15 from **Tepíc** (left) is at **K176+**. Turn (right) toward **Guadalajara** and a full service **Pemex**. Lots of trucks stop here and the place is messy. If you have enough fuel, it can easily be picked up ahead. One of the more interesting cargos we see is several hundred chickens in boxes stacked four-high on top of a bus.

The many roadside stands in Chapalilla specialize in honey. There are at least 50 different kinds of glass and plastic containers harboring numerous shades of the stuff. Tequila bottles seem to be the most popular, with plastic 2-liter milk containers a close second. Pottery and stone *metates* for grinding corn are also featured.

2.8   25.0   K173   We've outrun the honey stands and are heading south through alternating fertile fields and cactus-laden volcanic bluffs.

2.8   27.8   K167+   A signed, paved road east to **Amado Nervo**. At least the first half kilometer into **Tetitlán** is paved. Ahead and to our right are the **Sierra El Guamúchil**.

2.5   30.3   K163+   The land changes dramatically. Lava came through here about 120 years ago and left a huge area of sterile, uplifted lava monoliths reminiscent of Hawaii's lava fields.

1.2   31.5   K161+   The signed **Parador Ceboruco** is on the left. Completed in mid-1989, it presents the volcanic activity in a nice way. There is a tower for viewing the 1869 flow, Volcán Ceboruco and the vent from which the latest flow came. The trail to the tower has been landscaped with local cactus and other plants in *a jardín botanico*. There is obvious pride in what had been done, for it is well maintained. There is no charge, but the attendant smiled broadly when we bought sodas and a bag of chips from his little stand.

Shortly after regaining Mexico 15, we pass the shell of a burned-out truck loaded with Budweiser beer. *It appears to be like a total loss...Ironically, Bud is popular among the Mexicans and they snap it up at double and treble the price of their own excellent domestic brands. Miller is also a popular label.*

3.2   34.7   K156+   A little town features pottery and wood carvings in the roadside stands. Next, a few houses off to the right with a name, **Heriberto Jara**.

2.8   37.5   K152   Enter the town of **Ahuacatlan**. Most of it is off to the side and includes a building erected in 1550 as a convent. Historically, it has provided fine saddles and wrought iron work to the region. *From Ahuacatlan, a graded road leads south about 40km to the town of **Amatlan de Cañas**. Located on the banks of the river of the same name, this sugar town has a very fine museum featuring locally found artifacts. Nearby is a thermal water resort, **Agua Caliente**. Facilities include a restaurant and small hotel. Beyond Amatlan is a network of roads leading to ranches and villages in both Nayarít and Jalisco. As the roads are little traveled, local inquiries should be made before going further.*

Lots of rocks around here, and between them, little patches of corn. Obviously the clouds have lost most of their moisture by the time they get this far inland, for the area is more nearly a desert. The rocky hillsides sport only a few cactus and mesquite.

5.3   42.8   K143+   **Mexpan**. It isn't even on our maps. The stores along the road offer an excellent selection of the leather *equipale* furniture, plus chairs made from cane and pine. The baskets are some of the most unusual and well-made we've seen...from huge work baskets with rawhide reinforcing to small, delicate doll cradles. Several stores also feature locally-made pottery at very attractive prices.

1.4   44.5   K140+   Enter the town of **Ixtlan del Río**. Most of its 15,000 residents appear to live along Mexico 15. *The area is known for its fine bírria, a meat stew made with goat or lamb. We split a bowl at one of the small "no name" stands near the center of town. Excellent. They are also reputed to make very good ice cream, furniture, wood carvings and pottery. Nothing is for sale along the highway, but a tour of the back streets should bear fruit. We've found treasures in the past on less evidence.* Continue through town and on into open country.

3.0   47.5   K136   Entrance into the **Toriles** archaeological zone. *Cross the railroad tracks and park inside the fence. The ticket office is on the left. Being the only ones in the park the ticket-taker, **Jacinto**, had time to tell us of the people who created the temples a few hundred yards beyond the entrance. He speaks no English, but his dissertation should be of interest to anyone who has a grasp of Spanish. Toriles meant obsidian in the language of the local Indians and small chips are abundant throughout the site. Amidst the ruins is the Temple of Quetzalcoatl and temples to the sun and moon. The first has a base four meters high and 24 meters in diameter, with unique windows in the form of crosses. Artifacts gathered from here are housed in a museum in Tepíc and include clay bowls, figurines and stone objects. Jacinto showed us small pieces of clay monos of human figures he and his staff had found within the past few days. The patterns on the shards are well defined and* *recognizable.*

1.9   49.4   K133   There are many small settlements or ranches along here. The greater fertility of the soil is evident in the increased numbers and quality of the corn fields. Even the cactus looks healthier. *The mountains both north and south of Mexico 15 are full of tiny villages and ranchos. Many go back several hundred years and are serviced only by dirt roads and airstrips. Much of the handcraft found in such towns as Mexpan comes from areas like this.* Proceed east past a livestock and agricultural inspection station.

2.7   52.1   K128+   The signed community of **Ranchos de Arriba** is on the right. Continue eastward, then angle north as we climb toward a pass.

3.5   55.6   K123   We reach the summit and Nayarit's border with the state of Jalisco. Begin descending and winding toward the bottom of the canyon. *The trucks and busses climbing toward us create a hazard of sorts, for their slow speed encourages other drivers to try and get around at each perceived opportunity. We always drive with our lights on under these conditions.*

4.4   60.0   K116   A look over at the trucks, busses and cars crawling up the other side of the arroyo shows what we are in for. This will become a common sight over the next 40 miles. *The mountain ranges are at the heart of the program to create a new highway to bypass this portion of Mexico 15. Not only is there danger in having so much heavy traffic over a highway not designed for it, but it is very hard on the vehicles. Overheating takes its toll and there are few turnouts. A new road will make everyone happy.*

1.3   61.3   K114   The bottom of the hill...now, up the other side, topping out 2 miles, and 12 minutes later. We finally follow a less winding stretch toward the valley below and across a couple of bridges before starting the next grade.

7.7   69.0   K101+   The top of the grade, then down to **La Venta de Mochitlitic**, a well-bricked little town landscaped with cactus. Continue the ups and downs.

3.8   72.8   K95+   Top of another grade. Note the many stress lines in the rocks in the cut through the hill. There was a lot going on here millions of years ago.

4.1   76.9   K89   Signed town of **El Tequesquit**e. There is a bull ring, plus debris from a recent fiesta. A short distance beyond, a paved road (left) leads north into the mountains to a 15-letter town, **Hostotipaquillo**, 10km.

1.2   78.1   K87   La Quemada. This is definitely not a one-horse town...four of them are saddled and tethered in front of a small store. The terrain flattens out but remains rocky. There's enough for fences and corrals, and then some.

6.2   84.3   K77+   The center of the town of **Magdalena**. The cathedral with its large yellow-tiled dome is in front. The place is clean and the people well dressed. There are nearly 500 active opal mines in the region with about 4000 people working them and in related businesses. The opals from here are considered to be the best in Mexico, approachiong in quality those found in Australia and Brazil. If you are an opal fancier, a stop might be appropriate. The white flowers of the osites tree (which resemble a morning glory) have an extremely rich nectar, making the area famous for its honey. *Note: Mexico is the world's largest producer of honey.*

¡NIEVES!

As we leave town the **Restaurant Lupita** catches our eye. Clean and neat, they feature *carnes asadas*. Continue due east. Almost forgot...the **Pemex** in Magdalena has unleaded.

To the southeast is a tall, coned mountain, the top of which is often shrouded in clouds, Volcán de Tequila, 9300 feet. There is a road which goes almost to the top of the mountain to service a **microondas** station. No time to follow it up, but the trip could be a winner. A report would be appreciated.

4.4   88.7   K70+   If you have an obsidian obsession, or want a piece for a door stop, to carve an elephant, make arrowheads, etc., this is the place. The black bands of shiny rock in the cuts along the highway are obsidian. We finally find a wide spot and make the long walk back to pick up a chunk about the size of a baseball. The deposit continues for about a kilometer.

Note the gray-green color of the cultivated areas over on the other side of the valley. They are plantings of *maguey* cactus, the basic ingredient for **tequila**.

6.3   95.0   K60   We continue winding through miles of maguey cactus. Some plantings are new and the plants small...these often have corn planted between the rows. Others are in the process of being prepared for harvest. Most of the long leaves are removed in preparation for the final cutting, for it is only the heart of the plant which is of value in the making of tequila. There are some fine photo opportunities and places to pull off are relatively common.

1.1   96.1   K58₊   Enter the town of **Tequila**. The sign says 20,000 but we're told it's closer to 30,000. On the left a charro ring advertises competitions every Sunday. Here's the place to buy tequila. Everybody with a restaurant, store or roadside stand sells tequila. Many offer tastings. It is for sale in leather-covered flasks, wooden barrels, plastic jugs as large as one gallon, or plain old glass bottles. You can even bring your own. Some is labeled, much of it is not. There are several distilleries who still do it the old-fashioned way, with huge stone rollers, wood-fired steamers, copper cookers and tubing. Ask around, someone will fix you up. *Tom did it a few years ago and had such a rousing time he can't even remember where it was.*

TEQUILA...

By government decree tequila can be made from only one variety of the 400 agave species found in Mexico and it must be grown in a restricted area of the state of Jalisco and small areas of ajoining states. The name is protected by a "denomination of origin" designation and is under strict government control, similar to the way Cognac is controlled in France.

Long before the Spaniards arrived, the Indians fermented juices taken from the maguey cactus at the time when it is about to send forth the flower spike that will cause the death of the plant. (It is at this moment that the sugar content of the sap is at its highest.) After fermentation the product is called **pulque**. The Spanish added the distillation process, and a new beverage was born, **tequila**.

Today the hot, dry and rocky hills around the city of Tequila are blue with the agave cactus with the Latin name, **Agave tequiliana weberi**. At any one time there are several million plants in various stages of growth. The plant takes about ten years to mature from an onion-sized heart to one that weighs from 40 to 150 pounds at time of processing. Close-up views of the species in its various stages are found around the plaza and in the yards of some of the homes.

The hearts are picked, trimmed, cooked, shredded and the juice extracted. The sugary liquid is fermented then put through two distillation processes...the second producing 110 proof tequila. The alcohol content is then adjusted with distilled water to meet the requirements of Mexico, 84 proof and the rest of the world, 80 proof. The white tequila comes straight from the second distillation, while the gold is aged for from one to seven years in oak barrels.

Tequila is the national drink of Mexico. Drink it straight with salt and lime (in that order) or as a frosty margarita. Our margaritas are made with 1 part lime, 1.5 parts of Controy (orange liqueur) and 3 parts white tequila. Blend with lots of ice and give your car keys to a designated driver. Continue through Tequila past a full service **Pemex** and eventually back into the countryside.

4.2   100.3   K51+   To the right, a huge, walled enclosure with the name of

Rancho La Noria. Its high steel gates are closed and a guard stands outside.(???) Continue east past a railroad crossing. On the low hill ahead, spelled out in white rocks, is **Tequila Orendaín**.

    4.0 104.3   K45   Signed, **Amatitan**, this town of 10,000 has a full service **Pemex**.

If there is one signal or sign where all traffic halts in Mexico, you would expect it to be a stop sign or signal. Right? Wrong. It is at railroad crossings! And it is here that vendors seize the opportunity to get in a quick pitch for nuts, candies, fruit, homemade tamales, chicharones, potato chips or fruit juices in little plastic bags.

    5.4 109.7   K36+   **El Arenál**, another town of about 10,000, has a local **Pemex** only and appeared to have little to shout about until a serendipitous stop for lunch. *We are at the east end of Arenál about 50 yards short of where the highway widens for the bus stop. Our search for lunch ended here in front of a good-sized no-name restaurant in a brick building. Its windows are sparkling, the parking lot is crowded and most of the tables are filled. We find a table and sit down. A waitress brings the menu. The items listed are the normal fare. We opt for a half-kilo of carnitas with the usual condiments. Within a couple of minutes the food is on the table. We devour everything in sight, including a two-inch stack of handmade tortillas. The price is half what we expected. Here is the story as told by **Juan Guttierez Gonzales**, the manager...*

The restaurant is one of the enterprises of a livestock cooperative, or ejido, in El Arenál. The members grow their own pigs and make their own hams, salamis and chorizo. The cattle portion generates cheeses and meat for the restaurant and distriblution. And it's all sold here at very good prices. To find it look for the bus stop, then back to the tile-roofed brick building on the right. More clues...there's a restaurant sign, Camino Real...but that's not it. To the right of the sign is an ice machine. Find that, then walk a few steps west. There it is, Juan Guttierez Gonzales and his staff can be proud of what they have. You'll like it. Continue east up a small hill and into hundreds of acres of the grey-green maguey.

    4.1 113.8   K30   **Santa Cruz Astillero**. A small town with a bus stop. Continue east over a bridge and then up a short hill. The soil appears to be heavy on lime...bad for most crops, but the maguey likes it. After the crest we pass egg ranches and another railroad crossing.

    2.5 116.3   K26   **Crucero de Ameca**, a small town sited at the start of the four-lane portion of Mexico 15 into metropolitan Guadalajara. Continue straight, then gradually turn southeast.

    10.3 126.6   K9+   A large full service **Pemex**.

    0.9 127.5   K8   20.4 We turn (right) southwest onto the **Guadalajara Periférico** (bypass) road.

    End of log.

Guadalajara Hub Map

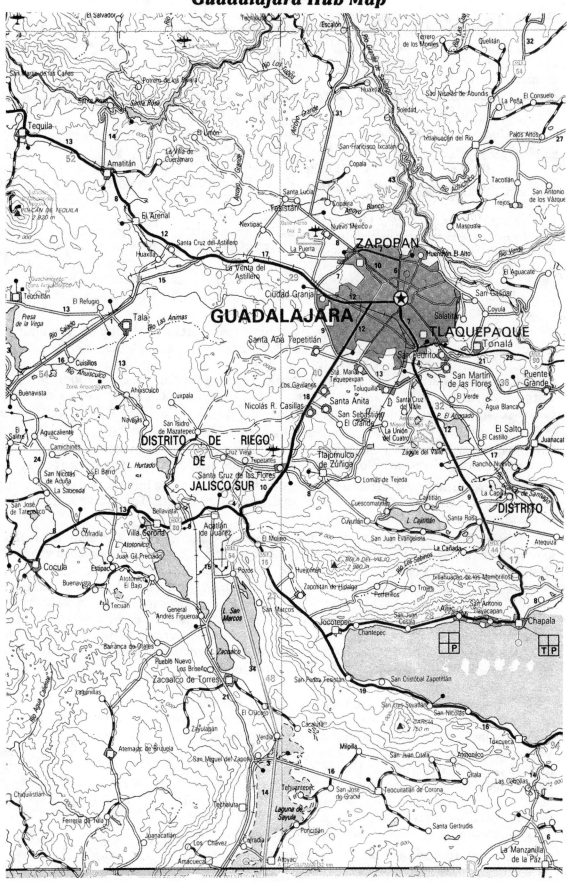

GUADALAJARA AND ENVIRONS...

Guadalajara, some might say, is a great name for a song, but it's a lot more than that to not only her five million residents but to the many visitors she entertains each year. Music, climate, business, history, the arts, architecture, furniture, pottery, glassware, shoes, clothing, food, tequila, retirement, friendship, and...because nothing is perfect, traffic jams, smog and spiralling prices.

*Here we try to outline some of what has drawn our attention over the years. As always, do not take this as a complete guide, there is a lot of material on Guadalajara and environs. (See **More Information?** at the end of the book.)*

It was not until the Spanish colonials moved north in the 1530s that the **Atemajac** valley, over which Guadalajara sprawls, had much in the way of a permanent population. Before then the region's Indians saw it as a neutral ground through which all passed without challenge. When the Spanish established a settlement there, the locals, especially the **Chimalhuacanos**, saw it as a threat and resisted. It took four tries in as many separate locations over a period of ten years before sixty European families and an appropriate garrison under the leadership of Nuño Beltrán de Gúzman became permanently established in the broad valley. The conquerors were so cruel to the Indians that Beltrán was finally expelled from New Spain.

Once established, Guadalajara grew rapidly in importance. Mining in the vicinity of **Laguna Chapala** and produce from the fertile valley made it a major center by the start of the 18th century. When the northern territories were combined to form a province, **Nuevo Galacia**, Guadalajara was selected as its capital. One of the earliest institutions of higher learning began here in 1701 as a seminary college. Today, as the **Autonomous University of Guadalajara**, it is one of the largest and most successful universities in the western world.

By 1810, Guadalajara's population had grown to 35,000, similar in size to Mexico City. Its power, too, was considerable. It would be difficult to overestimate the city's importance in not only the colonial era but during the struggles for independence.

There is much to see and do in and around Guadalajara. So much so that, after nearly 30 years of visits, we still find ourselves running out of time here. To best present our view of the city we divide it into several districts...

We center the city around the **Libertad** area, with its bullring, **Plaza de Mariachis** and huge central market with more than 2400 stalls. The Libertad is also one of the spots where you may hire a horse-drawn *calandria* carriage. For relatively little you can enjoy an evening tour of the residential streets. *Those to the north of the cathedral are particularly interesting.* On one such tour we were taken to a *carne asada* cart parked on a side street. Here we had dinner with our driver and maybe 25 other people. The *cocinero* produced beautiful plates of meat, beans, onion, tomato and tortillas at an incredible rate. He kept his two sons busy running back and forth to the house for clean dishes and supplies. When we got our plates, we did like everybody else...pick a hood or car roof, set the plate down and dug in.

If our shopping list has on it a pot scrubber, machete, party dress, furniture, onyx chess set, a big bouquet of flowers, even *peyote* (in the herb stalls), the **Libertad Market** is the place. We could also start or top off the day with a typical Yucatecan meal of *pibíl*, fried bananas and black beans from one of the hundreds of restaurants. For the shopper the experience is a fascinating one. Don't miss it. This market is indeed a world to itself. Selling native crafts and products from all over Mexico, most visitors cannot cover its 2400 stalls in a day.

MUSICA

In the **Juarez** district, the **Cathedral** presents the viewer with a half-dozen architectural styles...a result of its nearly-half-century (1571-1617) building phase under a half-dozen architects. Housed here are countless treasures from Spain and the New World. The painting of the **Assumption of the Virgin** is by the Spanish master, **Murrillo.** Fronting the Cathedral is one of the four beautiful plazas surrounding it to provide islands of benches, fountains and flowers, and each in turn are lined with historic buildings.

Another master, this time the native **José Clemente Orozco,** did the murals in the **Palacio Gobierno.** A son of Guadalajara, his home has been turned into a museum. Other buildings of note include the State Museum, only one of several worthwhile museums here; the **Degollado Theatre,** built from the same plans as Rome's La Scala Opera House, and hosting opera, ballet and theatrical groups from all over the world; the cultural center in the **Cabanas Hospicio,** a converted orphanage, contains one of Orozco's most famous murals, "Four Horsemen of the Apocalypse," on the ceiling of the chapel.

There are other churches of interest: the **Santa Monica** with its 18th century baroque stonework facade, and the **Templo de San Francisco,** completed in 1684 and with many unique exterior ornamental architectural trims.

And then there is the **Basilica of the Virgin of Zapopan** and its special story...

Located on the northern edge of the city is the suburb of **Zapopan.** Here in the basilica resides the "little one," a 450-year-old, 13-inch statue of the Virgin. A gift to the Indians from a Franciscan missionary, the **Virgin of Zapopan** is the patroness of Guadalajara and offers protection against storms and plagues.

Every year there is a great celebration when the "little one" returns home on October 12th from her yearly trek to all of the churches in the diocese. Escorting her are as many as 400,000 of the faithful, who walk, dance and ride all or part of the 16 miles between the **Cathedral** and **Zapopan.** The event inaugurates Guadalajara's month-long Octoberfest celebration, which includes artisan exhibits, charro competitions and other events.

The basilica itself is imposing, with twin towers and an interior decorated in blue and white to coordinate with the little Virgin. The tiny statue is credited with a number of miracles, one of which has to be that being made out of corn stalks and wood, she has survived for 450 years.

The **Hidalgo** district represents the upscale residential portion of central Guadalajara. But a Hidalgo address is no longer the only "in" residential area. More and more families are locating in the suburbs where there is enough room for a variety of recreational pursuits. One of these is the **Bosques de San Isidro.** Here in a nearby valley, an 18-hole golf course, tennis courts and pools are part of the country club life. There are also hot mineral springs and horse trails.

What else to do in Guadalajara? How about the zoo, an amusement park, a *charroeda* (Mexican rodeo) or soccer match...Guadalajara regularly fields some of the world's top soccer teams. Public libraries with English language departments, bridge clubs, etc., etc.

Oh yes, there is also a feminine predilection which is as well served here as anywhere in the world...shopping. You won't find the variety offered on New York's Fifth Avenue, the Via Venuto in Rome or Rodeo Drive in Beverly Hills, but there is choice and there are bargains. At times the choices are overwhelming...like the famous shoe street, **Esteban a La Torre,** where in seven blocks you can shop more than 100 shoe stores.

Guadalajara is one of those towns where tours do work. They seem to get filled up readily, away on time, and cover a variety of subjects. One tour includes the downtown cultural centers before going out to **Tonalá** and **Tlaquepaque.** Our strategy here is to bail out at the last stop, either Tonala or Tlaquepaque, look around some more and have a big late lunch. Busses or taxis bring us back to our hotel, along with all the stuff we've collected.

More things to check out, either with a rental car or guide, are the thermal water resorts southwest of the city just off the Mexico 80 highway. More thermal spring activity is found around Teuchitlan, where there is also a partially-explored archaeological zone.

WHERE TO STAY... Here in Guadalajara one would expect that every major hotel chain (cadena) in the world has built or thought of building a high-rise full of commodious rooms with central air conditioning, servibars and TVs with HBO and CNN. Among those that have done so are the **Hyatt Regency, Fiesta Americana, Holiday Inn** and **Camino Real**, each with their compliment of in-house bars, gift shops and restaurants. Some even have their own weekly Mexican Fiesta, complete with dancers. As their advertising implies...there it is easy to feel that you never left home.

The hilltop **Hotel Tapatío** is located south of the city on the way to the airport. This sports-oriented resort offers a country club atmosphere in what was once a tidy enclave surrounded by farmland...where one could smell the freshness as they walk the grounds in a silence broken only by the birds. Today the Tapatio is well within the megalopolis that Guadalajara has become. Unfortunately, between the many adjoining housing projects and the incessant traffic, much of yesterday's ambiance has evaporated. That which remains lies within the grounds, a friendly staff and good dining room.

In the downtown area of the city several hotels provide good accommodations at reasonable prices, the **Roma, Fénix** and **Aránzazu**. The historic **Hotel Frances**, just off the Plaza Liberación, is housed in a building from the early 17th century. It has been declared a national monument and oozes old world charm.

Out by the **Plaza del Sol** is another favorite, even though it is somewhat removed from the downtown area. The **Posada Guadalajara** is built around a five-story-high courtyard festooned with greenery. The guest are almost all Mexican families or business-men. The ambiance is great, and we can find our way out of town from here!

WHERE TO EAT... Over the years we've hit a lot of different eating places in and around Guadalajara. The choices are many, and come in all price ranges. The city has a reputation for restaurants serving a wide variety of ethnic cuisines. Italian and Chinese are, as expected, the most prevalent, with American-style foods close behind.

Top-quality Mexican foods came from many sources, from carts near the downtown area to Tlaquepaque's **No Name Cafe** and the very down-to-earth **Nuevo León** across from the bus depot. Here the preparation of *cabrito* (baby goat) is an artform. Another good bet, and without a big price tag, is the **Gemma** chain of *carne asada* outdoor restaurants. We found one across the street from the **Posada Guadalajara**. On avenida Mexico west of Lopez Mateos we've enjoyed excellent Italian food at **El Italiano**. They claim 25 different pizzas and pasta dishes. We particularly like the *antipasto mixto*, a combination of marinated and battered vegetables. Beer and wine are available.

Interestingly, one of the better values comes from the huge **McDonalds** near the **Plaza del Sol**..."just like home!" A double Big Mac with fries, really hit the spot after having been out of the U.S. for more than five months.

Off to Tlaqueaque and Tonala...

San Pedro Tlaquepaque is sometimes billed as the craft center of Mexico producing more folk art than any other place in the world. It is located 5 km southeast of downtown Guadalajara. In the mid-70s its tourism potential was recognized by government officials. Over a few years they renovated the inner city, turning the main street, Independencia, into a pedestrian mall. Most of the stores are located in beautiful old colonial homes, making shopping a double treat. Juarez, parallel to Independencia, also has many fine displays. The overall quality of the merchandise is excellent and the prices are generally reasonable.

Originally the town was a small center for glassblowers and artisans. Today the selections are many. You can find decorative and pre-Columbian artforms, clothes, the fanciful sculptures of **Sérgio Bustamante**, equipales and other rustic furniture, fine leather work, **Ken Edwards** pottery, table linens, woven rugs, famous red and blue glassware, brass and papier-mache animals, wood carvings, and on and on. We once spent four days here, in Tonala and Guadalajara, and bought everything needed to furnish our condominium in Barra de Navidad. Carol will never forget that shopping spree.

When the shopping energy wanes, she recommends a break under the arches in the plaza to take in a round or two of mariachi music.

A few miles beyond Tlaquepaque is another artisan center, the town of **Tonalá**. If at all possible go there on a Thursday or Sunday...these are market days when street vendors as well as shop owners offer special merchandise bargains. This has been a pottery center for centuries but today we find other arts and crafts too. The prices tend to be a little lower here, as it receives fewer visitors.

Laguna Chapala — Guadalajara's Gringo Gulch...

It is 1978, the lake laps at our feet, the sun is only a few moments from disappearing behind the mountains with a promise of pink, orange and red clouds to follow. Mariachi music comes from the restaurant next door and we wait for them to move our way. The waiter has brought a plate of tiny, crisp deep-fried fthiteish with our drinks. Nowhere on earth could we find greater peace and tranquility than here at Mexico's Laguna Chapala. In the early 70s we saw it as those who settled here saw it, those who came to write their personal chapters of the book, "Retire in Mexico on Not Much a Month."

Visually, today's Laguna Chapala is a disappointment. The level is way down due to the upstream diversion of much of the **Río Lerma**. Chapala's pier is several hundred yards from the water's edge. It is also polluted and the tiny, tasty whitefish are gone or inedible.

Despite the above, the area's near-perfect climate still attracts many retirees. It is also less than an hour from Guadalajara, Mexico's second largest city, and its excellent medical, shopping and cultural facilities. Guadalajara too has its own *norteamericano* enclave. By one estimate, 50,000 English-speaking retirees live between the two areas and there are branches of almost every service and social club you can think of...Rotary, Lions, DAR, AA (a number of 'em), Shriners, bridge, cultural and literary clubs, to name a few. Can you live there without being fluent in Spanish? Unfortunately, yes. *In a recent retirement publication, an author wrote that he had lived near Guadalajara for more than 20 years and still could not speak Spanish and neither could most of his friends!*

The *norteamericanos* have a tangible influence on the lifestyles in the north-shore towns of **Chapala**, **Ajijic** and **Jocotepec**. Their cultures mingle on the cobbled streets and in the local marketst, at the band concerts and fiestas. It is a generally happy mixture with something in it for everoyone. Each town has at least one American residential area made up of large, expensive homes, often with a tennis or yacht club nearby. They also each seem to have their share of expatriate writers and artists, thanks to the low cost of living and a ready market for much of their work. *Some call this area Guadalajara's answer to Puerto Vallarta's Gringo Gulch.)*

MAN FROM CHAPALA

There are obviously many things going for this region and most of the emigres we talk to exhibit satisfaction with their lives here. As **Mark Owens**, a retired oil company executive, said, "We are less than three hours from our children (they live near Dallas). We also have a better home and better life style than we could afford in the states." Then he smiled and said, "And the weather's perfect, particularly after Oklahoma City."

We stayed in Ajijic's *Posada de Calandria* a clean, older place with friendly guests. A small kitchen apartment with separate bedroom was rented for a few days for very little. The **La Cabana** served a good dinner to a clientele of Americans and Canadians. Questions directed to several of the old timers resulted in recommendations for the **Posada Ajijic** and the **Villa Formoso** apartments. Chapala and Ajijic both have many *gringo* restaurants, while Jocotepec seemed to be less affected.

A trailer park, the **PAL** (Parque Allen Lloyd) is located west of Ajijic on the road to Jocotopec. Clean and well organized with a heated pool, it is a popular stopping place. (There is another PAL park in southwest Guadalajara near the **Plaza del Sol** shopping center.)

What do we think of this part of Mexico? We can certainly see the advantages for many erstwhile full or part-time residents. It's definitely worth a look.

MEXICO 80 — GUADALAJARA — BARRA de NAVIDAD

*For reasons perhaps peculiar to ourselves, the city of Guadalajara presents monumental problems in logistics. We don't seem to be able to find the right one-way street to get us across town, or even into town. Most of the time we don't even know where north is, so we use public transportation and taxis. To transport ourselves in and out of this metropolis of 5,000,000, we pick a few spots we can get to, and away from, and take it from there. One such place is the **Plaza del Sol** shopping center because it is well signed and close to a favorite hotel. With our own limitations in mind, we begin our log from a known location, the Plaza del Sol.*

0.0   0.0   This log begins at the **Plaza del Sol** on Lopez Mateos Avenue (Mexico 15) and goes southwest past a variety of businesses, including several hotels catering to the Mexican businessman. Incidently, we've found this style of lodging to be both clean and inexpensive. They are in a similar category as one of our favorites, the **Posada Guadalajara**. They could be compared to motels in the United States which are relatively small and not part of a chain. You don't have to stay in a large chain hotel to have good accommodations in Guadalajara, or anywhere else in Mexico. There are also many places which offer suites at reasonable prices. If we are planning a stay of a week or more anywhere we always ask for, and usually receive, reduced rates.

2.5   2.5   Enter the *periférico* complex. Here we continue straight through the overpass following the signs calling out **Colima**. The road is four-lane, divided, and has nice feeling. Some hundreds of yards farther are signs indicating Mexico 15 and **Colima** via Mexico 54. About a mile past the *periférico*, look ahead and to the right for a distant view of some very large homes on the hills overlooking the valley. One of the names applied to the developments on the hill is **El Palomar**.

2.9   5.4   K141   We now have kilometer markers. To the right is the **San Jose del Tajo** resort and trailer park. With more than 200 spaces, it is one of the largest in the region. Its only drawback might be that it appears to be a bit out of the flight path of public transportation. A half-mile farther is the **Restaurant Los Gavilanes**. It specializes in *borrego al pastor*, a perfectly marvelous way of cooking lamb over charcoal. They also have good cuts of beef prepared in a variety of ways. Our recommendation is the *borrego*.

The "Campestre" type of restaurant is popular in this portion of Mexico. Usually with a standard array of Mexican dishes, its emphasis is often on grilled meats. They are usually well patronized, with seating for a hundred or more in an open-air format. Affordability is one of the secrets of success, for the campestre operates on volume. The atmosphere is friendly and family-oriented, the kitchens clean, and the service quick.

0.8   6.2   K139+   A full service **Pemex** is on the right. Next comes the **Club de Golf, Santa Anita**, offering golf, fine homes and condominiums in a country club atmosphere. This is popular with well-to-do locals, American and Canadian retirees. On the right is another of the series of *borrego al pastor* restaurants, **El Moro de Cumpas**. The place is clean-looking and well attended. Their charcoal pit is right there as you walk in. and we make our choice right there.

6.2   12.4   K129+   A road (right) is to **Balneario Río Escondido**, a small thermal spa. On the same corner is a full service **Pemex**. Now even the fringes of metropolitan Guadalajara are behind. Corn and other grains are on both sides.

3.4   15.8   K124   The road makes an easy turn (right) and upward toward the low mountains and out of the valley. The many corn patches on the hillsides make an interesting quilted effect with the brush, rocks, cactus and trees.

3.4 19.2 K0 We drop off the four-lane system of Highway 15 which continues straight ahead toward **Morelia** and **Mexico City**. The **Barra de Návidad** sign is hard to see, because it is right after a very sharp curve. We are now on our way to Barra via Mexico 80 and 54, and with new K markers.

2.3 21.5 K3+ Another intersection with the left branch, Mexico 54 going to **Colima**, while Barra de Návidad is to the right via Mexico 80. We go to the right.

2.5 24.0 K7+ This is sugar country. We are surrounded by fields of the tall canes while a mill across the valley belches its characteristic column of smoke. Shortly, there's a railroad crossing with its entourage of sales people...*cocos helados*, candies and sodas. There are even little dolls made from corn husks. The top entrepreneur is busy selling six-packs of beer iced down in a plastic bag along with a couple of sliced limes. It's a good "sizzle," and he's making money.

3.0 27.0 K12+ **Balneario Las Termas** hot springs is off to the right. Relatively small and with private baths it is more rustic than others ahead.

0.6 27.6 K13 The entrance (right) is into the town of **Villa Corona**. *We take a short tour of the town and note that every fourth or fifth vehicle has American license plates. No, they are not Americans wintering here, but Mexican agricultural workers home for the winter with their families. You might call them snowbirds, but with a twist. These people work most of the year harvesting all manner of fruit and vegetables. Then as the weather turns cold and the work stops they come home for the winter. The logic is there...look how many* **norteamericanos** *come to Mexico for the winter and go home for the summer.* Otherwise the town shows us little, only a dowdy church and a few small stores.

0.1 27.7 K13+ A signed road (left) leads to two several thermal water resorts including **Chimulco**. We turn south for a block or two, then west paralleling the highway. At 0.4 miles, Chimulco is on the left.

Chimulco's size is impressive. Not only does it have several large pools capable of handling many hundreds of guests, but its picnic areas cover acres. The facilities are spotless, the pools sparkling (the water is changed every day) and the thermal pools range up to 104 degrees F. There are about a hundred grassy trailer spaces with small cement pads and full hookups. There are also bungalows with kitchens. The trailerites we talked to are highly complementary about the management, the facilities and the atmosphere.

1.0 28.7 K15+ The **Agua Caliente** thermal baths have a similar setup for day guests...lots of pools, clean and organized change areas and many picnic benches. They can accommodate 30 units with full hookups. Bungalows are also available, with private pools, kitchens and bedrooms. This place has "return soon" stamped all over it.

3.9 32.6 K22 A graded road north leads past several small towns and ranches before connecting up with the so-called **Mascota** highway, Mexico 70. One of the stories going around is that the Mexico 70 route will eventually be modernized and extended to provide a more direct highway connection with Puerto Vallarta.

2.9 35.5 K26+ Top of a rise from which many acres of sugar cane stands out brightly against the more sombre hillsides and brown corn patches.

3.2 38.7 K31 We brush the northern outskirts of **Cocula**, a town dependent upon the lush sugar plantations in the valley, past a Corona beer warehouse, a hospital, a local **Pemex** and several restaurants. The hillsides sport a variety of cactus, mesquite and oaks, as the road winds westward over a low pass and out of the valley.

3.8 42.5 K37+ A small ranching community and, a half-mile farther, a signed road heads north from the *Crucero* to **Santa María**, 3km.

1.1 43.6 K39 The paved road (right) is to **San Martín Hidalgo**, 9km. Continue upward and southwest past a number of large and beautiful *higuera*s (fig trees).

The highway winds continually here and houses are around almost every corner. Watch for pedestrian traffic.

6.9   50.5   K50   Top out on a grade at **Quillilla**. A variety of buildings are scattered about in the valley ahead.

1.4   51.9   K52+   If you want to know what **Palo Alto, Jalisco** is like, take the cobbled road right. Continue up to the 5800-foot crest at El Mirador. The view is not as good there as it is a bit farther down the other side. The road then serpentines toward the valley below. Some oaks are evident, the perennial cactus and a large, shiny-leafed tree with a rough, nearly black bark. Some are fairly large, but we see no sign of their being logged, thus they are probably not good for lumber. The signed area of **Los Cuartos** goes by, then a fine view of the valley to the southwest. Mexico 80 flattens for a short time before resuming its meandering pattern through the mountains. Exercise caution for the road is narrow.

8.6   60.5   K66+   We come to the small, important town of **Ojo de Agua**. It must be important...it has a *plaza de toros*, bull ring.

Ojos to Make Your Eyes Water...

The maps of Mexico are full of place names containing the word ojo. Look it up in the dictionary and the translations include: eye, keyhole and hole. In most instances, the ojo refers to a hole in the ground from which one may take water. For instance, Ojos Negros refers to a dark water hole, and Ojo de Liebre was so named because the area was full of rabbit holes.

4.1   64.6   K73   **Tecolotlan**, a fair-sized town with a large church and a hotel. The central portion is off to the right. Graded roads to the north lead to many historical farming and ranching areas. The foothills known as the **Sierras Verdes**, particularly around **El Comalito** and **Jolapa**, lands are suited not only for corn and livestock, but marijuana and opium poppies. A trip into these and the other potential drug regions of Mexico should not be made without checking first with someone of authority...and for God's sake, go clean. A drug bust in Mexico is an automatic seven years...no questions. There's no plea-bargaining here and you'll get little help from the U.S. embassy.

Once past the town, farming again occupies most of the flat land, with *palo algodones* (cottonwoods) lining the streambeds, while cactus and mesquite dominate the hillsides.

2.7   67.3   K77+   Cross a small bridge and wind up the other side. There are a number of very large pitihaya-type cactus to the left and right. Some appear to have at least a hundred branches. In the fall the fruit is a delicacy to many of the locals. Their sweet-sour flavor is unique.

2.9   70.2   K82   A dirt road left is signed to another **Santa María**, 2km. Cross another streambed and up a grade.

1.8   72.0   K85   Top the grade, and straight into the next valley and out the other side. Plantings of corn cover the hillsides and much of the valley floor.

1.6   73.6   K87+   A paved intersection left and a short road leads to **Juchitlan**. Continue past and wind up out of the valley. A small *capilla* (chapel) is on a bluff to the right overlooking the town and the valley beyond.

2.5   76.1   K91+   We reach the top of the grade to see a small brick town, **Colotitlan**, and a lake in the valley to the west. Many small conical peaks are seen around here, sure signs of fairly recent volcanic activity...possibly within the last 20,000 years. The fences are made of rocks and the fields appear to be of marginal quality. A slightly detached western section of Colotitlan has what appears to be three ugly cement teepees. And that's what they are. During his time in office one of the presidents had thousands of them built throughout central Mexico for the storage of farm products. Gratefully, the idea never really caught on

4.9   81.2   K99+   Across a small lake is the picturesque village of **San Agustín**.

Its position near the water makes it a good camera subject.

2.2   83.4   K103   The paved road right is signed to **Talpa**. It also goes to **Ayutla** and feeds into the network of graded roads of the sierras of Jalisco. Continue southwest through the valley with little but brush and a few corn patches.

1.9   85.3   K106   We are passing a *campestre*-style restaurant, **La Hacienda**, with a state-of-the-art satellite dish perched on the roof. Here, in the middle of nowhere, could it be another sports bar? And it's crowded! The name of the wide spot in the road is **San Cayetano** (The Ramble).

4.3   89.6   K113   A few little houses and a small bridge over a streambed.

1.3   90.9   K115   We begin climbing out along the left side of the valley.

1.0   91.9   K116+   Signed intersection with a paved road north to **Union de Tula**. We can see an attractive church from the highway. Across from the local **Pemex** is a hotel, the **Brambula**. We looked at a room; it was neat and clean. The double bed would not hold two tall people, but with the price less than $6.00, we could afford two rooms! Lots of sugar cane to be seen along the valley floor.

2.6   94.5   K120+   The valley narrows as the hills close in from the north and the agriculture stops. Soon we begin winding up and out of the valley, topping out after a climb of about 500 feet.

4.8   99.3   K128+   The road continues down through a canyon. In the distance a valley with a sugar processing plant. Shortly we pass through a cut revealing vertical walls of dark red rocks. Far below is the **Río Armería** which eventually empties into the lagoon behind Manzanillo.

6.2   105.5   K138+   Intersection to the left with a paved road to **El Grullo**. If we were to follow it far enough we would pass through at least a dozen towns and skirt the **Parque Nacionál de Nevada de Colima** with its twin 14,000-foot peaks to eventually end up in **Colima**. We'd estimate the total distance to be just over 200 kilometers, and all on paved roads. **Adolfo Martinez Alvarez**, our amigo in Colima, speaks highly of the trip. Maybe next time.

1.5   107.0   K141   We pass through some dozens of large pitahaya-type cacti with their many vertical branches, then wind out of the valley and back into a larger valley with Autlan in the distance. There are many sharp turns; be careful of approaching traffic.

3.2   110.2   K146   The sign identifies the small brick town as **Mezquitan**. A couple of kilometers beyond is the signed **El Parador** restaurant, spa and pool complex. It looks very nice.

4.0   114.2   K152   Intersection. To the right is **Autlan de Navarro**, on the left is the *periférico* (bypass) signed to **Barra de Návidad**. With about 20,000 residents, Autlan has the appearances of a progressive, growing city, including a Lion's Club. Other signs are hotels, modern restaurants and a full service **Pemex** (up where the paved road goes due east to **El Grullo**). The valley is well irrigated and cane, citrus and row crops are plentiful. Follow the sign toward Barra at the next intersection.

5.5   119.7   K161   The climb out of the valley provides several opportunities to look back at the farm's lush green patches. It is obvious that there is more moisture available in this range of mountains than in those to the east.

2.5   122.2   K165   Another, even better view of the Autlan valley, followed by more views and a small turnout. We are literally climbing along the side of a cliff.

2.6   124.8   K169   We top out at a sign, **Puerto Los Mazos**, site of a small *capilla* and one building. Start down through forests of even larger trees, Tarzan vines, lots of bromeliads and a few orchids. There's no doubt about the rain here...they must average over 100 inches a year.

2.5   127.3   K173   The road is steep and winds along the southeast edge of a very

215

deep canyon. Below is the silvery ribbon of a river. Above, on the sides of the cliffs are *higueras* and all manner of huge trees, including *huanacaxtle*.

2.1 129.4 K177   A *mirador*. Here is a chance to look over hundreds of square miles of farms, mountains, rivers and cliffs. A large stand of kapok trees is growing right in front of us. Their yellow flowers are very showy and when the pods open later each will yield a handful of the cottonlike flotation and insulating material which was in such wide use before the development of man-made fibers.

2.1 131.5 K180   Continue winding down toward the long valley leading to **La Huerta**.

2.4 133.9 K184   A sign says **El Tigre**. There are no buildings, but at the curve a look to the left reveals a beautiful canyon. We turn out to take a longer look. *One could imagine all kinds of tigres living in there.*

2.6 136.5 K188   We are in downtown **El Zapotillo**. Beyond on the right is a marble factory. Huge chunks are lying about everywhere. Cut slabs are stacked along the highway. If you need a new floor, wall, counter top, or headstone this is the place to come.

1.9 138.4 K191   Paved road (left) is to **Casmiro Castillo**, 3km. We are now well into the floor of the valley amid a wide variety of vegetables, sugar cane and corn.

1.5 139.9 K193+   Paved road (right) goes northwest to **Purificación**, 23km.

3.9 143.8 K199+   Intersection (left) to **Tecomates** and another network of graded and unimproved back roads.Then comes a swampy area with hyacinths and water lilies. There is a miniature version of the tall wild palms *(cayacos)* seen closer to the coast in Jalisco and Nayarít. About 15 feet tall, they are quite attractive.

3.4 147.2 K205   A government agricultural research station is off to the right, followed by a similar one sponsored by the University of Guadalajara. There are sideroads everywhere to such places as **La Concha, Plazuela** and **El Tolote**. Continue westward toward **La Huerta** and the hills ahead.

7.2 154.4 K216+   We are now in the highway portion of **La Huerta**. The main part of town (church, plaza, market, etc.) is off to the left, or south. Up here on the highway we pass a local **Pemex**, small hotel, the **Gladys**, several restaurants and a Corona beer warehouse. There is also a small furniture factory making carved headboards, etc. It is on the right.

2.2 156.6 K220   We begin our climb out of the valley through more jungle.

1.7 158.3 K223   Start down the other side. The road winds a lot as it drops sharply toward sea level.

5.4 163.7 K231+   The signed little town of **Ejido El Rincón**. It is just mainstreaming with the world...there is a house with a *parabolica*, giving all residents around access to the troubles of the day.

6.6 170.3 K242   A first view of the ocean. Continue down toward the valley.

2.8 173.1 K246+   A sign points (left) across the arroyo to the small town of **Lázaro Cárdenas**. Just beyond is a bus stop, or *parada*, for the local residents.

1.9 175.0 K249+   The road straightens out and heads toward **Melaque/San Patricio**. We can see the ocean and beyond, **Isla Navidad** and the offshore rocks. The *primavera* trees growing along the highway put on a spectacular floral displays.

5.1 180.1 K257+   To the left, a full service **Pemex**. The road (right) is Mexico 200 from Puerto Vallarta.

0.7 180.8 K258+   Follow (left) east for **Manzanillo**. Straight ahead are **Melaque** and **San Patricio**, right is to **Bahía de Cuastecomate**. We are now on Mexico 200 heading south toward **Barra de Návidad** and Manzanillo.

End of log.

Yelapa...

If you have ever wanted to stop off on a south seas island to stay a few hours or days but don't want to put up the bucks for the 12-hour plane trip and high-roller accommodations, then you might consider Puerto Vallarta's version of a South Seas island, Yelapa. Though the days of the clunky old diesel bucket loaded with local freight and passengers are gone, it's still an adventure. Gone too are the dugout canoes and paddles have been replaced by motors, but you still take off your shoes and wade ashore.

Board the 120-foot excursion vessel, the **Princess Yelapa**, at 9:30 any morning, and we're 10 bucks and two hours away. During the trip south, **Captain Fernando Cosio** provides the passengers with a closeup view of the major PV beaches and resorts. We swing past the tiny town of **Boca de Tomatlán**, and a string of beaches...**Animas, Quimixto, Calleta** and **Majahuipa**, to name several. All have homes on them, including about 50 on Quimixto, and are all accessible only by boat.

The world of Yelapa is getting bigger by the day. With the increase in visitors...nearly 200,000 in 1988...the Yelapans no longer think of trapping a deer or handlining a giant *mero*. They are more attuned to the exchange rate, in both U.S. and Canadian dollars and the value of shrimp in the PV wholesale fish market. We run across two Aussie couples who are entranced with the "South Seas Island Adventure." They are staying for several weeks and having a "bonzer time."

The tour provides about two hours on the beach before the return trip to Puerto Vallarta. There are half a dozen restaurants vying for our pesos, with uniformly good food and reasonable prices. *We meet **Juanita**, the pie lady. She says she cooks ten pies a day and has been doing it for 20 years. Six delicious flavors: lime, pecan, banana, coconut, pineapple and apple. She puts out a tasty product, with Tom's vote going for the banana.*

Yelapa is an interesting place. No electricity during the night and the only access is by boat. Its 1500 residents are divided by the **Río Tuito**. During the rainy season the only path between the north and south sides of town is by boat. If you would like to stay a few days, the **Lagunita Yelapa** hotel has enough rooms to handle 40 or 50 people. It even has a pool. The cost is minimal and we sleep with mosquito netting securely wrapped around the bed. The hotel has a reservations office. Call 2-19-32 in PV.

Our stay in Yelapa was made easy by **Antonio (Tony) Romero,** who operates out of **Fanny's Restaurant**. He can arrange almost anything, from meals to horseback riding to boat rides and fishing. He also can also find you a house to rent for a long or short time for as little as $200 a month. Educated in Guadalajara and Arizona, Tony is a dynamo.

Yelapa is somewhat of a zoo while the tour boats are in (three of 'em). There is even a gaggle of iguanas riding around on the shoulders of kids waiting to have their picture taken with any *gringo* willing to part with a few thousand pesos. Once the boats are gone (around 2:30) everyone relaxes and does the things the tourists think they will see during their few hours on the **Island of Yelapa**. Even the iguanas go back to their cages.

217

Beaches of Cabo Corrientes...

The adventure contained in the following log is a great one, and it takes place within a short distance of one of Mexico's most popular resorts, **Puerto Vallarta**. Here in the peninsula extending west to **Cabo Corrientes** are some of the most intriguing places we've seen in a long time. If you decide to try it, be ready for a tough trip. Have a good rough-road vehicle, water and lots of time. And expect to get caught up in the sights and sounds of the beaches of Cabo Corrientes.

0.0   0.0   At K124 of Mexico 200, a half-mile south of the town of **Jose Pino Suarez**, a signed turnoff to **La Gloria** leads to a number of beaches scattered along some 50 miles of little-visited coastline. Our first surprise comes at 0.2 miles when we find a motel. Painted red, green and purple and with a large parking area, it is hard to miss. Next comes an irrigation canal. Cross it and go past cattle pastures and fields of corn and silage.

1.4   1.4   Cross another canal, this time following it on the right-hand side. The correct road is marked by its usage and surface (gray gravel). Ahead the road bears right toward the water tower and buildings of **La Gloria**.

0.5   1.9   Cross a stream and enter town. We don't see many cars or even pickups, but there are lots of saddled horses and burros. Several of the business buildings even have hitching posts. We'd guess there are enough houses for at least a thousand people...plus the ranchers. Follow straight ahead on the best-traveled road.

The action here is cattle. The natural vegetation includes some cactus, *guamúchil* and mesquite trees scattered over fairly flat plains. Altitude about 500 feet.

2.8   4.7   Another canal, then one more a couple of miles farther. Here, an elderly man assures us that we are on our way to **Mismaloya**. Our path is now carrying us in a generally northwest direction past more cattle and a few ranch houses.

5.4   10.1   Intersect with a better-graded road from the east. This likely comes in from **El Gargantillo**. We join it and go west.

2.4   12.5   Enter the town of **La Cruz de Loreto** past a pond of water lilies. We see a number of minor services directed toward the locals, and again, there are many more horses and burros than vehicles. Our California license plate is earning us a lot of waves as we go by the plaza, church and open air pool hall. Continue west and south through town.

1.2   13.7   We almost turn around. A wide pond is in front of us and, short of walking it, we can't tell how deep it is. We can see that large dual trucks have been across. but no other tracks are apparent. We back up to a wide spot and start to retrace when a pickup filled with people solves our dilemma by crossing without difficulty. Now we know. We follow and start looking for the turnoff to **Mismaloya**.

1.3   13.8   We're at a bridge over the **Río María Garcia**. On the other side we follow the trail that goes off sharply (left) along the riverbed.

The river is close-by on our left. Gradually the undergrowth yields to coco palms, mangoes and a couple of small farm plots. Ahead is the ocean.

At **2.7** miles we are in the yard of a family works on the plantations and fishes in the brackish lagoon just north of their house. With their permission, we park and check out the beach and the open cement buildings ahead.

Here we meet **Salvador**, his helper and several hundred baby turtles. Salvador is a graduate student from the state university at Guadalajara. His work has to do with the four varieties of sea turtles that come here to lay their eggs. Though it is late in the year, several hundred newly hatched **negra, careye** and **golfina** turtles were in small pens awaiting their turn to be tagged, numbered and measured. The project has been here for 14 years, and much has been learned.

Last year more than 70,000 eggs were located and transferred into large sandy beds

next to the laboratory. Here they are guarded from poachers and predators as the hatching process proceeds. The team has more than 70 kilometers of beach that they patrol on a daily basis between August and January. The species most endangered is the huge leatherback, which can weigh more than a thousand pounds. This year, Salvador expects that only about a hundred will return to these beaches to lay eggs, a far cry from the thousands of a few decades ago. Despite the problems our friend believes that progress is being made, as some of those turtles hauling themselves out of the breakers and above the tide line to lay their eggs, are ones which were checked, marked and measured by earlier teams from the University. We return to the car and a "gracias" to the family watching our vehicle. Back to the intersection.

0.0   13.8   At the intersection we turn northwest and inland. We come to a group of houses. A query confirms that we are on our way to **Peregriña** and **Ipala**. There are a number of trails which angle down toward the lagoon.

1.4   15.2   The vegetation along here might be classed as dwarfs of the tall jungle plants seen along Mexico 200 above and below Puerto Vallarta. The road is showing us more and more bad stretches. A standard car, motorhome or anything being towed would have been in trouble long before now. The little pickup is doing just fine.

3.3   18.5   A signed intersection, but it's so rusted that we can't read it. The right branch heads inland so we don't really care; we're staying on the coast. We've encountered some dozens of the large white *servieta* butterflies. The name means napkin, and is an apt description of the large floppy insects.

1.6   20.1   There are huge tuna cactus here. The top paddles are about 30 feet off the ground. Bromeliads too are plentiful...small red ones with tiny white flowers.

1.7   21.8   A well-traveled trail goes seaward at the intersection. *We follow it through sand and low brush. One of the brushy dunes is of red sand. At 1.0 miles we are on a grassy bluff with a spectacular view of a rocky point, then a beach curving to the north for several miles. It is windy, and whitecapped waves are smashing at the rocks with a vengeance. The beach is* **Playa Las Peñitas**. *Below are two tiny palapas and three divers. They gather oysters and lobster from the shore with fins, knife and spear. What they take goes into nets buoyed up by truck innertubes.*

Today is a day off because of the tide and the wind. Tomorrow, they say, will be a good one. There would be no problem with camping here. The problem would be getting in. A high clearance van or pickup with a low shell would be ideal. There is plenty of room. Be aware of the stickers growing on the "grassy bluff" mentioned above. The divers assure us that lots of fish patrol the rocks and beaches to the north and south and that casting **curicanes** *(jigs) is the way to go.* Back to the road.

0.0   21.8   Continue north past a warehouse and corral with few signs of life until we see a house to the right on a low bluff. To the left are grass and vine-covered sand dunes with the ocean just beyond. The hollows behind the dunes are full of low trees, shrubs and agaves. The agaves are about two feet high with sharp narrow leaves. They grow only in the heavy shade and show no signs of flower stalks.

1.4   23.2   Here's the tiny settlement of **Las Peñitas**. A sign says that it is **Ejido San Carlos,** but the cowboys we talked to call it Peñitas. Ahead are more beaches. This is a big area for tuna cactus.

1.5   24.7   A road branches left a few hundred yards to the beach and several nice camping spots. The drop-off is steep and the surf crashes in. The main road continues past houses scattered here and there, with more trails to the ocean before dropping into a small coconut planting.

3.7   28.4   Our poor road crosses another, even worse one. To the right is **El Realito**. Go left to the ocean?. We followed it for a short time, but it died and we were forced to back out. Continue past a pseudo-bridge and several houses with the name

Peregiña Gomez. At one of the houses something big must be going on. There are eight saddled horses tied under a tree in the front yard. Ahead we climb a low rise to overlook a beautiful lagoon populated with a variety of ducks and shorebirds.

With all of our comments one might expect to fall off the edge of the world into eternity. This is not true. This slow, single-lane, rutted trail is served by public transportation! We are looking at a full-sized bus with the name, **Transportes Costeños**, painted on the side. In white on the windshield someone has painted, **Puerto Vallarta!** It would be some kind of a trip.

*It is hard to imagine how the equipment, or the driver could handle many trips in a lifetime, much less on a daily, even weekly schedule. One of the names we've heard for these itinerant busses is **escoba** (broom), for as they creak, groan and leak their way through Mexico's back country it literally sweeps passengers up from under and behind every rock and bush.*

3.8   32.2   We enter downtown **Ipala**. Population, about 400. The residents work in the nearby fruit orchards. Again our presence draws attention among kids and adults. It was easy to ask for directions to the beach...any of several roads. Continue through town and up a gentle hill, then down to an intersection.

2.8   35.0   Intersection. The trail (left) goes up a hill and disappears into the bush. The road (right) continues up the coast. *The left track tops out at **0.2**, then drops steeply down a terrible bit of trail toward a beautifully protected small bay. As we descend we see sail boats anchored offshore and commercial pangas anchored closer in. On shore several pangas are being unloaded. We drop farther to see a few houses and a couple of palapa restaurants. We are looking at **Tehualmixtle**.*

At **0.6** miles we park the car just above the uppermost house and walk to the restaurant closest to the water. At the green wooden tables, we order beers and ask what they have today. The answer, *ostiones y huachinango* (oysters and red snapper), is perfect. An order of each, *"por favor"*.

In a moment the wheels are turning. **Candelario**, the owner walks to the shore, wades out a few feet and takes a dozen oysters from an onion sack and cleans them on the adjoining rock. The cook follows a minute later with two small red snappers. She scales them, makes the appropriate slits on the sides, rinses them in the ocean and goes back to the oil and garlic heating on the wood fire.

When we finally come up for air, the four beers, the huachinangos and the ostiones are gone, and we've spent a bit under $10.00! In January, 1990, Candelario's "gigante" lobster dinner is running $8 a person. (A note: In PV it is $24 and the lobster is smaller. It had also been boiled before it was frozen, thawed, split and grilled. A double-cooked, expensive lobster for the tourist trade.) Bad road and all, we will return. Back to the intersection and continue northwestward toward **Aquiles Serdán**, passing more west-bound trails.

1.5   36.5   We are in the town of **Maito** and several people are giving us names of places ahead, most of which are not on our maps. We pick up and continue north through a cattle guard. Two of the places mentioned are **Lopez Mateos** and **Ensenada Corrales**. The former is agricultural while the latter, and most distant, is a fishing cooperative. Only in operation a few years, our friend said that Corrales is very beautiful. We pass through a second cattle guard.

1.8   38.3   An intersection with a road coming in from the east. It goes back up to the highway at **El Tuito**. *We continue north toward **Aquiles Serdán** past **Ejido Morelos**, a farming center big on jamaica, a red flower which is used as a flavor in **aguas frescas**. Jamaica, a type of hibiscus, originally came from China. Aguas are similar to*

221

Koolaid and made in the home with sugar and a variety of flavorings. We find it very refreshing.

Two attempts to get to the beach from here ended up at gates and across a marsh from the sand. We go back and continue northwest.

We follow the trail to the southern bank of the **Río Tecolotán** *at* **3.3** *miles.* **Aquiles Serdán** *is a hundred yards away, on the other side. It is a running river with a solid sand bottom, so we cross. We are even more of an oddity here. Within seconds of our crossing the car was surrounded with young and old. Our questions are quickly answered and, after the amenities, we are on our way. After going almost a mile we reach a bluff overlooking a lagoon and miles of white sand. Part way down the hill an uncomfortably large washout looms. A check of the situation says we might need more traction to get back up through it than our little Toyota pickup can deliver, so we'll save it for another day. At* **4.1** *miles we back up, turn around and go back to the intersection into* **El Tuito.**

0.0   38.3   At the intersection we pick up two workers headed for El Tuito. With **Rogelio** and **Anselmo** as our guides, we will make no unnecessary detours. Now we go east into the **Sierra Lagunillas.**

2.6   40.9   Pass a ranch house and a corral on the left, a field of castor beans on the right, then continue a gentle climb into the foothills. As we progress the vegetation becomes more vigorous. The low trees are now taller, the vines larger. We are going up and down. The road gets better, then worse. W*e can't help thinking about that bus and how he might make this turn or ford that stream. We don't envy him.*

4.8   45.7   We climb into a little valley. Much of it has been cleared and planted in corn. A half-mile beyond are several houses and a soccer field. We are on the outskirts of **Los Conejos** (The Rabbits). As we pass through, a number of things become apparent. First, we see no power poles; second, it is a pretty big town...probably in excess of a thousand people; and third, nearly every house has a rack for storing saddles next to the front door. Again, the hitching posts are prominent. Out of town and on into the sierras.

The road winds a lot. By now we have worked our way up to about 1500 feet and much of our jungle vegetation is below us. Some, such as bromeliads and *higuera*s, are still around. We cannot get lost for there are no turnoffs. Oaks are now part of the scenery.

6.1   51.8   A cut in the road reveals bright orange-red rocks. Have never seen quite that color before. Continue through more oaks. Now we are getting occasional glimpses to the east and very tall mountains, some of which top 8000 feet.

3.1   54.9   Continue through little-changing territory until a corner is rounded, a tiny stream is crossed and past some bananas, then a couple of houses. Continue winding with change in altitude.

3.8   58.7   Fencing is showing more and more along the road, a sure sign of growth, for the wire and the posts are new. A small pile of trash was just seen along the road...indicating a town coming up. There are also a few fields of corn on the right.

1.5   60.2   Enter the west side of **El Tuito.** From the highway it seemed very small. Actually it is rather long and narrow, stretching nearly a mile along a cobbled street. We see several clean looking restaurants, the usual stores and even a *mueblería* (furniture store). Continue east toward the highway. *Incidentally, each January 7th, the town celebrates the end of the 12 days of Christmas with a parade, Indian dancers, cockfights and carnival. We also asked about the road indicated on our main map as going northwest from Tuito to the ocean at* **Chimo**. *One knew nothing about it, another said that it did go to the ocean. If anyone tries it, we'd appreciate a report.* We follow the main street to the highway.

0.9   61.1   We are back on Mexico 200 at K170.

End of log.

Chemla — Barra de Navidad Hub Map

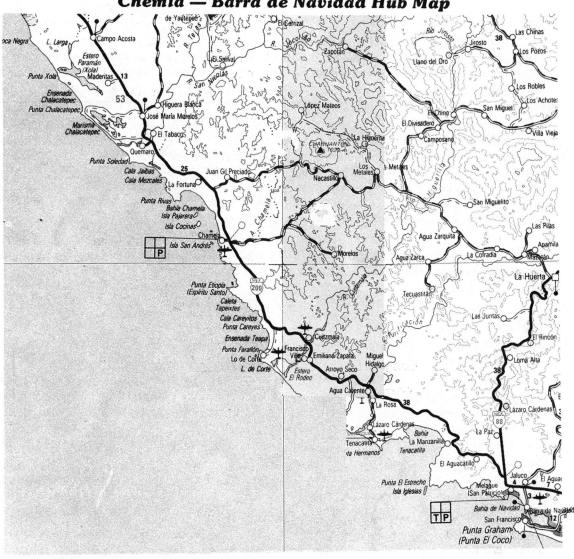

Playa Chalacatepec...

Near K88 of Mexico 200 south of Puerto Vallarta, watch for a white auto parts store with green Quaker State logos painted all over it. At this point take the road west, which goes straight over a slight rise and disappears. The target is **Playa Chalacatepec**. The road is rubbly with a number of less-used side trails. Continue past scrub, cactus, agave and cleared land used for grazing during the rains. Then come several low hills before seeing the ocean at **3.1** and dropping toward a lagoon. At **3.4** a road goes off to the left. We continue ahead past some mangos, arriving at the low dunes backing the beach at **5.5** where the road goes right, paralleling the water. There are a number of access spots, most of which are quite sandy. *Be careful, it took us an hour to dig out of one.* The short walk to the beach from any one of these spots is worthwhile. The beach is about two miles long in a graceful northwest-southeast crescent. Each end has a rocky point with broken pinnacles extending well out into the break area. We don't see many surfing angles.

The waves are not large today but the rocky point at the south end should provide some protection against heavy swells. There are several great camping spots on the point if you can negotiate a 50-meter patch of deep sand. Driftwood, some shells and piles of oyster shells are waiting for inspection. The Chalacatepec area would be an ideal place to kick back for a week or more. *And in the several places we stopped and walked to the water we saw no other footprints.* Back to the highway.

Playa Perula...

At K76 a signed dirt road goes southwest to **La Fortuna** and **Playa Perula**. This is the northern end of the large **Bahía Chamela** region. We arrive at the beach at **1.3** miles and go north past several nice homes, a number of uncompleted homes and multi-story buildings. The developers may not have finished their projects, but they did plant a lot of bougainvillas...it is everywhere.

There are several viable spots along here, the **Bungalows Playa Dorado** has quite a few rooms, some with kitchens, a pool and laundry. To the north are four or five clean-looking thatched restaurants. The **Perula Trailer Park** is at **2.2** miles. We count 15 serviceable spaces.

The beach is protected by a rocky bluff on the right and a fair-sized little offshore island. Here, behind the bluff and inside the island, birds are working and several schools of fish are breaking water. One school is made up of *sierra* mackerel while the others are from the tuna or jack families. A small boat and light spinning tackle would keep an angler busy for hours. The road comes to an end at **2.6** miles near two large private homes. Back to the highway.

Villa Polinesia...

At K72 a well-signed road goes right 0.8 miles to the **Villa Polinesia** motel and trailer park. The turnoff is marked with large brightly-colored carved tiki gods. The **El Tajaban** restaurant on the corner at the entrance road offers a variety of *antojitos* in a clean and friendly environment.

The complex is in about the center of **Bahía Chamela**. A look around reveals a 12-room motel, several dozen motorhome sites and lots of camping area. They also have little thatched lofts with foam mattresses, private toilets and showers on the beach. Much of their business appears to comes from residents of the inland portions of the states of Jalisco and Michoacan.

The place is lovely...lots of plants and trees, a beautiful beach but, from what we've heard, wonky management. The place should be filled with snowbirds, but it isn't. No matter...take a look around.

Playa Careyes...

A turnoff (right) onto a cobbled surface at K53+ brings us onto the extensive property of the Playa Careyes Company The road branches at **0.2** with the left side going to **Hotel Plaza Careyes**. Another branch (right) is signed to the Mirador restaurant and bar at **0.6**. The hotel comes into view at **1.0** miles, its ochre color standing out among the coconut palms and exotic shrubbery.

Built about 15 years ago, the hotel is a popular getaway spot with a variety of leisure activities. Should you be into it, there is even a polo field, ponies and all. Fishing, swimming, sunning and snorkeling, though, have many more devotees. The place is not cheap, and the meals even more expensive than we remembered, but it still has a lot going for it. Very nice. We return to the intersection toward **Club Med**. We follow the markers and arrive at their gate in **0.6** miles.

These two resorts share some of the most beautiful small beaches to be found in Mexico. A number of them are behind guarded gates, but the Careyes people welcome visitors as long as they think you are going to spend money at their bar, etc. The gates of Club Med do not open to casual visitors. The word *careyes* is a name for the sea turtles and the nearby beaches that hosted thousands of egglaying females each season. Today, few remain, but the resorts are making efforts to encourage their return.

If you have the time and interest, a brief run through the **Rincón de Careyes** real estate development provides a glimpse of palatial homes overlooking spectacular scenery. It is also an example of what unlimited water can do in the way of creating oases of rare and beautiful tropical plants. Back to the highway.

Arroyo Seco...

At K36 a dirt road west is signed to **Arroyo Seco**, 4km. We turn right past several papaya orchards. At **2.2** miles there's a soccer field and charro ring. **22.4** puts in the center of Arroyo Seco. In front of us is an open, shaded area or parties and meetings. At the moment there is a 15th birthday *(Quinciañera)* celebration under way. We pass the meeting hall on the right side, then bear right again past a rusty, dead tractor. After a short distance we follow the trail south along the west side of a long rocky ridge. At **3.5**, a view of a quarter-mile wide south-facing beach backed by coconut palms. The end of the road has no place to park...maybe two cars at the most, but the beach is beautiful and untouched.

We return to Arroyo Seco and take the road (left) past the other side of the meeting hall. This one goes south on the other side of the ridge mentioned above. This side is much different. There are a number of very nice houses, plus some palapa types. The beach faces south and a bit east, and from here the El Tecuán hotel is easily visible. The swells are large this day and swimming at either beach would not be recommended. Back to the highway.

El Tecuán...

At K33+ a little cement lighthouse invites us to turn right on a paved road and visit the resort center of **El Tecuán**, 10km. We've been here a number of times over the past 12 years and find it easier to return each time. The property is very large, and includes an extensive lagoon and mangrove channel ecosystem. And as it is mostly private, the lagoon has not been fished nearly to extinction. The hotel gathers its own shrimp and catches its own fish, among them the firm and tasty *robalo*, or black snook. The lagoon also attracts aquatic and shorebirds, making it a good destination for birders.

We come to the hotel at **6.2** miles, the lagoon entrance at **6.9** miles. The property includes two-plus miles of sandy Pacific beach backed with coco palms, an air strip and lots of room to camp. Water is available, but no electricity or sewer. Permission must be obtained from the hotel and if not always given...it's no reflection on the camper, but more on whether there is personnel available to police the area and collect the fees. Rarely will you find a more tranquil setting, in the hotel or on the beach. Surf fishing from the sand or the rocks at either end can be exceptional on early morning high tides.

During the rainy season many of the hotel's guests are fishermen. More specifically, *robalo* fishermen. El Tecuán has a reputation as having one of the finest snook fisheries in western Mexico. The best times are in July and August when the fresh water is coming out of the lagoon at a good clip. At this time fish weighing in excess of 20 pounds are not unusual, and monsters topping 40 have been taken here within the past five years.

The technique is relatively simple...cast lures from shore near the entrance or use live mullet around the mangroves. There is a group from Guadalajara, including several Americans, who have been coming here for 20 years. For those wishing more information and fish reports, contact the hotel at 7-0132 and ask for **Paul Siliceou**, the manager. Paul is not a fishermen, but it is in his interest to know.

Someday we see the region as an integrated retiree/resort community...all of the ingredients are there. There are properties available on the bluffs offering unparalleled ocean view opportunities. Back to the highway.

When You Run Out of Abalone...

*A shortage of abalone and conchs for ceviche and soups has prompted some Jalisco fishermen to harvest limpets found on the rocks at low tide. Little more than an inch in diameter, they have much of the flavor and texture of a young abalone. We have been eating them for years around Baja. Here they call them **gorritos**, in other parts of the coast they are known as **lapas**.*

Playa Tenactita...

At K28+ we cross the **Río Purificación** and take a signed dirt road south toward **Tenacatita**. *Aaaahhhh, Tenacatita. Here is one of those places where the beauty of the people and the ocean scenery match up well.*

There is an initial cluster of houses and a couple of businesses near the road but they have ended by **0.5** miles. The river is on the right as we pass a dirt road coming in from the left (it goes back to the highway south of where we entered) at **0.8**. Beyond is an abandoned zocalo and a crumbling kiosk. The town of **Revolcito** is at **3.6**, with a much better zocalo and meeting hall. *We attended a late-January saints day celebration here recently and were served spit-roasted pig and all the side dishes the hundred or so women in the town could put together. Music, dancing, open bar for cervezas and great conviviality.*

At the town we follow the road straight ahead into the salt flats with its mangroves and salty channels **0.4** miles beyond, we come to **Playa Tenacatita** at **5.1**.

The bay faces generally west, with the northern end hooking to face south. The offshore rocks in front of us are hard to describe, for they appear as though they might have been left over from some interplanetary movie set. We see hundreds of sharp pinnacles rising from a nearly flat sea. Around them fish break occasionally and pelicans dive for their breakfast.

A dozen or so thatched restaurants line the northern, most calm, end. The two farthest to the right, **El Puerquillo** and **El Riscál**, serve excellent seafood and quesadillas during our visits. They are also convenient to the rocks around which swim all manner of seagoing critters. The water is usually clear during the morning, clouding up with the prevailing breezes later in the day.

Camping is at the south end of the beach road, about **1.5** miles from the entry. There are a number of palapas which have rooms of a sort laid out under the thatch. We understand they can be rented. No more information than that right now.

When we have guests in this part of Mexico, Tenacatita is at the top of our list of places to visit for a kick back day. Back to the highway.

Melaque and San Patricio...

*At K258, Mexico 80 fades into oblivion in a beach town signed **Melaque**. At that* *intersection, if you turn south on Mexico 200, within a few yards there is a signed turnoff to* **San Patricio.** *Two names and one town?*

By some quirk the place acquired the two names and whatever the story, Melaque/San Patricio is another Mexican destination that is yet to become a byword north of the border. The streets and yards are more jumbled and less clean than neighboring Barra de Návidad.

Locals refer to it as Melaque, but when it comes time for the saints day for *San Patricio* (St. Patrick) everyone turns into *Santos Patricianos* from March 10-17 with dances, parades, fireworks and the wearin' of the green, Mexico style. If you are (or aren't) Irish, come join your brethren.

The town itself is not much, but it is located on a long golden crescent of sand which extends south to Barra de Návidad. At the far western end the swimming is excellent and snorkeling is good around the rocks. Facing that portion is the small **Hotel Legazpi,** a clean, rather new place with a beautiful pool. In the downtown area, the **Playa Trailer Park** is on the beach. The spaces are small, but the place is popular December through March. One block to the south the **Posada Pablo de Tarso** offers charming bungalows with kitchens (all utensils included). Another good value is the **Bungalows Mallorca,** eight blocks farther south.

Hotelwise, there are a number of moderate ones at moderate prices. One, **Coco's,** is pink, and the largest. Part of a chain offering all inclusive package accommodations, it also accepts walk-ins.

Melaque restaurant recommendations? We have none. *The several we've known have gone out of business, and why stray when we have so many good ones here in Barra. Even the Melaque people come to Barra for dinner.*

Fishermen might be interested in the fact that we've made several good catches of cabrilla, pargo and pompano around daybreak with small chrome lures cast near the rocks at the northwest end of the beach. Vary the speed of retrieve and depth until finding the right combination. Also watch for schools of cruising jacks near the sandy shoreline closer to town. Back to the highway.

Barra de Návidad...

From the moment a driver passes the maritime docks at the north end of Puerto Vallarta he is teased with a name he may not have heard before. And if he drives southwest from Guadalajara over Mexico 80, he will get the same siren message...Barra de Návidad. Even the most rudimentary knowledge of Spanish allows the driver to translate it to "Christmas Bar."

Expectations rise as the words are repeated regularly on the highway signs. They almost become a promise to a new and beautiful beach resort. "Let's stop at Barra de Návidad," becomes the password. And then the moment arrives...

The book says, "*K59 Road right (south) is to Barra de Návidad, a friendly little village with a great potential as a major resort destination.*" We make the turn and follow the road two kilometers into a quiet, cobbled village built on a spit of sand separating the ocean from a mangrove-lined lagoon. The buildings are not relics from the colonial days, nor are they modern high-rise hotels or condominiums. Instead, a surprisingly-large number of small hotels in the low to moderate price range stand elbow to elbow along a perfect sandy crescent, or scatter themselves through town. Two we've used and recommend are the **Delfín** and **Hotel Barra de Návidad.** Joining them are a number of excellent palapa-type restaurants which draw customers even from the posh Las Hadas Hotel, 20 miles to the south. The town's only 4-star hotel, the **Hotel Cabo Blanco** is located behind the town and fronts a budding marina. There are no trailer parks in Barra.

After scanning the town, most wonder why all the hype on the highway signs. It is because Barra de Návidad is well known to the Mexicans, especially those from Guadalajara. Gratefully, for the few in the know, the mainstream *norteamericano* has yet to discover the place.

Barra first showed up in a ship's log in 1535, but was not formally named until Christmas Day *(Dia de Návidad)* in 1540, thus the name. Puerto Návidad, as it was then called, was briefly involved in early expeditions to the Orient, including the 1564 departure of a fleet under the command of Adelantado Miguel López de Legazpi to conquer the Philippine Islands. With the movement of all of the Manila galleons to Acapulco late in the 16th century, Puerto Návidad faded, retaining only her position as a minor provider of coconut products and seafood to regional markets. It was not until the 1940s when electricity reached this part of Mexico, and, a few years later, when a road from Guadalajara to the coast was built, that anything began to happen. Its slow pace got a boost when Puerto Vallarta became a jet-set mecca, causing many Mexicans to seek quieter destinations.

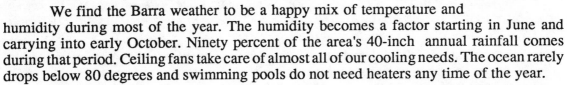

Sportfishing here is a reality as Barra boasts some of the best to be found outside of Baja. Panga fishing is the rule, with only a few cruisers available. Fish taken on a year-around basis include sailfish, dorado, tuna, blue and black marlin, wahoo and roosterfish...a big list for such a small destination. We divide our fishing time between two topflight captains, **Enrique Figueroa** and **Billy Scott**. Both may be contacted through **Rosco Scott** at the **Hotel Tropicál** or down at the sportfishing docks...ask for them by name.

We find the Barra weather to be a happy mix of temperature and humidity during most of the year. The humidity becomes a factor starting in June and carrying into early October. Ninety percent of the area's 40-inch annual rainfall comes during that period. Ceiling fans take care of almost all of our cooling needs. The ocean rarely drops below 80 degrees and swimming pools do not need heaters any time of the year.

When the word gets around, people will come from all over North America for the fishing and, like they did at Cabo San Lucas, end up returning not only for the fishing, but for the same kind of charm that Cabo had in those days. Barra reminds us of the Cabo of 20 years past.

Other daytime activities include a drive to any of a dozen isolated beaches to relax, snorkel or swim. There are restaurants on a number of them, offering the usual fare from

Mexico's abundant sea. *For suggestions see the Jalisco and Colima Beaches sections.*

Plans call for new marinas after the harbor entrance is deepened, and the first steps in that direction are already under way with an extension of the breakwater.

Our list of restaurants begins across the street from the church and behind a chain link fence where **Lupe** and her family provides some of the finest barbecued chicken anywhere. Just follow your nose. You cannot go wrong here.

On the east side of Vera Cruz street, a block back from the ocean, a charming lady opens her front door most evenings, puts a few tables out on the sidewalk and serves up some of the best pozole imaginable. Her tamales and tacos are also excellent. Her name, **Esperanza**; the name of the restaurant, there is none...just ask, or again, follow your nose. *Pozole is a marvelous mixture of hearty soup stock, hominy, mixed vegetables shredded pork, cabbage and sweet, fresh onions served with stacks of corn tortillas. One cannot go wrong at Esperanza's.*

Others to try, and we'll almost guarantee smiles as you leave, are **Pacifico** and **Nachos** on the ocean, **Bananas** and **Veleros** facing the lagoon. The **Cabo Blanco Hotel** serves the best tortilla soup we've ever eaten. A large bowl is a meal. The back-on-a-side-street **Los**

JALISCO BEACHES

Ārcos has fine breakfasts and *antojitos Mexicanos*. It is on Mazatlán a half block south of Zacatecas.

Another favorite among locals and visitors alike is **Bob Heaivilin's** restaurant. They have the best breakfasts in town and their hamburgers are unbeatable. Not normally open evenings, they announce an occasional evening special with a piece of cardboard stuck on a chair out on the sidewalk. Sometimes it is barbecued ribs, or Midwestern-style roast prime rib with horseradish, or roast pork and apple sauce, etc. The whole family is involved and the atmosphere is great. The honcho, Bob, is an expatriate electronics wizard, and whenever anything is happening in the world of sports, his *parabolica* is right on it. We watched the Super Bowl from a front-row table, drank beer and ate hamburgers.

There are also a number of restaurants across the lagoon on **Isla Colamilla** (or **Isla Návidad**). Here seafood is served as it should be served...fresh and cooked over wood fires. Access is best done by taking one of the water taxis over to the restaurant of choice. Ours is **Hermanos Figueroa.** *A note of caution...right now we feel that the pollution level inside the lagoon is too high. Thus we do not eat oysters, crabs and clams in Barra at this time.*

We can't forget **Rosita**, who has the best and cheapest tacos in town. Rosita also operates from a nameless building, though she usually has a menu out front. She is located on the corner of Sinaloa and Manzanillo streets. Walk two blocks toward the lagoon from the bank and look on the northwest corner. Not fancy, just good.

Barra is so well endowed with eating places that we can hardly go wrong anywhere. Something to keep in mind is that many are seasonal and open only from November through March.

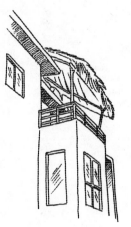

Most visitors driving along Mexico's 200 highway will go right past the paved road into Barra de Návidad, but if you like what you've read above, then make that turn for at least a look and maybe a stay.

We see this spot as having a great future if the city fathers decide to control and treat the raw sewage which flows regularly past one of the condominium areas and into the lagoon. Beside the smell, we see it as a very real health hazard. Hopefully it will clear up soon and we can once again enjoy the bounty of the beautiful lagoon.

And there's another if...

The whole area will prosper if the builders and developers will adhere to high quality standards and not leave this beautiful spot open to the blight so apparent in a number of other Mexican resorts, including **Santiago,** a few miles to the south.

BARRA CONDO

If you have thought about buying or building anywhere in Mexico, you will want to read **The Do's and Don'ts of Buying Property in Mexico,** in the back of the book.

You may wonder why we have allocated so much to space to Barra de Návidad...

We've been coming here since 1978 and, if you haven't already guessed, we own property here, a small penthouse condominium with a palapa-shaded terrace overlooking **Laguna de Návidad**. It is furnished with the flavors of Mexico and we spend as much time here as possible.

We have our own name for Barra de Návidad...**Home**.

Back to the highway.

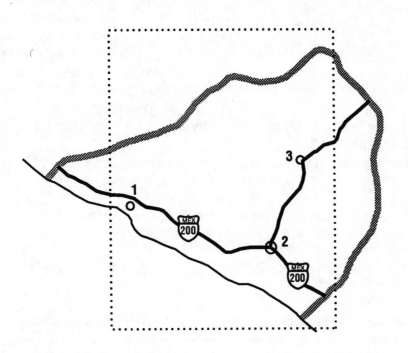

COLIMA

1. Manzanillo
2. Tecoman
3. Colima

COLIMA...

THE STATE

Halfway down Mexico's Pacific Coast lies Mexico's fourth smallest state, **Colima**. Its shape is roughly that of a triangle, with its base the Pacific Ocean and the upper and lower legs bordering **Jalisco** and **Michoacan** respectively. At the apex of the triangle are two 4,000 meter-plus, often-snowcapped, volcanic cones.

Within the triangle are tranquil isolated beaches, world class resorts, vast plantings of bananas, limes and coconuts, wild jungles and tropical lagoons. It also holds villages almost untouched by the centuries and a city, Manzanillo, striving to become Mexico's largest and most modern Pacific port. The weather is also diverse, from hot humid conditions along the coast to cool, sometimes freezing, temperatures in the high, inland valleys.

Thus far the oldest human settlement in the state has been found at Capacha northeast of Colima, and dates back 3,500 years. Other early relics found at Cihuatlán go back about 2,500 years.

A 100-acre site near Colima, El Chanal contains a number of palaces and pyramids with stones etched with shapes of animals and gods. The carvings are of particular interest, as they are very similar to ones found in the pre-colombian sites around Mexico City. El Chanal itself is an oddity, for the sites on the opposite sides of the river differ markedly in architecture and sculpture. There are also burial sites with underground shafts and tunnels. Found nowhere else in Mexico, they are similar to ones in South America.

The Colima Indians who lived around Manzanillo left artifacts which appear to have an oriental flavor, and some archaeologists believe they may have come in contact with Chinese traders as early as the 12th century.

The Spanish arrived in 1523 to make Colima the third Spanish city in New Spain. Its first mayor, a nephew of Cortéz, spent much of his time looking for the land of the Amazons, its beautiful women and hoards of gold and pearls he felt were nearby. Later, when Cortéz arrived, he ordered small ships to be built to continue the search into the Pacific. The caravels were built where Manzanillo is today.

The emergence of modern-day Colima did not start until the turn of the century, when a railroad was hammered through the rugged Sierra Madre Occidental to connect Colima with the rest of Mexico.

What was once a quiet corner of Mexico has become a tourist destination, with seaside resorts, surfing beaches and charming fishing villages. Colima, the state capital, has some colonial architecture and a number of museums. Nearby Comala is famous for its handicrafts, particularly its handcrafted furniture. In the Nevado de Colima National Park, two volcanos, the steaming Volcán de Fuego de Colima (3960 meters) and the extinct Volcán Nevado de Colima (4330 meters), can be climbed by foot, on horseback or in a 4-wheel drive. The archaeological sites of Comala, Los Ortices and El Chanal, and the fascinating new site of Tamalemapa, are all nearby.

We see Chiapas consolidating its touristic facilities over the next few years, then expanding into areas which will attract more long-term visitors, such as yachtsmen, fishermen and retirees from both the USA and Canada. It has great potential.

MEXICO 200 — BORDER TO BORDER

*From its entry into Colima at the **Río Cihuatlan** until it drops into Michoacan at another river, the **Coahuayna**, Mexico 200 wanders along estuaries and through miles of marshes, shipping and farming centers, lime trees and coco palms. Her touristic centers are concentrated around **Santiago**, with a great potential for expansion well into the 21st century.*

0.5   0.5   K43   Paved, signed road (inland) is to **Marabasco**. The land to the south and west includes low-lying marshes, swamps and tidal estuaries. It is fronted by a line of sand dunes, access to which is ahead. There are coconuts everywhere.

2.4   2.9   K39   The graded road (right) is to **La Centinela** (The Sentinel) 5km, a small coconut farming center located in an almost-swamp near the lagoon. The signed community of **Chavarín** is next with most of the activities centered around coconuts and bananas. We see a small church and not much else.

0.8   3.7   K37+   The **Playa de Oro International Airport** is signed off to the right. It is a pretentious-sounding name for a so-so airport serving the **Manzanillo-Barra de Návidad** region. The name comes from a defunct resort development just to the south of the airport. *The airport serves not only international and domestic airlines but one of the world's largest fleets of mosquitos.*

2.1   5.8   K34   The small signed community of **Emiliano Zapata** followed immediately by **La Cienega** (The Swamp). *The yellow, buttercup-like flowers seen growing along the road here and many places in Mexico, adorn one of the most vicious puncture weeds to be found anywhere. The seed capsules penetrate tennis shoes, thong sandals and bicycle tires with impunity. Around our Baja home we destroy them at every opportunity.*

2.0   7.8   K31   The cobbled road west is signed to **Playa de Oro**, 7km. *The road goes up into the hills, topping out with a view of the ocean at 1.2 miles. We reach the beach at 3.5, then turn northwest paralleling the water past several houses and a number of derelict buildings at 4.2. Continuing behind the dunes takes us past a number of camping areas and finally the airport fence at 5.8. The beach is beautiful, with lots of driftwood, but has a steep drop-off and is not recommended for swimming. The occasional big storm which hits the area would surely threaten almost anything built here.* Return to the highway. There are numerous kapok trees on the hillsides. Their cottony "wads" show up well, as do the large pods and the yellow flowers. The white flowering *osote* tree, or *palo blanco* is also prominent.

1.6   9.4   K28   **Ojo de Agua**. We continue winding through small hills, climbing, then descending.

1.6   20.8   K25+   A microondas station, **Cerro de Toros** is off to the right.

0.7   21.5   K24   Road (right) is to **Peña Blanca** (White Cliff or Rock). Here there's a gate and it's usually open, but we haven't explored.

2.3   23.8   K21   Near the center of **El Naranjo**, a road toward the beach is signed to **Vida del Mar**. *At 0.8 miles the road turns sharply left while a dirt road goes straight ahead. Follow the paving. The hills off to the right are well populated with the tall wild palm (coyucos), providing a green contrast to the springtime brown of the hills. At 1.5 miles, the lagoon appears off to the left. A few hundred yards beyond is the entrance into **Puerto Juluapan** (right), a hillside development overlooking the ocean, with some truly spectacular homes and vistas. A half-hour spent looking around there is time well spent. We continue straight along the side of a mangrove-lined lagoon.*

*The road (right) at 2.3 miles goes to **Le Recíf** restaurant and a condominium complex above. The restaurant is sited on a rock pinnacle overlooking the ocean. From our table we can watch the tropical fish move in and out of the rocks, while outside the larger waves boil on offshore pinnacles. Three visits to the place have left us unimpressed with the food...good, though overpriced...but in love with the views. A compromise is a drink and a plate of*

232

guacamole. Back to the intersection and off on the other (left) branch.

The sign says **Barefoot,** *and next to it is a smaller one,* **Paraiso Montemar.** *The cobbled road continues along the lagoon, then winds up the hill following the signs to reach the hotel at 3.1 miles. The place is well landscaped, with the buildings containing the rooms artfully inserted into the margins of the nearly vertical cliffs overlooking the ocean. We discover the reason for the two signs...the place is no longer officially the Barefoot, but the Paraiso Montemar. There are 52 rooms and suites, a beautiful pool and a restaurant/bar overlooking the ocean, the pinnacles, tropical fish and the Le Recif. What else can you say, its a find...didn't get time to try the food, but the prices are moderate.*

There are several roads leading to clifftop vistas and lagoonside lounging spots. Most are dirt and of interest only to the most curious. Back to the highway.

0.8   14.6   K19+   On the left, the intersection of a yet-to-be-completed highway bypassing the beach area and going toward Colima. A few hundred yards ahead is the prestigious **Club Santiago** golf course.

0.8   15.4   K18+   A large sign on an even larger stucco wall welcomes us into Club Santiago. *Once past the guard gate we go along the golf course. Here in an area roughly 3/4 by 2 miles, are a thousand or more homes, condominium units and a few condo-hotels. The development is one of the best laid-out we've ever seen. Most houses have lawns, gardens and pools, and all are well maintained. The owners come from all over Mexico, the United States and Canada.*

The beach, **Playa Miramar,** *is calm during the winter months, with high waves more likely during the summer storm season. The beaches are clean and open to the public. Guests are asked to observe parking restrictions and to use the designated beach access paths. At the far west end are several palapa restaurants, plenty of parking and the sea at its calmest. Accommodations are available through several of the condo-hotels near the center of the village. There is no camping or overnighting.* Back to the highway.

NET FISHERMEN

0.4   15.8   K18   We reach the ocean and a long sandy beach. *This is a good spot to watch the beach fishermen work their long nets on this westernmost section of* **Olas Altas** *beach. We've seen it several times, usually early in the morning. Using a small-mesh net up to 200 meters long and a small boat, they disperse the net in a rough semicircle out from the beach.*

When both ends are well attached to at least a dozen willing pullers, the net is retrieved with the catch inside. Once the last bit is above the waterline the fish are removed and distributed among the helpers. If you've been to an **Hawaiian hukilau,** *you will understand and appreciate the operation.*

The beach is fronted by palapa restaurants and several buildings in disrepair. *Hurricanes exact a terrible toll on buildings, particularly those not designed to take the punishment. Unfortunately, this is the story along much of Mexico's tropical west coast. It is also something to keep in mind should you consider buying into a timeshare or condo complex. If it is located in a storm zone, check the construction as thoroughly as you can and don't hesitate to ask lots of questions of the builder and others.*

0.4   16.2   K17+   An overpass connects the blue and white **Club Maeva** complex to a private beach club and restaurant. The complex operates somewhat similar to the all-inclusive Club Med concept. Most of their clientele come from Canada.

0.7   16.9   K15+   On the left is an attractive complex built around the small rocky hill, the **Hotel Vista Playa de Oro.** They too have a beach-side clubhouse, restaurant,

Colima City – Santiago Hub Map

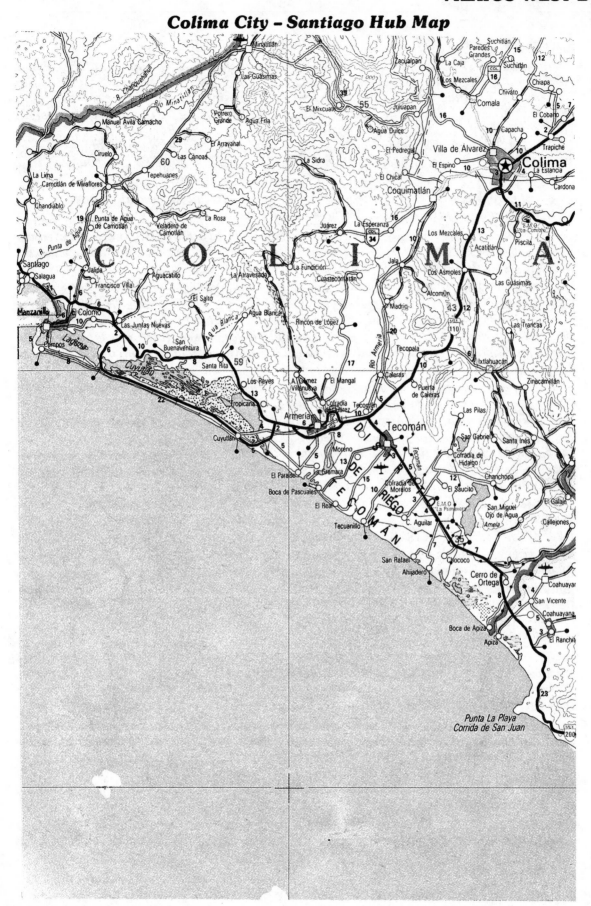

etc. We've had good reports on this one.

    0.6   17.5   K15   At this point, Mexico 200 goes inland while a small road (**Avenida Olas Altas**) continues on to parallel the central portion of **Olas Altas** beach. *The area is a mixture of older and nearly new buildings, but all seem to suffer from two things...they are not well maintained and we see few occupants.* A number of businesses front the highway including two nurseries, the usual auto parts stores (*refaccionarias*), restaurants, bars and a disco or two. . There are also several buildings featuring apartments or suites by the day, week or month. Some look good, others motheaten. The businesses increase as we close in on the touristic centers. There are a number of banks and a shopping center, **Plaza Santiago**.

    0.8   18.3   K13+   After crossing a small bridge, a paved road (right) signed to the beach goes past a number of decrepit condo buildings. *One look at these units illustrates why one should not make condo or apartment reservations without checking. Know what you are getting into, even if you have to spend a couple of nights in a hotel while looking around. There is always a room somewhere.* The road ends after about a mile at Olas Altas Beach and the **Hotel Santiago**. It too could use a paint brush and cleanup. Back to the highway and east past a number of businesses.

    0.5   18.8   K12+   Full service **Pemex**. The entrance to the **Las Hadas, Plaza Las Glorias** complex is just beyond. *Once past the golf course there are a variety of roads to the hotels, condominiums and private homes. Even if you do not play golf the Santiago course is worth visiting for the landscaping. A note of caution...if you go early or late, take along a good bug repellant. You may need it.*

    The gate into the Las Hadas complex ushers us into a different world. A world of comfort, conveniences and services found in few places outside of this enclave. The story began nearly 20 years ago when Bolivian tin magnate, Anteñor Patino, built the moorish-style resort. The concept immediately caught on with the jet set and the area has prospered ever since. Other luxury at luxury prices are the **Plaza Las Glorias** *overlooking the golf course, and the just-opened* **Sierra Intercontinental** *fronting the very attractive public beach,* **Playa Audencia**. *There are several other small beaches inside the Hadas complex but they are essentially private.*

    The road past Las Hadas continues to a mirador (lookout) showing the region in a most effective manner. From here you may continue around past more large homes, luxury condominiums and the Plaza Las Glorias hotel before reconnecting with the road back to Mexico 200.

    1.1   19.9   K11   This could be a positive addition for the region...a major shopping center, **Plaza Manzanillo**. It is under construction and scheduled for completion in late-1991. Just beyond, an attractive condominium project is under development, **Pacfico Azul** (Blue Pacific). The nearby **Posada del Sol** also invites attention.

    1.1   21.0   K9   The **Fiesta Mexicana** hotel is on **Playa Azul** beach. It is a well maintained older hotel and its good condition still commands top dollar for its rooms. *We recommend an ocean view room...those toward the highway tend to be noisy.* If you're into 'em, a nearby **Carlos & Charlie's Bar and Grill** will surely make your day.

    0.7   21.7   K8   Right at the K marker on the north side of the highway is a place you can easily miss, but shouldn't. **El Caporal** is a large palapa restaurant specializing in *botanas* (hors d'oeuvres). *Order a drink and they begin bringing small plates of beans, guacamole, soups, stews, ceviche, raw or pickled vegetables, etc. It seems almost endless. The more drinks you order the more "botanas" you get. By the time we work our way through a few cervezas we are so stuffed we can hardly waddle back to the car. Live music is also part of the attraction. We went in about 1:30 and by 3 the place was packed.*

    Now, to find it. El Caporal is located directly behind the **Carta Blanca** *beer distributor on the north side of the highway. The road in is narrow and jammed between two* *high walls. The vendor in the parking lot has excellent oysters, but they are expensive. He will shuck and serve them inside if you ask. Don't miss El Caporal. It is a blast.*

0.2   21.9   K7+   A *glorieta* intersection with the road straight ahead going to the **Las Brisas** peninsula and more of **Playa Azul**. *Actually a wide sandbar, it goes 1.8 miles south to form the northern arm of Manzanillo Bay. There are a number of hotels, suites, apartments and condo complexes facing a fairly well protected beach. Some appear well operated, others are lacking. Several of the better hotels along here are the pink **La Posada** and the adjoining **Las Rocas**. We retrace our route past another good one, the **Hotel Las Glorias**. Las Brisas is a bungalow area, a good place to find a spot with kitchen and beach adjoining, but we urge you to check them out personally...there are a lot of clinkers along with the goodies.*

Back to the *glorieta*. We go around one spoke to the east and end up on a viaduct over a swamp bracketing the northeast side of Manzanillo. There are all manner of dead snags with many shore and water birds in view.

1.2   23.1   K5+   The **El Palmar** trailer park is on the left. *It has lots of shade, courtesy of very high palm frond palapas and a few trees. A pool and barbecue area is also part of the scene. The only person at the park quoted the highest price we have ever heard of in Mexico. Hopefully he had his figures wrong, but if you are even thinking of staying there, get the price straight. We have overnighted in hotels for less.*

Another large, tile-roofed *campestre*-style restaurant is just ahead, and again on the north side of the highway, the **El Bigotes II**. It serves a variety of *mariscos*, and their *carne asada* comes highly recommended.

0.5   23.6   K5+   Another *glorieta*. This one takes off to **Colima** via **Minatitlan**. This route, though scenic, is 115 winding and tiring kilometers. We recommend the speedy, four-lane highway, Mexico 125, from **Tecoman** to Colima. A full service **Pemex** is at the intersection. Continue onto another viaduct past more of the **San Pedrito** lagoon (left) and the beginnings of the port on the right. *The port of Manzanillo is Mexico's largest Pacific port, and was one of the first to containerize much of its cargo. With the growing amount of imports from the Orient, and improved highway and railroad connections, this port can do nothing but grow.*

2.9   26.5   K1   A road (left) is signed to **Colima**. We begin a new set of K markers (K87) because we are now on Mexico 200D, a beautiful new toll road bordering the ocean and bypassing **Laguna Coyutlan**. The toll road reconnects with Mexico 200 and Mexico 110 (the new highway to Colima), bypassing the older, winding Mexico 200. We continue straight into **Mazanillo**.

MANZANILLO...

It would take a lot of flowery phrases, rose colored glasses and doctored photos to make the city of Manzanillo into more than what she is, the largest port and industrial center on Mexico's Pacific coast. Her downtown is crowded, jumbled and certainly hard to drive around in. Her stores are not geared to a slick, touristically-oriented lifestyle such as Puerto Vallarta, Mazatlán, etc. but they serve well the needs of her 70,000-plus inhabitants.

Manzanillo had its beginnings in 1522, only three years after Hernán Cortéz and his army of 550 men and 16 horses landed on Mexico's east coast near Vera Cruz. The name comes from the manzanillo tree, a type of palm, which grew in the area. Her importance began in the 16th century as a ship-building and provisioning center for the Manila Galleons.

The city itself is built on the hilly terminus of a narrow isthmus forming the south side of Manzanillo Bay. Its growth, landwise, is restricted by the San Pedrito swamps to the north and the large estero of Coyutlan to the south and east. The streets are narrow and most are one lane. Manhandling a motorhome through Mazanillo is an exercise in masochism.

COLIMA

The choice of fruits and vegetables in the downtown central market is good. Hardgoods which might be of interest are limited. A decorator might like to check out the shiny metal milk and cream cans, handmade baskets, tortilla presses, charcoal brazers, etc., but we don't see much here for the holiday visitors from Toronto or Wichita. Tourist goods and top-level restaurants are much easier to find in Colima's principal touristic area, Santiago.

Locals say that Manzanillo has great fiestas, especially the pre-lenten Carnival, May Day and December 12th (Virgin of Guadalupe).

We see the bottom line as...stay in Santiago, Barra de Návidad or San Patricio and give Manzanillo a visit if you find free time. We go back to the intersection and continue on Mexico 200D.

2.4   28.9   K83   Toll gate. *There are clean bathrooms just beyond the kiosk.* The road then follows the back bay past several spots designated as bird sanctuaries and over a bridge. Smoke stacks from the power plant are off to the right.

2.6   31.5   K79   A road on the right comes in from the road through the back streets of Manzanillo and past the power plant. It is not recommended. Continue south behind the dunes.

0.8   32.3   K78   An attempt at a beach resort, the **Villa Marina**.

2.0   34.3   K75   We are between the railroad tracks and the ocean. There are few turns to the beach along here, and those we tried are sandy and of little value to the casual traveler or camper.

3.1   37.4   K70   The dunes are a dark gray color, thus very hot during the midday hours. Despite this, much of the area is fenced off and farmers are raising *ciruelas* (a tropical plum) and *nopales* (paddle cactus) for the young leaves, or *nopalitos*. There is no apparent water here, thus all of this stuff must survive off the summer rains and the moist sea air. There are several miles of this type of farming effort.

2.0   39.4   K62   A large coconut plantation with lime trees planted between. We have heard that this is a profitable combination, as the lime trees respond well in this mixture of sun and shade.

1.1   40.5   K60   Intersection into **Coyutlan. (See Colima Beaches.)** We then cross the railroad tracks past a number of vendors selling coconut candies and small dolls made from the husks. We now head inland and swampy ground is less seen as we move toward Tecoman. Some cactus, mesquite and *guasimas* trees now dot the land not planted to palms and limes.

We are noticing blue plastic bags around cardboard boxes secured to low tree branches. After seeing a dozen or more we decide to stop and check. They turn out to be a part of a bug collection program monitoring the northward movement of the African honey bees. Popularly known as the "killer bees," they are considered a real hazard to livestock but of little danger to humans.

Thanks to several field investigators encountered later in the trip, we learned that the African bees have over the past 20 years moved from Brazil to as far north as **Tamaulipas** *on the eastern coast of Mexico and poised to invade Texas at any time. There is little evidence that they have come much farther north than Zihuatanejo on the west coast.*

2.2   42.7   K57   We come to a **mangrove** channel and recognize two types...the narrow-leafed **red** and the larger, taller **black**. The road continues almost due east.

1.9   44.6   K54   Intersection with another road (south) to **Coyutlan. (See Colima Beaches.)** The north branch goes to Colima.

2.8   47.4   K49+   Cross the railroad tracks and pass a charro ring. Continue east on the four-lane, divided road.

1.5   48.9   K47   A paved road is signed south to **El Paraiso** and eventually back to Coyutlan. The toll gate is a hundred yards beyond the intersection. New and modern, it provides rest rooms located about 30 meters beyond the toll booths.

    1.2   50.1   K45   A few meters beyond the K marker we cross the **Río Ameria**. It has a good flow and likely runs all year. The many canals bring water to fields of coconuts, limes, sesame seed, pineapples and mangos. Coconuts are very cheap around Amería. We see lots of roadside stands selling them by the bunch, iced, dried, cooked into candies, etc. They even have a special name, *Fabrica de Cocadas* (Coconut Factory).

    *Of special note is the very refreshing drink, **tuba de coco**. Dispensed from a large gourd through a nozzle, or **tuba**, it is made from iced coconut water to which a number of other ingredients have been added. They could be beet and/or lime juice, small pieces of pineapple and/or apple, etc., but always with a topping of a handful of coarse-ground peanuts. A vendor at a railroad crossing poured our first glass. Now we look for those telltale gourds whenever we're in the state of Colima.*

    3.3   53.4   K40   Intersection. Take the right lane to stay on Mexico 200. The main road continues inland toward **Colima. (See Colima Inland.)** The street into **Tecoman** is lined with *primavera* trees.

    1.2   54.6   On the right a restaurant serves *carnitas*, Uruapan style, and a few blocks farther on the left, the popular **Motel Real.**

    0.3   54.9   A large local **Pemex** is at the signed edge of Tecoman. In mid-1990 there is no **magnasin** gasoline being sold in Tecoman. Ahead are three signed turnoffs for **Boca de Pascuale** and **El Real**. The first two are cobbled, while the third is paved and much easier. **(See Colima Beaches.)**

    Tecoman is a typical prosperous Mexican agricultural city. It has a number of small to mid-sized hotels and motels; one, the **Bugambila**, is more than adequate. There are several clean, sizeable family restaurants in the northwest part of town and a number of smaller ones around the little park in the center of town. The grists for this mill are copra, coconut oil, limes and bananas. Mangos too will come into the picture as a major industry in a few years.

    We come to a "Y" and take the left branch (bypassing much of the downtown area), then drive past a small pedestrian mall, church and lots of cobbles. By following the traffic, the one-way streets and a sign here and there, we emerge on the opposite side of town and continue southeast toward the Michoacan border.

    1.2   56.1   K267   From here the road curves rather sharply from east to southeast past a local **Pemex**, the university and an **LPG** station.

    1.4   57.5   K265   The paved road (right) is to **Tecuanillo.** *We go south past plantings of cocos, limes and bananas, then an oil factory (lime and coconut). **Rancho Los Desmontes** is a farm for langostina , or fresh water shrimp, at **5.7**, a half-mile back from the beach. There is also a restaurant, **La Granja**, on the grounds with the personable **Francisco**, as the chef. It is not really surprising to find that the critters growing in the ponds around the restaurant are his specialty. His **Langostino Diablo Especial** is a very good one. So too are the ceviche cocktails.*

    *We meet the biologist in charge of the operation, **Rafael de La Torre**. A native of Colima, he has an aquaculture degree from the University of Alabama, one of North America's top aquaculture schools. He has also visited mariculture installations in Hawaii and Japan.*

    De La Torre filled us in on the progress of the project and what he sees in the future for aquaculture in Mexico, now that new laws encourage private ownership (even by foreigners) in areas where it had been prohibited before. People in the industry forsee a many-fold expansion of current facilities and a number of major new projects very soon. As to the possibility of aquaculture replacing the highly destructive shrimp trawlers which annually rip the shallow portions of Mexico's waters...time will tell, but de La Torre did say that banks are getting more reluctant to finance shrimp boats and more open to investing in land-based shrimp farms. We see it as a ray of hope for a return of sport and food fish to the Sea of Cortéz.

*The **langostina's** growth cycle, larvae to harvest, is rapid here...only about eight months. Thus, with regular plantings there is always a fresh supply. You can eat 'em here, or take frozen packages home.*

We reach the beach at **6.2**. There are a number of nameless restaurants. We meet a young man working in one who had lived in Acapulco most of his life. We ask why he chose to come to this little town. He smiled and said that in Acapulco he was only one in a million, while in Tecuanillo, he is one in a thousand. To him, and a lot of us, it makes a difference. A road (south) leads to the estero entrance. Back to the highway, through the toll gate and on toward the Michoacan border.

1.9   59.4   K262   A bull ring, for the town of **Cofradía de Morales,** on the north side of highway. Watch for *topes*. Note the vine-like growths in several of the *primavera* trees. It is a kind of parasitic mistletoe we had not noticed before.

1.3   60.7   K260   Paved road (right) is signed to **Colonia Aguilar**. An inquiry confirmed that there is no road from Aguilar to the beach.

2.3   63.0   K256   A paved road (right) is signed to **Ahijadero** (Maker of Protegees) and **La Manzanilla**. *The road takes off southwest past pastures of sementhal cattle and on to **Valle Nuevo** at **1.5** miles. The pasture grasses in some cases are waist high to the men harvesting coconuts. At **2.6** a branch right goes to La Manzanilla, which turns out to be a coconut grove, a couple of houses and the end of a road at a canal **1.7** miles from the intersection. No beach access. Back to the turnoff and we go toward Ahijadero (**4.6** mi), a gray/black sandy beach with a sizeable private development off to the right, "No Admittance". There is a newly graded road southeast down the beach 3km to **El Chupidero** and a small restaurant. We don't see this sidetrip as offering anything to write home about. Save your time and gasoline.* Return to the highway and southwest through increasingly-large cultivated fields.

5.0   68.0   K248   This region is known as **Valle Viejo**. Thanks to a new irrigation system the area is developing rapidly into a major supply center for winter cantaloupes, watermelons, baby squash and cucumbers (*melones, sandias, calabacitas* and *pepinos*, in that order). They have about 5 months of production, Nov-Apr, then during the 5-month Jun-Oct rainy season the same land yields crops of rice and milo-maize. Shortly, we top a low rise and look down onto miles and miles of coconuts.

3.1   71.1   K243   Intersection into **Cerro de Ortega**. A packing shed is at the "Y". For a treat, stop at one of the sheds and buy a couple of *maduro* (ripe)melons. Much of the product goes to the United States and Canada.

On the right, just past the intersection, is a yet-to-be-named little *carnitas* restaurant. **Ramiro**, the owner, cook, cashier, etc. has a butcher shop in Cerro de Ortega and he has decided that a restaurant located near the intersection should be a winner. The place is well attended, though he has been open only four days. We sit down with Ramiro and eat nearly a half-kilo of those juicy bits of pork. Curious about how much it costs to open a restaurant in Mexico? Ramiro gave us an insight...

He had the building constructed from scratch. It is roughly 20 by 30 feet. The sides are brick up to about 3 feet...above, the walls are open, with vertical pieces of hardwood saplings mounted for security and decoration. The floor is packed dirt. The roof is beautiful...made from reeds, it is called a **sacate**. The entire building cost less than $1100. He has two insulated ice boxes, one provided by Pepsi, the other by Corona. All the chairs and tables...12 tables and 48 chairs are supplied free by the beer distributor. The serving table and small

RAMIRO

239

refrigerator came from home and his **cuñado** (brother-in-law) put in the wiring and 3 or 4 lamps. The kitchen equipment consists of a tank of gas for the carnitas cooker, a large galvanized wash tub.

With the cuts of pork from his own shop in town, our friend got into business for a cash outlay of under $1500 including permits and deposits. And it's a first-class operation. A good sign...Ramiro is still open two months later, and he has painted the bricks a bright blue.

1.9 73.0 K239 This is another of the regions just coming on stream as a major agricultural production center. Irrigation is spreading rapidly with the brush-covered flatlands yielding to fields of melons, peppers, tomatoes, etc.

3.2 76.2 K234 A signed, paved road southwest goes 4km to **Boca de Apiza**.

We pass the usual coconuts and limes and cross a small mangrove channel at 2.6 miles. Another hundred meters brings us to the beach. The sand is a gray color. There is a lot of driftwood, but few shells. The currents are strong, but the beach angle indicates good surfing potential with a southwest swell. Free camping is easy here...but, as always, ask permission. There are a number of spider web-like roads radiating out to the northwest at and just before reaching the beach. No facilities at this time. Back to the highway. We continue on to the bridge over the **Río Coahuayna**.

1.2 77.4 K231 We come to the middle of the bridge over the Río Coahuayna and the boundary between the states of **Michoacan** and **Colima**.

End of log.

MEXICO 110 — TECOMAN — COLIMA

To many of the expatriate residents of Colima's coastal resorts, a trip to its capital city, Colima, is looked upon in the same way a resident of a small American town might look upon a shopping trip to Chicago, New York or San Francisco.

0.0 0.0 K38 We are at the intersection of Mexico 200 and Mexico 110, the highway to **Colima**. The four-lane highway goes northeast toward the hills past coco palms, mangos and the perennial lime trees.

5.4 5.4 K29+ A box factory (left), with a bit of a twist...the boxes start as logs delivered on trucks, and it's all done here.

0.6 6.0 K28+ **Tecolapa** is off to the left. A small church is visible over the tree tops.

2.1 8.1 K25 Intersection (right) on Mexico 98 goes down into a valley. It is signed as going to **Ixtlahuaca**. We continue uphill through scrub and cuts in the hillsides showing the volcanic involvement in this part of Mexico.

4.6 12.7 K17+ We start downhill into the valley of Colima past a rock quarry.

1.6 14.3 K15 A cement plant is on the right, amid miles of sugar cane.

2.0 16.3 K12 *When we came back through here during late April, there were a number of stands selling the melons grown a few yards off the highway. The competition is fierce, but our vote went to the lady who, when we stopped, came running over with an open melon and a knife. She had a juicy, sweet piece of canteloupe in our hands almost before the car had rolled to a stop. We bought a half-dozen.*

1.1 17.4 K10 **Cascadas de Tampumacchay, Campo Turistico** is signed off to the right. The sign promises natural caves, ruins, hotel, trailer park, pools and of course, the cascadas, or waterfalls. The turnoff is just east of the **Asamoles** bus stop on paved rural road #2. *Take the signed (left) turn at 0.3 onto a narrow, paved road and follow it until it ends at 3.0 miles, then right on the dirt road. Arrive at the complex at 3.3.*

And what a surprise. There is a small, modern six-room hotel, the **Tzatza Uaman**, a restaurant, bar, and several swimming pools. The whole complex overlooks a canyon with a flowing stream and a panorama of the mountains to the west and north.

There is also a 1500 year-old **Otomí** Indian city, the ruins of which are only 2 kilometers from the hotel. The hotel itself has a fascinating collection of pieces gathered from several tombs. More items from the ruins are used in the landscaping, including hundreds of stone carvings, **tales** (flat rocks) and **metates** (mortars) for grinding corn, pigments and other materials. There are also stone stamps and other miscellaneous items. Fascinating.

The area is large and trails are everywhere. One could hike and explore here for days. Caves with good displays of stalactites, stalagmites, etc. are nearby. Tours of the ruins and caves are available. Once out of sight of the hotel...a distance of only a few hundred yards, it is easy to imagine what life was like for the people of millennia past. Today the wind is blowing and the bits of dust raised add to the feeling of having dropped into the past.

The hotel is often full during the December-January, July-August and **Semana Santa** (Easter Week) periods. The sign says trailer park and there are several spots to park a unit without hookups, but with the use of the pools, toilets and showers.

And the cascadas? They exist only during the rainy season. We will definitely come back for this one.

The address is *Cascadas de Tampumacchay, Los Ortices, Colima, Mexico. Telephone for reservations, 2-51-59.* Back to the highway and on toward Colima past hillsides of scrub and some cactus.

3.3   20.7   K5   The pueblo of **Loma de Juárez** is involved in bee keeping, cattle and coconuts.

1.1   21.8   K3   A full service **Pemex** on the right. To the left is the entrance for the local golf course. We complete the four-lane part of our trip a mile farther on, then merge into the outskirts of the city of **Colima.**

1.2   23.0   K1   Intersection with a road to **Guadalajara**, Mexico 54, branching off to the right. Restaurant **Campestre San German** is on the left just ahead, then comes a soda bottling factory.

0.5   23.5   K0   Another *glorieta*, and another road (right) to Guadalajara on Mexico 110 (a toll road), another full service **Pemex** and the **Costeño** hotel. We continue toward Colima by bearing slightly left, then past car dealerships, tire stores, etc.

1.2   24.7   Cross a long railroad overpass and to a third *glorieta* and directly into town on **Avenida Rey de Coliman.** Coliman was a **Nauahtl** king, and the state and city bear his name. Welcome to **Colima.**

End of Log.

COLIMA, THE CITY...

In mid-May, when it is hot, humid and the breezes die along Colima's coast, a drive to the state's capital city could be the ticket. Here, at nearly 2000 feet above sea level, one usually finds lower humidity for about the same temperature levels. Breezes, even strong ones, are common in the valley of Colima. We are also in a city with a number of attractions, yet it is little-visited by the foreign tourist.

The early peoples, principally the **Nahual** Indians (who became known as **Aztecs** after they moved to central Mexico), built no religious or political monuments, concentrating instead on stone carvings and the production of a wide variety of pottery utensils and figures. It is easy to spend several hours in the **Museo de Las Culturas de Occidente** (Museum of the Pre-hispanic Cultures of the West) where the quality of the work and state of preservation is noteworthy. This large collection came from nearby burial tombs dating back

241

more than 2,000 years. The Indians produced pottery depicting animals that lived in the area...parrots, scorpions, armadillos and fat little dogs. The dogs especially, called **xoloitzcuintlis**, have caught the fancy of the Colimans, so much so that a pair of dancing dogs have become the symbol for the city.

The Nahuals also contributed greatly to the information coming down through the centuries by placing clay figures performing everyday activities such as grinding corn, dancing, playing ball, etc., into the tombs. Their models of houses and other building also gave powerful insights to the lives of the people. Even everyday items such as bowls, trays, etc., were adorned with animals, fish and insects.

Although its origin in 1522, as **San Sebastián de Colima**, goes back to the earliest days of Cortéz, its position in this mountainous volcanic portion of the Sierra Madre Occidente kept the city from reaching any sort of zenith during colonial times. The city's older buildings date only back to the late 19th and early 20th centuries.

A good place to visit is the **Museo de la Mascara y la Danza** in the University of Belles Artes on Manuel Gallardo at . Here the displays are of masks, dance costumes, handicrafts and a small amount of the pre-colombian Nahual pottery. The person with all of the answers here is the operator of the gift shop, **Ernesto**. Friendly and accommodating, he made several suggestions as to other places to visit.

Another worthwhile stop is at the downtown **Casa de Artesanias Colima**, where one may purchase fine handcrafts, including excellent reproductions of the clay articles found in the tombs.

Over February 2nd, Colima holds a grand celebration (*fiesta*) in honor of the **Virgin de La Salúd.** During the nine-day celebration, there are prayers, charity raffles and street festivals wrapped around that day. A similar routine is followed over March 19th, **Saint Joseph's** day. A third is near July 4th, when **Nuestra Senora del Refugio** is honored. All three fiestas are held at the churches of the same names.

Another big time in Colima is centered on the late-October, early-November **Colima State Fair**. Featured are agricultural, livestock, commercial and industrial exhibits, a fair queen, parades, sports and cultural events. The last fiesta of the year honors the Patron Saint of Mexico, the **Virgen de Guadalupe**, on Dec. 12th.

Most of Colima's amenities are directed toward business travelers and family groups. On the zocalo, but tending to be poorly ventilated, is the **Hotel Ceballos**. We can see it as a midwinter stopover, but not in the hot time of year. A better choice is the **Maria Isabel** on Camino Real in the northeast part of the city. Another large hotel, the **Los Candiles**, is next door, but appears rundown.

A pleasant dining experience came at the **Los Naranjos**. They are recommended for Colima dishes and filet mignon. Another pleaser was an Italian restaurant named **Giovanni's Pizzaria**.

A few blocks south of the zocalo is the central market. (We always seem to end up there.) This one was small, considering the size of the city, but we did find a fine handmade knife for chopping *carne asada*.

GREGORIO, SHOESHINE BOY

We've noticed it elsewhere, but here in the streets of Colima, the practice of saving a tree, even when it is necessary to put in a street, is a popular one. When there's a need, the two co-exist by paving the road around the tree and painting the trunk white. Sometime traffic goes on both sides. We guess that the practice doesn't come so much from conservation but from an early need for shade.

Prominent on the maps of the region are the two jagged peaks, **Volcán de Fuego** and **Volcán Nevado de Colima**. The best time for viewing is early in the day. Take Mexico 54

242

toward Guadalajara, turning northwestward at the sugar mill town of **Quesería**. Follow through town and into scenery reminiscent of Hawaii's Big Island as we drive around the slopes of Volcán de Fuego with its smoking top. When it erupted in 1985, it triggered strong tremors and scattered thousand of tons of ash. An eruption in 1941 has been classed as its most devastating, while the one in 1903 brought on the collapse of 100 meters of the top of the sharply-angled cone. It is interesting to note that most of the Nevado de Colima National Park and the Volcán Nevado de Colima are in the state of Jalisco.

Once around the volcano, the road angles back to Colima through **Comala** and **Villa de Alvarez**. Both towns are reported to have excellent Sunday markets for handicrafts. Comala has a fine furniture factory and showroom on the right as you leave town on the way back to Colima.

Isla Návidad and San Francisco...

A broad paved turnoff (right) comes at K52 of Mexico 200 north of Manzanillo (The turnoff is actually in the state of Jalisco) and is signed **Ejido La Culebra** (The Snake). We go past mangos, coconuts and a large orchard of *tamarindos. A tamarindo is a thick brownish bean pod. Four to six inches long, it has a high sugar content and is eaten as candy, or added to water and ice to make a refreshing drink. The tree is fairly large and resembles a mesquite, of which it is a relative*. A river channel to the right shows evidence of erosion from recent heavy runoffs and the repairs include some channelization.

After crossing a narrow bridge over the channel we come to a dirt turnoff (left) at **2.9** miles to **Playa de Cocos**. It is a long beach, and has two names. The southeastern end is known as **Playa de Oro** and is accessed via a cobbled/dirt road at K31. Our Playa de Cocos end continues northwest to the large rock promontory of **Colimilla**.

The crashing waves and steep drop-offs of Playa de Cocos makes it dangerous for swimming, but it does offer good beachcombing for driftwood and some shells. Here, and on a number of other dirt access roads, are potential campsites. The last oceanside access is at **6.4** miles where the sand and the cliffs meet. The Colimilla is an attractive, but currently dormant, development of hilly acreage offering many spectacular views. At the rocks, the road goes (right) on block paving north to a lagoon, then left to the small fishing and restaurant community of **San Francisco** at **8.0** miles. These are the restaurants which are served by the water taxis from **Barra de Návidad**. Several serve fine seafood, with the **Hermanos Figuroa** a personal favorite. Back to the highway.

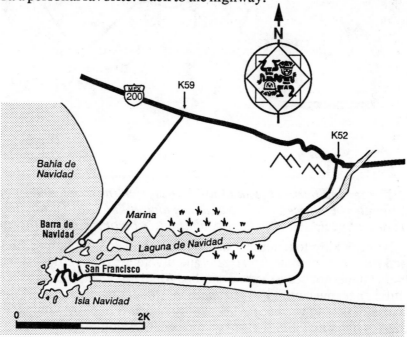

Cuyutlan and El Paraiso...

At K60 on Mexico 200D south of Manzanillo, a "Y" intersection (left) keeps us on the toll road while the straight-ahead portion is signed to **Cuyutlan.** The distance is minimal, less than a mile, but that mile brings us to the home of a natural phenomenon known the world over as the *olas verdes*, or green waves.

According to the literature, this larger-than-life phenomenon occurs between February and May when green phosphorescent waves as high as 40 feet(!) rise from the sea and roll toward Cuyutlan. One book even suggests that you rent a chair on the beach and watch the whole display.

It sounds as though Scotland's Loch Ness monster should be sharing her pedestal with Cuyutlan's *olas verdes*. And like Nessie, there is a measure of truth in the story.

In theory, abnormally large waves can result from a combination of changes in wind and current patterns offshore from Cuyutlan. Upwellings of colder, nutrient-laden water into the algae-rich surface waters can easily trigger a population explosion of algal growth, thus explaining the green color and the phosphorescent glow.

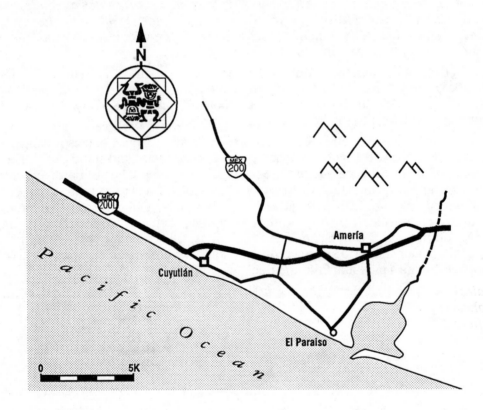

The second part of the equation comes from the moon and its effect upon the tides, plus anomalies in the ocean floor capable of amplifying a large standing wave pattern (such as from an Antarctic storm). The combination, in theory, could bring about the olas verdes.

After talking to a number of the local residents, including **Jack Shakespeare** and **Richard Baker,** expatriate Americans and inveterate olas verdes-watchers, it is reasonably certain that it has not occurred as described for at least a half-century. There may have been a few little ones, but certainly no *grandes* worth renting a chair for. The most likely reasons for the lack of the big waves are: 1) memory makes 'em bigger and; 2) the frequent offshore earthquakes have materially changed the ocean bottom.

Olas grandes aside, we see Cuyutlan as a find for those looking for a measure of isolation in a friendly, sunny beach atmosphere. But the word is getting out. In 1989 alone, the permanent American community grew by 50% when a woman from San Diego moved down and started building a home.

The town's hotels all have small rooms and most have *ventiladores de techo* (ceiling fans). They are for the Mexican weekend and holiday crowds and the prices are comparably low. The **Ceballos** is operated by a German lady, and comes highly recommended, as does her restaurant. Another nice-looking place is the **Hotel Morelos** a block back from the beach. A good buy for someone wanting to stay longer...a week, month or more are the apartments operated by Shakespeare and Baker. Write them at **Casa de Los Arcos, San Blas #140, Cuyutlan, Colima, Mexico** (phone 4-18-10 and ask for extension 118). To leave town, we can go out the way we came in, continue through town to an intersect with a signed road north to Mexico 200D, or continue past that intersection to **El Paraiso**.

We will visit Cuyutlan again soon.

PS: There really are chairs for rent. Hundreds of 'em. And umbrellas too. The real story is that the dark-gray sand gets so hot that lying on it without any air circulation underneath is akin to being in a frying pan. With the chairs you get ventilation...and a better view of the *olas verdes*.

El Paraiso is located about 10 kilometers almost due east of Cuyutlan. It has a number of palapa restaurants and beach houses in varying conditions. A few blocks to the east of the center of town is the only hotel, the **El Paraiso**. The rooms (*habitaciones*) are clean, minimally furnished and with *ventiladores* (ceiling fans). There is no hot water...not a big thing in this climate. The beach is long with heavy swells and a strong current, an uncommon occurrence during the winter, say the locals. The sand is dark, promising hot feet during midday. There is also evidence of recent summer storms having eaten at some of the beachfront properties, also not unusual on beaches facing south and west in these latitudes. Though nearly empty mid-week, the El Paraiso people say they are very busy on weekends and over the holidays.

We leave town by going north on the signed road to **Armería** and Mexico 200D.

Boca de Pascuales and El Real...

The scenery along the highway south and west to the two beaches of Boca de Pascuales and El Real pretty well sums up what Colima is about...an agricultural state with an emphasis on large plantings of coconut, lime and mango. The facilities in the two areas also reflect the fact that the people of Colima are mostly day trip beachgoers, while the many restaurants show that they really love their seafood.

0.0   0.0   We have found three signed turnoffs to **Boca de Pascuales** and **El Real** in Tecoman. The first is a short distance past the **Pemex** on the northern edge of town and is cobbled and narrow. A long block farther we find the second one, and it too is cobbled. The third is paved and a smooth **half-mile** through town to a signed east-west road. A **Conasuper** is on the corner. We turn right.

1.0   1.0   On the left is a *Plaza de Toros* (bull ring). Continue southwest toward **Boca de Pascuales**. The land is jammed with plants...principally coco palms with lime, papaya and tamarind trees planted in between. Cattle are grazing on the knee-high grasses growing among the trees.

4.1   5.1   The road makes a sharp turn to the west, then a mile later, back south. The scenery is the same...the coco trees and their leafy entourage. The blue plastic African bee traps are everywhere.

1.8   6.9   We pass a large processing area for extracting the dried coconut meats out of the split coconuts. *The white, meaty centers provide oil and a variety of other products. The husks are usually burned, often in conjunction with the making of fired* *bricks. It produces a very hot flame and is the preferred fuel for bricks in tropical Mexico. Our informant is **Idlefonso Marquez Castro**, a worker here in the plant. He, his father and grandfather were all born within "dos kilometros" (1.2 miles) of where he now works. As for his six children, only one son and a grandson live as far away as Tecoman, 10 kilometers to the north.*

EL VIEJO

0.8   7.7   *The road deadends at at the beach. We take the sandy right branch into **Boca de Pascuales (0.5 mi)**. There are a number of palapa restaurants and, as is the style in tropical Mexico, most come equipped with not only chairs and tables, a handwritten menu and lots of cold beer, but hammocks and shaded areas for the car.*

There is plenty of competition among the restauranteurs and everyone tries to outdo his neighbor in smiles and hospitality. Some of the restaurant names are...**Blanca Belin, Escondida, Balencon, El Marinero, El Jacalito, Las Palmas, Panda, Hamacas,** etc., etc. The **Larga Distancia** (long distance) telephone is located in the Hamacas, in case you want to tell someone where you are.

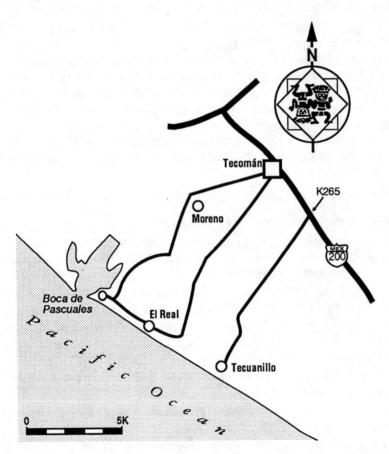

*The settlement of **Boca de Pascuales** is sited on a sandspit on the south side of the **Río Pascuales**. Behind is an estero where several pangas are beached. The point to the northwest is a favorite for surfers. The best time here for the big waves is during the hurricane season, August-November, but surfable waves are here year around, with early mornings the best. Back to the intersection.*

COLIMA BEACHES

0.0   7.7   From the intersection we head south toward **El Real**. The paved road passes just behind the dunes. Most of the property is fenced and some of the lots have houses, or better said, remnants of houses on them. The hurricanes here must be fierce. Construction techniques appear to lean toward the *keep-the-cost-down-and-I'll-rebuild-after-the-hurricane-if-I'm-still-interested* school of thought. An indication of the surf's danger to bathers is the fact that nearly every house, whether shipshape or derelict, has a pool of some sort for cooling off. Some are even under elaborate shades. Camping along here would be difficult, due to soft sand and many fences.

The beach seems well attended for a midweek morning and includes several fishermen with handlines and a *tiraya* (circular throw net). *The process begins by throwing the net into the surf for small silvery bait fish. They then bait larger hooks and cast them into the surf where fairly large members of the jack family take over by snapping them up. There are several jack cravalle, known locally as jurel, lying on the sand. Thought by some as usable only for bait because of the strong flavor and nearly-black flesh, the people here use it in surprisingly tasty soups, stews and grilled over coals after marinating the slabs in herbs and soya sauce. Other fish found are pargo blanco, a member of the snapper family, and a type of mackerel, the sierra.*

The fish are taken home and eaten or sold to the restaurants. *Where refrigeration is scarce or non-existent the fish which are not eaten immediately are usually salted and dried. Large displays of dried fish and shrimp are common sights in the central markets of the more remote towns.* Continue southeast.

2.8   10.5   The beach community of **Mascota** looms in the form of a dozen or so restaurants, the names of which all begin with the word, *Balneario*, which loosely translates to: *seaside-restaurant-where-you-can-swim-and-rest-in-a-hammock-while-your-car-sits-in-the-shade.* There are also a few houses. We return toward Tecoman via another road past many, many limes.

7.5   18.0   We're back where we started, in Tecoman.

End of log.

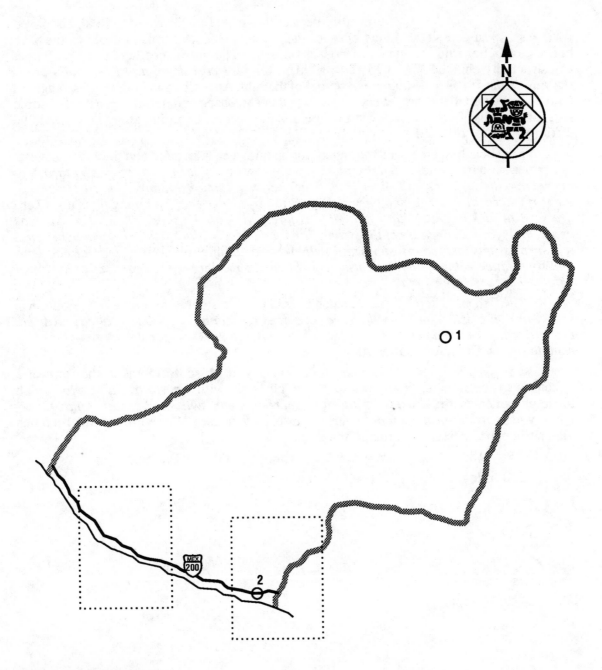

MICHOACAN

1. Morelia
2. Lázaro Cárdenas

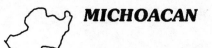
MICHOACAN
THE STATE...

Most Mexicans, when asked about **Michoacan**, will wax eloquently about this land of eternal spring, complete with descriptions of high mountains and beautiful streams, colonial cities and the people, their traditions and their hospitality.

Michoacan is a beautiful state and well worth the visit, but we aren't talking about that Michoacan. We are talking only about the 232 kilometers of Michoacan's new coastal highway connecting **Colima** with **Guerrero**. Over this distance we traverse some of the most spectacular coastline in Mexico and the many beaches along the way.

In a sense, we who go there today are the explorers, the pioneers, for there is no historical evidence of either Indian or Spanish settlements along this coast. A few may have visited, but they left no messages. We don't know what tomorrow might hold for this part of Mexico's Pacific Coast, but we hope that today's visitors can also step lightly and leave little evidence of having been there.

Mexico 200 – El Faro Hub Map

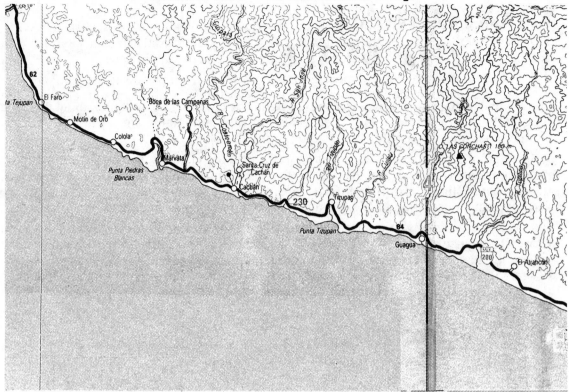

PARROTS...

From the time of the conquest until the present day, the new world's parrot family, *Psittacidae,* has fascinated bird fanciers. The appeal of parrots, macaws and parakeets lies in their beautiful colors and the ease with which they can be tamed, as well as the ability for many to imitate the human voice. The talking skills of African gray parrots is even mentioned in Greek and Roman literature. Another feature is their affection, not only for each other, but for humans.

Parrots can be traced to the Miocene Age and are thus relatively young in the bird kingdom, less than 15 million years old. Throughout the centuries, more species of parrot have been raised in captivity than any other group of birds.

In pre-Columbian Mexico, where all birds were considered magical, the parrot was valued for both its pet-like qualities and it plumage. The Aztec tribute lists included parrot feathers. Parrot plumage was used in making mosaics, shield decoration and clothing, including ceremonial robes and headdresses.

The first sight of a flock of these raucous, brilliantly-colored birds can be a memorable one. Bernal Diaz del Castillo, chronicler of the conquest, wrote, "It is enough to perturb the imagination." A legend tells of a Spanish cardinal in Puebla paying 100 gold coins for a parrot who could recite the Lord's Prayer.

The areas with the highest parrot concentrations in Mexico include Colima, Chiapas and Oaxaca. The king of the parrot family is the magnificent macaw, which lives in the rainforests of Central America and South America. The largest, nearly a meter from beak to tail, is the Scarlet Macaw. It is bright red with a long tail, rich patches of yellow, purple and blue on the wings and above the tail. Another common species is the Military Macaw. It has a green body with a red forehead and is slightly smaller than its scarlet cousin. Macaws usually travel in pairs.

In their natural habitat parrots are raucous birds which shriek, squawk or twitter, depending on their size. They develop their ability as mimics only in captivity. They can imitate a variety of sounds such as barking dogs and electric appliances.

One of the smallest and most common of the Mexican parrots is the parakeet, with some 70 varieties. In India and Australia parakeets are limited to mountainous environments and do not survive well in captivity, whereas the Mexican species do well in a variety of climatic conditions.

As pets, parrots are the most popular domestic bird. Exportation from Mexico was big business for many years until it was discovered that they might carry a viral diseases deadly to other avian groups. Though there's been some resumption of the movement of birds across borders, it is still difficult to bring any into the U.S.A. One thing lessening the availability of these beautiful animals is that their nesting habitat is being destroyed. Another thing is that man himself is taking so many of the young that few remain to reproduce. Thus a number of species are now in danger of extinction.

MEXICO 200 — BORDER TO BORDER

This log begins at K231 in the middle of the bridge over the Río Coahuayana, which serves as the border between the states of Colima and Michoacan...It is also a highway traversing a new land, for a roadbed was not punched through the rugged terrain to the south until early in the 1980s. Even today it has its problems with soil instability and heavy runoffs. Drive with caution, but try it...the scenery is worthwhile.

1.2   1.2   K229   An unmarked paved intersection. The right branch goes toward the ocean and **Apiza. (See Michoacan Beaches.)** *The inland branch goes to a number of small communities in the broad and fertile plain along the river before branching to a number of ranches and settlements in the Barranca Crustel region of the Sierra Madre del Sur, the dominant range of mountains in Michoacan's coastal region.* Our Mexico 200 continues across the flatlands of the alluvial plain toward the foothills.

3.0   4.2   K224   A local **Pemex.** Just past the station an unsigned paved intersection leads inland to **El Rancho** and **Coahuayana.** Then comes a signed bridge over the **Río El Ticiz.** We next exit the valley via a gentle, winding climb, bringing us more and more into natural vegetation and hillside cornfields. There are also examples of large primavera trees and the tall red-barked *papalillo* trees which resemble the *madrone.*

3.2   7.4   K219   Cross a bridge and up a low rise past a small red brick shrine. *A lot of energy is going into this one; the ground around is perfectly groomed and the contents are well maintained and exactly positioned.* We next see rainforest-type jungle, though not as verdant as encountered in Nayarít.

A road (right) toward the ocean into the town of Ojo de Agua, and beyond to **Playa San Telmo.** *We cross a one-lane bridge over a running stream at 0.3 and past many cocos and bananas. At 0.7, the small community of Ojo de Agua with its unfinished zocalo. We go out the other end on a dirt road to* Playa San Telmo *at 3.4 and a grouping of about a dozen ramadas, some with enough tables and chairs for a hundred or more guests.*

We are at the bottom end of a fine, gray sand beach which, with the exception of a break at Boca de Apiza, extends 80 kilometers north and west to Manzanillo. To our left a rocky headland towers a good fifty meters above the water. Perched on the cliffside a short distance above the sea is a house with a large, arched veranda. Back to the highway and small scraps of jungle in the lee of the many hills. Continue climbing and winding.

2.2   10.8   K213+   A dirt road (right) into the bush, and to the water at **Punta La Playa**. It is signed as leading to an oceanographic research station. (**See Michoacan Beaches.**)

0.8   11.6   K212   The start of a little town, **San Juan de Alima**, and the first of a number of roads to the town and the beach. The main part of San Juan also has several restaurants and what looks like two hotels, the **Parador**, and the **Hotel** hotel. The beach here is dangerous to swimmers and a number drown each year. For surfers it is a different story...

San Juan de Alima's rocky reefs help create waves to 15 feet during the August to November hurricane season, with big sets possible almost any time of the year. As a young Australian we met in a restaurant said, "It's spot-on, mate!" ("spot-on" meaning, perfect) According to **Estefan Ramirez**, shore fishing is good, though we didn't try it. The sand is gray, bordering on black where wet, and harbors fair numbers of sand crabs.

1.4   13.0   K210   There is a small *mirador* about a hundred meters ahead. *It is worth a stop for pictures if the sun and sea are right. The view to the northwest is of a rocky foreground yielding to several miles of sandy beach backed by palms. The other direction offers a forest of rock pinnacles jutting out of the sea. The early morning light silhouettes them perfectly against a silvery sea. At times of high waves, each rock sends up its own "signature" spray. On calm days the water is crystal clear. A sunset from this mirador, too, is memorable.* Yes, we have stopped here more than once. As the road goes back into the steep canyons its quality deteriorates in places, due in large part to heavy summer rains. There are a number of turnouts, more than normally found on most Mexican roads. We try and take advantage of them for hikes on the beaches below, or to gain a vantage point for photographs.

1.8   14.8   K207   There is a small white shrine with a red roof on the right. Again, a *mirador* with a superb view. We begin a descent into the valley past agaves clinging to the rocks. About *three feet in diameter, with sharp points and hairy sides to the leaves, their color is gray-green with reddish overtones. There are also a couple of small thick-trunked trees resembling the elephant trees of the Sonora deserts.*

1.2   16.0   K205   Just beyond, a fairly-well-traveled dirt road (right) goes to the water even though we are a distance into the hills. We call it **Tom's Beach. (See Michoacan Beaches.)** *In early May of 1982, Tom followed a bulldozer in a 4-WD pickup through a stretch only a few miles from one of our all-time favorite locales, **El Faro de Bucerias**. (See Michoacan Beaches.) He was among the first drive through. This part of Mexico 200 was officially opened in 1984.* A signed paved road (left) into the hills leads to **Aquila**, 15km, and a number of ranches. Another entrance onto the Aquila road is at K202.

2.3   18.3   K201   A drug check. *Several young soldiers are helping two or three civilians interrogate travelers as to destination, etc. We've been waved through twice and stopped twice during the past two years.* The road straightens out and is sided by palms and bananas.

1.3   19.6   K199   A small town, **La Placita de Morelos,** with a tiny hotel, the **Reina**, several restaurants and a way to the beach. *We enter the town and continue to the zocalo. At that point we go south a block, then west past a few homes. Next come bananas and coco palms all the way to the beach. At 0.5 miles we're in front of a thatched home/restaurant. Notice that the peak of the roof is capped with a wash tub! It isn't a good-luck talisman, or anything like that. The metal tub provides an easy way to solve the problem of how to keep the water from coming through the spot where the palm leaves come together. We never did stop a leak at the same spot in our Baja beach house.*

Javier, his wife and kids live here. They open their the restaurant on weekends and holidays only, a logical move, for this little spot is hidden

INDIAN GIRL

252

from all but the locals.

The southwest-facing beach has fine dark sand and the water is rough. Wood is everywhere and includes some of the exotic hardwoods sought by cabinet makers and wood carvers. Javier points out the safe places to swim. He said that only a few weeks ago five people lost their lives 10 miles to the north at San Juan de Alima when they became caught in the undertow.

Javier is a fisherman...he fishes the beaches in front of his house and, according to his stories, with good results. He tells of shoulder-high pargo (pargo colorado, or dog snapper), of the smaller, and tasty, pargo blanco, roaming schools of sierra mackerel and jack cravalle, and all from the surf. Lisa (mullet) are snagged for the big ones, while small silvery sardine-type school fish are netted for the pargo blanco, toro, sierra, etc. During the rainy season the catch is sweetened with the appearance of *robalo*, or black snook.

This is as Javier tells it...we will come back and confirm it someday. Camping, at least overnighting, shouldn't be a problem...check with Javier. Back to the highway.

3.8   23.4   K193   A one-car *mirador* looks back over the same beach we had seen from the *mirador* at K207. Continue south along the coast. There are a few white-flowering plumeria trees on the hillsides to the left.

3.9   27.3   K187   A signed dirt road inland to **Ostula**. In a moment we cross the **Río Ostula**.

2.6   29.9   K183   Signed road (right) is to a popular surfing spot, **Playa La Ticla**. **(See Michoacan Beaches.)**

1.5   31.4   K180+   A bridge over the **Río Ixtapilla**, a small, currently-dry wash. *The beach is a hundred yards away. The road leading in that direction goes to a locked gate, but one could easily park down by the river and walk.*

2.2   33.6   K177   A small ranch and little restaurant.

1.7   35.3   K174+   A sampling of the original forest is found here, including *huancaxtle*, *primavera* and *higuera*.

0.5   35.8   K173+   A wide, graded dirt road (right) goes to **El Faro de Bucerias**, one of our favorite beaches. It is signed going north, but unsigned going south. **(See Michoacan Beaches.)** Continue across a bridge and past more big trees.

2.8   38.6   K169   A small thatched ranch house to the right overlooks the ocean. There are several large cactus along the road and corn patches on the hillsides. Small turnouts offer views, or a chance to climb down to the beach.

1.3   39.9   K167   Road to the right is to **Motín de Oro** (Mountain of Gold). *There is no beach access due to the lagoons between us and the* ocean. *Next come* two bridges and a climb over a low crest before returning to sea level.

2.5   42.4   K163   A bridge, **Puente Ximapa**, then a tiny road (right) on the south side of the bridge which leads to a locked gate. A short distance beyond, we've a view of a long beach stretching out to the southeast. It would appear to be a fine beach for turtles. There is a small turnout to get a look, but no motor trails leading there.

2.1   44.5   K159+   A hard-to-see turnout to the beach. It angles back to the right rather sharply next to a small hill. *The beach is about a hundred yards from the highway, and would surely get considerable day use with a larger parking area.* Continue east past the beach and enter the outskirts of a group of houses signed **Colola**.

MICHOACAN COAST

1.0   45.5   K158   A signed turnoff (right) into **San Isidro.** The road goes past several houses and directly to the water. There are large gray granite boulders on the south end of the light-gray sand beach, while the main portion is fairly steep with rocky ridges showing just offshore. It then arcs off to the northwest. We see some driftwood.

1.4   46.9   K156   A turnoff toward the ocean. This beach has rocky margins with plants growing down the sides. The beaches and vistas which greet us as we continue south will be sites for fine homes someday. The road continues to wind back and forth...first along the coast, then inland to cross a bridge or two before coming back to the Pacific.

2.4   49.3   K152   A dirt road (right) angles back to a small cove. We go through *an opening in a fence, cross and recross a shallow wash and on down to the sand at 0.6. West-facing, it is maybe a hundred yards wide and well protected by high cliffs on each end little swell when compared to nearby beaches. There is some room for camping and the family living there can use the small fee charged for overnighters. Motorhomers should prerun this.* Back to the highway and continue parallel to the beach, winding gently through tall scrub and cactus.

1.3   50.6   K150   Cross the second of two bridges, then look for a turnoff (left) down and under the bridge toward the water at **Playa Marvata. (See Michoacan Beaches.)** The same turnoff also serves a road (left) into the hills to **Pomaro,** 16km. A kilometer or so beyond is a paved airstrip, then the road turns inland to cross more bridges.

3.8   54.4   K144   Signed bridge, **Paseo de Noria.** Cross and go up and out to the next small arroyo.

3.8   58.2   K133   A dirt road (right) precedes the bridge over the good-sized **Río Cachan.** *The road goes past a small number of houses, then, for us, a pig crossing. Three unattended sows and at least 25 piglets take precedence over auto traffic for several minutes. We continue to the water, arriving at **1.3** miles. The dark sand beach has lots of driftwood and several palm frond lean-tos. The water looks dangerous, in that the drop-off is sharp and currents are evident, even in this day's moderate surf conditions. There are miles of beach to explore. Conditions also appear right for dawn and dusk surf fishing. We'd recommend a full day here, overnighting if possible.*

Continue southward and inland. Note the vertical lines in the highway cuts. They are from sedimentary deposits and thus were horizontal some millions of years ago. Consider the incredible pressures required to wrinkle these miles of rocks up onto their sides.

6.3   64.5   K123   *It has taken some distance to figure out why there are not as many ocean views as we remember in years past. When we first drove this highway it was new and the bush had been cleared to facilitate construction. By 1985 it had not fully regrown, nor had it in '88. Now the underbrush is indeed vigorous and effectively blocks many of those graphic views.*

1.7   66.2   K120+   A turnout allows us to check out a line of rocks and water to the northwest. Truly beautiful. It is reminiscent of the views we've seen along Hawaii's northeast coast. The summer of 1989 was hard on this part of the road and crews are still making repairs (May 1990).

8.4   74.6   K107+   We pass a cut in the hillside revealing veins of a beautiful marble-like white stone. A turnout ahead is right across from one of the best bands.

0.6   75.2   K106+   Cross the Puente Tizupa and continue back and forth between the coast and the inland bridges.

2.0   77.2   K103   A dirt road (right) is to a kilometer-long beach of dark sand and pebbles. There is a parking area and several sombras.

3.9   81.1   K97   Cross the **Puente Cuichua.** On the south side, a road to the beach. It *is **0.9** miles on a dusty road to where we parked to check this one out. We are short by about 150 yards. The place has a sand/pebble mix with a good assortment of driftwood.*

MICHOACAN

The water is rough...at least on a large southwest swell. The April water temperature is in the 80s. Overnighting should be OK. Back to the highway.

1.4   82.5   K95   A cluster of houses and a restaurant, the **Pichilinguilillo**. Then across a small bridge and a road (right) to a small beach with a palapa on it. There are more ocean vistas as we continue south past a house here and there, coco palms and scrub.

1.9   84.4   K92   A bridge, the **Puente Aguijote**. Beyond is a mirador, or turn-out, with an excellent view.

4.0   88.4   K85+   The **Puente La Huahua** precedes the town of **La Huahua**. One of the largest we've seen for some time, it has well over a hundred buildings and access to the ocean. Overnighting should be no problem...just ask.

3.1   91.5   K81   **Puente La Manzanilla**, then a road (right) to the beach. It angles sharply back toward a group of houses, a volleyball court and at 0.3, the beach. *We are at the north end, where a cliff and a jumble of rocks make an effective barrier against northwest swells. To the left the beach extends for at least a mile. We can see lots of driftwood and the light colored sand is scored with the trails of land crabs. A panga is up on the beach. A small tienda has sodas. The white-haired lady living in the house next to the beach is all smiles when asked if permission could be obtained for camping. There is not a whole lot of room for many rigs, but those that fit will have an almost-private domain.*

Several teenagers fishing by the rocks to the right are catching jurel (jack cravalle). The system is to first catch a baitfish, which is done by casting hooks with small weights out into the school herded into the shallows by the jurel. After snagging one of the little guys, they rehook it and toss it back out. A strike is almost immediate. Then comes the tug of war. The fish landed are in the 3 to 4-pound class.

There surely is an official name for this beach, but we neglected to ask. At only 0.3 miles from the highway it's worth a visit. And if you like kids...there are a bunch of 'em here. Back to the highway.

A piece of the original Michoacan jungle is seen in the small valley off to the side.

3.6   95.1   K75   The road (right) just past the bridge accesses the riverbed only. Note the large, shallow cave on the inland side of the bridge.

4.9   100.0   K67   A somewhat obscure dirt road (right) just before the **Puente Mexiquillo**. *It goes uphill past a tiny cemetery on the left and on toward the coco palms. At 0.3 the road forks. The right one deadends at a gate and house. The left fork also goes to a house and fence, but there is a small parking area, (0.6 mi) and a path leads left past the house and fence to the ocean. A five-minute hike on the beach revealed only our footprints...nothing else was there to disturb the firewood or the many hermit and land crabs. There were several huge tree trunks of a dark and hard wood. Eventually the logs will be cut up, hauled off and sold. Much of the lumber in this region comes from the beaches.* Back to the highway. We next go past a busy coconut and papaya operation.

1.5   101.5   K64   **Puente Majahuita II** followed by **Puente Bejuco**, and just beyond, a dirt road (right) to a house.

4.7   106.2   K56   Dirt road (right) goes over a hill and down toward **Barra de Nexpa**, and a great adventure. **(See Michoacan Beaches.)**

0.2   106.4   K56   Cross the bridge over the **Río Aguililla**, which empties into the ocean at **Barra de Nexpa**. There is a huge, bright pink bougainvilla by the south end of the bridge on the right. Continue almost due east along the coast. There are scattered palm groves and an occasional driveable trail toward the water, but most appear to access the palms only.

2.4   108.8   K52   There is a way to the beach here, but through a gate. *The 200*

255

yard beach is lined with palms and bracketed by large volcanic rocks. Camping, with permission, is OK.

    0.6   109.4   K51   Cross a bridge signed **Boca de Campos** and climb toward the town of **Caleta de Campos**, population about 2000. *The place is surprisingly large considering its location on the edge of nowhere. There is a small hotel, the **Yuritzi** (private baths, fans, 24 rooms). The town is situated on a bluff and encompasses several beaches. A rather spectacular **bufadora** (blowhole) is near the point in front of the town. Unfortunately, we had time only to touch lightly on Caleta. We will try and headquarter there for a few days on another trip.*

    0.7   110.1   K50   We've left the metropolitan area of Caleta de Campos and are back to the country, and right in the middle of many yellow-flowering kapok trees. Next a road (right) leads to a paved landing strip.

    1.5   111.6   K47+   Cross the **Puente Teclan**. To the right, the beach is visible through the coco palms, a beautiful sandy beach with driftwood, rocky headlands and no apparent road. Continue along the bluff overlooking the ocean.

    0.8   112.4   K46+   There appears to be camping access on the right. As we continue east there are more beautiful spots with foot trails leading to them. Turnouts are almost nonexistent through here.

    1.6   114.0   K44   Here we have a small beach community and a restaurant, the **Paraiso Escondido.**

    1.4   115.4   K42   **Puente La Manzanilla #1**. To the right are several houses and a *panga* on a small, sandy cove. Access appears to be only by foot. We continue to get glimpses of similar little beaches. There are also several small houses on rocky points overlooking the sea, surely signs of what may be in the offing for this portion of Mexico's Pacific coast.

    0.8   116.2   K40+   A poor road goes south to a gray, sandy beach liberally studded with black volcanic spires both in and out of the water. The graphics are marvelous. A couple of days here would be a dream.

    1.4   117.6   K38+   A bridge, **Puente Mexcalhuacan**. A restaurant, **Puesta del Sol** (sunset) is nearby overlooking the beach and ocean...but it is so situated that a sunset into the Pacific is not possible. No beach access.

    0.3   117.9   K38   A restaurant, **La Flor de Costa**, is on a bluff facing southwest over the ocean. A *cerveza* and *mariscos* stop here is mandatory for a number of reasons.

*Let's start with **Vicente**, a young fisherman, and his family who operate the restaurant. Vicente is maybe 18 and already has a decade of fishing experience. He operates one of the **pangas** pulled up on the beach a short walk down the hill from the restaurant. The beach is pebbly with a number of tidepools below the cliff on the left.*

Vicente catches nearly all the fish, lobster and caracoles (sea snails, or conchs) that the restaurant serves. The people are charming, the food excellent and very inexpensive. Vicente will also take rod and reel fishermen out for marlin, sailfish and tuna, which he says occur only a few miles offshore.

    1.3   119.2   K36   Cross a small bridge and take a road (right) about a hundred yards to **Playa Solidad**. The turnoff is signed going north, but not going south. *Here is another of the "indescribable" beaches so common here. There are a few thatched cottages and some hundreds of yards of beaches to enjoy.*

    1.1   120.3   K34   Just beyond is **Puente La Solidad**. Once across the bridge there's a marginal trail down to the right toward a few thatched cottages. A better one is at K33. *Here the road angles sharply back and down off Mexico 200 for about a hundred yards to a number of trees and*

MOTHER'S PRIDE

256

Lázaro Cárdenas Hub Map

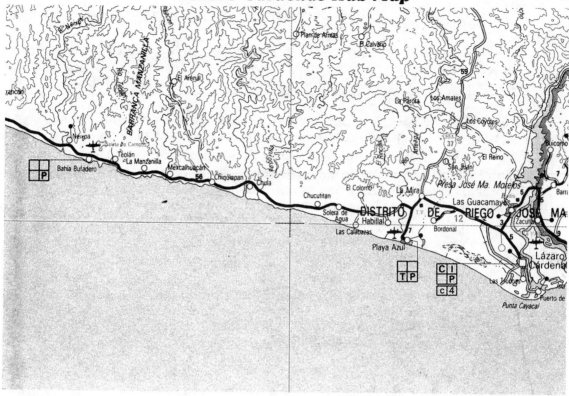

a house. *It is one more of those special beaches. About 150 yards wide with rocky margins left and right, it is pristine in all respects.*

Meet **Manuel Orozco** *and his family. They live behind the beach known as* **La Salada**. *He is around 50, married and has at least four children, the youngest only a couple of weeks old. We ask permission to park and check the beach. His response is a wave of the arm and a loud* **"bienvenidos!"** *We walk the beach and watch one of Manuel's sons fishing from the rocks to the left while another comes back from the other end with a bag of oysters.*

As we help him put wooden frames up for palm shelters, Manuel talks about his beach, and his life here at **La Salada**. *Two of his children still go to school and he is very proud of his new baby. Later he shows off a beautiful new adobe brick and mud cooking center with wood burners of various sizes arranged in a manner similar to what you would find on a manufactured stove. It is truly a work of art.*

Why the palm shelters? They are for his friends who come to visit. Does he charge for their use? He shrugged and doesn't quite know how to put it, "How can you charge your friends. They bring things, and that is appreciated."

Want to camp here? The area is small but everyone is welcome, says Manuel. (We suggest that you avoid weekends...that is when his friends come.) Facilities are nonexistent, but what a beach. Back to the highway.

0.9   121.2   K32+   A road (right) to the beach leads to some palms, a few thatched houses and half a dozen *palapa*-type restaurants. A fishing *panga* is pulled up on the beach. Continuing east, we pass a small school and the town of **Chiquiapan** near the bridge over the **Río Chiquiapan** and several coconut staging areas where they are split and dried. *The discarded husks are stacked in large piles waiting for some brickmaker to haul 'em off for fuel.* There is a road through town to the beach. Many large willow-like trees with beautiful yellow flowers line the river banks. The trees look at least 70 feet tall.

2.2   123.4   K29   There is a private road (right) to several houses but no public access.

1.1   124.5   K27   A dirt road (right) signed, **Playa Bocaseca**, has a gate across it. We move inland up a narrow valley and back into the jungle. In a few hundred meters the road goes over a small rise, and the jungle is gone. Ahead are more access trails toward the beach.

1.0   125.5   K25+   A bridge, the **Puente Chuca** and a road which provides access to the river only. Farther on we cross a long bridge over the **Río Popoyutla**.

3.4   128.9   K20   A little road toward a bluff and several small houses. It is the private **Club Vejuca**. A quarter mile beyond the club look to the right for a 200-meter wide grey sand beach, **Playa Vejuca**, with rocks on the ends. There is also a restaurant operated by the fishermen's families. The prices are reasonable, and they're anxious to please.

1.3   130.8   K18   A small group of houses on the south side of a short bridge. Its name, **Las Peñas**. Below are several *pangas* and a *palapa* or two. More access roads follow. Some have houses, some palapas, others nothing.

0.5   131.3   K17   The road (right) leads to the southernmost of the Las Peñas beaches. The 100-yard road deadends in a coconut grove with a sandy base. *The beach is long and loaded with all of the ingredients for great surf fishing...huge sand crabs, some clams and small silvery baitfish which are taken with the **tiraya** (a circular throw net). There are also many fish to be seen feeding in the shallows and outlined in the long breaking waves. We took a croaker family member they call a **roncador**. It closely resembles a species we have taken from the shore in Baja. We also snagged a threadfin pompano and a member of the snapper family called **pargo blanco**. All of the fish ranged from 1.5 to 4 pounds...great sport on light tackle. My new surf fishing friends also say that sierra mackerel to 2 and 3 feet are common. Most of their fishing activity is from pangas over nearby reefs, where they catch the more marketable **huachinango**.*

Unfortunately our time here is limited, so another trip will be planned sometime after we get the book out. Motorhomes and trailers should be very careful. The road heads away from the sea into mango and banana orchards, etc., then past **Chucutitan**. A few miles farther we cross a bridge into the small community of **Solera de Agua**.

5.8   137.1   K7+   Road right is signed to **Villa Dorada**, a beach development scheme some 3 miles from the highway. *We pass through a small town on the way in. The project is aimed at the upper middle class Mexican family, but they appear expensive even for them. The several miles of beaches we passed coming in here are open to camping, according to one of the sales people.* Beyond, on the left are huge dark gray piles of what look like tailings from a mine.

1.7   139.0   K5   Intersection with a paved road to **Habillal**. The straight road goes into town, the one curving to the left is the one we want. A bridge over the **Río Acalpican** is next.

3.0   142.0   K0   Road right is to **Playa Azul**, 7km. The road is about 5 kilometers and goes past palm and banana plantations and a local **Pemex** before entering the somewhat-faded beach resort.

*There are numerous restaurants to choose from here in Playa Azul, and all the names begin with **Enramada**. When we were in Boca de Pascuales, they all started with the word, **Balneario**. The buildings look the same in both places...same hammocks, same palm leaf-covered car ports, etc. Even the beaches are similar, but here enramada is in and balneario is out.*

The first time we noticed Playa Azul, it was through Spanish-language descriptions in a travel brochure. How marvelous we thought, here is a first class resort area as yet unspoiled by the gringo tourist, but the first visit brought up the question as to whether we were even in the right town. Nothing seemed to add up. The glittering hotels and the plush dining rooms eluded us, so we opted for Zihuatanejo.

A later visit rekindled the same thoughts, but we decided to stick it out. The hotel selected turned out to have a pool problem...it was a dull green. The air was hot, the ocean had large waves and heavy currents and the sand was blowing. That night we had bolillos and cheese because the beachfront restaurants were closed due to the wind. Not a good beginning. And then there were the roosters...

The block across from the hotel was encircled by a high brick wall. Unbeknown to us, the people on the other side raised and trained fighting cocks. And that particular night, the wind, coupled with a perfectly full moon, gave the hundreds of roosters an excuse to have an all-night crow-fest. If those birds could fight as well as they could crow, the owner had the chicken world by the **cojones***.*

Now, after two more visits, we may have found a limited comfort zone in the facilities of the **Playa Azul Hotel and Trailer Park***, plus a couple of restaurants along the beach. During our last visit there was no wind, and the water was perfect. That also helped.* Back to the intersection and east toward **Lázaro Cárdenas**.

1.6   143.6   K334   The signed intersection at the entrance into **La Mira**. A road straight north (Mexico 37) goes into the **Sierra Madre del Sur** and such towns as **Arteaga**, **Nueva Italia** and **Uruapan**. *A number of side roads branch off Mexico 37 before it reaches the highlands, and these should not be traveled without checking as to their safety...for this is a fine climate for raising marijuana, opium poppies and other "recreational stimulants". As in some of California's northern counties where marijuana is a big cash crop, the highways themselves are little problem, but you stay off the side roads.* The road east and south through town is Mexico 200. We also pick up another set of K markers.

1.5   145.1   K120   A local **Pemex**, followed in a couple of miles by some *topes*. The land to the south and west is prime coconut country...*one wonders how the world can absorb so much coconut oil, but it's properties make it valuable in a variety of soaps, foodstuffs, etc.*

6.0   151.1   K110+   An American freeway-type entry into **Lázaro Cárdenas**...watch the signs and traffic. Lázaro is to the south, our Mexico 200 path is to the northeast.

Lázaro Cárdenas is the largest city on the coast of Michoacan, but has little to offer the tourist...not even unleaded gasoline. The city has grown to its present size since the damming of the **Río Balsas***, the construction of power generators and the Sicartsa steel works in the 1970s. High hopes for an industrialized center based on the steel produced have faded. (Poor quality steel is one of the reasons given.) Recently expanded port facilities have done better, and the industrial base is slowly growing. The town has a number of business hotels and several restaurants serving good* **carnes asadas***, etc.* We continue past a paved airstrip, right.

1.2   152.3   K108+   The fairly large town of **Las Guacamayas** is straight ahead. The bypass road goes slightly to the right and parallels the river. We take the bypass.

2.7   155.0   K104   We continue slightly uphill toward the dam across the Río Balsas. We know we are officially out of Las Guacamayas when the smelly, smoking, city dump is behind us.

0.7   155.7   K103   Cross the top of the small dam for the power plant, then the larger, cobble-surfaced dam and into the state of **Guerrero**.

End of log.

MICHOACAN BEACHES...

There could be a book on Michoacan beaches alone. In the main they are pristine, productive and plentiful. Here we meet the local fishermen and divers, the visiting surfers and few tourists. When we get here, we too slow down and soak up the atmosphere, check out the surf, the fishing and the driftwood. It is easy to spend days, weeks, even months along Michoacan's beaches.

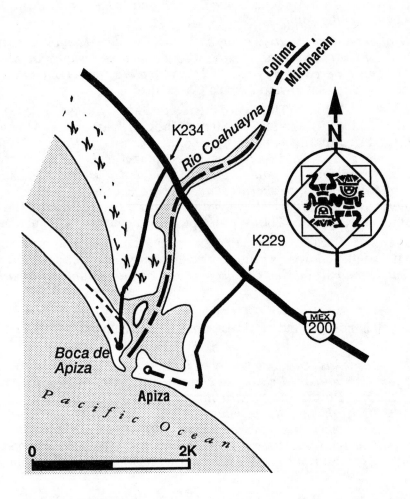

Apiza...

Just south of the Michoacan-Colima border, at K229, a signed turnoff southwest goes through coco palms and bananas to **Apiza**...

At **2.1** a water tower on the left is followed immediately by a lagoon. The ocean is at **2.6** miles. The town has a small **Conasupo**, a school and a dozen restaurants facing a rather pretty gray-sand beach and lots of driftwood. Each restaurant has a complement of *sombras* (shades), for both the sun and the sand are hot here.

A freshwater lagoon is off to the northwest with a supply of shrimp, crab and mullet. Overnighting is possible for the self contained. A nice, quiet place. Back to the highway.

MICHOACAN BEACHES

Punta La Playa...

At K213 of Mexico 200 a road (right) is marked as going to an oceanographic research station. At **2.2** miles, an entrance into a private club with its own beach. Follow the road (left) a half-mile to the public **Punta La Playa** beach, staying on the best-traveled branches. Once there we strike it rich...a long sandy crescent to the left, a jumble of rounded boulders and sharp cliff faces on the right. The beach looks almost due south, resulting in gentle waves on all but a vigorous south swell. A few rocks directly ahead around the break line also lend to the beauty of the scene. There are a number of likely camping places, though getting stuck here is a viable likelihood unless you know what you're doing. A better possibility might be to go back about 200 meters and take a less-used road west toward the rocks. This is definitely not a motorhome or trailer road. Back to the highway.

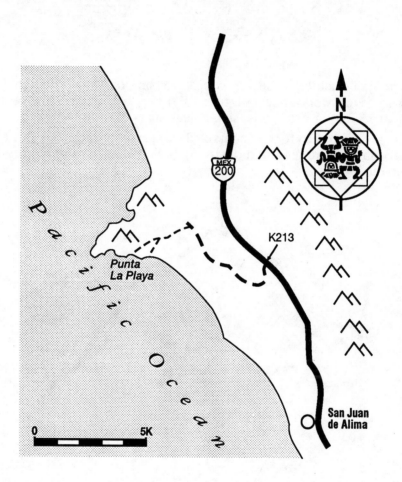

Tom's Beach...

From just beyond the K205 marker of Mexico 200, a road (right) goes down through a small canyon and eventually to a small group of houses at the far right end of the beach. *We ran out of time for a visit during the logging phase of the book, thus have no distances, but remember it to be about two miles.* Tom has been there several times over the years and found the people hospitable, and with a love for fresh fruit...the first time there he and his hosts devoured a 10-pound *sandía* (watermelon) in only a couple of minutes. On the next visit he took in another sandía, plus several *jícamas*, with the same result.

On the west, the beach is butted against a high cliff with a jumble of rocks at the bottom, while the other end extends for a mile or more before disappearing into another cliff. The sand is light gray and easy walking, with some driftwood. Several years ago we had a

memorable hour of catching white *pargo* (snapper) on small lures and light line just off the rocks. The pargo were working schools of small silvery fish within a few yards of the beach. We kept about 15 for our hosts, releasing at least an equal number.

There is no problem for self contained campers. Motorhomers or trailerites should pre-run the road if you are serious about trying it. Someday we will return for an extended stay. Back to the highway.

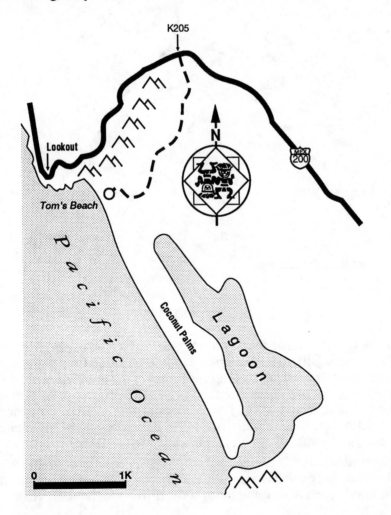

MICHOACAN BEACHES

La Ticla...

A signed road (right) at K183 is to **La Ticla** and the beach. We cross a small irrigation canal **(1.3)** and pass a large tract of land being cleared and prepared for planting. We are heading northwest about a quarter-mile behind the beach. At **1.7** the road forks...take the best-traveled (left) branch. At **2.0** miles a basketball court is on the right. Turn (right) at the end alongside the court, and then a final left to the southwest. We are at the beach at **2.2** miles.

Ticla is principally a surfer's beach with the main break a short distance to the west. A small "sometimes" restaurant provides some shade from the hot sun and several hammocks, a couple of pop-tents, five cars (three from California) and eight or nine surfers are taking advantage of it. One of the Californians, **Sandy**, now lives in nearby Tecoman, Colima where he operates a surf shop. Two boys from San Diego have been coming here for several years and are finishing their second week, with no plans to go home. The waves have excellent form and movement. The boys rate it as good as **Barra de Nexpa**, but without the crowds.

Once past the immediate camping area, the beach is loaded with driftwood. The sand is gray and soft. Accommodations range from hammock hooks to a spot to park a vehicle or pitch a tent. No facilities beyond that. *Several years ago the area was pretty involved in the drug scene and there was a drug-related murder. We understand that things have quieted down, but, be aware.* Back to the highway.

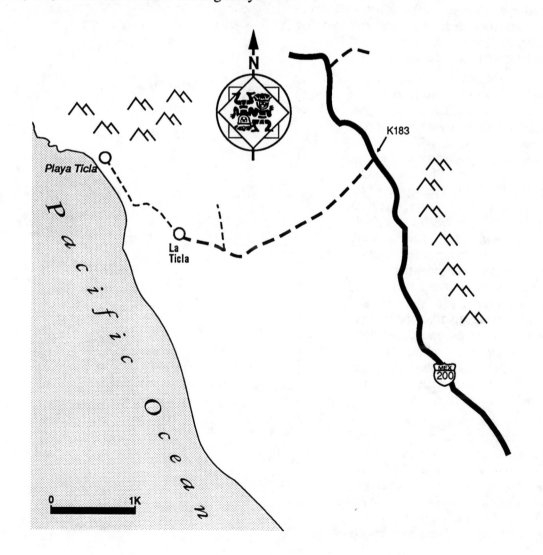

El Faro De Bucerias...

At K173+ a well-traveled road goes down a small arroyo toward the ocean. Shortly before it empties into the sea (**0.9** miles) we enter the town of **El Faro de Bucerias** (Lighthouse of the Divers) and a basketball court. We go past and on to one of the most charming sites we know of in Mexico at **1.3** miles.

The beach itself is a pleasing mix of rocks, gently-washed pools and open sand with crashing waves. One can spend hours here climbing around shooting pictures, or just relaxing.

There are no facilities beyond the several restaurants, although to the west along the beach are buildings intended to be the humble beginnings of a tourist industry. They look like goners, as it seems to be disintegrating into rocks, sand and scraps of wood.

Aside from the views, Bucerias offers friendly people and some of the freshest seafood in the world. Several times we've been able to watch the divers return to the small cove, walk over to inspect the catch, make a choice of the lobster, oysters, conch or octopus and carry them over to the restaurant to be cooked on the spot.

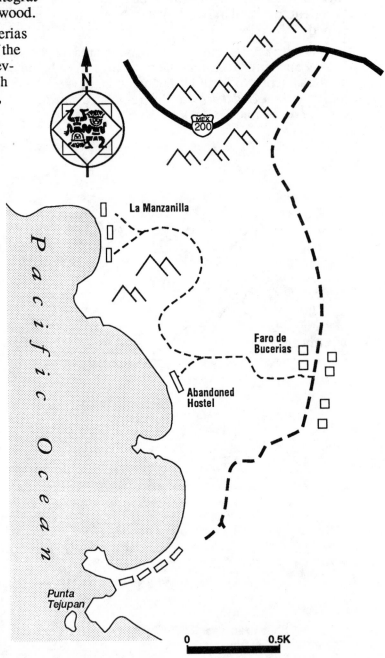

There is another little beach accessible from the Bucerias road...**La Manzanilla**. It is to the west over a very rough road that takes off from the northwestern corner of the basketball court. The trail goes around a hill to end up just past the west end of the Bucerias beaches. Here we find a couple more restaurants and a small building for commercial fishermen to clean and store their catch. The beach is south-facing and very pretty. Off to the west and within walking distance are several more coves separated by low, rocky ridges. Fishing is good around the rocks to the west according to one of the local boys. Back to Bucerias.

Bucerias is worth not only a stop but a meal if you can take the time. Though our last trip left a bit to be desired in the way of cleanliness, the litter may have been from the Easter Week holiday. Don't try to take a motorhome in. Back to the highway.

Playa Marvata...

At K150 of Mexico 200, just after crossing the second of two bridges, we turn left (not right) at the signed **Playa Marvata** and **Pomaro**. The Marvata part of the road immediately turns left again down and under the bridge. At **0.5** we pass a huge *higuera* tree. Covering several thousand square feet, there are actually two with the roots and trunks are intimately intertwined. Next come some of the houses which comprise Marvata. At **0.8** we enter the common area for three small beaches separated by rocks, (almost islands), with cactus, agave and small trees growing on them.

The beach to the left backs up to a small freshwater lagoon and sweeps south and east in a long white arc. There is only a small surge here next to the rocks and is calm enough to launch pangas.

The center beach is bracketed by huge rounded boulders, several of which are laced with caves and arches open to the sea. There is a strong surge with today's southwest swell, but may well be flat under other conditions.

The show put on here by the interaction between the sea and the caves and the arches in the granitic monoliths is a spectacular one. Whistles and booming noises intermingle to announce the explosion of tons of green and white water through the openings. To one standing nearby, it seems as though you are about to be engulfed in a wall of water, but it dissipates quickly on the sand.

The third, and largest, beach is open to the northwest. Here, the surge is the strongest, and the drop-off steepest.

A number of palapas are along the beaches, offering the typical seafood and Mexican-style meals. Camping is a popular pastime here, especially during the December-to-March period. Being self contained is a real advantage as there are few facilities. We have seen motorhomes here, but check the road first. The area is very clean compared to most well-visited beaches, and both residents and visitors work to keep it that way. We hear that campers organize clean-up days and assist in the hauling away and burning of unwanted material.

The majority of the residents of Marvata are **Nayuhtl** Indians. In fact, the community is owned by the tribe, and all members are the collective owners. Thus land cannot be sold, only leased under a rather complicated set of rules.

Many of the residents still speak their tribal dialect rather than Spanish and hold to old customs.

Playa Marvata is surviving nicely under the increased camping pressure. Hopefully it will continue to do so. It is a very special place. Back to the highway.

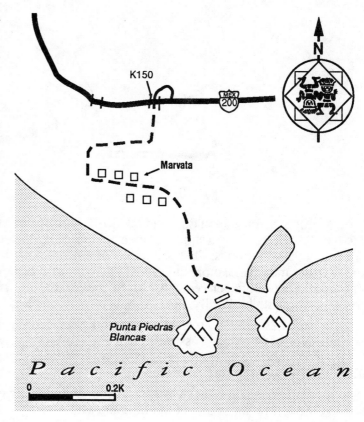

265

Barra de Nexpa...

Barra de Nexpa has to rank near the top of our serendipitous adventures list.

We were running behind schedule and the sun is getting low. We should have been off the road an hour ago. Now there is little alternative but to find a campsite quickly. We took the first turn toward the ocean and landed right in the middle of a number of houses and 25 to 30 travelers from all over the world! Watch the K markers on this one.

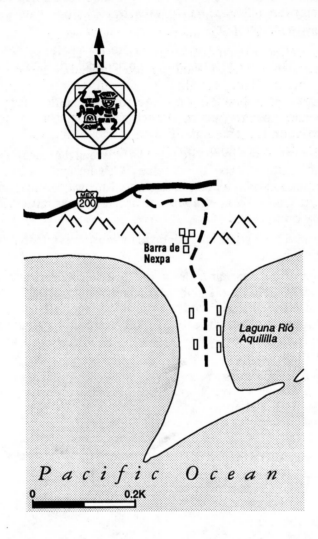

A rough, semi-graded dirt road takes off (right) from Mexico 200 at K56 and over a rise to parallel the highway a short distance, then south to the edge of low bluffs and perhaps a dozen thatched buildings. One is marked as a restaurant. The road continues down to a coconut grove and several more buildings. There are also a few campers and vans and a small motorhome. Our odometer reads **0.7** from the road, and according to **Efraim "Brian" Mendoza**, who with his family, operates this picturesque locale, we are in **Barra de Nexpa**.

Brian is about 17, an avid surfer and skateboarder who speaks English with a California-North Carolina-Aussie-English-French-German accent. It might be best to categorize the mixture as **surfereese**. He communicates perfectly with 99% of his guests. And his guests come to surf...period.

Surfing magazines have been writing about Nexpa for several years. They've described the left break as one of the best anywhere.

MICHOACAN BEACHES

Photographers have shot and sold many sequences of the long smooth rollers which come from as far away as the storm-tossed Antarctic. Tubes here are commonplace, as are rides of a minute or more. Waves of 10 feet and up are not uncommon. With all of the coverage, one might expect the place to be overrun. Not at all, for the name is commonly omitted from the copy. *We thought long and hard before mentioning Nexpa here, but there's a lot of room and it is about time the family has a chance to cash in on land they have been holding for generations.*

As a first-time visitor from North Carolina drawled, *"Ah neva, eva thought ah'd see suf lak this. The fust day made the treeup wuthwaahl."*

The "treeup" mentioned began in North Carolina before dawn with a flight to Dallas, then Mexico City and on to Zihuatanejo. From Zihuat they caught a bus 120 miles north to Caleta de Campos, a small, busy town with a hotel. The next day they found someone who would bring them here, southern accent, surfboards, camping gear and all! Such is the dedication of a surfer. We wondered how the word had gotten back to North Carolina...

BARRA DE NEXPA

Several years ago one of them heard about Nexpa from a surfing buddy, who got it from a friend of a friend who worked for a surfing magazine in California. With no real confirmation of the story, three of them loaded a van and headed for Mexico. After reaching the Pacific Coast, it took another week of wandering between Puerto Vallarta and Acapulco to locate Nexpa.

Once here, the weather kicked up and they couldn't get out for over a week. But they weren't alone, 20 other surfers were also waiting out the rain. When it ended, they were hooked. The North Carolina contingent has grown each year since.

As non-surfers, we kept busy: watching the surfers, walking the beach, rummaging through heaps of exotic driftwood, casting lures for a variety of fish, and swimming in the freshwater lagoon.

As of this writing there are no conveniences other than the restaurant with its limited menu and a first-rate view of a setting sun. This is a surfer's beach. We loved every minute of it, and will return at the first opportunity. Back to the highway.

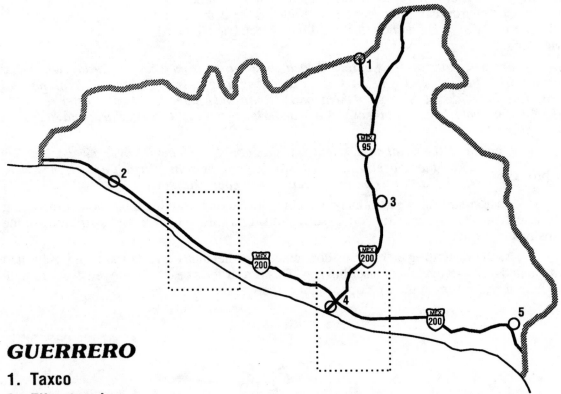

GUERRERO

1. Taxco
2. Zihuatanejo
3. Chilpancingo
4. Acapulco
5. Ometepec

GUERRERO... THE STATE

It was in 1948 that a newly-elected president, Miguel Alemán Velasco, called for an all-out effort to bring the sleepy port of Acapulco on stream as a world-class tourist destination. And the mandate changed the face of the nation. Today our southern neighbor is one of the most visited countries in the world with over six million visitors annually. And, surprisingly, one out of five tourists still include Acapulco in their itinerary.

Historically, the state of **Guerrero** has been the home of a dozen or more resident groups. Some of the earliest left paintings on the walls of their caves, pottery shards at their campsites and wooden utensils near fishing grounds. Centuries later other indigenous groups built great fortifications and cities. Pyramids and platforms near El Cerro de los Monos (Hill of the Figurines) in the northern part of the state date from the 7th and 8th centuries, A.D. The ruins of a fort at Otumba include a large 15th-century arch from a fort built by the Aztecs as a defense against the Tarascan Indians. The Aztecs also occupied Taxco from 1440 until the Spanish conquests.

And from this mix came proud and independent citizens who did (and do) not hesitate to fight for their rights. One, appropriately named Vicente Guerrero, became a president of Mexico, and the state was named after him.

Four mountain ranges and numerous watersheds which regularly turn into raging torrents kept much of Guerrero isolated until President Alemán's Acapulco directives brought about the development of highways, bridges and airports. Since that time the region has moved steadily forward.

Today's access channels include the excellent four-lane highway from Mexico City to Acapulco, and the *Camino Costal*, Mexico 200, which runs along the coast past Ixtapa-Zihuatanejo and Michoacan to the north and through the states of Oaxaca and Chiapas on its way south to the Guatemala border.

The beaches of Guerrero are not found only around Acapulco and Zihuatanejo. Watch for more jewels at Playa Ventura, El Atracadero, Troncones and Riscalillo, where life of a different richness awaits those willing to travel beyond the normal touristic destinations.

Today Guerrero is a state with a rich economy in which tourism plays a major role. Chipancingo, the state capital, is home to the state university, paper manufacturing plants, an agricultural center and lumber mills producing much of Mexico's plywood. Iguala is an industrial city manufacturing a wide variety of equipment and parts to service factories all over Mexico. Another bright spot is Taxco, a colonial hillside town with red-tile roofs. One of the most famous silver working centers in the world, it offers the visitor more than 300 shops to browse in search of that perfect piece. Acapulco plays a dual role, that of being a major Pacific Rim import and export center, and as Mexico's oldest world-class beach resort.

Statewide, farms grow sesame seed, coffee, tropical fruit and vegetables. There is mining of gold, silver, copper, tungsten and iron. The forests provide fine woods and fishing fleets patrol the Pacific continental shelf. Colorful thread and yarns come from a number of areas. Another important product is the fiery mezcál, a beverage similar to tequila, which is distilled in the central mountains.

The future for this flagship state would appear to be in honing their spirit of welcome, and in utilizing in a measured way the many miles of yet-untapped coastline. Their brackish lagoons can also serve as sites for a variety of mariculture programs, thus taking some of the pressure away from offshore fishing grounds.

MEXICO 200 — BORDER — ACAPULCO

Once you take your vehicle south of Mazatlán it is surprising how little has been written about the roads, beaches and the people of Mexico's west coast. And that dearth of information becomes even more evident once Manzanillo disappears from the rear view mirror. This section has been open since 1983, yet until recently less than one thousand **norteamericano** *vehicles traversed it annually. And there were considerably more American and Canadian cars and motorhomes visiting Acapulco and points south each year than that, but they came in from the Mexico City area via the beautiful and modern Mexico 95 highway.*

0.0   0.0   K102   We cross the cobble-surfaced dam across the **Río Balsas** and enter the state of **Guerrero** on Mexico highway 200.

1.6   1.6   K100   A signed wide spot in the road, **Las Tamacuas**, then **Zacatula** and a drug check. *The Zacatula portion of the Río Balsas complex is the one which carries most of the water through the delta and on into the Pacific.* There are coconuts, mangos and bananas everywhere. We head southwest over a well-maintained highway.

6.7   8.3   K89+   A large construction program is underway off to the left. It appears to be a coal or oil powered generating station.

0.7   9.0   K88+   The town we are entering is **Petacalco**. Watch for the *topes*; they are big ones. Restaurants line the beachfront and offer the usual *mariscos*. Access is via any of the side streets. Most of the beach is pebbly and pangas with nets are plentiful. Want to stay the night? There's the **Hotel Campos**. We'd rate it OK in a pinch.

0.9   9.9   K87   We cross the **Puente Zorcua**, a mini-laundry river, then a small town, **Zorcua**.

4.2   14.1   K80   A couple of dirt roads come in from the beach side, but they are farm service roads.

4.1   18.2   K73+   Signed road (left) 1km to **La Salada**.

5.9   24.1   K64   At **Joluta** a signed road goes (right) to **El Atracadero** and the beach. **(See Guerrero Beaches.)** The road continues fairly straight past papaya orchards and several tiny settlements. A number of roads stray off in both directions, but we are some distance from the ocean.

3.7   27.8   K58   The small, signed community of **El Chico**.

2.4   30.2   K54+   **Puente La Union**. The riverbed is large and well formed. There appears to be water all year.

0.2   30.4   K54   A local **Pemex**. *A road leads south to a bleak and dreary beach at 2.5 miles. There are several scruffy seasonal fishing shacks and one family in permanent residence. The place is dirty and not worth the trip.* Back to the highway.

1.3   31.7   K52   A signed, paved intersection with a road north to **La Union**, a fair-sized agricultural town, and on into the mountains and an assortment of small towns and villages. To the right is a dirt road to **El Capire** and **Boca Los Cuches**. Continue southeast a mile or two behind the beach, going slightly up and down past various cultivated enterprises. A few huge trees are visual reminders of the jungle which was cut down to accommodate the farms.

3.0   34.7   K47   We intersect with graded dirt roads north to **Chutla** and south to **Boca de Chutla**. *The south road goes along the right-hand side of the river and past a house with a huge bougainvilla. Beyond is scrub and newly cleared land and, at 0.5, a three-way fork. We begin with the center of the three. That branch then forks at 1.4. We go right and into a grove of palms. The trail gets fainter, but brings us to the shore at 2.1. It is a beautiful beach with signs of having been occupied on at least a seasonal basis. Lots of driftwood and many, many coco palms under which to relax. The water looks fishy, with several channels and bars to provide feeding troughs for nearshore species. The place should be navigable for most cars and drivers with common sense but not for motorhomes or trailers.*

We didn't take the other branches, leaving them for others to explore and to give us a reason to return. The Boca de Chutla area looks like a good get-away-from-it-all spot. Back to the highway and over the **Río Chutla** bridge.

2.0   36.7   K43   A dirt road (right) goes to an oyster beach. *We turn west and head toward the ocean, passing through the small agricultural development of **Hixtapa** at 0.7. A dusty road continues beyond several less-used turnoffs around 1.6, then between barbed-wire fences to the beach at 2.1. For all practical purposes the road ends about a hundred yards back from the actual beach because of a wide expanse of soft sand. Several rock reefs outside the breaker line yield enough oysters to attract up to a dozen divers on calm days. To get the oysters they must dive to **tres brazas**, three fathoms (18 feet). Any way you look at it, that's a hard way to make a living.*

The waves are nondescript while the beach is gray sand with patches of small stones. Driftwood is scattered and not plentiful. It really doesn't have a lot of special features. Though the distance is only 2.1 miles, we may have saved you even that. Back to the highway.

A short distance beyond, a road (right) is signed to **Rancho Huapinolar**. It goes in *1.8* miles to a locked gate...*we had to back up a long ways before finding a turn-around.*

2.0   38.9   K40   A signed community, **Los Llanos**, (The Flat Land) with the ocean off to the right. (**See Guerrero Beaches.**) Next comes a small bridge. *This area seems to be particularly well endowed with iguanas. Should you wish to cook one yourself, there are usually some for sale along the side of the road. And you know they're fresh because they're still alive.*

4.3   43.2   K33   **Puente Lagunillas.** Off to the right, a graded dirt road to **Playa Majahúa. (See Guerrero Beaches.)** The hillsides are cleared for the rainy-season corn crops. Small plantings of papayas, mangos, etc., lie in between.

1.5   44.7   K30+   Paved road (right) is to **Troncones**. It is un-signed from the north, so watch the K markers. (**See Guerrero Beaches.**) It's worth a visit.

2.9   47.6   K26   The pueblo of **Buena Vista**.

3.5   51.1   K20+   A bridge, then **Pantla**. Most of the homes have tiled roofs, as contrasted to the reed-thatched ones a few miles back. A road goes east to the ocean and a most interesting beach. (**See Guerrero Beaches.**)

2.1   53.2   K17+   The turnoff (right) to **Barrio Nuevo** eventually leads to a beach only a mile or so north of **Ixtapa's Playa Linda** hotel and trailer park. *The beach is strewn with wood and backed with many coco palms. The road to the water from Barrio Nuevo is rough, dusty and complicated to track with a log. It differs little from the Playa Linda beach and we recommend you drive there and walk back if you are really committed.* Continue southeast to a permanent drug inspection station. We have yet to be inspected here...a question or two and we're on our way. A few yards beyond, a paved road inland is signed to **Ciudad Altamirano**. This highway, Mexico 134, continues on to Toluca and the Mexico City basin.

1.0   54.2   K16   Bridge over a fair-sized river.

4.4   58.6   K8+   Intersection, the road (right) is into **Ixtapa**.

IXTAPA, The Planned Community...

Ixtapa actually began in 1970 in a bureaucrat's office in Mexico City, when **Fonatur**, the government agency created to implement the growth of tourism in Mexico, began a search of the west coast for an area close in air miles to the U.S., with an average temperature in the 80s, lush vegetation and most important, beautiful beaches. The objective was to create a planned resort community designed to tap the upscale American Midwest and West Coast markets and Canada's central snowbelt.

Eventually they settled on the Zihuatanejo area and, rather than rebuild, expand and

Ixtapa – Zihuatanejo Hub Map

disrupt the town, wisely picked a beach five kilometers to the north and bought the coconut plantation facing it.

Within a year Fonatur had designed and built the current infrastructure of water, sewers, electricity and streets. Next came an international airport and invitations to luxury hotel chains to lend their names to this new and beautiful destination.

Today the four-mile-long Ixtapa development is lined with luxury hotels in a vacation playground offering a full spectrum of activities. The golf course is an especially fine one. Designed by Robert Trent Jones, it goes from surfside inland past lakes and trees. Here's a tip or two on playing the course...

Early starting times are best, but take along a good insect repellant as some of the little critters can be very ornery if awakened by golfers tramping on their grassy homes. The same holds true after about four in the afternoon, with the problem increasing as it approaches sunset. Properly prepared, the course is a good one. One more thing...don't play through the caimans, western Mexico's version of an alligator.

Consistent with the image, the hotel's elegant restaurants are augmented by bistros, cafes, pizza/pasta parlors and the food chains found in other resort areas. Discos too have taken root, along with shopping centers and boutiques.

The thought of a row of high-rise hotels facing some of the most beautiful sunsets in the world may make you want to rush right in and register, but their size and cost might also turn you off. The jury is still out with the traveling public, for the region has not yet realized the potential envisioned in that Mexico City office 20 years ago.

Back to the beaches of Ixtapa. Here there is no argument...the beaches are truly beautiful.

Starting at the turnoff from Mexico 200 highway at K8+, we go west toward Ixtapa. At the next intersection a left takes us into the center portion of **Playa Palmar**, Ixtapa's main beach. *Palmar faces the open Pacific and can be dangerous. The northernmost end of the main beach is usually calmer; we've had some fine body surfing sessions there. The gray sand beaches offer lots of strolling space, plus a few shells, sand crabs and some driftwood.*

A right turn at the intersection points us toward **Playa Linda**. At **2.5** miles from the highway a dirt road (left) goes sharply back through an open gate in a chain-link fence. Once inside, there are three choices; left, right or straight, and each leads to its own small cove. In several visits over the years, we've seen only one other group, a local family with a number of children.

At **3.0** the paved road (left) is signed to **Playa Quieta**. At **3.6** it deadends at the south end of a beach stretching north into the **Club Med** complex. When parking take a look over to the south...another beautiful little beach, **Playa Cueta**.

The rocky, protected end of Quieta has a small pier where *pangas* debark for a special experience...a visit to **Isla Ixtapa**.

The short run to the island takes about ten minutes, with shuttles every quarter-hour between 9 and 5. (And hang on to your tickets, they are collected on the way back.)

Isla Ixtapa is a wooded wildlife sanctuary, presumably with exotic birds and animals. The boats unload at Playa Baradero. Here, facing the mainland, the water is almost a lake and excellent for swimming. Snorkeling is fairly good at the north end, though it is better off the south-facing beach, Playa Carey. Baradero has a number of palapa restaurants with tables, chairs and lounges on the beach. Here an afternoon can go very fast, what with snorkeling, swimming, eating and drinking. It was not until just before we retired for the day that a hike west and north introduced us to several other restaurants (including El Marlin) and another beautiful beach. Back to the mainland.

At 4.0 miles the paved road ends at Playa Linda, its hotel and trailer park. The hotel has a clean Olympic-size pool, bathrooms and outdoor restaurant. The trailer park, sited on the hotel grounds, offers pool privileges, etc. *A May, 1990, rumor had it that the hotel's new owners are going to phase out the trailer park. We hope not, for it is one of the best in Mexico.* Back to the way we entered and south on Mexico 200.

Mexico 200 winds along behind hills which variously front on the water and back up the Ixtapa portion of the resort complex.

2.6　61.2　K4　A wide *mirador* offers an opportunity to take in the beauty and layout of **Ixtapa**. Note the buildings sprouting on the high bluff on the left, and the beginnings of a full-blown marina on the right end of the beach. Exit the *mirador* and pass the intersection with the lower road in from Ixtapa, then continue east down the hill toward town.

2.2　63.4　K0　Enter the glorietta which spins the Zihuatanejo traffic off to the southwest.

ZIHUATANEJO, The Good Life...

From the *glorieta* it is a short distance into the rapidly growing town/city of **Zihuatanejo.**

Tourism may have started here at **Zihuatanejo** around the year 1000. For it is from that time frame that artifacts have been recovered. This is in itself not unusual, but the material found represents a variety of indigenous cultures, thus making it a region of transient visitations. Even the name, Zihuatanejo has linguists arguing among themselves as to what language it may be derived from.

At the time of the Spanish conquest the population of the entire **Costa Grande** was thought to be several hundred thousand, but disease, wars and slavery drastically reduced the number. The Indians of the area worked for the landowners, growing coconuts, cocoa, cotton, sesame seeds and coffee. Zihuatanejo was involved with the Orient trade until around 1570, when Acapulco was declared the only importing/exporting harbor on Mexico's west coast.

The region's large plantations continued after the Spanish were expelled from Mexico but the status of the Indian changed little. Contemporary Zihuatanejo began as a port and village around the turn of the century, through the exportation of fishery and agricultural products and lumber. In 1935, an airport was built and by 1945 the road to Acapulco was completed. This was the beginning of the tourist trade, but the beauty of the area remained a well-kept secret until Fonatur created **Ixtapa** in the 70s.

Today the two cities are a study in contrast...both have tourism as their main activity, but with a different approach...

Although Zihuatanejo has grown from the muddy/dusty fishing village of 4,000 in 1972 to the cobbled and paved town of 30,000 today, it has retained much of its original charm. Burros still bring their owner's produce to market, fish are sorted on the beach near the pier, and the string of sparkling beaches encircling this beautiful bay still attract locals and visitors alike. Add to this the number of older, less expensive hotels and excellent restaurants and Zihuatanejo is our kind of destination.

But there are a few cracks showing...a new marina is becoming a reality and hillside condominiums are under construction. The sleepy part of town is getting smaller, but it's still there. Lets look closer at Zihuatanejo, beginning with the waterfront.

From the main street through town, Calle Jose Morales, make a turn toward the bay on 5 de Mayo and down to the **Playa Municipál**. This is the heart of Zihuatanejo. On the right is the pier, the best spot to charter sportfishing cruisers, for you can not only check the boats out but usually arrange better prices than through the hotels. It is also the place to catch the shuttle boats to **Playa Las Gatas**. A walk along the *malecón* takes us past some of the restaurants and shops which dominate this central portion. Some streets have been closed to traffic, slowing the pace and increasing the enjoyment of the sights. The best place to swim is the far end of the beach, away from the pier. The downtown section has a number of clean medium-priced hotels. They include the **Suzy, Posada Citlali** and the **Zihuatanejo**. There

274

are apartment rentals, too. Several people we talked with say they have been staying at the same hotel in the same rooms for years. They can think of no better way to avoid the rigors of a snowy winter.

Almost anything from *carnes asadas* to fish, from pizza to yogurt, is available at reasonable prices in the central part of town. On the *malecón*, the **Cafe Marina** for *tortas* or pizza; back a block and around the corner, **Kapi-Kofi** has a daily lunch special built around fish. Always good. They also make a great hamburger. Another winner if you are looking for chicken is the **Pollo Loco**, a very local version with rustic seating and a downhome atmosphere.

The Fat Mermaid, **Sirena Gorda**, is more tourist-oriented, but recommended for breakfast and fish tacos. Dinners at **Garrobos** are good and reasonable. Their specialty is *paella*, which must be ordered at least several hours in advance. **Coconuts** is Zihuat's most pricey restaurant, but it does a fine job with its menu. International cuisine is the thing here. The setting too is superb, a beautiful patio and the refurbished customs building from the 20s with both indoor and patio dining available. Two others with good reputations are **Casa Elvira** and **Puntarenas,** located on the other side of the entrance into the lagoon/marina. *A former favorite,* **La Mesa de Capitán** *appears to have succumbed to the Ixtapa mentality and we found prices inflated and service slow.*

We'd be remiss if we didn't mention at least one gift shop, the **Embarcadero.** The owner is a beautiful lady named **Natalia Krebs**, whose skills as a clothing designer have put the place on the map and made her label a familiar one. Natalia's artistic eye also serves her well as she travels through the remote towns in Oaxaca, the Yucatan and the mountains south of Mexico City. Over the years, some of our finest weavings have passed through her hands on the way to honored positions in our home. Don't miss the Embarcadero, or Natalia.

Calle Jose Morales is the conduit to another beach, but in the opposite direction. Follow the signs to **Zona de Hoteles** and we come to **Playa La Madera**. The name is a leftover from when *madera* (lumber) was floated to the waiting ships in the harbor from this spot. It is a small beach with a few thatched restaurants and steep rocks on either side. Backing the beach on the hillsides are several good hotels and small apartment units. The hotels begin at the bottom of the hill...

The **Palacios**, an older structure on the beach with small clean rooms with ceiling fans. Next is the **Villas Miramar**. Located on both sides of the street with large rooms, beautiful gardens and pools, it is one of the nicest hotels in the area. The **Posada Caracól**, a favorite on previous trips, is slipping on maintenance and is temporarily closed. Their bayfront rooms offer fabulous views. Up the hill and adjoining the Caracól is the **Hotel Irma**. It is doing well, with newly decorated common areas, bayside pools and terraces. At the top of the hill (and the top of the pile) is a six-unit guest house, **Nicole's**. The owner, a French lady of the same name. Nicole's rates include continental breakfast, superb views and siesta hammocks.

At the top of the hill above the hotels, try the sunset happy hour at **Mamacitas**. We enjoy the sunset, the happy hour and the *botanas*. The **Bay Club Restaurant** across the street has a good-looking, but expensive, menu.

On the west side of the small *arroyo* forming **Playa Madera** a street running along the top of the bluff, **López Mateos**, is loaded with bungalows, apartments and small condominium complexes. (Go right instead of left at Calle Adelita, then left up a short, steep hill.) The **Allee, Ley, Grupo Pacific, La Madera, Sotelo** and **Bahía** all have their regulars, but we choose the lady with a Baja connection...**Anita Hahner** and the **Bungalows Pacificos.**

In the early 1950s Anita lived in a small Mexican mining town. Her best friends there were a couple named Antero and Cruz Diaz. One day Antero announced that he was going to Bahía de Los Angeles, Baja California, to work in a mine, and that he was taking his family. The many friends of the Diaz's were apprehensive for the destination was a stark, hot desert, much different from the town they were leaving.

The mine project soon failed, but Papa, Mama and the eight kids stuck it out to carve their names into the minds and hearts of thousands of Baja visitors and fishermen. Though "Papa" died recently and Cruz spends much of her time now in cooler climes, their names will always be connected to Baja.

Anita's six units overlook the bay with the living and dining areas partly covered, full of plants and open to the air. The atmosphere is superb. Anita is booked almost solid from November through Easter but give her a try. Write to Bungalows Pacificos, Zihuatanejo, Guerrero, Mexico. Phone, 4-21-12.

If you have been traveling in Mexico for more than a couple of weeks, you're probably pretty hungry for a hamburger. If the description fits, you might like to save that hunger for **Rubin's**. It is located at the bottom of the hill leading into the Zona de Hoteles. A bit funky, laid back and functional, their hamburgers are out of this world. And that is all they serve...hours, 6 to 10 every night. No, Ruben is not another displaced *norteamericano*, he is **Ruben Akali Roncalli**, from San Luís Potosí, and he makes a helluva burger.

Follow the hotel zone road upward to the crest overlooking **Playa Ropa**. As we drop toward the water we pass the **Hotel Sotovento-Catalina**, a beautiful hotel with the best views in Zihuatanejo. Just beyond on the beach is the **Fiesta Mexicana**. *Playa Ropa got its name when an 18th-century sailing ship wrecked near here and its cargo of Chinese silks and clothes washed up on the beach.* The beach is beautiful, with white sand and gentle waves. The hot restaurant here is supposed to be **La Perla**. Big, and with lots of items on the menu. It failed to impress. There's a trailer park, **Pepi's**, out behind the beach. At least that is what the signs say. We find it weedy and nearly abandoned.

The farthest-south beach on the bay is **Las Gatas**. Accessible from the pier only by boat, its name comes from a benign, whiskery shark which used to be found here. There is a coral reef just offshore, which is reputed to have been installed by a **Tarascan** king to keep dangerous fish and waves out of his "swimming pool," and the remains still protect the white sand beach. Snorkeling is good and equipment can be rented on the beach, as can pedal-boats, sailboats and water ski equipment. Swim, snorkel, eat seafood and relax. It is a nice, but crowded, spot.

The last beach is **Playa Majahúa** a good 2 or 3 kilometers out of town to the west on a dead-end road. Billed as a nude beach, the only nudes we saw were two young children cavorting on the not-too-attractive pebbly beach with fully-clothed mama and papa watching. . There are no facilities, not even a serviceable palm frond for shade.

Zihuatanejo...is it a winner? We think so and we'll continue to return.

We go around to the second exit of the *glorieta* and continue southeast on Mexico 200 toward the airport and Acapulco. The Chrysler, Ford and Chevrolet dealerships are along the way, then the usual numbers of auto-parts stores. *Refacciones* **Garcia, Ramirez, Beto, Barato** and **Camionero** are but a few names on the store fronts. Next comes the beautiful new bus depot...one of the nicest we've seen in Mexico. *Almost makes you want to park and ride. We also change K markers.*

0.3   63.7   K240+ A full service **Pemex** is on the left.

1.8   65.5   K236 An obscure dirt road right at the brick wall leads to **Playa Riscalillo**. *It would be unfair to say that the road is good, or well graded, or not rocky. It is dusty, lumpy, narrow, and would be a bear after a rain. Take a motorhome in and you'll probably leave it there.*

We reach the beach at 1.9 after traversing the last 200 yards through a hail of flying coconuts...workmen are harvesting the nuts and tossing them onto the road.

What can you say about a beach which is 70 yards of white sand, backed by coconut palms and anchored on each side by 50-foot cliffs topped by a variety of flowering trees, vines and cactus? Nothing. Just enjoy.

The water is about 82 degrees and as clear as you can imagine with waves coming in as large turquoise tubes. Diving and fishing around the points is excellent according to what we saw and heard from **Israel**, *the caretaker of this idyllic spot. We talked to him as he was leaving to dive on the point for "4 or 5 kilos" of fish for dinner. Asked if he expected any trouble, he laughed and said that he has trouble only when the waves are very large.*

We ask if camping is permitted and he replies that he often had **huespedes** *(guests) as he calls them. They bring him things he can use and/ or provide a small fee for his servicing of the beach. We've promised to bring some beef for carne asada when we return. There are no facilities other than shade, sun, sand, magnificent water and tranquility.*

Today Riscalillo lies fallow. But maybe not for long...the owner is a hotelier. In the meantime, don't miss it. Back to the highway.

We are now back in the country, with tiny enclaves of thatched or tiled houses among the thousands of acres of palms, mangos, bananas and papayas. Many of the towns have recently installed speed bumps, or *topes*, to slow the truck traffic. Some bring everything down to a crawl, unless the driver wants to leave car parts behind. Pay close attention.

4.7   70.2   K230   Paved road (right) is to the Zihuatanejo International Airport. There is a beach behind it that you should know about, **Playa Los Pozos. (See Guerrero Beaches.)** Continue southeast on Mexico 200 through coco palms.

2.5   72.7   K226   Here is a wide turnout under a huge, shady *huanacaxtle* tree (in this part of Mexico they are also called *pirote*).

0.5   73.2   K225   The bridge, **Puente Los Achotes**. On the east side a signed, graded road goes right to **Laguna Potosí** and on to **Barra El Potosí** and **Playa Blanca. (See Guerrero Beaches.)** The road winds and climbs, providing occasional glimpses of the ocean or intervening lagoons between the many palm trees.

2.6   75.8   K221   A dirt road (right) will take you on a merry-go-round of locked gates...*nearly five miles of frustration and no beach access*. Continue on to drop into yet another bunch of coconuts. A half-mile or so beyond, a well-graded road goes off to the right. Though it looks like a good prospect it divides and ends up at: 1) a closed coconut plantation with a number of large buildings and a cement cross; and, 2) a small evaporative salt works sited on a lagoon. Nine miles of learning where not to go.

2.4   78.2   K217   A cemetery by the side of the road at the entrance to the small community of **San Jeronimito**. Again there are *topes*. Cross over a river, **La Tigra**. It is well used by the local women for the family wash and the kids, sans clothing.

1.5   79.7   K214+ The next *topes* belong to **Palos Blancos** (White Trees) just beyond the bridge. We see more cactus and less green vegetation. The rainy season in this portion of Mexico is confined almost entirely to the period from June to October, leaving the vegetation to fend for itself the rest of the year. If you go back into the foothills a dozen or more miles, it is a different story; more rain over a longer time frame, thus more greenery.

3.9   83.6   K208   We are on the outskirts of **Petatlán**. A good-sized town it has topes, bridge and a laundry river. There is almost clothes-drying room along the banks, but they keep washing more and more *ropa*. There are even small, temporary palm-leaf shelters in the middle of the riverbed. The south side of town has a fine new bus station, then comes an LPG station and local **Pemex**.

LAUNDRY RIVER

4.5   88.1   K201   A fairly large lumber mill processes pine from the hills to the north and east. Next comes the local gun club's target range, *Campo de Tiro*. We continue past another small group of houses, several ponds with water hyacinths and more orchards.

3.0   91.1   K196   A small community of **Juluchuca** follows. Continue through coco palms, up a slight rise and back toward the lagoon.

1.9   93.0   K193   If you are into 100% natural sea salt, this is the place. **La Salina** not only has its own evaporative salt works but their product is sold in little bags along the side of the road. It looks good, maybe a bit granular, but it rims a margarita glass well. Take some home to the neighbors. The price is right.

1.6   94.6   K190   Proceed up and down, in and out of small valleys solidly planted with coconuts. Thatched and tar paper houses are found in small clusters within walking distance of the plantations. **Puente La Barrita**, a bridge, comes and goes.

1.6   96.2   K187+   We take the northernmost of several turnoffs into **La Barrita** beach. *The beach faces southwest, with rock formations scattered through its mile frontage. The surfing is good here, with the hottest spot coming on a left break off the rocky boiler about 50 yards offshore.*

*The **Enramada La Barrita** is popular with the surfing crowd, both Mexican and American. Its ambiance is good, with a low, cool palm roof over well-raked sand, and the usual wooden tables and chairs. There are even a few spots to shade your car. As elsewhere, the action is on Sundays and over holidays. Several signs in Barrita claim to have bungalows for rent...but don't think you'll like 'em. We climb out of the arroyo to enjoy a fine view back along the beach. The highway continues east and up a slight rise.*

2.0   98.2   K184+   A dirt road (right) is marked with a hand painted arrow on the pavement. *It winds rather steeply past at a well-used foot trail (0.6), then clockwise up and around a group of rocks and brush. The end comes in a very small turnaround at which there is a poor foot trail. It looks so little used that we opt to try the first path.*

*The trail passes along the edge of a near-vertical drop into the water some fifty feet below. At 75 yards, a tiny cove comes into view. We are looking down on two houses, a half-dozen pangas pulled up on rocks cluttered with driftwood. From above, the water is a perfectly clear iridescent blue. We wave to the people below and are invited down to say hello. The name of the place is **Puerto Aputica**. Their catch here includes huachinango from the nets, a few lobsters, oysters and limpets (**lapas**) from the rocks. Two families live here at least part of the year, while the others hoof it in from homes several kilometers away. Puerto Aputica is not your surfing beach, nor your camping beach, it is a looking and photogenic beach. And, if the fishermen haven't already carried their catch up the hill and out to the market, you can likely buy very, very fresh fish.* We continue through a signed scattering of houses, **Cayacal**.

1.0   99.2   K183   A restaurant is perched on a cliff overlooking the ocean. There are steps down to the beach next to the restaurant's patio leading to another palapa restaurant, **Brisas del Mar**. Over the next half-mile we pass several more restaurants.

1.0   100.2   K181   A *mirador* overlooks a stunning crescent beach stretching to the southeast. The water is shallow and we see a few riptide channels. This lookout even comes with a small restaurant, and they're fixing a batch of tamales as we make our stop. The road continues near the ocean past a few houses.

3.1   103.3   K176   We cross a bridge named **Arroyo Seco**, then the town of the same name. It's still coconut country...more thousands of the palms are encountered with each turn.

3.8   107.1   K170   *Topes* tell us that we are in a town...this time it is **Coyoquilla Norte**. Then comes another laundry river. There are cornfields on the hillsides, coconuts and mangos in the narrow valleys.

*Over the last few miles we've gone by a number of good-sized obviously-handpainted signs on rocks. **Vota por Jávier** is the message. As there are no political logos and as some of his messages are painted halfway up a cliff, we would profile Jávier as an energetic, independent thinker. We wish him and his supporters well...obviously they care.*

GUERRERO

3.2   110.3   K165 We are entering the municipality of **Papanoa**. *The core of Mexico's urban and rural administrative processes is embodied in the political entity known as a* **municipio**. *Roughly equivalent to counties or provinces, most were created as the country grew and regions became settled. And like everywhere, the boundaries are usually based on political considerations. Some are very large or are densely populated, while others are small or sparsely inhabited. And the champion state in terms of municipios is Oaxaca.*

There are more municipios in Oaxaca than in all of the rest of Mexico put together! The 324 of them range from Oaxaca City to several containing less than 25 families. Once one is established, like any bureaucracy, it is hard to change. For example, lands which were once important parts of logging operations, but now have only a few scattered families, still levy taxes, elect officials, etc.

There are several impressive homes off to the left about midway through town. Papanoa is large enough to have a number of open air markets offering all kinds of things. It is also a town of *topes*. Several small sawmills are on the left. The highway moves closer to the water.

3.0   113.3   K160 The signed road (right) is to the beach and **Cayaquitos**. Beyond is a hotel, **Club Papanoa** resting on the edge of a rocky promontory overlooking the beach to the northwest. A rather well-kept structure, the hotel is often full over the weekends and on holidays. But if you want a whole hotel, pool, restaurant and bar almost to yourself, come during midweek and savor the isolation.

The hotel is independent of the development below along the beach. There are only a half-dozen homes built and a few more under construction. It appears that the infrastructure is falling into disrepair. So much for another spurt of optimism on the part of someone. The initial energy expended putting in roads, etc. has left campers with numerous opportunities to pick a beachfront spot. Ask at the hotel. We return to the bluffs, then back down past another small beach.

2.1   115.4   K156+ The paved road (right) is signed to **Puerto Vicente Guerrero**. *The road passes quickly through the town and winds upward beside a papaya orchard. Past the crest, we drop sharply to sea level and the signed community of* **Puerto Escondido** *at 1.2 miles. There are a hundred or more houses, a manmade harbor and a half-dozen scuzzy-looking restaurants. Built in 1981, the harbor appears to have been chiseled right out of the surrounding hillsides. There are docks holding upwards of 40 pangas and a small commercial gillnet boat. The area is congested with gear and the rather scummy harbor is full of baitfish and diving pelicans. There is no indication of any interest in sportfishing, nor in catching fish other than with a net. That about covers the waterfront.*

But don't give up yet...we're headed for **Claudio's Pizza Hut**. *We leave the harbor and follow the road south to a dirt trail (left) across from the small Navy station, then over a small rise to another little beach. Watch on the right for a sign and 50-yard trail to Claudio's. Now here's a guy who puts together a damn good pizza out here in the middle of nowhere. The waves crash in front, the sand is white and sparkling and he has a fine collection of musical tapes, including the old American classics. What an atmosphere for an afternoon or evening. We'd suggest registering at the nearby* **Hotel Papanoa**, *then splitting for Claudio's. He and his family have a nice new house and the best of life. Back at the barracks, if you go straight ahead you will come to several more palapa restaurants with fine seafood, but no pizza.* Back to the highway and continue past a group of hills to a long beach fronted by dunes.

4.1   119.5   K150 A dirt road south to the beach is signed to **Piedra Tlalcoyunque** and the **Carabelas** restaurant. **(See Guerrero Beaches.)** Mexico 200 straightens out and continues east through more coco palms.

2.8   122.3 K146 **Pascuela**, a permanent drug check station. Be prepared to stop.

3.8   126.1 K140 We are being welcomed into the municipality of **San Luís de La Loma** by *topes*. A restaurant, **Los Jarochitos**, is on the right. Offering homestyle meals, it is upstairs, picking up the breezes. The kitchen smelled good and the place is clean and the *cerveza* cold. Beyond and on the other side of the highway, the **Río Vista** restaurant also beckons. We cross a long bridge over a sizeable river and continue east through **San Luís San Pedro**. A road north into the mountains just past the bridge is signed to **La Laguna**, 54km. Then comes a local **Pemex** and a surprise...no *topes*.

3.1   129.2 K135 A road goes south toward the ocean but our map shows a lagoon in between. We believe the map.

3.1   132.3 K130 Signed paved road (right) is to **Fraccionamento Costa del Sol**, 4km. As *Fraccionamento* loosely translates to "lots for sale," it is not hard to guess what we're going to see... *After 1.3 miles we pass a small swampy spot and a number of cattle in a lush pasture. The pueblito of Los Tarros is next at 1.8. We go through with the basketball court on the right, do a couple of little jogs and we're on our way. The road comes to the beach dunes at 2.6. Several hundred yards ahead a bumpy road takes us close to the beach. To the left about a mile are some trees and buildings. This is obviously the headquarters for Costa del Sol. We went and looked...another one that didn't get off the ground, nor, as we see it, is it likely to do so in our lifetimes. But thanks to their subdivision efforts we have a wide choice of camping sites with few chances of seeing anyone. Driftwood is plentiful, the currents strong and the sand soft in some sections.* Back to the highway.

The road, straight for so long, finally makes a small break to the east. Soon we can see a lagoon to the south and a long, narrow strip of land covered with coco palms on the other side. There has to be at least one road out to the palms, but we never found it.

3.2   135.5 K125 An unmarked fork in the road. The left branch goes almost due north and circumnavigates **Nuxco**. Then it rejoins Mexico 200 on the other side of town. We follow the bypass.

3.6   139.1 K119 The *periférico* road rejoins Mexico 200 and we go past more coconuts. Then comes a road (right) which beckons us to visit **El Carrizál** and the restaurant **Billa Mar** with two swimming pools, etc. *The road is well graded and we pass quickly through coco palms and bananas and come to El Carrizal at 0.8. This time don't go to the basketball court but stay left of it, bypassing most of the town. Continue through coconuts and up a small rise, then down the other side at 2.0.*

At 3.2 we come into another bit of a town, La Zara. It is some hundreds of yards from the ocean, yet it is here that the palapa restaurants are located, including the by-now-famous restaurant with two pools, the Billa Mar. The beach is long and uniform, with crashing waves and little driftwood, shells, etc. The sand near the water is pretty soft, discouraging camping. We think we've saved you a trip.

4.4   143.5 K112+ Road right is paved and signed to **Tenexpa**. Our maps do not indicate that it gets beyond a lagoon.

2.4   145.9 K108 **El Suchil**, followed by **Colonia Ramos**. Then comes a long bridge over the **Río Tecpan** and the bigger town of **Tecpan de Galeana**. Tecpan is a major supply center for the coconut industry. There are offices of *copra* (dried coconut meat) buyers along the main street and the hardware stores also reflect the industry. Watch the *topes*. A full service **Pemex** is located near the far edge of town.

6.3   152.2 K97+ A nice looking restaurant, the **Diana**. Then comes a paved road (right) signed to **Tetitlan**. The map shows it continuing to **Boca Chica**. **(See Guerrero Beaches.)** We continue to drive east past an **LPG** station and more palms. We are now seeing a few of the fan palms, some organ pipe-type cactus and several small mesquite trees.

7.4   159.6 K86 A coconut oil factory on the right. Continue southeast to the marked entrance into **San Jerónimo**. *We follow the road through town toward the beach.*

GUERRERO

*A sign had announced that the **Miramar Trailer Park** is looking forward to our visit. After several miles of zigging and zagging to the ocean, then chasing a mile south along the beach we come to a dilapidated clubhouse, a green swimming pool and a few poorly-delineated parking spots. The operators are friendly and acknowledge that things aren't going too well. (We take that to be an understatement!) They also know no reason why anyone could not park and camp anywhere on the miles of beach along here. No motorhomes. The total distance in and out is less than eight miles. That's the story.* Back to the highway.

2.5   162.1   K82   The river and a local **Pemex**. Just beyond, a paved road (right) is signed to **Paraiso Escondido**. (This is one we didn't check out.) We are skirting closer to the foothills of the **Sierra Madre del Sur**. Our directions are northeast then back to southeast at the intersection with Mexico 196.

4.2   166.3   K75   **Alcholoa** is on the south side of a bridge. Coconuts are everywhere during harvest times, which seems to be all of the time. The little towns are lined up; **Colonia Lalaja** is followed by **Cacalutla**, then **Colonia Cuauhtémoc** and **Zacualpan**.

10.3   176.6   K58   We climb a small hill and have a view of the large **Laguna Miltla** to the south and west. **Rancho Vista Hermosa**. A real surprise. A palacial *hacienda* here in a world of tiny thatched houses.

2.6   179.2   K55   **El Cayaco** and **El Papayo** are two more coconut pueblos. The hillsides are cleared for the corn, beans and squash to be planted with the first summer rain.

6.0   185.2   K45   The road follows the contour of the hills crossing several small arroyos in the process.

1.8   187.0   K42   The town of **El Zapote**. A road (right) is signed to a beach development, **Playa Las Palmas**. *It turns out to be a private membership club with several buildings and a nice beach.* There is a good view of the broad marsh to the right.

3.2   190.2   K37   **Penjamo** has sideroads both into the hills and toward the ocean. The "ocean" road turns out to be to a small farming area. Penjamo itself is a center for hammocks...the ladies hang them from tree branches along Mexico 200. *We've found the hammock quality good and the prices reasonable. We bought several for ourselves and friends.*

1.3   191.5   K35   Bridge over the **Río Coyuca**, a big laundry river. The good-sized town of **Coyuca de Benitez** follows. It is a busy place, and very typical of the Mexican towns that see few tourists. A small factory makes folding and non-folding wooden chairs similar to those seen in the palapa restaurants. Beyond that, a full service **Pemex**.

4.0   195.5   K28+   A local restaurant advertises *Pollo de Leña*, or Tree Chicken, as one of their specialties. Pollo de Leña is another name for iguana. In case you're interested, it tastes much like tough, fishy chicken when done over coals.

2.8   198.3   K24   A small unnamed community on the right, then a bit farther, **El Embarcadero**.

3.1   201.4   K19   Mexico 95 goes east and north to intersect with the Mexico 95 toll road to Mexico City (**See Guerrero Inland.**) There is a permanent drug check here in all directions. We continue southeast toward Acapulco. Another laundry river is upcoming, the **Río Conchero**, followed by the town.

2.6   204.0   K15   A marvelous name for a town...**El Cerrito de Oro**, The Little Mountain of Gold. There are more tiny settlements as we continue past more coconuts and a restaurant or two.

2.9   206.9   K10+   The turnoff into **Pie de La Cuesta** (Foot of the Hill). (**See Guerrero Beaches.**) Continue around the curve to the left and along the beach for a short distance before starting the climb to the *cuesta*, or top. The road winds southeast along the edge of a series of sharp dropoffs into the Pacific. *Here and there houses have found niches on which to insert sturdy foundations into the rocks to afford their owners some of the most spectacular seaview vantage points imaginable. There is a wide divergence in building*

281

styles, etc. from luxury homes to tarpaper hovels within only a few hundred yards of each other. Trash abounds along the road, detracting from the desirability of this portion of Acapulco's spectacular coast.

We would guess that in the not-too-far-distant future the city fathers will come up with solutions to the area's problems...then watch the area boom!

0.4   207.3   K10   The first of a series of bungalow or cottage developments which appear to have been built during the 60s. A road (right) is signed to **Santa María Acapulco,** a residential project.

2.2   209.5   K6+   An **ISSSTE** resort development...it is a low-cost tourist project for less-affluent Mexican families. We've seen several of these resorts scattered through Mexico.

2.8   212.3   K2   There is a full service **Pemex** on the right at a "Y", the left branch of which drops down into the the center of the city. The right branch winds through more traffic and lights and eventually ends up near the *zocalo* in the old part of Acapulco.

End of log.

ACAPULCO...

Archaeologists and anthropologists are still working to provide accounts of the this region through the sculptures, rock paintings, hieroglyphics and the thousands of small ceramic heads being unearthed in the 2000-year-old ruins of a **Tlahuica** Indian city near **La Sabana,** just north of Acapulco Bay.

More decipherable accounts began when the Spaniards arrived in 1550 and found a small fishing and agricultural village on the shore of the protected bay. It expanded when Hernán Cortéz designated Acapulco as the home port for his Pacific expeditions and began building boats there. By 1565 the Manila trade routes had opened and Acapulco became the most important western port in the new world when, a few years later, it became the only port allowed to handle the Oriental trade goods. Here, treasures of silk, spices, silver, gold and pearls were stockpiled for transshipment over the mountains to Mexico City, Vera Cruz and eventually, Spain.

Its importance as a port made Acapulco a key ingredient in Mexico's struggles for autonomy. Blood was spilled in 1810 as she struggled to free herself from Spain; the city was attacked by Santa Ana during the reform era and she was shelled by the French in 1864. Without the Orient trade, activities slowed in Acapulco, especially after more Pacific Coast ports opened in the United States. By the turn of the century, this former center of western commerce had regressed back to a sleepy Mexican fishing town. It was not for another quarter century that her fortunes took a turn for the better.

In 1927, a road was built through the mountains to connect Mexico City with the Acapulco coast. Then came a landing strip in 1928. The first tourist hotel, the **Mirador,** opened in 1933 overlooking the spectacular cliffs at **La Quebrada.** But the big break came in the early 1950s, when President Miguel Alemán made Acapulco his personal project. The broad street circling the bay appropriately bears his name.

Today, when we look at Acapulco, we see it as having three faces...

The first is the line of high-rise hotels, restaurants, discos, shops, and more shops. It presents itself as a fast-paced, glamorous, swinging resort, attracting visitors from Chicago, Boise, Los Angeles and New York; Toronto, Manitoba and Montreal; London, Paris and Stuttgart; and Mexico, too.

Another face is presented by the more traditional, downtown Acapulco, the places where it all began more than a half-century ago. Here it is quieter and the buildings have fewer amenities, but they have a personality often lost in a 22-story, 400-room hotel catering to "package" tourists. It is here that many of the true *aficianados* of Mexico's resorts, lifestyles and ambiance gather. It is here in traditional Acapulco that one can still sit on the edge of a cliff, watch the ocean pound onto the rocks below, see the birds diving on schools of bait and savor a perfect sunset with no vendors, no highway noise and no shoulder-to-shoulder crowds.

The city itself and its million residents is the third face. Here, on the hillsides, in the valleys away from the beaches and the burgeoning suburbs live the taxi drivers, waiters, bartenders, chefs, maids, shopkeepers and streetsweepers who keep this world-class resort functioning. Their attitude and the way they do their jobs are have a strong influence in helping a visitor decide to return.

Lets look at a few of the things each has to offer...

The La Quebrada area belongs to the daring cliff divers and the old **Mirador Hotel** (now the **Las Glorias**), with its unobstructed views from the terrace. To the south, another lovely old hotel, **Los Flamingos**, sits perched on the cliff's edge overlooking the sea to the south and west. It is a favorite, and we headquarter here during our Acapulco stays. The **Hotel Casablanca** is another up here with a grand view.

Playa Caleta and nearby **Caletilla** are popular beaches in the older section of town. From Caleta, the "morning beach," boats will take you to **Isla Roquet** for snorkeling and scuba diving. Or take a glass-bottom boat. And there's a bullring nearby. Sundays at 5PM.

On the hillsides above the beaches are numerous hotels, motels, bungalows and suites, and most are excellent values, such as: **Villa Las Hadas, Linda Vista Suites, Hotel Nao, Hotel Sherazada Suites, Bungalows El Rosio, Punta Peñasco Hotel,** and **Motel La Jolla**. Here too are many of the finer old homes built in the 40s, 50s and 60s. A look into the cool courtyards reveals murmuring fountains, spreading trees and tranquility.

The thatch-roofed **Mitla** near the yacht club serves the cheapest beer in town and a good luncheon menu of typical Mexican food.

The busy *zocalo* area sports a number of excellent seafood restaurants, shops and budget hotels. Take a relaxing stroll through the tree-shaded **Plaza Juan Alvarez** or sit at a sidewalk cafe and people watch. West of the plaza are the seafood restaurants, the **Mariscos Silva, Nachos Cevichería, El Amigo Miguel** and **Sr. Pipos**. Pipos, which goes back to the days of Johnny Weismuller and Errol Flynn, still serves some of the finest seafood in the city.

One of the best meals in the city is found up a flight of stairs overlooking the plaza at a German restaurant, **Terraza de Las Flores**. Try their *chamorro de cerdo* (German sausage), sauerbraten, or steaks. They have their own slaughter house in Mexico City. Expect to wait for a table...it is a busy place.

Tamales Licha, near Pipos, has the best tamales in town (open evenings only). North of the zocalo on Calle Felipe Valle, the 200 year old colonial **Hotel Misión** not only has charming rooms off a plant-filled courtyard, but puts on a Thursday lunch buffet that is reputed to be the best around; however...twice a Thursday came and went, and no buffet. Better check first.

Northeast of the plaza is the **Mercado de Curiosidades**. It is full of little shops selling all the usual handicrafts at lower prices than the downtown area. Even the most reserved visitor is likely to stagger out with all sorts of treasures. Nearby, at the corner of 5 de Mayo and 2 de Abrfl, **Goyo's** serves an excellent *comida corrida* for very little. This day's special is Azteca soup, barbecued beef, beans, *guacamole, bolillos* and stewed prunes. Add a soda or *cerveza* and you're set for the day. *The busy, smiling waitress here is **Liliana**. She has been a waitress for 22 years and loves every minute of it.*

Across the **Costero** from the plaza are the docks where fishing trips are arranged and you board the larger ships for the sunset and harbor cruises. The **San Diego** fort, with its fine regional museum, is to the east of the plaza.

Move east around the bay to **Los Hornos** beach. Named for the ovens where lime was burned to make mortar during the construction of **Fort San Diego**, both Hornos and **Hornitos** to the east are lined with *palapa* restaurants and fronted by clusters of beach chairs and umbrellas or thatched palm shades. They are for rent by the hour or day.

Acapulco Hub Map

The names of the public beaches change at every street, so you'll find a lineup like **Hamacas, Dominquillo, Suave, Bocana, Tamarindos, Karabali** and **Bocanita**, if you care to keep track. On the land side of the Costero, restaurants, hotels and shops share space with a children's park and several large retail supermarkets. There are some good places to eat along here too...though prices tend to be higher. We've had good dinners at **La Bella Italia** and friends recommend **Super Hamburguesas** on **Avenida Cuauhtémoc** for large American-style hamburgers..."better than they can make in Detroit."

The city's only metropolitan trailer park is the **Playa Suave**. Located behind the **Doral Playa Hotel**, it offers a convenient, well-fenced and guarded location from which to visit Acapulco. The park is shaded by huge mango trees, and each space has its own bathroom and shower. No hot water...but who needs hot water in Acapulco. Spaces are limited and they do not take reservations.

Now comes the area known as **La Condesa**. About three miles long, it is wall-to-wall four and five-star hotels, chic shops and pricey restaurants. Here's where you find the fashionable cafes, swinging bars and lively discos. Sports fans can find identity at the **Cheers Disco**, as they feature all manner of sports daily until the 9PM start of discomania.

The downtown Costero portion of Acapulco ends at the **Centro Cultural de Acapulco**. Built in 1976 and set in 35 acres of beautifully landscaped gardens, it is the home for numerous conventions, cultural events and expositions.

The fiestas around Acapulco tend to be nonreligious. The **NAO de China** commemorating the start of the galleon trade with the Orient, is in November, and the **Expo-Acapulco**, an industrial and commercial expo, from Dec 20 to Jan 7, are examples. To many visitors, any time is fiesta time in Acapulco. Enjoy.

284

GUERRERO

MEXICO 200 — ACAPULCO — BORDER

The highway below Acapulco has less to offer than Guerrero's portion of Mexico 200 north of the city, but there are several very special jewels located a short distance off the highway. We begin this log several miles east of downtown Acapulco where Mexico highways 95 and 200 intersect. To get there we leave the hotel zone via the Diana Glorieta and go east over the hill.

0.0   0.0   K0   Now in front of us is another *glorieta* sporting a statue of **General Lázaro Cárdenas**. We take the south exit onto Mexico 200.

This route doesn't mean we are getting rid of the traffic...it is jammed...but we don't have to deal with miles of taxis, pedestrians, signals and the many, many side streets which make Acapulco frustrating for the driver passing through. **(See Acapulco City.)**

One can become inundated with the possibly-thousands of vendors lining both sides of the already-narrow highway. Foodstuffs of all kinds...chickens, meats, fruits and vegetables are everywhere. Not even a place to park, so they obviously deal mostly with pedestrians. It looks like a zoo, but all things seem to be working. We pass a local **Pemex** and follow the road south.

1.7   1.7   K2+   **El Coloso** trailer park is on the left. It appears to be well off the beaten track and probably pretty warm. It does have a pool and a fair amount of shade. During a mid-February visit it was about half full. There is only one trailer park remaining in Acapulco proper, the **Playa Suave**. Two others are in Pie de La Cuesta, 6 miles north of town and there are two out this way on or near Mexico 200.

We have always been fascinated with the ability of women and girls to carry things on the tops of their heads, and after over 30 years the mystique is still there. We recently watched a woman in Acapulco weave through traffic with a full case of Coca-Cola balanced on her head. Laundry, buckets of water and bundles of firewood are common sights. So too are the day's dishes. This balancing act is carried out even while the woman is going up or down a steep river bank.

A recent addition to the list is the lady who carried two armloads of washing while balancing a large pot topped by a wheel of cheese. Another was a mother in high heels who balanced the week's washing, tub and all, while carrying a baby in one arm and a large plastic bag of detergent in the other.

The best thus far is the middle-aged woman near Pinotepa Nacionál who carried on an animated conversation while walking briskly with a wooden dining-room chair under each arm while her head balanced a large tray with a bucket of dishes on it. And directly in front of the bucket on the tray was a glass bottle of tomato catsup! A walking restaurant, maybe?

1.0   2.7   K4   The intersection to **Puerto Marques** (right) and the region of the **Acapulco Princess/Pierre Marques** complex. This cutoff is just over 7 kilometers. It does have a trailer park, the **La Roca**, near the 5 kilometer marker. Otherwise, it is just that...a cutoff. It will also take us to the airport and the beaches near and beyond it. **(See Guerrero Beaches.)**

To the west in **El Coloso** are dozens of 8 to 10-story white and pastel apartment buildings. They are the housing for many of the people who work in touristic services along Acapulco's **Costera Alemán**. We continue southeast past a Coca Cola bottling plant. *In the early days of traveling and camping in Mexico, the sight of a soft drink bottling plant was a welcome one, for here we were allowed to fill up on potable water. It was a marvelous gesture that was extended with a smile. Today, we buy the bottled water in one-gallon plastic containers at a nearby store. Just ask for "agua potable".* Next comes a long bridge and the entrance to the signed town of **Tunzingo**. We've finally broken away from the city and are back into coco plantations and small towns.

2.3   5.0   K8   This is the locality known as **La Sabana**. *Sabana is the site of a little-publicized archaeological zone that has yielded numerous ceramic heads, the* *remains of several sculptures and ruins of buildings. Some of the containers found here resemble human figures and are inscribed with writings as yet undeciphered. There is some disagreement among anthropologists as to whether the work was that of the* **Tlahuica** *Indians, who were known to have lived there, or by an earlier group.*

1.6   6.6   K10+   A clean-looking restaurant, **Las Palmeras**, is on the north side of Mexico 200. Then come the signed communities of **Nicolás Bravo** and **San Pedro de Las Playas**. A large lagoon, **Laguna Tres Palos**, is immediately to the south.

8.1   14.7   K23+   The small town of **San Antonio**. We continue east-southeast through low rocky hills and gentle curves. **Laguna Tres Palos** to the west is about gone, replaced by ever more palm trees. Next is the appropriately-named little village, **Cerro de Piedra** (Rock Hill). Several houses sport signs announcing the availability of *queso de rancho*, ranch cheese. As we move toward the valley ahead the rocks thin out and corn is back on the hillsides.

4.6   19.3   K30+   We reach, and cross, the **Río Papagallo**. It is a good-sized river with a *pueblito* on the southeast side.

1.8   21.1   K33₊   A little household on the left is taking advantage of the abundant small trees nearby by cutting and selling wood for cooking fires. It is all cut to length and stacked neatly in long rows by the highway. There is easily enough here to fill a big truck.

1.0   22.1   K35   On the left is **Tejoruco**, a tiny collection of houses and a white and blue church. The church surely cost more to build than all the houses in the area put together. Beyond, on the right, is a small, rustic poultry ranch. The paved road south used to connect with the beach road south of the Acapulco airport, but no longer. The bridge is out. **(See Guerrero Beaches.)**

4.0   26.1   K41+   A permanent drug and weapons inspection station. We are usually closely inspected here. *Incidentally, by now the highway traffic has thinned way out and is very light.*

1.3   27.4   K43+   Here's a rare one-lane bridge over a nameless laundry stream. Just beyond is the signed community of **El Cortés** and a graded road into the hills. The town is typical of the region, with tile roofs, brick and adobe walls and a small church.

1.1   28.5   K45+   There is a busy roofing tile (*tejas*) factory on the left. All of the work is done by hand, and if you have time and are curious about how it's done, they are happy to show you.

2.8   31.3   K50   The signed pueblo of **La Estancia** and two more brick factories before another one-lane bridge.

5.0   36.3   K58   We enter the outskirts of **San Marcos**, population 15,000. The action here is principally livestock, agriculture and fishing, with some production from the nearby evaporative salt works. Take a few minutes and turn (left) into town and go to the central market. Not only do they have excellent fruits and vegetables but also a variety of pottery items, some baskets, burro saddles and iguanas on the hoof. The people are friendly and demonstrate a fine sense of humor.

A Friday visit to the San Marcos mercado netted us a wooden tray almost three feet in diameter, with a handle carved on one side. It is made by **Rudolfo**, *a charming gentleman in his sixties with large and powerful hands. Rudolfo lives some miles up the Río Estancia and walks to town whenever he has something to sell. Our interest in the tray and the negotiations for it caused the nearby women considerable amusement but we dismissed it as a result of our poor Spanish.*

A bargain was finally struck and the large, beautiful and lightweight tray was ours. A triumphant march through the market to our car brought more laughs.

Finally someone explained. What we bought from Rudolfo is used by the women to carry laundry to the river. Once there the concave, slightly uneven surface serves as a washboard. The joke was over the likelihood of gringo Tom getting gringa Carol to carry laundry to the river on her head...and then wash it!

We wondered aloud why the laundry board would be made round rather than rectangular. The answer should have been obvious...so it will balance on Carol's head more easily!

Rudolfo's marvelous washboard is headed for our Baja house and will undoubtedly serve many salads, tostadas, etc.

Back out to the highway and past a Superior/Dos Equis beer warehouse and a small hotel with a pool, the **Lecarma**.

Years ago the **mariachis** *from San Marcos were famous for their renditions of Mexico's folk music. Today, based on the several signs we see along the highway, they have been replaced by such "grupos" as "Galaxie," "Penultimo" and "Panteón Azul (Blue Cemetery)." But then, where else in the world is it any different?* We continue south, winding gently through the hills past corn fields and coconuts.

7.7   44.0   K70+   A small, signed group of houses, **Caridád** stretches along the highway for about half-mile.

4.4   48.4   K77+   The signed pueblo of **San José**. The paved road turns left here while a signed dirt road goes straight ahead to **Espinalillo de Tenante**. Shortly we come to **Las Vigas**, a community large enough to have a few *tiendas* and a local **Pemex**. It also has its own river, though not much of one.

2.9   51.3   K82   On the left is what may be a new, low-cost housing development...only time will tell.

2.0   53.3   K85   We cross the **Río Nexpa** on a high and wide bridge. It is a laundry river, thanks to the pueblo of **El Porvenír** on its east bank. The road continues southeast through a marshy area jammed with water hyacinths and coconut plantations.

4.4   57.7   K92+   A graded road (right) does not go to the ocean. Forget it.

2.2   59.9   K96   The outskirts of the town of **Cruz Grande**. The main portion of the town is to the north of the highway. It serves as a junction for a paved road north into the foothills of the **Sierra Madre del Sur**. Passing through **Ayutla de Los Libres**, it eventually connects with other highways into Chilpancingo and Mexico City. There is a local **Pemex** as we leave town. Next comes a small laundry stream and a few houses.

5.9   65.8   K105+ A few more houses and lots of turkeys. *This portion of Mexico seems to have a love affair with turkeys, or guajolotes. Every house seems to have a flock scratching around. They come in all colors...from the typical gray/black to reddish to white and combinations thereof.*

1.6   67.4   K107+ An unsigned collection of houses big enough to have a soccer field.

1.6   69.0   K110+ **Las Peñas**. A road (right), presumably to a lagoon. *And it does go to a lagoon. The road is rough, dusty and about 2.5 miles in to the water and a ramshackle collection of stick and mud houses. It is a colony of the black* **Costeños**, *who have inhabited this portion of Mexico since the mid-1500s.*

The Costeños are believed to have evolved from Africans brought over as slaves who escaped from the Spanish at Huatulco more than 400 years ago. Their history and true origins have been the object of several recent studies. There are a couple of restaurants and a number of boats are pulled up on the shore, but the people do not appear friendly. A car must be a true rarity here; we didn't see any, or even tire tracks in the dust around any of the several hundred houses. Maybe we've saved you a trip,..or piqued your interest.

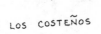

LOS COSTEÑOS

287

3.3   72.3   K116 A single-lane bridge over a wide laundry river. The road divides, the left section goes to **Copala**, the right bypasses it. We log the bypass. The town is not large, but it's big enough to have a furniture (*muebles*) store, a couple of *abarrotes* and a *farmácia*.

2.8   75.1   K120 A good-sized brick factory is on the left. The large pink-flowering trees around here are said to be a variety of *primavera*, whose showy yellow flowers are common each spring around Manzanillo.

2.3   77.4   K123+ A dirt road south is signed to **Playa Ventura**, 5km. **(See Guerrero Beaches.)** There are a couple of houses directly across from the intersection. This part of Guerrero doesn't appear to get much rain, but what it does receive probably comes in big gulps. The road continues east in long, straight stretches over fairly flat land.

5.2   82.6   K132 Road (right) to **Las Salinas**. Next comes **Islatepec**. Both are predominantly brick-and-roof-tile communities.

1.8   84.4   K135 We come to a school, a bridge over a swampy area, then another laundry river. The fair-sized town, **Marquelia** (K137), on the east side of the river provides the dirty clothes. Wednesday, Friday and Saturday are the big market days. There is a road to the beach that leaves from near the center of town. On the right, near the end of the sales stalls, is a building with the name Dr. Zarate on it. Turn just past here and go back a few meters to a graded road south. We are headed for **La Bocana**.

*We begin by going past a number of houses, then zigzag toward the south along property lines through coconut and lime trees. The vegetation is abundant as we are very near a small freshwater lagoon fed by the **Río Marquelia**. We arrive at the water at 1.9 miles. This is the mouth of the lagoon, and the water is very shallow...a couple of feet or less. On the other side are about 20 small restaurants. They are flimsily built, because each rainy season they have to be picked up and moved to higher ground or they will be lost.*

Talked to a charming lady named **Sara** who showed us fresh oysters, huachinango and shrimp. The shrimp are taken all year from the lagoon. The oysters come from the offshore rocky reefs, as do the huachinangos. Her stove is made of adobe and would be too heavy and fragile to move...thus a new stove has to be made each year. Where the adobe comes from we don't know.

The beach beyond the bocana is very pretty, with a good wave pattern. We see some driftwood and shells. There's no place to camp and very little parking, but it has a special charm which will draw us back, if nothing else but to see Sara's new stove. Back to the highway and the *topes* leading us east past a local **Pemex** and out of town.

1.8   86.2   K138 Just as Marquelia ends, a signed road points us toward **Barra de Tecoanapa**, 15km. This one we decided to pass up in favor of **Punta Maldonado**. Maybe next trip. Continue east past a number of tiny settlements.

4.4   90.6   K145 The signed community of **Barrio Nuevo**. The area is dry, but must be some humidity for there are bromeliads in most of the trees. The green and red leaves and tiny flowers look strange on otherwise leafless trees.

3.7   94.3   K150+ A bridge over a small stream.

4.0   98.3   K157+ Signed town of **Juchitan**. Watch for **topes**. Tamarindo trees are common here. *Tamarindos are a sweet, edible bean pod from this member of the mesquite family and is a popular flavoring for the low-cost **aguas frescas** so common in rural Mexico.* A road (left) goes north to **Azoyu** and several other farming centers. Continue east along a row of high-tension towers.

5.8   104.1   K166+ At the top of a small rise is a panoramic view to the south and west. Looking north we see line after line of hills, then mountains as the full 6000-foot height of this portion of the **Sierra Madre del Sur** is revealed. An impressive sight, particularly with thunder heads looming high over the tallest peaks.

*At one point (**K168+**) we stop under a very large, densely-leafed tree to relax and*

288

move around a bit. Shortly a man came across the highway to see if there was a problem. When he realizes that there is none, he asks where we are from and where we're going. As we get back into the car he wishes us well on our trip and we thank him for the use of the tree. A win-win situation.

Continue through the hills, catching occasional glimpses of small green valleys off to the right and hillsides mottled with the corn fields on the left.

3.7   107.8   K172+ The **Río Quetzala** is nearby on our right. Then comes into the town of the same name, and a bridge. This one is another laundry river, with kids by the dozen playing above where the women are washing. It appears to be a tumbling, diving form of soccer played in water about a foot deep.

1.6   109.4   K175   A signed road (left) into **Ometepec, 16km**, *and a bridge over the Río Quetzala. Ometepec has an interesting archaeological background. Two small heads made of stone have been found nearby. They are formed in the style of the Olmeca culture. Not far away is a spot known as **Piedra Labrada** (Carved Rock), where there are many ceramic pieces similar to those found in Monte Alban. There are also several zoomorphic sculptures made of basalt; an ocelot and a turtle. The scientists, have also unearthed several stele. The largest is about 15 feet high and 3 feet in diameter. Some of the glyphs have been deciphered and are expected to provide further insights into the spread of Olmec culture through **mesoamerica**.* Mexico 200 bends here at a local **Pemex** and heads south across a valley of coco palms.

4.1   113.5   K181+ To the right, a small lake and marshy area. Two men in a dugout canoe are moving slowly across the lake. Water hyacinths are common through here. *It is unfortunate such a beautiful plant can be so destructive. The water hyacinth originally came from Brazil and gained popularity as a decorative plant in ponds. A rapid grower, it can quickly cover the surface of a shallow pond, cutting off the lifegiving light to the plants and animal life below. Many things have been tried to control the water hyacinth, from manatees and dugongs to harvesting it for the manufacture of paper and animal fodder. Nothing yet has proven satisfactory, and it continues to spread.*

1.9   115.4   K184+ We cross a sizeable river with lots of moving water. Our maps indicate that it is the **Río Santa Catarina**, which flows into the Río Quetzala. We continue into a lush valley with lots of cattle, green pastures, well-kept coco palms, mangos and bananas. All of this beauty is a result of the hard work of the people of **Comaltepec**.

3.0   118.4   K189+ This graded/paved road right leads not to the ocean but to a couple of small farming *ejidos*, according to the local farmers. We've a pig farm off to the left. The odor is unmistakable.

1.6   120.0   K192   Next comes a bridge across another laundry river and more of the verdant land we've been seeing over the past miles. Every bit of ground here has something on it. Even bananas and papayas are growing wild along the highway.

4.4   124.4   K199   A rather incongruous sign, **Lenny's Restaurant and Bar** adorns a restaurant and it looks pretty good. Just beyond is a local **Pemex** and a sign welcoming us to **Cuajinicuilapa**. Vendor stalls line the highway on both sides. Watch for the unmarked **topes**. Every day is market day here. *We notice a store selling Singer Sewing Machines. Yes, they still make treadle machines and distribute them widely in the developing countries. We went in and priced them...the equivalent of $165 American dollars as of March, 1990.*

CALABASAS

1.6   126.0   K201+ An intersection with a signed and paved road south to **Punta Maldonado**. It's hard to miss this turnoff...the road is paved, signed, has a drug check station. *We said that it is paved...well it is...at the start. There are detours and washouts along the way. The soil in this rolling terrain is bright red.*

*After passing several small settlements we arrive at Maldonado, and a surprise...**Punta Maldonado** has lost its beach! Once a wide one with lots of sand and many, many pangas*

289

pulled up on it, it is no more. During the end of 1988 and into 1989 a change in the current patterns had completely obliterated the half-mile beach. Now it is only a jumble of small, rounded boulders, making it almost impossible to safely bring in a boat. What will happen here in the future is anybody's guess, according to one fisherman. Many of his friends have already moved out.

We are sorry. Though it never was a beautiful find which would live forever in your mind, its loss is being felt by some very nice people. Back to the highway and continue east on a very straight road through fairly flat country with little or no plant life to decorate the skyline, only a few cattle here and there.

We've noticed that many of the horsemen through this portion of Guerrero and south to Pinotepa Nacionál wear felt hats rather than the straw **sombreros**. *Not sure why, but it gives a Texas-like atmosphere to the landscape.*

4.0   130.0   K208   We've come to the border between **Guerrero** and **Oaxaca**. The Mexico 200 highway continues straight southeast over a good two-lane roadbed.

End of log.

THE ACAPULCO BYPASS

If you are driving a large motorhome or pulling a trailer, it is not too swift an idea to try to negotiate the crowded and winding northwest entrance into the city. It is far easier to get to the southern part of Acapulco, or bypass it entirely, by taking the route described below.

      0.0   0.0   K19   We turn off Mexico 200 at K19 north of **Pie de La Cuesta** and take Mexico 95 east and north to connect with the Mexico 95 toll road from Mexico City. After passing through a somewhat ramshackle collection of houses we begin winding through the low hills backing this portion of the coast. Brickmaking is a popular business here...the right kind of dirt and lots of coconut husks come together for good product in a ready market.

      2.3   2.3   K18   Bridge over **Río Valle**. Continue east up past a number of roadside coconut stands and along the left side of a narrow valley full of coco palms. The hillsides are, again, set aside for corn. There are even little palapas scattered about in the clearings, apparently so the farmers can rest in the shade.

      3.3   5.6   K13   The road goes farther into the hills and away from the palms. Scrub brush from the mesquite family and other small deciduous trees (including kapok) cover the hillsides.

      2.1   7.7   K9   One of Acapulco's many trash dumps welcomes us. A relatively small one, it is followed by a much bigger (and messier) one at K7. Then comes a descent toward Mexico 95 and the rest of the Acapulco bypass.

      2.4   10.1   K5   **El Zapote** is a signed grouping of about ten houses up on a hill. As there is no apparent road, all supplies, including water, would have to be packed up.

      1.7   11.8   K2+   There are several attempts at restaurants here. Continue on over a bridge and an attractive little stream cascading over jumbles of rocks.

      1.2   13.0   K0   We intersect with the Mexico-Acapulco highway. The road (right) goes south into the back section of Acapulco, while a left turn leads eventually to Mexico City. As noted earlier, this is a preferred route to the The Mexico 200 highway and southern portion of Mexico's west coast for those entering Mexico from Texas. We turn toward the ocean.

      1.5   14.5   K115   We briefly follow along the left bank of the river, then cross and follow the other side.

      1.5   16.0   K117+A small community that's loaded with coconuts. The next wide spot is **Los Organos**.

      1.7   17.7   K120   Beginning about here and the rest of the way into the city, there are countless roadside stalls selling coconuts in any form you can imagine. *Green and icy-cold for a refreshing drink; brown-husked; dried and shredded; cooked in syrup and made into candies; etc. etc. One place even had nativity scenes glued into the hollow shells.*

      1.5   18.2   K122+ A Corona beer agency is on the left. Continue straight toward town. We come into the industrial section of Acapulco and a six lane boulevard. To the left, a full service **Pemex** station...the first in a while.

      2.0   20.2   K126   We are now in the middle of the *glorieta* circling **General Lázaro Cárdenas** who stands overlooking the traffic snarls, maybe wondering whatever happened to the good old days. This traffic circle is supposed to sort the traffic heading north to the upper parts of Acapulco, west into the tourist section and south along the coast into the proper lanes and channels. It is only partially successful, but on the second go-around a space opens and we head south, avoiding the metropolitan district entirely.

    End of the Acapulco bypass.

PUERTO MARQUES — MEXICO 200 JUNCTION

0.0   0.0   We leave the intersection shunting cars to Acapulco, the airport, **Puerto Marques** and the intersect east with Mexico 200.

3.1   3.1   On the left, someone is putting in the infrastructure for a trailer park, though this doesn't look like a particularly good spot for this use. Our belief is reinforced by the fact that the **La Roca** trailer park up the street is open, but empty, just before Easter.

2.1   5.2   The numerous apartment buildings on the left are accessed by this turnoff to the left. The development is called **El Coloso**.

0.7   5.9   We intersect with Mexico 200 at K4. To the right is the road to **Pinotepa Nacionál**, left is to Acapulco Centro and points north.

End of Log

GUERRERO BEACHES

Playa El Atracadero

At K64 north of Zihuatanejo, a dirt road branches right toward **El Atracadero**. At **0.8** a road (right) appears to go toward the central portion of the beach...it is principally a farm road with very poor road conditions near the water. We did not try it all of the way for fear of getting trapped but returned and took the left fork. At **1.7** we go past some good-looking mango and papaya orchards. Near the beach coconut palms predominate. We arrive at **1.9** to see a half-dozen *palapas* scattered just above the tide line. Most offer *hamacas* and car shades. At high tide they are either out of business or have a captive audience because you must drive over the wet sand to reach the restaurants.

OYSTER DIVERS

We are looking at sacks full of oysters, only minutes out of the water. We order a platter of *ostiones cruda en su concha* (oysters on the half-shell), then a *ceviche* of oysters marinated in lime, chiles, tomatoes and onions. They also serve fried fish.

The beach is beautiful. The south end is rocky for some distance beyond the breakers. This is where most of the oysters come from, and 25 divers make their living gathering them. Staying in the ocean as long as three hours at a time, diving, swimming to new grounds and hauling around the catch in large innertubes, their bodies are muscular and lean from the heavy exercise. Their attitude is positive and expectedly a bit raucous when they finally finish their work for the day.

The oysters are fantastic...five minutes out of the ocean and they are being opened for our table! Here we can buy three dozen for what a plate of six cost in a trendy Ixtapa restaurant. Back to the highway.

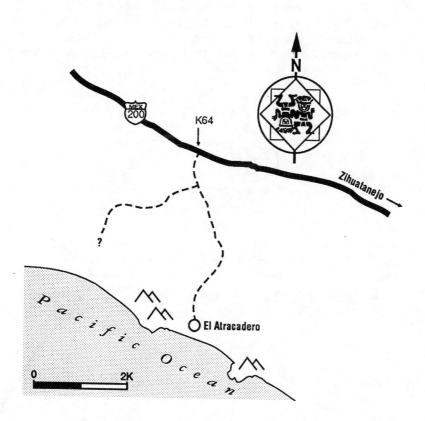

293

Playa Los Llanos...

At K40 north of Zihuatanejo, we go right through the town of **Los Llanos**. *This particular beach is well known for its excellent lobster dinners at very low prices. We made a couple of wrong turns before getting it straight.* At **0.2** turn (right) just before the basketball court. At **3.1** we are at the beach. Of the half-dozen restaurants along here we have chosen the one on the far right, **Palapa Jacalyn**. Named after one of the daughters, it keeps the whole family busy.

RURAL SCHOOL HOUSE

The gray beach sand has a fine texture and the lagoon entrance is on the south end next to their restaurant. There is some driftwood, but not much close to the road. The break is good enough to attract a fair number of surfers. It also enjoys a small enclave of refugees from the Pacific Northwest.

A couple from Montana were camped in a coconut grove several hundred yards to the south. It was their fourth winter here. Three Canadian surfers and their girlfriends were jammed into a van which didn't look large enough to hold all six of them, much less the boards, tents, ice chest, stove, chairs, table, etc. needed for their wintertime adventure.

The combination of fresh and brackish lagoons and an ability to get out on the open sea makes for a marvelous variety of seafood. There are crabs and pargo from the lagoons, while the boats going outside load up on lobster, oyster and *huachinango*. They sell only what they catch...nothing else, and are proud of it. Back to the highway.

Playa Majahúa...

At K33 north of Zihuatanejo we take the signed turnoff to **Playa Majahúa** and follow a dusty road west past papaya trees for **0.8** miles. At the fork we take the left branch as instructed by a worker at the papaya orchard. There is a low crest at **1.8**, then a descent to the ocean. Several small stands of the original forest are scattered about, but some of them are being cleared...more signs of "progress." A small waterhole is on the left at **3.2**. On the

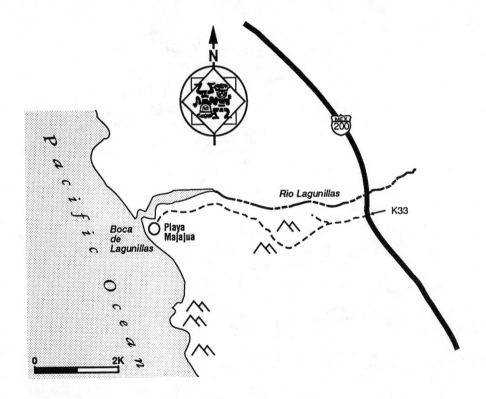

right, more papayas and a power line, then the ocean at **3.5**. There are a few palapa restaurants, a dozen or more houses and a small building for processing seafood. The beach is very pretty, with rocks dominating the southeastern end, while a small *estero* and a palm plantation back a sandy beach to the north. Driftwood is plentiful and shells scarce. The locals say that they do well on jack cravalle and pargo from the beach. There is little room to camp, but people do it.

We haven't found Majahúa on anybody's list of surfing spots but there were some great, empty, left breaks off the point on a high west swell during this visit. Back to the highway.

Playa Troncones...

Turn southwest at K30+ of Mexico 200 on the intersection to **Troncones**. The road is paved for **2.2** miles. Then follow the dirt road through town and on to the beach at **3.5**. A left turn takes us to a small lagoon entrance and a low bluff and rocky point which would make a marvelous homesite. Just beyond is a small beach and intertidal area studded with black lava spires.

*Our first time here was in the mid 70s, when we were brought by a Zihuatanejo resident, **Natalia Krebs**. At the time it was completely uninhabited and a perfect spot for pictures. One part has really not changed much...that second beach...it was, and still is, stunning.*

Palapa restaurants dot the beach front and there are many spots for camping. Check with the nearest resident.

There are also the remains of a well-intended touristic complex. Actually it is not that bad...most of the rooms still have doors and most of the plumbing and much of the community kitchen complex is intact. A crumbling water tower and delapidated well casing fill out the infrastructure. It is sited almost perfectly, a couple of hundred yards west of the

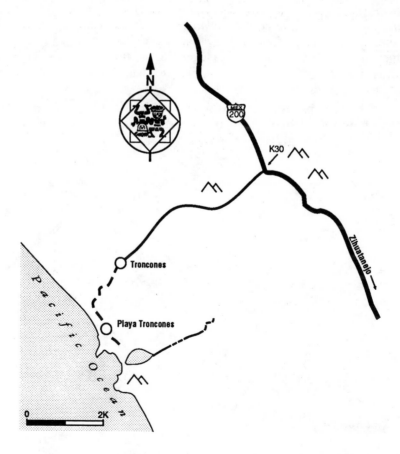

small beach mentioned above and back far enough from the water to be reasonably safe from storm waves. There it sits...a monument to someone's imperfect planning...whether it was financing, ownership of property, poor construction (that seems unlikely) or what...it is a sad sight.

To the right of the intersection the road extends for at least a mile through sometimes-rough terrain past a number of homesites and marked lots. The beach is rocky with some sand, thus making it less likely to wash away during storms. The underbrush is heavy but there are access spots to the beach and possibly a campsite.

Though the entire beach area shows signs of having been masterplanned, it is definitely in limbo...but one of these days it will happen; the area is too beautiful to stay undisturbed. Back to the highway.

Playa La Capilla...

At K20+ a road (right) is signed to **Pantla**. We go through town past the basketball court on the left and toward the riverbed, turning into it at **0.8** miles. Go out the other side and follow west to a gate at **1.5**. Permission to pass is easily obtained, just be sure to leave the gate in the position you found it. At **2.4** we are at the ocean, parked in the middle of thousands of coco palms. Nearby is a beautiful small church (*capilla*), a house under construction and the home of a caretaker, a charming lady by the name of **Giselda**. When we arrive Giselda is cooking the midday meal for about a dozen workers on an *Estofa de Tierra*. Translated literally, it is a stove of dirt. Made of adobe, it is nine years old and looks brand new. Fascinating.

*The chapel and the large and luxurious home here in the middle of miles of coconuts is owned by the woman who used to own the **Huerta de Ixtapa**, the site of the tourist complex, Ixtapa. When she sold it to the government she bought these miles of beach and its many thousands of coconut palms. When the house is completed she will move in and the place may be closed to visitors, but in the meantime, if you have the time, the beauty of the **capilla** alone makes it a worthwhile trip.* A word of warning...it is unlikely that you will ever run into more dust than is found along the last portion of this trip. Right after the rainy season up into January it is not bad, but by March and April...it is something else.

The beach itself is long, beautiful and pebbly in places. It is well stocked with driftwood. The house and chapel are positioned near the southern end of the beach. No motorhomes! Back to the highway.

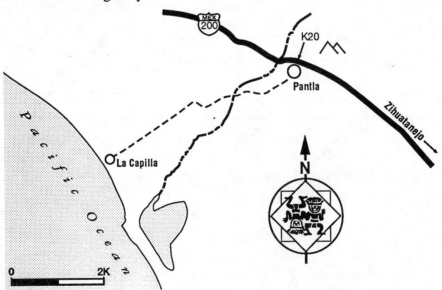

GUERRERO

Playa Los Pozos...

There is a beach you should know about. Its name, Los Pozos...

We begin by taking the paved road (right) to the **Zihuatanejo** airport at K230. Begin looking for a dirt road (right) at the green chain-link fence just before the *topes* and the parking lot entrance. A good road, it follows the fence **1.2** miles to the beach, where we are greeted by a lineup of 7 or 8 palapa restaurants.

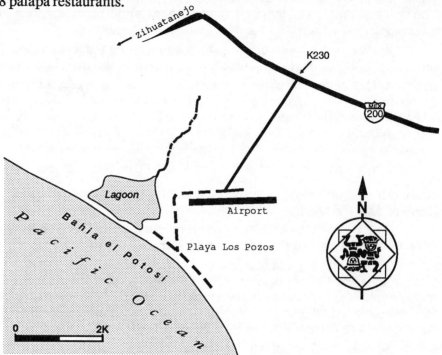

The beach is a beauty, stretching for 10 miles between the rocky hills just south of Zihuatanejo and Barra de Potosí. The fine sand is light gray and we detect little current during this time of small (2 to 3-foot) waves. How many people on the beach right now? Four. The two of us and two other people just barely visible to the north.

Playa Los Pozos has all of the ingredients to make a surf fisherman think he's in heaven. Ready supplies of live mullet and shrimp are in two adjoining freshwater lagoons; you need only a throw net (*tiraya*) or a working agreement with one of the locals. One lagoon is loaded with pargo to two pounds, and snook to four pounds are common. Live bait or lures cast to just outside the breakers are resulting in roosterfish as large as 25 pounds, jack cravalle (*jurél*), sierra mackerel and a couple members of the croaker family. Near the end of the rainy season when the lagoons are overflowing into the ocean the handliners will take snook from the surf to 20 pounds. The top times are dawn and dusk. Dawn in the surf, dusk in the lagoon. If this report isn't of interest, then you're not a fisherman.

Camping is possible with permission. The best locations are at the south end of the line of palap*as*, though there are a couple of possible spots at the north end. If you do camp on Los Pozos and find your private beach suddenly turned into a zoo, it's Sunday, or a national holiday, times of family trips to the beach.

We suggest you drive to the northernmost *enramada* and meet **Ernesto** and **Myrna Gomez Campos** of the **Enramada Netos**. After nearly falling asleep in a hammock we polished off a pair of Myrna's *huachinangos fritos, mojo de ajo*.

MYRNA & ERNESTO

They have a daughter who, though only two, is out-maneuvering, out-splashing and out-yelling everyone up to three times her age. A truly remarkable bundle of energy.

Ernesto once worked in the United States as a farm laborer, but stopped after being deported twice. He was also fleeced by farm operators who, in one instance, made him sign a receipt for a large amount of money and then gave him only $10 for a week of backbreaking labor, with the warning that if he made trouble he'd be turned over to the authorities.

Today they operate the restaurant, catching some of what they serve and taking care to give good service and excellent food. They are happy with their life and hope to do well. You will like them...and there are many Ernestos and Myrnas throughout Mexico. To find **Enramada Netos**, turn right and go to the end of the road.

A fresh breeze is coming off the ocean making the hammock the perfect place to be, and we've brought out the Toshiba laptop to record the mood of the moment...

A half dozen children ranging to six years are playing around the edge of the freshwater lagoon which comes up to within a few feet of us. The play is typical. They run and chase each other, then crash into the water; climb in and out of a boat on the sand and take imaginary voyages, then tumble into the water. By now it is time for sand rolling. When completely unrecognizable...back to the water to repeat the whole pattern.

Playa Los Pozos is a prime destination...and once there, don't hurry. Back to the highway.

Barra De Potosí...

At K225 of Mexico 200, just beyond the **Puente Los Achotes**, a signed graded road (right) goes to **Laguna Potosí** and on to **Barra de Potosí**.

The road is in good condition with many of the low spots cobbled and cemented to prevent erosion. Coconuts are everywhere. We pass a few houses and a couple of small mango orchards. At **3.1** we drive between two sizeable lagoons. Numerous egrets and herons can be seen perched along the margins. A number of side roads are evident, but appear to go to houses or orchards rather than the ocean.

At **4.0** cross a small one-lane bridge and arrive at the beach at **4.3**. In front and to the left are several large houses with water tanks (*tanacos*) prominent above the roofs. We turn to the right and follow the road past a series of large fenced beachfront lots. Some have houses on them, some beginnings of houses, and some the remnants of a dream. In about a mile the road ends at a locked gate into a coconut grove.

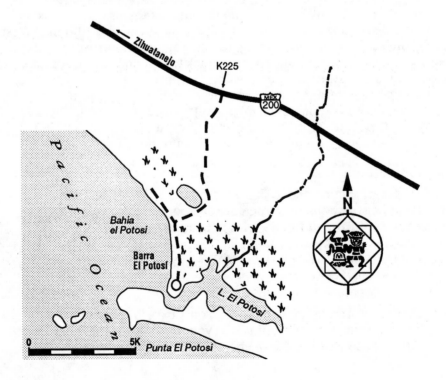

Back to the intersection and southeast past more homesites and homes. Some are truly impressive. The owners are both Mexican and American. To us it looks like all have a very good deal, for the beach is beautiful, the sun sets into the ocean year around and the landscaping possibilities seem unlimited. We are told that the people at the **Enramada Los Amigos** can give us information on property, but there's a wedding reception is going on when we are here...not a good time to intrude.

At **1.4** from the intersection, Barra de Potosí has the appearance of a well-organized community with a school, a number of "look-alike" brick and tile houses, tiendas, etc. *Palapa* restaurants line the ocean front and extend back some distance along the banks of the lagoon. Again, all of the names begin with the word *enramada*. We visited the mother of Myrna of Playa Los Pozos at her restaurant, **Enramada La Condesa**. Her name is **Edelmira** and she too is a charmer. Here, mama, three daughters, two nieces and a cousin make up the work force. The stove is typical of the region...made from adobe and fired by yard-long lengths of hard wood from the nearby scrub. Each meal, including the tortillas, is prepared as it is ordered. Hammocks are a fixture, and are there to be used. Don't feel self-conscious...they expect you to stretch out and relax. Return to the highway.

Piedra De Tlalcoyunque...

Even when you know the kilometer marker, K150 north of Acapulco, you have to watch for this one. It's on a curve and comes up quickly...the dirt road south to the beach signed to **Piedra Tlalcoyunque** and the **Carabelas** restaurant. It first crosses a wooden cattle guard, then passes several buildings, a corral and a grove of mangos. The road arrives at the beach at **1.5**. Again, a lovely sight. The people who operate and live in the **Carabelas Restaurant** have a good thing here.

This site in California would either be priced in the millions or a national monument. Here you can have it by the hour for as little as 60 cents American, the price of a beer. We pick up our orders and take them over to little tables set in the shade overlooking a beautiful mixture of large and small granite boulders, pounding surf, pinnacled islets, each with a complement of pelicans.

Take a walk along the beach and look at the 10-foot diameter tree trunk, or pick up a few driftwood pieces of more manageable dimensions. There are several men casting handlines into the eddies around the rocks and we watch one man bring in what appears from a distance to be a jack cravalle.

The sea is a cauldron here, and is likely to be all year-round. Photographs taken near the point during or just after a heavy storm should be prize winners. The beach extends for miles to the south and east past countless coconut palms. **Piedra Tlalcoyunque** is well worth a visit. Back to the highway.

Playa Boca Chica...

A paved road (right) just past the K98 marker north of Acapulco is signed to **Tetitlan**. Our map shows the road continuing on to **Boca Chica**. The road gains a bit of altitude as it winds south and east. Past the first hill, we follow the foothills with cocos on the right and the hills on the left at **1.1**. The small town of Tetitlan is at **3.3**. The pavement ends here and we leave on a graded trail past the cemetery and through several *vados* in poor repair. At **5.1** we are in **Boca Chica**.

There is little showing except for one very marginal

RIVER FERRY

299

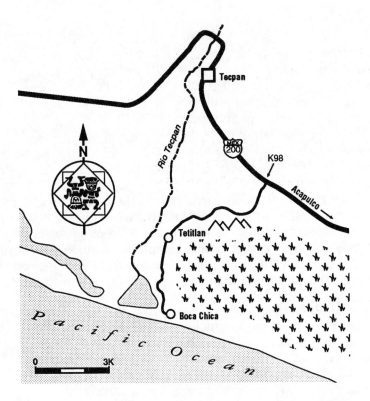

palapa that serves sodas and *cervezas*. But don't turn around yet, look to the south...

Out on the other side of the *estero* on a sand bar are a number of nice, shady *palapas*. That's where the action is, and for under a buck you can be part of it. If **Mario** is not waiting for you, he'll be right back to ferry you and anybody else over to this incredible little spot.

The beach is beautiful, with some driftwood and shells. The waves are a bit heavy at this moment but we've been assured that it does calm down. Besides, there's the fresh water lagoon right behind us. The restaurants serve nothing but what they catch, and much of it from the surf. Sierra mackerel are on the menu today, minutes fresh and broiled over coals! The place abounds with charm and beauty. It is high on the "return soon" list.

There's no room at Boca Chica to camp, but one might get permission to stay overnight. But as a day trip...it is a sure winner. Back to the highway.

Pie De La Cuesta From Downtown Acapulco...

Never, in the half-dozen times we've driven out of **Acapulco** via **Pie de La Cuesta**, have we done it without having to backtrack at least once, and twice ended up on our way over the mountains to the east with little recourse but to go to the end and turn around. Sooooo, we took a good part of a morning to research this critical issue for all concerned...

First, get yourself onto **Costero Alemán**, the road which borders the bay, and head north and west toward the Zocalo. Just before the Zocalo, you'll find a signed intersection with Javier Mina. (**Sanborn's** is on one side, **Emil** on the other.) There are signs indicating most of the required turns, but we've found that by zigzagging north and east we finally run into the road bordering the river channel. At this point go to the north or east side, and turn left (upriver). We leave the river when we see the central market on the right hand side. At the far corner of the market, turn right and slightly uphill for **0.3** miles and a Y. Take the left branch. There is a **Ferretería Ortíz** on the east side of the street, a paint store, **Comex Pinturas**, is on the northwest corner. From that intersection it is about **1.4** miles until we are at the full service **Pemex** mentioned in the Zihuatanejo to Acapulco log. Once there bear right and follow the traffic, or read the log backwards to Pie de La Cuesta.

At K10+ we are at the signed turnoff into **Pie de La Cuesta**. Turn left.

0.0   0.0   Intersection into Pie de La Cuesta. **Steve's Hideaway** is a restaurant a few yards around the bottom end of the lagoon. On pilings over the water, it has a southseas atmosphere. Lagoon trips are also available here. Several of the bungalow units appear to be clean and reasonable. Among those are **Bungalows Cristina**, **Ukai Kim** and the **Tres Marias**. The Tres Marias restaurant also comes well recommended.

1.0   1.0   The **Acapulco Trailer Park** is on the left while a barefoot skiing school and beer bar is across the street. A few yards beyond another trailer park faces the lagoon, the **Quinta Dora**. We found the Acapulco Trailer Park well attended and restful. *It is guarded and fenced. This is a fact of life in this area. Your car should also be in a guarded area, as it should be in almost any metropolitan area in the world. We have heard of theft problems from couples who had their rigs at Quinta Dora (it is not fenced.)*

0.2   1.2   We turn (right) shortly before the entrance into the military base and skirt around it, then parallel the north side of the paved landing field.

1.9   3.1   On our right are a number of well laid-out little brick buildings which were probably part of the military base at one time. Now they have no roofs, doors or windows. Ahead, topes near several houses and *tiendas*. All of the land on both sides of the road is fenced or marked for ownership in some other manner. Little has yet been developed, but the territory has been staked out. *This part of the peninsula has the name, **Luces en El Mar** (Lights in the Sea). This may come from the presence of phosphorescent plankton in the water at certain times of the year.*

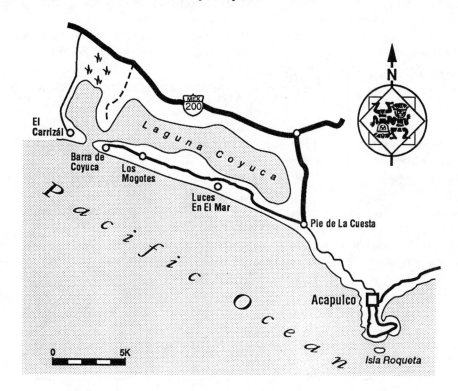

3.5   6.6   **Playa de Club Maebba** is on the left. A family sports resort, there's a pool, a zoo for the kids, shaded eating and relaxing areas along a pretty stretch of beach. The paving ends near here. We continue past several houses and an increasing number of restaurants.

2.7   9.3   We are now about a hundred meters past the basketball court and at the end of the road. The name of the restaurant in front of us is **Dos Vistas**. Offering a view of both **Laguna Chocua** and the Pacific, it is owned by **Chencho Cruz** and his family. There are lots of tables and plenty of shade. They even water down the sand to increase the cooling effect of the breezes.

Thanks in large part to Chencho's son, **Arturo**, the place is jumping. Arturo went to the university in Acapulco, majoring in business. In the six years since, he has opened a travel agency and become a tour operator. He also serves as program director and organizer for the family enterprise here. His English carries a perfect California accent, though he's never been out of Mexico. Arturo's lagoon tours, with an open bar, lunch and swimming included, have proven to be a great attraction and on occasion fills several tour busses a day. As you get off the bus you are handed a huge coconut full of coco loco (a mixture of rum, gin, coconut water, etc.) with refills available. The food is served buffet style and includes fish, chicken and the works.

COUNTRY KITCHEN

The trip into the lagoon is something to write home about as Laguna Coyuca is three times larger than Acapulco Bay. We are seeing a wide variety of aquatic birds, large expanses of lilies and hyacinths, and small enclaves of fishermen along the way. The water is clear and very shallow in places, providing opportunities to pole quietly through the aquatic plants while fish dart from the shadows.

The lagoon hosts a wide variety of fish, including mullet, largemouth bass, catfish, snook, snapper, mojarra and carp. There are also blue crab (*jaiba*) and traps for their capture are abundant. Fishing for snook is particularly good during the rainy season. The only problem here is that it is sometimes difficult to get out around the entrance because of flooding. Snook to 10 and 15 pounds are common, according to Arturo Cruz. He has knowledge of the bass fishing potential and says he has seen them to 3 kilos (6.6 lbs) in the nets. Arturo's phone number is 2-33-85. Back to the highway, and Acapulco.

Barra Vieja From Acapulco City...

*Many times over the years we've driven up the hill leading out of Acapulco Bay wishing for a breath of air...and as we near the top, like magic it appears. There is a unique resort there, the world renowned **Las Brisas** (The Breezes), where most rooms have their own private swimming pool and pink jeeps are available as part of the accommodations. Note too the many nearby homes which also benefit from "las brisas".*

From the crest of the hill the spectacular bay of **Puerto Marques** is sure to catch your eye. There are several m*iradores* (lookouts) along here...take advantage of them. Note the solid line of *palapas* along the beach in Puerto Marques. By unofficial count there are 63 restaurants, each sharing walls with their neighbors. You want to get to the beach, you gotta go through a restaurant...and that move leaves you open for a lot of pressure to have a seat. Actually, that's an understatement...every few feet someone will test your will power.

JUANITO

*If you have checked the highway options on your Mexico road maps and decide to leave Acapulco via the highway past the airport and south along the beaches, you will be in for a surprise. The road does not go through. In fact it has been closed for more than 10 years! Why the AAA and Mexico's map makers haven't picked up on it is beyond us. Our maps do show that this road is **closed**. But come along, there are things of interest down that way.*

0.0   0.0   K0   We are now at the **Puerto Marques** *glorietta*. If we go northeast 7 kilometers, we are on **Mexico 200**; straight ahead (southeast) is to the **airport**, and **Barra Vieja** and the end of the road. The Marques beach area is on the right. Just beyond the circle is a signed road (right) to **Playa Revolcadero**, a not-particularly attractive complex of restaurant and touristic services. The beach near the rocks is reputed to be a fine summer surfing beach. It is also the northern end of the beach in front of the **Acapulco Princess** and **Pierre Marques**.

Continue toward **Barra Vieja** past a full service **Pemex**. There are a number of restaurants and other businesses on the left while the greens of the Acapulco Princess golf course take up much of the right side of the road.

1.2   1.2   K2   Paved road on the right leads to the **Acapulco Princess** and **Pierre Marques** hotels. Take the time, go in and look around...everybody does...the architecture and landscaping of both are worth the price of a *limonada* or *cerveza*.

2.5   3.7   K6   There are still a few restaurants catering to tourists scattered along the highway. The land is flat with lots of coco palms in view.

3.5   7.2   K13+ Road straight ahead is to the **Acapulco International Airport**. We swing to the right and take the road past **Los Amates** toward Barra Vieja, coming rather close to the beach and paralleling it a hundred yards or so back. Between us and the water are enterprises offering apartments for rent, condo occupancy, restaurants, etc.

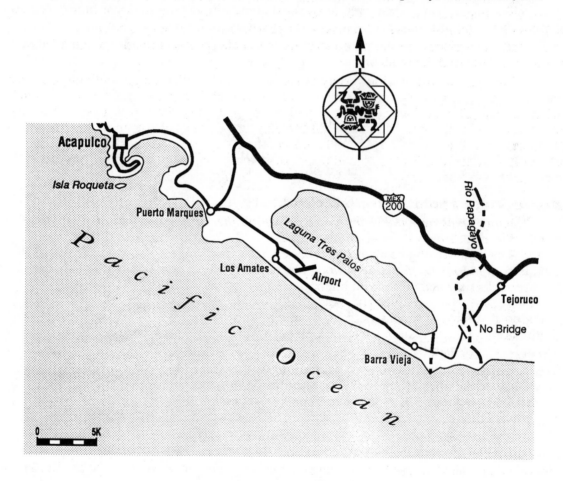

4.5   11.7   K21   A development named **Tres Vidas de La Playa**...a rather strange name, but the buildings look good and the gate guard is awake. We did not go in. At this point the road goes inland past a number of small farms.

4.2   15.9   K28   The road returns to the ocean. There is beach access near an old house. As we go by more *palapa* restaurants, it occurs that some of these places probably get more visitors off the quality of the shade than the quality of the food. There are some, however, who provide both, and very well.

2.4   18.3   K31₊ **Club de Playa**; it is also signed, **Playa Encantada**.

1.0   19.3   K33   The entrance into what passes for **Barra Vieja**, a not-too-impressive collection of houses, *tiendas* and a **larga distancia**. (*We called the U.S. from* *here, got right through and the operator was charming. Spanish is not required...see section on telephones.*) There is a lagoon inland from us and the Pacific is on the right. Each side has its own complement of ocean or lagoon-side eateries.

0.3   19.6   K33   On the right is **Beto's Condesa**, a large complex featuring several eating areas, a big pool and parking. The food is expensive, but the services are great. We went through the kitchen...spotless with three preparation areas. The three *cocineros* (cooks) say they serve as many as 1000 meals in a day!

The last restaurant on the right before the single-lane bridge is also named **Beto's**. It too is spotless and though it has no pool or large parking area, the *huachinango* is exceptional. *We select our own from a dozen or more which look as though they should still be moving. It is then weighed and fixed in whatever manner we choose. The prices are considerably lower, and the ambiance good.*

The second Beto's however, has almost no beach, no pool, and less breeze because it faces the lagoon rather than the ocean. We spent the day enjoying both places.

If you wish to see where the road ends cross the single-lane bridge and go about 3 miles. It's there in dull monochrome. Back to Acapulco. (And when you get home, tell the AAA.)

Playa Ventura ...

At K123+ of Mexico 200 south of Acapulco a dirt road south is signed to **Playa Ventura**, 5km. The road is fairly well graded and not too dusty. We see a number of *agaves* near the road. At **0.9** a large *higuera* and some *huanacaxtles*. A few meters beyond the road forks. We take the best traveled left branch. Coco palms begin to predominate at about **2.4**. The beach is directly in front of us at **4.4** miles.

PLAYA VENTURA

The south-facing beach is open to the ocean. The sand is fine and the beach has driftwood and sand crabs. We see rocks here and there, with major outcroppings to the southeast. From the angles off a sandy point about two miles north of us, it should be a an excellent surfing destination. If not, no matter, the place is so beautiful that a visit is almost mandatory.

The area is currently on few people's must-visit list only because they haven't seen it. The sites for homes and small four-to-eight unit-bungalow apartments are legion. And much of it is for sale.

The road extends for several miles to the east and south past a number of perfect camping spots for vans, campers, etc., but not motorhomes or large trailers...they'd never make it. A couple of miles beyond where we've driven we can see another point with a long left break.

Fishing from the rocks and over the sand is good for a variety of fish including pargo, sierra and several members of the jack family. Snook to three feet are a bonus during the rainy season. At times small silvery bait fish are abundant in the surf and are taken with throw nets. All the fishing at Playa Ventura is done from the shore, as the water is very rough. We did not see any pangas. There are several restaurants and the people are friendly and accommodating.

Playa Ventura will be discovered one of these days. It cannot miss. If we could afford another home in Mexico, this would be at the top of the list. Back to the highway.

OAXACA

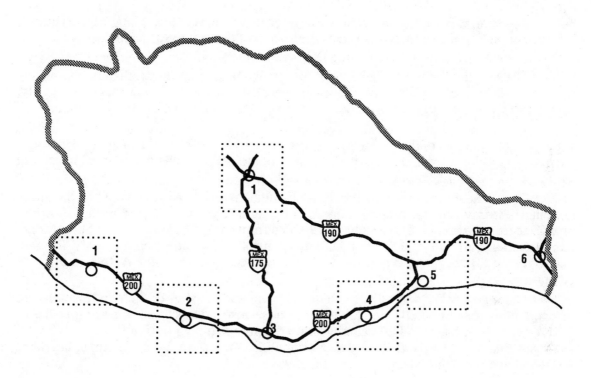

OAXACA

1. **Pinotepa Nacionál**
2. **Puerto Escondido**
3. **Puerto Angel**
4. **Salina Cruz**
5. **Juchitán**

OAXACA...
THE STATE

Much of the character of Mexico's state of **Oaxaca** is influenced by two major mountain ranges, the rugged Sierra Madre del Sur and the higher, even more intimidating volcanic Sierra Madre de Oaxaca, a southern extension of the Sierra Madre Oriental, which parallels it to the east.

Between the two ranges is the lush, mile-high central valley, which in early times, was the home of several of mesoamerica's finest civilizations including the **Zapotec** and **Mixtec**. Today it is home for a majority of the states more than 3.5 million residents and its beautiful capitol, Oaxaca city. At the eastern end of the state is the low-lying, windy Isthmus of Tehuantepec, while its west and south-facing 570 kilometer coastline has many isolated beaches, coves and lagoons.

The state is loosely connected by an admittedly-inadequate network of roads, but one which is growing daily. Air transportation has come to its major centers such as Oaxaca City, Salina Cruz and the burgeoning touristic centers of Puerto Escondido and Huatulco.

The history of the Indian in Oaxaca State has deep roots, particularly in the central valley where a number of the new world's most advanced civilizations had their beginnings. Archaeologists have located more than 300 sites of the peoples who had roamed in and out over a period of more than three thousand years.

One of the richest archaeological sites in Mexico, Monte Alban, is situated on a high, flattened hilltop only 9 kilometers southwest of Oaxaca City. It appears to have had its origin as a Zapotec religious center around 600 BC and at its zenith a millennium later, Monte Alban itself had around 25,000 inhabitants and controlled the entire central valley. In about 1200 AD the Mixtecs took control and were in turn conquered by the **Aztecs** in the 15th century.

Other groups of Indians lived along the coast and the sites of their civilizations are just beginning to be studied. One such group, whose descendants live in the salt marshes of the Laguna Inferior, are the **Huave** Indians. Anthropologists are now coming to the conclusion that this group arrived by sea from either Nicaragua or Peru, for their language resembles the Sinubar dialects of those regions.

When the Spanish *conquistador* rode into the mountains and valleys of Oaxaca they received a hostile reception from people who had been fighting for their existence for centuries. As the white man's diseases, famine and mistreatment decimated the ranks of the inhabitants the invaders took more and more of the land, driving the survivors into the mountains where they continued to resist.

To this day Oaxaca is known as a cradle of rebellion and the cries of its citizens for social justice have historically impacted Mexico's constitutional and social systems. Two of the 19th century's truly significant figures in Mexico's struggles to maintain independence and become a viable nation were born in Oaxaca, Benito Juarez and Porfirio Diaz.

After the Spanish conquest, the protected coves of Oaxaca's coast became favorite spots for English pirates to hide while waiting for returning Manila galleons. One of the pirates, Sir Francis Drake, relates in his ship's log how, in 1579, they ransacked the area of Huatulco and captured a 100-ton galleon.

Due to their remoteness, the people living in the mountains of Oaxaca had little contact with the Spanish, and later with the Mexican national governments. Even today these people are little connected with contemporary Mexico.

Though the independent attitude of the Oaxacans contributed materially to Mexico's evolution into an autonomous nation, it also has led to many problems for the Oaxacans

306

themselves. Today it is one of Mexico's poorest states. There is very little industry and much of its natural resources, including the beautiful tropical hardwoods and the mountain confers have been over-exploited.

Despite some land redistribution under the *ejido* program, actual ownership remains a serious source of friction. Often the land parceled out to the Indians has been of the poorest quality and their population centers are only marginally included in road and irrigation development programs.

The literacy rate is low due in part to the difficulty of establishing even rural schools in the tiny, nearly-inpenetrable, mountain enclaves where many of the state's 16 different indigenous groups still live, and who often do not even speak Spanish. Most housing consists of one-room buildings without indoor plumbing or running water. Also, many retain their traditional dress, worship their own gods, and are leery of outsiders.

Most of the economy is one of subsistence, through the growing of corn, beans and squash on otherwise-worthless hillsides. Some families also generate a small amount of cash from handwoven fabrics, mats, baskets and bracelets or the production of a wide variety of clay products, including the famous black Oaxacan pottery.

While helping us edit the book, longtime Mexico travelers, Paul and Mary Pierce shared this story: "We had to camp one night in a poor village on the highway from Tehuantepec. The villagers made sure we were safe all night and gave us gifts of fruit when we left. The ones with the least are often the most hospitable."

In recent years thousands of families have left Oaxaca to pursue lives as migratory farm workers in other parts of Mexico, including Baja California, Sonora, Durango, Vera Cruz and Michoacan.

The visitor to Oaxaca is presented with a fascinating kaleidoscope of things to see and do. Arts and crafts abound, particularly in and around Oaxaca city. Mats, baskets, sandals, hammocks, machetes, amber, gold and silver reproductions of archaeological treasures, leather goods and wood carvings are but a part of the things to admire, bargain for and cart away. Even if you specialize in handcrafted ox muzzles, you are in the right place.

We have friends who have been coming to Oaxaca City for years, sometimes for several months at a crack, and each time find new cultural and artistic experiences without leaving Oaxaca's central valley.

You will want to explore the many sites of the ancient world's most advanced civilizations: Monte Alban, the Acropolis of the western hemisphere, which grew and flourished under a number of ruling civilizations; and Mitla, a very important Zapotec center. Other lesser-known sites, Dainzu, Lambityeco and Yagul are worth a visit. It is an unending quest here in Oaxaca...discovering the lifestyles of the early ones.

The fiestas in Oaxaca are among the most well-attended in North America. From the holiest days of the Christian calendar to the traditional pre-columbian observances of time-honored deities they are celebrated with enthusiasm.

Though Oaxaca's Pacific Coast has for years been popular for Europeans as a place to get away from it all at bargain prices, only now is it gaining attention from many American travelers. Under the umbrella of Mexico's touristic development department, Fonatur, the picturesque coves in the region of Huatulco are now getting international attention.

Moving more slowly are the beach towns of Puerto Angel and Puerto Escondido. Here it is still OK to practice *manana*, to watch the fishermen come in, buy a *huachinango* off the boat and carry it up to a beachside restaurant for lunch. Here you can still find a room with only a *ventilidor* (ceiling fan) in a 10-room family hotel with no hot water. In our view, these are the true stars along Oaxaca's Pacific coast.

There is little doubt that Oaxaca has the potential to become a colorful and enriching jewel in an ever-searching world's list of prime travel destinations. They have all of the ingredients, now comes the hard part, getting the word out. We wish them well.

MEXICO 200 — BORDER TO HUATULCO

We pass from a state with a strong touristic background to one who is just realizing its potential. The infrastructure here is beginning to come on line. We will be watching, for the beaches of Oaxaca are exquisite.

0.0   0.0   K208   A sign out here in the bush tells us we are leaving **Guerrero** and entering **Oaxaca**. The two-lane road continues southeast.

2.5   2.5   K212   The countryside is relatively featureless, with cattle pastures dominating the landscape.

6.1   8.6   K222   A fair-sized community, **La Estancia**, is off to the right. Most of the homes are adobes with tile roofs.

1.5   10.1   K224   A graded dirt road right is signed to **El Ciruelo** and **Coralero**. *The road winds toward the south and into the small community of El Ciruelo at 1.9. At 2.3 turn left past a brick building and a large higuera. 2.8 miles sees us at a sandy arroyo, followed by lime trees and several corrals and pasture land. After a small grove of tropical forest come more mangos and coconuts. At 8.7 a brick yard is followed by a rocky ridge with several white-barked higueras growing out of it. We drop into a flat area past a few more houses and a basketball court. Go past the right side and on to a singularly unimpressive beach at 10.9. Coralero is a bust as far as we are concerned.* Back to the highway and east on Mexico 200 into the hills.

1.7   11.8   K227   A wide spot along the road with a huge *huanacaxtle*, or *pirote* tree growing right in the middle of it. There are a number of small and large *higueras* (wild fig) through here. We are climbing more now as we continue east.

2.0   13.8   K230   The top of a grade, and on to another alluvial plain.

8.1   21.9   K243   A small unsigned grouping of houses with the largest *huanacaxtle* we can remember seeing.

0.9   22.8   K245+   A drug check and intersection with a paved road into the hills. Our map shows the highway to be Mexico 125, leading to Pinotepa Don Luís (**See Oaxaca Inland.**) and eventually Oaxaca City. Continue on Mexico 200.

1.5   23.3   K248   A small saw mill on the right. In another moment we are entering the outskirts of a city. Watch for *topes*. There are several full service **Pemex** stations as we enter. Welcome to **Pinotepa Nationál**.

A busy town of least 50,000 residents, Pinotepa Nacionál has a unique background. Her original name, **Pinotepa Real**, came from the early colonial period, so when Mexico won its independence from Spain in 1810, the inhabitants renamed it to reflect Mexico's new-found independence. Twenty-five kilometers inland is another Pinotepa, **Pinotepa Don Luís. (See Oaxaca Inland.)** It, being much the smaller of the two, is often referred to as **Pinotepa Chico.**

There are many **Mixteca** Indians in and around the valley, and though some of their traditional customs and dress remain, they are fading rapidly. One which is nearly gone is the practice of both men and women going nude from the waist up as they go about their work. We saw this practice here as late as 1982, and it is still seen among the older people in the outlying villages.

The traditional skirts of the women, *pozahuancos*, are hand woven in Pinotepa de Don Luís. The dye used in coloring the material purple comes from a sea snail common to the region. Skirts can be purchased in the central market here in Pinotepa.

Another claim to fame is the excellent quality of the *machetes* made here and in the town of **Huaxolititlan**, 20 kilometers to the southeast. Their machetes have a reputation for quality both as a working tool and as weapons...the later coming from battles the peasants have had over the years regarding land rights.

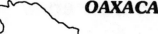

Pinotepa Nacionál Hub Map

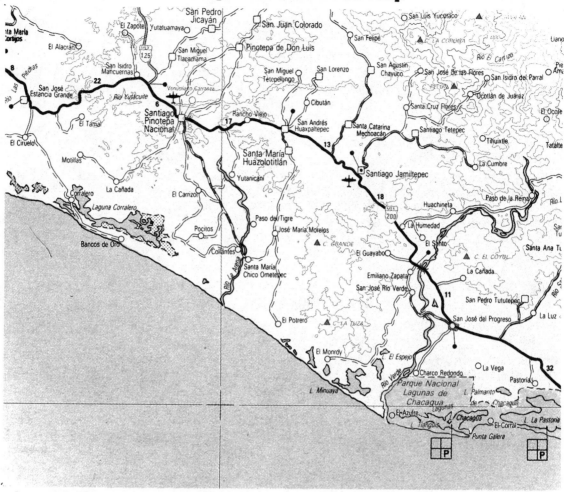

Jicotepec, a small town about 5 miles north of Pinotepa, was, for a few years, the subject of a unique, inadvertent, experiment in linguistics. It seems that an American couple visited Pinotepa and, finding the area to their liking, settled in Jicotepec, some thousand feet above the valley floor where they found cooling breezes to go with a great view of the area.

The interesting thing is that the town's 900 inhabitants were Mixtec Indians, and very few could speak Spanish. In order to communicate with their neighbors, the American couple began learning Mexteco and, in the process, a number of the Mextecs learned English, making them bilingual, yet still unable to speak Spanish.

Now that a graded road has replaced the old burro trails, things are beginning to change in Jocptepec. On our visit we saw many of the old ways in clothing, houses and implements but we also saw teenage boys dressed in Levis, T-shirts and tennis shoes, but still carrying machetes and water gourds as do their fathers to this day. The road is graded most of the way, getting quite rough the last mile. Once there there's little to see except groupings of houses with ill-defined roads or trails connecting them.

Pinotepa's original church has been almost destroyed by earthquakes, services are now held in the new steel and concrete building next door. The central market district begins a few blocks past the church.

The central market in downtown Pinotepa offers products brought in from the outlying ranches on an everyday basis, but on Thursday the supply multiplies several times over. Pottery, baskets, clothing and hand-woven yardage are on display, as are plums, tomatoes, chickens, turkeys, etc. It's a festive day.

A very serviceable hotel, the **Carmona** is near the center of town along Mexico 200. It has a beautiful pool, comfortable rooms with *ventiladores* (fans) or *climas* (air conditioners). The kitchen was adequate, but we found the **Bora Bora**, a sports club located directly across from the first **Pemex** as you enter town, more to our liking. *Go through the arch and up the hill to the large palapa.* All of the dishes we tried in two nights were excellent and very inexpensive. Our waitress is **Dometila**, a beautiful lady with a sparkling personality.

During the first logging of this portion of Mexico 200 our camper developed an engine problem...it refused to go over 45 miles an hour and almost stopped on even the slightest hill. We limped into town and inquired at the first auto supply store, refaccionaria, about a mechanic. We were told to go to the second Pemex, look across the street for a small mariscos restaurant and the maestro (expert) would be just to the right. And he was. After a short test drive Manuel Orosco diagnosed it as a gas pump/line/filter problem. Back at the shop Manuel and his helper began to check the lines while a third employee set out in a taxi to locate parts. Within an hour from the time we stopped we were ready to go. The cost, including an extra set of filters...less than $20! And the marisco restaurant, serves a fine pulpo (octopus) cocktail...but you might want to have them go lightly on the chiles.

1.6   24.9   K0   This is an undefined spot one kilometer back from the K1 road marker in the next entry...

0.6   25.5   K1   We leave the eastern outskirts of **Pinotepa** and wind a short distance up, then down into a canyon and a bridge over a good-size river, the **Río La Arena**. On the left about 300 yards beyond the bridge, a stream comes cascading down the side of a rocky promontory. *Several years ago we drove past here right after it had been raining heavily and the water was roaring off the top into the boiling cauldron below. Add the tumultuous roar of the water and the scene was a memorable moment.* Today we see a bus-type motorhome parked across from the falls with a couple of chairs and a table nearby.

4.2   29.7   K7+   A small unidentified group of houses.

2.9   32.6   K12+   Another gathering of houses. There are many bromeliads in the trees. We are beginning to see more of the high ridges which form the backbone of the **Sierra Madre del Sur.**

3.2   35.8   K17+   A sign welcomes us to **San Andrés Huaxpaltepec**, a rather typical village of maybe 4,000 people. If you are interested in carved wooden masks you might want to drive 5km south of here to **Santa Maria Huazolotitlan**. They say this is where the good ones are made. **(See Oaxaca Inland.)** The town has a local **Pemex** and a few small stores. Continue through into a valley several miles wide that sports a good population of cattle with the white sementhal predominating. The pastures are green and healthy looking.

4.7   40.5   K25   A graded road goes (left) back into the hills to **Santa Catarina Mechoacan** and a number of ranchos. The road stands out because its surface is white. We continue gradually upward in a southeasterly direction. Enter a canyon and wind up to a ridge, then down the other side.

3.2   43.7   K30   We are entering the southern fringes of **Santiago Jamiltepec**. *There is an artisan's center on a rise (left) just as we enter town. Temporarily closed, it is a "must" stop when open, for the skills of the **Mixtec artesanias** are widely known. There is another shop, sponsored by the tribal council about a mile into town on the same road which goes past the other center. Its name is **Yukuuku chakuaa**. And what a find...*

Here, in one small store, is a cross-section of the products of the Indian artisans of Oaxaca's southern coastal ranges. The collection has been assembled by a charming man who obviously not only knows his business, but loves every moment of it. His name is **Santiago de La Cruz Velasco**. The craft centers have been his baby since day one, and his knowledge of who does what and where is enormous. Need furniture? Stop by and see Santiago. Chances are he can locate it for you. Special orders for weavings, carvings and a

310

myriad other things are all within his capabilities. We bought a unique chair brought in the day before by burro from a ranch a full day's journey back in the mountains.

The central market in Jamiltepec is also a place to check for items of interest. Thursday is market day, when people by the hundreds come in from the mountains with all manner of items to sell or barter. This is a busy and interesting town which is little visited by people other than buyers from fine gift stores all over Mexico. Put it on the itinerary. Back to the highway. Markets aside, the principal activity appears to be cultivating the many hillside cornfields.

Since leaving Jamiltepec, the road has climbed gradually, ultimately presenting a view to the southwest with the ocean in the distance. We head back down at a slow pace through sharp curves. The near views are of tall scrub on the hillsides and several corn patches, while some of the small *arroyos* (valleys) have a variety of tall trees or plantings of coconuts, papayas or mangos.

7.8   51.5   K42+   We are now in the pueblo of **La Humedad** (The Humidity). The tree on our left, should it die, is large enough to provide everyone in town with wood for years to come. There are a lot of burros in Mexico, but they seem particularly prevalent here, and they like to wander along the highway. Exercise caution.

3.6   55.1   K48+   **El Charquit**, a small signed community next to a small lake. A box factory is on the right, about midway through town.

0.9   56.0   K50   Come to a bridge over a good-sized river, the **Río Verde**. This seems to be a wintering spot for swallows, as there are thousands darting in every direction this late February afternoon. We now enter a verdant valley of pastures and well-blooded cattle.

5.7   61.7   K59   **San Jose Progresso** is the name of the town coming up. Watch for a hellacious speed bump (*tope*)...then several more. A signed road goes to **Chacahua**, 29km. This road leads into the **Parque Nacionál Lagunas de Chacahua**, an incredibly rich combination of bird and animal life in a pristine swamp environment. Some believe that this spot could be the last bastion of survival for a number of the more reclusive species of tropical birds and amphibians.

*The mouth of the **Laguna Chacahua**, more specifically **Punta Galera**, is reputed to have some of the best summer surfing waves in Mexico. Often written about, but little identified, it is an exercise in determination just to get there. Located in the middle of the aforementioned Parque Nacionál Laguna de Chacahua, it is reached by 1) a terrible road which is virtually impassable during most of the year, or 2) hiring a boat out of **Zapotalito** to take you, or 3) finding somebody to drop you off by helicopter. (We were told in Puerto Escondido that this method is under study.) Anyway, it must be something else again to elicit such attention.*

1.4   63.1   K61   We are back out of town going east past a lime packing plant. We've passed a dozen or more miles of almost solid lime orchards. And the sight of one huge truckload after another makes us wonder how the world can possibly use all of the limes grown in Mexico.

4.3   67.2   K68   A full service **Pemex, magnasin** and all, is at the entrance to the small town of **Santa Rosa**. It is unusual to find unleaded in such a small town but the owner claims he always has it.

1.9   69.1   K71   Lots of coco palms, and even more limes.

6.8   75.9   K82   Road (right) is to **Zapotalito,** a small Indian village on the edge of **Laguna La Pastora**, the largest lagoon in the Lagunas de Chacahua National Park. *It is from here that the boats to Punta Galera are supposed to depart.* Continue east back into scatterings of the tall wild palms (*cayacos*) associated with Mexico's west coast jungles. The area is lush with many shades of green.

1.9   77.8   K85   We come into a valley with three types of palms growing profusely...the coconut, *cayaco* and short fan.

    3.1   80.9   K90   A road right, though not signed, should go to **El Encanto**. *After more than an hour of hunting and asking we give up. There is no discernible road beyond it to the ocean.* Next comes a bridge over a multipurpose river. Laundry, swimming, playing and car washing are all going on at the same time. A number of houses are on both sides of the bridge, as are several seafood restaurants. There is also a local **Pemex**. The name of the town, **Río Grande.**

    5.4   86.3   K98+   Road (right) goes off in the direction of the ocean. After several inquiries we find that it does go to **El Venado**, but not the ocean.

    2.4   88.7   K102+   A signed collection of thatched houses, **Cacalotepec**. Next comes a small bridge over a riverbed and, finally, the Pacific Ocean.

    4.1   92.8   K109   Immediately after crossing a bridge a road (right) goes through a gate and toward the beach. We move in and out of palm plantations and low hills.

    4.0   96.8   K115   The bridge here has inconsistencies in its surface which can make a large vehicle bounce rather violently if you go at a certain speed...it's known as harmonics. Take care. Beyond, the hillside corn fields above the highway look like exercises in rock climbing.

    0.8   97.6   K116+   A graded road (right) leads to the east edge of the **Laguna San Juan Maniatepec.**

    5.2   102.8   K125   We are now skirting the north edge of the very beautiful San Juan Maniatepec lagoon. A number of restaurants offer seafood...some of the names...**La Alejandria, Aguaje, El Zapote, Las Hamacas**. Tours of the lagoon can be arranged, but if you want an English-speaking guide, trips are best arranged through the **García Rendón** travel agency in Puerto Escondido. Early morning departures are best as bird activity decreases markedly after the first few hours of daylight.

    2.7   104.5   K130   A small community, **Baja de Chila** is off to the left. Continue east toward Puerto Escondido.

    4.5   109.0   K137+   Road (left) is into the Puerto Escondido airport complex.

    1.2   110.2   K139+   Signed turnoff right on a rough dirt road to the **Puerto Escondido Trailer Park** and **Playa Carrizalillo.**

    0.8   111.0   K141   Intersection into **Puerto Escondido .**

PUERTO ESCONDIDO...

    If we thought we could get away with it, we wouldn't put this one in the book...it's one of our favorites. Puerto Escondido is growing, but it still retains much of the charm of a small village. It was founded as a coffee exportation center in 1925 and by 1965 had a population of 400. Electricity and the telegraph arrived in 1969, then, a few years later, the telephone. It is a fishing village in an area still rich with giant oysters and lobsters. One of the farmers says that eleven different varieties of bananas grow here. Now in the 1990s, this small resort town still features lovely beaches, reasonable accommodations, good restaurants and plenty to do and see.

    At the upper end of town sandy **Playa Bacocho** stretches northwest in a graceful arc. Open to the ocean, its sometimes-abrupt dropoffs make swimming dangerous at times. Overlooking the beach is the most expensive hotel in the area, the **Posada Real**. Now a member of the **Best Western** chain (*cadena*), its lovely grounds extend down to the beach below and **Coco's** restaurant and pool. Also in this area are the **Fiesta Mexicana** and **Villa Sol** hotels. The latter has a beach club on Playa Bacocho.)

    The most stunning beach in the area, **Playa Carrizalillo**, is in front of the **Puerto Escondido Trailer Park**. By stopping and working there both coming and going, we got six full days under a large tree on a breezy bluff overlooking that perfect beach. Carrizalillo hosted us to an hour's snorkeling each morning and a break for body surfing before sunset. The only price was the walk down the hill and over perfect golden sand to the water. And this is where we met **Hombre Verde**.

It could only happen here in Mexico...We drive into a modern campground and get challenged on our right to be there by a chicken! And an American-hatched (gringo) chicken at that. His name, Hombre Verde...

Hombre has adapted well, and with puberty his feathers have developed a green metallic sheen which turns the girl chickens on wherever he goes, and has presumably helped him leave a trail of little hombre verdes along the way. His ability to scavenge has eliminated the need for Dave to carry chicken feed, and he does a fair job of drinking out of a dripping spigot. While traveling, Hombre has even learned to accept confinement in an ice chest so the windows of the van can be left open.

sheen which turns the hens on wherever he goes and has presumably helped him leave a trail of little hombre verdes along the way. His ability to scavenge has eliminated the need for Dave to carry chicken feed and he does a fair job out of a dripping spigot. While traveling, the chicken has even learned to accept confinement in an ice chest so the windows of the van can be left open.

During the three months he's been in Mexico, Hombre Verde has acquired the street smarts to become a topflite guard chicken. Nothing within 50 yards of his station gets by him, until it gets dark. Then he finds a perch...chair, stepladder, tree branch, etc., and goes to sleep.

It has taken a couple of days for Hombre to get used to our being around. Now he greets us with a loud crow and a sideways dance. It's a great relationship. When we take a walk on the beach, Hombre comes along. When we eat, he expects his share...even fried chicken! Several evenings we've gone to bed with Hombre sound asleep on the hood of the camper.

What lies ahead for Hombre Verde? It's a bit uncertain, as the boys don't know when they're going home..."maybe in a couple months," they say. And, as it is illegal to import birds into the USA, Hombre may be housed on a ranch near the border, so they can pick him up next fall for another "endless summer."

TOM & HOMBRE VERDE

313

Closer to town is the jewel-like, **Puerto Angelito**. With calm water clean sand and rocky points, it's perfect for snorkeling. Equipment, including hammocks, can be rented at the kiosk in front of the palapa restaurants.

Playa Principal is in the main section of town. Adjoining are many good restaurants and budget to moderate-priced hotels. A steep hill leads down to the main street, the center of which is closed to traffic. We are staying at the **Villa Escondido** with a hammock-sized balcony overlooking the downtown area and the ocean. It's 96 steps down into town, but it has a wonderful breeze. We put the small kitchenette to good use and also enjoy the rooftop restaurant. Two other hotels, **Las Palmas** on the beach and **Paraiso Escondido** on the hill are clean, and good values.

Mario, the owner of **Pizzaland**, has a few clean, basic rooms behind the restaurant and is a fountain of information. He also serves an excellent pizza and tasty pastas.

We get good vibes from Bob Taylor's **La Parrilla de Guitano** (The Gipsy Grill). Taylor, who lived in Brazil and Paraguay for some years, serves an excellent dinner with a South American flair. In the middle of the *malecón*, on the hill side of the street, a little no-name taco stand serves Argentine-style beef...excellent. One night we sat on a wall and enjoyed our tacos and *cervezas* while talking to two locals and petting their dog.

The **Hotel Santa Fe** at the south end of the main beach is a charming older hotel with an excellent *palapa* restaurant overlooking the raging surf on **Playa Marinero**. This area is slated to have several hotels here and on adjoining **Playa Zicatela**.

Beside the sparkling beaches and their attendant swimming, snorkeling, surfing sailing, etc. there is also an excellent fishery a short distance offshore. We've been out a number of times, but none will ever top a trip made in February of 1986 when we took three sailfish in less than two hours, but in a very unusual way...we went hookless.

*We met **Baltasar** on the beach in front of the family restaurant, the **Tangaroa**, had the gear stowed and were off to the blue water within minutes.. Baltasar's brother, **Mario**, was our guide for the day. On the way out we talked about what fish were working, the best lures, etc. Mario said we were going for sailfish and handed me one of the hot lures. With that he turned back to checking his outboard, leaving me to inspect the "sure thing".*

The lure was handmade. A four-ounce egg sinker served as the head and had a groove cut in for the wire used to retain the 18-inch skirt made from a piece of nylon rope. The heavy monofilament six-foot leader was secured to the lure with a tight double overhand knot under the skirt where the hook should be. That's right, no hook! This was what our guide was waiting for. With eyes sparkling, he said "Not to worry," everything was OK.

We relaxed, presuming that the hooks would be attached when we stopped. But it didn't happen...instead they went on our lines just the way they were. On our trip we had three strikes and the pleasure of working all three up to the boat. The things worked like a charm. How did it come about? Mario explained...

*Several evenings before he and **Baltasar** were putting gear together for a sailfish charter when they discovered they had no large hooks. A canvass of friends yielded no hooks suitable for trolling lures. While wondering what to do Baltasar began weaving the end of a nylon rope to keep it from raveling. As he progressed he noticed that the rough skin of his fingers kept catching on the super-fine filaments. Suddenly, a light flashed. He picked up a marlin bill and drew the frazzled rope ends across the rough surface. It stuck like Velcro!*

Why not give it a try, they said. They did; and it worked. After blowing the first two hits the next morning, they learned to drag the lure in the normal manner, but when a fish hit at the trailing tail they stop the boat and let the line run free. In this manner, the sailfish gets his bill irretrievably tangled in a maze of loose filaments. After the first two blown fish, they had five strikes and brought five sails to the boat. We gave it a name, "RagMop."

BALTAZAR

314

Not only does the RagMop work like a charm, but it's ideal for catch and release. No hook to remove or cut off. At worst the billfish will be left with some bits of threads hanging from its bill. and when using a RagMop, you know that billfish will be the only fish you will bring to the boat (well, maybe a needlefish). Action for tuna, dorado and roosterfish can also be fast and furious.

Another recommended activity is the guided tours into fascinating **Manialtepec Lagoon.** They are best booked through the **García Rendón** travel agency on the Malecón as they can often supply English-speaking guides. As usual, we enjoyed the central market located north of the highway, particularly for its fruits, vegetables and delicious comb honey.

0.0　111.0　K141　From the westernmost entry into town from Mexico 200 we continue southeast past a lineup of *topes*. There is an excellent overview of the downtown area with close-ups of the beaches and the houses, hotels and restaurants rimming them.

0.5　111.5　K141+　On the right is the **Villa Marinera** complex. At the far corner of the property the road toward the beach is to **Playa Marinero**, site of the **Hotel Santa Fe.** A half-mile farther on the left is the impressive **Villa Las Brisas.**

2.5　114.0　K145　Turn off to **Playa Zicatela**. *This beach is said to have the best waves in all of Mexico and has earned the nickname "Mexico Pipeline". The breaks are either left or right. Another popular spot is at the rocks on the lower end of the beach. Breaking around and through the rocks, it is left only. We've watched the action at both spots several times and have not been disappointed. When you look at all of the **cabinas** (cabins) scattered along the beach to house the surfers, you can see that they too have found a home away from home.*

0.8　114.8　K146+　A small signed town, **Barra de Colotepec** precedes a bridge over the **Río Colotepec**, a laundry river. *A short distance past the bridge a dirt road (right) leads up to a cross on a hill (at the left fork) and onto private property. There is no easy beach access.* The Mexico 200 highway continues straight through coco palms and scatterings of the small fan palms.

5.5　120.3　K155　The beach is not far away. There are some turnoffs toward the water but most, if not all, are gated.

2.5　122.8　K159　Shortly before arriving in **El Tomotal**, a small group of houses a mile back from the ocean. There is beach access via a dirt road. *It goes past a small round no-name restaurant and on into the main part of town at 0.3. We zig right, then left across a small streambed. Next comes cultivated ground with well-tended coconuts and bananas. The beach is at 0.9.*

Parking is about 75 yards back from the water. There are a few palms under which one might camp, but check the footing first. It is an open ocean facing southwest. The surf is fairly small, on a day when it was booming into Zicatela. It is a long flat beach with some driftwood, lots of sandcrabs at the surf line and few neighbors...thus far, we've seen a motley dog and two boys of about 10. Back to the highway. A large *higuera* with many trunks is on the east end of town. There are patches of jungle in some of the areas between the low hills.

1.9　124.7　K163　A road south goes to a long sandy beach with areas to camp. *We go straight at the fork, following the most traveled branch. There is a photogenic higuera on a little rise to the right with at least 25 trunks or major air roots. Continue past more cleared land and on to an ocean view at 0.8.*

YOLANDA

315

The fine gray sand beach faces southwest. Driftwood is every-where. A road (left) follows behind the low, brush-covered dunes for some distance, affording a number of camping opportunities. The water appears clear of heavy currents, but small channels and sand bars are apparent. This condition, along with sand crabs usually mean surf dwellers by the bunches. A few days here could be a rewarding experience for a variety of species. The road is not particularly bad, though motorhomes and trailers should do a pre-run. We couldn't find anyone to ask what name this stretch of sand might have, so we're calling it **No Name Beach**. Back to the highway.

1.8 126.5 K166 A dirt road (right) goes to houses but not the water.

0.8 127.3 K167+ A signed wide spot in the road, **Valdeflores** and a road (right) to the beach and, according to the sign, the **Restaurante Rita**. *We start past a few scattered houses and higueras on a rather easy road. At* **1.0**, *a fork and, if we understood a youngster correctly, both go to a beach. The left branch is farther, while the right one has the restaurant.*

We opt for Rita and her promise of sustenance. At **1.9**, *as we approach the beach, the road becomes very soft and shows little use or promise of getting us to the water, so we toss in the towel. The other, longer branch, was not attempted during this run. Maybe another time. If you find Rita, tell her we tried.* Back to the highway and continue toward Puerto Angel.

2.1 129.4 K170+ Signed on the graded road to the left (north) are **Cozoaltepec** 14km and **San Bernardino** 7km. The highway continues about a mile back from the ocean, then drops toward a bridge and back up the other side.

4.9 134.3 K178+ A bridge over a flowing river. The ocean is about 500 yards to the south.

5.5 139.8 K187 Another bridge, **Puente Lagartero**, (Bridge of the Lizard Catcher). There are not many houses through here, and they tend to be isolated from each other. The hills have few corn patches, probably due to inconsistent rainfall and/or poor soil. In the uncleared areas the vegetation consists of many small hardwood trees up to 8 inches in diameter, a few paddle cactus and small brush.

4.8 144.6 K195 We come to the small community of **San Isidro** but it is large enough to support a church and a couple of *tienditas* (very small stores). Next, a bridge over a laundry river, then **El Venado** (The Deer) another contributor to the crowd of people below the bridge. Continue east past lime and papaya trees, irrigated corn and squash.

2.2 146.8 K198+ The road (right) is an interesting dirt trail which eventually ends up in Puerto Angel. (**See Oaxaca Beaches.**) We continue going almost due east past several houses and a small school.

2.6 149.4 K202+ A cluster of houses on the left is signed, **Tonameca**.

4.4 154.8 K209+ A major paved intersection. Toward the right is the fishing and resort town of Puerto Angel. (**See Oaxaca Beaches.**) A turn inland toward the mountains will put you on a paved road to **San Pedro Pochutla** and ultimately, the city of Oaxaca. *Traversing some rugged mountains and offering spectacular vistas, about a hundred kilometers of the 250K highway is incredibly winding, thus very, very slow and tedious. It is an interesting, all-day project, and much better done from Oaxaca to the sea. Later we'll have other suggestions getting to Oaxaca.* (**See Oaxaca Inland**) We continue east toward **Playas de Huatulco** past a small military camp and a few houses. The land changes a bit, with more jungle and a few more houses.

4.4 159.2 K217 After a crossing of the **Río Aguacate** we move slightly uphill to a view of the area. On the south side of the bridge a road angles back and goes to the beach through a coconut plantation. At this writing the way is clear to visit...no gate.

2.7   161.9   K221   A small community here with a single restaurant and *tienda*. The name...**Los Ciruelos** (The Plums).

1.1   163.0   K223   A dirt road (right) goes toward the beach. We are some distance from the water, but it looks well-traveled and does make it, "shouldn't take more than a half-hour," says a local farmer! (**See Oaxaca Beaches.**) Continue east on Mexico 200.

3.0   166.0   K227+   We swing to the north around a hill for an unrestricted view of the heavily-forested sierra above. A dominant landmark here is the distant 10,200-foot **Cerro La Sirena**.

3.3   169.3   K232+   A winding descent brings us past a couple-dozen houses and a bridge over a small stream.

2.2   171.5   A restaurant, **El Chole**, is at the intersection with a signed paved road north to **Santa María de Huatulco**. A few more houses appear a kilometer farther, along with a local **Pemex**.

1.0   172.5   K238   The **Huatulco International Airport** is on the left. *We check it out and return to the highway.* The highway continues to wind through low hills some distance away from the water.

3.4   175.9   K243+   Graded road (left) into the hills to **Piedra de Los Morros**. Continue winding, maybe even more than before.

4.5   180.4   K250+   Road (right) is signed into **Santa Cruz de Huatulco**.

End of Log.

SANTA CRUZ DE HUATULCO...

If you try to find Huatulco in a guide book written before 1986, you probably won't. But if you do, it will likely read something like this: "A small fishing village with few touristic amenities, surrounded by a dozen crystal coves rimmed with white sand." Today, we find an international airport, and three of those coves are under intensive development.

This portion of the Oaxacan coast was settled in the pre-hispanic era by **Zapotecs** and **Mixtecs** who were outcasts from elsewhere in Oaxaca. The English pirates Francis Drake and Thomas Cavendish headquartered here in 1578 and 1587. Some records indicate that African slaves were imported here. There is little more to chronicle...at least until **Fonatur** began its touristc development program in 1987.

The program currently is centered around the three main bays of **Santa Cruz**, **Chahue** and **Tangolunda**. All have nice sandy beaches, with Santa Cruz being the most tranquil. Chahue to the east is slated to receive a **Fiesta Americana** while the last, Tangolunda, already has three large hotels, the 348-room **Sheraton**, the equally-large **Club Maeva Royale** and 752-room **Club Med**. Offering lots of tennis courts and free-form swimming pools, they share a nearby golf course and a beautiful, but practically-unswimmable, beach. *When we asked Arsenio, our guide, about it. He shrugged and said the locals have always known it as Olas Altas (Place of High Waves). He says that the red flag is up most of the time. If you wish a swimming beach, he suggests taking the excursion boats leaving from Santa Cruz beach.*

Tangolunda also has two shopping centers (one is half-full and the other nearing completion) and a small marina (in Club Med). Also under construction are villas, condominiums and, back against a hill, the **Hotel Virrey del Pacifico**.

When we arrived we considered staying in one of the beachfront Tangolunda hotels for a few days but...

Neither Club Med or the Royal Maeva would take anyone off the street, even for cash. They also wouldn't allow a walkthrough. Both said that admission is by reservation only and suggested we contact a travel agent!

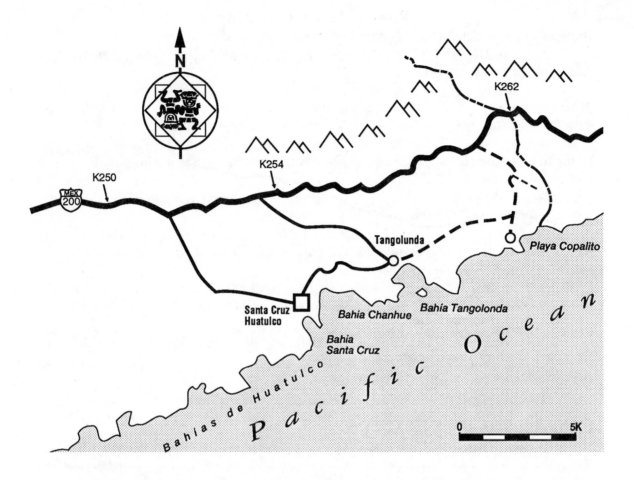

The Sheraton, however, opened the door a crack by "allowing" us to register if we are willing to pay a rate inflated (by the desk clerk's own admission) by about 50% over what we would have had to pay if we had gone through an American travel agent ahead of time! The gouge comes about by an on-site rate of $115 American per night (extra for ocean front). This really doesn't sound too bad because this a beautiful property, but until we asked there was no mention of the 15% IVA tax on top of the room rate. *It is our understanding that Mexican law (at least common courtesy) requires that the IVA be included in the quoted price.* He then "mentioned" that there is also a 10% service surcharge, so presumably, tipping is unnecessary.

When we said we had no American dollars he said he would have to tack on an exchange fee which amounted to about 10% for our payment in Mexican pesos! To his credit, the clerk was embarrassed and said that he could only follow orders. *It was he who suggested the place where we finally stayed, the* **Hotel Busanvi** *in* **La Crucecita.**

The Sheraton's lounge is beautiful and the 5-piece combo talented, but the tab for a so-so margarita is $5.50 each! As we happened in at happy hour we get two for that price. The crowd is less than overwhelming. We share the lounge with a couple from Monterey, Mexico for nearly an hour before someone else comes in!

Eight-thirty is a fashionable time for dinner in Mexico, yet there are only about 30 guests in the hotel's main dining room at that hour, plus an equal number of waiters, busboys and hostesses.

Touring the Huatulco area is best done by boat, and well worthwhile. In this manner one can visit a half-dozen otherwise-unreachable bays with shady restaurants, good swimming and some of the finest snorkeling to be found anywhere in the eastern Pacific. For more private couples with their own *refrescos*, food and recreational pursuits, there are 23

318

Puerto Angel Hub Map

uninhabited beaches ranging in size from several meters to several hundred, to laze on. *And don't forget to make arrangements for someone to come back for you. It happens more often than you might imagine, and the zancudos (mosquitos) are too hungry to allow any overnighting.*

Here are a couple of the bays you might want to try...**Maguey** has seven restaurants and excellent snorkeling. **Entrega** is nearby and offers rental facilities too. The most distant is **San Agustín** (25 miles) and requires a day-long charter.

Sportfishing can be very good here, especially for sailfish and dorado. Roosterfish patrol the shallow reefs and sandy beaches, as do jack cravalle and pompano. Members of the pargo family are also common in a variety of nearshore habitats. Boats may be chartered from the marina at the main beach, Santa Cruz. *A word of warning...we find the effort poorly organized and very, very expensive. Today we would not rate it as a prudent investment of time, money or patience.*

We like the Santa Cruz Bay area, for it is here that the locals have their central plaza, open air markets and small commercial center dotted among numerous apartments, some homes and several condo complexes. We check out the in-town hotels, the **Binniguenda** and **Castillo de Huatulco**. Both have restaurants, pools, lovely gardens, air conditioning and moderate rates.

There is also a budding Santa Cruz suburb by the name of **La Crucecita** (Little Crossroad) with a number of small hotels, including the **Busanvi**. We found the ceiling-fanned Busanvi clean and inexpensive. Be sure to ask for a room on the street side...more air. Another budget hotel is across and up the street, the **Hotel Grifer**. We had a good breakfast at **Palma Real**.

Just south of Crucecita is the beach of **Chahue**. At present there is a miserable trailer park with filthy restrooms and broken showers behind the dunes (*Easter week and two customers!*). The beach is beautiful with rocky headlands. It is slated to have a public beachfront park with hotels, residential areas and condominiums nearby.

What's in the future? It is hard to tell, but they are projecting a development covering 52,000 acres (approximately 18 by 4 miles) with nine bays and 10 miles of white sand beaches ultimately involved .By the year 2000 it's supposed to have 7800 hotel rooms, a population of 100,000 and a hoped-for 875,000 visitors annually. Ultimately the plan is for 22,000 rooms, 200,000 population with 2 million visitors! This will create 50,000 permanent jobs and 75,000 more related to the construction. These aren't our figures, we got 'em from the Mexican Tourist Department.

319

MEXICO 200 — HUATULCO — BORDER

0.0   0.0   K250+   We are at the intersection into **Santa Cruz de Huatulco** and Mexico 200. We continue east toward **Salina Cruz**

2.5   2.5   K254   Intersection, and another paved road (right) into the **Bahias de Hualtuco** resort area. This one takes us directly into the **Tangolunda** beach area.

0.9   3.4   K256   The road winds a lot, even though it stays fairly level. There is still a heavy growth of small trees, cactus and vines on the low hills.

4.2   7.6   K262+   Graded dirt road (right) leads to **Playa Copalita**, a beautiful beach with charming inhabitants and excellent photo opportunities. **(See Oaxaca Beaches.)** Drive east on Mexico 200 past the bridge over the **Río Copalita**. This river not only is hosting a bunch of launderettes, but three cars and a horse, all in the process of being washed. There is probably a saying in Copalita..."If you want rain, wash a horse." The small town of **Copalita** is sited on the east side of the river. We continue winding east.

GIRL FROM COPALITO

4.3   11.9   K268+   Cross a bridge.

2.9   14.8   K273   The **Río Zimatán** is a small rocky one, with a *comedor familiar* restaurant serving *cervezas* at the east end of the bridge. Here we go into the hills past a few agave cactus on the left and a good view of the ocean to the right.

1.3   16.1   K275   Signed road (right) over a rise into **Barra de Santa Cruz**. There are a hundred or more houses here and no road to the beach. *It does go 1.7 miles south to the pueblito of Barra de Santa Cruz, but no farther.* The highway continues to turn every chance it gets, making for slow driving.

1.9   18.0   K278   **Río Chacalapa**. A pretty little river with tall green trees along its banks.

4.0   22.0   K284+   The trees here have an unusually large number of bromeliads growing on them. We are used to seeing them on trees with some leaves...these trees are bare, making the sight all the more noteworthy.

0.3   22.3   K285   If you have noticed large dark masses in the forks of trees earlier on this journey and not known what they might be...they were probably termite nests. The *nests are occupied by an entire colony of termites, queen, workers, nurses and all. The migrations come during the rainy season. From their tree top empire it is easier for the termites to gather the cellulose they need for survival. It's tough on the tree, but good for the termites.*

3.1   25.4   K290   Ahead a large rock sticks up well above everything else. As we come closer we realize how big it is and that it has a fully grown cactus perched on its apex. *Several cactus types predominate along in here...the Mexican organ pipe and a pitahaya-type with three sides on its branches and a tendency to take on a purple color as it ages. There is also a very spindly cactus that gets 30 feet high.*

1.3   26.7   K292   We begin a downgrade leading to the **Río Ayuta**. There are a dozen or more cattle and several burros wandering around in the river bottom, but no people.

1.4   28.1   K294+   Off to the left is a collection of about 120 homes. It is likely **Morro Ayuta**.

1.5   29.6   K297   A small dirt road (right) in the direction of the ocean. There is another one a half-mile farther on. Neither one makes it.

0.7   30.3   K298   A bridge over the **Río Coyol**. The town of **El Coyol** is a short distance off to the right. Most of the houses are adobe with tile roofs. Watch for the *topes*. The fences are made of small tree trunks dug into the ground, one against the other. They look like they could stop almost anything. *There is a road to the ocean from here. According to a man in the tienda, you enter town on a dirt road with a soccer field on the left. Then go left past the cemetery and follow that road to the ocean. He says it is only a couple of miles. We didn't take time to check him out, due to our earlier* **Half Hour Beach** *adventure.*

2.1   32.4   K301   A graded dirt (right) goes to the salt lagoon. We continue over a series of viaducts and small bridges, then onto a wide flood plain. The area is called **Arroyo Seco**, as is the *pueblito*.

2.3   34.7   K305   The road into the small town of Arroyo Seco. Add a yellow-flowering paddle cactus to the list of plants common through here. The farther we penetrate into the region of the **Gulf of Tehuanapec**, the drier the hills appear. The winds are also much stronger through here.

2.6   37.3   K309   A small group of picturesque, thatched roof adobe houses is on the left. Note how far the palm leaves hang down...this is to protect the adobe walls. If the overhang weren't there the walls would melt away in only a few rainy seasons.

0.4   37.7   K310   **Tapanala** is the signed name of a sizeable grouping of thatched houses. Widely scattered, it appears to have no specific center. We saw no evidence of electricity here either. The highway jogs a bit, then we pass through tile roofed **Santa María Huamelula**.

3.2   40.9   K315   **Puente Santa María**, over an *arroyo seco* (dry riverbed). The road begins to angle toward the ocean, following the arroyo.

1.9   42.8   K318   **Santiago de Astata**, one of the largest towns we've seen for some time. An organized business section is off to the right, along with a church and small *zocalo*. It also shows evidence of recent storm damage.

1.3   44.1   K319+   A paved road (left) goes to **San Pedro Huamelula**, then north into the hills. We cross a bridge, then drive past a huge black monolith with hundreds of small agave cactus clinging everywhere. There are also a number of large and small *hiqueras* (fig trees) clinging to the cliffsides, their white roots and trunks standing out starkly against the black rocks. Continue east onto a plain with small trees and a few fan palms. Ox carts are common here. They travel parallel to the highway on narrow dirt trails. Most of the carts have wooden wheels with metal rims. The axles fit into the chocks just as they did hundreds of years ago. Locating the *maestros* who make them would be a fascinating project.

5.9   50.0   K329+   A well-used road goes south to the ocean at **Playa Colorada**. *We pass the edge of a salt lagoon at* **0.5**. *The water is a reddish color from the special kind of algae able to live in water with high concentrations of salt. Thus the name* **Laguna Colorada** *(Red Lagoon). Just beyond we take the better-traveled right fork. The plant life is typical of what we have been seeing along the highway, small trees, etc.*

At **1.2** *we are by the water with an abandoned sombra (palm-leaf shade) in front of us. The road continues west, disappearing around a dune. The sparkling white beach arcs off to the left. A small island in front and rocks off to the right complete the scene. The prevailing winds come from the southeast through the* **Isthmus of Tehuantepec** *and can be fierce, however we have been assured that the winds are often less along the water than a short distance inland or a mile out to sea. Today it is perfect. The wind is blowing only enough to be refreshing and the water is about 85 degrees, a perfect temperature for early April.*

This is **Semana Santa**, *Easter Week, one of Mexico's busiest beach holidays, yet we are the only people here! Camping should not be a problem, but no motorhomes. The structure of the beaches makes one think of fishing...inshore rocks, sand bars and channels, lots of beach crabs and some bird activity.* Back to the highway and east past another little road to the Laguna Colorada salt works. Farther on, we've a good overlook of the many little salt ponds, the lagoon, **Estero San Diego**, and beyond, the ocean with its collection of rocky islets.

2.2   52.2   K333   We continue to skirt the base of the foothills past several houses, a few ox carts and beautiful views of the ocean. We then turn inland past a dense grove of fan palms.

1.5   53.7   K335+   We cross a bridge, then encounter for a dirt road on the right and back toward the ocean. *We go over a little ridge and past a number of adobe, thatched houses. This is an ox-cart community. We continue on the truck road past a huge huanacaxtle tree (left) and down a small arroyo toward the water and a fork at **0.4**. We take the right branch to follow a fence to a salt flat and a dead end at **0.9**. Retrace back to the intersection and take the other fork.*

*The left fork goes through a small grove of higuera trees and past the remains of an adobe house. After **0.7** miles it too dead ends, this time at a schoolhouse, basketball court and about 30 houses. In the process of turning around we back over a sharp little stump and rupture a tire. Gratefully, a gang of the local teenagers take it upon themselves to give a hand with the changing process. We are very grateful, especially to the two sparkling teen girls, **Norma** and **Andrea**, who conned the boys into it. We have no name for the place, but from the reception it could well be **Amistad** (Friendship).* Back to the highway and east along Mexico 200.

7.5   61.2   K347+   To the rear we have an excellent view of the preceding beaches, lagoons and marshes. Continue a short distance to the pass and drop toward the ocean through a narrow valley. Ahead is a river mouth and an array of sand dunes.

0.9   62.1   K349   A poor road (right) is signed **Sanjon**. *As far as we can tell it goes to the ocean at the northwest end of the beach we visit at K351+.*

1.5   63.6   K351+   Intersect with a roads (left) to **Santa Cruz Bomba** (Pump) and right to **Concepción Bomba**, 1km, several rock quarries and the beach. *Concepción Bomba is laid out along the edge of a dry arroyo at 1.0. The road continues to the beach at 2.1. Here two breakwaters provide calmer water for launching pangas. We also see several shady restaurants.* Back to the highway and continue to the top of the grade and on to the next valley.

4.0   67.6   K358+   A dirt road (left) to a cluster of houses. Then just down the road a signed, graded road right is to **Ensenada Chipahua,** 3km. *We follow southwest into a small town, **Santa Gertrudis Miramar**, and a school and basketball court at **0.5**. A road branches left at **1.3**, while we continue west behind the coastal dunes to some houses and several restaurants facing a beautiful white beach, **2.4** miles. It extends west beyond a wall of rocks on the right and to the east as far as we can see.*

Though beautiful and facing a turquoise sea, Ensenada Chipahua is in a wind tunnel and its waves and currents look to be a hazard for water sports. We can see it as a day or overnighting destination, with an eye on the weather. Not recommended for motorhomes or trailers. Back on the highway, we go east past the **La Palapa** restaurant on the left.

2.2   69.8   K362   A signed graded road goes inland to **Aguas Calientes, Santa Clara** and **San Vicente**. We continue over a dry river bed and into a broad valley where the signed community of **El Morro Mazatan** is sited. Here we have a local **Pemex** and large *topes*. At the end of the *topes* is the **Comedor Maríe**. *The lady taking our order, cooking, serving and making change is a charmer named **Braulia**. She is a person who calls it the way she sees it. As the restaurant is hers and it's in her home, she has a few ground rules... There's only one brand of beer in one bottle size...**Superiór** in **liters**. Why? Because Braulia sees Superior as the best beer, and a liter bottle as the best value! So if you want a cerveza, be sure you're thirsty. And she makes a mean plate of pork chops.*

About 200 yards beyond the Comedor Maríe, a road takes off west through Morro Mazatan to **Playa Cangrejo**, (Crab Beach)...

*We start out past a number of houses, most of which have solid wood fences. At **0.7***

Salina Cruz Hub Map

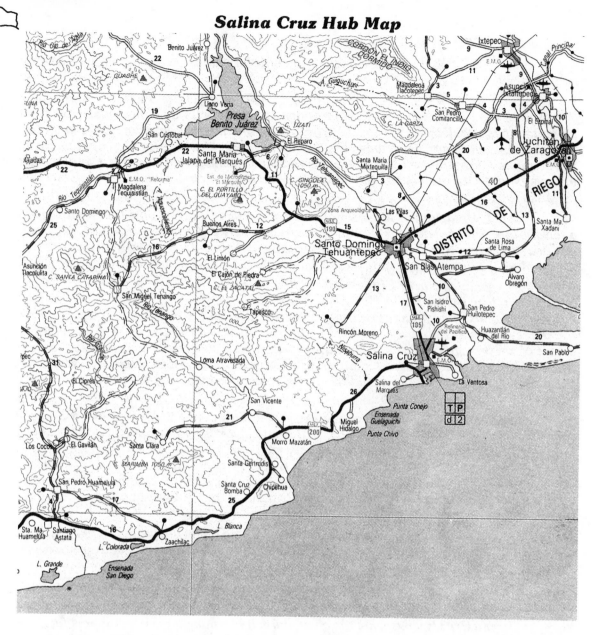

go right and past a soccer field. There are still houses around here. If you have any doubt, ask anyone you see, "A la playa?" or follow the best-traveled trails south and east past irrigated fields, including several plantings of papayas. We make a sharp right at **2.5** and wind through an alluvial delta area. Mesquite, guasimas and several cacti predominate. We are at the beach at **3.6**.

The beach faces almost due east, has white sand, some driftwood and rocks. There are about a dozen restaurants, replete with hammocks. The parking area is behind the beach and a small fee is charged. The breeze is refreshing, the food inexpensive, the cervezas cold and the water warm. Good ingredients for a pleasant afternoon. Permission for overnighting is available and inexpensive. Again, it is not for motorhomes or trailers. Back to the highway. (On the way back out we see a jitney-bus marked to Cangrejo from Morro Mazatan and it is jammed.) After Mazatan we ride along the foothills with a great view of the ocean below. There is a small turnout about halfway up the hill. A good spot for pictures.

6.6   76.4   K372+   The road turns around a bluff and presents a super view of what is ahead, the **Salina Cruz** basin and harbor. Home of a large oil refinery, it always has tankers offshore loading up on the various refinery products. The refinery itself is fed by a

323

pipeline from oilfields in the state of Vera Cruz.

  2.9   79.3   K377   Signed bridge, **Puente Coralitos**, over a dry wash. Continue northeast.

  1.3   80.6   K379   A road (right) to **Ensenada Guelauguichi** and **Playa Escondida**. *We go through a small community with a school, water tower and at 1.5, the ubiquitous basketball court. We turn (right) toward Playa Escondida at the basketball court, go one block along the power lines, then (left) past a small brick church. A right turn past more houses follows. We continue zigzagging along the most-traveled trails until we are going west between two fences with power lines in view.*

  The road moves into a flood plain and numerous mesquite trees at 2.7 miles. The beach is at 3.2. Up against a tall, rocky point with a road leading to the lighthouse, it has a restaurant and some parking. The sand is white and extends for miles to the east. The water is a beautiful turquoise, but rough and heavy with currents. Back to the highway.

  0.8   81.4   K380   A signed road right is to **Playa Azul**. *The road is graded, somewhat gravelly in places, dusty in others. The first 0.2 miles is accompanied by a fence on the right, then swings into the flood plain and a vegetation mix of mesquite, brazilwood, agave and cactus. We continue to the beach at 2.0 and a number of palapa restaurants built for shade, they sport a number of hammocks, and shade-covered sand. A sign makes us aware of another spot, Bahía Chipahúa, off to the right. We gird for another kilometer or two of driving only to find that it is the name of a restaurant behind some trees less than 50 yards from where we were parked! We celebrate by ordering a plate of tacos and several cervezas.* Back to the highway.

  4.8   86.2   K388   Signed road (right) to **Salinas de Marquez**. *We follow the road straight to the water where it "T"s. Left is into a nondescript town centered around a harbor and a (right) turn presents an unremarkable beach broken by rocky groins and a couple of restaurants. The round-trip distance is under two miles.* Back to the highway. We continue toward Salina Cruz. The plants around here look like they had been transplanted from the desert around La Paz, Baja California Sur...they consist of scrubby members of the mesquite family, several deciduous hardwoods, copals and three or four kinds of cactus.

  1.2   87.4   K390   A portion of the city is laid out on the right. Frankly, it is not an especially memorable sight. As we drop toward the entrance into the city the *refacciones* (auto parts stores) proliferate, along with the *topes*.

  1.9   89.3   K393   We are at the intersection into **Salina Cruz**. A right turn takes us into the downtown area.

  Salina Cruz is a busy, not too clean port city. Although the present port facilities were originally built in 1905 and have been added to and improved over the years, it was always a port. Cortéz sailed from here on his expeditions to Central America and the Sea of Cortéz.

  Today it has a number of industries which are tied into the petroleum industry, for Salina Cruz is the western terminus for Mexico's abundant oil. The pipeline from Vera Cruz brings petroleum to storage tanks and refineries. From here both petroleum products and crude oil are shipped along Mexico's west coast to Pacific Rim countries. Salina Cruz is also a fishing and trade center, with packing and freezing plants for a variety of products.

  From the intersection we bear left and follow signed Mexico 185 due north to **Tehuantepec**. *Yes, we do lose the designation of Mexico 200 for a while, but it rejoins us later.* The highway, with new K-markers (beginning with 298), takes us past a variety of businesses, including a local **Pemex** and an **LPG** station; signed turnoffs to *colonias*, or suburbs; and a lot of *topes*. There is also a hospital and considerable cookie-cutter-row-housing with lawns as we work our way through the corridor between the two cities.

  8.8   98.1   K284   There is a major intersection here. Mexico 190 highway goes west and north into the mountains toward **Oaxaca City**, while Mexico 185 goes northeast

324

through **Tehuantepec**. There is a full service **Pemex** at this intersection and a good-looking, large restaurant, **Gujexhoba**, with lots of business, next door. Remember the *topes*.

0.4　98.5　K283　The first street on the north side of the long bridge over the **Río Tehuantepec** takes us into the town, the central market and zocalo.

It is a bit after five and there are a number of food carts, stands, etc. in the process of setting up along the eastern edge of the zocalo. We are told that each night about 25 entrepreneurs serve food all night, "6pm to 6am." Our informant says that they keep very busy. If we ever stay the night around here, the zocalo at Tehuantepec will be on the menu.

*This area was peopled by the **Zapotec** Indians. They were such fierce fighters that the Aztecs were never able to conquer them, and even the Spanish soldiers were hard-pressed to gain a foothold. Another interesting feature of the people of the Tehuantepec region is the importance of the women. The native society here is matriarchal with women of Tehuantepec taking a leading role in business and politics. Although the younger ones wear western clothes, many of the older women still wear traditional costumes of embroidered **huipiles** and full, printed skirts. At fiesta time the dress is even fancier. Some wear a strange lace bonnet with sleeves hanging down the back that is said to originally have been a baby's christening dress. There are numerous fiestas as each **barrio** (neighborhood) has its own, and they may last a fortnight. One curious celebration is the **Tirada de Frutas** where the women stand on roofs and throw fruit at the men below.*

We continue northeast on the *periférico* past numerous plantings of mangos, bananas and papayas. There are fruit stands offering several varieties of ripe mangos. *Imagine, juicy ripe mangoes in February. A California friend, Fred Greenwood, will surely book a flight south the February after he reads this...such is his mango obsession.*

1.9　100.4　K280　Here comes the **Hotel Calli**, *con clima*, (air conditioned), and the only one recommended for the area. It also has a dining room if you don't want to go back to those zocalo restaurants..

3.1　103.5　K275　We are now going straight across a broad flat plain rimmed by high mountains on the west and north. *Between the two ranges a low (600-foot) and narrow (three mile wide) pass leads north 140 miles to **Vera Cruz** and the **Gulf of Mexico**. The area looks seared, and it is, both by the sun and the perennial winds which whip through the valleys below the **Tehuantepec Venturi**.* The small trees, cactus, brush and occasional areas of sedge grass all look ready to find a more salubrious environment. A large and modern 2-story white stucco and brick house is to the left.

4.3　107.8　K263　The signed town with the intriguing name of **Pepe y Lolita** is off to the left. *There has to be a story on that one.*

4.0　111.8　K258+　A signed bridge, **Puente Los Perros**, a livestock river. It is actually the **Juchitan River** that it bridges, and though the river's proper name is the Juchitan, it is locally known as the **Río Los Perros** (River of the Dogs).

0.5　112.3　K257+　Paved road left is signed to **Ixtepec**. From there it goes for many kilometers past dozens of villages and ranches. *Though **San Jeronimo Ixtepec** is a rather young city it is busy developing reasons for visitors to come and visit. The buys in gold and other jewelry are reputed to be good and its saint's day celebration, September 29 and 30 has a nighttime calenda (parade of lights). A few meters past the Ixtepec turnoff is the entrance (right) into **Juchitan de Zaragoza** and a bit of a surprise...a full service **Pemex**, magnasin and all.* We continue straight northeast.

1.6　113.9　K255　An **LPG** station, then a new suburban housing tract of brick, block and adobe, **Los Pinos**. A lot of sugar cane is grown near here, if the many pieces scattered along the highway are an indication.

3.0　116.9　K250　A signed location, **El Porvenír**, is interesting only in the fact that it and the road sign for traffic coming the other direction are only about 5 meters apart. This usually indicates a bus stop or a trail leading off somewhere. In this case we can find nothing, not even a wide spot. The hills to the north are called **Cordon La Cordillera** and range to a bit over a thousand feet.

    4.4   121.3   K243   Intersection and a local **Pemex**. To the left is the **Transisthmus Highway, Mexico 185.** *At this point Carol brought up the subject of how far we are from the United States Border. Tom guessed, and was almost a thousand miles off the mark. By heading north here on Mexico 185 and taking the main federal highways, we are only 902 miles from Brownsville, Texas! That's less than the distance from Tijuana to La Paz on the Baja Peninsula! It is hard to believe.* The (right) branch is Mexico 190, complete with a new set of K-markers. We take it and proceed east past cattle grazing in rich, green pastures. Where undeveloped, the land looks like a desert.

    3.2   124.5   K5   Here is a marshy area with several small lakes scattered about. Various species of reeds predominate. There are also several stands of the small fan palm. When the marshes clear up we are back to dull, deciduous brush and cactus.

    6.0   130.5   K15   A signed paved intersection south is to **La Venta** and **Union Hidalgo**. We continue due east along the northern edge of a wide, flat plain. The high mountains to the north and east are the **Sierra Atravesada**. Behind the six and seven thousand feet mountains there should be a lessening of the winds which plague the region to the north and west.

    1.8   132.3   K18   Sugar cane is beginning to show, particularly to the south toward the lagoons.

    1.9   134.2   K20   On the left in **Santo Domingo** is the stack of a sugar refinery. They also manufacture alcohol. There are miles of sugar cane extending in all directions. Where the land is still uncultivated it is covered with mesquite-types, palms and other scrub. Much of the roadbed is raised, probably to prevent flood damage, but it has settled unevenly and is lumpy in places.

    4.7   138.9   K27+   **La Blanca**, a signed road inland. We see sheep grazing in nearby fields...the first in a long time.

    0.9   139.8   K29   Intersection with roads leading to **Cerro Iguana** and **Santo de Abajo**.

    3.7   143.5   K35   We top a short rise to see a pyramid-shaped mountain directly ahead. Continue east through the edge of the city of **Niltepec**. This seems to be a city of *comedores* (restaurants). A few of the names...**Lorena, Rosa, Diana, María**. We'd guess the population at about 20,000.

    5.3   148.8   K45   The landscape is changing. The plants are holding their leaves longer, indicating a different mix of plants, and/or more rain.

    8.6   157.4   K59   **Puente Ostuta**, a bridge over the river of the same name, next to the town of the same name. *There is something going on in the riverbed by the bridge. It is not laundry, or horse and car washes, but restaurants! We can see several palmleaf shelters very near, or in, the shallow water. On a warm evening, imagine dangling your feet in the stream while downing tacos and beer.* A paved road (right) to the sugar communities of **La Reforma** and **Ixhuatan**. On the left the two closest mountains are the 5000-foot **El Bejucal** and the somewhat shorter **Cuscumate**.

    5.0   162.4   K67   A bridge over the **Río Zanatepec**, a year-round river on the western edge of **Santo Domingo Zanatepec**, a sugar cane town. Signed as 13,000 inhabitants, it looks a bit larger. The town boasts the first airconditioned restaurant we've seen in many miles, the **Comedor Lonchita**.

    1.3   163.7   K69   The new, small **Posada San Rafael** motel is located a half-mile or so from town. *We loved the hammock on our own little patio. The rooms are with ceiling fan or air conditioner, and very inexpensive. It tends to fill up with transients well before sunset, so an early stop is indicated. The restaurant next door is a good one...but traditional meals only.*

326

4.3   160.0   K75   Well-cared-for mango orchards are a feature here. We begin angling more to the south.

2.6   162.6   K79+   A couple of clean-looking restaurants, **Mary Ann**, then across the highway, **Alex**, while another, **Comedor Yessy**, is the most picturesque of the bunch.

3.5   166.1   K85   We see piles of driftwood in many places well above the normal level of the nearby riverbed. From the looks of it, the storm that left all of that stuff was a big one.

2.1   168.2   K88+   An **LPG** station, then **Tapanatepec** is the signed community ahead. The town is big enough to have *topes* and a number of stores. To the north are the **Sierra La Jinetas**. The tallest visible peak in the group is **Cerro El Baul** at 6900 feet.

1.1   169.3   K90+   Intersection with a local **Pemex**. Here Mexico 190 continues north to Tuxtla Guttierez, while the road southeast is our old friend, Mexico 200. At this point we get another set of K markers. Start at K0 and follow Mexico 200 out of town past mangos, limes, and coconuts.

4.4   173.7   K7   Intersection with a road straight ahead into **Chahuites**. We branch to the left and follow Mexico 200 southeast. The corn is back on the hillsides...a sign of better weather conditions.

7.1   180.8   K19   Sadly, more and more of this part of Oaxaca is being cleared for agriculture. The road is rapidly approaching the hills to the south.

4.3   185.1   K26   We are at the border between **Oaxaca** and **Chiapas**. End of log.

AROUND PINOTEPA NACIONAL

Jicotepec, a small town about five miles north of Pinotepa, was, for a few years, the subject of a unique, inadvertent, experiment in linguistics. It seems that an American couple visited Pinotepa and, finding the area to their liking, settled in Jicotepec, some thousand feet above the valley floor where they found cooling breezes to go with a great view of the area.

The interesting thing is that the town's 900 inhabitants were Mixtec Indians, and very few could speak Spanish. In order to communicate with their neighbors, the American couple began learning Mexteco and, in the process, a number of the Mextecs learned English, thus making them bilingual, but still unable to speak Spanish.

Now that a graded road has replaced the old burro trails, things are beginning to change in Jicotepec. On our visit we saw many of the old ways in clothing, houses and implements but we also saw teenage boys dressed in Levis, T-shirts and tennis shoes, but still carrying *machetes*, as did their forefathers. The road is graded most of the way, getting quite rough the last mile. Once there there's little to see except groupings of houses with ill-defined roads or trails connecting them. Back to the highway.

Pinotepa Don Luís...

We begin at the signed intersection of Mexico 125 with Mexico 200 at K245+ and go northwest. Destination, **Pinotepa Don Luís.**

An intersection comes at **1.2** miles. It is signed to Pinotepa Don Luis (right).

At **2.9** miles from the intersection we are in **San Miguel Tlacamama,** a small Indian town with much the same dress and activities as Jicotepec, except, being on a road and having electricity, it is more advanced. A dirt road (left) near the end of town is signed to **La Catalina.**

The road becomes a single lane, but graded and easy driving. We cross a very narrow bridge and descend northwest into the valley with fine views of mountains, homesites with their gardens, and an occasional streambed with a ribbon of green trees marking its path.

A huge shady *huanacaxtle* tree at **6.3** miles offers a chance to cool off. We continue across a mile-wide valley, out the other side and begin climbing. Now the views are of the valley behind and another off to the right.

The **8.6** mile mark brings us high enough to see the ocean a good 30 miles to the south. A mile beyond we enter **San Pedro Jicayan,** another village with a strong Mixtec flavor. The town has a basketball court, church and small *zocalo.*

At the far end of town, **10.0,** the road splits. The left branch goes to **San Pedro Atoyac** while the right, and most traveled, is to Pinotepa Don Luis.

We are climbing again, but more to the east with views of row after row of mountain ridges until they disappear into a blue haze. Corn and beans are on the hillsides.

We come to a small school on a ridge at **12.3.** Around the bend we begin dropping into the valley of Pinotepa Don Luís. *Just before entering town, we see three women weaving with backstrap looms on the veranda of the house on the right. We stop to ask permission to look at their work, but our initial questions cause so much confusion that we leave. (Later we realize why...they don't speak Spanish.)*

The *zocalo* is at **13.6** miles. The central market and the main portion of the town is just beyond. As it is late in the day, the market is almost deserted. A lady shows us some beautiful loomed cloth. As we go through town we see several other houses of weavers. Considering our experience and the shyness of the people, it would appear that the central market would be the best place to buy. Their work is very intricate and precise. The weavings are rarely seen anywhere else, and then at very high prices. A piece from here might be used to set off a room decor. Back to the highway.

328

Santa María Huazolotitlan...

Just east of Pinotepa Nacionál, at K17+ of Mexico 200, a sign welcomes us to **San Andres Huaxpaltepec**. *Just beyond the entrance a graded road south goes to* **Santa María Huazolotitlan**. *(It is not signed going south, but is signed coming north.) If you are interested in carved wooden masks this is one of the carving centers for the state of Oaxaca.*

At **1.4** miles we wind back and forth up to the top of a ridge overlooking a beautiful little town. A stream reflects the morning sun. Smoke from cooking fires curls up from the houses. The hills are splashed with green and brown.

We enter past the *panteón* (cemetery). It looks like a miniature town in itself, for the tombs replicate houses and churches in miniature. The valley has a wide variety of fruit trees...mango, coconut, banana, papaya, *círuela* and others. Continue into town past the zocalo at **2.7**.

It is Sunday and the dress of the parishioners reflect the Indian heritage. The women here wear their hair coiled tightly on top of their head, not like the long flowing styles of many other parts of Mexico. We stop at the **Tienda Rosa** to ask directions.

Here we meet **Sylvia de Santos Banos**. The señora quickly named one of the town's better-known carvers, and dispatches two of her children to lead the way.

To reach the home of the wood-carver we must climb a winding, zigzag trail past many other homes and eventually to the top of a hill overlooking the valley. Now we see why we need the children as guides.

Here we meet the *maestro,* **José de Luna Lopez**. He is self-taught and his style unique. The majority of his masks are centered around the *tigre*, or jaguar. He does both miniatures and full-sized. He rarely has much to show, for his work is sold almost as fast as it is made to stores in Oaxaca.

Despite his success, Señor Luna Lopez sees it as only something to do when he is not tending his hillside during the summer, for tradition says that the corn, beans and squash raised there will feed his family for the next year, thus they have priority. A thoroughly charming gentleman. *The decor in our Baja house will feature some of the work of Don José.*

Silvia knows another carver and about where he lives, but cannot remember his name. She does know though that his uncle's name is Antonio. With these clues anyone should be able to find him! Back to the highway.

THE VALLEY OF OAXACA CITY...

Nestled in the mountains of southern Mexico is the mile-high **Valley of Oaxaca**. When one sees the rich land, the clean air and sparkling water, when one goes through the central markets and sees the bounty of fruits and vegetables this benign climate yields then it is easy to see why clans of hunters and gatherers roamed this verdant valley more than 4000 years ago and, with succeeding migrations, built one of the world's unique civilizations...

The story of 3000 years of continuous occupation is told high on a mountaintop nine kilometers west of the city of Oaxaca in what we now call **Monte Alban**. It is told in the temples, the tombs, and yes, the trash dumps of this city which was as large as 25,000 and whose influence was felt as far away as **Teotihuacan** in the Valley of Mexico.

The first people to build temples, carve gods and systematically draw on the wealth of the region, arrived around 1500 B.C. when branches of the **Olmec** tribes settled here. The stone and clay messages left behind indicate that they held sway for nearly a thousand years, yielding finally to the **Zapotecs**.

The Zapotecs were builders, accomplished builders who not only created great temples, courts and residential complexes, but did it with a flair. At one point the top of the mountain which dominated the valley became too small, so they flattened it off. How many millions of baskets of dirt and rock were removed, one can only guess, but they did it. They also terraced hillsides, built dams, a drainage system and a network of cisterns.

Some of the terraces are still in use, providing corn and other staples to todays residents much as they did 1500 years ago. And the history of Monte Alban is still being written as the terraces yield more pieces of the past.

Monte Alban reached her zenith between 250 and 750 A.D. when 25,000 people occupied about 6 square kilometers and exercised control over several hundred outlying towns and villages. Her influence was felt as far as Chiapas, Vera Cruz, Puebla and the Valley of Mexico. The partially excavated site of **Lambityeco**, 29 kilometers east, is an example. The signature of the Zapotec is there, on its tombs and in its architecture.

The end of an era came for the people of Monte Alban around 750 A.D. when the greater part of her population left to occupy other communities in the valley. The movement came in part because the population had simply outgrown the ability of the mountain to provide basic needs...food, firewood and, especially, water. At first water came from the hills they lived on, for the forested lands sustained numerous small springs. But as the population grew the need for wood increased, and with the forests went the springs. The dam and cisterns worked until the demand again became overwhelming. Eventually the ability of the population to hand-carry water up from the valley floor was outstripped by the numbers to be served. And the migrations continued until a balance was reached.

Today nearby cities such as **Mitla**, **Yagul** and **Zaachila** house many of the descendents of that migration.

In the 11th century the **Mixtecs** invaded the Valley of Oaxaca and added their pottery and jewelry-making to the skills found in the valley. As a complete assimilation of the two groups never came about, many towns still hold to either Zapotec or Mixtec customs and artisanal specialties.

When the **Aztecs** began to move toward Central and South America in the 15th century, they swept into the valley and, in 1486, set up an administrative center where the city of Oaxaca is today. As conquerors, the Aztecs forced the vanquished peoples to pay tribute in the form of textiles and cochineal dye.

In the 1520s when the Spanish began to consolidate their empire of New Spain, they met with strong resistence from the people of the Valley of Oaxaca. **Hernán Cortéz** founded the city, named himself **Margues del Valle de Oaxaca** and then took title to most of the valley.

Oaxaca Valley Hub Map

Despite intermittent rebellions and earthquakes Oaxaca became the most important town in southern Mexico during the early colonial period. Numerous churches and monasteries were built. The Indians, who had prospered for so many centuries declined in numbers...from 150,000 to under 50,000 by 1640 as the benevolent word of God was spread among the residents.

Earthquakes continue to plague the region. In 1854 much of the city was destroyed, in 1931 70% became uninhabitable and again in 1957, one lasting three minutes did extensive damage. In a way, it is a miracle that any of the early buildings have survived.

Today's Oaxaca is an exciting city with colonial architecture, beautiful churches, a bustling central market, lively music in the *zocalo*, colorful fiestas, spicy regional dishes and a rich Indian culture. The environs provide archaeological ruins and small villages producing exquisite handicrafts. Family-run *mescal* distilleries and ox cart trails through shoulder-high corn fields are also part of the experiences which fuel an increasingly-important part of the region's economy...tourism. Oaxaca is also one of the least expensive tourist destinations in Mexico.

The **Cathedral**, started in 1533, had a long construction phase, due in part to earthquakes, and was officially completed nearly 200 years after the cornerstone was laid. With its adjoining *zocalo* it is located on the north edge of the central plaza, one of the most attractive in Mexico. With huge laurel trees, shaded benches, an ornate kiosk, balloon vendors, strolling musicians and sidewalk cafes, this is a perfect setting for a 24-hour diorama of Oaxacan life. It ebbs and flows here in the center of the city.

OAXACA

A few blocks from the cathedral the 16th-century church of **Santo Domingo** has one of the most ornate interiors to be found in Mexico. Particularly noteworthy is a carved genealogical tree of the family of patron Saint Domingo de Guzman. It also includes the entire lineage from Abraham to the Virgin Mary. The figures are intertwined with flowers and leaves, with the styles of dress changing from generation to generation.

The **Museo Regional de Oaxaca** is located in the monastery adjoining the Santo Domingo church. It contains pre-Columbian artifacts from Monte Alban and a fine collection of masks, jewelry, textiles and utensils used by Oaxacans over the past century. There are also examples of contemporary craftsmanship based on these historic skills.

Another museum, sponsored by and sited in the family home of the famous Oaxacan artist, **Rufiño Tamayo**, is well worth a visit. Its emphasis is not so much on the culture and lifestyle, but deals principally with the tremendous skills exhibited by the early settlers of this valley.

An interesting tale of Oaxaca has to do with a church, **Santuario de La Soledad**, a muleskinner, and one of his mules...

Legend says that a driver noticed a strange mule in the pack train he was bringing to town, and when they arrived at the edge of town the mule refused to go any farther. Unable to budge the beast the driver decided to redistribute the load among the other mules. When he opened the pack, his eyes fell upon a statue of the Blessed Virgin. And with that, the mule dropped dead.

The episode prompted the construction of a church on the exact spot, and La Virgin de La Soledad (The Virgin of Loneliness) has been worshiped there ever since.

*Shortly after the church was completed a duplicate image of the grieving Virgin was placed on the balcony overlooking the street. It was located there so that the mule drivers could worship her without leaving their mules to run loose in the streets. The **Virgen de la Soledad** is now the patron saint of the city.*

The history of the **Convento de Santa Catalina**, a monastery built by the Dominican friars in 1576, is one of diversity. For nearly 300 years its fortunes rose and fell with the

OAXACA INLAND

Dominican order. Then it was confiscated by the government and became, variously, municipal offices, jail, warehouse, art school and movie theater. Finally in the late 60s the structure was declared a national treasure and preservation work began. A team of experts took on the job of restoring the frescoes done by the friars, replacing floors and rehabilitating the old monastery to its original splendor. Since 1975 it has been a luxury hotel, the **El Presidente Convento.**

Like the plaza, the central market is where the action is. Located just south of the plaza and covering a full city block, it epitomizes the universal Mexican market. And, as in every native market you can bargain to buy most anything. Though better prices are sometimes found in the individual outlying villages, here there is everything...from green and black pottery to wooden bowls, blouses and wall hangings to the fine local hammocks. We even watch a few women weaving baskets to add to the piles in front of them.

Another good local market, the **Mercado de Abastos,** is located southwest of the city's center. It is also called the **Oaxaca Tianguiz.** Though open every day, it comes into its own on Saturdays, when hundreds of vendors arrive from the outlying villages to offer their wares on the sidewalks, curbs, or anywhere there's a bit of space. The fresh produce is some of the best to be found anywhere in Mexico. The vegetables are often picked that morning, washed and packed off to market to be sold at very low prices. If you're going to be around over a Saturday, save a couple of morning hours for this one.

There seems to be little to worry about here in Oaxaca when it comes to accommodations, with the exception of trailer parks.

The only one remaining out of a number a dozen years ago appears to be the **Oaxaca Trailer Park** in the northeast part of the city. Go east on Calizada Chapultepec (Mexico 190) and look for Escuela Militár and head north a few blocks to Violetas. Turn left a couple of blocks, and it's on the left. (*This is where Tom and a rug merchant road tested the mescal, El Minero Pechuga some years ago with interesting results*). The place is large (94 spaces) with full hook-ups, showers, well-planted with trees and surrounded by a brick wall.

The choice of hotels in the Oaxaca area is many and varied...

Three of the best hotels are located on the north side of the city's center, the **Victoria, Misión de Los Angeles** and **San Felipe Misión.** Also in that direction are several bungalow/ apartment complexes including the **Villas de Sol,** (with full kitchens, patios and 1 or 2 bedrooms on attractive grounds). They are for those planning to stay for a while...a month or longer. A country club is adjoining, and special memberships are available. We met people there who had been wintering in Oaxaca for a dozen or more years. A great value.

More modest accommodations are scattered throughout the center of the city. A personal favorite is the **Marques del Valle.** Located on the north side of the *zocalo* directly adjoining the cathedral, many of its rooms face out onto the plaza where we can watch the happenings below. The last stay provided us with front row seats for a folkloric group from **Guanajuato,** a drum and bugle corps and an orchestra, church bells and mariachi groups, children and young lovers, families and balloon vendors. All contribute greatly to our fascination with this marvelous city.

Another hotel on the plaza is the **Senorial,** but with fewer rooms overlooking the action. A nearby hotel, the **Gala,** is new, clean and modern (in a 200 year old building). Another older one, hotel **Principal** comes recommended and is also nearby on 5 de Mayo. It is clean and built around a central courtyard.

Mentioned in the history of Oaxaca, the **El Presidente Convento** hotel in the old Dominican monastery offers an architectural uniqueness seldom seen. Tapestries, frescos, balconies and verdant courtyards are all there, and it's open to the public. It is well worth a visit.

Many say that Oaxacan food takes some getting used to. And if you go strictly with the native cuisine we'd agree. However, because of the large number of visitors from other parts of Mexico and the world, a number of the dishes have been toned down in some restaurants, even in those claiming authentic Oaxacan cuisine. A reminder...if you get a hot one, it can take the top of your head off.

El Asador Vasco is one of two favorite restaurants. Upstairs overlooking the *zocalo* (plaza) from the west side, it has won many accolades for its cuisine, which is the modified Oaxacan mentioned above. It also has a good assortment of specialties from other parts of Mexico. Of special interest are the tortilla and french onion soups. The salads are crisp and well presented, the entrees hot and attractive. All portions are very large. We usually order one soup, one small salad and one entree for the two of us. Ask for a table overlooking the plaza, and the evening's entertainment is set.

The **Cathedral** is a block north and west of the cathedral. It has several eating areas, including an open patio with a bounty of green plants and a fountain. The food is varied, well prepared and attractively served. The Caesar's salad this far from its original home in Tijuana is a pleasant surprise. The pork and beef dishes are well prepared. Portions, again, are large enough to split an entree.

*Meet **Hugo**, a waiter at the **Cathedral Restaurant**. He speaks some English, is about 24 and very proud of his newborn, first child. He and his wife have an apartment nearby and he is very happy with his job. We wondered how he has made such a good start on his life. He said that several years ago he decided to go to the United States and make enough money to start a family in a good way, so he caught a bus north to Tijuana and snuck across the border. He went no farther than San Diego and an auto repair shop. Though caught and deported to Mexico twice he returned each time to his old job in San Diego. After a year he had enough money, and came back to Oaxaca. Hugo appears to have a leg up on the rest of his life, much of it thanks to a bus trip north. He likes what the system did for him, and so do we.*

In more down-to-earth categories, we find the **Pizzeria Alfredo de Roma** north of the cathedral on Alcala to have good pastas and pizzas. Alfredo, the owner might be from Roma, Italy, but he might also be from Roma, Zacatecas. Whichever, he does a fine job.

Nothing works out every time and Oaxaca is no exception...the **Mi Casita**, located on the north west corner upstairs overlooking the *zocalo* comes highly recommended for its authentic regional dishes but we found the maitre'd indifferent to whether we ate or left...so we left. The Mi Casita is open only for the midday meal.

A real disaster was **Nino's**. Just off the *zocalo*, it touted itself as having been from Ixtapa...that they moved here because they wanted a "more relaxing" atmosphere. They seem intent on relaxing themselves out of business. Our order was handled by a teenager in the kitchen, and the results were inedible...we sent it back and paid only for two very mediocre bowls of soup. There were no apologies, only a disinterested "que sera" shrug of the shoulders.

Breakfasts have been a bit of a disappointment in Oaxaca...on the *zocalo*, an old favorite was too busy to even hand out menus or take an order. If you are in a hurry the **El Meson**, just off the northeast corner did a better job, though at a stiff price. We are lost for breakfast, except for the juice bars in the central market. The Sunday brunch at the El Presidente is reputed to be a good one, and at El Presidente prices.

From our balcony at the **Marques de Valle** it seems as though there is always some kind of festival going on, however there are several of special note...

The full flavor of the diverse Oaxacan Indian cultures can best be observed in July during the **Fiesta Guelaguetza**. Based on the ancient custom of honoring **Centeotl**, the god of maize, it attracts celebrants in full costume from all over the state to dance and present offerings of fruits and flowers.

December is another big time here. First comes the fiesta honoring the city's patron saint, the **Virgen de la Soledad** with costumed processions of Indians, fireworks, floats and dances. From December 16-24, the traditional *posadas* of the Christmas season dominate, culminating on Christmas Eve in the *zocalo*. And, if there's still any celebrating energy left, on Dec 23rd the **Fiesta de Los Rabanos** is held in the zocalo with displays of elaborately-carved platters of radishes.

Other times of the year have their days in the sun too...*Semana Santa* (Easter Week), with concerts, processions, fireworks and fairs, and on August 31 everyone brings their animals to the **Church of Merced** for the **Blessing of the Animals**.

If you've gotten the impression that we like Oaxaca, then we're communicating. It is a fascinating spot.

Itinerary Around Oaxaca City...

There never has been enough time to do **Oaxaca** in the manner we'd like, but here is a routine we tried during the preparation of the book which jams a lot in over a period of only five days...

We suggest that you park your vehicle for a few days and take a direct flight from nearby Puerto Escondido or Huatulco on Oaxaca's coast, or more distant Acapulco or Tuxtla Gutierrez. In all cases we fly over the imposing **Sierra Madre del Sur** peaks on the way to the verdant Valley of Oaxaca. *If you have several weeks, we recommend that you put up with the hours of hairpin mountain roads, as the valley is easy driving, given the time to get there.* Once there our travels are by tour bus, taxi and rental car. Based upon previous trips, plus suggestions from friends, we arrive intentionally on Wednesday, and will fly back to Puerto Escondido the following Monday.

A principal reason for coming to Oaxaca is to visit the many small native towns where each features its own particular handicraft skills. We also want see several of the sites of the cities of the Zapotec and Mixtec cultures. So, after settling in at the **Marques del Valle** hotel, we rustle up a car and driver for the next day and the **Thursday Market** towns.

Thursday is market day in **Zaachila**, 15 miles southwest of Oaxaca on Mexico 175. This is not really a place or day for artisans but there is a wealth of items which are in everyday use, such as ox yokes, heavy wooden plows, baskets, brooms, cooking pots and *varras* for water. You can buy alfalfa bouquets for your ox, and muzzles too, for when they shouldn't be grazing. *Note...Ox muzzles are not sold singly, you must buy them in pairs.* Handmade ropes from the fibre, *ixtle,* are common and in all lengths. *Ixtle* comes from the leaves of the *maguey* cactus grown in Oaxaca and elsewhere.

On an earlier trip we bought an ox yoke from **Pedro Dominguez***, one of the maestros in the field. About 70 years old, he had been making and selling the things for more than 40 years.* Currently $40 is the going price for a first-class yoke for ploughing, $60 for one for pulling carts. And a pleasant surprise, Pedro is still here.

A few kilometers off the same road is the town of **Cuilapan**. Here we find the ruins of a Dominican Monastery built in the middle 1500s. Cuilapan is principally inhabited by the descendants of the **Mixtec** Indians.

The town of **Arrazola** is located 5km to the north of Highway 175. Here we meet **Santos Pino Santiago,** who makes the fancifully shaped and painted wooden animals that are so popular right now. The process is interesting in that the wood must be carved when it is green. Then, when the shaping is completed and the pieces fitted they are put in the sun to dry. Why? Because it carves readily when green but sands poorly. When it is dry it is well-nigh impossible to carve, but sands well. Santos is working on one which will be an assemblage of 19 pieces when done. He classifies it as a "first ever" design in wood. Most impressive.

After a drive up a narrow, winding road we come to the largest of the Zapotepec ruins, **Monte Alban**. Here a small museum and diorama prepares us for what is outside and up the hill. There are refreshments, snacks and restrooms. There are also guides available. An hour or two here is time well spent. Expect to be approached by furtive vendors with artifacts "found" in the terraced hillsides nearby. The pieces might be genuine, but if they are it is illegal to possess them. If they are imitations, they are greatly overpriced. But we found it interesting to see what they have and hear their stories.

Our next stop is **Atzompa**, the home of the green glazed pottery. The entrance to town is from Mexico 190 in the direction of Mexico City. The turnoff is at the southeast corner of a country club, which is several miles out of town. The road is marginal and we find very little there. (Two days later at the Saturday Market we found a wide array of beautiful green pottery.) This is enough for one day anyway...back to the hotel.

The big outside market day is Friday and several operators offer comprehensive tours...or you can hire a taxi. *Here you will want to be sure that he understands what you want to do and where you want to go.*

The key destination has to be **Ocotlan**. Our minds boggle every time we go there.

One of the prizes from this trip is a finely crafted machete in a beautiful leather scabbard. It is made by **Palomino "Angel" Aguilar** who has been making them in his home in **Ejutla** and selling them in this central market for nearly 40 years. It is obvious that this man is respected. The men who come by speak to him with respect, with many calling him *maestro*, or *Don Angel*, for they know his work. We watched them come up to his display and heft several blades before settling on the proper length and weight. Then they test the temper, feel the edge and check for flexibility. Finally, the price is discussed. We followed the routine, and could not resist. **Don Angel** appeared to be particularly pleased that some *norteamericano* would select one of his best blades to take to his home somewhere in America.

Another of the good buys here are wooden burro saddles, or *fustes*. Made of hard woods, including oak, they lie around in stacks waiting for a burro owner to have a need. The best looking piles belong to **Enrique Martinez**, who makes *fustes* all week at his rancho in the mountains, then brings them on the bus to Ocotlan's Friday market. Did we buy one? Not this time, because a long time ago a lady told us that one should always buy the saddle before selecting a burro. Her reasoning never was fully explained, but we own a *fuste* made by her husband. Maybe another *fuste*, after we fit a burro to the one we have.

If you have never been to one of Mexico's jails, Ocotlan might be a good place to start...to check out the handicrafts made by the inmates. The *carcel* (jail) is located to the left of the municipal office buildings which are just south and east of the market area. Here we find dozens of varieties of cane baskets...big ones, little ones, some for your head, others for your arm. When you've made your selection you go over to the bars and call for the owner. He comes over and completes the transaction. We found inmates busy, cheerful, and anxious to get out. One of the better craftsmen said that we should buy now, because next year he wouldn't be there. We bought.

The last of the peso-parting stops is at the shops of the **Aguilar** sisters on the edge of Ocotlan. The four sisters have shops in the same block on the right hand side as you enter town. Each offers different types of painted clay figures. **Guillermina** likes nativity scenes, while **Josefina** is more into female figures performing everyday tasks, particularly carrying stuff around on their head. The third sister, **Irene**, makes bells with painted animal heads on the top. *We already have two of her bells, having bought them in Newport Beach, California, several years ago.* Don't know what the fourth sister's specialty is, her store was not open.

Santo Tomás Jalieza puts forward its best cotton belts, table runners, place mats and purses on Fridays. *They also have a bang-up saints day celebration in honor of Santo Tomás each December 21st. Tom has been invited to attend as an honored guest because of his name, and if he will agree to dance with three of the weavers...Elena Mendoza, Dorotea Vasquez and Efenegia Gomez. The offer, they say, holds good for three years. Absolutely charming ladies with beautiful weavings.*

336

At about K28 a road west takes us to **San Martín Tilcajete** and its painted wooden animals. Again they are carved green, dried, sanded and painted. There are no shops here...all of the work is done in the homes and sold from them. We see no signs anywhere, but have no trouble lining up half a dozen "showings" by merely stopping at the nearly-abandoned *zocalo* and getting out of the car. Within a couple of minutes we have two basketball players and a man with a wheelbarrow offering to show us where we can buy *Las Figuras*. One of the carvers is **Candido Ortega**, who with his cousin, **Magdalena Mendoza** specialize in animals playing musical instruments. Most are rather small and all show a pixie-like quality. They were the best of what we saw, but we probably missed 20 other home workshops.

San Bartolo de Coyotopec is world famous for its black pottery. The legendary person in the black pot biz is **Doña Rosa**, who in the early 1950s developed the process whereby black clay pottery can be made to have a sheen to it. Though she has been dead for some time, her process has been successfully promoted by the family, and the whole town has prospered.

Dona Rosa's is located about a half-mile east of the highway as you enter town from the north. Along the way there are a number of other, smaller showrooms.

At the same corner, but on the west side is the **Centro de Artesinas** (Artesans Center). Strangely, we have seen a number of black pottery items in stores outside of the Oaxaca area which we have been unable to locate here where all of the black pottery is supposed to be made, including mid-sized *chimineas* for use with charcoal as a space heater on a patio. Everyone says that they make them here, but nobody has one.

Our favorite store in San Bartolo is in the Artesania Center. The booth is operated by a charming lady named **Rowena**. About 70, she is several inches shorter than 5-feet, but with a smile and sparkle that makes her stand very tall. Rowena makes all of what she sells, seems to specialize in whistles and will gladly demonstrate any or all of them. Before she completed her repertoire she had gone from a tiny bit of toe tapping to shoulder shrugs and energetic hip-swaying. Her quality and prices are comparable. Don't miss Rowena. Back to the hotel.

Saturday is well spent in the city itself, starting with an early visit to the Saturday market. First, its size will blow you away. There are literally acres of fruits and vegetables, and aisles of bakery goods. A hundred or more little restaurants are waiting with ready glasses of orange, watermelon or papaya juice; barbecued goat, pork or beef; chiles rellenos, chicken mole, enchiladas and tacos. There are also several dozen versions of *menudo, pozole, sopa azteca* and *birria con papas*. Hundreds of meters of clothing, thousands of pots and bowls, dozens of music cassette booths (with examples blaring). Then there are booths full of handmade hemp ropes, burro saddles and hammocks. It is all here in a bewildering array. Located a short taxi ride south west of the plaza, the Saturday market is not to be missed.

The rest of the day can be spent browsing the numerous stores near the *zocalo*. The temptations are many.

Sunday is a busy day, and an early start is recommended. Today a car and guide is a big help. To the east of the city on highway 190 we start at K48 in the town of Matatlan...home of many family-operated *mescal (Oaxaca's version of tequila)* distilleries. Little stores are everywhere. Look around and ask where you can visit a *fabrica*.

*Some years ago, following an exhaustive survey of bartenders in Oaxaca City as to who made the best **mescal**, we arrived in Matatlan to visit the factory making the most-recommended brand, **El Minero Pechuga**.*

We stopped at several of the small stores offering a variety of mescals...both with and without worms...with no success, until a resident who overheard our question, confided that the fabrica for El Minero Pechuga did exist. It was right next door!

We went over and entered a sizeable courtyard through a large, open gate. The scene was totally unexpected.

We saw a large pile of wood and two large brick ovens. A high, thatched roof stood over a large, circular area around which a mule was placidly plodding. Inside that a large stone wheel was going around in a circular cement trough full of a steaming, smelly substance. There were also a small stack of wooden barrels and piles of a fibrous material which a worker was transferring to the back of a burro cart. The rest of the visual image was filled with animals...chickens, ducks, turkeys, burros, pigs and dogs.

As nobody seemed to take any interest in our being there, we wandered around looking at the process.

The trimmed hearts of the maguey cactus were brought in by burro cart and transferred into an oven where they were baked, or steamed until soft. At that point a man shoveled the large, steaming carcasses into the cement trough where the mule's rolling stone reduced them to mush. The liquid drawn off and put in tanks is very high in sugar and ferments rapidly (in this environment we'd judge it would be impossible to keep it from fermenting, what with the clutter and the numerous animals).

The second fire was under what turned out to be the still, complete with the traditional array of copper coils and condensers. The final product, the elixer we were looking for, poured out of the bottom in a tiny stream into a five-gallon bucket sitting in a hole dug in the ground. Why the hole? Because the tubing was too low! Around this precious bucket chicken scratched, pigs grunted and dogs snored. We looked at each other and decided that if this was, indeed, what we had come for we didn't really want any.

At that moment a woman came up to fill our order. Not knowing how to get out of it we ended up buying two liters for the equivalent of $1.50, American. We supplied the bottle from our motorhome and watched them siphon our currently-not-so-attractive firewater out of an oak barrel. When asked how long the stuff had been in the barrel she shrugged her shoulders and indicated that it had been put in there, "**ayer**" (yesterday)!

Deciding to accept our loss, we thanked the lady and went back to Oaxaca.

Now, the rest of the story...At the trailer park we ran into a vendor pitching anyone who'd listen on an arm load of handwoven, wool blankets. Still wondering about the mescal from Matatlan, we decided to try it out on the vendor. At first he politely demurred, but when he heard the name, he brightened and accepted. We watched as he tasted, then took another sip and smacked his lips. There was nothing to do but join him.

The stuff was good. In fact, it was great. El Minero Pechuga was so smooth it might as well have been **agua mineral**. Tom's last memory for the evening was of his vendor friend carefully walking his bicycle over to an empty, grassy space where he laid out one of his blankets and immediately collapsed.

When we got back to Huntington Beach a chemist friend did an analysis on the stuff. When told that it was 123 proof, we knew what happened to that night in Oaxaca.

For the next stop we take the **Mitla** turnoff at K44 and go east for five kilometers to the town of Mitla. Here, almost in the downtown area are the ruins of another **Zapotec** stronghold. A visit to the ruins, which are from a later period than Monte Alban, is well worthwhile. There are also numerous stores well-stocked with quality weavings.

Another stop if you are into antiquities is at **Yagul**, another of the Zapotec strongholds during the 250-750AD cultural zenith. It is off to the north as we head back toward Oaxaca. The origin dates back to 400 BC with most of the ruins dating around 900 AD. The remaining walls, etc, though generally Zapotec, shows some Mixtec influence.

The big Sunday market at **Tlacolula** has a wide variety of crafts from which to choose. Made up of Zapotec descendants, it has an even greater feeling of the Indian cultures than Oaxaca. Here's another jail where baskets can be bought from the resident guests. The best time in Tlacolula is in the morning, as the vendors begin to pack it in right after noon.

Santa Ana del Valle, 3km east of Mexico 190 at K33, is a textile village that dates back to pre-Columbian times. It is one of the towns that, in the 15th century, paid their taxes to the Aztecs in the form of weavings. Today they weave woolen blankets, sarapes and bags for the tourist market. And do very well.

At K31, we turn into **Lambityeco**, a small Zapotec burial site. Several thousand people lived here before 1400 AD. The gentleman who sells tickets is knowledgeable, in Spanish, and is enthusiastic about the site. The tombs here are built in the manner common in Peru, but found in a very few locations in Mexico, leading to speculation that there may have been some contact.

Teotitlan del Valle is off to the east at K25. This is another weaving town and well worth a visit. **Hermilo Ruiz**, at Ave Juarez No. 61, is one of the premier weavers of blankets, rugs and hangings. His material is different in that there is an oriental feel about it. They use pure wool and natural colors. Very nice.

Another interesting one is **Casa Hipolito**. It is just off Juarez on the east side. **Casa Gonzales** is another on Juarez with fine material. There are several hours of browsing here if you are in the mood. There are many "canned", or oft-repeated designs, while others are unique, and it takes time to find those reflecting personal tastes.

Given the time, there are three other spots on the way back to Oaxaca which might be of interest. The ruins at **Dainzu**, the church of **San Jeronimo** in **Tlacochahuaya** and the huge *Ahuehuete* tree, a type of cypress, in the town of **El Tule**.

This trip we added the town of **San Antonio** here as it also has a Sunday market and nothing the rest of the week. The town is 30 km south of Oaxaca on highway 175. It is known for its embroidered dresses, decorated crosses and birds. Though of interest, it is a time consumer.

For Monday, there are museums to catch up on and a dozen or more fine stores within walking distance of the *zocalo*. Then there is the problem of figuring out what to do with all the things you bought, and how they are going to fit on the plane. Don't worry...the airlines have dealt successfully with that one before.

Enjoy Oaxaca.

Back to the coast.

Beaches West of Puerto Angel...

The K198 turnoff led us on one of the most interesting trails we have experienced. The stories from here have several messages, though we haven't sorted out all of the meanings, or what to do about them. This road is not an easy one, and we do not recommend it to anyone who has not had experience on steep and sometimes-soft roadbeds, and certainly not for big rigs. Even a standard car is risky. It also can take the best part of a day.

After checking with several locals for confirmation of directions, we leave Mexico 200 at K198+ and go south between fences on a one-lane road past several houses. Cultivated fields are to the left. At **0.5** a road comes in sharply from the right and goes back to **San Antonio**. Then pass under several big shady trees, a favorite stopping spot for cattle from the looks of the ground. A little-traveled trail branches (right) up a hill at **1.8**. We stick to the main road and continue to wind through the hills past occasional fields of corn, finally coming back to the flood plain of the river around **2.7**. The land here is being cleared in increments. We pass a large thatched house on the right and continue south.

At **3.3** we check with two workers in a field. They confirm that we're on course. The road then works its way up to a point from which, at **3.7**, we can see the ocean. The road then drops into a town large enough to have electricity, a *zocalo*, school and basketball court. Just beyond is a turtle research station and a small restaurant at **4.9**.

*In the process of getting to the beach we meet **Doña Porferia**, three of her daughters and at least six grandchildren. She fills us in on the name of the beach, **Mazunte**, and insists that we park under her tree and pass through her kitchen to get to the beach. In return, she cheerfully made cervezas y sodas available. A win-win situation if we ever saw one.*

The beach is a beauty, with striking rock formations bracketing a curving south-facing beach. The sand is light colored and we see very few shells. Only a bit of driftwood is evident, possibly because of its proximity to the pueblito (little town). There are good picture angles here, and at times we'd guess the waves would be very large.

In the process of seeing the beach, drinking the cervezas and talking to the kids we find that they do not have one picture of any family member, so the next thing is a family photo session. The results are to be mailed to Doña Porfiria after processing.

When the energetic Senora finally lets us go, we continue east past the entrance to the turtle research station and over a hill into another beach community. Here on **Playa San Isidro**, at **5.5** they catch fish and lobster. They used to take turtles from here, but that ended in mid-1990, when the government made it illegal to catch or possess sea turtles. Again, the beach has a measure of protection thanks to resident rocks and a small island or two. We find the beaches clean of trash and the water clear. The surge might preclude swimming, but shallow-water splashing is a popular sport for the few kids and one adult within view.

On the right at **5.9** laborers are pouring cement for what looks to be a hotel. It appears to have been started and stopped several times. Following the "hotel" we return to the hills to twist and turn toward another beach. At **6.2** a sign says *Se Venden Hamacas* and points up and around a hill. Then we pass a house and see someone on the veranda busy making a bright red hammock. The next beach, **Zipolite**, begins at **8.3**.

Here there are lots of hammocks for sale. You can also rent them by the day or week, or bring your own, and rent only the hooks. A shore walk through the area and a listen to the people talking tells us that Zipolite is still popular with German and French visitors.

*About 10 years ago **peyote** and **marijuana** were sold on this beach much in the manner of the Acapulco beach vendors...they would even bargain. We hear it still goes on, though not as openly.*

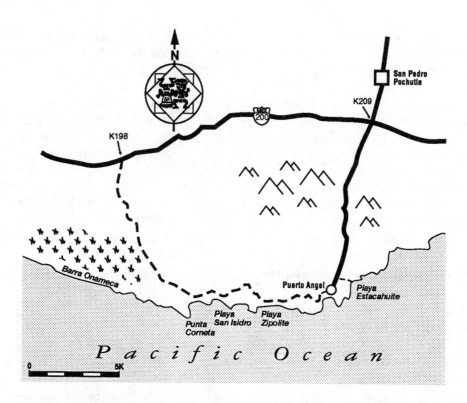

A look around confirms that many of society's dropouts still congregate here.

As we move east along the beach there are signs offering cabins, hammocks and rooms. Small, then larger restaurants are seen facing the beach. At **9.6** we are at the end of Zipolite and about to bump and rumble over the hills into Puerto Angel.

At **10.3** we are at the intersection just outside **Puerto Angel**. The town is to the left, while a right turn takes us to **Playa Panteón** (Cemetery Beach) and the cliffhanging **Hotel Angel del Mar**. Panteón is unquestionably the best beach in the town. It is now bracketed with restaurants, each with their own huckster who won't hesitate to flag you down, even if you don't intend to stop. A half-mile on the left branch puts us in downtown Puerto Angel.

End of Log.

The Beaches of Puerto Angel...

The K209 post on Mexico 200 marks the paved turnoff south into the fishing and resort town of **Puerto Angel**. The road goes past scattered homes as it winds from about the 500-foot level down to the sea. A beach is off to the left (east) as we descend into town. Near the K250 marker watch for the sign, **Club de Playa** on the east (left) side of the road.

The dirt road to Club be Playa drops rapidly down to a fork at **0.2**. Follow it to the right and drop further to **Playa Estacahuite** at **0.4**. And what a jewel, or better, a series of jewels. We step inside a *palapa* restaurant with several dozen chairs overlooking a tiny white sand cove bracketed with huge rocks. To the left of the main beach are a couple of beaches only a few meters wide, yet they offer protection from all but the worst water conditions. On the hill behind the main beach are a number of small *cabañas* built into the hillside in a regular manner, and comprises the Club de Playa. The sites are open to most breezes, and with the beach and the view, plus those breezes, a membership here should be a valuable item. Back to the highway and south into the town of Puerto Angel.

The town of Puerto Angel is an enigma to some classes of tourists. We know people who cannot get away fast enough, others who revel in the laid-back lifestyle. Mike, a friend from San Diego cannot get enough time here, and has been coming for more than 20 years. His roots go back to the 60s and his lifestyle has changed little since. And it is that way with

341

many of the habitues. The town, too, has changed little since our first exposure in 1982. A few new buildings maybe, but the beaches and general demeanor of the citizens remain pretty constant. What keeps the town going? A combination of tourism, fishing, coconuts and coffee.

The action around town is minimal, except what might be generated during the day along beaches such as Zipolite. The largest and best hotel in town is the Angel del Mar which overlooks the entire bay from its perch high on a hilltop behind Playa Panteón. It has one of the better restaurants in town, a pool and spectacular views. Another hotel with clean rooms and ceiling fans is the **Soraya** which is located on the hill behind the pier. You can also find at least a dozen other small units offering varying levels of accommodations. As far as restaurants are concerned, we have little to say, having eaten only at the hotel and one of the beachfront restaurants (without a name) on Zipolite Beach during our brief stay.

The town beaches are not as attractive to most as the outlying ones to the west...Zipolite, etc., but they do deserve a mention...

The downtown beach, **Playa Principál**, comes complete with pier, pangas, palapa restaurants and, unfortunately, the pollution attendant with downtown beaches and fishing boats. It is within walking distance of many of the small pensions scattered about on the hillsides above town.

Playa Panteón (Cemetery Beach) is located on the west end of the bay in front of the port. It is calm, clean and offers good snorkeling. It is also a hangout for many laid-back Europeans who comprise much of the town's tourist business.

A word of comment...there are a number of stories floating around about loss of property, even from locked cars, and we talked to a young man who was recovering from knife wounds received on a beach just west of Zipolite. Another story had to do with the indifference of authorities to act on a reported burglary and a robbery at knife-point. Be especially careful here if you decide to stay anywhere but in one of the major hotels. Back to the highway.

Half-Hour Beach, or Playas Chicomolco and Tahuca...

At K223 of Mexico 200 south of Puerto Angel we take a dirt road right toward the beach. How do we know it goes to the water? Because a local farmer assures us that it is only a half-hour away. *This is how many of our side trips start...by asking around about an unmarked sideroad, or a line on a map.* The road is very dusty, rough at times and a sure loser for motorhomes or trailers. We pass an occasional house or piece of cultivated land as we wind our way through the hills. At **2.7** we can see the beach about a mile ahead...but the road goes to the left. After more winding and more time we are in the center of a heavy growth of mesquite and small hardwood trees.

At **7.7** forward progress stops at the gate of a yard containing a house and another small building (which turns out to be a school house). While trying to get our bearings and realizing that we already have invested well over our half-hour, a man of about 30 comes out of the house and asks if he can be of help. Following introductions, **Domingo** locates us on our map, points toward the beach "just beyond the *mesquite*s." And he will guide us.

DOMINGO AND HALF-HOUR BEACH

Before we know it Domingo has us parked under a huge tree, out of the car and on our way. It is like trying to follow a jackrabbit as he as he bounds barefooted through the brush toward an unknown horizon. It is hot, it is dry and the pace is a killer. When we finally get Domingo under rein we are completely out of sight of any landmark. We can't even hear the ocean. After about a half-hour of sloughing through burning sands, thorny mesquite and bristling cactus, we come to clear dunes and the faint sound of the surf.

Another hundred yards and we have our sizzling feet in the Pacific under the watchful

342

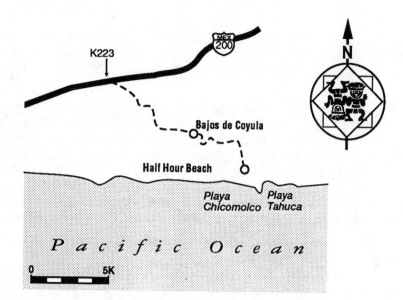

eyes of nearby land crabs and shore birds. The beach extends for a number of miles to the west but it stops abruptly about a quarter-mile to our left at a rocky bluff. Even though it is out of season for turtles, we saw the nests and tracks of several recent visitors.

After giving us a chance to cool our feet, Domingo suggests that we hike to the rocks and go over and look at the "swimming beach." After several polite refusals to budge, he gives up and we head back for the car...in a different direction! "It's shorter," he says.

The car comes back into view and we both say a hallelujah and dive for the ice chest and something cold. We offer to share with Domingo. After one *no gracias*, he finally accepts a soda. Ours are downed in seconds. His remains unopened.

We said our goodbyes and headed back for the highway. The intersection was finally regained, a full 17 miles and 205 minutes after we left in search of Half-Hour Beach. Incidentally, the given names of the beaches are **Chicomolco** and **Tahuca**.

Playa Copalito...

The graded turnoff south from Mexico 200 to **Playa Copalito** comes only a few miles east of the main turnoff into **Santa Cruz de Huatulco** at K262. Keep to the well-traveled portion of the road, ignoring the several small branches (left). The road turns more westerly as we pass several water pumping stations at **2.1**. At **3.0** watch to your left for a narrow road dropping sharply just before crossing a small filled section of the graded road. In less than a hundred meters we are in the middle of a half-dozen houses and three small restaurants. We ask the woman in the nearest restaurant if it would be possible to have dinner and stay overnight in our camper. She said yes to the overnighting, but unfortunately she had already closed the kitchen.

THE COPALITO SCHOOL

With the help of every kid in the settlement, we are guided to a level spot on the basketball court. As there is no electricity, the community is in bed about an hour after dark.

The next morning we met the school teacher, **Enrique**. He teaches the dozen children living here, and he loves it. He roams the beach through a maze of driftwood and huge boulders and fishes from the shore. His lifestyle here, he says "*es muy tranquilo.*"

It would appear that this place cannot last long, for Huatulco's **Bahía Tangolunda** with its Sheratons, Club Meds and Maevas is only a couple of miles west of here. Back to the highway.

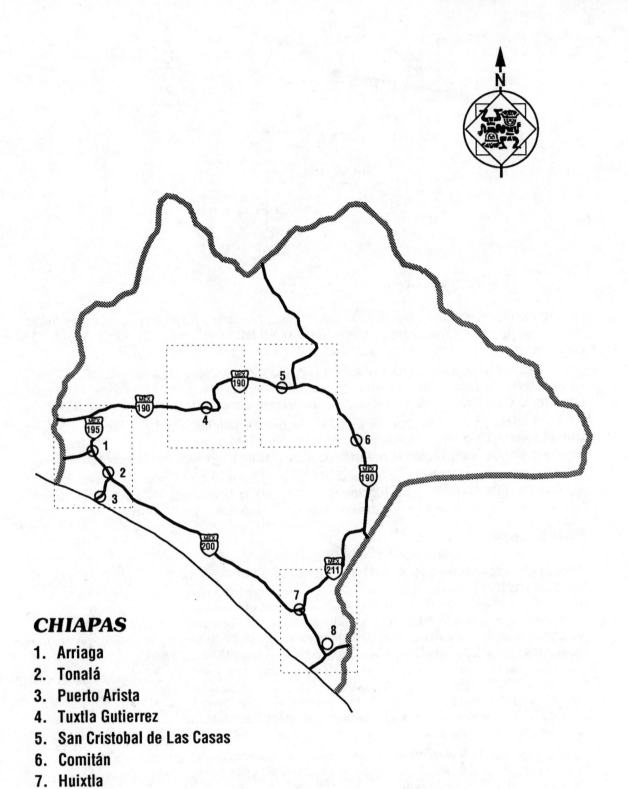

CHIAPAS

1. **Arriaga**
2. **Tonalá**
3. **Puerto Arista**
4. **Tuxtla Gutierrez**
5. **San Cristobal de Las Casas**
6. **Comitán**
7. **Huixtla**
8. **Tapachula**

CHIAPAS...
THE STATE

The isolated position of **Chiapas**, Mexico's southernmost state, left it little affected by contemporary Mexico's social and economic changes until recently. And it is that preservation of historic Indian and Spanish traditions which attracts many of today's visitors. Other factors attracting tourists are the economic and cultural diversities brought about by the variety of climatic zones within its borders.

The lowest region, known as the Soconusco, is a narrow stripe of fertile land between the steep Sierra Madre range and the Pacific Coast. Only 15 to 30 kilometers wide and 280 kilometers long, it was populated as early as 1600-1500 B.C.. Agriculture and fishing supported the coastal villages of both Chiapas and Guatemala. The **Olmecs** flourished from about 1300 to 400 B.C. Izapa near Tapachula is thought to be a link between the Olmecs and the **Mayas** who occupied the area from 200 B.C. to 200 A.D. After the Mayan collapse the **Toltec** influence was felt on the coast from 1000 to 1200 A.D. The region's abundant *cacao* (chocolate) trees attracted the Aztecs near the end of the 15th century, shortly before the area was overrun by the Spanish in 1524. Under the Spanish those natives who didn't die from diseases were heavily taxed, sold into slavery or put into forced labor camps.

The second region of Chiapas begins above the coastal plains in the Sierra Madre. As with the coast, the Olmec, Toltec and Aztec cultures came and went, with the remnants being taken over by the Spanish as they moved inland from the Soconusco.

The third, or central, region is known as El Depresión. Located on the north and east sides of the Sierra Madre this long valley forms the heart of the state and its pre-colonial history closely parallels the Soconusco. Chiapa de Corzo, for example, dates from about 1500 B.C. Under the Spanish the peoples here did not retain communal land and have been almost totally assimilated into the Mexican culture. The state capital, Tuxtla Gutierrez, is located here in El Depresión.

It is in Zone Four the mountainous Sierra Norte de Chiapas, that the Spanish had the least effect on the people. Even today many of the Indians maintain their traditional ways. The colonial cities of San Cristobal de Las Casas and Comitán dominate the area but do not have much influence in the nearby **Tzotzil**, **Tzeltal** and **Tojolabal** Indian communities. Uncharacteristically, the Catholic missionaries when they introduced Christianity, also permitted the inclusion of a surprising number of native beliefs.

Both the Tzeltals and Tzotzils are decendants of the Mayas and were amoung the most oppressed of the indigenous peoples during the colonial period. That any of the groups

345

survived at all has been attributed to their fierce independence and strong tribal bonds. To this day that pride is still strong and is reflected in the costumes worn in many of the *pueblos*.

In the north and east portions of Zone Five lies one of Mexico's few remaining rainforests. It was in this environment that some of the finest examples of Mayan culture flourished, including Palenque, Bonampak, Tikál (just over the border in Guatemala) and Yaxochilan.

And it is also here that the Mayan heritage has remained the most pure, for it was into these forests that the **Lancandón** branch of the Mayas fled at the onset of the conquest and the Spaniards never really tried to catch them. There in the jungles, the traditions and the language carried well into the 20th century. Now, even that is disappearing as the rainforest is being dismantled by loggers and farmers.

It was not until after the Revolution of 1810, in 1824, that Chiapas voted to leave its alliances with Guatemala and become a part of the new Mexican Republic. Even today the hearts of many Chiapañecos lie with their Indian brethren to the south, for it is there that they find their identity.

Most of Chiapas was part of Guatemala during the Spanish reign, being adminis-tered by the prefect of Antigua in the province of Guatemala. After the Spanish lost out in the Mexican Revolution of 1810, Chiapas was given the opportunity to choose its own destiny through a plebiscite. In 1824 it voted to become part of the new Mexican Republic but it wasn't until 1882 that all of the legal documents were filed.

Though the changeover came nearly two centuries ago there are still many very strong feelings bonding Guatemalans and Chiapanecos, such as tribal, familial and religious affiliations, climatic and geological similarities.

Today the coastal plain provides a wide variety of agricultural products. The government has built a deep water port at Puerto Madero and the coast offers only a few beaches. With its rich soil and dependable rainfall the mountains of Chiapas produce some of the world's finest coffee. The region grows 40% of the nation's coffee and it is the state's most important crop. Coffee plantations require substantial acreage to be successful and many of the traditional Indian lands have been usurped over the years for this use. At harvest time, September - December, workers come even from Guatemala to pick the beans.

The mountains surrounding the valley of the great depression empty their rivers into the large Grijalva River. Recently harnessed by three dams, it provides more of the nations electricity than any other river. The area grows sugar cane and other commercial crops. The mountainous fourth zone is principally made up of small villages and individual farms where subsistence farming is predominant. The principal supply center for the Indians, San Cristobal de Las Casas, is also developing a tourism base which contributes more and more to the economy of the region.

The emergence of Chiapas as a touristic destination continues as access improves. Even with only 34 of nearly 500 buildings excavated, the ruins at Palenque are said to be the best in Mexico. Other outstanding sites are located at Bonampak, Yaxchilan, Chinkultic and Tonina.

The capital city of Tuxtla Gutierrez and its magnificent Sumidero Canyon is worth a visit. For sheer beauty visit the Laguna de Montebello region and the 60 or so nearby lakes. Agua Azul and the Misol-ha waterfalls in the jungle south of Palenque are other visitable spots. There is also the magnificent Río Usumacinta, which flows through the spectacular rainforest along the border between Mexico and Guatemala.

The states only overnightable beach destination is Puerto Arista, a somewhat laid-back beach community with minimal facilities.

Our time in Chiapas has been woefully short. We would like to return for a month, or two, or three.

MEXICO 200 — BORDER TO BORDER

The western portions of Chiapas come under a different weather pattern than those lands north of the Isthmus of Tehuantepec. Here the rainy season begins in late March and early April in the high mountains behind the long central valley. The activity spills over into the valley in a couple of weeks, and ending up in the Soconusco in early May with the cyclonic storms sweeping into the state from the Pacific shortly after.

The areas near the highway are dominated by various farming enterprises...coffee, dairy and beef cattle, fruit orchards and chocolate. The region is fed by many streams and small rivers which come tumbling out of the mountains. To the west, sugar cane and cattle predominate where there are no lagoons or marshes. Due to all of the high water areas, there is little activity and almost no access to the Pacific Ocean between Tonalá and the Guatemala border.

0.0   0.0   K26   We are at the border between **Oaxaca** and **Chiapas**. A few yards farther a road (right) is signed to **La Gloria**, a village on the shores of the **Mar Muerto** (Dead Sea) in the state of Chiapas. Just beyond that is a small military camp. We head east away from the border with the railroad on our left shoulder.

2.8   2.8   K30+   Just off to the right is **San Ramón**. The highway continues east with only a small detour toward the north.

1.5   4.3   K33   Continue along the foothills. The view to the right is of nothing but flat land.

3.7   8.0   K39   A signed road (right) is to **Colonia Azteca**. There is evidence of road damage throughout the region. We've been seeing it since before Tapanatepec. Then comes a new bridge, rebuilt because of a flood.

2.6   10.6   K43   The intersection into **Arriaga**, population over 25,000, is to the left. The several hotels and car dealerships tell us that it is a busy trading center.

1.8   12.4   K46   A local **Pemex** is here at the intersection with Mexico 35 to Tuxla Gutierrez. Mexico 200 continues east past a hotel, the **El Parador**.

1.3   13.7   K48   A produce and livestock inspection station here. We can see several tall mountains. Due east is 8500-foot **Cerro Tres Picos**, while **Cerro La Placa** is southeast.

8.7   22.4   K62   **Colonia San Francisco Ocotal** is signed and off to the right by the railroad tracks, then comes another new bridge.

2.8   25.2   K66+   **Tonalá**, signed as having 50,000 people, has the reputation of being the hottest spot in Chiapas. As usual, there are *topes*. The long business district has various hotels and we see several attractive restaurants. One, the **San Francisco** is near the **Bancomer**.

1.6   26.8   K69   A small clean park or *zocalo* (they call it **El Parque**) is on the left. From here a road (west) goes to the **Paredón** beach resort and **Laguna Mar Muerto**, the Dead Sea Lagoon...

Paredón, a moderate-sized fishing village on a large body of water called Laguna Mar Muerto, has been described as a place not worth 10 minutes of any body's time. And on the surface this would appear to be the case, however...there are things about Paredón which do not appear on the surface...

We begin at El Parque by heading west on Calle Francisco Madero past a kilometer of businesses and houses before leaving Tonalá behind. The road is not signed, but it identifies itself as we reach the end of Madero with a painted white line. It curves slightly (right) almost immediately past a long hedge of magenta bougainvilla on the left and a soccer field.

*The region offers a variety of landscapes, including the coastal jungle trees, green pastures and plantings of mangoes, corn, bananas and tamarindo. At **3.5** we pass **Rancho***

*Los Sergio on the left, then make a lazy "S" maneuver at **5.7** and past several houses. The entrance to **Paredón** is past a distinctive orange house on the left. The open waters of **Laguna Mar Muerto** are in front of us at **8.7**.*

The pavement ends at the rock-walled turnaround. Boats are everywhere. Most are the fiberglass pangas of varying ages with powerful outboards. There are still a few dugout canoes in use, and one is equipped with a new 5-horsepower Evinrude! These log-canoes are not little things, a couple are nearly as long as the 24-foot pangas. Consider the size of the tree, and the work involved. They are true classics.

BEST OF BOTH WORLDS

The water is muddy, somewhat choked with mosses and aquatic weeds. A pig is wandering around in the mud rooting out edibles. We drive down the road behind the boats, worksheds and primitive houses where fish are being cleaned, shrimp sorted and clams washed. Shortly we are at a breakwater with a roadway along the top. More boats and nets. We look at each other and wonder why anyone would want to spend a day here...

*Meet **Manuel**. He has the answer. The playa at Paredón is where people go to get to another, and better, playa...*

They hire Manuel and his boat, or others like it, and motor across the Mar Muerto, Dead Sea to the sand island facing the Pacific Ocean where the water is clean and clear, the clams abundant and the breezes cool. The boats involved are not fancy, don't even have shades, and we could find no signs advertising the taxi services offered, but it seems to work. You'll find Manuel next to the breakwater on the left side. Back to Tonalá.

Tonala's *mercado centrál* (central market) is several blocks south and west, and it's a big one. Things to look for include pottery, baskets, hammocks, palm-leaf brooms and needlework. At the far end of town is a local **Pemex** followed by an **LPG** station. If you look to the east you can see the 8500-foot **Tres Picos** mountain with its three peaks in perfect view.

*The Tonala region raises a lot of beef and dairy cattle but is probably best known for the fiery distilled cane alcohol produced here, **Aguardiente**. The town's biggest fiesta follows the rainy season, when they honor their patron, **Saint Francis**, the first four days in October. Another big time is December 20-31 when the Christmas celebrations are combined with a livestock fair.*

MEXICAN CLAMDIGGER

2.5   29.3   K73   A signed intersection. Straight ahead is to **Puerto Arista. (See Chiapas Beaches.)** We curve gently left on Mexico 200 and continue southeast. The long range of mountains off to the left is the **Sierra Madre de Chiapas.** Many of the peaks exceed 6000 feet.

2.8   32.1   K77+   A bridge over a small stream is signed, **Quetzalapa.** There are cornfields once again on the hillsides. *This portion of Mexico must deal with a situation which few other areas of the world will ever have to worry about...fence post trimming. The tree used here in the construction of barbed wire fences roots very easily. Thus, shortly after digging the post holes and rigging the wire, little sprouts begin appearing around the upper ends of the fence posts. Soon the sprouts become branches, and within a year or so the fences are adorned with a very pretty pink flower. We checked the posts out and find the wood to be soft and pithy. The answer must be that there are no hardwoods readily available, and, as long as the "post" is alive the bugs won't eat it. The condition does bring up one extra task for the farmer...he must go out and trim his fence.*

2.5   34.6   K81+   An as-yet-unsigned new bridge over a streambed. The river is

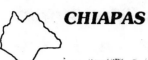

the **Oquilapa**. The cattle business through here is intensive. Feed lots, loading pens and ramps all tie in with the pasturage and hay fields to present a well-integrated picture of Chiapas' beef cattle industry. The small mountain peak ahead and to the left is **Cerro Bernál**, altitude 3500 feet. We are climbing a bit as we approach the pass between Bernál and the hills on the left.

  6.5 41.1 **K91+** Bridge over the **Río Horcones**. (An *horcón* is one of the up-right posts which are used to hold up thatched roofs.) Farther down the road the hills on the left provide a bright yellow February-March display of flowers on the many *primavera* trees. Next come the twin bridges over the **Río Pedregal**.

  5.5 46.6 **K100+** The paved road (right) is signed to **Tres Picos** 4km, a maintenance station for the railroad. *A dirt road continues 11km past Tres Picos to **Santa Elena** near the edge of a swamp.*

  0.8 47.4 **K102** **Cruce de Ganados** is a small grouping of houses nestled among large granite boulders. The alluvial area below the hills offers small stands of the fan palms, an occasional large tree and many types of grasses.

  4.4 51.8 **K109** The **Río de Jesus** is crossed. Beyond, a graded road goes left to a small community, **Las Piedritas 2**. Herds of both dairy and beef cattle are common through here. There are more primavera trees on the hillsides to the left.

  3.3 55.1 **K114** The bridge over the **Río Los Patos**, another of the numerous small streams which come tumbling out of the Sierra Madre de Chiapas. A rock quarry on the right follows. A bit beyond is the **Río Siete Cigarros**. We are still gradually climbing.

  4.5 59.6 **K121+** The mountains are now much closer than they have been, making them appear taller. The actual height of the tallest peak visible here is just over 5000 feet, **Cerro Santo Tomás**. We now come up on the **Paraiso** restaurant, a popular stop for the *camioneros* (truck drivers).

  1.1 60.7 **K123** A signed paved road (right) says **Cales de Chiapas**. It leads nearly 5km to a small railroad station and maintenance center.

  1.3 62.0 **K125** Paved road (right) is to **San Isidro** 4km, then on to several small lagoon-oriented communities. We next cross a small river and go by several large *higueras*.

  2.9 64.9 **K130** The terrain becomes a bit more hilly as we wind through hillside stands of small trees, while the arroyos harbor *higuera*, *huanacaxtle* and other large trees. We are also moving away from the mountains on the left.

  2.6 67.5 **K134** The beautiful **Río San Diego** comes tumbling out of the hills and under the Mexico 200 highway. *The streambeds in this part of Chiapas are as pretty as you will find anywhere. Most are lined with boulders, between which clear water cascades from one pool to another. There are numerous trees, large and small, overhanging the water, making a perfect oasis for a short break.* Cattle raising is the activity here, with some pastures and a number of hillside grazing areas visible. Houses are few and far between.

  2.6 70.1 **K138+** The signed **Río Urbina** bridge. We are coming back into the hills, and an increase in winding roadbeds.

  3.4 73.5 **K144** A graded road (right) signed to **Colima**, 8km, is followed by a restaurant and a bridge over the **Río Pijijiapan**. Most of the town is south of the highway where a number of services are available including a central market. There is a local **Pemex** on the highway. A graded road out the south end of town is supposed to take us 18 kilometers to a beach at **Embarcadero**. (We did not investigate.) The bus depot is on the highway near the end of town.

  5.3 78.8 **K152+** The restaurant **Donde** offers *piguas*, a type of **langostina**, or freshwater crustacean. We cross the **Puente Echegaray** over a very pretty stream. There are a couple of small restaurants nearby.

7.1   85.9   K164   A signed graded road right is to **Margaritas** 6km and **Las Brisas** 15km. We continue across the bridge over the **Río Margarita**. *We are seeing something new on the hillsides...a dwarf palm with a crown little more than 4 feet in diameter.* To the south the ground is flat and descends gradually to the many *esteros* and *lagunas* between here and the Pacific. The farming efforts are principally of a subsistence nature, with bananas, mangoes, etc. found only in small plantings near buildings.

4.3   90.2   K171   We cross a nameless, but active laundry and bathing stream.

6.0   96.2   K180+   A signed graded road (right) is to **Las Cuates, Valdivia, El Zapotál** and **Palmarcito**. Just beyond is the bridge over the beautiful **Novillero** river.

5.1   101.3   K188+   We enter **Mapastepec**, a town of more than 30,000. There is a local **Pemex** on the highway and the town is off to the right. *Its plusses include a small but good central market for perishables and some nice-looking Mexican-style beef. We bought an excellent piece of pork loin here. Several of the stalls had pottery and other handmade items such as baskets, brooms, etc. Two abarrotes and an ice plant rounded out our stops. One of the local specialties is cheesemaking and several stalls feature it.* Next, a bridge over a small laundry river, followed by a small rocky one. We continue along the edge of the foothills with the road running in nice long, straight stretches...a welcome change.

COWBOY

3.8   105.1   K195   We enter an area where a fire has just completed its journey through the low trees, shrubs and annual grasses. There are several spots where dead tree trunks, etc., are still smoking. Even the rainy tropics have their problems with fires. It extends more than 2.5 miles along Mexico 200, but all outward signs will disappear once the summer rains begin.

1.7   106.8   K197+   Cross a small rocky streambed with a healthy flow of crystal water under large shady hi*gueras*. Cattle feeding on rich grasses in manicured pastures are the landmarks along this portion of Mexico 200.

2.8   109.6   K202   The boulder-strewn little **Río Ulapa**. Another stream follows shortly, the **Río Madre Vieja** (Old Mother). The lushness of the grasses and the trees, the abundant water and the rolling hills are reminiscent of the Atherton Tableland region of Australia's tropical Queensland province.

4.6   114.2   K209+   A picturesque little restaurant with a high-peaked thatched roof and spotless interior. Next we come to a hill covered with a thick growth of vines, huge trees, orchids, etc. One could easily become lost or trapped in the tangled thickets.

2.6   116.8   K214   The **Río Doña María** is another of the rocky streams typical of our last 30 kilometers. There are several children playing in a pool just above the bridge. A couple of kilometers beyond is the town of **Acacoyagua** where artifacts in the form of black, red and orange ceramic products have been found. A couple of unique items are bowls with rims and figures with holes for the eyes.

2.8   119.2   K218+   Another beautiful stream, the **Cintalapa** leads us past a local **Pemex** and into the outskirts of **Escuintla**. Its 8000 to 10,000 citizens are active in raising cocoa, mangos, bananas and avocados. *Several mounds from early civilizations have been found nearby and large numbers of ceramic artifacts recovered.* The road continues southeast, climbing gradually in long easy turns between straight runs.

4.6   123.8   K226   A graded road (left) goes up a hill and disappears into a valley. Soon we pass four or five of the largest mango trees we've ever seen. Under them, in an almost impenetrable gloom, stands a small house. When the fruit ripens one would imagine that the inhabitants would take their lives in their hands each time they step out the door. There appears to be no way that the trees could be effectively harvested.

2.2　126.0　K230　We are getting tired of saying it, but here's another bridge over another beautiful stream.

2.7　128.7　K234　**Villa Comaltitlán**, population 5000, is on the right just past a bridge over the **Río Comaltitlán**. A typical small farming supply center, it even has a sign for an air-conditioned hotel, the **Narcia.** We continue past more *higueras* and more streams. Everything is a rich, light green. Large plantings of sugar cane are now part of the scene.

5.2　133.9　K244+　**Rancho Santa Elena**. An impressive ranch operation with some good looking horses in the pastures.

1.5　135.4　K247　Swiss dairy cattle (*ganados suizos*) are featured on the signs of several ranches. They are the brown variety and look very well fed. The larger houses in this area are of a different style...there are wide verandas encircling the entire house.

1.2　136.6　K249　We come to the top of a hill and look down into a valley and the town of **Huixtla**. A guess would put Huixtla at 30 to 40 thousand inhabitants and still growing. We cross the rather large and fast-moving **Río Huixtla**. This is a major laundry river with dozens of little drying racks arranged along the water's edge. *Huixtla is an important commercial center for coffee and cocoa. Offices and warehouses for these commodities are everywhere. Another major crop is bananas followed by rice, coconuts, livestock, lumber and dairy products. As in all of the Soconusco region, here too are archaeological sites containing stone carvings and ceramic pieces.*

1.2　137.8　K251　Mexico 211 intersects from the left across from a large local **Pemex**. It is signed to **Motozintla** and would take us to **Comitán** and **San Cristobal de las Casas. (See Chiapas Inland.)** The **LPG** station is next, followed by a Chevrolet agency and a Coca Cola bottling factory. It has ice...go to the rear of the building and ask for *hielo.* Next to the factory is a little restaurant, **La Bahía, Mariscaría Familiar**, with an impressive lineup of seafoods. Continue southeast through beautiful green hills and valleys. We go past a short paved road inland to **Tuzantan**. Then comes the bridge, **Puente Tepuzapa.**

4.5　142.3　K258+　A large banana planting is on the left. A bridge over another river comes a few hundred yards later. Then comes a huge *huanacaxtle* along with several other large trees. **Chamulapa** is signed on a bridge, then on a small collection of houses.

2.6　144.9　K263　A *Larga Distancia* phone office is on the right. Beyond this small collection of houses is the railroad. Mangos and bananas are plentiful, and if you look under them and under the forest trees you will see many many coffee bushes. Some are beginning to bloom, leaving a heavy perfume in the air.

2.6　147.5　K267+　A paved road (left) goes to **Huehuetán**. Next comes a large local **Pemex** and the beginnings of a 4-lane road. We cross the **Río Huehuetán**. It is a wide and beautiful meandering piece of clean-looking water with a few laundry doers squatted on the upstream side.

4.5　152.0　K277　We have been passing a number of large homes surrounded by well-kept lawns and gardens. The rich soil supports dairy cattle, pastures and mango orchards.

2.1　154.1　K280+　You cannot miss the concrete block house on the right if they don't repaint it. It is a bright, bright pink with vivid green stripes around each window and door. To top it off, the artist has put another band of bright blue under the eaves. The railroad tracks are to our right, sometimes within yards of the roadbed. *Just beyond, on the northeast side of the road, is an incredibly bright purple double bougainvilla.*

4.8　158.9　K288　An **LPG** station lets us know that we are near a sizeable town. Sure enough, we top a hill and right in front of us is the city of **Tapachula**. It appears to be just off to the right as we take the *periférico*. Several paved entries are on the right.

*The **Hotel Loma Real** is up a small hill on the left. It comes well recommended, as does the **Kamico**. The city is a business and agriculture center where products from the*

Soconusco region are distributed to other parts of the country. The region produces coffee, bananas, cocoa, and livestock and dairy products. There are coffee processing plants, cotton gins, aguardiente plants and sugar mills. Another indication of the success enjoyed by the Tapachula region of Mexico is seen in the row of new car dealers.

Tapachula was a meeting place of pre-hispanic cultures. **Olmec, Aztec** and **Maya** all contributed to this region. The mounds, burial sites and ceramics of the ruins at **Izapa** contain examples of an Olmeca/Mayan city which flourished between 200 BC and 200AD. Ceremonial platforms, altars, stele and a ball court have also been unearthed in Izapa.

More recent fusions of cultures have come from German immigrants, and another infusion came from Chinese refugees during the 1940s. Today refugees from Guatemala and El Salvador are crowding into the area and setting up little tent cities in the surrounding forests.

1.2   160.1   K291   Signed intersection. To the right is **Puerto Madero** and the airport. *After checking with several sources we decided not to go to Puerto Madero...the consensus was that it's a loser as a beach resort, but the port is very active.* Next comes the bus depot and beyond, the clean palapa restaurant, **El Maracate.** We are now blessed with a new set of K markers.

2.5   162.6   K0   We have followed Mexico 200 through Tapachula to its southeastern outskirts. Here we see a large full-service **Pemex,** and across the street an even larger supermarket/discount store. Just beyond is a *glorieta.* Follow the signs and take the road southeast toward the Guatemala border. Then comes the **Puente Caoacan,** a bridge over a beautiful little river. This day it is populated with swimming kids.

1.7   164.3   K2+   The restaurant **Bugambilas.** The **Finca La Chinita,** an attractive home with well-kept grounds, follows on the left. Continue past a restaurant/bar, **Villa de Lobos,** also on the left. It is enclosed and *con clima* (air conditioned).

3.1   167.4   K7   Intersection. Mexico 200 is signed as going to both **Ciudád Hidalgo** and **Talisman.** Actually 200 goes only to Talisman no matter what the signs say. Both are ports of entry into Guatemala. We are going to Talisman.

1.1   168.5   K8+   An archaeological zone is signed to be on the left in **Izapa.** You can see it from the road. Beside the buildings, tombs and other burial sites have been located. The bridge over the **Río Izapa** is next. To the left are a number of tents and crude shelters built in the forested area. The occupants have cleared out the underbrush, gathered piles of cooking wood and look to be semi-permanent. We are told that they are refugees from political strife farther south in Central America.

1.1   169.6   K10   There is a local **Pemex** on the right, the signed small town of **Tuxla Chico** on the left. It is noted to be 420 meters (1400 ft) in altitude. There are many bananas, all with coffee growing under them. We then come to a paved, signed intersection to **Cacahoatan** (left). We continue straight, coming to an arroyo which faces into Guatemala and the high mountains in their northernmost *cordillera.*

3.1   172.7   K15   The Guatemala border is here along with its maze of governmental offices that can keep you going back and forth like a ping-pong ball for an hour or more, even when there is no one else waiting. But that's a story for another edition.

End of log

Telling Time In Mayaland...

When reading through literature on the Mayas one notices references to so-and-so having died/arrived/born on specific dates (eg: September 4, 1094) and one wonders how today's scientists can be so specific.

The Mayas too had a calendar which assigned certain dates to natural phenomenon (eg: an eclipse of the sun or moon). Using the chart below we can convert their dates into the Gregorian calendar used by most countries today. Should you wish to convert your birthdate to the Mayan calendar you might begin with the the fact that July 6, 292 AD converts to 8 *baktuns*, 12 *katuns*, 14 *tuns*, 8 *uinals* and 15 *kins*. Then by using the following chart:

20 kins	=	1 uinal (20 days)
18 uinals	=	1 tun (360 days)
20 tuns	=	1 katun (7200 days)
20 katuns	=	1 baktun (144,000 days)
20 baktuns	=	1 pictun (2,880,000 days)
20 pictuns	=	1 calabtun (57,600,000 days)

Tom discovered that his Mayan birthdate was 12 baktuns, 14 katuns, 5 tuns, 1 uinal, 3 kins, plus or minus a day or two!

About 1500 years ago these marvelous people computed the length of the year to be 365.2420 days, while our modern scientific community has come up with 365.2422 days. A difference of only 17.3 seconds!

The synodical revolution of Venus (the amount of time between alignments of Venus and Earth) is 583.92 days days according to our atomic clocks, lazers and computers. The Mayans calculated it to be 584 days, and knew they were just a little bit off and adjusted for it!

For the Mayans, an eclipse of the sun or moon was a piece of cake, their records are filled with references. Most of us, calculators and all, haven't the foggiest how to even start on that one.

WAITING FOR THE BUS

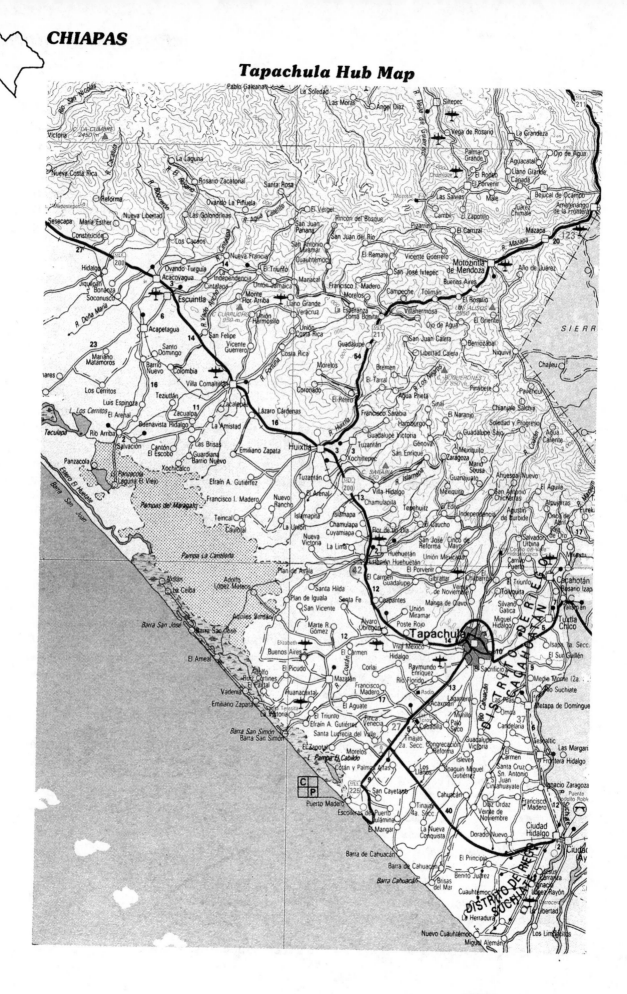

HUIXTLE — SAN CRISTOBAL DE LAS CASAS

The transition from the relatively cosmopolitan coastal plain to the land of the Tzotzil and the Tzeltal Indians is a big one in many respects. We turn off the air conditioner within the first half-hour, pine replaces huanacaxtle, many of the residents live in small enclaves on the hillsides with no trails for motorized vehicles. Human power replaces even burro power in some areas. The Indians are in the majority and Spanish is often a second language. Clothing not only reflects the need for warmth but colors and styles tell their own story of a homeland in ways little changed in centuries. It is a winding, fascinating highway which should be taken at a leisurely pace, for safety and to absorb new insights into the many faces of Mexico.

0.0   0.0   K0   At K251 of Mexico 200 in Huixtla there is a signed turnoff left to **Motozintla**. Across the street is a large local **Pemex**...a last chance to check your supplies. We are now on Mexico 211. The road goes uphill northeast past a number of businesses pertaining to coffee, then an abandoned hospital. The arroyos along the route are still heavily forested, but the underbrush has been cleared and coffee bushes planted. It is in this part of Chiapas that some of Mexico's best coffee is grown. The upper portions of the hills are planted in corn and what looks to be a silage grass.

1.9   1.9   K3   The road twists and turns as it rises into the mountains. With every turn of the wheel we are treated to a new and different perspective of the mountains enveloping us and the narrow, paved road. You could say that we are now officially in the tropical forests of Chiapas. All appears primeval with the exception of the few collections of thatched houses and (you must look closely) the coffee bushes.

3.9   5.8   K9+   A small group of houses is gathered around a small bridge over the **Río Huixtla**. Beyond are another few houses and a basketball court, this time with a sign so badly rusted we couldn't read it.

1.2   7.0   K11+   We cross the Huixtla again. It is a beautiful scene...crystal water flowing in cataracts over huge rocks into many pools. Some are natural swimming pools, others are cauldrons inviting disaster.

0.9   7.9   K13   The town of **Chipingo** is signed. In fact the *rotulero* (sign-maker) for Chipingo even added that it has 26 families and 145 people. The cobbled road to **Morelos** is also signed, but only with the distance, 9km.

2.8   10.7   K17+   A perfect little stream comes in from the left down a steep arroyo. It drops in waterfalls from one level to another over rounded boulders and past bright green plants. Unfortunately, there is no turnout.

1.0   11.7   K19   A small coffee village which has numerous cement slabs scattered around for drying the beans.

0.9   12.6   K20   The road continues winding upward past a lot of coffee beans, or potentials thereof. We come to a little cobbled entry to a road in the direction of the river. It turns out to be private property. This Mexico 211 highway is literally carved out of the the walls of the several canyons forming this Pacific watershed and is almost always being worked upon. Keep an eye out for workers.

1.6   14.2   K23   There is a sizeable group of houses perched along the opposite side of the river. Their only access is by a narrow suspension bridge. We stopped and looked at the thing...at our age there is no way we would even walk across, let alone live over there. It would be different if we were born to it, but we weren't. The tenacity and survival skills of these people are admirable.

1.4   15.6   K25   A fine view of the river. There are several hundred houses, a small school and several tiendas. We continue to see suspension bridges. The place is signed as **Colonia B. Dominguez**. There is a cobbled intersection (left) to a number of pueblos and pueblitos. This area of Mexico has had its problems with drug production and trafficking and such roads are not recommended unless with a local guide. Just be aware.

356

2.0 17.6 K28 There is already a marked temperature drop. We have climbed at least 4000 feet since leaving Huixtla. The plant mixture is also different, though there are still lots of coffee plants. The corn fields, maybe better described as cliffs, are everywhere. On one near-vertical spot we see bananas! Bromeliads and orchids by the thousands are in the trees. Some are loaded while others of the same species are devoid of these air plants entirely. Why?

3.6 21.2 K34 We see about 50 houses across the river, plus an equal number, and a basketball court, on this side.

2.5 23.7 K38 We are now high enough to have pine trees, some with Spanish moss.

1.1 24.8 K40 The climb has steepened perceptibly and it is cooling off to the point where the windows have been raised a bit. We are also high enough that views of the canyons below are evident. The mountains around us are also in better perspective and we can even better appreciate the energy put into raising corn at these altitudes.

As we pass more and more of the hillside houses an appreciation of the difficulty of the lifestyle of these people becomes paramount. The fact that miles of foot trails are the only thing which connect entire colonies of people should be of particular interest to those who are driving and using this book. These people are true survivors.

3.2 28.0 K45 We are in **El Rosario** across from a restaurant, **El Sagitario**. If you are into it, this might be your lucky day. There is a big satellite dish at a restaurant on the other side. A sports bar maybe? Check the canyon off to the left...there is a group of five or six houses connected to somewhere via a foot trail which winds down into the deep canyon and disappears. We continue winding upward. The side streets of El Rosario are nonexistent because the town straddles a narrow hogback with near-vertical drop-offs on either side. No basketball court here...it would be tough to get the ball back if it went out of bounds.

2.1 30.1 K48 A paved intersection is off to the left. We continue following Mexico 211 to the crest of the Sierra Madre de Chiapas. Sheep keep the hillsides cropped short. We come to a house with a number of large melons for sale. They look like a cross between a watermelon and a squash and grow on the nearby hillsides. The woman calls them a *chivocoyote*. The meat is firm, white, very sweet and is boiled before eating. The view from the front yard is spectacular. We see range after range of mountains as far as the eye can see and a good 3500 feet below, the city of **Motozintla**.

CHIVOCOYOTE MELONS

0.8 30.9 K49 On the left, a basketball court. We then run into a small group of trees covered with Spanish moss. Continue downward into the canyon leading into the **Depresión Centrál de Chiapas**. Below are silvery threads of water coming out of the canyons and coalescing into a fair-sized river. The highway tips over the edge and according to the map we will be twisting and dropping for about 8 miles.

7.5 38.4 K61+ The grade comes to an end and we are at the top edge of Motozintla, the center being off to the left. We continue ahead on the bypass, or *periférico* past a basketball court.

The canyon sides have only a thin carpet of grasses on them. Again, sheep. Little hillside corn is raised around here...not enough water. The plants to be seen around the highway are cactus and plumeria plus various host trees for bromeliads. As we continue to drop we see several small stands of tropical trees in protected side canyons.

0.9 39.3 K63 Here is the signed community of **Mazapa**. It is on the left with the main portion down in the canyon. It has a *Larga Distancia* office; watch for it on the right. Down in the river bottom there are numerous little plots of vegetables. From above we can identify onions, corn, melons, peppers, beans, tomatoes and several leafy plants, and all should thrive year around. We cross a bridge over a river...a kid's river. There are a half-dozen of them, splashing, tossing rocks, etc...all of the things we did at that age.

        1.7   41.0   K65   There is an immigration inspection station. *Over the years we have found that when we have passports and tourist permits in full readiness, the officer is less likely to inspect the vehicle. When he has to wait while we rummage through the glove box he takes more time to check us out.* Cross a bridge and continue along the right side of the river. Note that the hundred or more houses on the other side of the river are not connected by anything more than foot paths. Also see how neat and well-kept they appear.

        1.7   42.7   K68   We pass a basketball court and enter **Villa Hidalgo**.

        1.9   44.6   K71+   About 300 yards past the K71 marker there is the tiniest bit of a vegetable garden on the right in a miniscule side canyon. We can see onions, beans, chiles and several other vegetables. It is no more than 15 feet wide, terraced and well tended. See if you can pick it out.

        2.3   46.9   K75   **Amantenango de La Frontera** says a marker on the highway. If you look on the hills to the south (right) you can see a number of houses. They are full of Guatemalans for we are at the border and Mexico doesn't own that piece of turf. We continue past an immigration check point. Have the papers ready.

        3.1   50.0   K80   Watch for rocks on the highway. This is a landslide area with material occasionally tumbling down from the cliffs to the right.

        3.7   53.7   K86   A view (left) presents a microcosm of the area we have been going through...at the top are pine-covered peaks with cliffs plunging down to the next level, a plateau with oaks, a few pines and scrub. Next, after another set of cliffs a grove of coastal trees (*huanacaxtle*, *higuera*, etc.) extends down to the flood plain of the river.

        1.3   55.00   K88   We come into a grove of the large trees mentioned above. They extend for nearly a half-mile.

        1.4   56.4   K90+   To the left are some 200 houses spread along both sides of the river along with numerous truck gardens. We can also see coffee bushes under the trees.

        2.9   59.3   K95   About a dozen adobe houses with tin roofs have corn growing in the yards and a beautiful river in front of them. The surrounding wooded hillsides and arroyos are used to grow coffee. They appear to be family operations where much of the drying is is done in the front yards and every other available flat spot, including the cement rain gutters along the sides of the highway. One yard has even pressed the family wheelbarrow into service.

        More environments for coffee bushes are created with plantings of bananas. Several of them are off to the left. The drying and shipping process appears to go on much of the year while the harvest season is complete by the first of the year. (We're here in mid-March.) The beans we see drying along the side of the road are a whitish color, however we have seen several batches which are a very dark brown or black.

        1.8   61.1   K98   A taro patch is off to the left. Didn't know that it was in use in our hemisphere. How do they use it? We'd like to know.

        2.1   63.2   K101   A *balneario* (water and sports center) is to the right. It has pools, basketball courts and picnic area. We continue past coffee plants under bananas and another stream. **Agua Zarca**, a small signed group of houses is next. The houses here are mostly brick, some even have brick walls around them.

        1.5   64.6   K103+   **Las Brisas**, a nice-looking little restaurant is on the west, or left, side of the highway.

358

CHIAPAS INLAND

An Overnight Sensation...

What would you do if someone were to drive up to your house and, in very poor English ask permission to camp in your front yard? This in essence was the position we put a Chiapas family in...

We were well south of Tehuanatepec on the way to San Cristobal de Las Casas when it became obvious that we had miscalculated on where we would be for the night. This was coffee country, miles and miles of up and down mountains, canyons and tiny villages too small to even have a basketball court. The watch word became, "Find a place for the camper."

A half-hour into the search we see a well-traveled dirt road to the right which appears to go toward a stream. With luck, a place to camp.

The road did go to the river, and across it on a very narrow bridge without even a place to turn around. We rattled the camper up the other side, now just looking to turn around. The only wide spot was at the end of the road...in someone's front yard. While trying to figure how to make the maneuver, we saw two men standing off to the side watching our antics. Realizing that we could not turn around without going well into the yard, we mumbled an apology and asked for, and received permission to turn around up by the garage.

In the course of things we asked for suggestions where to find a spot for the night. They looked briefly at each other, gave "why not" shrugs and waved us into the driveway.

Shortly after we got settled, the owner sent his superintendent to invite us up to the big house for coffee.

Our host turned out to be **Don Everardo Soto López**, a dynamic man in his early 70s with a strong grip and steady eye. A native of Chiapas, he knows its mountains and valleys intimately. He has also spent considerable time in Guatemala. He began rattling off and describing the places we should visit so rapidly that it was useless to try and take notes.

The conversation turned to his coffee plantation of 250 **hectarias** (670 acres) and its hundreds of thousands of coffee bushes. He described how he had acquired the property more than 25 years ago and the pleasures of living in the mountains of Chiapas. During his tenure, in addition to a wide variety of fruit trees, Don Everardo has planted many exotic plants from all over the world...palms from Madagascar, ginger from Hawaii and the South Seas, pine trees from Russia and the Indian continent, etc. It is truly a Shangri-La.

Does he have many foreign visitors? He said their last **norteamericano** visitor was three years earlier and he came in the form of a backpacker hiking his way through Mexico. His arrival must have been somewhat of a culture shock for the local residents, for he ate only fruits and vegetables because he could not kill anything. For the same reason he would allow mosquitos to chew away without even a swipe to move them. He vigorously maintained that all creeping, crawling and flying things had a right to live and must not be disturbed. The visitor had long hair, wore filthy red head and waist bands, leather sandals and ragged clothes. He stayed for several weeks, sleeping under a tree by the stream or in one of the outbuildings. He will forever be remembered as **"Carlos Cristo,"** and stories of him will be told and retold for generations.

As we lie here at night we hear the owls call from the nearby trees. Raccoon, armadillo and iguana abound, and some parrots remain in the forest; they are more heard than seen.

The next morning Don Everardo's plantation manager, **Mario Culebro Marín** gave us a tour of the property. Mario has a degree in agriculture from the university in Salina Cruz and his love for his work is obvious.

Our tour allowed us to see how the coffee is cultivated (often on near-vertical hillsides) and where the beans are dried, sorted and graded. Mario's nursery of new plants...to replace those no longer producing or to expand the plantings...are all neatly

359

organized under palm-leaf shades.

He also takes us by the several streams on the property, the swimming-size pool in the adjoining river, a natural shower fed by a small spring and the pond where he raises tilapia and mojarra, both excellent food fish.

For the September-to-November harvest time they hire up to 300 workers who stay in the rooms provided, or camp under the trees. During the three months they pick, sort, grade and bag many thousands of pounds of Mexico's finest coffee and eat Mario's fish.

The hospitality of Don Everardo, Mario and his wife Madelaine will remain an ever-bright highlight of our adventures in Chiapas. We toasted their health for several months, thanks to a generous gift of their finest blend of coffee.

1.0   65.6   K105   **Frontera Comalapa**, population 15,000 is a coffee town with graded connections into the country north and west of this small city. Here too the beans are laid out everywhere there is a flat spot and a bit of sun. When one looks at where coffee is grown, sometimes on near-vertical hillsides, and the way the beans must be selectively picked and dried, it is a wonder that coffee is as inexpensive as it is. A local **Pemex** station is located on the east end of town.

6.3   71.9   K115   We've been seeing a tall, pink-flowering tree scattered here and there near the hills. Their early-March blooms are spectacular. We had been told that it is a variety of **primavera** tree but it is not. It seems that many spring-blooming trees are called primavera because that is the Spanish word for spring. We are now climbing gradually away from the coffee and into more cattle. A tree the locals call *roble*, (oak) predominates, along with a healthy scattering of the trees with the pink flowers. Next, a sign indicating an upcoming hotel.

4.3   76.2   K122   The entrance into **Paso Hondo**, and the answer to the hotel sign...it appears very minimal. Next come topes. In the square on the left is an unusually bright magenta-colored bougainvilla.

1.4   77.6   K124+   An intersection. To the right is **Cuauhtémoc** and the **Guatemala** border, while **Comitán** and **San Cristobal de las Casas** is to the left. This marks the end of Mexico 211 and our beginning of Mexico 190. Note the new kilometer markers.

0.0   77.6   K251   We now go due north past a couple of *fincas de cafe* (coffee plantations) **El Dorado** and **Copacabaña**. Then comes a small town off to the right, **El Jocote**, with a local **Pemex**. This land appears to dry out thoroughly before the summer rains. The hillsides in April are reminiscent of Southern California's summer landscapes.

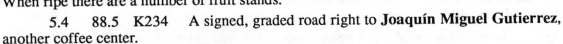

INDIAN GIRL

5.5   83.1   K242+   On the right a few small ranches with *círuela* trees (a delicious, acidic, fruit resembling a plum). When ripe there are a number of fruit stands.

5.4   88.5   K234   A signed, graded road right to **Joaquín Miguel Gutierrez**, another coffee center.

2.1   90.6   K231   In **San Gregorio** we stop at the Mexican government immigration (*migración*) station for passports and tourist permits to be checked and recorded. Then we cross the **Río San Juan**, a sizeable tributary to the **Rio San Gregorio** river system. The San Gregorio ultimately feeds into the gigantic hydroelectric and irrigation system of **La Angostura**. This huge reservoir has been formed in the long natural depression between the two mountain ranges, **Sierra Madre de Chiapas** and the **Meseta Central de Chiapas**. The entire complex makes Chiapas the largest provider of hydroelectric power in Mexico.

*The building of the dam, **Presa Belisario Dominguez**, was not without controversy* *as the waters behind it cover 14 towns whose residents were moved to new locations. In addition 176 archaeological sites were inundated. Though the sites are now under water, some representative material was saved. One of the lost sites, **Copanahuastla**, was an ancient Indian ceremonial center. Here the remains included mounds, platforms, plazas and foundations. Tombs in which the cadavers were placed in clay jars under the houses, were also studied before the lake covered the site.*

The colonial history of Copanahuastla also has interesting facets. When the Spanish arrived in the 16th century they built a major religious center, including a large temple and convent. The story, as related in early books on Chiapas and Guatemala, was that the Indians managed to hide an idol in the altar behind the statue of the virgin. Thus when they were taken to the temple to worship the new God, they were able to direct their prayers and incantations to their own deity. When word got out of the subterfuge the furious priests exacted a heavy penance and many of the Indians fled. Interestingly enough, a few days after the confrontation an epidemic struck down and killed most of the city's remaining population.

0.5   90.8   K230   The road continues north and west. To our left is a broad irrigated plain, a corner of the much larger **Depresión Central de Chiapas**. The hillsides here were denuded many years ago and their value for even subsistence corn and bean crops is minimal. There is also less rainfall than on the ocean side of the **Sierra Madre de Chiapas**. Sometimes this region is referred to as the *tierra blanca*, white earth, referring to its limestone origins.

3.1   93.9   K225   A small community of **Villa Elena**. We begin to climb into the hills along the side of a small stream. The trees we see in the arroyo are the roble, higuera, primavera and huanacaxtle.

3.1   97.0   K220   The road levels out in another flat area some hundreds of feet higher than the large valley we just left. We pass several non-irrigated cornfields as the highway goes north through the valley.

0.9   97.9   K218+   A graded road branches (right) to **Las Delicias**, 20km. At the intersection is a large yellow and orange bus with a huge luggage rack. It looks to be designed for at least 10 goats. Don't laugh...five are tethered on top with room to spare.

3.9   101.8   K212+   **Puente Santa Inéz**, a bridge over a stream followed by a small school and a few pink buildings. Ahead on the left is a factory which does something with, or generates, what looks like cotton.

1.4   103.2   K210   There are some rather tall examples of the fan palms we are used to seeing near the sea-level lagoons. Limestone predominates and *tierra blanca* still describes the land. In a little bit we go by an unsigned graded dirt road east leading to **Buena Vista** and a number of other ranches or communities.

3.1   106.3   K205   We continue uphill, taking a brief jog to the northeast. Here and for the next several miles the cuts made in the hillsides for the highway show the stressed condition of this region during previous millennia. Keep in mind that this is limestone, which was formed at sea level and in a horizontal plane.

2.5   108.8   K201   Here is a turnout and a good place to catch up on the views of the mountains and the valleys. There are some four or five species of the agaves along the rocky hillsides. The road continues to climb. Though not extremely steep, it is quite a pull over these several miles. Be sure to check your temps, etc.

5.0   113.8   K193   A *microondas* road off to the left.

2.4   116.2   K189+   We are in **La Trinitaria**, a town of 15,000 people, altitude 1530 meters (just over 5000 feet). We pass a rather unusual-looking church, a local **Pemex** and several rock-walled houses. We see lots of burros, a few ox-carts, and several oxen tethered to trees.

1.2   117.4   K187+   A signed paved road (right) is to **Lagos de Montebello.** The *lagos* are a series of lakes beginning about 40 kilometers from Mexico 190. *There are about 50 lakes scattered over an area of about 15 km. The region is reputed to be very beautiful and unspoiled. There are several camping areas and a couple of shelters, according to a young couple from Germany we met in a taquería in Comitán. They had spent a week there and claimed to have hiked to at least a dozen lakes and visited the nearly-unknown ruins of* **Chinkultic.**

Across from the intersection are more of the teepee-shaped warehouses. Continue straight northwest through a broad valley with a few low hills breaking the flatness.

3.2   120.6   K182   On the right is a **LPG** station.

2.6   123.2   K178   We have an immigration (*migración*) check point. Passports and tourist papers will be checked and recorded. Next, **Tzimol** is signed off to the left on the paved intersection. A local **Pemex** is also on the left, then the outskirts of **Comitán de Dominguez,** population, 80,000.

2.7   125.9   K174   The road through town divides as we pass a variety of businesses. The center divider is well landscaped with especially-vibrant shades of bougainvilla. A fairgrounds is signed off to the left and the central portion of town is on our right as we pass through the outskirts.

Originally the area was Mayan and known for its beautiful pottery. It was given the name **Comitán,** "Place of the Potters", by Aztec military scouts in the 15th century when they passed through on the way to Central America. There are foundations, steles and various other ruins in the area. Comitán is the birthplace of **Belisario Dominguez,** a local doctor and patriot who was put to death by the **Huerta** dictatorship in 1913. His home is now a museum.

Comitán, which began as a logging center, now directs its attention to livestock, bananas and corn along with high quality thread, textiles and the fiery, sugar alcohol-based beverage, aguardiente.

The town is also known for its many fiestas and for the enthusiasm developed during those celebrations. January, February, August, November and December all have 10 or more days dedicated to one fiesta or another. There are several local **Pemex** and a bus depot on our route through Comitán.

Today's Comitán is becoming a stopping off place for visitors to the Montebello Lakes district, 56 km to the east. There are several recommended hotels; the **Real Balun Canan** and the **Internacionál,** with the Real reported to have a good dining room. Continue North past a few more businesses including the modern looking, **Hotel Los Lagos de Montebello,** on the right.

0.8   126.7   K171   An ice plant (*hielería*) is signed off the *periférico* one short block to the right. As we leave the metropolitan area the corn plantings resume. A migración inspection station is next...have passports and tourist papers ready.

2.5   129.2   K167   We begin to descend through a small valley past more corn plantings and a few houses.

1.2   130.4   K165   The signed pueblito of **Chabaljocom,** then northwest and into more scattered pines.

0.8   131.2   K163+   Intersection, **Soyatitan** is signed to the left. There are a few wood-framed houses, indicating the existence at one time of a lumber industry. Another signed group of houses, **El Roble** is next.

3.0   134.2   K159   Semi-graded road off to the right to **Ogutzil.** The scenery is reminiscent of the piney mountain areas north and east of the Los Angeles basin or the hills east of Sacramento, California. Another graded road follows to **Zaragoza La Montana** at K155. Continue northwest past more groupings of houses.

5.6   139.8   K150   The soil in this end of the valley is almost jet black. More houses and a sawmill are on the left. The signed settlement of **El Durazno** (The Peach) includes a number of peach trees on the south west side of the highway. The road winds gently through the hills with little change in altitude.

      4.9   144.7   K142+   A small pond, **Laguna Chamula** is off to the right. We climb slowly out of the valley over the next 2 miles to top out and overlook a small town on the right, **Cruz Quemada**. This area is principally pine forest, with a scattering of agaves, bromeliads and deciduous scrub. Continue through pines, small groups of houses and a fair number of burros.

      7.8   152.5   K130   Soon we come upon the signed hillside scattering of houses, **Tulanca**.

      There is something different here at Tulanca. We have entered that special, almost ethereal world which surrounds the San Cristobal de Las Casas region. It shows in the small painted church; even before seeing the residents one gets the feeling that something is different here...the houses are widely scattered, the usual groups of playing children are missing. When you do see the residents many are dressed in tribal costume. The town itself is small and could easily go unnoticed, except for that aura. There will be more places like this to come. Continue past Tulanca and begin a descent into the next valley.

      1.9   154.4   K127   This valley is loaded with horses and dairy cattle. On the left is the reason...the large and well organized **Establos de San Nicolás**. We continue northwest to the edge of the valley and then descend into a larger one with the town, **Amatenango del Valle**, in the near end.

      1.6   156.0   K124   Well up on the hill near the first scattering of houses are roadside displays of pottery. The shapes and painted designs are unique to the region. Go slowly and be ready to stop, for they are truly beautiful. Continue down into Amatenango de Valle where there is usually a large display of pottery adjoining a parking lot.

      2.2   158.2   K121   An intersection. To the left is a paved road southeast to **Villa Las Rosas, Pijiltic** and several more sizeable towns. It eventually bends back to the west and north and rejoins Mexico 190 about 50 kilometers west of San Cristobal de Las Casas. We continue on Mexico 190.

      1.8   160.0   K118   A signed town, **Teopisca**, population 19,000, altitude 5600 feet. There is a local **Pemex** at the entrance into town...where the road divides. It also has a **Bancomer**, and several restaurants. The stores and the benches in and around the zocalo are covered with hand-painted tiles. One of the stores is that of a saddlemaker. We step in to look around and discover that everything displayed (even the saddles under construction) are for burros! The town is clean with well-painted buildings and sparkling streets, despite the many burros in the area. We come out the north end and resume our trip up the highway.

      1.5   161.5   K115+ On the left is another of the cement "teepee" grain storage complexes which was built some years ago by one of Mexico's presidential administrations.

      1.7   163.2   K113   A small hotel is on the right, but is closed at this writing. Across the highway and down 300 yards appears to be another loser, the **La Amistad** trailer park. Facilities seem limited and deteriorating, though the site among the pines is beautiful. We continue northwest, a little up, a little down.

      1.4   164.6   K108+ There's a small mirador offering an almost unlimited view to the south and east. Well to the west, about 15 miles away is the **Río Grijalva**, a river vital in the generation of electric power and responsible for much of the irrigated land in Chiapas. Continue northwest through more of the small lumbering and farming villages. Most of them are populated by the Indians, with very few mestizos.

      1.2   165.8   K106+ **Guadalupe**, a signed collection of wood houses. Several of them are sporting small orchards of peaches or similar fruit. A number of the houses are built from upright logs imbedded into the ground. Their fences are constructed the same way, just shorter and with no roof. Very interesting.

  1.1 166.9 K105 This is **Betanía,** another example of the ability of these people to use what is around them. Some of the houses are of adobe, others of wood, while the church is rock. The houses are scattered over the hillside with interconnecting foot-trails. Continue past more little enclaves of houses on the sides of hills or strung along a convenient walking trail. Most of the women in this part of the sierra wear blue rebozos. The color and the design is unique to this particular group. In other regions the color might be red, pink or black. Here and there you might see water still being carried in clay ollas (pots), often with the help of a head strap. Small garden plots are behind some sturdy fences, otherwise the goats and pigs would have a field day.

  3.0 169.9 K100 There are many black sheep in the flocks through here. The reason is found in the fact that black wool is widely used in the homespun tribal dress patterns and growing it black is better than dying it black. We continue past the signed community, **Mitzitón.**

  2.6 172.5 K96 The paved road (right) is Mexico 199. It goes to **Palenque,** about 200 kilometers to the northeast. The hills are well populated with pine trees of all sizes, though there appear to be few remaining which could be economically converted into lumber.

  1.1 173.6 K94 One of Mexico's National Parks is one kilometer off to the left, **Parque Recreativo Grutas de San Cristobal.** Grutas means caves, thus there are caves. *About 500 meters are open to the public, while another 15 kilometers are not. The stalactites are impressive, though not lighted to the best advantage (that may come with time). There is a restaurant and horseback riding, picnic and camping areas among the thick groves of towering pines. The camping fees are reasonable and the atmosphere, superb.* Continue northwest past small fenced plots of ground. When the rains begin they will be planted in corn, beans, etc. Eventualy the road begins dropping into the valley, and it's slippery when wet.

  3.1 176.7 K89 Intersection with the western *periférico* around **San Cristobal de Las Casas.** We continue straight toward town.

  0.6 177.3 K88 A branch (right) goes up into the hills and skirts around the north and east portions of San Cristobal to rejoin Mexico 200 on the other side. It is signed to **Tenejapa,** one of the more colorful Indian villages in the area. **(See Chiapas Inland.)** We continue toward the city, which is signed as having 82,000 residents. After a local **Pemex** on the left, watch for the signed entrance into the Centro. Welcome to a fascinating experience, the world of San Cristobal de Las Casas.

  End of Log...

SAN CRISTOBAL DE LAS CASAS

They came and went here in the **Joval Valley** high in the pine forests of central Chiapas. It began early in the history of the tribes of Mexico when small clans of hunters and gatherers left their calling cards, arrow points, *metates*, etc. Later, during the height of their empire, the Mayas established several outposts in the region. The Aztecs too came and went during their expansion into Central America. The visitors were many, but few stayed until the **Tzotzil** and **Tzeltal** branches of the Mayas arrived about the time of the collapse of the Mayan Empire in the 9th century.

When the Spanish arrived in 1524 they were met with resistance from the city-states of **Chamula, Zinacantan** and **Huixtan**. Not having the forces to subdue and rule, the Spanish withdrew to return four years later under the command of Diego de Mazariegas. Once in control they built a cathedral and administrative buildings around the site of the present *zocalo*. The effort to bring the scattered Indians into town was successful to a degree and *barrios*, or neighborhoods, were established around smaller churches and plazas.

Over time outlying villages were subdued and controlled through the system known as *ecomiendas*, where large tracts of land and the natives who lived there were assigned to a Spaniard. In return the "owner" was supposed to "take care" of his Indians. This he did by forcing them to convert to Christianity and to work on the land they no longer owned. This, plus starvation diets and plague after plague of the white man's diseases brought the Indians down from an estimated 350,000 in 1528 to 95,000 in 1600.

Through these difficult times the Indians had few champions. One, **Bishop Bartolome de Las Casas**, spent more than 50 years championing their cause. His efforts earned him lasting affection and later, **San Cristobal** was renamed in his honor.

During the colonial period the principal crop was wheat and much of it was shipped to other parts of the Spanish Empire. The administration of Chiapas came under the jurisdiction of Guatemala during much of the time before 1824, when **Joaquín Miguel Guttierez** led the negotiations with Guatemala that brought Chiapas in as a state in the new Mexican republic.

Though Chiapas was part of the Republic of Mexico by choice, the lives of the *Chiapanecos* were barely improved, if at all. Virtual slavery under *ladino* landowners was not finally addressed until the 1917 revolution. Even today the state's average per-capita income is the lowest in the country.

Contemporary San Cristobal is a cool and misty highland city with a mixture of Colonial Spanish plazas, churches and narrow cobbled streets. Substantially altered over the years a visit to the 1528 **Cathedral** is still reminiscent of a stroll through one of the grand cathedrals in Madrid or Sevilla. The **Templo de Santo Domingo** is another from the 16th century which demonstrates the fine craftsmanship of the workers of the era. Around the *zocalo* (plaza) are several buildings which served as homes and offices for the conquering Spaniards. You can even stay in one if you choose...the **Hotel Santa Clara**, for instance.

The Santa Clara is but one of the old buildings which have been modernized and are being used as hotels. All are clean, have center courtyards, 3 and 4-foot walls and an ability to take you back in time. They include the **Posada Diego de Mazariegos**, which now has a covered courtyard and occupies two city blocks. The **Hotel Español** has fireplaces in every room while the **Mansión del Valle** is newer but done in the colonial style. The **Ciudád Reál** has a beautiful open-air patio restaurant and the **Moctezuma** has one of the better dining rooms in the city. Another plus for the Moctezuma is **Sandra García de Meyer**. She is knowledgeable and speaks very good English. Born and raised here, she has absorbed much of the lore of the region.

FLOWER LADY

Others which attracted our attention were the **Fray Bartolome de Las Casas** which

365

offers very clean basic rooms at a good price. The **Bonampak** is located at the northwest end of town on the Tuxtla highway. It is more typical of an American-style motel. The last is the **Hotel Molino de La Alborada,** which is sited on a hillside west of the city. It presents a panoramic view of the valley, especially at night. The rooms are spacious, with fireplaces, and rent for very low prices. There is also a salon and spotless dining room.

Motorhomers or trailer campers are faced with decreasing numbers of available spaces for their rigs. The only trailer park we saw with a semblance of organization is behind the Hotel Bonampak.

Dining in San Cristobal de Las Casas is a pleasant surprise, particularly after looking at recent menus in Mexico's tonier west coast resorts. Here we can buy a full dinner for less than the price of an hors d'oeuvre in an Acapulco tourist hotel. Here are a few success stories...

La Misión del Fraile is located on the east side of Insurgentes one and a half blocks south of the zocalo. This has to be one of the best finds in Chiapas. We hit the place three times and had three winners. An excellent value on a wide variety of Mexican dishes including a mixed meat grill which comes to the table on a charcoal brazier.

Restaurant La Familia looks to have survived from the days of Alice's Restaurant. It offers a vegetarian-and-chicken array of dishes with notable success. They are three blocks north of the zocalo on Calle Gral. (General) Utrillo and are often crowded.

Tuluc Restaurant does a fine job on steaks (a specialty is a thin piece of beef wrapped around cheese, spinach and other ingredients). The soups are excellent. The address is Madero #9 south of the zocalo. The **Plaza** restaurant overlooks the plaza. It's staff is friendly and anxious to please. As of now they have some work ahead of them to be among the top ones, but we wouldn't hesitate to try them again soon. A baked pork dish and a so-so filet mignon are not the right choices at this time. They are on the south side of the zocalo.

The **Galería**, a few doors off the plaza is a beauty. The decor of this spacious downstairs restaurant is laced with some of the region's finer handicrafts. The menu was attractive and the reports good. Unfortunately we ran out of time, but it is on the list for the return trip.

La Phaisan restaurant turned out to be the only loser on our tour of San Cristobal...the people were friendly, service a bit slow but the food, a fried chicken and a mole of pork, should have never been allowed out of the kitchen. Several customers were eating heartily, but we weren't the only ones picking at our plates.

We mentioned earlier that the **Hotel Moctezuma** has a good dining room. And they do...pork chops, *antojitos* (hors d'oeuvres), chicken, soups (try the Azteca) and salads are tasty and fresh. The Moctezuma is three blocks from the *zocalo* on the corner of Leon and Juárez.

San Cristobal is home to **Na Bolom**, a unique sanctuary for the contemporary Maya peoples living in the surrounding hills and jungles. This effort has been particularly helpful to the **Lancandón** Indians from the jungles bordering Guatemala, many of whom still live in the ways of their ancestors before the Spanish conquest. Started shortly after World War II by Franz and Trudi Blom, it has preserved the records and the folkways of these fascinating people and serves as a research center for academicians from all over the world. The displays of artifacts, the library and the grounds of Na Bolom are well worth a visit.

LANCANDON CHILD

There is a wealth of handicrafts available in San Cristobal. They not only arrive daily on the *Collectivo* busses but are imported from Guatemala. The center for much of it is uphill to the east around the church of **Santo Domingo** and the nearby central market. Here the women and children in tribal costumes sell fruit, vegetables and display a wide array of woven pieces. Ranging from friendship bracelets to belts; potholders to wall hangings, they are hard to resist. So too are dolls, dresses, pottery and *rebozos*. Bargaining is part of the game

366

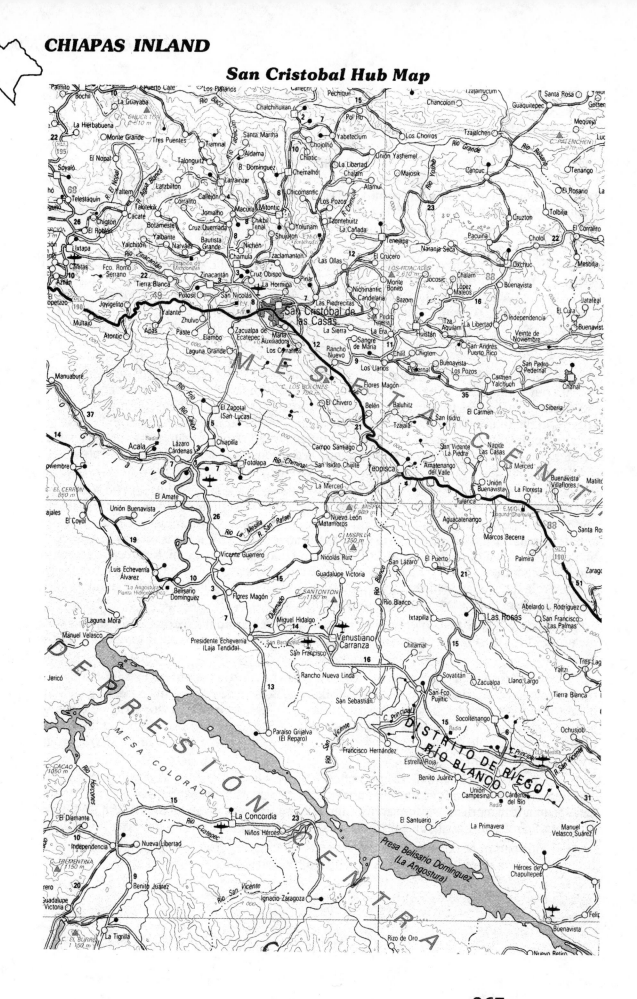

and is expected. We did find some resistance to photography here, so take either long shots or ask permission.

Between the entrance into Santo Domingo and the museum which takes up the left side of the building is the store, **Sna Jolobil**. Here you can peruse a collection of some of the finest weaving products to come from the villages. Each piece is selected individually and attractively displayed. It's worth a visit. On the street behind the church, Calle Gral. Utrillo, look for a much smaller store which also has very fine weavings, the **Galería de Artes**, where a young Indian woman named **Rosa** showed us a variety of weavings and described the meanings of the patterns typical of each village. Though she speaks little English, she came across very well.

More native crafts are found in the many stores on Calle Real de Guadalupe, which goes east from the north side of the zocalo. Of the stores we shopped, the most memorable has to be the one owned and operated by **Abelardo Cordero** and his wife **María Elena**. Their store, **Casa Malena** is undoubtedly one of the most jam-packed bits of space we have ever seen. There are things layered on walls and stacked on top of other stacks. Apparently-unopened boxes are stacked upon more boxes. Abelardo and Maria Elena themselves make the place look full. But...nearly anything you might want from any specific village will be under, over, beside or inside something. Their ability to come up with our wants is amazing. Abelardo has been traveling to the villages throughout the sierras of Chiapas for almost 30 years and claims to have somebody in every village on the lookout for him. We do not doubt it. Thanks to this charming couple and their incredible store we now have two complete tribal *trajes* (costumes) for very small children for our new Baja home. Casa Malena is located at Calle Real de Guadalupe, #24A.

Nearly every surrounding village is served by transportation of some sort. Most of it is centered around fleets of *colectivas,* VW Combis, pickup and stake bed trucks, who shuttle in and out of the central market area. They serve the area in a unique manner, hauling not only people but whatever they might want to bring along. Corn, pottery, firewood, even small animals are part of the cargo. If you want an adventure, pick a town such as **Magdalena** or **Tenejapa**, then go to the east end of the central market and ask which *colectivo* to board and when it comes back. No guarantees, but we know of several people who do it regularly. A more relaxed way to visit the surrounding towns is to drive your own vehicle, hire a taxi, or maybe best...take a tour. Any hotel or travel agency can fix you up.

Each village has its own traditional *traje*, or dress, and it's recognizable throughout the area. The weavings of each village are also unique and considered among the finest in Mexico.

By tradition the Indians grow *maize* or corn, but this is becoming less productive as their slash and burn methods deplete the soil. The forests are also taking a beating as their need for wood increases. Those who are no longer able to survive on subsistence farming and the sale of a few handicrafts are now being forced to leave home and work in the coffee plantations or as field hands in other parts of Mexico. *We have seen Chiapanecos as far afield as San Quintín, Baja California.*

Here in San Cristobal, as in no other place we know, visitors are being beautifully imprinted with the colorful tribal costumes and customs in an atmosphere of colonial Spain. European and American visitors are finding it a place to remember and to return to. Surely a profitable mix of tourism and culture, plus this incredible variety of handicraft products.

This part of Mexico is changing at an ever-increasing pace...Come to **San Cristobal de Las Casas** before it is too late. You will not be sorry.

AROUND SAN CRISTOBAL...

As we try to get a feel for this region our senses are bombarded with many new impressions. The people and their dress, the way they live and how they react to our intrusions (yes, intrusions, for this is the land of a private society and we are outsiders). This is a world apart, and we are the aliens. Let us try to observe the courtesies we would want should they be guests in our homes.

One of the big no-no's is photography, for many of the Indians believe that the capture of their image on film takes away part of their soul. The beliefs are strong and must be respected. On rare occasion someone will agree to allow pictures for a fee. It is not only a way to supplement the income, but the money allows them to recover their soul by burning candles in the church. Unauthorized photographs have resulted in attacks, and in at least one case, death. No pictures, particularly close-ups, without explicit permission.

Tenejapa...

*One of the more remote, yet accessible Indian villages, **Tenejapa** should not be missed. Whether you drive or take a tour, the experience is a positive one. We see a people who, despite tremendous hardships imposed by Spanish and Mexican overlords since 1528, have maintained their tribal integrity and only little by little are changing their lifestyle to accommodate the world around them. In essence they have their own world and are making it work. The road begins as a paved one, but eventually turns into a graded and sometimes-rough trail through stunning scenery.*

From K88+ on the eastern outskirts of San Cristobal the paved periférico goes north into the hills to service outlying suburbs. After passing through a number of settlements and past a half-dozen rock quarries it will reconnect with Mexico 200 on the other side of the city. After **3.5** miles of climbing, descending and winding we come to the road (right) which is signed to Tenejapa while the periférico continues (left) down through houses and back to the valley floor.

0.0   0.0   K0   We turn (right) at the paved, signed intersection to Tenejapa and climb up out of the valley past scattered houses and a view of some hillside cornfields.

3.4   6.9   K5+   At **Las Piedracitas** there is a bright blue and white church on the left. It appears large for the number of houses around it, but also serves hundreds of families living back in the mountains.

1.0   7.9   K7   The road winds up and down with different sights around every corner. Just beyond, a dirt road (left) goes to **Zontehuitz**, 12km.

1.2   9.1   K9   We come into the village of **Cruzton** where blue dominates the costume. If you are an equine-fancier you might appreciate the fact that Cruzton is the home of a yellow burro! It is a strange mixture of shadings varying from white to a definite pale yellow. The locals don't appear to think he is special for he is hauling wood right along with his darker brethren...As we go along we pass a large amount of wood along the road. All cut to length and carefully stacked, it waits for a buyer. We also note that the burros have little or no hair on their tails. The hair is "harvested" to make ropes and other products.

1.4   10.5   K11+ This is the signed entrance into **Romerillo.** There are terraced gardens and a small irrigation project. We see potatoes, cabbage, corn, chiles and squash. A unique cemetery is ahead on the top of the rise. The plots are raised soil covered loosely with boards and marked with wooden, painted crosses. On the highest part of the cemetery there are eight very large blue crosses. Fully 15 feet high, they are decorated with long pine branches, making them appear to be in a forest. Their function is to mark points of access into the spirit world.

369

Another oddity, at least to us, is the fact that many of the pigs have long shaggy coats of fur. No explanation, just an observation. We exit the town and go north, winding up and down through magnificent forest and mountain scenery. There are little houses with wisps of smoke rising from stone chimneys. We watch men in tribal costume working in the fields while women and children tend small herds of sheep. It all makes for memorable scenes, particularly today, for the clouds are in perfect harmony with the land below them.

1.8   12.3   K14+ A bus stop, **Paraje Yutosil**. Note the houses hard to the right...of adobe and with high-peaked reed roofs, they appear to be from another century, yet just above them is a power line, a paradox of incongruity.

0.4   12.7   K15   We have run out of pavement as such...a few more scattered patches and it gives up entirely. At the entrance to another group of houses there are several families farming an attractively-terraced hillside planted in potatoes, peas, beans, etc.

1.3   14.0   K17   **Nishnamtic** is 5km to the right on a signed, semi-graded road which disappears quickly around a hill. A few more yards puts us in **Las Ollas**. About 50 houses, plus garden plots, pastures and more of the hairy pigs are between the two signs marking its boundaries.

0.9   14.9   K18   **Matzam** is 16km off to the right.

1.3   16.2   K20   **Baluncanal** is another signed group of houses. The setting with the houses, the nearby cultivated hillsides and the more distant forested mountains form a marvelous vista.

0.9   17.1   K21+ A faint car trail goes to the right to **Rancho El Coralito**. Off to the left at the top of the rise is a small blue church...but with a difference. It is of the Seventh Day Adventists. The presence of Adventist congregations in this part of Mexico is relatively new, and very controversial. The dichotomy of the Catholic Church has been threatened by the aggressive missionaries, and zealots from both sides have had many clashes with hundreds, likely thousands, having been killed or ostracized from traditional homelands. It is an ugly situation, and not likely to be settled for some generations. Continue winding upward.

1.5   18.6   K24   A government warehouse for foodstuffs is on the right. Just beyond we catch a first view of Tenejapa far down to the left. On the sides of the cliffs we see some small spots of purple orchids. The plant is about 2 inches across while the bloom is nearly an inch. Continue downhill on a steep, winding course toward the valley below.

1.3   19.9   K26   Just before the road levels out and the town begins, we come to a small building on the right. Signed, **Escuela de Tejeda** (School for Weaving), it serves as an education and marketing center for the production of the *tejedas*. We are invited in by a charming **Tzeltal** Indian woman who explains the function of the school. There are some weavings here, but there is a much better selection below...

0.2   20.1   K26+ Downtown **Tenejapa**. The town is good-sized, around 10,000. It serves as the cultural and business center for about 20,000 Indians. There are also a few Ladinos (people of mixed blood). The language most heard is the musical Tzeltal, not Spanish, though Spanish is gaining rapidly as the children complete school and enter tribal society. Market days, when people come in from the remote ranches and villages, are Thursdays and Sundays. Principal fiesta times are Christmas, Easter, and the day of their patron saint, Idelfonso (January 23rd).

The first thing we come to after parking is a museum, **Museo Regional de Tenejapa**, displaying the textile arts of the area. The contents of the building is a major reason for coming to Tenejapa. Here all manner of woven and embroidered items are on display and for sale. The women are friendly and helpful, despite a lack of English. The two we met,

Juana and **Patrona**, were not only a great help but shared a bag of roasted cacahuates (peanuts), with us. The prices here are firm and extremely fair.

It is hard to describe what we see upon entering Tenejapa's zocalo. It is the Thursday before Easter and the town is crowded with families from outlying villages and ranches, and all but a very few are dressed in full tribal regalia...the men in black or white ponchos with short embroidered pants. A colorful cloth belt holds the whole thing together. The men holding positions of prominence wear necklaces with silver medallions or coins. Some also wear straw hats with colored ribbons trailing.

The women too have unique costumes...white huipiles or blouses with brightly-colored embroidery, dark blue wrap-around woolen skirts and maroon and white sashes...a handsome combination. They also wear a blue rebozo and are invariably carrying something in it. Most of the time it is a child, but may include food, laundry or firewood.

Signs of cracks in the facade of tribal dress here and in other Indian centers become apparent when looking at their feet. Instead of wearing sandals or going barefoot, a number of the men and children, even a few women, are wearing tennis shoes, including **Reebok** and **LA Gear**.

As it is also the Thursday market day we see dozens of items which have been carried into town for sale or barter. It is going on everywhere...tomatoes exchanged for candied hearts of maguey; shoes for a toy; another is exchanging a small handful of coins for plastic plates.

We watch the separate groups of men and women as they talk of their world. The scene is fascinating and we wish that photography were possible...prints would be a prominent part of any gallery.

A basketball court is adjacent to the zocalo, or town square, and two half-court games are going on. The obvious hotshot is a youngster of about 14 named **Agustín**. When he found out we are from Los Angeles his eyes popped wide and he said, "Conoce Magic?, Conoce Los Lakers?"

Each word about **Magic Johnson** and the **Lakers**, and how they are doing, is gobbled up by the youngsters, with some of it even being translated into Tzeltal. Agustín and his amigos are a great audience.

One wonders how such household names in America's contemporary sports scene can possibly become such a popular item in this small enclave of Indians in a remote valley where Spanish is spoken by only a minority, radio and television are rarities, and newspapers nonexistent. The world is indeed becoming smaller. Back to San Cristobal de Las Casas.

Chamula and Zinacantan...

In the two communities of Chamula and Zinacantan we have an opportunity to observe two very different tribal villages. Though both are from the same branch of the Maya, Tzotzil, they have adopted strikingly different dress. The Chamulans tend to be more directed toward the land and provide vegetables to much of the San Cristobal area while the the Zinacantecos have historically been traders and still provide much of the salt used by the mountain people of Chiapas. In recent years they also have established a highly successful cut flower business. The skills of the women in weaving are now recognized as a major asset and their work receives high praise in the gift and specialty shops of the area.

COLECTIVO

Incidentally, all of the above has not made either town prosperous. The people still are on the bottom rung of Mexico's economic ladder. But maybe it's a start.

The log begins at the north end of San Cristobal and we turn northeast at the signed intersection off the northern periférico toward Chamula and Zincanatan. The first sign we see after making the turn is one which forbids the taking of pictures of the people or the towns ahead. The request is a serious one, and should be respected. The road winds upward in a northerly direction.

At **1.9** miles we clear the suburbs of San Cristobal and are among scattered small houses, terraced garden plots and a healthy supply of pigs and sheep. **Inchintón** is the sign on one little group of houses. It is also signed as being part of the municipality of Chamula. The women's costumes here consist of blue skirts and rebozos.

Intersection at **2.9**. The road (left) is to Zincanatan, go (right) for Chamula. We continue on the right branch, with the other to be taken upon our return. Continue past a group of well-built homes, more garden plots and sheep. The blue clothing still predominates. In the distance there are more views of hillside farming.

An abandoned church and graveyard is on the right at **4.3**. Below is the town of **San Juan Chamula**.

At **5.3** we are parked about a hundred meters from the large open space in front of the church. It is mid-morning of Good Friday. The town is crowded with people in their best tribal dress. The walled area immediately in front of the church is the site of a ceremony depicting the last days of Christ...

We stand watching the many candles in the procession burn brightly, despite a light rain. The painted images and the music, the boughs of pine, incense and cascades of flower petals, the native costumes and the brightly-painted church all combine to make an unforgettable scene which can only be recorded in the mind.

Slowly the procession circles the courtyard and disperses, then the participants reform in a line to enter the church. *On a previous trip we were given special permission to enter the church, providing that we stayed in the rear and made no noise. The interior holds the trappings of the Catholic religion, yet it is different in many ways. The first thing of note is that there are no seats or pews. The parishioners kneel among pine branches scattered on the floor. The light inside stems only incidentally from the few small windows. Most of it comes from the hundreds of lighted candles attached to the cement floor by their own wax. The low sound of prayers in an unfamiliar language is in the background.*

MAN FROM CHAMULA

During their prayers the men occasionally reach for something from a small pile of offerings, a fruit, a small piece of bread or other edible. We are told that the sessions may last for hours and many candles burned before prayers are completed. During the ceremony we notice something which appears to be completely out of context...beside almost every offering is a **Pepsi Cola** *bottle and from time to time the men would take a swig! When we asked about it, we are told it contains a homemade alcoholic beverage,* **posh**. *Somehow, some years ago the Pepsi bottles and the firewater became part of the ceremony. Exactly where it began seems to be lost in legend, but a number of the municipalities in this portion of Chiapas have similar attachments to Pepsi Cola.* We return to our car and go back to the intersection leading to Zincanatan

Back at the intersection we take the left branch toward Zincanatan past more hillside gardens. In the uncultivated areas are oaks and an occasional pine tree.

The top of the grade comes at **1.0**, then descends toward the town. From up here we have a remarkable view off to the left. As we approach there is a distinct pinkish hue to the area surrounding the church. As we get closer the hue becomes small pink dots, then individuals with pink-colored jackets. The difference in dress between two towns, though separated by only a few kilometers, is amazing. It reenforces the differences

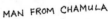

MAN FROM ZINCANATAN

brought about by being in a highly regionalized society for centuries.

We arrive at **2.4**. Aside from the differences in dress there are other dissimilarities between Chamula and Zinacantan. This town is much cleaner than Chamula...not only the streets and buildings but the people. Things here are better organized, with rather well laid-out streets, sidewalks in some places, and a church which is more traditionally maintained. (*The interior still follows the mixing of the Christian and the old religions, but in less striking ways.*) Our visit here is also on Good Friday, but the ceremonies have been completed and the town is now in a more festive mood, with booths offering foods, religious mementos, etc. We buy an *elote*, a boiled ear of corn topped with butter, salt, lime and a bit of salsa (excellent). The rain is still with us so we decided to head back to San Cristobal de Las Casas.

Return to the intersection...then to San Cristobal where it isn't raining.

We notice that the hands of the Indian women and children are never still. While walking they will be carrying a variety of things...while tending sheep they are busy carding or spinning wool, weaving the small belts and friendship bracelets later sold in the markets and along the streets of Mexico's tourist centers. It is surprising how much product is generated in this manner. And to many families it is necessary, for the challenge of adapting to a monetary society is difficult at best. Our hopes are that their children, and their children's children, will have it easier.

LIVING MAYA

MEXICO 190 — SAN CRISTOBAL — TUXTLA GUTIERREZ

When you travel from the mountain enclave of San Cristobal de Las Casas down to tropical Tuxtla Gutierrez you begin to understand why there can be such a diversity of life-styles over such a short distance, for those mountains are a true challenge. Imagine if you will, standing at the top of the canyon wall with a burro laden with everything you own. Now, nobody in their right mind would tackle that hill without the roadbed as it now stands. This is at K63, 12.5 miles from San Cristobal on Mexico 190

0.0   0.0   K83   We are on the northwest side of the city of **San Cristobal de Las Casas.** The highway to Tuxtla Gutierrez goes west out of the valley past a military camp and up a rather steep hill. There are scattered houses and a large church, along with several peach and plum orchards. (Incidentally, they begin to ripen in March.) We're seeing what might be considered to be dalmatian sheep...they're white with at least a dozen black spots scattered over their bodies and heads.

4.2   4.2   K76+   We are at the top of the pass. Then start down the other side.

2.0   6.2   K73   **Nachig.** A small Indian village offering a variety of items for sale...weavings based on their tribal costumes (a finely striped red and white hand loomed cloth which has the appearance of being pink), firewood, squash, cabbage, fruits in season, etc. *Note the many small gatherings of houses on the hillsides, sometimes far from any kind of road. This is typical of the region. In many instances the Indians choose this kind of existence as it brings them closer to their land. But even these conditions are beginning to change as the children become better educated and their awareness of the outside world increases.*

3.8   10.0   K66+   Top of the grade and the signed village of **Navenchuac**. Here is a place to stop and look down into the long and deep *barranca* (canyon). There is also a little store. *Note the houses perched on the hillsides on the opposite side of the canyon and the terraced hillsides ahead. It looks as though they've had to pack in every ounce of topsoil in order to make those few square meters of level ground.*

2.3   12.3   K63+   A cobbled entrance to a dirt road (left) leads to **Apaz** 4km. *These side roads in the Chiapas highlands often go to small communities, sometimes with completely different customs than a village only a few kilometers away. If you are of an adventurous nature and willing to respect the customs of the inhabitants, a quiet walk is sure*

373

to yield some memorable moments. Remember this means no pictures and no entry into the local churches without an OK.

0.2　12.5　K63　We begin down the southeast side of the canyon's wall. This is a spectacular descent for everyone in the car except the driver...he will have no time to look at the panorama below and on the other side of the canyon. If you do take a bus to or from San Cristobal to Tuxtla Gutierrez be sure to get a window seat on the right side going down, left going up.

1.9　14.4　K60　There is a small turnout about 300 yards beyond the K60 maker. (Note the agaves on the rocky cliff just before the turnout.) One more comes in about a half-mile, then another.

1.5　15.9　K57+　**Chainatic**, a small signed community. Here the men and women wear reddish jackets loomed by the people here. There is a mirador with a small store containing weavings. The materials are beautiful, and the view, magnificent. As we move down the mountain toward **Tuxtla Gutierrez** look across and above...there are almost solid cornfields. Again it boggles the imagination and inspires admiration for these hardy people laboring long and hard on those hillsides.

2.2　18.1　K54　A small adobe brick operation, one of a number to be seen along the roadside. We are still enjoying wide vistats off to the right as we continue winding downhill. At one point we pass a bus stop signed **Parada Piedra**.

3.8　21.9　K48　A signed graded road left to **Chiquinivalvo**.

1.9　23.8　K45　There are several small turnouts along here. Take advantage of them for a brief rest, pictures or just looking. Continue downhill.

3.1　26.9　K40　There are probably ten varieties of agaves on this stretch of highway. There are several views of the path the highway will be taking us during the next half-dozen miles on our way to the bottom of the mountain. The cliffs we are traversing on the way down are limestone, which means that this area was pushed up very very high during the formation of this portion of the earth's crust.

3.2　30.1　K35　Intersection. A road goes back sharply to **Pichucalco**. Continue straight ahead toward Tuxtla. Next comes a cardboard sign, **Rancho El Diesisiete** (Seventeen). Hopefully the ranch is more longlived than the sign is likely to be.

6.2　36.3　K25　A small turnout. **El Choreadero** is signed back sharply (right) on a paved road.

1.6　37.9　K22　Here's the bottom of that winding piece of road. We now go north past mango and lime orchards, and a growing number of small towns.

1.1　39.0　K20+　**Colonia Grijalva**, a small community on the left. We see perhaps a half-dozen ox carts in the nearby yards, plus several tethered oxen. Next **Villa de Acala** is off to the left on a paved road. Next comes the outskirts of **Chiapa de Corso**. Shortly we come to an archeological site right at the intersection where we would officially enter the downtown area. *(See Chiapas Inland.)* We continue right past the foundations.

4.0　43.0　K14+　To the left is the northern entrance into Chiapa de Corso. Continue west toward Tuxtla past many *ciruela* orchards. Another local **Pemex** follows. A four-lane road is under construction paralleling the road we are on...today confusion, tomorrow a smoother, faster ride.

3.4　46.4　K9　We cross the bridge over the **Río Grijalva.** To the right is the entrance into **Sumidero Canyon**, a national park with an unforgettable boat ride through the canyon to the large hydroelectric development at the other end. With the crossing of the bridge we are officially in the outskirts of **Tuxtla Gutierrez**. Continue west on the four-lane road past a **Pemex** and a number of businesses.

2.0　48.4　K6　An LPG station is on the left followed by the signed perifericos left and right. We continue straight toward the center of Tuxtla Gutierrez. End of Log.

TUXTLA GUTIERREZ and CHIAPA de CORZO...

It is a clean, modern city of nearly a half-million, yet it gets lost among Chiapan images of mountain pueblos peopled by descendents of the Maya. It is a prosperous city of the 90s sited at the west end of the hot central valley of Chiapas known as the Depresión Central de Chiapas. Around it are tropical forests, deep valleys and vertical canyon walls. It's numerous nearby natural attractions include several waterfalls, the kilometer-deep Sumidero Canyon and one of the world's finest zoos. Meet Tuxtla Guttierez.

The original Indian settlements were along the **Grijalva River** to the east of today's Tuxtla. The name **Tuxtla** is from the Indian, meaning place of rabbits. The image continues as rabbit is featured in some markets, and a version of rabbit stew, *sihuamont*, is considered a regional specialty.

The name **Guttierez** was added in 1852 to commemorate the liberal patriot, Joaquín Miguel Gutierrez. Gutierrez was one of those instrumental in bringing the Chiapas region of Guatemala into Mexico's fledgling republic in 1824. Several years later Gutierrez died when he threw himself off the cathedral tower to avoid being taken prisoner by conservative government forces.

As the fertile central valley area of Chiapas developed, Tuxtla Gutierrez gained in size and stature until it was named the state capital in 1892. Today as a distribution hub for major portions of the country's tobacco, chocolate and coffee industries, plus corn, tropical fruits, cattle and forest products, the city has become one of Mexico's principal commercial and political centers.

Despite those credentials, few think of Tuxtla as a major touristc destination, and it probably never will be. Yet within the city and adjoining area lies the essence of the land and the people who make up this unique state which geographically, ethnically and historically is closer to Guatemala and Central America than it is to Mexico.

After several visits to Tuxtla we're prepared to suggest a rather busy two-day itinerary of what to see and do. A weekend is preferable for there are more things going on...

Plan for a mid-morning arrival at the central plaza in nearby **Chiapa de Corzo**. Once parked there is no need to move for the rest of the day...

Historically Chiapa de Corzo dates back to the mid-16th century when the Spaniards perceived a strategic importance and built a church and administration buildings around a large plaza. They also erected a unique brick fountain which is in the form of the crown of the King of Spain. It is remarkably preserved and dominates the plaza. Some of the other early buildings now contain shops offering the work of local artisans, much of which is rarely found outside of Chiapa de Corzo. Items warranting a good look include woodcarvings in a wide variety of woods, subjects and sizes. The quality is excellent and several of our favorite Mexican carvings have come from here.

CHIAPA DE CORZO

Another group of *artesenías* showing remarkable talent are those who, using brightly-colored lacquers, transform ordinary gourds into valuable pieces. The process is unique to the area and is taught in the school connected to the *Museo de Laca*. The school and museum are located at the northeast corner of the plaza. Some of the best work of the students and teachers are for sale here.

There are generous supplies of regional clothing and dolls, much of it relating to the dances and processions of **Los Parachicos** (For the Children). *The Parachico is a January festival relating to the giving of food during colonial times to the hungry by the maids of a very wealthy woman. In it, boys masked and wearing a white ixtle-fibre wigs dance with girls wearing beautiful flowered dresses. The dances take place on the 15th, 17th and 20th of January, though **folklorico** shows featuring Parachicos are performed throughout the year* *here and in Tuxtla Guttierez.*

It is a short walk from the plaza to the broad Grijalva River where launches take passengers down river into the Sumidero Canyon, one of the narrowest and highest river gorges in the world.

The attraction is a recent one as it was not until the 240 meter-high Chicoasen dam was completed in 1981 and the lake covered the canyon's impassable cataracts, that the trip became possible. The speedy boats cover the canyon's 20-plus kilometers, and back—photo stops included—in about 2 hours.

SUMIDERO CANYON

The boats also takes passengers to small riverside beaches. On holidays many family picnics are celebrated in this manner. The landing area has gathered around itself a lively group of restaurants featuring a variety of menus. Several also have *marimbas* and guitars going full blast on weekends and holidays. A snack and a few spirited tunes make a pleasant break after the canyon trip.

A return to Tuxtla leaves enough time to check out the *Museo Regional de Chiapas* located in the new museum/theater/park complex called *Parque Madero* in the north east section of the city. The museum is particularly well done, with fine exhibits of Mayan artifacts, colonial pieces and a good collection of costumes and handicrafts.

A salon is set aside for traveling exhibits from the nation and the world. This time there are turn-of-the-century photographs from several of the Indian villages. Beyond the museum is the **Teatro de la Ciudád**, a public swimming pool, and a children's park.

For those with the time and the interest, a botanical garden is located nearby with a wide selection of jungle plants labeled not only as to their name, but their industrial and medicinal uses.

An early evening visit to the *zocalo* at **San Marcos Cathedral** in the central district is a treat. Here, under numerous Indian laurel trees trimmed into huge umbrella-like shades, food and toy vendors have staked out territory and are looking for customers. It is a family activity, with weekends a melting pot of cultures. The open air restaurants around the square are busy serving everything from icy *jamaica* to steaming pizzas. The cathedral's bell tower gets into the picture by putting on an hourly parade of apostles accompanied by tunes played with its 48 bells.

Four blocks east of the zocalo along Calle Centro is the **Restaurant Las Pichanchas**. Highly regarded for its regional dishes, it has a pleasant courtyard setting. There is nightly marimba music, while *Parachico* dancers are featured on Thursdays, Fridays and Saturdays.

Given the energy, get an early start—at the gate by 8:30—for the **Parque Zoologico Miguel Alvarez del Toro**. It is a winner. Sited in the *bosque*, or forest, on a hillside just off the south *periférico*. The turnoffs are well signed.

The zoo is rated among the finest regional zoos in the world, and the early start allows the viewing of most of the animals in an active state before the heat sends them, and you, to cover. The animals are in large natural enclosures, with the presentation of the spotted and black jaguars and the puma particularly impressive. On the other end of the spectrum, the spider and insect displays were fascinating. Of special interest are the large diagrams showing their anatomy and how they make the webs.

The zoo features only those animals indigenous to Chiapas, and fittingly so because, Chiapas has the highest concentration of animal species in North America due to its wide range of environments. One figure impressed us particularly...there are more than 1200 varieties of butterflies flitting around Chiapas! Allow at least 2 hours, 3 or more if you are a zoo-buff. Incidentally, the admission is free but there is a donation box.

Now, how about lunch. In the restaurant *El Mixiote* we feel we have located one of

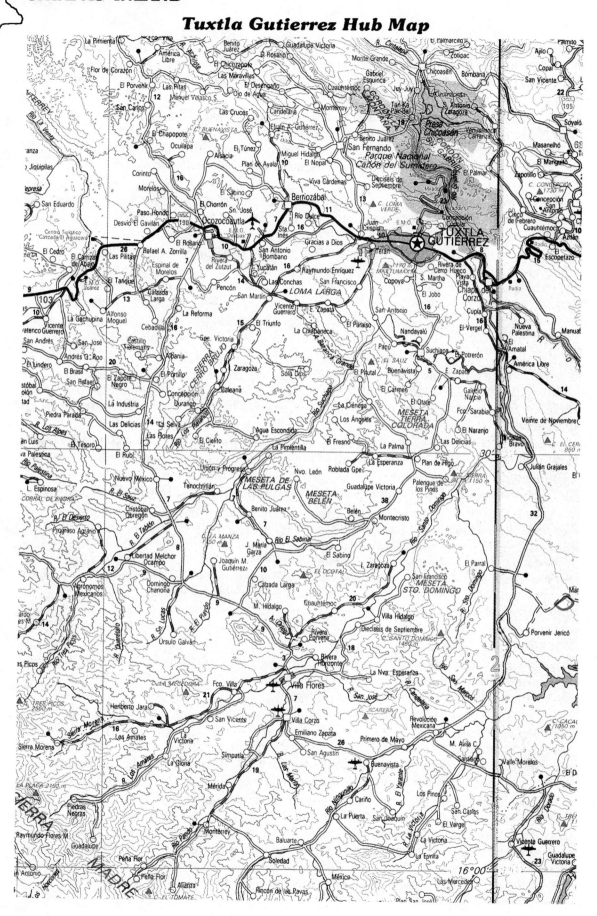

the best midday restaurants in town if you are interested in typical Chiapan meals centered around lamb and chicken. The place is small, family run and in a residential portion of Tuxtla. Everything is very good and reasonably priced, with the lamb *barbacoa* plate getting a top rating.

The tip came from a taxi driver who said that every taxi driver knew where it was. Well not exactly...it took four tries before a driver was located that did know how to get to **El Mixiote**. His name is **Jorge Limón** and he's a fountain of information about things to do and see. He even gave us his home address and phone number in case we needed anything!

El Mixiote's address is Calle San Martin #6 in Colonia Santa Ana in the southeast part of the city. It is open Saturday and Sunday (with special dishes on Sunday) from 7am to 5pm. Tuesday through Friday it's 9am till 5pm. Are they successful? How about the fact that they cook and serve as many as 25 lambs on a Sunday.

For another midday restaurant we found the *La Palapa de Amado* near the east end of the south *periférico* a fine alternate. La Palapa is a huge open-air affair serving seafood and *carnes* (meats). The atmosphere is family-oriented with lively music and a small dance floor. They close at 6 o'clock.

For the dedicated handicraft hunter, here are two more places to squeeze in somewhere...

1) The central market is located three blocks south of the cathedral and *zocalo*. As expected, there are many booths offering a wide variety of fruits, vegetables, meats and household essentials, including baskets and pottery. The mood and excitement of the typical Mexican marketplace is here at *El Mercado Central* and special can't-do-without-'em items are a likelihood.

2) Don't miss the *Instituto de la Artesanía Chiapaneca* located across the street from the **Bonampak Hotel** in the western end of the city. The operation is run by the government and features the finest work of dozens of artisan centers throughout the state. It is difficult not to buy out the store, for the prices are fair and the quality good. It is well worth a visit.

Just outside the entrance to the Instituto we ran into a Lancandón Indian who was trying to sell some clay pots he had made back home in the jungle near the old Mayan city of Bonampak. He was carrying a number of boxes tied with fibrous pieces of bark over to a bus stop. Tom, recognizing him as a Lancandón, went over to help and found out that Antonio Chun-kin had brought several months worth of clay pitchers and other handmade pieces into Tuxtla hoping that he could sell them to the gift shop.

LANCANDON MAN

The effort was unsuccessful and Antonio was preparing to get back on a bus (dozen boxes and all) for Bonampak and then a 2-day walk to his home. He showed us some of the pieces and we could understand why they didn't want them...they were very crude, but not too crude for us...we bought a jarra (pitcher) for display in our Baja home.

An excellent late afternoon destination is the *miradores* on the road along the top of **Sumidero Canyon**. To get there take the road north off the northern *periférico* where it dead-ends into the *Parque Madero*. The road winds steeply up to the edge of the canyon and the five viewpoints. At least one restaurant, the **Atalaya** serves regional and international dishes. It also has a small exhibit area and gift shop.

It was up here at the top of the cliff that the fiercely independent Chiapa Indians made their final stand against the invading Spaniards early in the 16th century. In the last prolonged battle of El Sumidero, with their backs to the precipice, they held off the Spanish with arrows and spears. The Spaniards called for their surrender, but the Chiapa refused, answering with sticks and rocks. Out of food and with no recourse other than surrender and slavery, first the wounded, then the women and children and finally the warriors threw themselves into the canyon.

378

A dinner favorite of Tuxtla resident and good friend, **Laura Camacho Diaz**, is the **Los Arcos Restaurant**. It is located at the corner of 7th and Central Poinente. It specializes in Chiapaneco cuisine right out of the countryside. We found it rich, tasty and spicy.

Laura also has a sleeper...a hotdog cart which sets up shop every evening at 5pm just south of the Los Arcos on 7th. It has no name but **Pancho** is the chief cook and bottle washer—actually he has two helpers. He usually has a crowd around right up until he closes. Laura claims that he makes the best hotdogs in Mexico. We'll try him next time.

Laura also filled us in on a couple of the local drinks which can be ordered in many of the local restaurants. **Bozol** *is* **masa** *(corn meal) mixed with water and sugar. It is sometimes flavored with cinnamon.* **Tazcalate** *is a mixture of ground, toasted corn, cocoa and achiote chile mixed with hot water or milk. The bozol didn't do it for Tom, but the tazcalate was good for a second cup.*

Now, as to places to stay. We've overnighted in Tuxtla four times with the following results....

The trailer park on the grounds of the **Hotel Hacienda** is minimal, and we look to it being phased out, but today it is the only game in town. It is located at the western *glorieta* where the *perifericos* rejoin Mexico 190.

*Rooms (**cuartos** or **habitaciones**) **con clima** means airconditioned in this part of Mexico. Generally speaking, from Mazatlán north, the word is* **airecondicionado**.

On the hotel side we found the downtown **Gran Hotel Humberto** to be noisy, not too clean and overpriced. If you want to stay in the downtown area the **Maria Elena** and **Avenida** are possibilities at a lower price and appear better organized. After that one night we opted for something quieter out of the downtown area.

Once past the above-mentioned western *glorieta* we found better accommodations and values in the hotels **Flamboyant** and the **Arecas**. Across the divided highway from each other they both have pools, good food and clean rooms with *climas*.. The Arecas is less expensive and has a disco. *Friday and Saturday nights it booms out, so ask for a room in the rear. Then it's no problem.*

Those Red-Flower Trees...

The flame tree (*arbol de fuego*), also known as *flamboyant* and *tabachín* tree is a native of Mexico...its pods can be as long as 2 feet. When dry, they rattle and are a popular souvenir. Their bright red flowers begin in late spring and continue through summer.

Several hotels visited but not stayed in include the **Bonampak** near the tourist office and artisan center. There is a good kitchen and some fine *folklorico* entertainment. Another impressive one is the **Real de Tuxla**. It is located on the main street, **Calle Central** to the east of the city center and is popular with tour groups.

Miscellany: There are two waterfalls in the area, **El Chorreadero** (The River-runner) and **El Aguacero** (The Downpour) on the **La Venta** River 53 kilometers west of Tuxtla off Highway 190 between **Ocozocoautla** and **Cintalapa**. Flights can be arranged to **Palenque, Bonampak, Yaxchilan, Montebello Lakes, Presa de la Angostura** and **Presa Netzahualcoyotl**. Check at the airport.

MEXICO 190 -- TUXTLA GUTIERREZ — SAN PEDRO TAPANATEPEC

*Here, between the long valley which spawned Tuxtla and the broad coastal belt lies a formidable range of mountains, the **Sierra Madre del Sur**. These rugged mountains had a profound influence on the integration of the people of this part of Mexico into the country's economic mainstream.*

0.0   0.0   K150+   There is a full service **Pemex** as we leave the *glorieta* on Mexico 190 at the west end of **Tuxtla Gutierrez**. This is the point where the periférico come in. *If you get on the north periférico...you will find a **Blanco** supermarket to the east of the Madero Park complex. The selection is great...even frozen green peas and sticks of imported Italian salami.* We head due west past the hotels **Flamboyant** (left) and the **Arecas** (right). Just beyond the hotels are a number of luxury homes.

2.3   2.3   K147   The road (right) is signed to **Chicohasen** as we begin a gentle climb west out of the valley.

1.9   4.2   K144   The road divides...passenger traffic is directed to take the left branch, a wide roadbed with ample shoulders.

1.0   5.2   K142   A house on the right has several dozen piles of white-painted rocks scattered around the yard. We know not why.

5.3   10.5   K134   Intersection. We go left on what appears to be a bypass of the airport and head toward **Ocozocoautla**, a lumber, livestock and dairy products center. Here the road loses its extra width and its shoulders. We now wind through low hills past something of a first...a number of long, rock walls. *The walls are beautiful. The mason's work must have gotten him more jobs, or imitators, for there are a number along here.*

2.9   13.4   K129   We come to a Y in the road. The signed road (left) is to **Cintalapa** while the (right) branch is back toward the airport and Tuxtla Gutierrez. *We are being issued a new set of K markers while on this Ocozocoautla bypass. (Our confusion level was so high we discarded them and will resume at the other end of the bypass.)* After the intersection we wind down into the valley below. *Note that the sedimentary layers of rocks in the cuts for the highway are horizontal and unbroken...indicating that this portion of the earth's crust has come from the ocean's depth to this 3000-foot plateau with a minimum of disruption.*

4.7   18.1   K124   Pass a local **Pemex** and go north and west through the southern portion of **Ocozocoautla**.

2.1   20.2   K120+   Another road (right) to Ocozocoautla. Continue west and back onto the regular Mexico 190 route.

5.4   25.6   K112   Signed settlement of **Rivera El Gavilán**. We are going by here shortly after the region has been set afire in order to clear the land, control the brush and encourage the growth of grasses. *This is common practice throughout Mexico and it helps make April and May the hazy months along Mexico's southwest coast. Controlled burning has been practiced by civilizations throughout the world for millennia. (Not only did the Australian aborigines burn the forest grasses thousands of years ago, but today's Aussies are world leaders in the practice.)*

Strangely, the United States is only awakening to this method of modern (ancient) forest management. Our scientists are now beginning to experiment with this type of "preventive maintenance" in our national forests. Maybe with too many of us, Smokey (The?) Bear lives on. We continue to wind west.

5.5   31.1   K103   We complete a short climb to a low crest, then down about a mile later toward a large valley.

5.1   36.2   K95   The road continues to twist and turn down the face of the bluff toward the valley. At the bottom we cross the **Puente Rogelio Anza**. The craggy mountain off to the right is 4000-foot **Cerro La Puerta**.

5.0   41.2   K87   We come around a hill and are greeted by a wide panorama of mountains and m*esas* (tabletop plateaus) to the south and west.

1.0   42.2   K85+   **Jiquipilas** is the small town off to the left on a paved road. The granitic rocks along here are a somewhat unusual rose color. Next comes another road into Jiquipilas, then a bridge, **Puente La Cintal** over a broad *arroyo seco* and past a truck-stop restaurant, **Las Vegas**.

4.3   46.5   K78+   An **LPG** station, then the entrance (north) into **Cintalpa**, a small city of about 15,000. The restaurant **Don Gabi** is next. We squeeze in with a group of truck drivers for breakfast. They all know where California is, but not one can pinpoint Huntington Beach. A good breakfast and they make their own *chorizo*.

0.9   47.4   K77   A local **Pemex**, then another just down the highway. The town overhangs a bit onto the south side of the road. Most of the homes are adobe with tile roofs.

4.5   51.9   K70   The road begins to climb as we enter the rolling hills. Continue in a westerly direction.

3.8   55.7   K64   This small settlement is signed as **Colonia Lázaro Cárdenas**. The buildings are painted white or light pastels...most picturesque with their tile roofs. There is a small *zocalo* on the left. We see a large sign offering *quesos* for sale. This portion of Mexico 190 is gratefully straight. The tall mountain to the north is 5000-foot **Cerro Cachimba de Oro**.

4.3   60.0   K57   Intersection with Mexico 195. The road (left) goes almost due south to **Arriaga** on Mexico 200. **(See Chiapas Inland.)** We continue straight southwest toward **San Pedro Tepantepec**.

A bit of commentary on the highway ahead...the last 40 kilometers of Mexico 190 before it enters Tepantepec is very winding at best, and it is currently undergoing a major reconstruction program due to a deluge associated with a late-summer, 1989, hurricane. We found it barely passable in February 1990, but better in May. There is still work to be done. We recommend Mexico 195 south to Mexico 200, then west to Tepantepec as the way to go. As we've taken the road twice, we pass on the log for this portion of Mexico 190 for those who wish to take the "shortcut." Mexico 190 continues straight in a southwesterly direction

4.4   64.4   K50   High on the hill to the left is one of the *microondas* stations, **Villa Morelos**.

5.0   69.4   K42   We come to a network of canals and large irrigated fields. Note that oxen are common power sources through here. The road makes a turn after some miles of going straight. Next comes a bridge over the **Río Macuilapa**.

1.2   70.6   K40   We have started climbing into the foothills. The small arroyos between the hills are well stocked with *huanacaxtle* trees of varying sizes.

0.9   71.5   K38+   To the left is the very tiny signed community of **El Horizonte**, which doesn't show on any of our maps. We are climbing toward the crest of this small group of low mountains, **Sierra La Jineta**.

1.4   72.9   K36   We come into a few pines, then go around a corner to see several small lakes and a sizeable village below on the left. Next comes a paved/unpaved road (left) into the village. There is a livestock inspection station on the right. You must have your cows, horses, goats and sheep inspected here.

2.2   75.1   K32+   We have been going through pines, mesquite, a few *agave* and *higueras*, then a surprise...a small marginal hotel with lots of hammocks hanging out in front. It looks to have more hammocks than rooms. There is also a small restaurant.

1.1   76.2   K31   Here is a view of a very large monolithic hunk of granite extending several hundred feet above the material which has sloughed off of its sides over the millennia. Note how the farmers plant corn right up to the bottom of the cliff. We continue toward the ocean on a Pacific-facing watershed.

2.6   78.8   K27   A local **Pemex**, then we are a short distance from the **Oaxacan** border in **Rizo de Oro**. There are a couple of small restaurants just past the gas station. We leave town and head up another canyon. After reaching the top we start down toward the Pacific side of the sierra. *Check your brakes and plan to use engine compression to ease their burden.*

3.7   82.5   K21   There is a turnout here offering a fine view of the Pacific Ocean and the broad plain some 3000 feet below. We continue to wind abruptly through one small canyon after another, many of which show signs of damage from the giant rainstorm mentioned earlier.

0.7   83.2   K20   We come onto the **Puente Umoa**, a bridge built after the previous one disappeared. *We strongly suggest that this road is best taken from top to bottom because the incline is prolonged enough that overheating could be a problem and there are few turnouts. Also, uphill traffic can be very, very slow due to trucks and busses.*

1.1   84.3   K18   On the side of the hill is another variety of agave. It is narrow-leafed, very "spiky" and about 3 feet in diameter with a tendency to turn reddish. Continue toward the valley below. The scars from the 1989 floods will be obvious here for many years to come. It gives one an idea of the power of the crippling Hurricane Hugo. Continue dropping toward the wide valley below and **San Pedro Tapanatepec**.

6.5   90.8   K8   The road follows several stream beds as they drop through the foothills toward the valley below. Then comes a *parada* (bus stop) signed **Las Minas**.

1.9   92.7   K5   We're almost down and about to be swallowed up in a sea of mango trees.

1.8   94.5   K2   Intersection with Mexico 200 in the outskirts of **San Pedro Tapanatepec**.

End of log.

MEXICO 195 NORTH OF TUXTLA INTO ARRIAGA

One might look on this log as one of an alternate route because of the mountain range to the west. It was difficult to build a road through and is prone to heavy rains. Thus, if we continue on Mexico 195, we are less likely to encounter problems with the highway.

0.0   0.0   K0   We turn left off Mexico 190 at K57 onto Mexico 195. The road takes off almost due south toward **Arriaga**, on Mexico 200, but about 50 kilometers south of **San Pedro Tepantepec**. *This road is faster and with less kilometers of winding road, but if you are heading north it is 40 kilometers longer.*

0.7   0.7   K1   The road proceeds straight through a long valley broken slightly by small hills. The area appears to be dry-farmed, principally for corn.

3.4   4.1   K6+   A beautiful home on the left with the name, **El Carrizál**. Note the wide verandas on this and other homes in the area.

2.0   6.1   K10   The land is barren, with only an occasional *higuera* (wild fig) or *huanacaxtle* tree breaking the monotony of low scrub and grass.

2.6   8.7   K14   The community of **Nuevo Chiapas**. At the moment of our passing, a red-hot soccer game is going on in the field adjoining the highway. We next cross a small bridge over a stream and start to climb out of this valley and into another, higher one. As we pass the fields we see a number of oxen being worked, either plowing or pulling wooden-wheeled carts. *You surely will need to know that the heavy wooden yokes come in two basic sizes...the smaller one is used for plowing while the larger, wider version is for pulling carts and range in cost from $40 to $75. (You won't find that in any other guide book!)*

4.1   12.8   K20+   The road begins to wind and enters foothills leading to yet another valley. Again, corn is the name of the game.

1.9   14.7   K23+   **Tiltepec** is the signed community off to the right. The principal landmarks here are the tepee *bodegas*, or warehouses. The next community, **Ejido Tierra y Libertad**, has them too. The hotel/restaurant **Santa Cruz** is on the right in case you get stuck. Toward the west end of town on the left is a church, *zocalo* and basketball court.

2.0   16.7   K27   A paved intersection (left) is to **Villaflores**. We are now climbing at a good rate and can see pine trees ahead.

1.8   18.5   K29+   There is a small chapel on a rise at **La Sepulcura**. Continue westward and begin descending into a canyon...and it is some canyon. The sides are steep with many pines. We can also see vertical cliffs and occasional smaller canyons. This road also took a beating from the deluge of 1989 but the amount of mountain terrain we traverse on this road over the other, Mexico 195, makes it much easier.

3.5   22.0   K35   A small signed community of **Monte Bonito**. We continue to drop and wind, crossing a small stream bed and past a roadside shrine.

2.4   24.4   K39   We have just about cleared the canyon and are now in the flood plain. How long the piles of tree trunks will remain is moot...today they are here, eight months after the flood. A number of the hillsides show huge pale scars where landslides have cleared away all cover.

3.8   28.2   K45   The stream bed on the left is attractive with a good amount of water tumbling past logs and boulders.

1.4   29.6   K47   We've entered the outskirts of **Arriaga** and are at the intersect with Mexico 200. To the left is **Puerto Arista** and points south while the right turn takes us toward **Salina Cruz, Oaxaca**.

End of log.

Puerto Arista...

Puerto Arista is considered the finest ocean beach in the state of Chiapas. (In fact, it and Paredón are the only beaches we are covering in Chiapas. Puerto Madero was described by several well-traveled Tuxtla residents as not being worth the long drive for the beach...though it is a major shipping port, so we've skipped it.)

About two long hours from Tuxtla Guttierez, Puerto Arista is on the minds of many Tuxtlans during the hot and humid rainy months. "**Vamos a Arista**," becomes a rallying cry to help people survive until the next weekend or holiday period.

Unfortunately for Puerto Arista, not many come the rest of the time, making the resort business here a particularly difficult chore. Fully two thirds of the tourism comes during the two-week Christmas holiday period, the 14 days centered about Easter and a half-dozen three day holiday weekends. The rest of the year is a time of survival until the next holiday. To those of us who drive to Mexico and want a taste of a true, ungringoized Mexican beach resort, Arista is one to check out. We found it frayed around the edges and a bit faded, but charming and very inexpensive.

0.0   0.0   K0   At the signed intersection at K73 on Mexico 200 below **Tonalá** we go west to **Puerto Arista** while Mexico 200 curves to the southeast.

1.4   1.4   K2   A railroad crossing.

1.9   3.3   K5   The impressive entrance into **Rancho Nueva Roma** is on the left, a large cattle ranch.

1.9   5.2   K8   The farmers are busy along here with sugar cane, mangoes, bananas and a few papayas, plus scattered pastures for beef and dairy herds.

2.4   7.6   K12   **Colonia 20 de Noviembre**, a small signed community. Kids are everywhere, working on their national pastime...soccer. Watch for darting youngsters as much of the action takes place near the highway. *Huanacaxtle*, *higuera* and the small fan palms dominate the plant scene after the few acres of mangoes near town are passed.

0.8   8.4   K13   More Simmental cattle in rich, green pastures. There are a few trees spotted around, probably to provide shade. Shortly, we see shrimp ponds on the right. *Though not yet in full production, the locals are optimistic that the new industry will give a boost to their flagging economy.*

1.3   9.7   K15   A paved road east extends for 12 kilometers to **Belisario Dominguez**, then another 24K of dirt past a half-dozen other little fishing colonies. *All are sited along the inland margins of a very long and narrow lagoon, thus offering limited ocean access.* We continue a short distance, then cross a small bridge over that narrow lagoon.

1.3   11.0   K17   Enter **Puerto Arista** at the lighthouse. Our stay is at the **Bugambilas**, the only place in town less than 10 years old. And the only one with *clima*, air conditioning. It was not necessary this time, but we hear it is usually needed in Arista.

The town is arranged along about a mile of beachfront, with another mile of homes, partial homes or vacant lots split between each end.

The town is nearly empty. During our stay (a weekend in mid-February) we share the 24-room Bugambilas with 2 families and 2 couples. The **Puesta del Sol** restaurant is supposed to the be the best in town, yet we didn't eat there because at 8-pm on a Saturday night there is nobody in the place and they are stacking the chairs. The only action is at a little *carnes asadas* street stand a half-block back from the empty restaurants. We get in line with the locals, grab a table and have a choice of beef, pork, liver and *tripa de leche* tacos with **Superiór**, **Tecate** or **Dos Equis** to wash it down. Marvelous.

The beach at Arista is one of those horizon-to-horizon kind that take your breath away. It really does disappear into the line where the earth meets the sky on both ends. The waves are generally large due to the weather conditions of this part of Mexico and its south-facing position. Heavy storms are common during the summer rainy season, May—October.

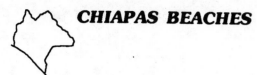

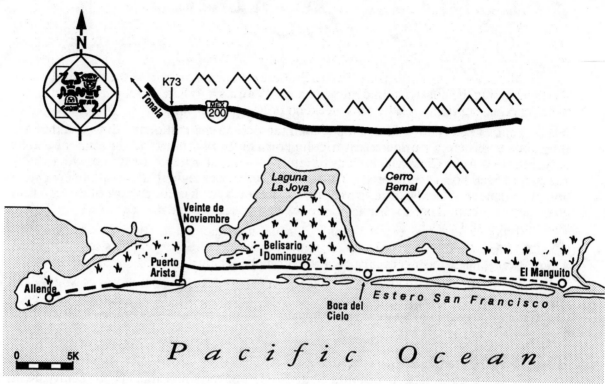

During the season shrimp trawlers often anchor a half-mile offshore and sell to those sturdy enough to go out through the surf in *pangas* to get them. Net fishermen place gill nets perpendicular to the shore and bring in a variety of species. The most common is *bagre*, or catfish, which spawns in the lagoons behind the long beach and moves into the sea to grow. And grow they do...the ones we checked weighed between 4 and 10 pounds.

Another fish taken in quantity, particularly during the early rainy season (June-July) is the black snook. These also come from the lagoons and range to 10 pounds. Sportfishing here from the beach is unknown, with only a few of the residents using handlines when the fish are especially plentiful and they don't want to set a net.

Our stay in Puerto Arista has been relaxing and interesting-we would come back again, given the opportunity. Back to Mexico 200.

BROTHER & SISTER

BEYOND THE BORDER...

Some of the reasons for Tom's leaving the coat-and-tie-nine-to-five world of engineering in the early 70s are outlined over the next few pages under the categories of **Beaches, Fishing, Handicrafts, Fiestas** *and, eventually,* **Retiring in Mexico.**

THE BEACHES OF MEXICO WEST...

It is not often that a beach will get past us without being given at least a cursory inspection and rating for a return trip. Given the time, Tom will come up with a detailed inventory of the flotsam and jetsam deposited on a given beach and the animals inhabiting its margins. Within an hour he will have returned with an armload or two of wood and a pocket full of shells and pebbles. He will have also staked out several likely surf-fishing spots and if needed, will bring back a fish or two for dinner. Tom has spent most of his free time since childhood doing just what he does now, and never tires of it.

Where Baja beaches are big on shells and not much on driftwood, Mexico's west coast beaches are the opposite and our reports reflect it. From toothpicks to entire trees, Mexico West has it, especially the beaches of Michoacan.

Shell collectors will find their avocation best served along the shores of Sonora and Sinaloa with various augers, clams and snails fairly common. We have directed a good portion of the roadlogs to the exploration of Mexico's marvelous beaches. We have let those logs do most of the talking.

THE FISHING...

There is little question that nearly anywhere you go along Mexico's coast line, if you can get to the water you can get to fish. Certainly some spots are better than others, the Baja peninsula and the Michoacan coast for example, but fishing of one kind or another is available almost anywhere. And we've tried to keep track as we go.

Go Easy on the Tackle...

A long time ago we gave up on taking a ton of tackle because, after packing it all along we'd still end up without some "essential" item. Over the years we've boiled it down to the following, keeping in mind that surf fishing is a favorite method.

For the beaches we have settled on seven-foot spinning rods and reels designed to handle up to 10-pound test line and lures to two ounces. The fish we are looking for with this gear rarely exceed five pounds and are less than 50 yards from the shore. Much of the usage will be with small lead weights and hooks baited with sand crabs or other edibles.

For inshore panga fishing we carry six-foot jig rods and conventional reels designed for 20 to 40-pound test lines and they do a fine job on 95% of the fish we might take. Most of the fishing effort will be through trolling, thus feathers and Rapala-type lures are a must. Drifting and casting, especially yo-yoing around reefs, are still new to most fishing guides along this coast, but we've found the iron and Scampi-type lures effective throughout the area when we've used our own boat or found an understanding guide.

It is not necessary to bring heavy tackle in case you decide to go marlin fishing, as it is now standard equipment in most tourist areas. The serious billfisherman, however, will still want to bring his own gear, with fresh, lighter line and smooth-working drags.

Fishing tackle stores have yet to make much of an appearance in Mexico West so plan to bring whatever terminal tackle you might need.

A short check list should include hooks with wire leaders and a few short wire leaders for use with jigs along with plenty of regular hooks in a variety of sizes. There are a lot of "toothy" fish around, ready to slash even the heaviest monofilament.

You are likely to come up with many types of fish that you have never seen before, plus the more familiar species. For identification, one book we'd suggest is **Angler's Guide to Baja California.** (See **More Information?...**)

DIVING MEXICO WEST...

The reefs and coves along Mexico's west coast number among the premier places in the world for the diver. Hundreds of species of sealife may be found in sometimes bewildering abundance. There are, however, several restrictions that must be heeded.

1) It is illegal to possess a speargun if you are using Scuba equipment; however, it is permissible to use one when free diving (but not CO2-powered.)

2) You may not take lobster, abalone, pearl oysters or cabrilla.

3) It is necessary to have a valid Mexican fishing license in order to take any form of sealife by any method.

The rules are not strictly enforced, but when they are, the penalties can be severe, so confine most of your activities to looking.

SURFING AND WINDSURFING...

Judging from the number of surfboards seen year around along Mexico West's roads and beaches, it is obvious that this sport is here to stay. Mexico is truly the home of the "endless summer". Also growing rapidly is the subculture of windsurfing. Though their needs are a bit different - reliable breezes and small waves - they too are finding their version of year-around action.

Some of the more out-of-the-way breaks are listed as we visit the beaches of Mexico West. Some are nameless, others well publicized, and all offer good breaks at times during the year. From what we saw, the coastal points of Michoacan will be of particular interest to surfers.

MEXICAN ARTS AND CRAFTS...

One of our fascinations with Mexico comes through the wonderful handmade hardware, utensils and clothing found throughout the country. We make mention of many out-of-the-way marketplaces and artisan centers in the road logs, whether it be a village or an individual home. Here we step into a world of traditions dating back to pre-hispanic days. The beautiful pots that we see as art are cooking soups in a Mexican kitchen while treasured hand woven baskets stand outside the door filled with produce for the morrow's market day.

The marketplace provides an exciting, vibrant glimpse of Mexican life and an excellent place to find unique crafts such as baskets, brooms and blankets, serapes, sandals and shawls, rugs, pottery, hammocks and wood carvings. We've purchased a wooden washboard in a *mercado central*, and use it as a large platter. Carved *masa* containers have become salad bowls and chile baskets, laundry hampers. The man living next door to a small museum in Colima made us a figurine in the manner of the early people and we treasure it highly. Carved burro saddles and ox yokes, handmade ropes and chairs from palm fronds, they all have a value to many of us other than their original intent. We find it part of the charm, and the excitement, of a week, a month or a year exploring the backstreets of Mexico. We hope you'll come along.

FIESTAS

Some years ago, Carl Franz, author of that marvelous book, **The People's Guide To Mexico**, got enthusiastic about doing a book on the fiestas of Mexico. His first step was to contact the Department of Tourism for a list. The answer caused him to rethink the whole project...there are between 5,000 and 6,000 specific, documented *fiestas* in Mexico each year!

Suffice it to say that this is a land of celebrations and each day has a fistful of *fiestas* waiting and ready. National holidays and saint's days, weddings and anniversaries, births and deaths. The visitor need only to stop, look and listen. He will rarely be disappointed.

A typical *fiesta* may go something like this...

It starts with a parade led by decorated trucks full of children portraying the reason for the celebration. Whether it be Pancho Villa's birthday or the Day of the Virgin of Guadalupe, the children will be in costume, complete with rouge, lipstick and painted mustaches. Then come more kids packed into and on-top-of pickups, taxis, tractors and horses. Stir in some cheer leaders and a band or two (lacking a band, a ghetto blaster with fresh batteries) and march them around town to end up in front of the church or city hall.

Later come the *charredas* (rodeos), bullfights and *palenques* (cockfights). The plaza is decorated with streamers and colored lights. The air is filled with the smells of steaming *tamales* and *elotes*, savory tacos with char-broiled beef and pork, potato chips, hot dogs, cotton candy and mangoes on a stick. For the thirsty there are limitless servings of *aquas frescas*, sodas and beer.

Music and happy voices highlight the food, the confetti and the glitter...until the fireworks. And these are not ordinary fireworks, but a pyrotechnic display designed and supervised by the local *maestro*, or expert. Near the end of the evening, after an appropriate speech or introduction, someone lights the fuse and the skeletal bamboo frame with its pinwheels and rockets, sparklers and firecrackers comes to life. Sparks fly and the children dance with excitement.

THE MAN WITH THE MATCH...

Fireworks all over the world tend to have their own individualistic styles, their favorite kinds of noisy, spitting and sputtering displays, and Mexico is no exception. Though the following happened in Taxco, it could have been anywhere...

The end of February found us wandering south of Mexico City in a car we had rented for a few days of "just lookin'." It was late afternoon when we approached our stop for the night, Taxco. The traffic was heavy but we could think of no particular reason.

That something unusual was going on became pretty obvious when we saw a man in a business suit directing traffic! He came over, apologized for the confusion and welcomed us to Taxco.

A new kind of welcoming committee? Not really. We had lost track of the days, and it was Shrove Tuesday, the last day of Mardi Gras and Taxco was putting on a fireworks show. When our greeter found we didn't yet have a place to stay, he suggested the Santa Prisca. They had a room, and we were set for the night...and the fiesta.

After dinner the *señora* directed us to follow the crowd high up the side of the canyon to the church. As we approached a number of little stands offered tortilla-wrapped *carnes asadas*, *elotes* (steaming ears of corn slathered with thick cream, crumbled goat cheese and chili powder) and *tamales*. Tempting, but after the exertion a *cerveza* sounded better so we started following the strolling beer drinkers back to the source.

As we reached the edge of the small plaza our eyes took in a 75-foot haphazard web of bamboo, ropes, cords and wires. Attached to almost every piece of the cane edifice was some sort of pyrotechnic device, promising hundreds, maybe thousands of sparks, whistles and bangs. Kids were everywhere...their readiness for the big event being measured by a frenzy of running, jumping and yelling.

We soon found our man...tucked in a rear corner of the churchyard, he was cheerfully popping the caps from bottles of icy Superior. The demand slowed as the 9 o'clock starting time approached so he accepted our offer to buy him one. The conversation came between sips and sales of his brew. As we talked the kids kept sneaking up and taking the cardboard cartons that had contained the beer and as they did, one of the men would make a half-hearted attempt to stop them. Later we found out why.

His name is **Alberto** and he operates a local *ferretería* (hardware store) and our talk covered a variety of topics...*Taxco is indeed having a fine celebration...Tourism is down...He likes the man who is now president...He did not like the previous one...and, yes, there are too many cars in Mexico City.*

Alberto is also interested in Los Angeles...*What we think of Mexico...what ferreterias are like in the Estados Unidos, etc.*

The time, and two more rounds, go quickly. Nine o'clock has long passed...in fact it is after 10. We try to excuse ourselves (this was his round) but he waves it away, saying that the fireworks could not start until he's ready. "I have the match," he said with a smile. Then he reached into his pocket and showed us a wooden match.

A few moments later, beers in hand, Alberto escorted us under and through the tangled maze toward a flight of stairs leading to a house overlooking the churchyard. After introductions and getting us settled on the narrow lawn, our host grinned, took the match from his pocket, said, "Now we are ready," and turned on his heel to go down the stairs.

A moment later the crowd cheered as the match touched the beribboned fuse. His work done, our benefactor retires to the corner of the church to watch.

In seconds the sky above was full of streaking sparklers and bright flashes as bombs exploded, and fiery bits of paper fluttered down into the crowd.

Little by little the many twirling, jumping, whistling, spurting and exploding displays self-destructed to the delighted shouts of the crowd. Each burst of cosmic energy seemed to be presaged by about 30 suspenseful seconds of a sputtering fuse that would almost go out, then leap forward, only to almost die again. Alberto seemed to revel in the suspense.

At one point a green and white whistling pinwheel went around so fast it flew apart, showering the first few rows of onlookers. There was no panic and no apparent permanent damage, it was just part of the show. *Imagine that happening in the USA...suit-happy personal injury lawyers would be counting their fees as they ran around gathering names.* Sparks continued to fly, particularly as the upper portions of the display ignited. Now the reason for the cardboard became apparent. The kids, holding pieces over their heads, took turns running back and forth through the showers of fire.

After more than an hour and a splashy finish, in which a large crown lit up the night sky, our amigos once again went to the launchers and unleashed two last cannonades of a dozen rockets each. The explosions reverberated through the tiny valley, surely waking anyone silly enough to have already gone to bed. A wonderful evening.

Someday we will have to see how one of these pyrotechnic displays is put together. The skills that go into the design and construction of the 75-foot skeleton of bamboo, wires, ropes, cables and strings, would not appear to be part of modern technology. Just looking at it would tell you that it cannot be there any more than a bumblebee can fly...yet there it is, with a full compliment of fuses, pinwheels, fountains, rockets, etc. Truly a wonder of the ages.

With the last salvo everyone goes home happy and tired...and, as they walk back along the dark, dusty streets, the talk is of the next fiesta.

The major religious festivals celebrated in Mexico include the following... the week prior to Lent, or *Carnival*; Easter week, *Semana Santa*; the day of the Dead, *Dia de los Muertos*; the day of the Virgin of Guadalupe, *Dia de la Virgen de Guadalupe*; and the Christmas holy days, or *Návidad*.

Some of the *fiestas* are a mixture of Christian and pagan rites and vary from region to region. The stronger the Indian influence the more native costumes and dances are incorporated into the rituals. Of the nonreligious holidays the most popular takes place the night of September 15th and all of the next day, commemorating the revolution of the Mexican people against the Spaniards in 1810. As our narrative takes us through Mexico

West we've attempted to describe these and other celebrations as we've experienced them.

El Carnivál...

Carnival is a joyous, boisterous celebration that culminates on the Tuesday before the beginning of Lent (*Martes de Carnival*) in a great celebration, or *Mardi Gras*. Each village or city participates in their own traditional way.

Mazatlán's *Carnivál* is reported to be the best in the country, with parades of floats, dance groups and bands. Dancing and masked balls are everywhere. In **Manzanillo** we find similar activities on a smaller scale. In **Culiacán**, **Sinaloa**, exhibits and a variety of shows. accompany the parades, while **Acapulco** hosts national and international groups who dance through the streets in an endless parade. The elegant hotels there also have their own elaborate balls and shows.

Some of the more unusual pre-Lenten rituals are performed in several Oaxaca villages. **Pinotepa de Don Luís** has dances and costumes honoring *La Paloma*, *El Toro*, and *El Tigre*. In **Zaachila, Oaxaca**, the main event is the battle between the *curas*, priests, and the *diablos*, devils. The devils use lariats to catch the priests and the priests fight back with wooden crosses and buckets of water. Both groups wear wooden masks and when all the fighting is over the priests will have won to the delight of the onlookers. In **San Juan Chamula, Chiapas**, Indians cover themselves in *maash*, monkey hair, and wear Napoleonic type coats and caps and perform a variety of dances. Another ceremony is performed in front of the church when Indians jump through fire as an act of purification.

Easter Week...

Easter week, *Semana Santa*, is a week-long national holiday and many families take the opportunity to travel, and resorts are crowded. Religious ceremonies center around the churches and cathedrals with reenactments of the last week of the life of Jesus Christ.

As with other religious holidays where Indian cultures are still strong, the rituals carry pagan undertones In **Potam, Sonora**, the special rites are performed on the *Dias Santos*, Wednesday, Thursday and Friday. One is called *Tinieblas* (Darkness), an old Catholic ceremony where the church is darkened and chains are rattled to signify the taking of Christ. On Saturday effigies of Judas are burned while dancers perform the *Pascolas, Matachines* and *Venado* dances. In **Pinotepa de Don Luís** the Indians carry poles decorated with fruits and flowers in Good Friday processions. They also burn effigies of Judas accompanied by fireworks. *Semana Santa* in **Pinotepa Nacionál, Oaxaca**, is a week dominated by a fair attracting thousands of colorfully costumed Indians from the outlying areas. Youths called *Judios*, Jews, whitewash their bodies and carry decorated bows and arrows which they shoot into the air while chanting in Mixtec. On Good Friday the faithful don shrouds and carry huge crosses. Sunday night ceremonies include a lively dance, the *Chilenas*.

Dia de Los Muertos...

(The following account of *Dia de Los Muertos* was written by Paul "Panther" Pierce several years ago and has become a classic. We thank Paul for his permission to reprint it here.

When I am dead, meet me somewhere in Mexico in the last golden days of October. If you have coins of sorrow, spend them for candles and bring the bright orange flowers of the dead. Spread a small altar feast for hungry spirits and, with the comfortable happiness that true Mexicans share with their beloved departed, come in solemn joy to Dia de los Muertos, the great fiesta for the dead.

Down the misty pathways of the Mexican centuries have come the beliefs of three great cultures - Indian, Spanish and Mestizo. Gradually they have blended into one comfortable and comforting concept: "Life emerges from death, and death from life. The cycle is unending." There is no escaping that firm belief when October becomes November and the people celebrate Dia de los Muertos.

In ancient times, believers performed rites for returning spirits as early as the middle of October, and in remote places they still do. With Christianity, the old customs and death festivals merged with the traditions and holy days to become the solemn revelry of today, beginning with the harvest days of October and reaching its nationwide climax on All Saints Day, November 1, and all Souls Day November 2. No matter where you are in Mexico, the time will be celebrated somewhere not far away, and you shouldn't miss it, for it is an unforgettable outpouring of affection and respect for the dead.

The weeks of preparation provide a time for Mexicans to play and joke with death. Death, a friendly death, is on every hand. Bakery windows are filled with pan de los muertos, the bread of the dead, baked in the form of human and animal skeletons. Candies come in the shape of skulls, some with bright tinsel eyes. Holiday toys for children include coffins from which skeletons jump when their strings are pulled.

This is hardly worship of the dead, but rather an uncomplaining acceptance of mortality. The earliest Indians treated death as an important part of life, believing that somehow the personality continues after death in much the same way as before it.

Thus to the revelers, the dead are still one with the living, sharing the fears, the sorrows and the loves of this world, and it would be unthinkable to exclude the dear departed from the pleasures of the fiesta. So Dia de los Muertos has evolved as a blend of rituals and beliefs, a joyous folk pageant, a drama played from the hearts of the people, and a brave and eloquent statement of faith in the human continuum passed on from generation to generation.

The candlelight vigils of All Saints Day Eve or All Souls Day Eve are most important to assure that returning souls may find their way back in time for the great family feast. Long ago a multitude of candles would provide a beacon so they would not get lost. The souls of little children, inexperienced spirits that they are, may need something as visible as fireworks.

With the spirits safely back, it is time for the great climax of the fiesta. Some families have their feasts at home. In remote villages, Indians hold jungle processions, light sacred fires and give impassioned speeches to the visiting spirits. Most local residents...and a few fortunate tourists...eventually wind up at the local panteón where family members are buried. The one great tradition, subject to local variations, is that the souls of the dead must be received as honored guests. Food is always provided for the visiting souls and is served in ceremonial fashion.

Altars of food and drink called ofrendas are placed on graves, in private homes and even at memorial crosses and shrines along the road. The altars are elaborately decorated with the ubiquitous **zempasuchitl** flowers and lit with candles. The flowers resemble marigolds but are grown only to decorate the Dia de los Muertos season; their use for that purpose dates back to the days before the Spanish conquest. Some graves in first-class cemeteries have permanent shrines, but all have special altars set up for the ofrendas with fine tablecloths and dishes used only for that day. In the poorer sections of the graveyard there may be only mounds of dirt with wooden crosses, but every grave is decorated with the orange flowers, candles, or a few scattered petals if that is all the family can afford. Here and there, one sees a toy for the spirit of a child.

Outside the cemetery gate, vendors offer candles, flowers, food drinks and desserts, and people stop for snacks and lively conversation before moving on to the more subdued atmosphere within the walls. Nowhere are there signs of sorrow. The mood is reverent but lighthearted, festive but without the raucous abandon of Mardi Gras or Carnival. Priests set up outdoor altars and celebrate mass. Cash contributions buy special responsories or the blessing of a grave as the living and the dead join together for a family fiesta. Once the dead have taken their share of the food and drink in spirit, the real feast for the living begins. The rest of the day is spent in eating, drinking and remembering departed loved ones, not as they were when they were dying, but in the fullness of life.

I have been there. When I am a spirit I will be there again in the golden days when

October becomes November. There will be ofrendas, bright with zempasuchitl. I will find my way by orange petals scattered in the sunshine, or by the glow of candles in the dark.

You and I, and those we love, will be joyful as we feast on memories and drink to the good times. There is no sorrow when the spirits come, in the autumn time, to the great fiesta. Dia de Los Muertos.

(Please remember...loud voices, photography and intrusive actions are no more appropriate than they would be at a funeral or high mass...and in some places, could have disastrous results.)

Day of the Virgin and Návidad...

December 12th, the *Dia de La Virgin de Guadalupe,* is a national holiday with processions of the faithful coming in from the outlying villages to the shrines of the Virgin. As with other fiestas, there are parades, regional dances and fireworks. The children of **Acapulco** dress as Indians and join floats, musicians, and folk dancers in a parade through the streets. One of the country's most colorful celebrations takes place in **San Cristobal de Las Casas, Chiapas** where thousands of **Tzotzil** and **Tzeltal** Indians come to town wearing their hand embroidered costumes. The processions include horseback riders and carts decorated with flowers and cypress branches while musicians play marimbas and string instruments.

In some parts of the country the Christmas celebrations begin with the day of the Immaculate Conception, December 8th. The time is marked by lines of worshipers placing flowers and candles on the alter of the shrine of the Virgin. In some towns, such as **Tequila**, a fair is built around this and other activities, including cockfights, rodeos and fireworks.

December 16 to 25 brings forth nightly *posadas*...processions in which couples dressed as Joseph and Mary go through the streets singing, carrying candles and knocking on doors from time to time seeking a room for the night. At the last house or at the church, a happy fiesta ends the pilgrimage.

The evening ends when the *piñata*, a brightly-colored paper-maché figure covering a clay pot filled with candy, money, small toys or fruit, etc., is brought out for the children. Hitting and breaking that dangling effigy full of goodies is not easy, for the youngster with the stick is blindfolded and the person on the rope keeps the figure dancing, and the crowd cheering. When a solid hit finally breaks the piñata, there's a great scramble to pick up the fallen prizes.

Another Christmas tradition is the displaying of Nativity scenes...

Christmas at Christmas Bar...

The air is calm. The temperature in the high 70s. A glowing sun is readying itself to present us with another last-second green flash before retiring for this rather special evening.

It is Christmas Eve. A special Christmas Eve, for we are in a town which was named on Christmas day in the year of our Lord, 1540. As we replay our thoughts during the hypnotic moment of the green flash, the sounds of the Barra de Návidad enter our consciousness. They are Christmas carols sung in Spanish by a sizeable group of young, soprano voices...their tones melding with the lazy splash of a calm ocean.

The somewhat discordant church bells toll for the final nightly procession of La Posada in this the 449th celebration of the birth of Christ here in the community named for Him. We stand with Lupe and her family (they operate the town's top restaurant for pollo asada) and watch the procession carrying the figures of the Nativity along the malecón, around the zocalo and back to the church.

Here, the repositioning and blessing of the figurines in the Nativity scene is supervised by the priest as a choir sings softly in the background. With the last statue in place the songs are replaced by a protracted pealing of the bells, then a final round of songs and the Piñata. Yes, the Piñata, it could not be complete without the highly-decorated donkey with its stomach full of candies and a dancing desire to avoid destruction.

The parade-watchers then become the parade as they move from home to home exchanging best wishes and admiring each family's own diorama of the birth of Christ. Usually set up next to the front door and lit by candles or small lights they reflect the personalities of the family living there. Closer inspection may reveal figures of great age...we are told the ceramic kings in one scene are more than 150 years old. In another, the carved wooden pieces seem to show the wear of centuries, with bits of bright paint still clinging to some of the figures.

We stop by Anselmo's house for a toast. and a visit with his mother, sisters and the children. Angela, the lady who squeezes us a liter of orange juice every morning waves us over. We meet her mother and grandmother and drop off a couple of small bags of cookies for the children.

The encounters continue throughout the evening. Many of the people we do not know, but each smile and greeting is returned in kind. It is like being part of a family with several thousand members. The food, the favors, the toasts and the Felíz Návidads continue until we head for home and a small celebration around our own Christmas tree...a potted ficus with strings of lights and straw ornaments.

At midnight we go out on our terrace, exchange toasts and watch the fireworks. Barra de Návidad, Jalisco, Mexico, has observed its, and His, birthday, just as it has for 450 years.

Christmas Eve in **Oaxaca City** is particularly impressive. There will have been nightly *posadas* all over the city since December 16th and on the 24th a solemn torchlight procession leaves several churches carrying the Baby Jesus to the central plaza (*zocalo*), where a parade with floats circles the park. Later they return to the church to replace the Christ Child in the manger.

For many the Christmas season continues until January 6th, *Dia de Los Reyes*, when the three Wise Men (*Reyes Magos*) arrive with gifts for the Baby Jesus. That morning, the children who put out their shoes will find small gifts from the Magi, and in many towns the day is marked with cockfights, rodeos, folk dances and fireworks.

Looking for a Fiesta?...

There are few of us who can resist going to a party. And in Mexico it is a pretty easy affair...

Nearly every population center with a name, no matter how small, has a time of the year when it's citizens go all out to celebrate a day which is special to each and every resident...their ***Dia de Santa*** (Saint's Day). Sometimes lasting a week or more, the festivities usually include rodeos and cockfights and certainly, food and music, dancing and parades.

When we're in a party mood we watch for the indicators in the towns and cities as we pass. For things such as posters, balloons, a beer truck, palm-frond shelters, folding chairs around a zocalo. With luck you will come across the parade or a circus. Whatever the signs, they're worth taking a few moments to check out.

Though this list touches only a few of the thousands of celebrations, consider it a start, for the trail of the Mexican fiestas is, indeed, a happy one.

Mexico's Sleeping Policemen...

The practice of placing *topes*, or speed bumps, in and around Mexico's population centers has gained in popularity over the years.

We first became aware of the word in the Yucatan during a trip from Mérida to Chitzen Itza in the early 1970s. It seemed that almost every house had their own set, and our driver was becoming more impatient with each gearing down and reacceleration. As it turned out we all survived, even the driver, and he had regained his good humor before we got back to Mérida.

That evening we were telling the hotel manager about the many, many topes and were wondering if they were accomplishing their purpose. He replied that yes, they were doing their job...slowing traffic, particularly trucks and busses, through population centers. He added that here in the Yucatan they had a special name...*policias dormiendos* (sleeping policemen).

We've passed the name on to others over the years and it seldom fails to get a laugh and the acknowledgement that the *topes* are indeed a very efficient police force...24 hours a day.

Do's and Don'ts of Buying Property in Mexico...

Interviews with others traveling the highways of Mexico West show that many are looking to retire in Mexico. For some retirement is a reality, or nearly so. For others it is a dream helping to shape their future. We too have those dreams and anticipate making them come true some day soon.

There are a number of ways to become a Mexican resident without surrendering your American citizenship. The easiest is to merely go there and live on a tourist permit, returning every six months or less to renew your papers. Though possible everywhere, this method is particularly easy to accomplish in Baja because the peninsula is currently a "special status" zone under Mexican law. We are among the many who have established "vacation" homes in Mexico and find the procedure easy and pleasant. Under this informal, "unofficial" residency you are not allowed to work without official permission.

Should you want to work you must apply for immigrant status for an *imigrado, imigrado rentista,* or *visitante rentista* permit. Check with a Mexican Consulate as requirements change often.

Land Ownership in Mexico West...

The issues of land ownership in Mexico have been points of contention and confusion since the 1876-1910 reign of Porferio Diaz. During this time nearly 15% of Mexico's land area came to be owned by foreigners. This changed with the adoption of a new constitution following the revolution of 1910-14. Mexican law now specifically bans foreign ownership within 100 kilometers of its borders and 50 kilometers of the coasts...but there is a new and creative way to legally get around it.

In 1971 the government made it possible for foreigners to control property within the prohibited zones. The specific regulations became law in 1973 and have opened many areas for development. The tool created to accomplish this is a **"Fideicomiso"**, or beneficial trust. This provides the benefits of property ownership to the investor, while it is held in your name at a bank. The ploy meets constitutional requirements, while the purchaser has essentially the rights of ownership. The bank administers the property, paying taxes, title search, transfer fees, etc. in return for a reasonable maintenance fee. Once the fideicomiso is established you have control of the property for an apparently indefinite time in segments of 30 years duration, You can retire on it if you wish, improve the property, sell it or leave it to your heirs.

Today there are many examples of 30-year purchases of Mexican beach front property. Beginning just below San Diego at Playas de Tijuana, they extend throughout the Baja peninsula, along Mexico's west coast and the Yucatan peninsula.

Good People to Know...

Here is something you can do before leaving home which can make any search for property in Mexico a more productive one. Write to Horacio Ramirez at the address below for a list of the licensed realtors stating the area you are interested in. We've been friends for

394

years, and there's no obligation.

Mexican National Association of Realtors
PO Box 433346
San Diego, CA 92143

Thoughts on Buying Property in Mexico...

At a recent party the host's next-door neighbors had just returned from their first extended trip to Mexico. While previous forays below the border had been weekends in Ensenada and a 7-day cruise along Mexico's west coast, this time they had flown to Puerto Vallarta, stayed at a beachfront hotel, eaten at the tourist spots, sunned in perfect weather, and bought a condominium on the beach. "We're going to retire there," they announced.

The pronouncement became the topic of the evening.

The Joneses described Vallarta in glowing terms, the furnishings selected and the American colony who would soon be their neighbors. Eventually, the subject of money came up...

"It's all paid for....we got a great deal,...the salesman said prices were going up the next day,...we saved a lot of money,...we'll be living in style."

The fact that it wasn't finished didn't bother them at all..."They told us we could stay in a *corporate guest house* for a week at a time until ours is completed. And," he added brightly, "when we're not there they'll rent our unit for us and we'll make money."..."We're really lucky."

Ouch!

An update...The units were completed, but almost two years behind schedule; the guest accommodations were always "full," and they didn't get the corner unit as promised. Finally, in spite of the disappointments, the Joneses did move to Puerto Vallarta, became part of the American colony and are glad they made the move.

You may have heard similar experiences and are now shying away from thoughts of wintering or retiring in Mexico. But please don't jump to hasty conclusions, for if done right the acquisition of property in Mexico can be just as simple, straightforward and secure as a similar transaction in your home state. The illustrations below are to show what can happen, but understand that there are also many offsetting success stories.

Here we offer our set of commandments for getting a share of the **Mexican Dream**, for we believe that there is something out there for everyone with a yen for a slower, more economical lifestyle in a friendly, sunny climate...

1) When purchasing property in Mexico, hang on to your money until you know what you're getting.

The practice of paying cash up front for property in Mexico is something that foreigners do, not Mexicans. The locals make a down payment and appropriate progress payments, holding a good chunk until the transaction is complete.

Take a page out of their book and don't pay it all up front, no matter what they might say. Realistically you probably will have to make a 5% deposit to hold a particular unit for a period of say, 60 days to allow you to make a decision. This may or may not be refundable, depending upon the agreement.

Once you've decided to go for it, another payment will be appropriate, but in no way should the entire purchase price be paid until everything meets the conditions of the contract. (Keep in mind how little money changes hands until the completion of escrow in the United States and Canada. Here in Mexico you might equate the receipt of the fideicomiso to the completion of escrow. Our Mexican friends recommend that no more than 50% of the purchase price be paid prior to having the fideicomiso signed, sealed and delivered. You will also want to check carefully to see that the terms of the contract are being met. For this, we recommend consulting an attorney or notary.

If necessary, you can offer to put the balance due on the contract in a savings account requiring both signatures before it can be released. This arrangement too is perfectly legal, enforceable, and recommended by the Mexicans themselves.

2) Know the area under consideration, its weather patterns and topography. Keep in mind proximity to transportation, medical and shopping facilities. Check up on the contractors and sales agents. How do they stand in the community? Talk to others who may have bought or live nearby.

There are condominiums in Barra de Návidad, Jalisco that have been built in a coconut grove which is subject to flooding. The whole town knows it, yet the contractor built 24 units right in the middle of it, raising the level of the ground only a couple of feet as a feeble precaution.

In June of 1990 a heavy runoff overran the buildings and damaging some ground-floor units. Unfortunately, the locals say that it will happen again, and again. Our units, built in the same coconut grove, were untouched because they were built up on a walled, landfill six feet above the original level.

Now the same builder appears to be starting another 24 units in the same flood zone. Has he learned? Check back in a couple of years.

3) Don't buy the first thing you see. Nothing moves that fast, particularly if the salesperson is offering free breakfast, lunch or dinner to get you to listen to the pitch. For most of us, a house, condo or timeshare anywhere represents a major investment decision and should not be done on the spot. It pays to do your homework and look around.

Pete and Sharon first visited Cabo San Lucas on a cruise. They hired a cab and took the brief tour of the region. Back aboard their Love Boat two hours later, they compared impressions and discovered that both were silently rehearsing arguments to convince the other that they should dump their California Contemporary lifestyle and come to Cabo.

Within a couple of months they were on their way, having sold the house and quit their jobs. They now live on a sizeable piece of ground overlooking the Sea of Cortéz in a beautiful home they built themselves. Would they do it again? Without question. But maybe with a bit more preparation.

4) Purchase contracts should be in English if you are not comfortable with Spanish. If they are selling to Americans and Canadians, reputable sales agents will have legal English versions available.

*Have everything checked by an attorney (**abogado**) or notary (**notario**) before making any kind of commitment. You can also write in changes in the contract if a portion is not agreeable.*

5) Ask for your Fideicomiso, or trust ownership papers, immediately. It will take some time, but keep pushing. Anything over six months indicates that somebody is not doing their job or that something is wrong with the title. Stay in contact with your agent for progress reports and hang on to your money.

*We are part of the many who didn't give it a thought when we paid off our Barra de Návidad condominium before receiving the **fideicomiso** on the property. We had to wait more than three years for the final papers because the builder and sales agent failed to follow up. After two years the buildings had not even passed final inspection! Though it has all worked out, it has been a hassle and the delay caused many administrative problems for the complex. Next time we follow our own rules.*

6) If a unit is not completed, be sure you have in writing what it is you are getting. If stoves, refrigerators, etc. are included, settle on the additional cost. Get the makes and model numbers, and check to see that they will be adequate. Negotiate on upgraded appliances, and make any changes part of the contract. Ask that all electrical outlets be

396

grounded with double three-prong outlets installed. Lacking this, make sure that all major appliances are grounded. Water, gas and sewer installations should be carefully inspected, as Mexican contractors are often lax and building inspectors have a tendency to approve projects without checking things too closely. Before taking possession, check carefully to see that everything works

People we ran into in Oaxaca told of paying several thousand dollars for a furnishings package represented as being equivalent to that in the model unit. When they arrived in Cancun for their first extended visit, they were met with the powerful odor of gas. Despite opening the windows the smell persisted, so they went to a hotel for the night. The next day the condo operators denied that anything was their fault and refused to do anything. They wouldn't even say where the stove was purchased.

As for the refrigerator...it never got cold enough to make ice...they kept perishables in the freezer! Again no help from the management. Several hundred dollars spent on repairs didn't solve either problem and they eventually junked the stuff.

Three years after our condo was built, Carol almost became a statistic when a fan fell out of the ceiling, missing her by only a couple of seconds. A check of the others showed one to be only days from falling due to a broken and corroded bracket! A check of the fans in the other units in the complex revealed several similar deficiencies.

7) If given a completion date, get it in writing. You might even try for a penalty clause for missing the date. If you are in a hurry, a bonus for early completion sometimes works.

Most major touristic centers in Mexico have a number of partially-completed or rundown condo and timeshare facilities. Thankfully, recent, stricter regulations are making new problems less likely.

8) Don't be an absentee buyer. If your unit is under construction, frequent visits to the site will make the contractor more likely to stay on the ball. And when it is done, be there to make the final inspection.

This was a major reason why the couple we met in Oaxaca had such problems with the kitchen appliances.

9) Get acquainted with Mexico's Consumer Protection Agency, *Procuraduría Federal de Consumidor.* These are people you can go to if you have a problem which has defied solution. This does not mean that they will always make things work, but we've seen some good things happen after they have been contacted.

There are offices all over Mexico. In Guadalajara it is located at Heroes #128-1er Piso, phone 14-94-16. The one in La Paz, Baja California Sur is at Hidalgo S/n entre Aquiles Serdán y Revolución, phone 2-80-77, while the main office is in Mexico City at Carmona y Valle No.11, Colonia Doctores, Mexico, DF, Mexico. You don't even have to file your grievances in Mexico, your nearest Mexican Consulate can act in your behalf. There are special forms which have to be filled wherever you file, thus a visit or letter first is appropriate. Then, when filing, be sure to include copies of all of papers pertinent to the case.

We learned about these people when trying to complete the paperwork on our Baja homesite. They reviewed all of our paperwork and showed us how we could speed up the process, and it has worked nicely. A success story for the ninth commandment.

10) The tenth commandment is to go back and reread the first commandment.

There is no need to let the above intimidate you for when given the opportunity, the system does work. After all, there are over 100,000 foreigners living in Mexico and the count goes up daily.

WHOM TO WRITE

MEXICAN GOVERNMENT OFFICES

TOURISM OFFICES

Los Angeles, CA 90067
10100 Santa Monica Blvd., Suite 224
(213) 203-8191 Fax (213) 203-8316

Houston, TX 77008
2707 North Loop West, Suite 450
(713) 880- 5153 Fax (713) 880-1833

New York, NY 10022
405 Park Avenue, Suite 1402
(212) 755-7261 Fax (212) 753-2874

Miami, FL 33156
11522 S.W. 81st Road
(305) 252-1440

Chicago, IL 60601
70 East Lake Street, Suite 1413
(312) 565-2786 Fax (312) 606-9012

Washington, D.C. 20006
1911 Pennyslvalia Ave N.W.
(202) 728-1750 Fax (202) 728-1758

Toronto, Ontario, M4W 3E2, Canada
2 Bloor Street West #1801
(416) 925-2753 Fax (416) 926-6061

Montreal, Quebec, H3B 3M9, Canada
One Place Ville Marie #1112
 (514) 871-1052 Fax (514) 871-3825

DIPLOMATIC OFFICES...(a partial list)

EMBASSY:

Washington , D.C., 20006
1911 Pennsylvania Ave. N.W.
(202) 728-1600

CONSULATES:

Denver, CO 80203
707 Washington Street, Suite #A
(303) 830-0523

El Paso, TX 79901
910 E. San Antonio Ave.
(915) 533-3644)

Los Angeles, CA 90012
2401 West 6th Street
(213) 351-6800

San Diego, CA 92101
1333 Front Street
(619) 231-0337

San Fransisco, CA 94102
870 Market St., #528
(415) 392-5554

Seattle, WA 98101
1425 4th Avenue , Suite 612
(206) 682-3634

CRANKING UP THE SPANISH

Though some English is spoken by many of those with whom the Mexico traveler ordinarily comes into contact, Spanish is still the language of Mexico and you can enjoy the country more if you learn, and use, even a few words and phrases.

Mexicans, unlike some other nationalities, are not scornful of mispronunciations and errors in grammar. Rather, they welcome even the most halting attempts to use their language as a sign of respect It is relatively easy to make yourself understood if you keep it simple and employ only the words needed to make a point. At first keep to the present tense, adding others as they are learned. And don't be afraid to bring out the dictionary and use it.

For an English-speaking person, Spanish is one of the easiest languages to learn because so many words have the same root source: **family**—*familia*, **restaurant**—*restuarante*, **cathedral**—*catedral*, etc.

Another plus comes from the fact that Spanish is an almost-phonetic language. With few exceptions consonants are pronounced as they are in English. The pronunciation of the exceptions, as well as the vowels, are given below:

A — as the *a* in father

E — as the *e* in they

I — as the *i* in machine

O — as the *o* in over

U — as the *u* in rude

Y — as the *y* in yes

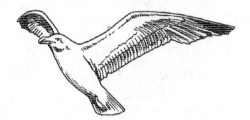

G — (with *i* or *e*) as the *h* in home

G — (with *a,o*, or *u*) as the *g* in go

H — always silent

J — as the *h* in home

LL — as the *y* in yes, with a slight *j* to it (jyes)

ñ — (with a ~) as the *ny* in canyon

Q — as the *c* in come

R — has a single trill

RR — has a double-triple-quadruple trill

V — often pronounced *b* or as a combination of *b* and *v*

Almost all words have the accent on the next-to-last syllable, with the exceptions usually noted by accent marks. For example, *José* is pronounced, **Ho-SAY**, not **HO-say** and *cardón* is **car-DON**, not **CAR-don**. With no accents *Pepe* is **PAY-pay** and *biznaga* turns out to be **biz-NA-ga**.

Another variant with English is that Spanish words have a sex, or gender. Nouns or adjetives ending with an *o* are masculine, and are preceded with *el*. Those ending with *a* are feminine and will be found the with a *la* in front of it. There are numerous examples in the lists of words on succeeding pages. *There are also exceptions...but don't worry about them...just be aware.*

399

Some Starters...

Hello — *hola*
My name is — *Mi nombre es*
Please — *Por favor*
Thank you — *Gracias*
Good morning — *Buenos dias*
Good afternoon — *uenas tardes*
Good evening, good night — *Buenas noches*
Good-bye — *Adios*
How are you? — *¿Como esta usted?*
What's happening? — *¿Que pasa, Que tal?*
Excuse me — *Perdoneme*
Yes, No — *Si, No*
I don't speak Spanish — *No hablo español*
I don't understand — *No comprendo*
I need — *Necesito*

Who knows — *Qúien sabe*
Why not — *Como no*
True — *Verdad* or *De vera*
You're welcome — *De nada*
I am sick — *Estoy enfermo*
Where are you going? — *¿Adonde va?*
Where are you from? — *¿Adonde viene?*
We want to eat now — *Ya queremos comer*
I am thirsty, hungry — *Tengo sed, hambre*
Is there, Are there, Have you — *¿Hay?*
Have you a beer? — *¿Hay una cerveza?*
Have you a soft drink? — *¿Hay un soda?*
What is your name? — *¿Cual es su nombre?*
Let's go — *Vamanos*
What time is it? — *¿Que hora es?*

Please speak more slowly — *Habla mas despacio por favor*

The Numbers...

1. *uno*
2. *dos*
3. *tres*
4. *cuatro*
5. *cinco*
6. *seis*
7. *siete*
8. *ocho*
9. *nueve*
10. *diez*
11. *once*

12. *doce*
13. *trece*
14. *catorce*
15. *quince*
16. *diez y seis*
17. *diez y siete*
18. *diez y ocho*
19. *diez y nueve*
20. *veinte*
21. *veintiuno*
30. *treinta*

40. *cuarenta*
50. *cincuenta*
60. *sesenta*
70. *setenta*
80. *ochenta*
90. *noventa*
100. *cien*
200. *doscientos*
500. *quinientos*
1000. *un mil*
1,000,000. *un millon*

The Days...

Sunday — *domingo*
Monday — *lunes*
Tuesday — *martes*
Wednesday — *miercoles*
Thursday — *jueves*
Friday — *viernes*
Saturday — *sabado*

The Colors...

red — *rojo*
pink — *rosa*
orange — *naranja*
yellow — *amarillo*
green — *verde*
blue — *azúl*

purple — *purpura*
brown — *café* or *moreno*
white — *blanco*
black — *negro*
gray — *gris*
dark — *obscuro* or *prieto*

Directions and Places...

right — *la derecha*
left — *la izquierda*
straight ahead — *el derecho*
back up — *el atrás*
north — *el norte*
south — *el sur*
east — *el este*
west — *el oeste* or *oriente*
street — *la calle*
road — *el camino*

highway — *la carretera*
avenue — *la avenida*
corner — *la esquina*
block — *la cuadra*
town — *el pueblo*
city — *la ciudad*
mountain range — *la sierra*
canyon — *el cañon, la barranca*
hill — *el cerro*
valley — *el valle*

lake — *la laguna*
river — *el río*
wash — *el arroyo*
point — *la punta*
cape — *el cabo*
port — *el puerto*
bay — *la bahía*
sea — *el mar*
beach — *la playa*
island — *la isla*

400

BEYOND THE BORDER

In Hotels and Cafes...

bedroom — *la recamara*

bathroom — *el cuarto de baño*

single room — *un cuarto sencillo*

double room — *un cuarto doble*

dining room — *el comedor*

hot water — *aqua caliente*

ice water — *aqua con hielo*

key — *la llave*

towel — *la toalla*

soap — *el jabón*

breakfast — *el desayuno*

lunch — *el almuerzo*

dinner — *la comida*

menu — *la carta*

the bill — *la cuenta*

daily special — *especiales del dia*

waiter — *el mesero*

waitress — *la mesera or señorita*

Where is the ladies room? — *¿Donde esta el lavabo de damas?*

Where is the men's room? — *¿Donde esta el lavabo de señores?*

Shop Talk...

groceries — *los abarrotes*

beer — *la cerveza*

market — *el mercado*

bakery — *panadería*

cold — *frío*

hot — *caliente, el calor*

hot (spicy) — *picante*

clean — *limpio*

dirty — *sucio*

for sale — *se vende*

large — *grande*

small — *pequeño*

bad — *malo*

good — *bueno*

expensive — *caro*

cheap — *barato*

more — *mas*

less — *menos*

high — *alto*

low — *bajo*

SNACKING IT UP BELOW THE BORDER...

The Mexicans are great snackers. We sometimes wonders where they put it all. After some study we see an ingestion pattern which falls into three categories...

The Carts...

There is what we call walkaround food, which if eaten sitting down might qualify as a meal. It comes from the sidewalk carts and stands found wherever there is a reason for people to congregate. You name it and they're there...next to a school or office building, at the *zocalo* or on a residential side street.

The snacks include small tacos of grilled beef, pork or chicken to which you add condiments such as beans, tomato, salsa and cabbage. American-style hamburgers and hotdogs are growing in popularity, typically with process cheese on the burgers, bacon on the dogs. When there are several close-by carts we often order a bit from each, returning to the the tastiest for the last round.

Other favorites are *ceviche* and seafood cocktails from a variety of ingredients, including clams, shrimp, octopus, scallops or oysters. We watch these places carefully, patronizing them only if they are clean, organized and already busy. And we've had some marvelous meals. (There are references throughout the book as to the freshness of these critters. In our opinion shellfish constitute the greatest potential health risk wherever you might be in the world...more than ice or drinking water.)

Watch for the boiled ears of field corn called **Elotes**. Served with lime, salsa or chili powder, salt and often a brushing of butter or margarine, (In come areas they come slathered with thick cream, crumbled goat cheese and chili powder.) they are available year around almost anywhere in Mexico. As a snack they rate high with young and old, native and tourist. The next time you're around a public gathering check how many people are munching on *elote*s.

The Raw Stuff...

Fresh fruits and vegetables are a major part of the Mexican diet and much of it is consumed as they go about their daily routine. Big sellers include fruit and vegetable cups found in glass-enclosed carts, and served with a choice of lime juice, salt or chili powder. A personal favorite is a combination of cucumber, jícama, orange and papaya with lime, salt and chili powder. If the mix lacks vegetables we usually stick with lime and a bit of salt.

When *mango* season begins, it is easier to understand why there are so many mango trees in Mexico. Everybody is munching, chewing or sucking on a mango. Out of hand, peeled and sliced in a fruit cup or candied in sugar, the consumption is staggering. Mangos are also eaten green. Cut to resemble a flower and served with lime and chili, the unripe ones have an unusual, tart flavor.

Another source of fresh fruit products are the juice bars, or *jugeterías*. Here you may order a wide variety of drinks from a combination of fruits and vegetables.

First come the straight juices: orange, grapefruit, pineapple, papaya, mango, *sandía*(watermelon), etc. and identified as *jugo natural*.

Next are the *licuados*, a combination of fruit, sugar and water mixed in a blender. You may ask for them be be made with *leche* (milk) to give a richer texture. Other options include eggs, *canela* (cinnamon) and vanilla.

Aguas or *aguas frescas* are made with juices of a variety of fruits, herbs and other materials such as tamarindo, rice, wheat and grenadine. They are rarely seen outside of Latin America. In essence they contain a smaller amount of juice or extract, sugar, lots of water and ice. The combinations are inexpensive and quenching. One of the aguas, the dark-red *jamaica* has become common around our home. Actually a dried flower of the hibiscus family, it is steeped like tea. Its tart, refreshing taste is unlike anything we've had before.

The coconut is a quenching and essential part of the *refrescos* scene...and it comes in its own container. We find the clear liquid refreshing and a great mixer...ever tried a *coco loco*? The meat in a mature nut is excellent plain or with a bit of chile, lime or salt. We're told that the soft meat in green coconuts is a natural laxative, while the juice is just the opposite.

We rarely hesitate to eat almost any fruit or vegetable we might encounter, but we do take the precaution of peeling those fruits or vegetables when such a processes is appropriate, and we do soak lettuce and most unpeelables in chlorinated water. The problems of the past, though, are little seen in most of contemporary Mexico.

Plain Junk Food...

The third group on the snacking scene is the one it shares with the rest of the world...racks and racks of junkfood. From the smallest tienda to giant supermarkets, central markets to roadside stands, there are literally thousands of brands, types and packages of pastries, cookies, chips, candies, gum, sugared fruits and squashes, etc., etc. There are even candy warehouses where anyone can buy it by the case, wholesale! Needless to say, the sugar consumption in Mexico is extremely high, and their teeth show it.

One place Mexico really shines is in the quality and flavor of their potato chips. The **Sabritas**-brand chips are easily as good as those made in Australia, and we had classed them as the best we'd ever eaten. *Even better are the fresh ones made by the vendors in the zocalo in front of the Cathedral in Tuxtla Gutierrez, Chiapas.*

Roasted garbanzo beans dusted with salt and chili powder is popular with us, as are the old reliable hot-roasted peanuts, especially when they come piping hot off the charcoal braziers in the zocalos and central markets.

If you are a junkfood junkie and have a weight problem, stay away from Mexico. On the other hand...there's no better place in the world to be if you like year-around fresh fruit in literally hundreds of shapes, sizes, colors and flavors.

EATING YOUR WAY THROUGH MEXICO...

The meals(Las comidas)...

el desayuno — breakfast
el almuerzo — a light lunch or snack
la botana — a snack, especially the food served (sometimes free) in bars
la comida — food in general, or the main meal of the day
la cena — supper, the evening meal

The people (los gentes)...

el gerente — manager
el mesero, la mesera — waiter, waitress
el cantinero — bartender
el cocinero, la coninera — cook, he or she
el cajero, la cajera — cashier, ditto

Miscellany in the restaurant...

la carta — menu
la cuenta — the bill
la propina — the tip, *normal is about 15%*
la ensalada — salad
el plato fuerte — the main dish
la sopa — soup
la sopa de arróz — it's steamed rice, not a soup
la torta — a sandwich made on a bun
los totopos — tortilla chips, or appetizers
la comida corrida — the daily special, also called *el lonche comercial*

The cooking (La cocina)...

la barbacoa — barbecue
la bírria — barbecued on a spit
el asado — barbecue or roast
asado a la parilla — broiled over coals
el frito — fried
la empanizada y frito — breaded and fried
el mojo de ajo — fried in oil and garlic
el cocido, el herventado — boiled
el ahumado — smoked

The tools (Los utensilios)...

la cuchara — spoon, soup spoon
la cucharita — teaspoon
el cuchillo — knife
el tenedor — fork
la servilleta — napkin
el mantel — table cloth
el plato — plate
la tasa — cup
el vaso, la copa — glass

FRESH EDIBLES...

There is often a large selection of *frutas* and *verduras* (also called *legumbres*) in the *supermercados* or central markets, but the varieties can range widely. Listed below are what are most likely to be found...

En Español, when a bean is uncooked (*cruda*) it is called *frijól*. When it is cooked (*cocido*) it becomes *frijoles*. Not even a Mexican could tell us why...it just is.

Vegetables (Las verduras)...

las acietunas — olives
el apio — celery
los cacahuates — peanuts
la crema de cacahuates — peanut butter
la calabaza — pumpkin or squash
la calabacita — baby squash or zucchini
la cebolla — onion
la cebollita — green onion
los champiñones — mushrooms
los chícharos — peas
los chícharos en lata — canned peas (ugh!)
los ejotes — green beans
el elote — corn on the cob
el frijól — dried beans

los frijoles — cooked beans
los garbanzos — garbanzos or chick peas
la lechuga — lettuce
las lentejas — lentils
el maíz — corn off the cob
las palometas — popcorn
la papa — potatoes
las papitas fritas — potato chips
el parejíl — parsley
el pepino — cucumber
el rábano — radish
el repollo — cabbage
el tomate — tomato
la zanahoria — carrot

el chayote — a mild, light green squash-like vegetable.
los nopales — very young "leaves" of prickly pear cactus.
la jícama — looks a bit like brown turnip, tastes like an apple. Try chunks of it as a snack with lime and chili powder.
el tomatillo — small green tomato with leafy outer skin or husk, used in sauces.

Fruits (Las frutas)...

la ciruela — plum
el chabacano — apricot
el coco — coconut
el datíl — date
la guayaba — guava
el higo — fig
el limón — lemon or lime of varying sizes
la mandarina — tangerine
el mango — mango
la manzana — apple

el melón — melon
la naranja — orange
la piña — pineapple
la papaya — papaya
el plátano, la banana — banana
la sandía — watermelon
la toronja — grapefruit
las tunas — fruit of the prickly pear cactus
la uva — grape
las uvas pasas, las pasas — raisins

Spices and condiments (Especias y condimentos)...

el ajo — garlic
el aderezo — salad dressing
el azafran — saffron
el azucar — sugar
el chile — chile or chile pepper
la canela — cinnamon
el cilantro — fresh, green coriander
la crema — cream
el comino — cumin
los fideos — noodles
la mantequilla — butter
la mayonesa — mayonaise

la miél, el jarabe — syrup
la miél de abeja — honey
el oregano — oregano
el parejíl — parsley
el queso — cheese
la sal — salt
la salsa — sauce
la salsa de tomate — catsup, tomato sauce
la vainilla — vanilla
el vinagre — vinegar
la panocha — an unrefined brown sugar, usually in cone shape
la pimienta — ground pepper (often white pepper)

404

BEYOND THE BORDER

Land animals (Las carnes)...

la carne de puerco — pork
el jamón — ham
el tocino — bacon
la carne de res — beef
el higado — liver
el borrego — sheep
el cordero — lamb
la cabra — goat

el cabrito — baby goat
el pollo — chicken
los huevos — eggs
el guajolote, el pavo — turkey
el conejo — rabbit
el pato — duck
la codorniz, la chaquaca — quail

Sea animals (Los mariscos)...

el pescado — fish
el dorado — mahi-mahi, dolphinfish
la cabrilla — a type of sea bass
el pargo — snapper
el huachinango — red snapper
la langosta — lobster
la caguama — turtle

el calamar — squid
el congrejo, la jaiba — crab
los callos — scallops
los camarones — shrimp
los ostiones — oysters
la almeja — clam
el abulón — abalone (a rarity today)

To drink (Para Tomar)...

el agua — water
el cafe — coffee
el té caliente — hot tea
el té helado — iced tea
la leche — milk

la cerveza — beer
el jugo de naranja — orange juice, etc.
el refresco, la soda — soft drink
con hielo — with ice
el vino blanco, -rosado, -tinto —wine, -white, -rose, -red

Mexican Beer and Wines...

It didn't take long for beer to come to Mexico. Shortly after 1542 Alfonso de Herrera, accompanied by permission from King Carlos V of Spain and a group of Flemish braumeisters, was on his way to constructing the first brewery in Mexico. And it was an immediate success.

Today Mexico's breweries all produce an excellent product. Among the better known of the light brews are Carta Blanca, Superior, Pacifico and Corona Extra. Dos Equis and Modelo are dark and rich. Bohemia is more of an ale and very popular with urban upper-class Mexicans.

Wine making in Mexico began on a limited scale when the Spanish monks brought cuttings from home. It was not until 1937 that the wine industry began in earnest with the introduction of European varietals and the learning of modern wine making techniques. Today it is a growing and profitable industry though we haven't found their vintages comparable to the California varietals, the product is enjoyable. Some that we and others have found to be good are — whites; Chenín Blanc from Santo Tomás, LA Cetta, and Calafia; and for the reds; Cabernet Sauvigñon from Hidalgo. Another popular drink both in the U.S. and south of the border is *Sangria* — one-third red wine mixed with lemonade. Usually laced with crushed fruits, it can be bought by the pitcher.

The grocery store (La tienda de abarrotes)...

la tienda — store (any kind of store)
la tienda de abarrotes — a small "mom and pop" type grocery store
el mercado — market, marketplace, either open air or in a large building where many sellers have separate *puestos* (stalls)
el supermercado — like our supermarkets in variety, but not necessarily large

Conasupo, Conasuper — Government subsidized grocery stores which sometimes have lower prices on recognized staples.

ultramarinos — a delicatessen-like store, selling fancy or imported foods, canned goods, liquors, etc.

licores — liquor store

Baked goods...

One of the bonuses of travel in Mexico is the opportunity to consume some of the best baked goods to be found anywhere. Prepared with ingredients rarely used in the United States - unrefined flour, raw sugar, and lard *(la harina, el azucar y la manteca)* - they are rich in calories and flavor. The prices are low, thanks to heavy government subsidization. If you are looking for a big bakery with modern ovens and white uniformed workers, forget it. They are found north of the border and in a few large supermarkets.

It is more likely that the bakery will be in a building with a *Panadería* sign and a large pile of firewood alongside. Here traditional brick ovens *(hornos)* are heated by building a fire inside the oven. The coals are later swept out when it reaches the right temperature.

The baker then puts those goods requiring the highest cooking temperature — usually cookies in first, followed by cakes and, finally, the bo*lillos*.

Ahhhh *bolillos*, nowhere in the world are rolls made the same.

el bolillo, el birote — a football-shaped roll, it is our all-time favorite bakery product.

el pan — bread; a loaf of bread is simply *"un pan"*

el pan de barra — sliced loaf of bread, gringo style. It is found in plastic bags under the name Pan Bimbo. This stuff is made in modern ovens and is no better than the mass-produced U.S. equivalent.

el pastél — cake, pie

el pay — pie

el pan de dulce — sweet rolls

las tortillas — round and very thin cakes of corn *(maíz)* or wheat *(harina)* that come from the tortillerias

Places to...

The ending *-ería* means a place where you can get whatever is in the first part of the word — *tortillaería* — tortilla factory; *taquería* — taco stand; *cervecería* — beer bar or a brewery; *carnicería* — butcher shop; *zapatería* — shoe store, etc.

Educated guesses...

The prepared dishes *(los platillos)* you'll see on menus (when there are menus) are too numerous to list here. You'll get to know the different sauces and cooking methods as you try them. If you want to know before ordering, look for the main ingredient (*pescado, aquacate, carne de res, etc.*) and ask the waiter *"Como se prepara?"* How is it prepared? (Of course when he answers you might not understand. We have that problem.) Where there are no menus there are often only one or two entrees anyway. Then there's even less of a problem.

Below are a few of the basics...

For breakfast (Para el desayuno)...

El desayuno is usually rather simple. In the smaller places you might be served a cup of hot water and be expected to mix your own from a jar of instant coffee on the table. They

406

may have only 2 or 3 alternatives available. If you don't want coffee and have doubts about the water, consider a plate of *huevos rancheros* washed down with *una cerveza bién helada* (very cold beer). It is a personal favorite.

la avena — oatmeal

el cereal — cereal

los huevos — eggs

    cocidos, huevos duros — hard boiled

    estrellados — sunny side-up

    tibios — soft boiled

    volteados — over easy

    revueltos — scrambled

    mexicanos — scrambled with tomatoes, onions and chiles

    rancheros — fried, served on a crisp tortilla and covered with sauce

el jugo — juice

la marmelada — marmalade, jam, jelly

pan tostado — toast

los chilaquiles — tortilla strips cooked with a sauce of tomatillos, chiles, onions and cheese

What's In It?...

In the smaller places there is usually no menu and only a few lunch or dinner entrees are available. Usually they will be in the following list. (Even if it's not, you can ask by using the *Carnes* and *Legumbres* lists shown earlier.)

los antojitos — snacks of *frijoles, guacamole, cheeses, tortilla chips, salsas,* etc., in a variety of combinations

el burrito — a flour tortilla wrapped around refried beans, *machaca* or other fillings seasoned with *chile.*

el chile — green, yellow or red peppers. There are many kinds of chiles — *jalapeño, serrano, ancho, california, fresno, de árbol, poblano, pasilla, etc.* Before diving in, get to know your tolerance levels or you may get burned, literally.

los chiles rellenos — a relatively mild pepper stuffed with cheese or other material, dipped in egg whites and deep fried.

la enchilada — a corn tortilla wrapped around chicken, beef, cheese or other fillings and baked with a sauce.

la flauta — a small corn tortilla wrapped tightly around a small amount of meat and sometimes a condiment. It is the usually fried crisp.

el guacamole — sauce, salad or paste made of avocado, tomato, onions, chile and other ingredients

el menudo — a spicy soup of beef tripe (and often beef or pork knuckle), garlic, chile. and a scattering of vegetables.

el mole — the famous sauce from the Yucatan made with chile, chocolate, peanuts and more.

el pozole — a soup similar to menudo but with hominy (nixtama) with more meat and vegetables

la quesadilla — wheat flour tortilla filled or covered with cheese and heated

la salsa, salsa casera — the sauce of the house - usually of tomatoes, onions, chiles and cilantro, and placed in a *salsera* (special sauce dish) on the table

la salsa picante, picoso — a very hot sauce - try a little bit before slathering it on

los tacos — the all-purpose fast food of Mexico. Basically it's one or two small corn tortillas (soft or crisp) folded around a filling of any kind of meat, fish or whatever else is handy.

los tamales — *masa* or corn dough filled with meat, pineapple, an olive or two (watch for the pits!), or other ingredients, then rolled in corn husks or paper and steamed. (Note singular is *tamál* not tamale as we norteamericanos call it).

la tostada — a flat, toasted tortilla covered with beans, tomatoes, lettuce, cheese, etc.

la torta — a sandwich made on a *bolillo*, or roll. It is often heated, and sometimes hollowed out to accommodate the filling.

FISHING SPANISH...

A day on the water among some of the world's hungriest fish can be made even better if you are able to establish some measure of communication with your host, even if he does speak your language. You might call it is an expression of respect for the culture and the people...

What is your name?	*¿Cuál es su nombre/Como se llama?*
My name is...	*Mi nombre es*
Stop	*Alto*
Go ahead	*Adelante*
Back up	*Para atrás*
Return to same spot	*Vamos al mismo lugar*
Turn left	*A la izquierda*
Turn right	*A la derecha*
Let's go	*Vámanos*
a little faster	*poco mas rápido*
a little slower	*poco mas despacio*
Just a second	*Un momento*
Hurry up	*Apúrate/Andale*
Bring in the line	*Enrolla la lineas*
Change the bait	*Cambie la carnada*
I would like to fish for...	*Quiero pescar...*
something else	*algo diferente*
near shore	*en la orilla*
out deep	*en la hondo*
What kind of fish are here?	*¿Que classe de pescado aquí?*
Let's anchor	*Tira el ancla*
Can I cast here?	*¿Puedo lanzar aquí?*
How deep is it here?	*¿Que tan hondo aquí?*
I want to set my own hook	*Yo quiero anzuelear*
Bigger hook	*Anzuelo mas grande*
Smaller hook	*Anzuelo mas chico*
Don't touch the line	*No tiente la linea*
Don't touch the rod	*No tiente la caña*
Boat the fish	*Enganchalo*
Release the fish	*Dejelo ir*
Tag the fish and release	*Marcalo y sueltalo*
What kind of fish is it?	*¿Que classe de pescado?*
How much does it weigh?	*¿Quanto pesa?*
Is it good eating?	*¿Se come?*
I would like lunch	*Quiero lonchar*
I would like a soda	*Quiero refresco*
I would like a beer	*Quiero cerveza*

BEYOND THE BORDER

What place is that? (pointing)	*¿Que lugar es ese?*
Where is the head?	*¿Donde esta el sanitario?*
Let's go home	*Vamanos a la casa*
How much do I owe?	*¿Cuanto de debo?*

And more...

water — *agua*	line — *linea*	flying fish — *volador*
boat — *lancha, panga*	swivel — *destorcedor*	sardines — *sardinas*
oar — *remos*	leader — *empate*	mullet — *lisa*
outriggers — *tangones*	hook — *anzuelo*	gaff — *gancho*
engine — *motór*	feather — *pluma*	rocks — *rocas*
bow — *proa*	artificial lure — *cúrrican*	shore — *orilla*
stern — *popa*	bait — *carnada*	island — *isla*
reel — *carrete*	live bait — *carnada viva*	good — *bueno*
rod — *caña*	cut bait — *pedazo de carnada*	bad — *malo*

Zip Verbs

Here are four simple verbs which can be combined with the infinitives of other verbs to put forth a wide variety of meanings. The system was brought to our attention many years ago by Paul Fisher and has served us well.

Tengo (tenemos) que — I (we) have to
Voy (vamos) a — I am (we are) going to
Quiero (queremos) — I (we) want to
Puedo (pueden) — I (we) can

For example: *Puede llevar la maleta,* — You can carry the suitcase.
Or, you can state it as a question:
  ¿Puede llevar la maleta? — Can you carry the suitcase?

The following verbs are representative of what can be added to the above...

buy — *comprar*	find — *encontrar*	make (or do) — *hacer*
carry — *llevar*	fish — *pescar*	need — *necesitar*
camp — *acampar*	give — *dar*	open — *abrir*
change — *cambiar*	go — *ir*	park — *estacionar*
drink — *tomar*	help — *ayudar*	sell — *vender*
drive — *manejar*	know — *conocer*	etc...
eat — *comer*	live — *vivír*	

THE MECHANICS OF TRAVEL...

One of the critical links between you and a great time while traveling the highways of Mexico is having a trouble free vehicle. As problems do arise, even at home, we've translated a list of repair and maintenance operations and the parts that could be involved.

This section is arranged alphabetically in both English and Spanish so that you or the mechanic need only to point to what might be a problem and both parties will understand. We and others have used the system for years and it works.

Spanish to English...

abrazadera — clamp	*alineanación* — wheel alignment
acelerador — accelerator	*alternador* — alternator
aceite — oil	*anillo* — rings
acumulador — storage battery	*apretar* — tighten
afinar du motor — tune-up	*arbol de levas* — camshaft
aire — air (tire)	*arcanar de* — hacksaw
ajustar — adjust	*arrancar* — to start

409

arranquedora — starter
arreglar — to repair
baleros — bearings
banda — fan belt
barrillas de dirección — tie rods
bloque — block
bobina de encendido — coil (electric)
bomba de agua — water pump
bomba de gasolina — gas pump
buje — bushing
bujía — sparkplug
cable — cable
cable de acumulador — battery cable
cambiar de aciete — oil change
carburador — carburetor
cardan — universal joint
chequear — to check
cigueñal — crankshaft
cilindro de frenos — brake cylinder
cilindro maestro — master cylinder
cinta — fan belt
cojinete de la rueda — wheel bearing
condensador — condenser
curceta — universal joint
defensa — bumper
desarmador — screwdriver
desarmador de cruz — philips screwdriver
diferencial — differential
direccionales — turn signals
distribuidor — distributor
eje — axle
embolo — piston
embrague — clutch
empaque — gasket
empaque de cabeza — head gasket
engranajes — gears
engrasar — to grease
engrase — lubricate
escofina — file (metal)
espetusa de uña — tire iron
faros — headlights
filtro — filter
flecha cardán — drive shaft
flotador — float (carburetor)
frenos — brakes
gato — jack

generadór — generator
grasa — grease
grua — tow truck
herramientas — tools
lima — file
limpiadores — windshield wipers
liquido de frenos — brake fluid
llantas — tire
llave — wrench in general
llave de astrias — wrench, closed end
llave de española — wrench, open end
llave de estilson — wrench, stilson
mangera — hose
mangera — tube (small)
martillo — hammer
mofle — muffler
muelles — springs
multiple — manifold
palanca de cambios — gear shift
palanca de engrañe — gear shift
parabrisas — windshield
parche — patch
pedal de frenos — brake pedal
perico — crescent wrench
pinzas — pliers
pinzas de presión — vice grips
radiadora — radiator
refacciones — auto parts
regulador de voltage — voltage regulator
rotulas — ball joints
rueda — wheel
ruido — noise
salirse — leak
soldadura — weld or solder
suspensión — suspension
tambor de frenos — brake drum
tanque — tank (gas)
tapón — cover
termostato — thermostat
tornillo — bolt, screw, clamp
tubo camera — innertube
tubo de escape — exhaust pipe
valvula — valve
ventilador — fan
volante — steering wheel
zapatas de frenos — brake shoes

BEYOND THE BORDER

English to Spanish...

accelerator — *acelerador*
adjust — *ajustar*
air (tire) — *aire*
alternator — *alternador*
auto parts — *refacciones*
axle — *eje*
ball joints — *rotulas*
battery — *acumulador*
battery cable — *cable de acumulador*
bearings — *baleros*
block — *bloque*
bolt — *tornillo*
brake cylinder — *cilindro de frenos*
brake drum — *tambor de frenos*
brake fluid — *liquido de frenos*
brake pedal — *pedal de frenos*
brake shoes — *zapatas de frenos*
brakes — *frenos*
bumper — *defensa*
bushing — *buje*
cable — *cable*
camshaft — *arbol de levas*
carburetor — *carburador*
clamp — *abrazadera, tornillo*
clutch — *embrague*
coil (electric) — *bobina de encendido*
condenser — *condensador*
cover — *tapón*
crankshaft — *cigueñal*
crescent wrench — *perico*
differential — *diferencial*
distributor — *distribuidor*
drive shaft — *flecha cardan*
exhaust pipe — *tubo de escape*
fan — *ventilador*
fan bel — *banda, cinta*
file — *lima*
file (metal) — *escofina*
filter — *filtro*
float (carburetor) — *flotador*
gas pump — *bomba de gasolina*
gasket — *empaque*
gear shift — *palanca de cambios,..de engrane*
gears — *engranajes*
generator — *generador*
grease — *grasa*
hammer — *martillo*
head gasket — *empaque de cabeza*
headlights — *faros*
hose — *mangera*

innertube — *tubo camera*
jack — *gato*
leak — *salirse*
lubricate — *engrase*
manifold — *multiple*
master cylinder — *cilindro maestro*
muffler — *mofle*
noise — *ruido*
oil — *aciete*
oil change — *cambiar de aciete*
patch — *parche*
philips screwdriver — *desarmador de cruz*
piston — *embolo*
pliers — *pinzas*
radiator — *rediadora*
rings — *anillo*
screw — *tornillo*
screwdriver — *desarmador*
spark plug — *bujía*
springs — *muelles*
starter — *arranquedora*
steering wheel — *volante*
suspension — *suspensión*
tank (gas) — *tanque*
thermostat — *termostato*
tie rods — *barrillas de dirección*
tighten — *apretar*
tire — *llantas*
to check — *chequear*
to grease — *engrasar*
to repair — *arreglar*
to start — *arrancar*
tools — *herramientas*
tow truck — *grua*
tube (small) — *mangera*
tune-up — *afinar du motor*
turn signals — *direccionales*
universal joint — *cardan*
universal joint — *curceta*
valve — *valvula*
vice grips — *pinzas de presión*
voltage regulator — *regulador de voltage*
water *pump* — *bomba de agua*
weld or solder — *soldadura*
wheel — *rueda*
wheel alignment — *alineanación*
wheel bearing — *cojinete de la rueda*
windshield — *parabrisas*
windshield wipers — *limpiadores*
wrench — *llave*

"Muchas gracias" works wonders in Mexico, just like "thank you" brings a smile in the U.S. Use it often...and have a great time.

411

MORE INFORMATION?...

Over the past couple of decades we've referenced a lot of books during our forays into mainland Mexico. In fact, they have become the nucleus of a collection of Mexico travel guides. One we picked up recently was written in the early 1930s (the population of Tijuana, Baja California was 2,500, Mexico City, 400,000). Below are a few titles that could help set the stage for your adventures in Mexico.

...**Mexico West Travel Club.** PO Box 1646, Bonita CA 91908. These people deserve to be on the top of any list for the excellent information and services available to members. A well-written, informative newsletter deals exclusively with Mexico travel. They also provide tourist permits, fishing licenses, insurance, etc., and carry a variety of reference books.

...**Mexico, a Travel Survival Kit** by Noble, Spitzer, Wayne and Scott. Lonely Planet, Box 2001A, Berkeley, CA 94702, 1989. IBSN 0-86442-047-1. Written with backpacks and bus tickets in mind, it contains an astounding amount of material. The prices listed were outdated before the book was printed, but it would be a mistake not to take it.

...**The People's Guide to Mexico** by Carl Franz and Lorena Havens. John Muir Publications, Box 613, Santa Fe, New Mexico 87504. 1988 ISBN 0-912528-99-0. One of our favorites. Well written, it mirrors his and Lorena's quixotic view of life and we'd be lost without it. Full of useful information about traveling and living in Mexico. We wouldn't think of crossing the border without it.

...**The Shopper's Guide to Mexico** by Steve Rogers and Tina Rosa. John Muir 1989 ISBN 0-912528-90-7. Good information on shopping for folk-art, handicrafts and typical Mexican products in the larger cities. It is part of our travel kit.

...**The Baja Book III** by Tom Miller and Carol Hoffman. Baja Trail Publications Box 6088, Huntington Beach, CA 92615. 1991. ISBN 0-914622-0-8.0. A Map-Guide to Today's Baja California it has been through many printings and updates. When you want another adventure try the "Baja Bible" for a enlightening trip down the Baja peninsula.

...**Angler's Guide to Baja California** by Tom Miller. Baja Trail Publications. ISBN 0-914622-04-8. Though directed toward Baja, its fish identification drawings and tackle tips are valid throughout Mexico West.

...**Birnbaum's Mexico** by Steve Birnbaum. Houghton Mifflin, Boston. ISBN 0-395-51140-2. A popular basic guide to Mexico's oft-visited tourist areas.

...**Hidden Mexico, An Adventure's Guide to the Beaches and Coasts** by Rebecca Bruns, et al. Ulysses Press, Box 4000-H, Berkeley, CA 94704, 1989. IBSN 0-915233-16-9 A sometimes-sketchy guide to many out-of-the-way beaches on both coasts. It includes areas to camp, things to do and places to stay.

...**RV Camping in Mexico** by Carl Franz with Steve Rogers. John Muir 1989. ISBN 0-912528-56-7. The guide fits well with the budget RVer and offers many suggestions.

...**RV Travel in Mexico** by John Howell. Gateway Books, San Francisco, CA 1988, ISBN 0-933469-08-X. Has good material. A number of the parks listed are no longer open, but that happens to all of us

...**Choose Mexico** by John Howell and Don Merwin. Gateway Books ISBN 0-933469-04-7. 1987 It says "Retire on $400 a month," and you can't do that any more, but it does have some good guidelines.

...**National Parks of Northwest Mexico II** by Richard Fisher. Sunracer Publications, Box 40092, Tucson, AZ. 1987. ISBN 0-9619170-0-8. A large section on the Copper Canyon with beautiful pictures and descriptions of the area, Indians, flora and fauna. It also does credit to the Seri Indians and the Pinacate National Park. A favorite.

...**Insight Guides to Mexico,** APA Publications (HK) LTD, Singapore. 1989 ISBN 0-13-466442-6. A good introduction to life in Mexico, its history, its people, its cities; its arts, crafts, fiestas.

...**Frommer's Budget Travel Guide...Mexico '91...on $35 a Day.** Prentice Hall Press, 15 Columbus Circle, New York, NY 10023. ISBN 0-13-337114-x. Much of their information is dated, but there are recommendations for moderately-priced hotels, and a section on walking tours.

...**Distant Neighbors** by Alan Riding. Random House, New York. 1986. IBSN 0-394-74015-7. Gives an excellent insight into Mexico of the 1980s and how they evolved from their past.

...**Travel Guide-Mexico,** American Automobile Association. This small light-weight book has limited information on lodging and restaurants with a bit of history tossed in. It tends to be conservative and outdated, but it's free to members.

...**The American Express Guide to Mexico.** Well organized with a comprehensive restaurant and hotel section.

...**Fiestas in Mexico,** 1978. An interesting compendium of fiestas throughout Mexico. It's out of print but you might check the library.

...**Zihuatanejo-Ixtapa, A to Z Guide** by Linda Fox-Sullivan. A locally-written guide with a lot of information on the area. Self Published. We found it in Zihuatanejo.

If You Like What You've Read...

You will note that we've listed two of our other book in the material above, and in the hope that you might like to order one, or both, we've slid in more information, prices and ordering details below....

The Baja Book III by Tom Miller and Carol Hoffman. ISBN #0-914622-08-0. The oft-revised satellite-imagry maps and body copy of this third **Baja Book** reflects the coming of age of the Baja California peninsula. With more than 160,000 copies of the Baja Book series in print, **The Baja Book III** continues to be the "Baja Bible" for first-timers and old hands alike. Soft cover,180 pages. **List price, $11.95 US.**

Angler's Guide to Baja California by Tom Miller. ISBN #0-914622-04-8 In its fourth edition, the author has packed 40 years of Baja angling expertise into this up-to-date fact-filled book. In ways available nowhere else the where's, when's and how's of Baja California fishing are presented in the maps, tips, charts and the nearly-100 fish identification drawings. The **Angler's Guide** is as important to the Baja angler as is his tackle box. Soft cover, 128 pages. **List price, $7.95 US.**

Mexico West Book by Tom Miller and Carol Hoffman. ISBN #0-914622-09-9. We shouldn't have to say any more about this one. We hope that you have enjoyed it and will recommend the book to others. **List price, $24.95.**

Shipping and handling on all books is $4.00 in the United States. ($5.50 to Canada). Add $1.00 for each additional book. California residents must add 7% for State and Local taxes.

Send your orders to:

BAJA TRAIL PUBLICATIONS
PO Box 6088
Huntington Beach, California 92615
(714) 969-2252

We accept Visa and Master Charge, but cannot ship COD

INDEX

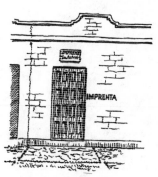

PRINT SHOP

NOTES...

In the event that we make available update sheets on the **Mexico West Book** and you would like to receive same, please send your name and mailing address to Update, Baja Trail Publications, P. O. Box 6088, Huntington Beach, CA 92615.

Thank you for coming along...